Shojo Beat

Millennium Snow

A Thousandth Snow

Vol. 1   Story & Art by **Bisco Hatori**

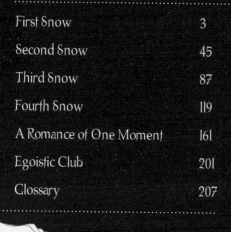
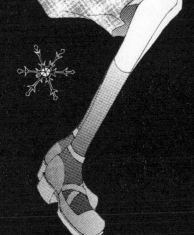

Table of Contents

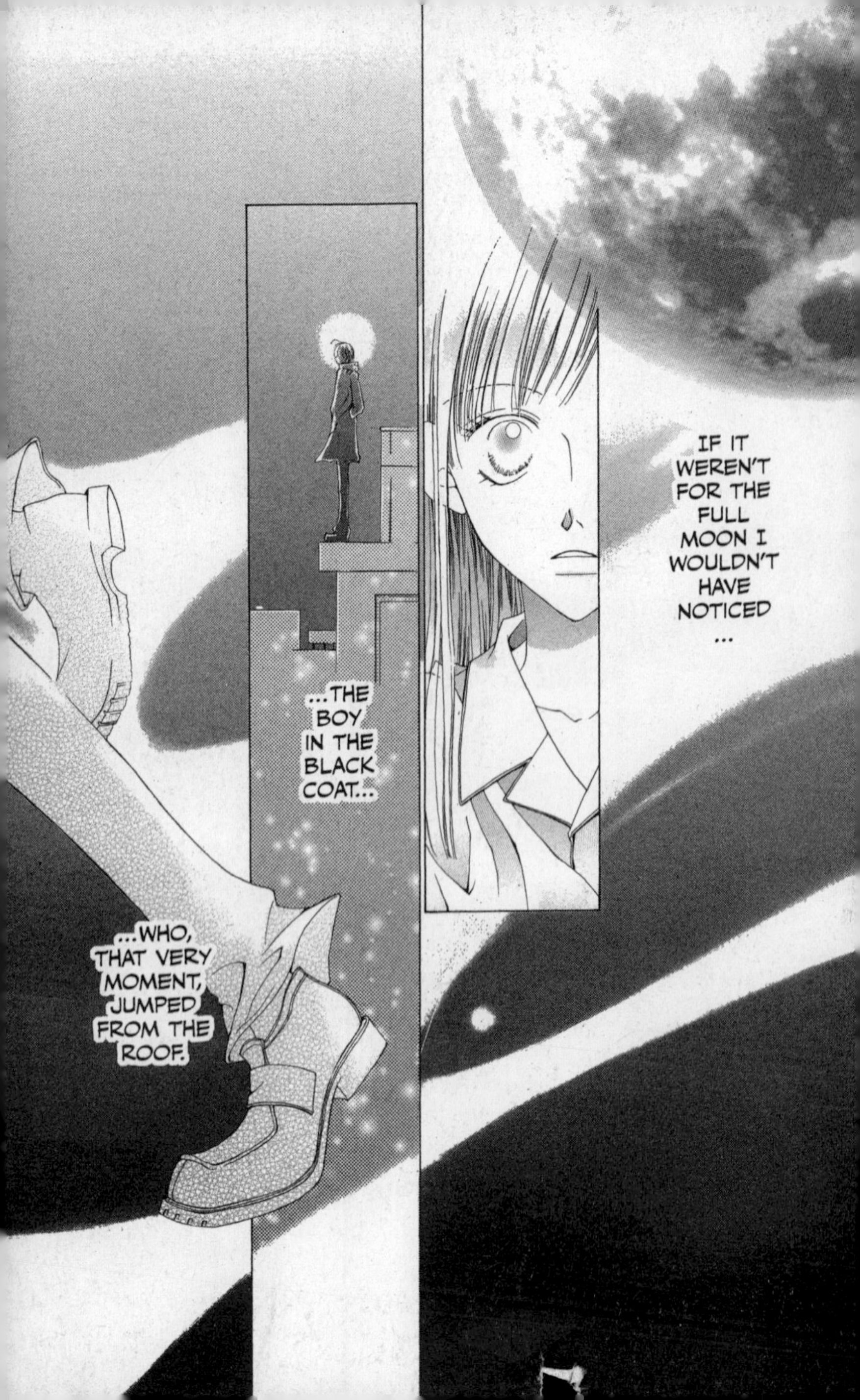
IF IT WEREN'T FOR THE FULL MOON I WOULDN'T HAVE NOTICED ...
...THE BOY IN THE BLACK COAT...
...WHO, THAT VERY MOMENT, JUMPED FROM THE ROOF.

Millennium Snow

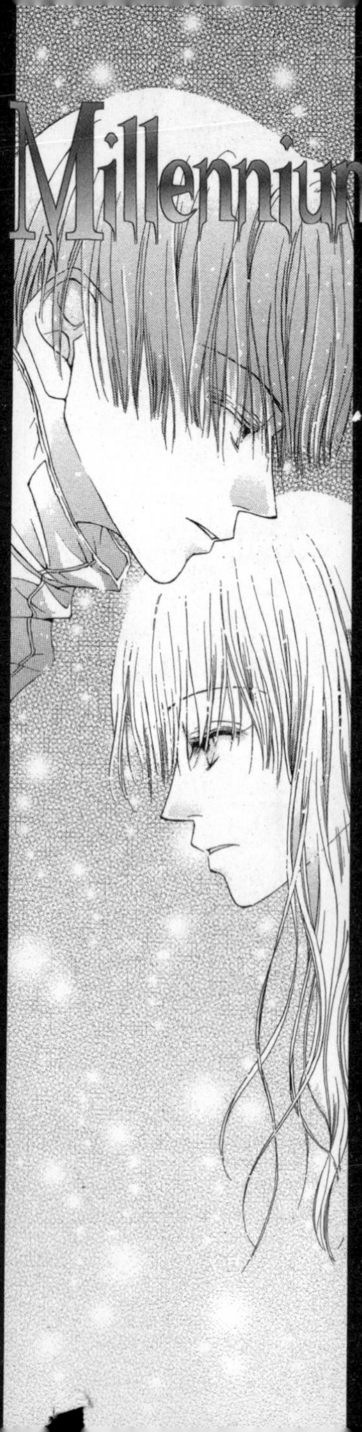

First Snow

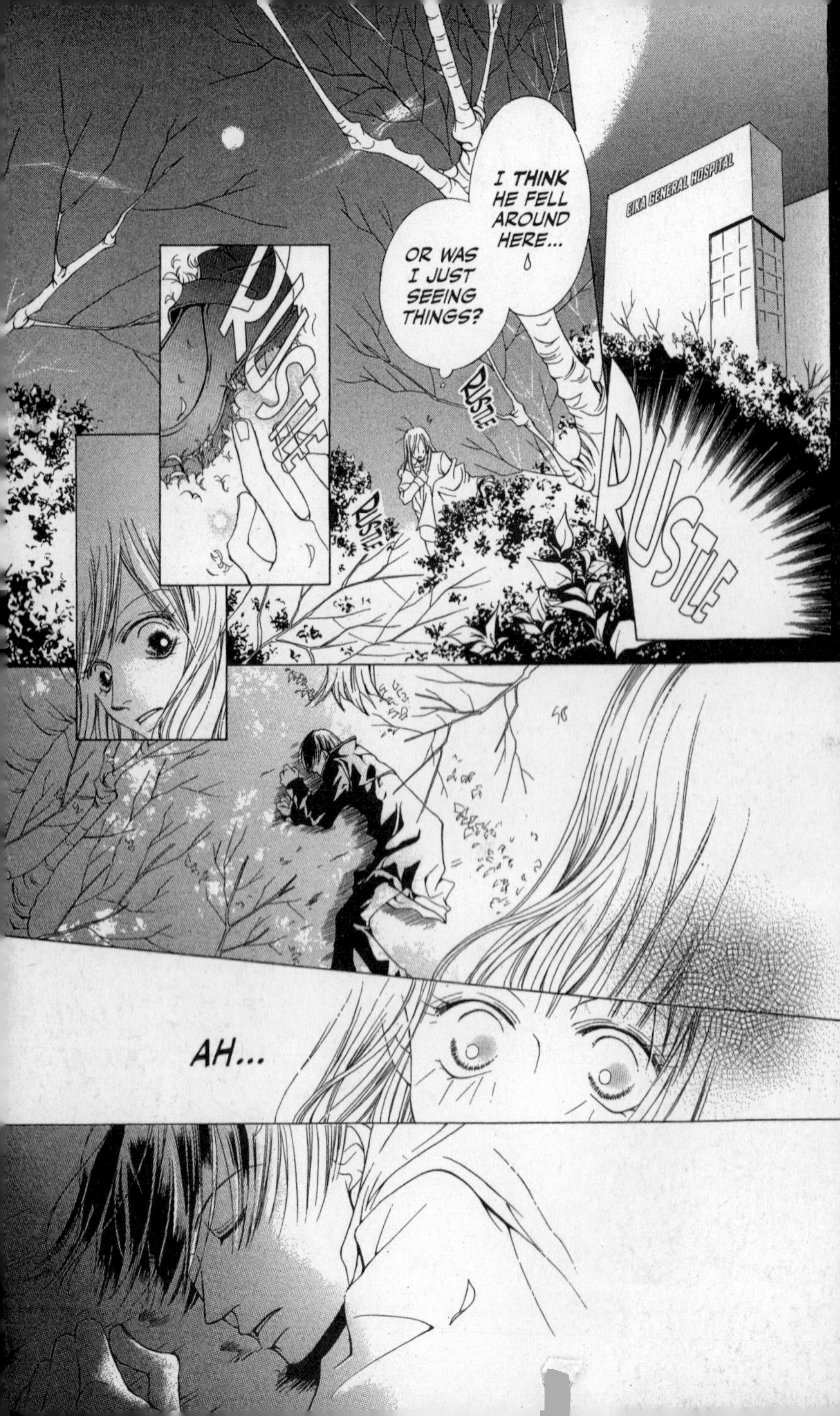
EIKA GENERAL HOSPITAL
I THINK HE FELL AROUND HERE...
OR WAS I JUST SEEING THINGS?
RUSTLE
RUSTLE
RUSTLE
RUSTLE
RUSTLE
AH...

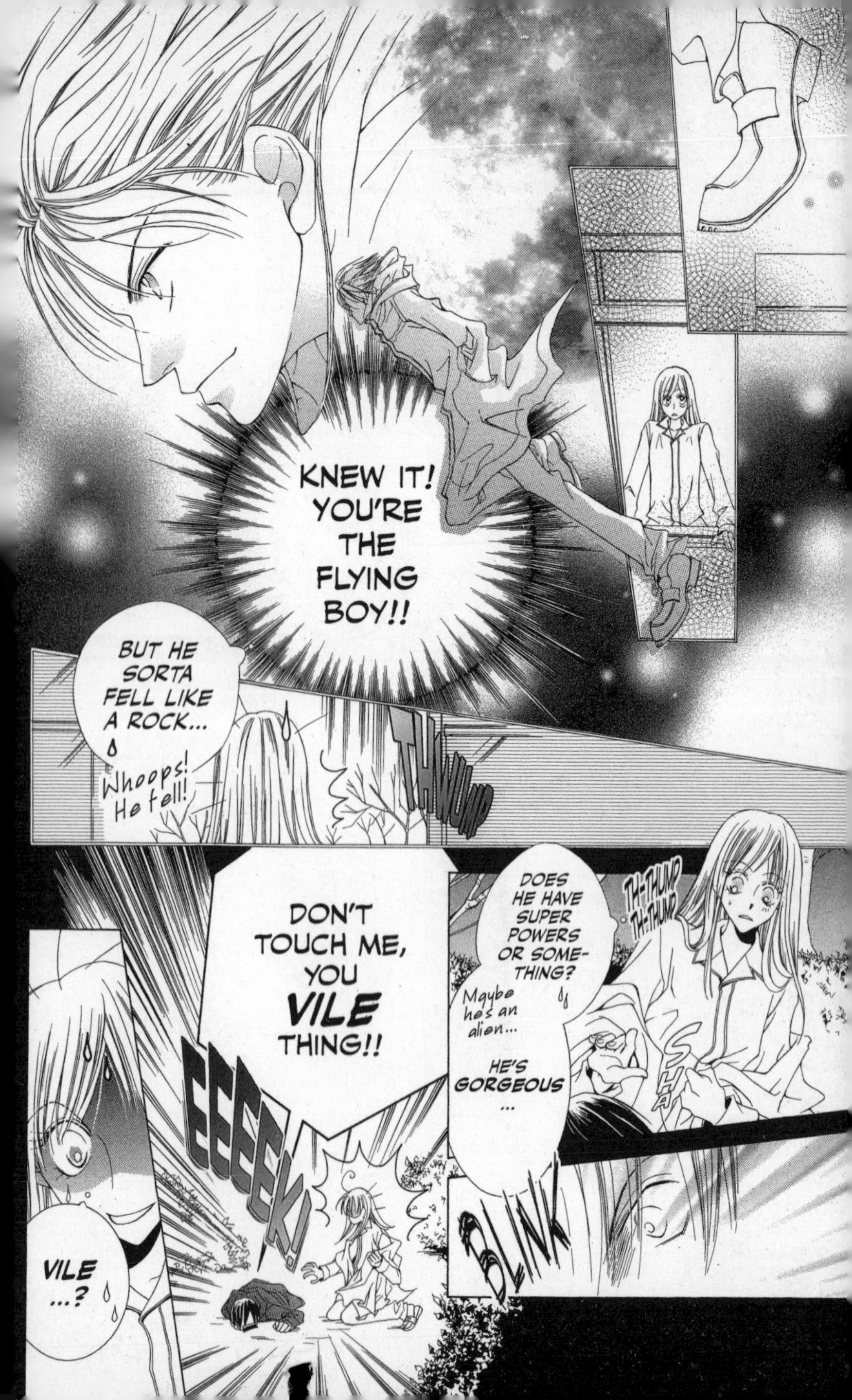
KNEW IT! YOU'RE THE FLYING BOY!!
BUT HE SORTA FELL LIKE A ROCK...
Whoops! He fell!
THWUMP
TH-THUMP TH-THUMP
DOES HE HAVE SUPER POWERS OR SOME-THING?
Maybe he's an alien...
HE'S GORGEOUS...
SHA
BLINK
DON'T TOUCH ME, YOU VILE THING!!
EEEEK!
VILE...?

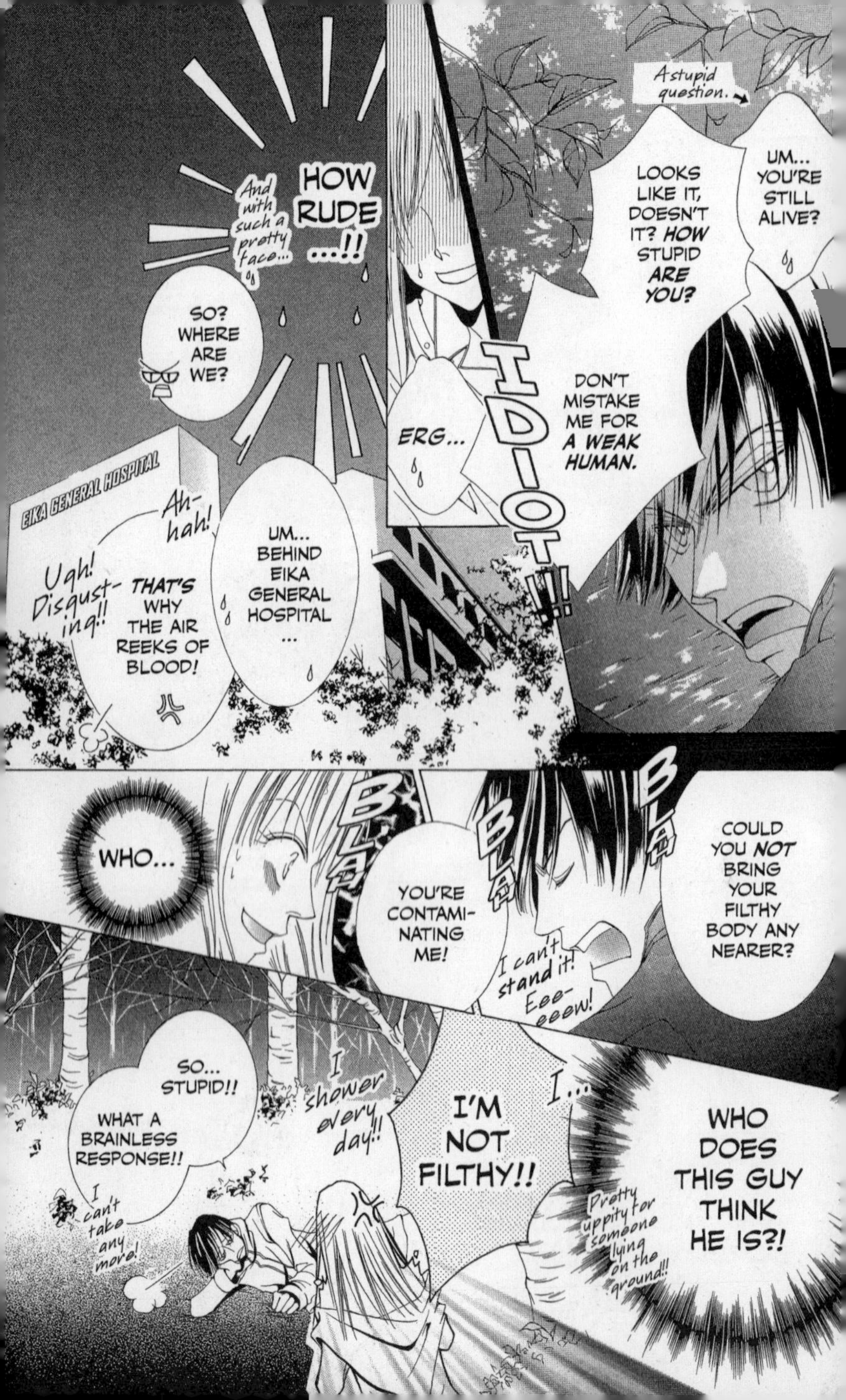
A stupid question.
UM... YOU'RE STILL ALIVE?
LOOKS LIKE IT, DOESN'T IT? HOW STUPID ARE YOU?
DON'T MISTAKE ME FOR A WEAK HUMAN.
IDIOT!!!
ERG...
HOW RUDE ...!!
And with such a pretty face...
SO? WHERE ARE WE?
EIKA GENERAL HOSPITAL
UM... BEHIND EIKA GENERAL HOSPITAL ...
Ah-hah!
THAT'S WHY THE AIR REEKS OF BLOOD!
Ugh! Disgusting!!
COULD YOU NOT BRING YOUR FILTHY BODY ANY NEARER?
BLA BLA BLA
YOU'RE CONTAMINATING ME!
I can't stand it! Eee-eeew!
WHO...
WHO DOES THIS GUY THINK HE IS?!
Pretty uppity for someone lying on the ground!!
I...
I'M NOT FILTHY!!
I shower every day!!
SO... STUPID!!
WHAT A BRAINLESS RESPONSE!!
I can't take any more!

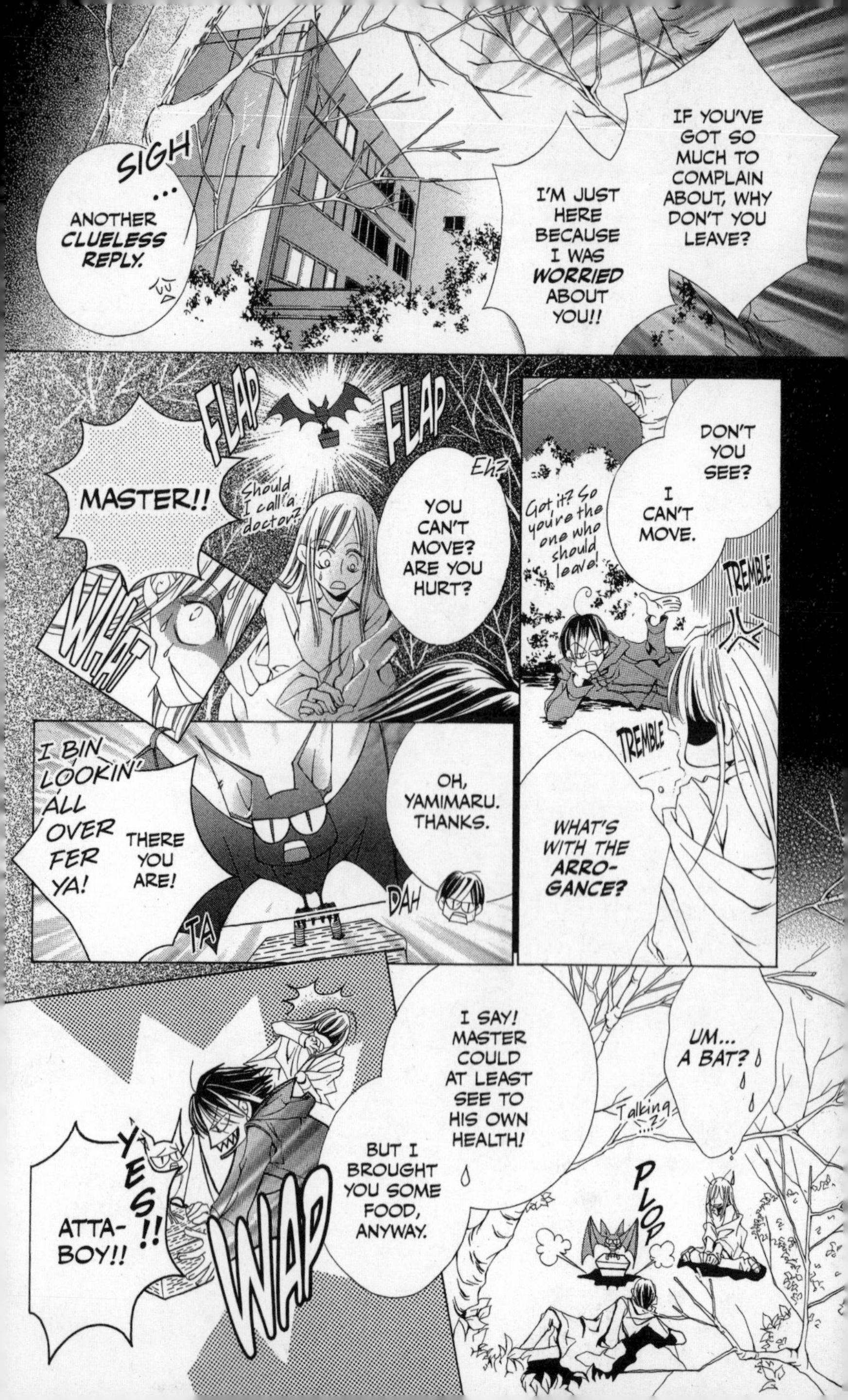
IF YOU'VE GOT SO MUCH TO COMPLAIN ABOUT, WHY DON'T YOU LEAVE?
I'M JUST HERE BECAUSE I WAS WORRIED ABOUT YOU!!
SIGH...
ANOTHER CLUELESS REPLY.
DON'T YOU SEE?
I CAN'T MOVE.
Got it? So you're the one who should leave!
TREMBLE
TREMBLE
WHAT'S WITH THE ARROGANCE?
Eh?
YOU CAN'T MOVE? ARE YOU HURT?
Should I call a doctor?
FLAP
FLAP
MASTER!!
WHAT
OH, YAMIMARU. THANKS.
DAH
THERE YOU ARE!
I BIN LOOKIN' ALL OVER FER YA!
TA
UM... A BAT?
Talking...?
I SAY! MASTER COULD AT LEAST SEE TO HIS OWN HEALTH!
BUT I BROUGHT YOU SOME FOOD, ANYWAY.
PLOP
YES!!
ATTA-BOY!!
WAP

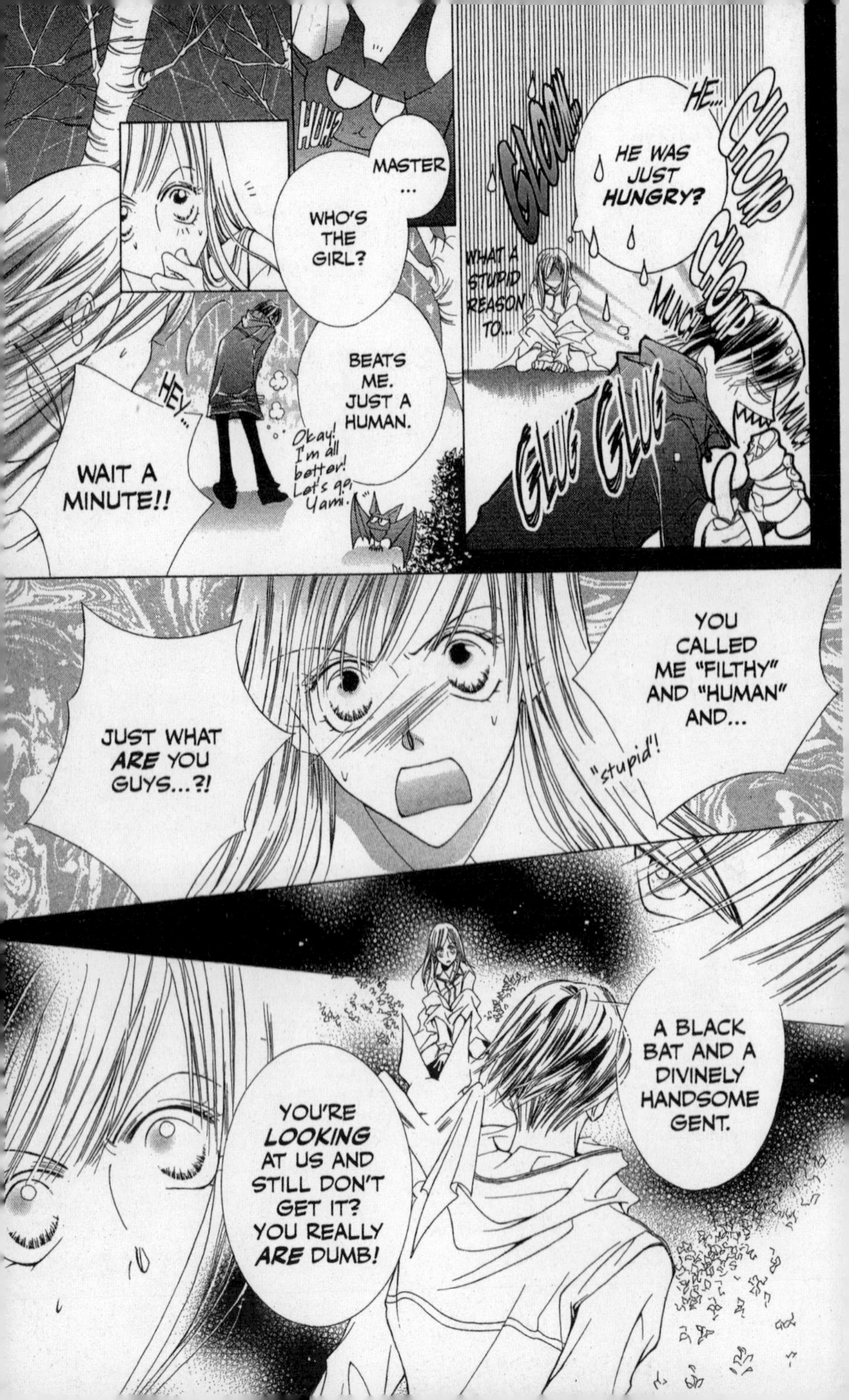
GLOOM
HE...
HE WAS JUST HUNGRY?
CHOMP CHOMP
MUNCH MUNCH
GLUG GLUG
WHAT A STUPID REASON TO...
HUH?
MASTER...
WHO'S THE GIRL?
BEATS ME. JUST A HUMAN.
Okay! I'm all better! Let's go, Yami.
HEY...
WAIT A MINUTE!!
YOU CALLED ME "FILTHY" AND "HUMAN" AND...
"stupid"!
JUST WHAT ARE YOU GUYS...?!
A BLACK BAT AND A DIVINELY HANDSOME GENT.
YOU'RE LOOKING AT US AND STILL DON'T GET IT? YOU REALLY ARE DUMB!

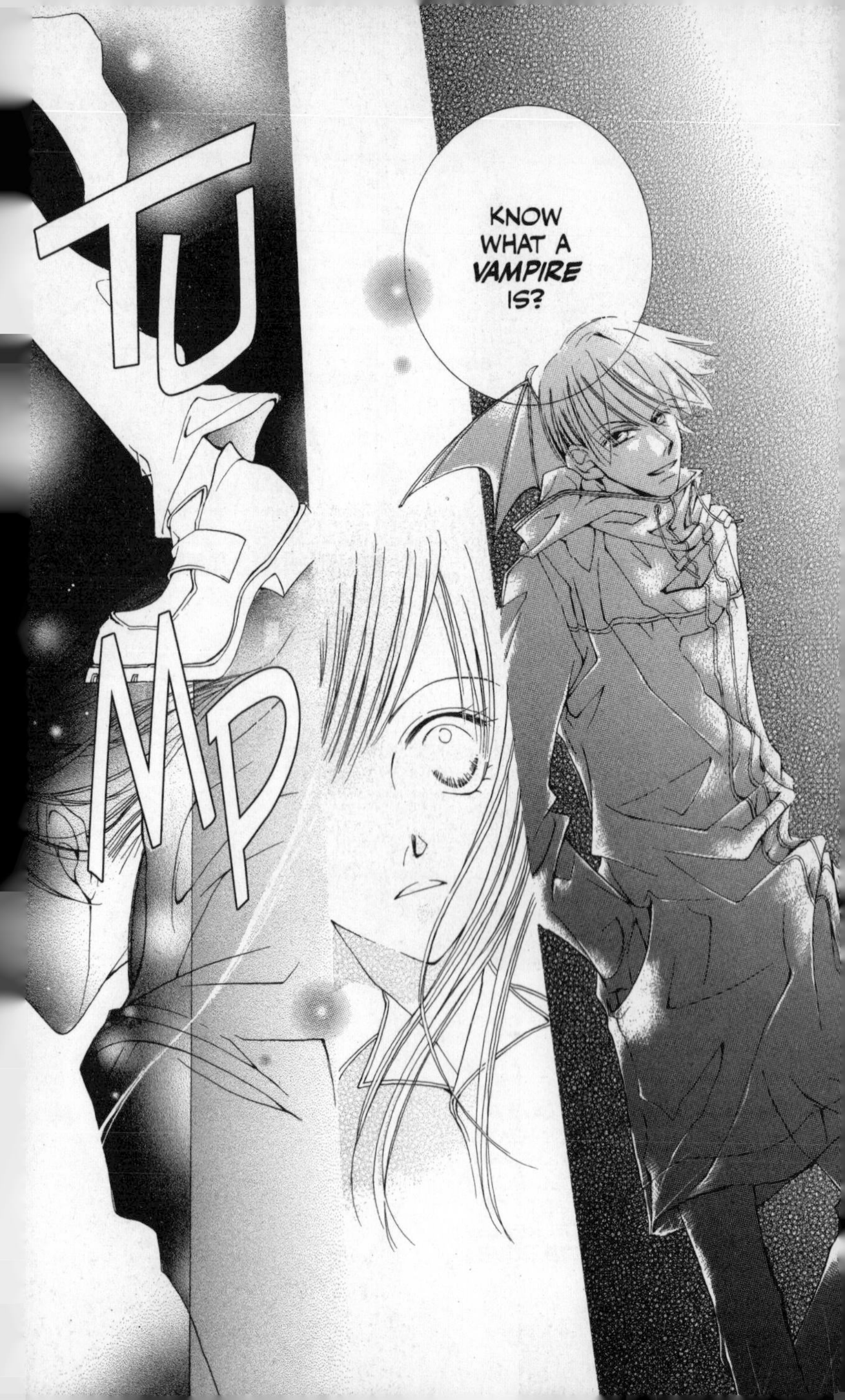
KNOW WHAT A VAMPIRE IS?
TUMP

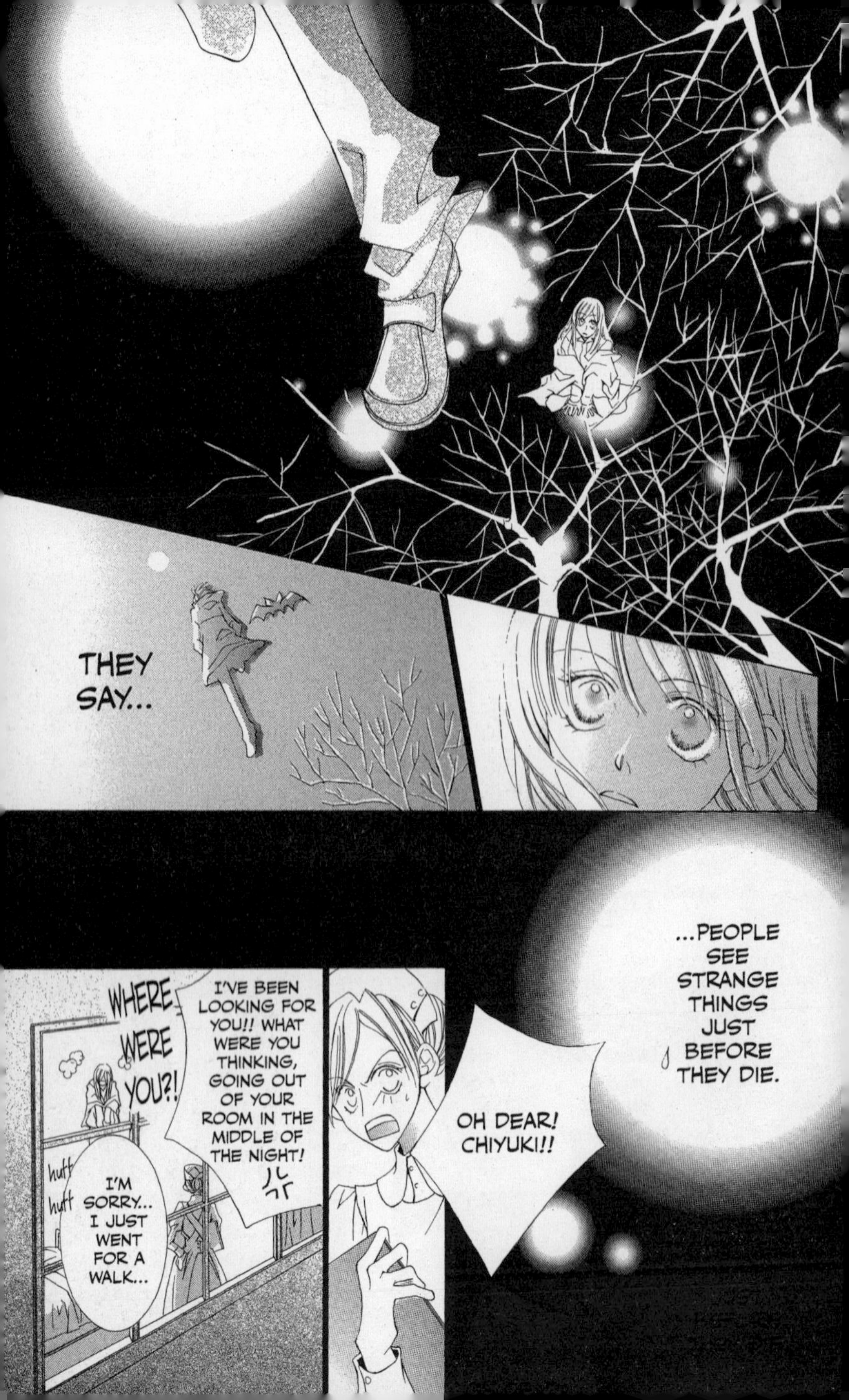
THEY SAY...
...PEOPLE SEE STRANGE THINGS JUST BEFORE THEY DIE.
OH DEAR! CHIYUKI!!
WHERE WERE YOU?!
I'VE BEEN LOOKING FOR YOU!! WHAT WERE YOU THINKING, GOING OUT OF YOUR ROOM IN THE MIDDLE OF THE NIGHT!
huff huff
I'M SORRY... I JUST WENT FOR A WALK...

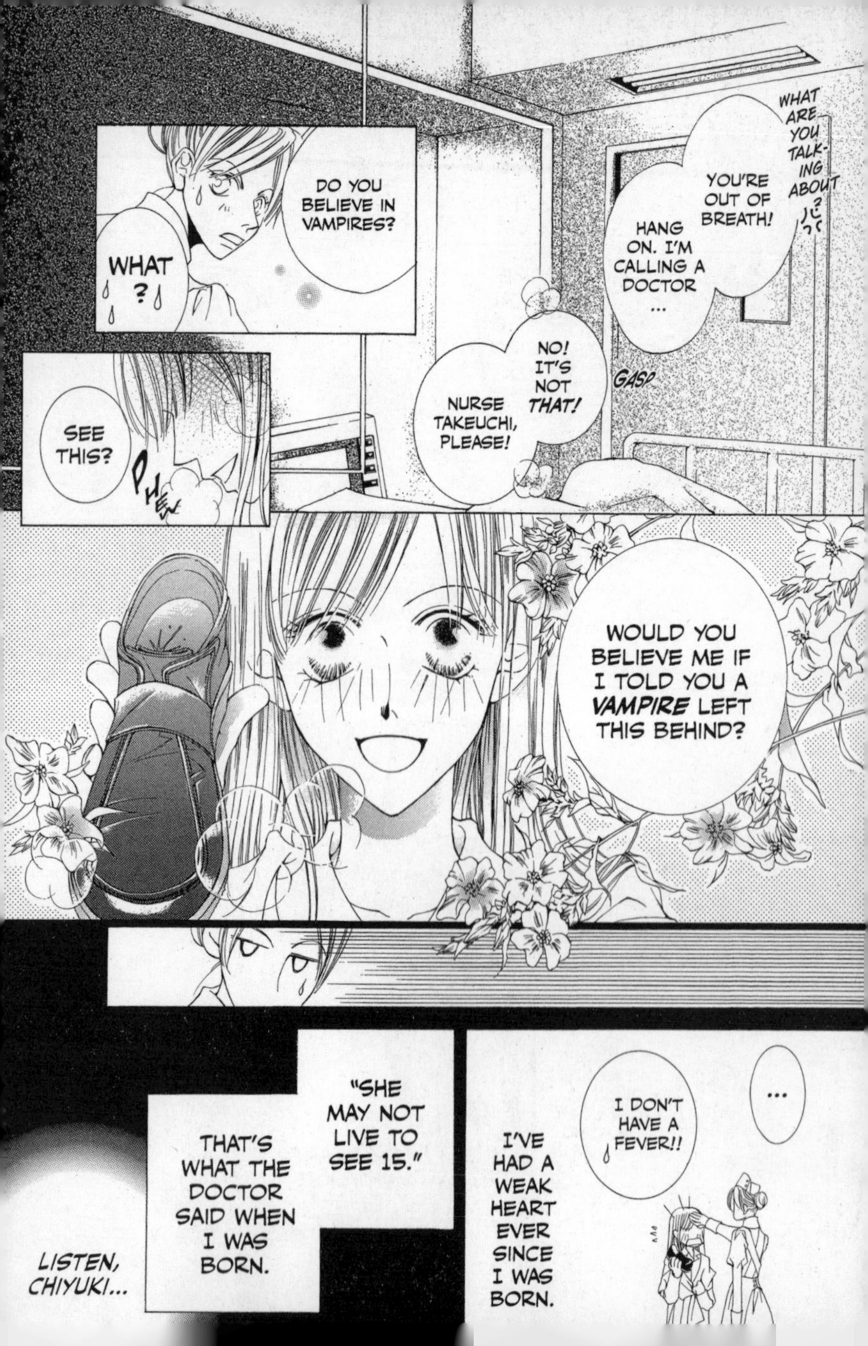
WHAT ARE YOU TALKING ABOUT?
YOU'RE OUT OF BREATH!
HANG ON. I'M CALLING A DOCTOR ...
GASP
NO! IT'S NOT *THAT!*
NURSE TAKEUCHI, PLEASE!
DO YOU BELIEVE IN VAMPIRES?
WHAT?
SEE THIS?
PHEW
WOULD YOU BELIEVE ME IF I TOLD YOU A *VAMPIRE* LEFT THIS BEHIND?
...
I DON'T HAVE A FEVER!!
I'VE HAD A WEAK HEART EVER SINCE I WAS BORN.
"SHE MAY NOT LIVE TO SEE 15."
THAT'S WHAT THE DOCTOR SAID WHEN I WAS BORN.
LISTEN, CHIYUKI...

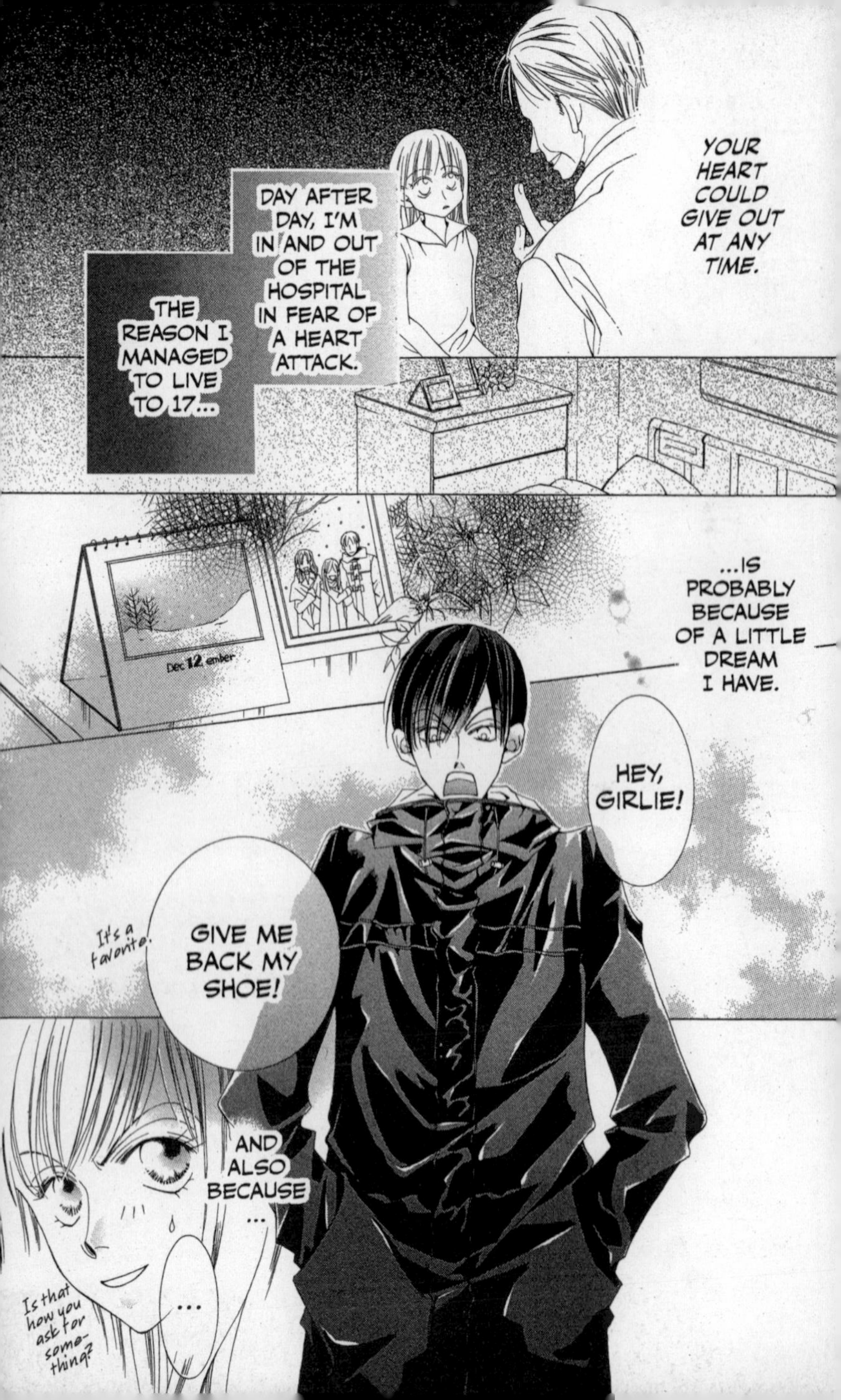
YOUR HEART COULD GIVE OUT AT ANY TIME.
DAY AFTER DAY, I'M IN AND OUT OF THE HOSPITAL IN FEAR OF A HEART ATTACK.
THE REASON I MANAGED TO LIVE TO 17...
...IS PROBABLY BECAUSE OF A LITTLE DREAM I HAVE.
Dec 12 ember
HEY, GIRLIE!
GIVE ME BACK MY SHOE!
It's a favorite.
AND ALSO BECAUSE ...
...
Is that how you ask for some-thing?

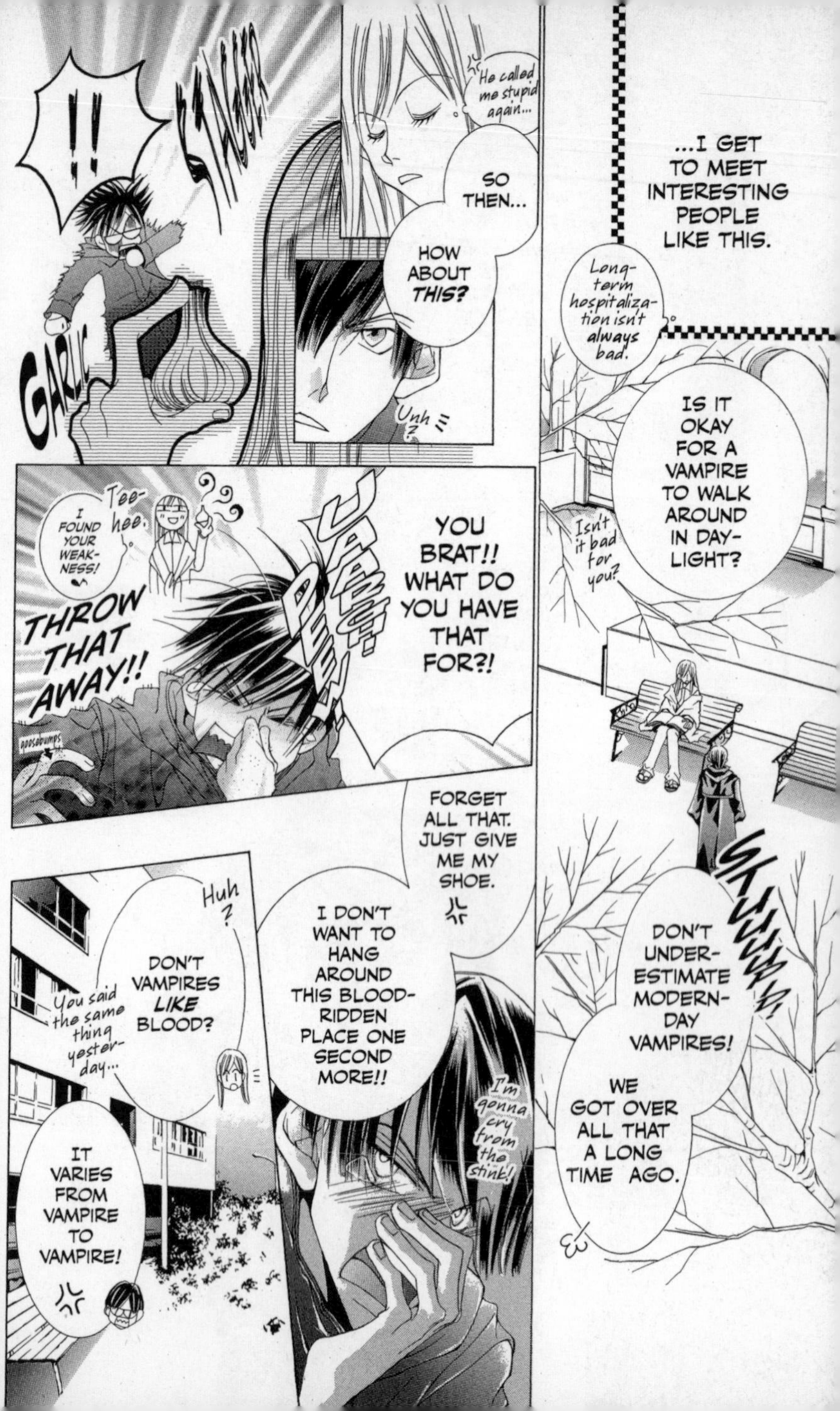

Long-term hospitalization isn't always bad.
...I GET TO MEET INTERESTING PEOPLE LIKE THIS.
IS IT OKAY FOR A VAMPIRE TO WALK AROUND IN DAYLIGHT?
Isn't it bad for you?
SKUUUUN
DON'T UNDERESTIMATE MODERN-DAY VAMPIRES!
WE GOT OVER ALL THAT A LONG TIME AGO.
He called me stupid again...
SO THEN...
HOW ABOUT THIS?
Unh?
!!
GARLIC
YOU BRAT!! WHAT DO YOU HAVE THAT FOR?!
THROW THAT AWAY!!
Tee-hee.
I FOUND YOUR WEAKNESS!
goosebumps
FORGET ALL THAT. JUST GIVE ME MY SHOE.
I DON'T WANT TO HANG AROUND THIS BLOOD-RIDDEN PLACE ONE SECOND MORE!!
Huh?
DON'T VAMPIRES LIKE BLOOD?
You said the same thing yesterday...
I'm gonna cry from the stink!
IT VARIES FROM VAMPIRE TO VAMPIRE!

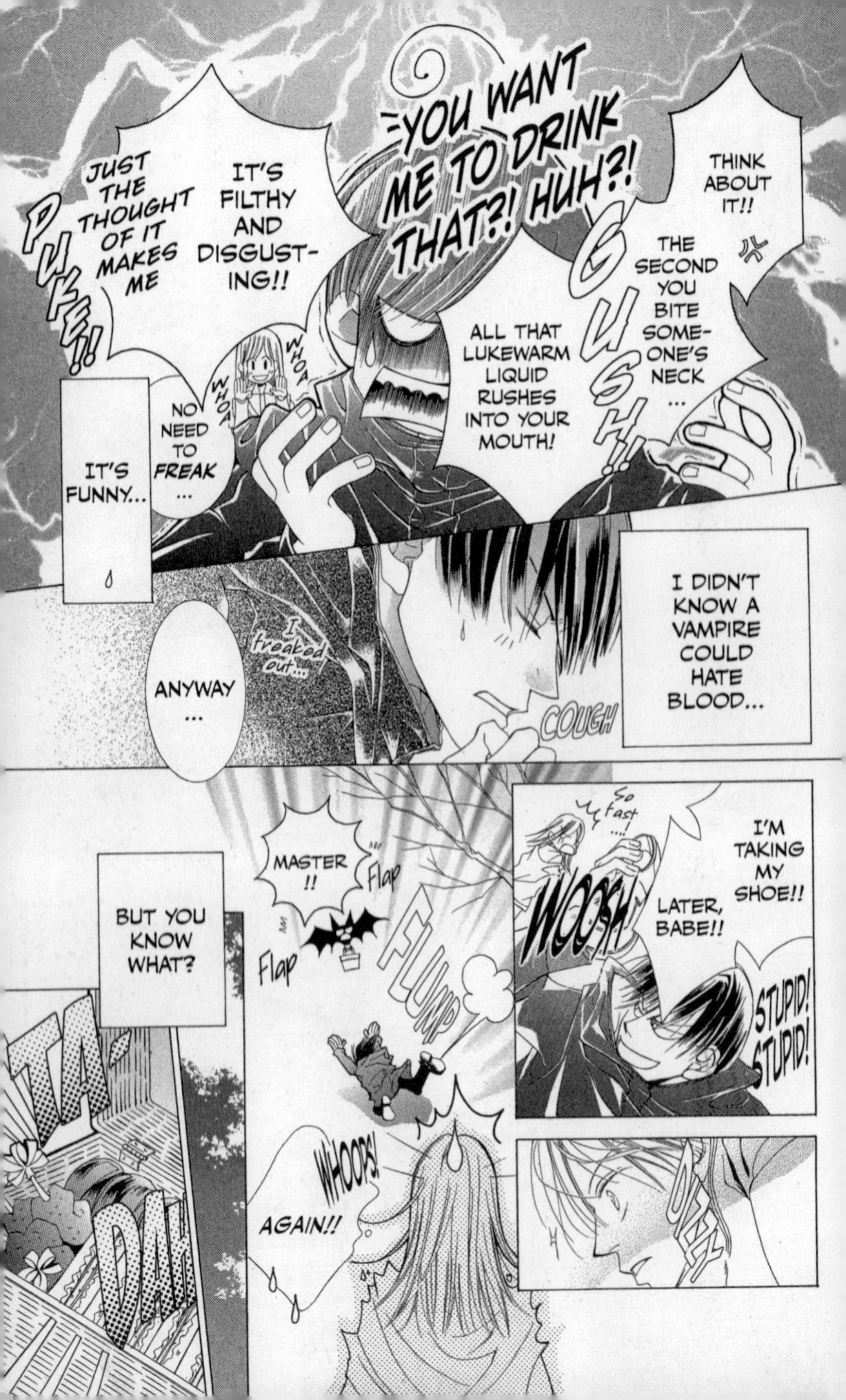
THINK ABOUT IT!!
THE SECOND YOU BITE SOME-ONE'S NECK ...
ALL THAT LUKEWARM LIQUID RUSHES INTO YOUR MOUTH!
GUSH!!
YOU WANT ME TO DRINK THAT?! HUH?!
IT'S FILTHY AND DISGUST-ING!!
JUST THE THOUGHT OF IT MAKES ME
PUKE!!
WHOA WHOA
NO NEED TO FREAK ...
IT'S FUNNY...
I DIDN'T KNOW A VAMPIRE COULD HATE BLOOD...
COUGH
I freaked out...
ANYWAY ...
I'M TAKING MY SHOE!!
So fast ...!
WOOSH
LATER, BABE!!
STUPID! STUPID!
FLUMP
MASTER !!
Flap
Flap
BUT YOU KNOW WHAT?
WHOOPS!
AGAIN!!
TA-DAH

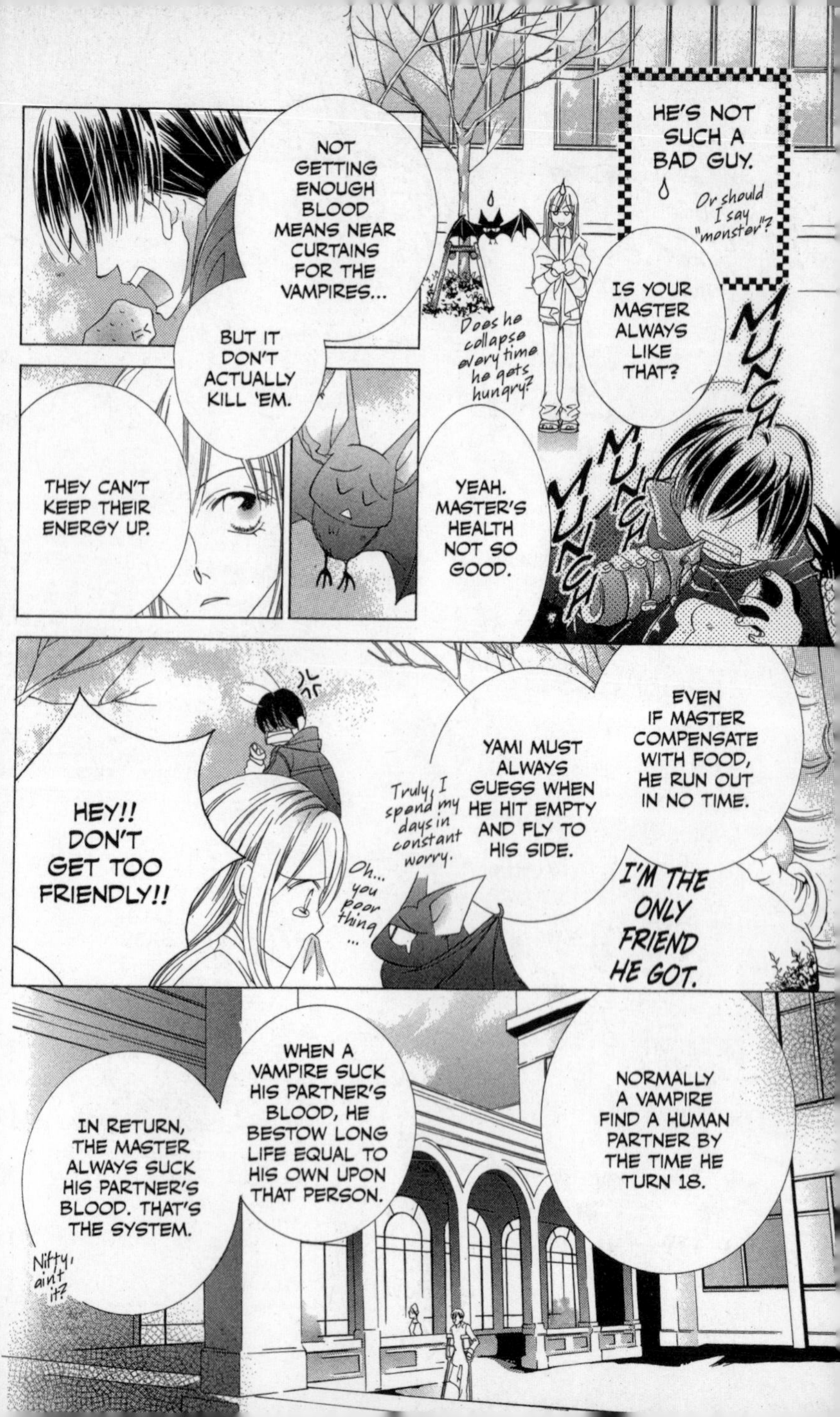
HE'S NOT SUCH A BAD GUY.
Or should I say "monster"?
IS YOUR MASTER ALWAYS LIKE THAT?
Does he collapse every time he gets hungry?
MUNCH
MUNCH
MUNCH
YEAH. MASTER'S HEALTH NOT SO GOOD.
NOT GETTING ENOUGH BLOOD MEANS NEAR CURTAINS FOR THE VAMPIRES...
BUT IT DON'T ACTUALLY KILL 'EM.
THEY CAN'T KEEP THEIR ENERGY UP.
EVEN IF MASTER COMPENSATE WITH FOOD, HE RUN OUT IN NO TIME.
YAMI MUST ALWAYS GUESS WHEN HE HIT EMPTY AND FLY TO HIS SIDE.
Truly, I spend my days in constant worry.
I'M THE ONLY FRIEND HE GOT.
Oh... you poor thing...
HEY!! DON'T GET TOO FRIENDLY!!
NORMALLY A VAMPIRE FIND A HUMAN PARTNER BY THE TIME HE TURN 18.
WHEN A VAMPIRE SUCK HIS PARTNER'S BLOOD, HE BESTOW LONG LIFE EQUAL TO HIS OWN UPON THAT PERSON.
IN RETURN, THE MASTER ALWAYS SUCK HIS PARTNER'S BLOOD. THAT'S THE SYSTEM.
Nifty, ain't it?

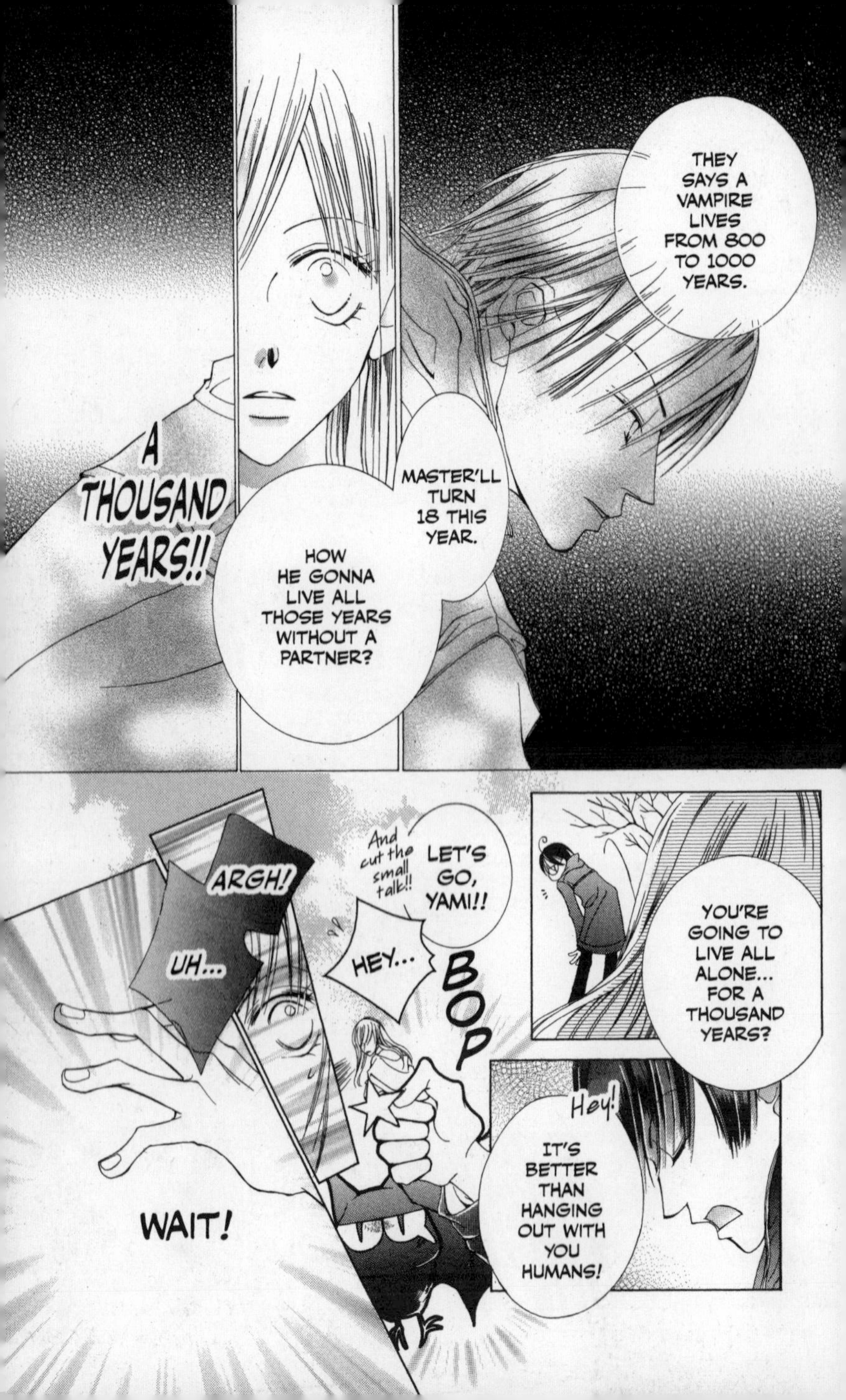
THEY SAYS A VAMPIRE LIVES FROM 800 TO 1000 YEARS.
MASTER'LL TURN 18 THIS YEAR.
HOW HE GONNA LIVE ALL THOSE YEARS WITHOUT A PARTNER?
A THOUSAND YEARS!!
YOU'RE GOING TO LIVE ALL ALONE... FOR A THOUSAND YEARS?
Hey!
IT'S BETTER THAN HANGING OUT WITH YOU HUMANS!
LET'S GO, YAMI!!
And cut the small talk!!
HEY...
BOP
ARGH!
UH...
WAIT!

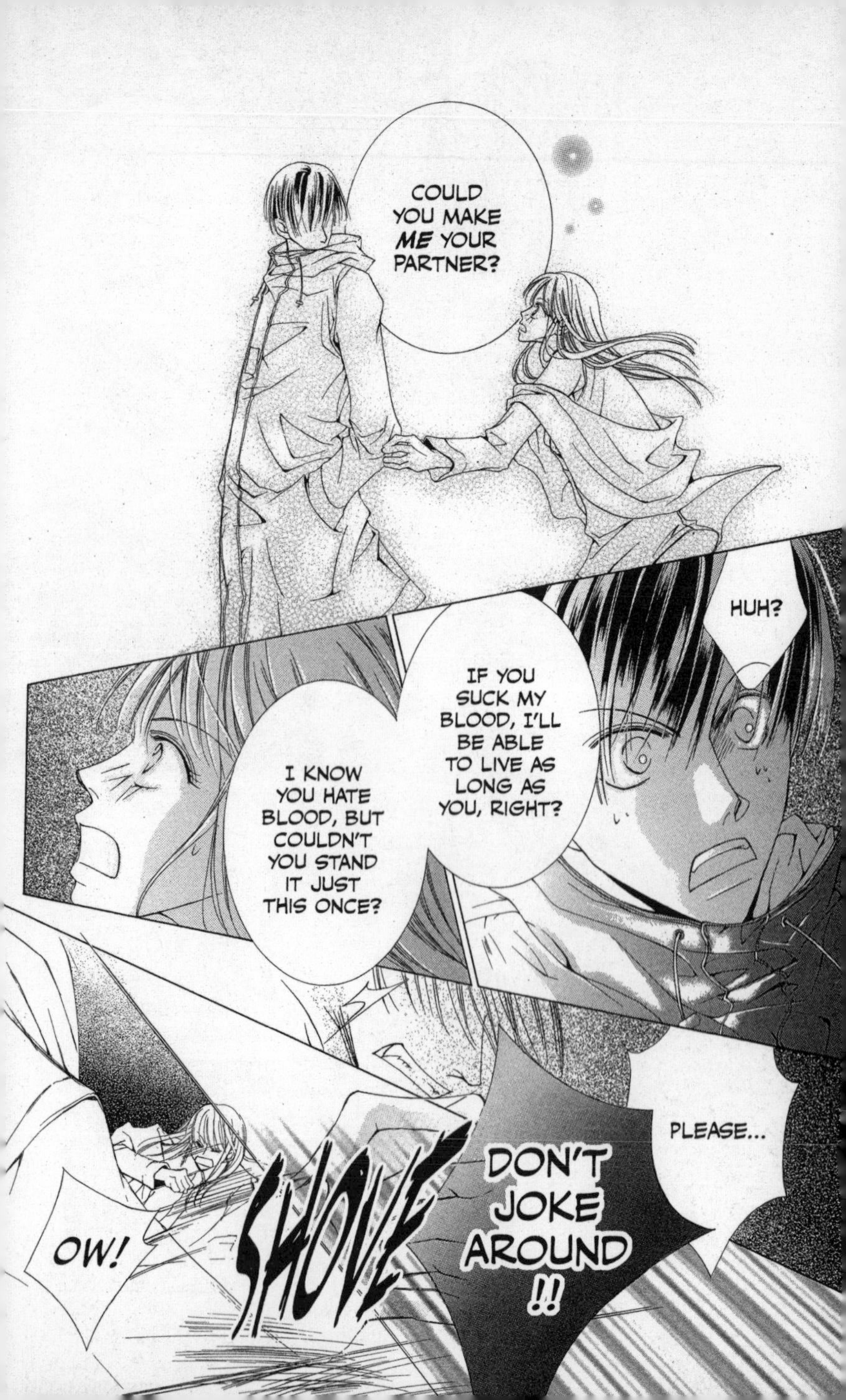
COULD YOU MAKE *ME* YOUR PARTNER?
HUH?
IF YOU SUCK MY BLOOD, I'LL BE ABLE TO LIVE AS LONG AS YOU, RIGHT?
I KNOW YOU HATE BLOOD, BUT COULDN'T YOU STAND IT JUST THIS ONCE?
PLEASE...
DON'T JOKE AROUND!!
SHOVE
OW!

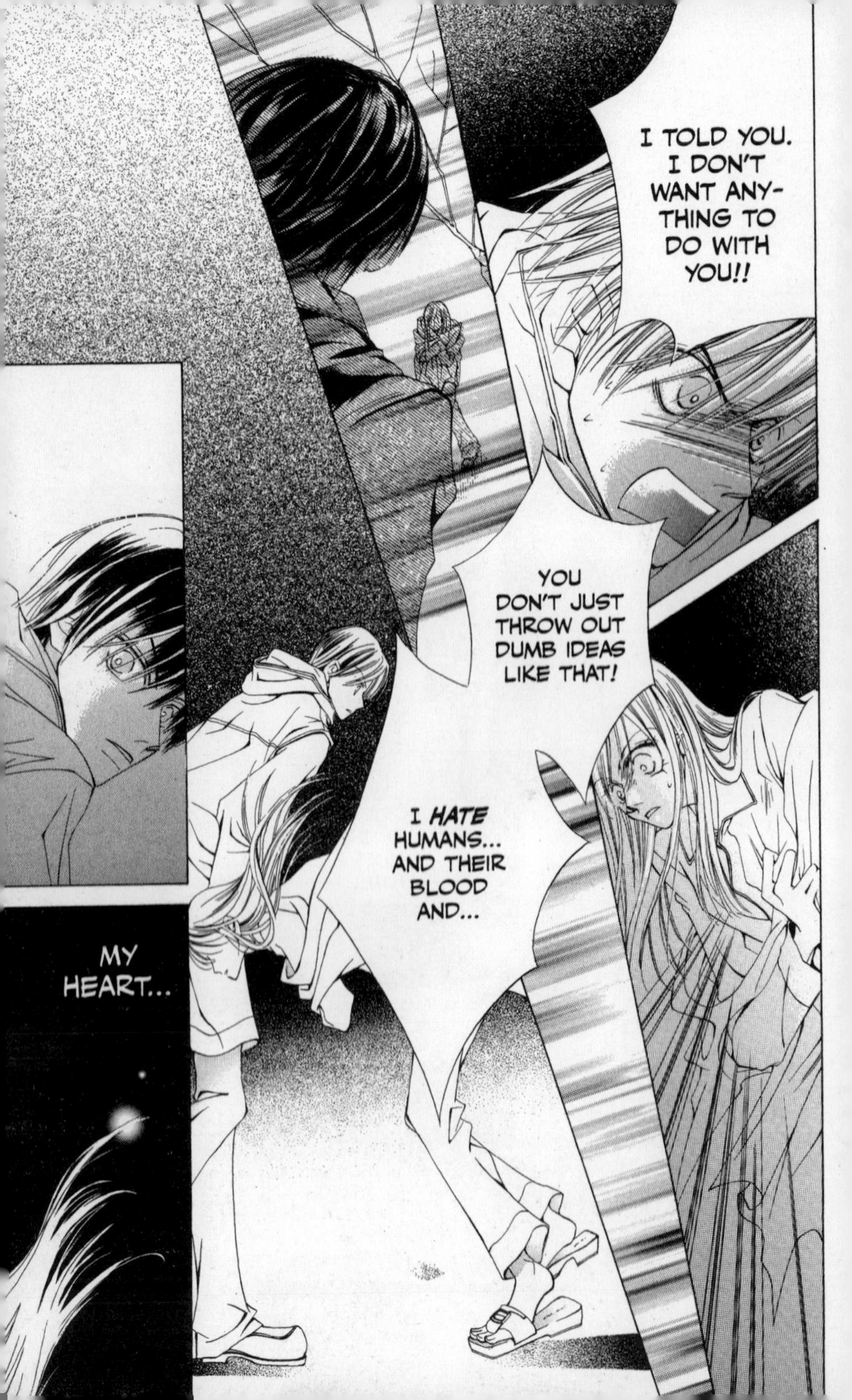
I TOLD YOU. I DON'T WANT ANY-THING TO DO WITH YOU!!
YOU DON'T JUST THROW OUT DUMB IDEAS LIKE THAT!
I *HATE* HUMANS... AND THEIR BLOOD AND...
MY HEART...

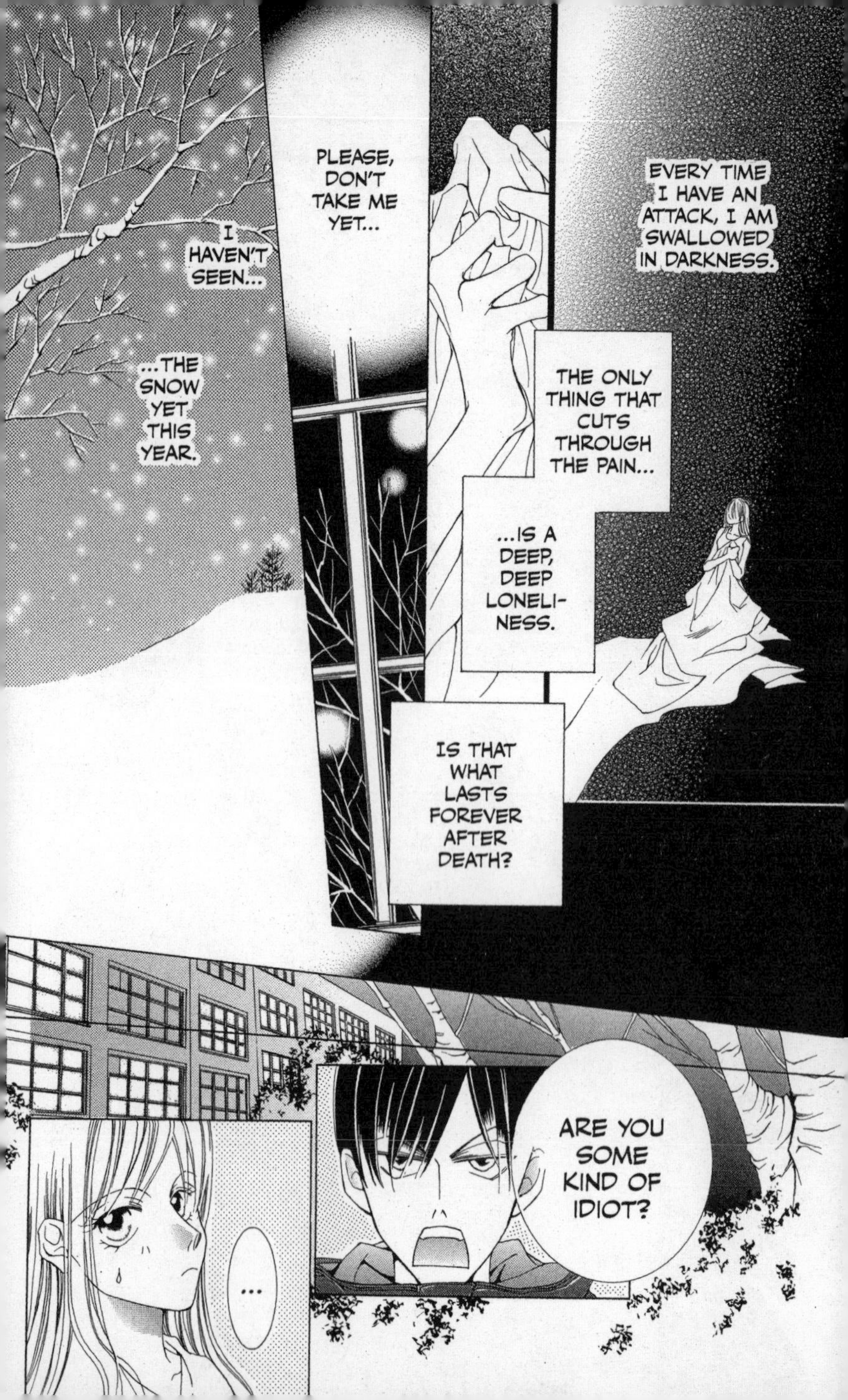
EVERY TIME I HAVE AN ATTACK, I AM SWALLOWED IN DARKNESS.
THE ONLY THING THAT CUTS THROUGH THE PAIN...
...IS A DEEP, DEEP LONELINESS.
IS THAT WHAT LASTS FOREVER AFTER DEATH?
PLEASE, DON'T TAKE ME YET...
I HAVEN'T SEEN...
...THE SNOW YET THIS YEAR.
ARE YOU SOME KIND OF IDIOT?
...

01

THANK YOU VERY MUCH FOR PICKING UP MY FIRST MANGA.

MILLENNIUM SNOW WAS FIRST PUBLISHED AS A STAND-ALONE AND THEN SERIALIZED A HALF A YEAR LATER.

WHEN I LOOK BACK NOW, MY DRAWINGS HAVE CHANGED A LOT... SORRY ABOUT THAT! (SWEAT)

THAT'S BECAUSE OF MY INEXPERIENCE, BUT I HOPE YOU WILL ENJOY THE MANGA—ALONG WITH ITS CHANGES—ALL THE WAY TO THE END.

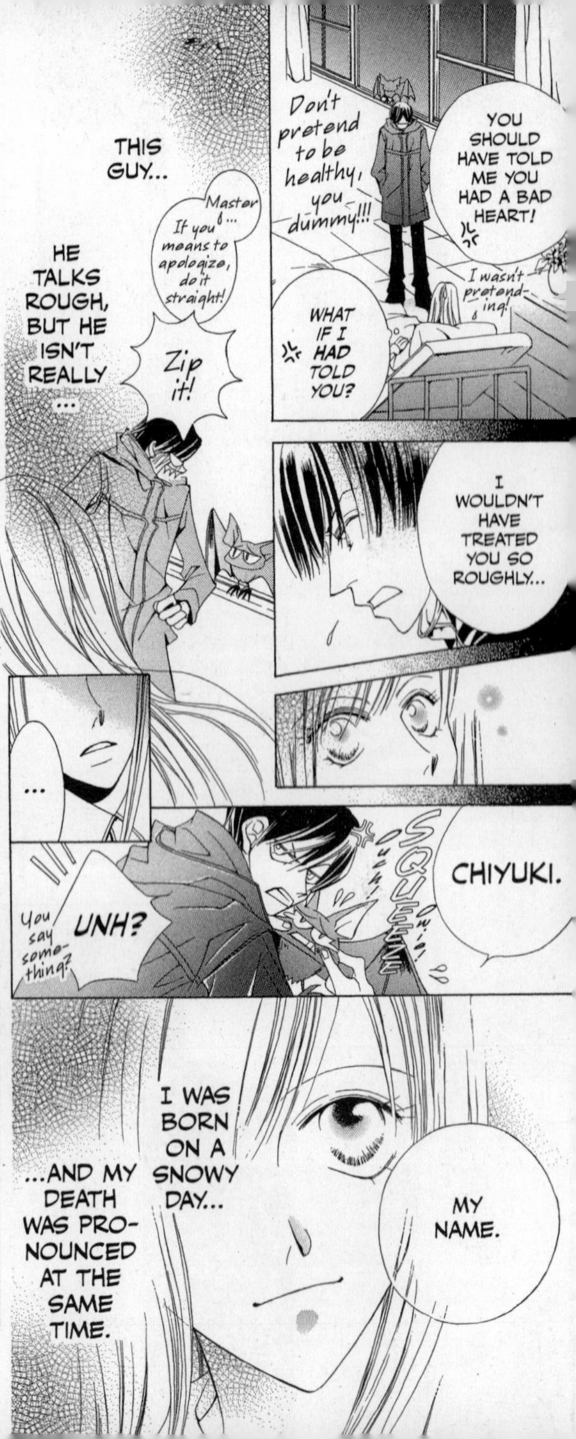
YOU SHOULD HAVE TOLD ME YOU HAD A BAD HEART!
Don't pretend to be healthy, you dummy!!!
I wasn't pretending!
WHAT IF I HAD TOLD YOU?
I WOULDN'T HAVE TREATED YOU SO ROUGHLY...
THIS GUY...
Master... If you means to apologize, do it straight!
Zip it!
HE TALKS ROUGH, BUT HE ISN'T REALLY ...
CHIYUKI.
SQUEEEEZE
Ouch!
Owww!
UNH?
You say something?
...
MY NAME.
I WAS BORN ON A SNOWY DAY...
...AND MY DEATH WAS PRONOUNCED AT THE SAME TIME.

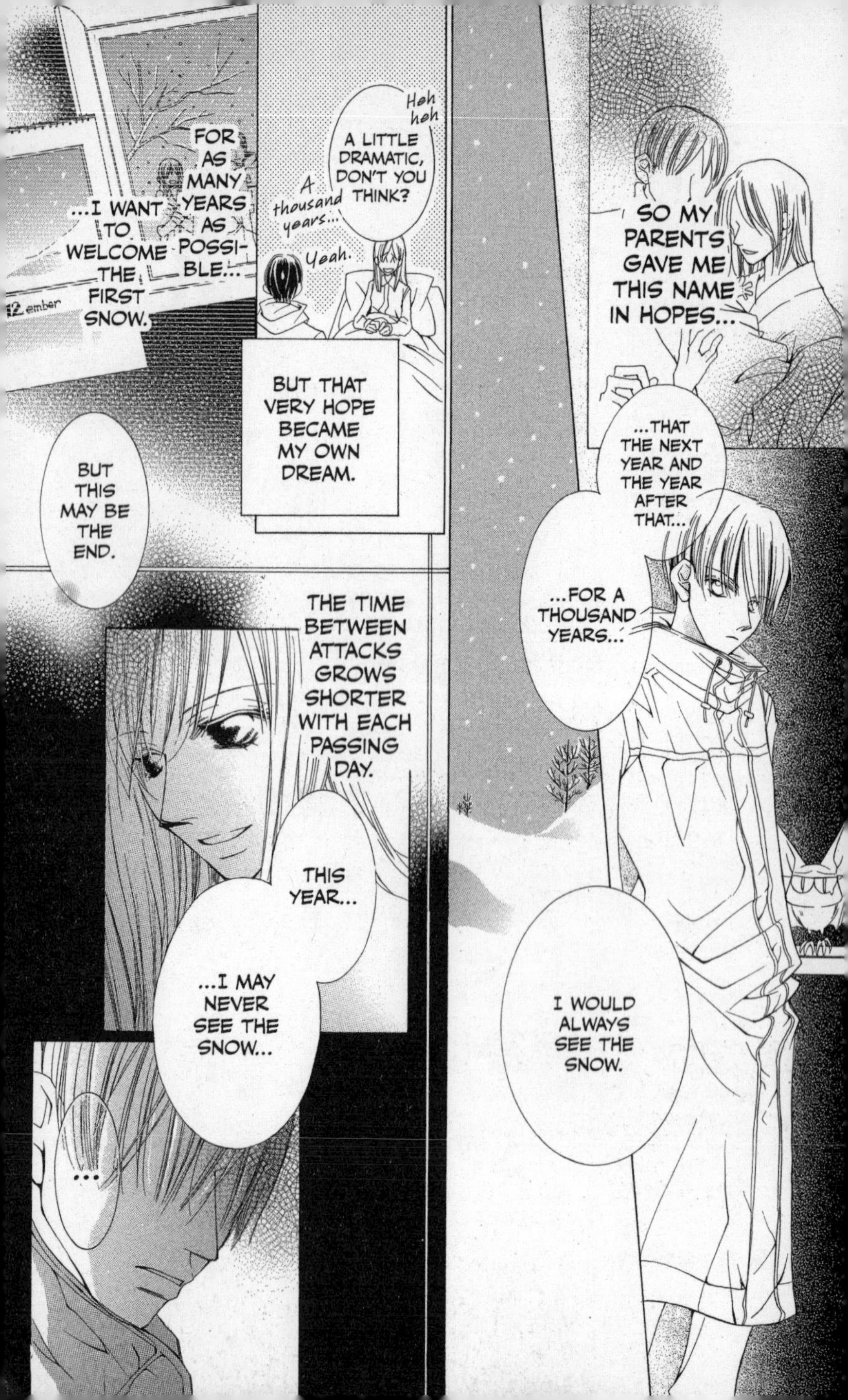
SO MY PARENTS GAVE ME THIS NAME IN HOPES...
...THAT THE NEXT YEAR AND THE YEAR AFTER THAT...
...FOR A THOUSAND YEARS...
I WOULD ALWAYS SEE THE SNOW.
Heh heh
A LITTLE DRAMATIC, DON'T YOU THINK?
A thousand years...
Yeah.
FOR AS MANY YEARS AS POSSI-BLE...
...I WANT TO WELCOME THE FIRST SNOW.
BUT THAT VERY HOPE BECAME MY OWN DREAM.
BUT THIS MAY BE THE END.
THE TIME BETWEEN ATTACKS GROWS SHORTER WITH EACH PASSING DAY.
THIS YEAR...
...I MAY NEVER SEE THE SNOW...
...

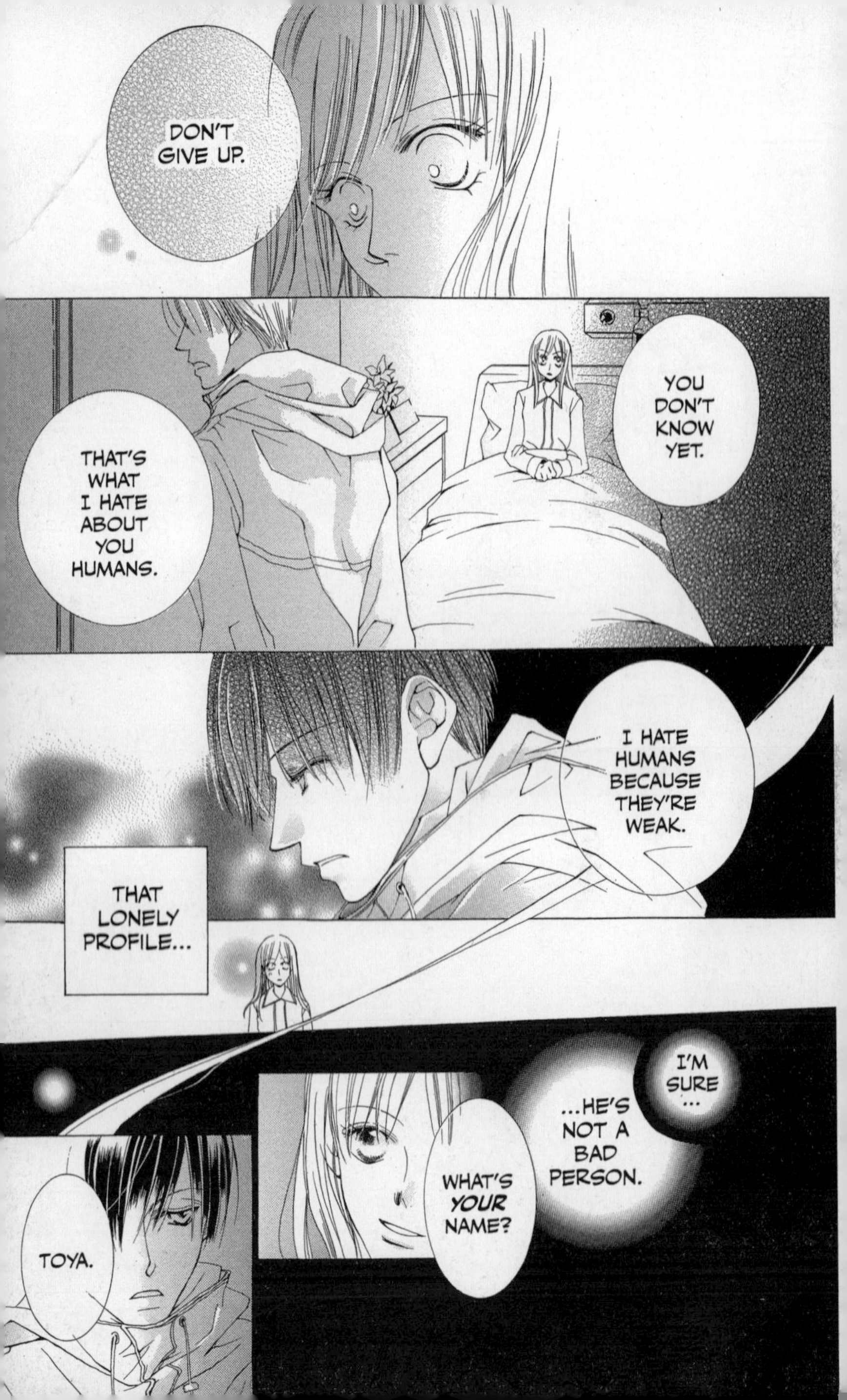
DON'T GIVE UP.
YOU DON'T KNOW YET.
THAT'S WHAT I HATE ABOUT YOU HUMANS.
I HATE HUMANS BECAUSE THEY'RE WEAK.
THAT LONELY PROFILE...
I'M SURE...
...HE'S NOT A BAD PERSON.
WHAT'S *YOUR* NAME?
TOYA.

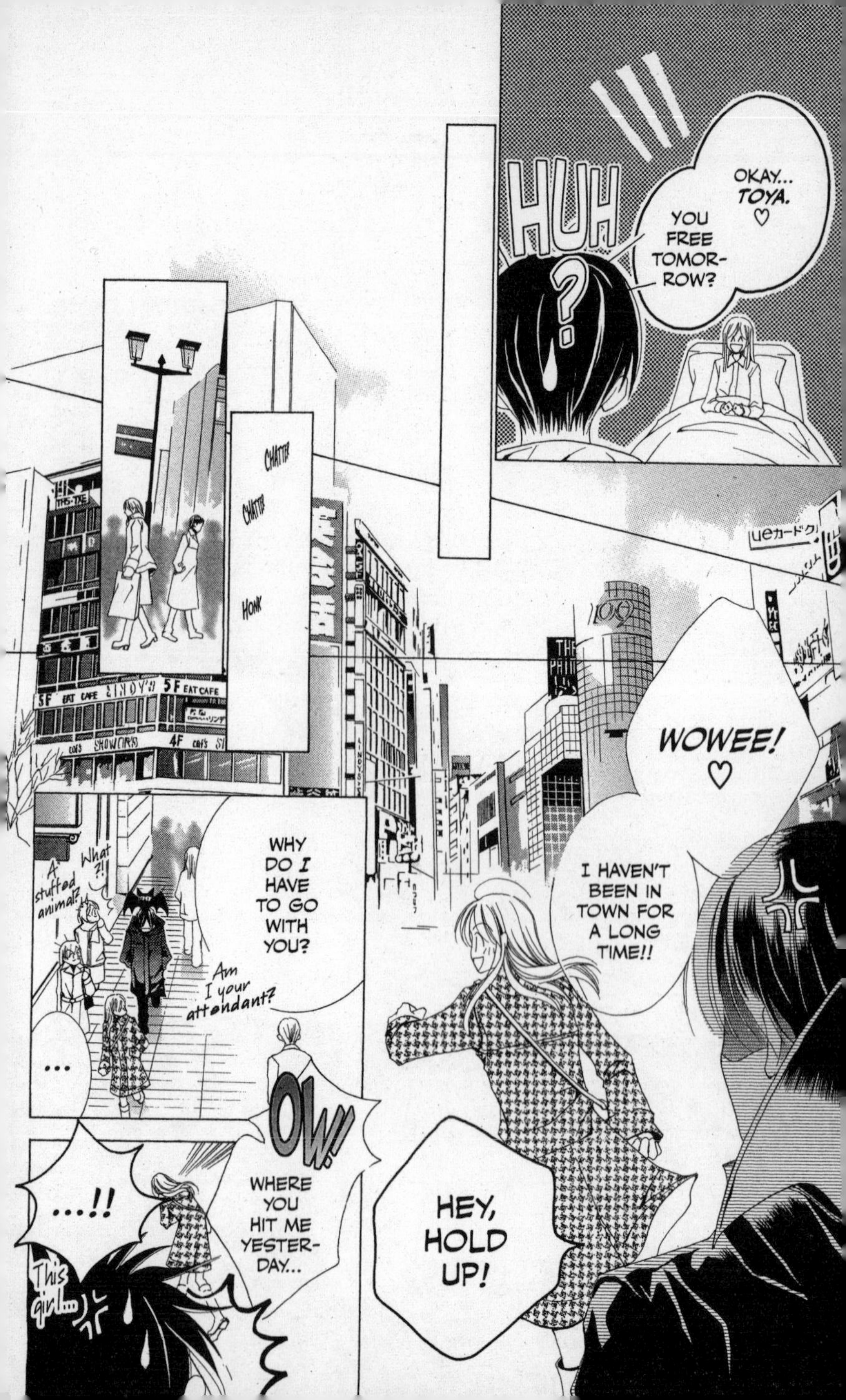
OKAY... TOYA. ♡
YOU FREE TOMORROW?
HUH
?
CHATTER
CHATTER
HONK
WOWEE! ♡
I HAVEN'T BEEN IN TOWN FOR A LONG TIME!!
WHY DO I HAVE TO GO WITH YOU?
Am I your attendant?
What?!
A stuffed animal?
...
HEY, HOLD UP!
OW!
WHERE YOU HIT ME YESTERDAY...
...!!
This girl...

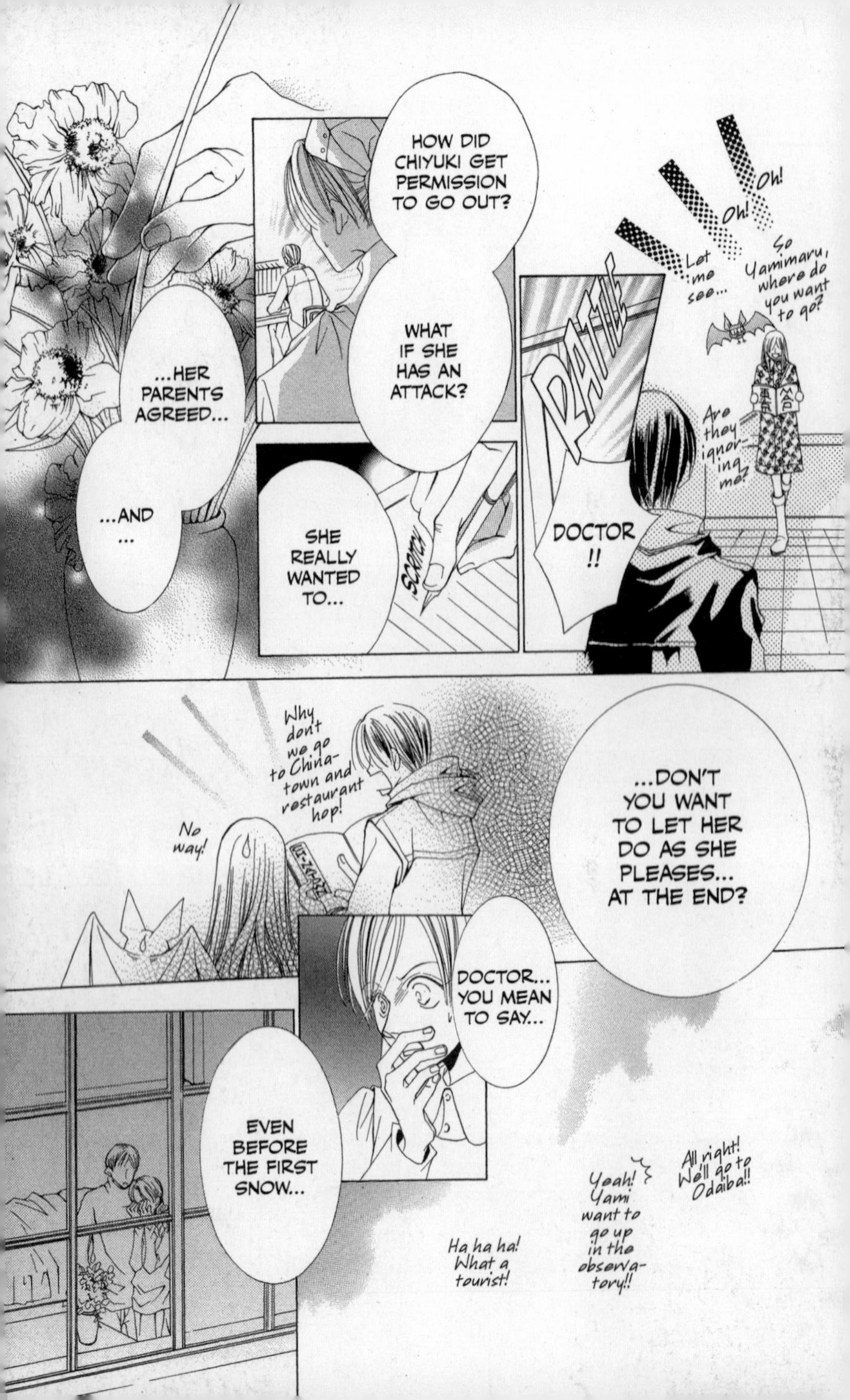
So Yamimaru, where do you want to go?
Let me see...
Oh!
Oh!
Are they ignoring me?
RATTLE
DOCTOR !!
HOW DID CHIYUKI GET PERMISSION TO GO OUT?
WHAT IF SHE HAS AN ATTACK?
SHE REALLY WANTED TO...
SCRITCH
...HER PARENTS AGREED...
...AND ...
...DON'T YOU WANT TO LET HER DO AS SHE PLEASES... AT THE END?
Why don't we go to China-town and restaurant hop!
No way!
DOCTOR... YOU MEAN TO SAY...
EVEN BEFORE THE FIRST SNOW...
All right! We'll go to Odaiba!!
Yeah! Yami want to go up in the observa-tory!!
Ha ha ha! What a tourist!

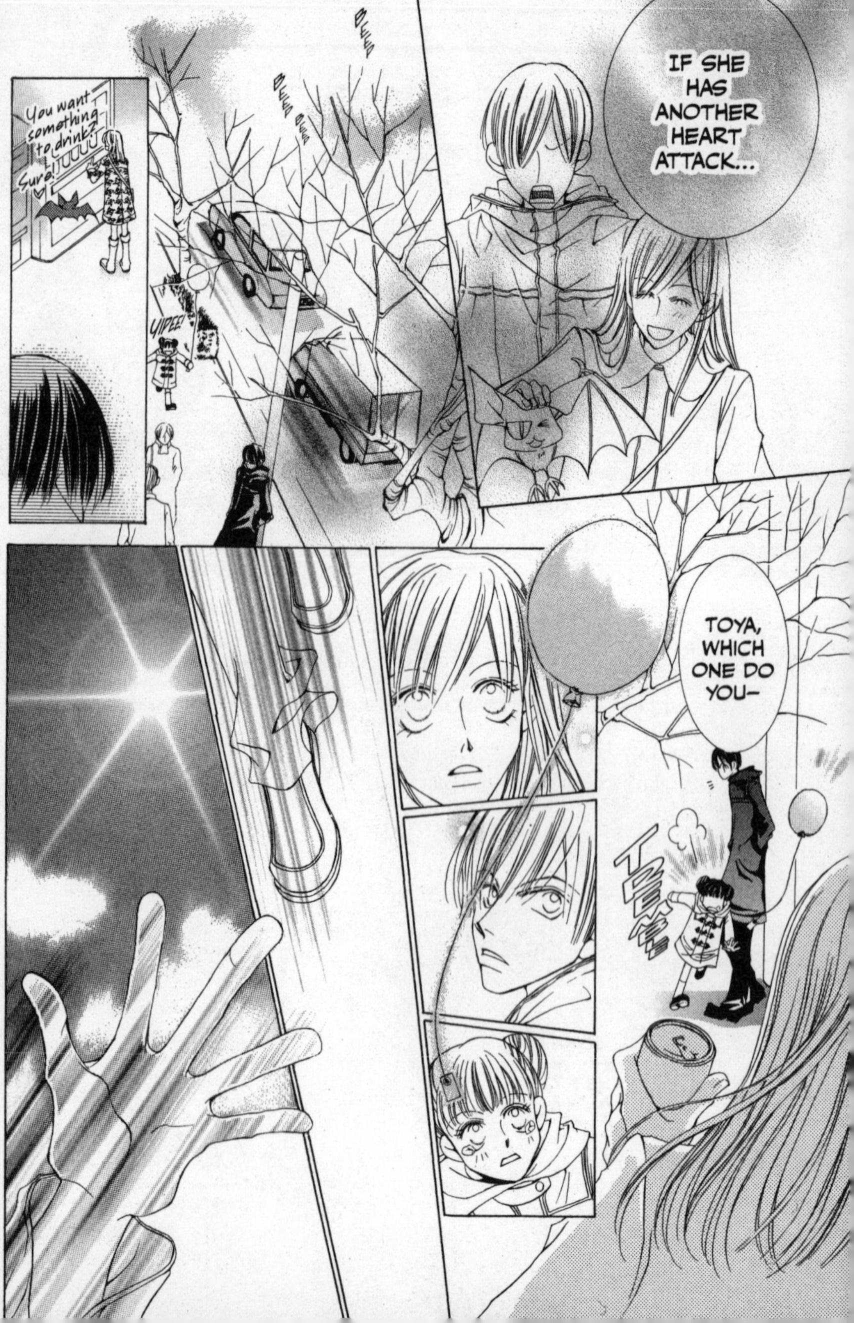
IF SHE HAS ANOTHER HEART ATTACK...
BEEP
BEEP BEEP
You want something to drink?
Sure!
YIPEE!
TOYA, WHICH ONE DO YOU-

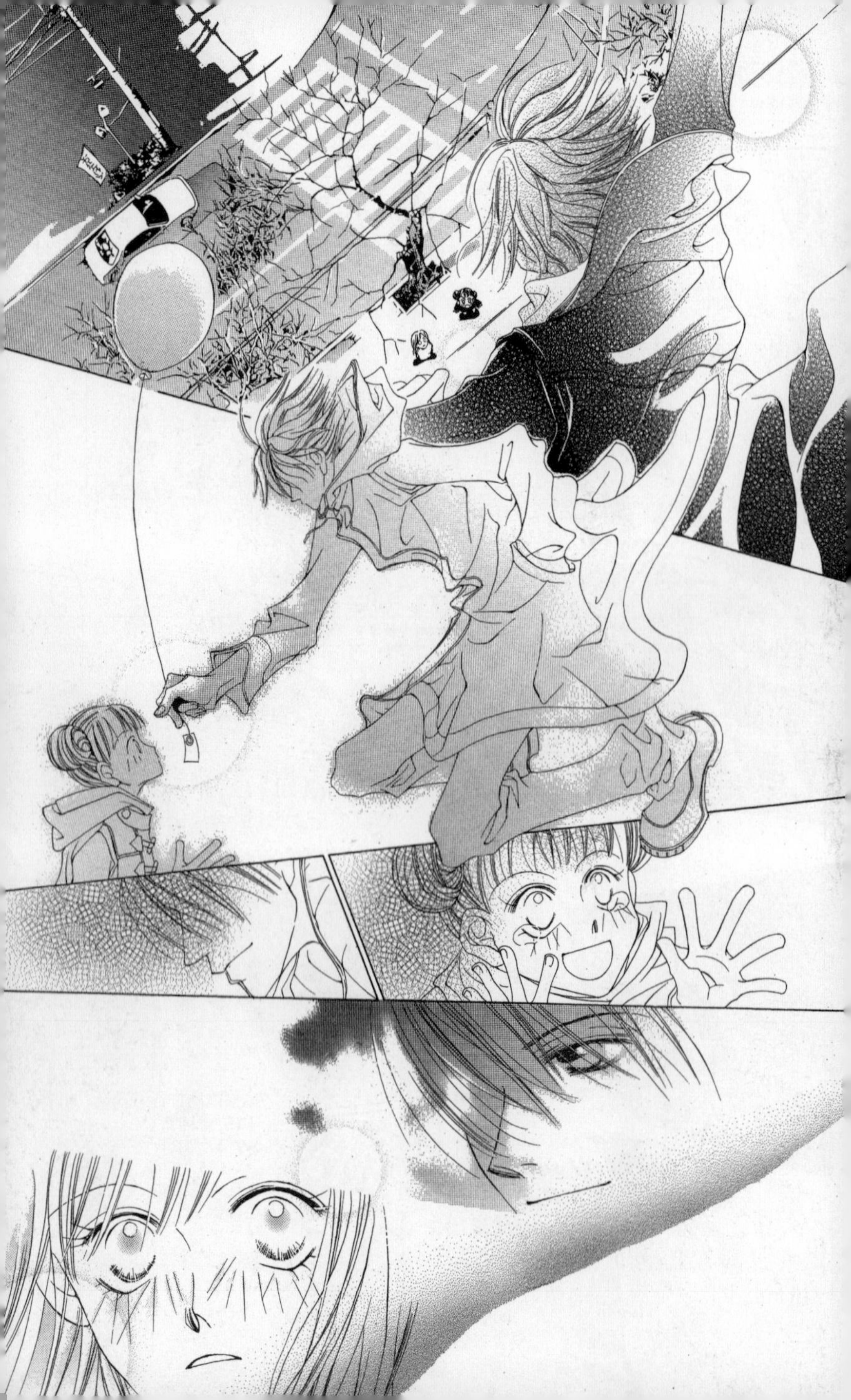

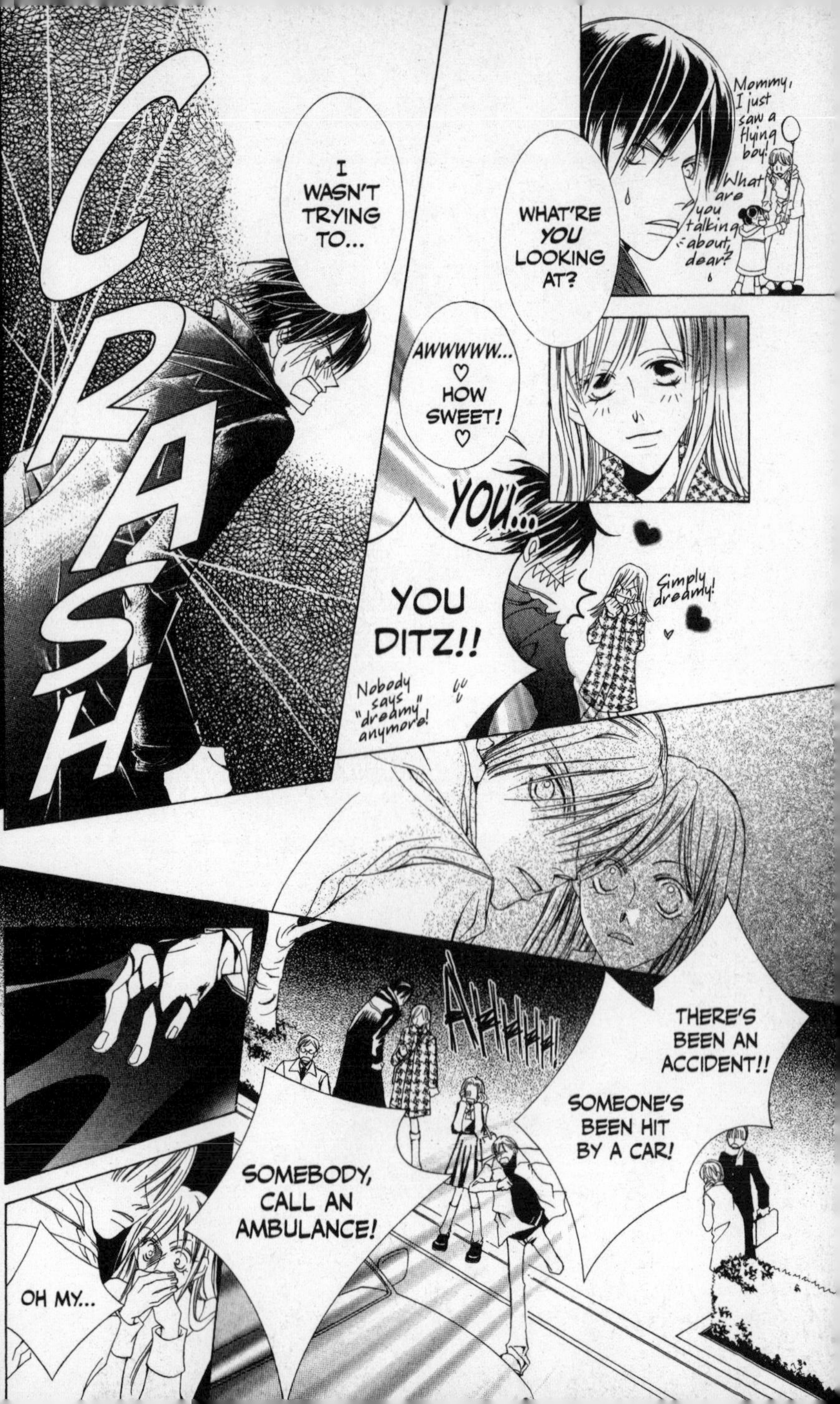
WHAT'RE YOU LOOKING AT?
Mommy, I just saw a flying boy!
What are you talking about, dear?
AWWWWW... ♡ HOW SWEET! ♡
YOU...
YOU DITZ!!
Simply dreamy!
Nobody says "dreamy" anymore!
I WASN'T TRYING TO...
CRASH
AHHHHH
THERE'S BEEN AN ACCIDENT!!
SOMEONE'S BEEN HIT BY A CAR!
SOMEBODY, CALL AN AMBULANCE!
OH MY...

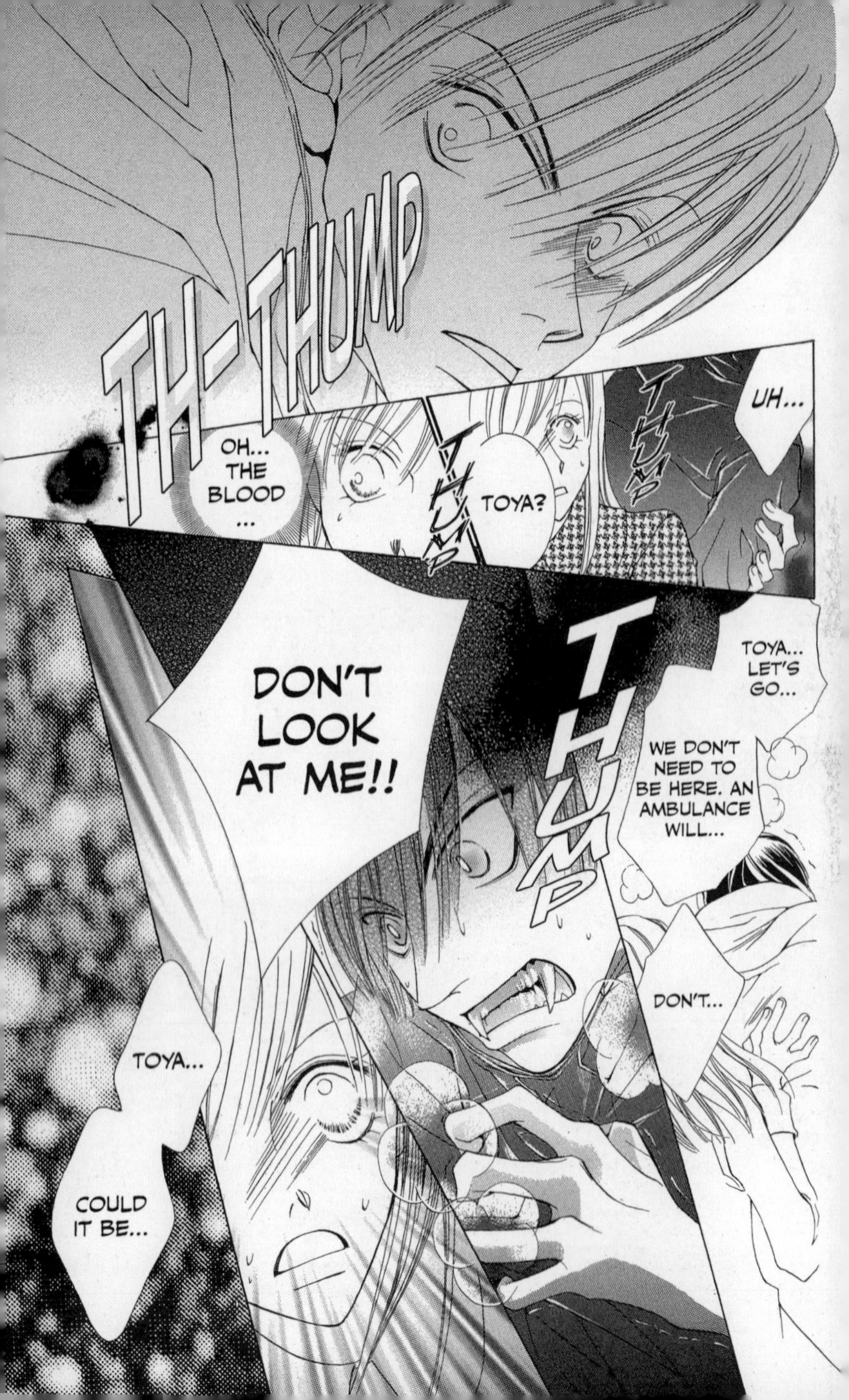
TH-THUMP
THUMP
UH...
TOYA?
THUMP
OH... THE BLOOD ...
THUMP
TOYA... LET'S GO...
WE DON'T NEED TO BE HERE. AN AMBULANCE WILL...
DON'T LOOK AT ME!!
DON'T...
TOYA...
COULD IT BE...

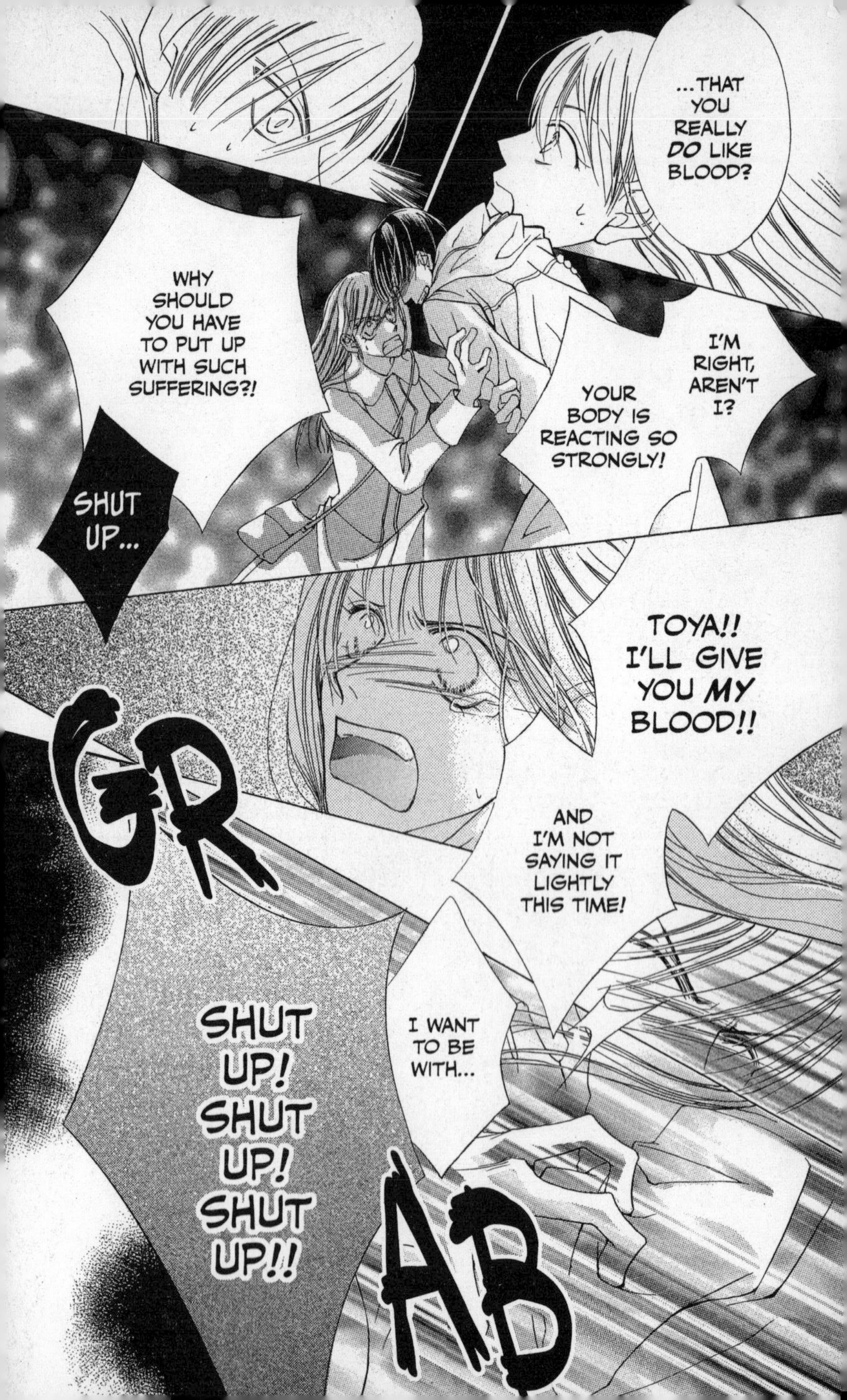
...THAT YOU REALLY DO LIKE BLOOD?
I'M RIGHT, AREN'T I?
YOUR BODY IS REACTING SO STRONGLY!
WHY SHOULD YOU HAVE TO PUT UP WITH SUCH SUFFERING?!
SHUT UP...
TOYA!! I'LL GIVE YOU MY BLOOD!!
AND I'M NOT SAYING IT LIGHTLY THIS TIME!
GR
I WANT TO BE WITH...
SHUT UP! SHUT UP! SHUT UP!!
AB

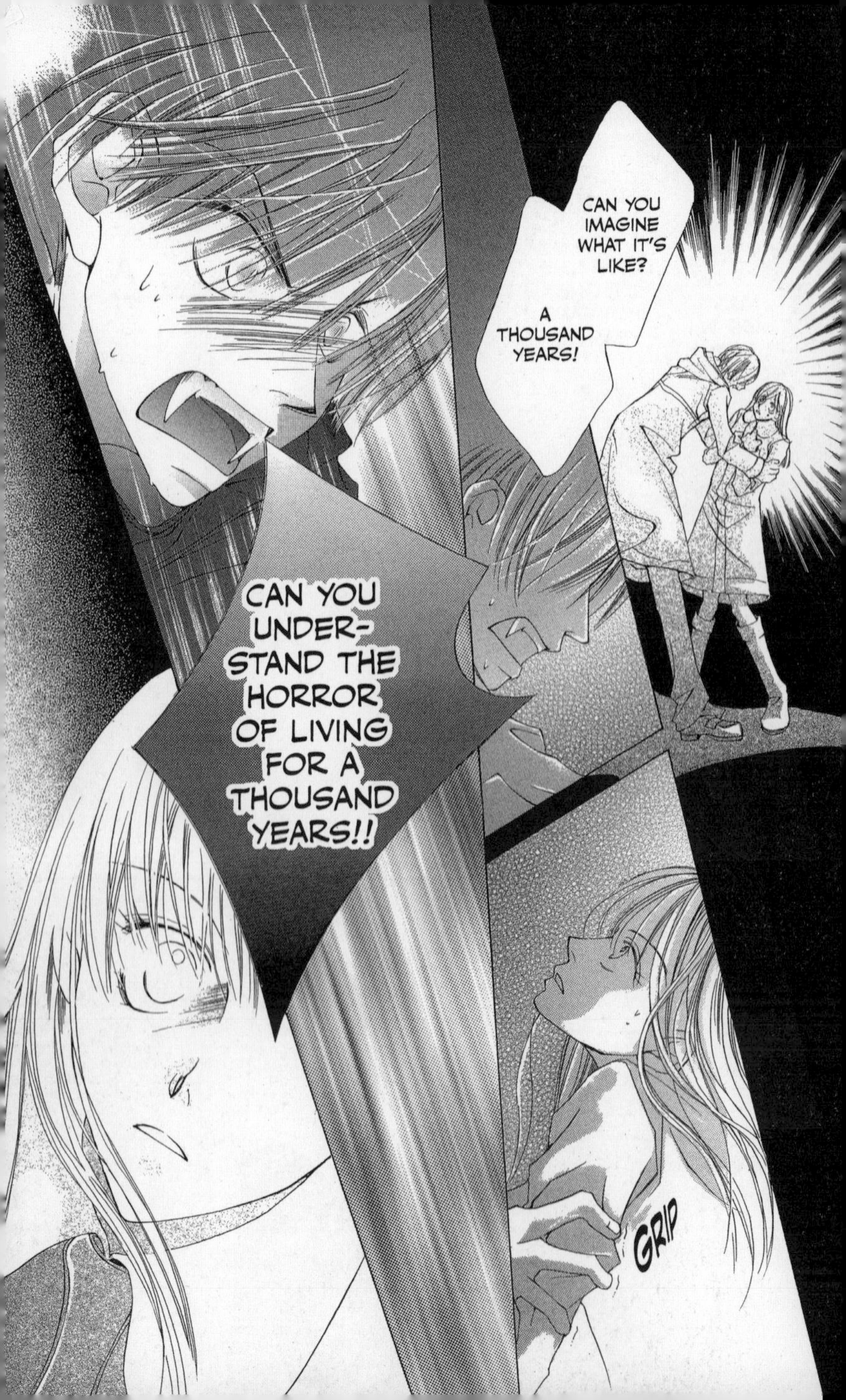
CAN YOU IMAGINE WHAT IT'S LIKE?
A THOUSAND YEARS!
CAN YOU UNDER-STAND THE HORROR OF LIVING FOR A THOUSAND YEARS!!
GRIP

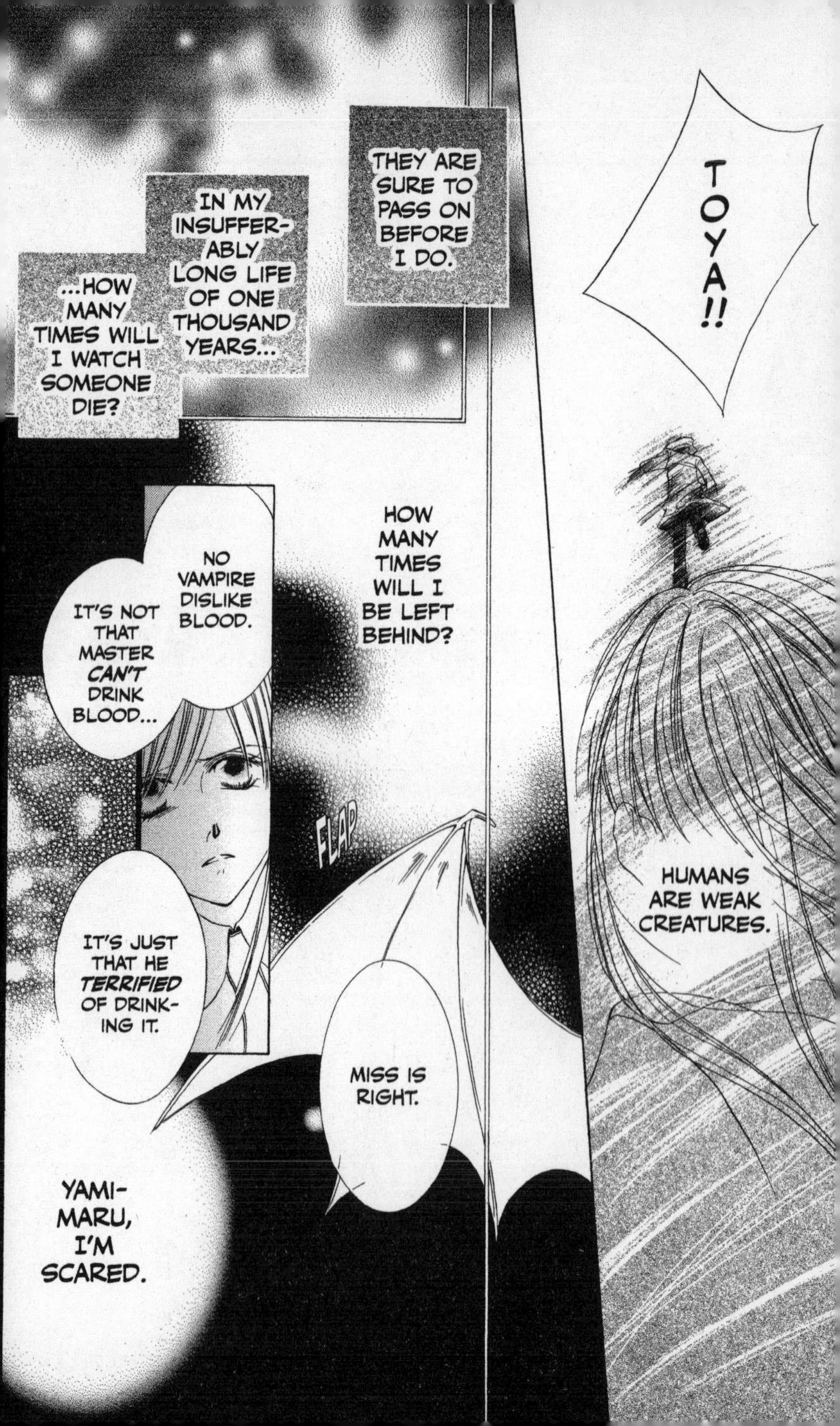
TOYA!!
HUMANS ARE WEAK CREATURES.
THEY ARE SURE TO PASS ON BEFORE I DO.
IN MY INSUFFER-ABLY LONG LIFE OF ONE THOUSAND YEARS...
...HOW MANY TIMES WILL I WATCH SOMEONE DIE?
HOW MANY TIMES WILL I BE LEFT BEHIND?
NO VAMPIRE DISLIKE BLOOD.
IT'S NOT THAT MASTER *CAN'T* DRINK BLOOD...
IT'S JUST THAT HE *TERRIFIED* OF DRINK-ING IT.
FLAP
MISS IS RIGHT.
YAMI-MARU, I'M SCARED.

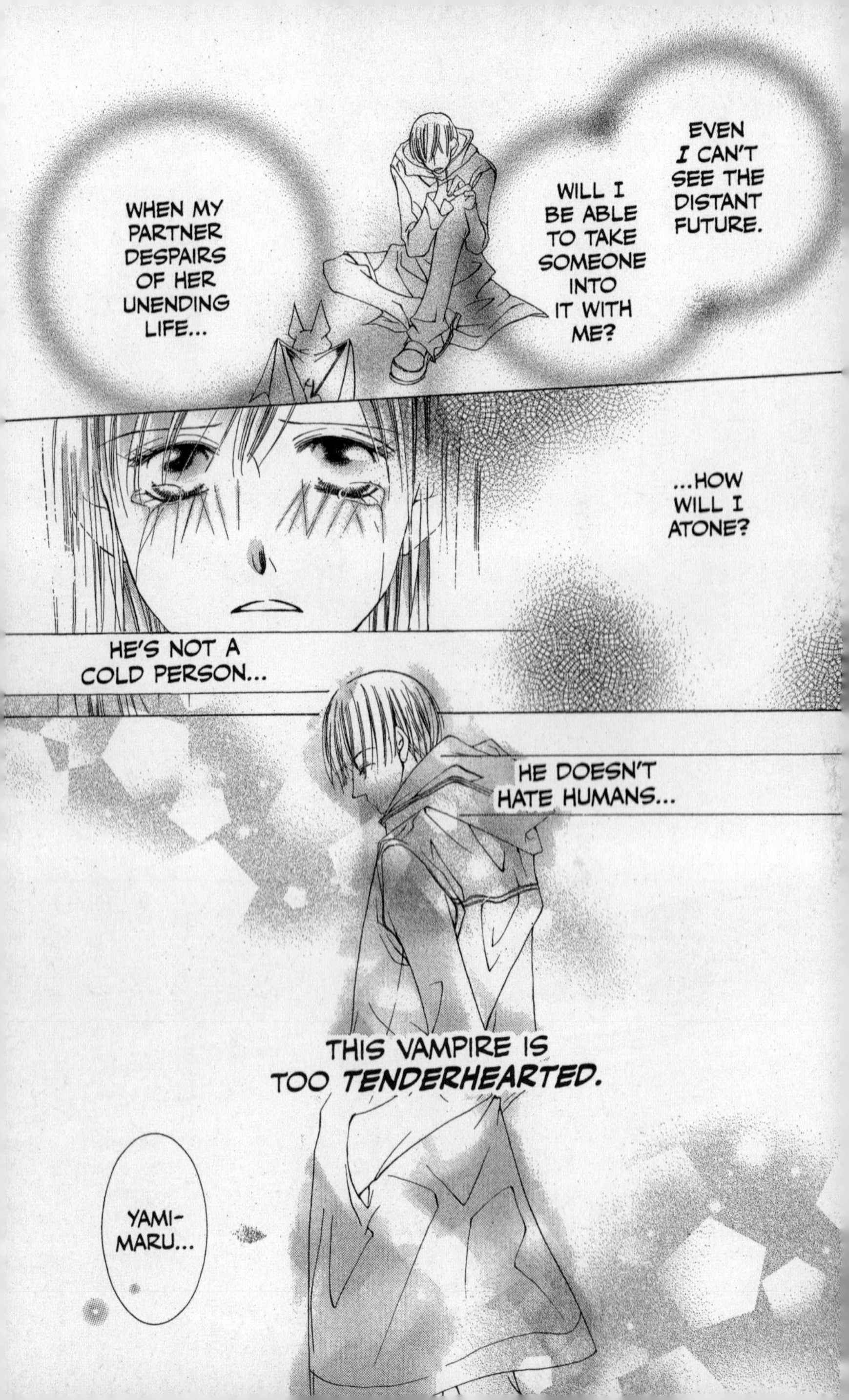
EVEN I CAN'T SEE THE DISTANT FUTURE.
WILL I BE ABLE TO TAKE SOMEONE INTO IT WITH ME?
WHEN MY PARTNER DESPAIRS OF HER UNENDING LIFE...
...HOW WILL I ATONE?
HE'S NOT A COLD PERSON...
HE DOESN'T HATE HUMANS...
THIS VAMPIRE IS TOO TENDERHEARTED.
YAMI-MARU...

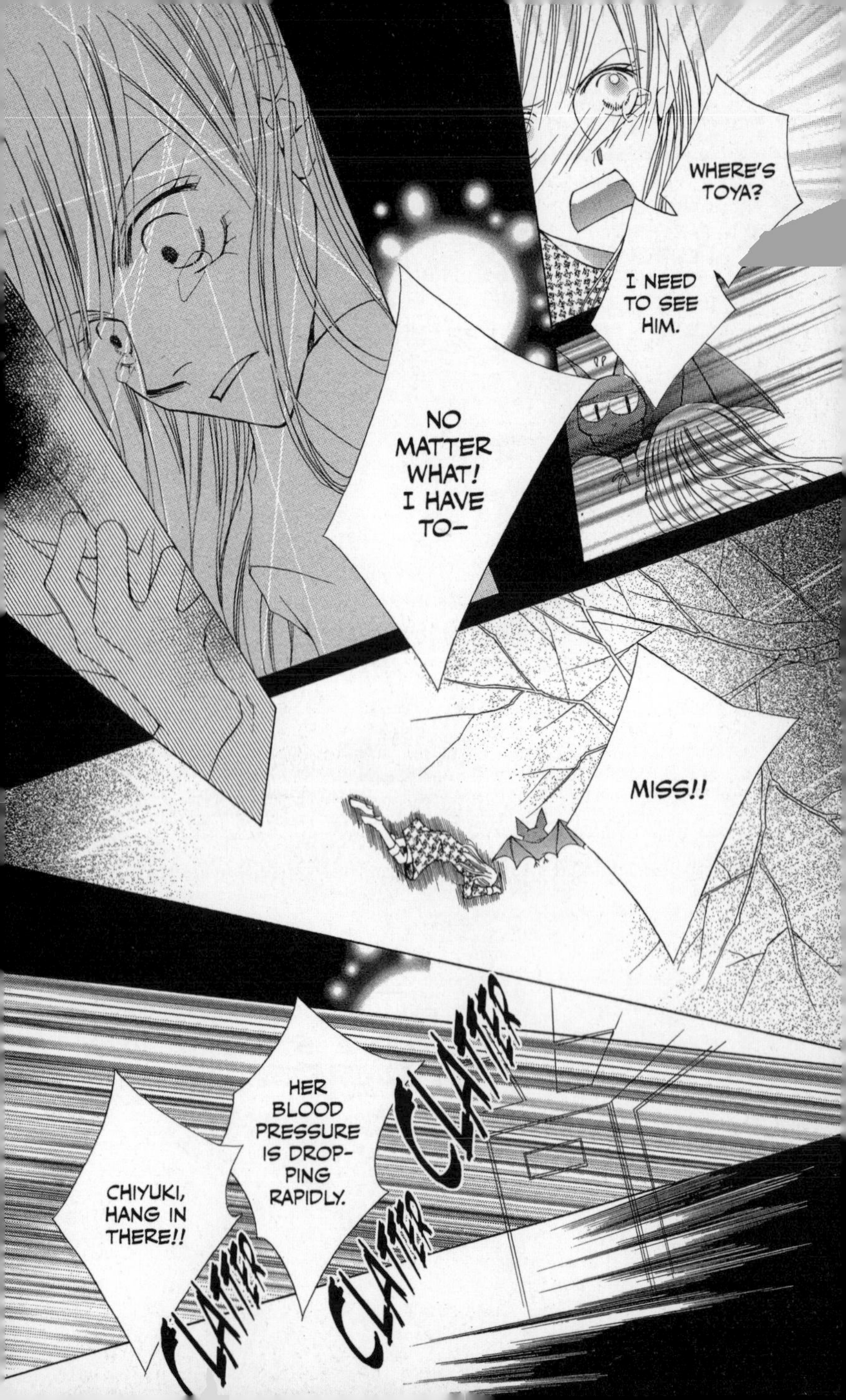
WHERE'S TOYA?
I NEED TO SEE HIM.
NO MATTER WHAT! I HAVE TO-
MISS!!
CLATTER CLATTER
HER BLOOD PRESSURE IS DROP-PING RAPIDLY.
CHIYUKI, HANG IN THERE!!
CLATTER

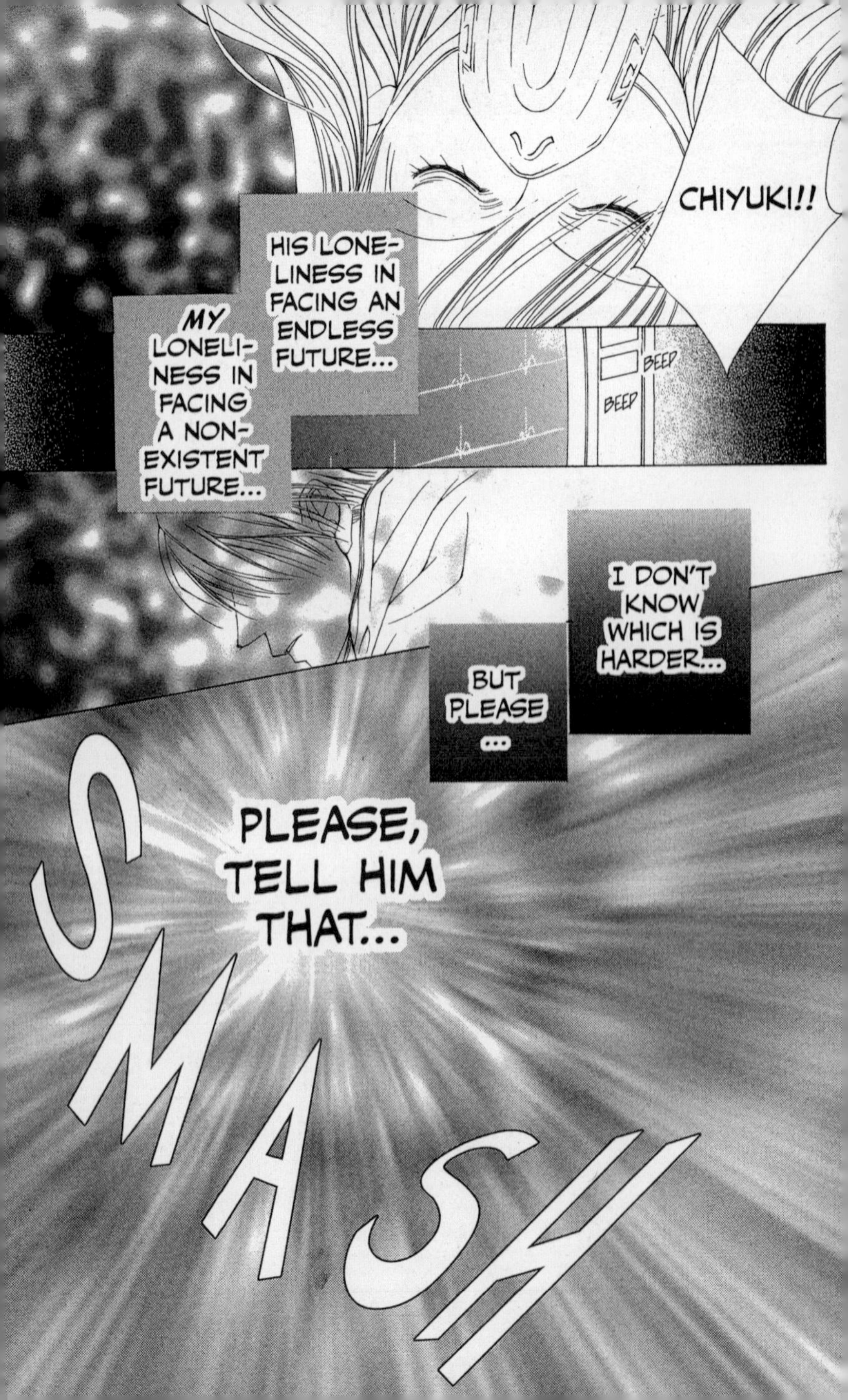
CHIYUKI!!
HIS LONELINESS IN FACING AN ENDLESS FUTURE...
MY LONELINESS IN FACING A NON-EXISTENT FUTURE...
BEEP
BEEP
I DON'T KNOW WHICH IS HARDER...
BUT PLEASE...
PLEASE, TELL HIM THAT...
SMASH

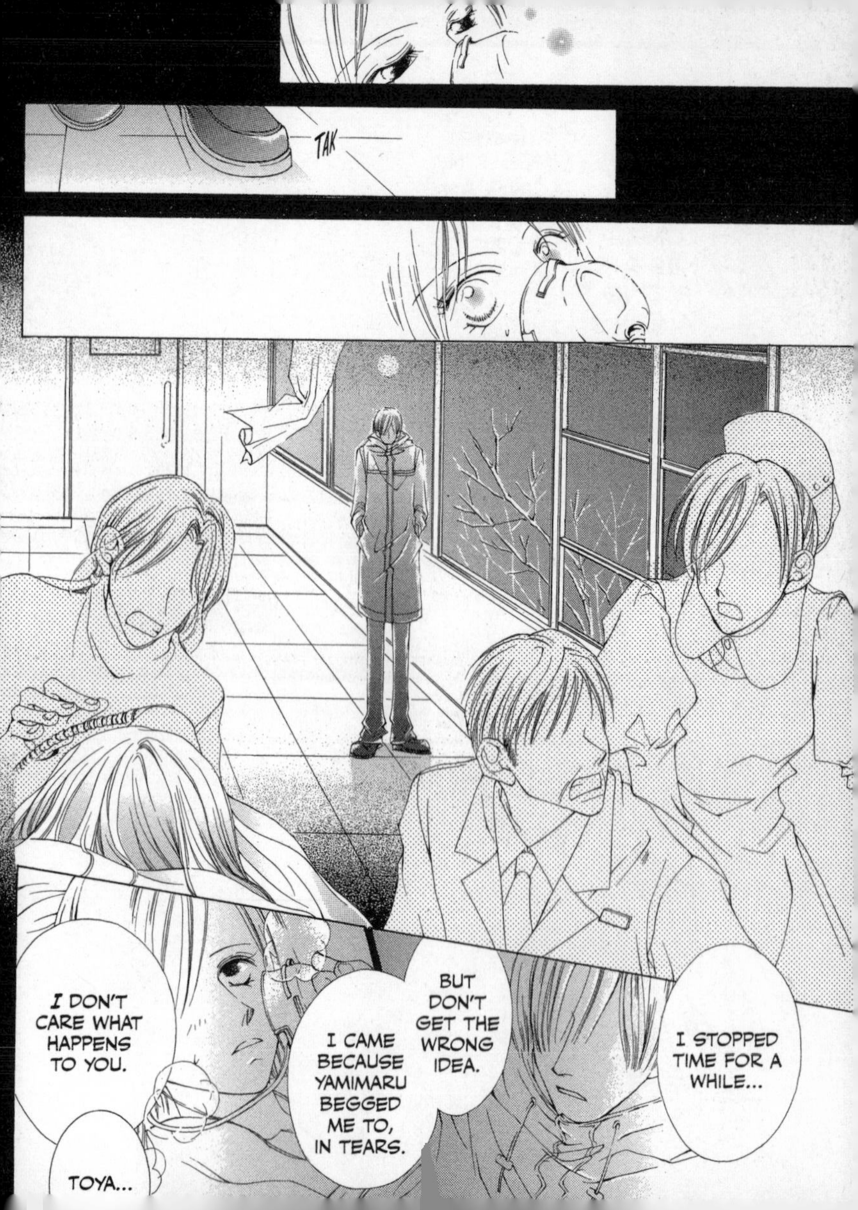
TAK
I STOPPED TIME FOR A WHILE...
BUT DON'T GET THE WRONG IDEA.
I CAME BECAUSE YAMIMARU BEGGED ME TO, IN TEARS.
I DON'T CARE WHAT HAPPENS TO YOU.
TOYA...

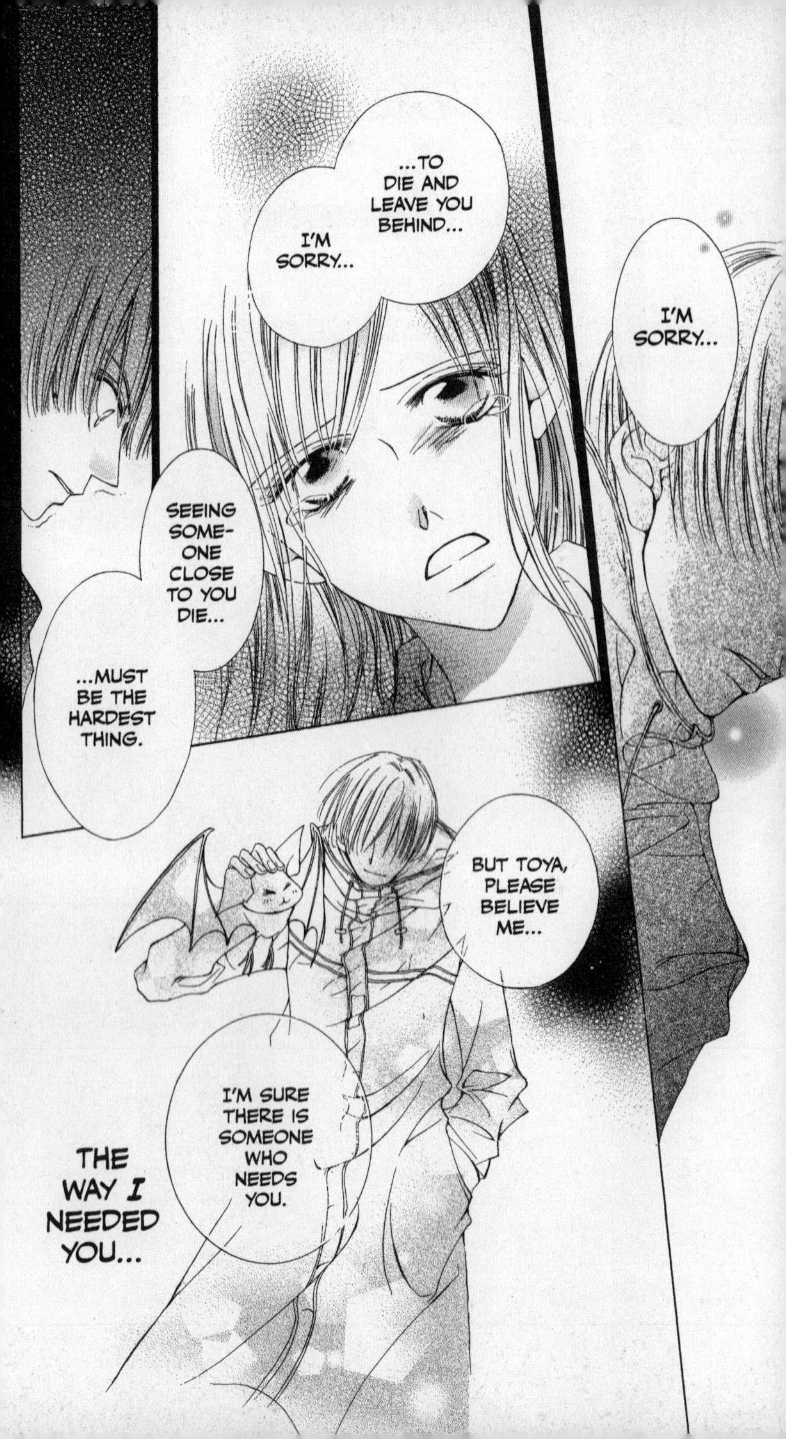
I'M SORRY...
I'M SORRY...
...TO DIE AND LEAVE YOU BEHIND...
SEEING SOME-ONE CLOSE TO YOU DIE...
...MUST BE THE HARDEST THING.
BUT TOYA, PLEASE BELIEVE ME...
I'M SURE THERE IS SOMEONE WHO NEEDS YOU.
THE WAY *I* NEEDED YOU...

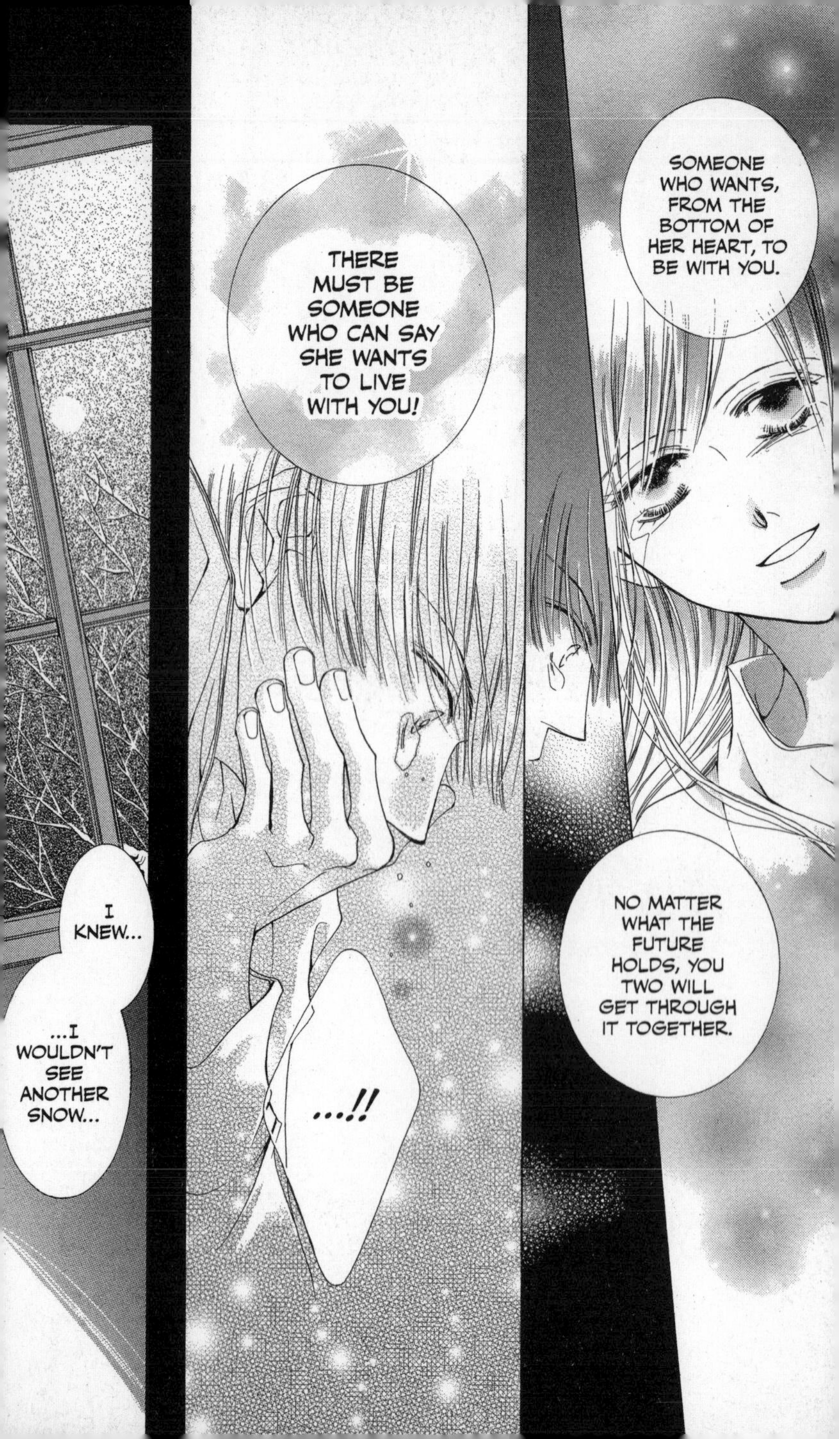
SOMEONE WHO WANTS, FROM THE BOTTOM OF HER HEART, TO BE WITH YOU.
NO MATTER WHAT THE FUTURE HOLDS, YOU TWO WILL GET THROUGH IT TOGETHER.
THERE MUST BE SOMEONE WHO CAN SAY SHE WANTS TO LIVE WITH YOU!
...!!
I KNEW...
...I WOULDN'T SEE ANOTHER SNOW...

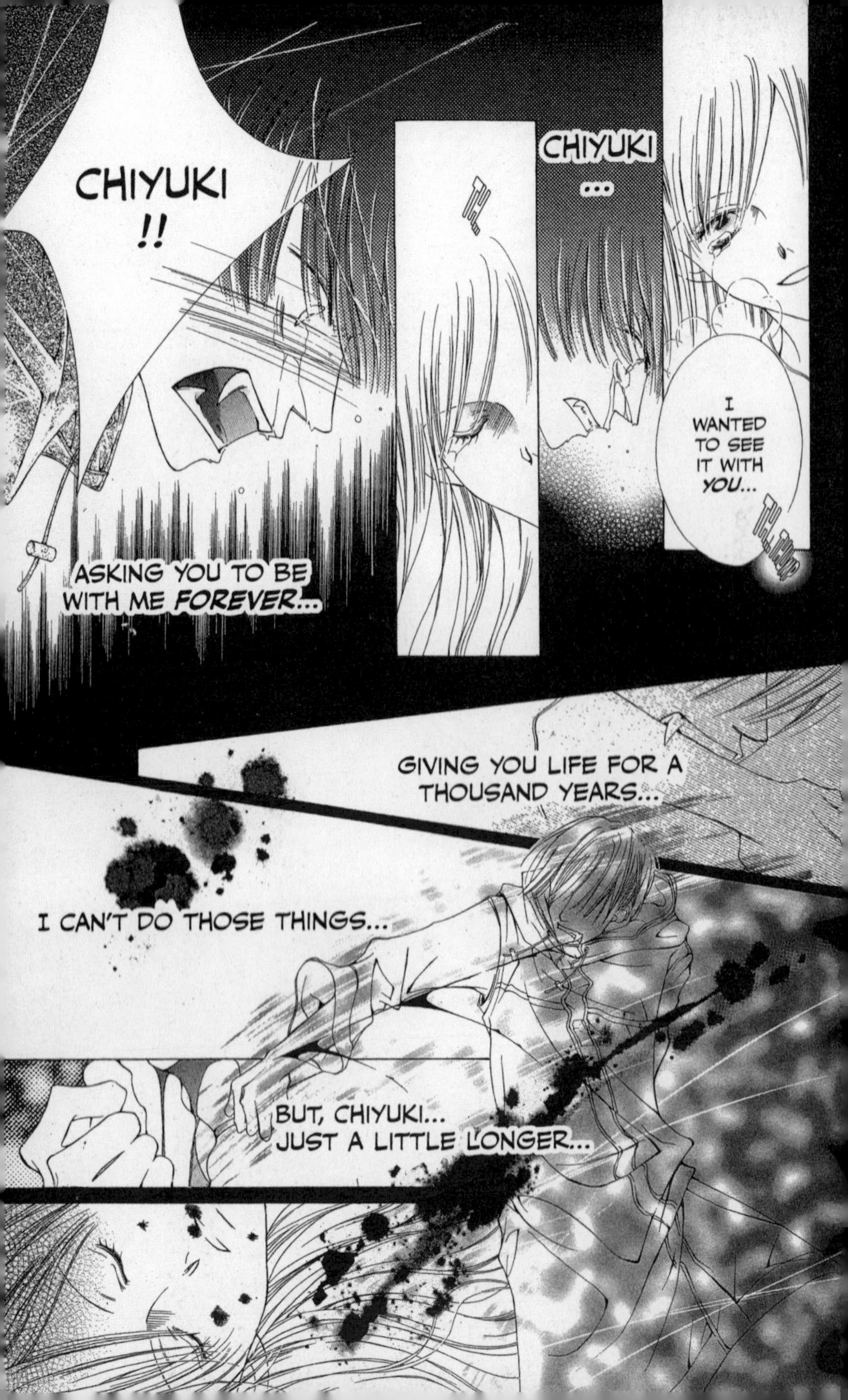
I WANTED TO SEE IT WITH YOU...
CHIYUKI...
CHIYUKI!!
ASKING YOU TO BE WITH ME FOREVER...
GIVING YOU LIFE FOR A THOUSAND YEARS...
I CAN'T DO THOSE THINGS...
BUT, CHIYUKI... JUST A LITTLE LONGER...

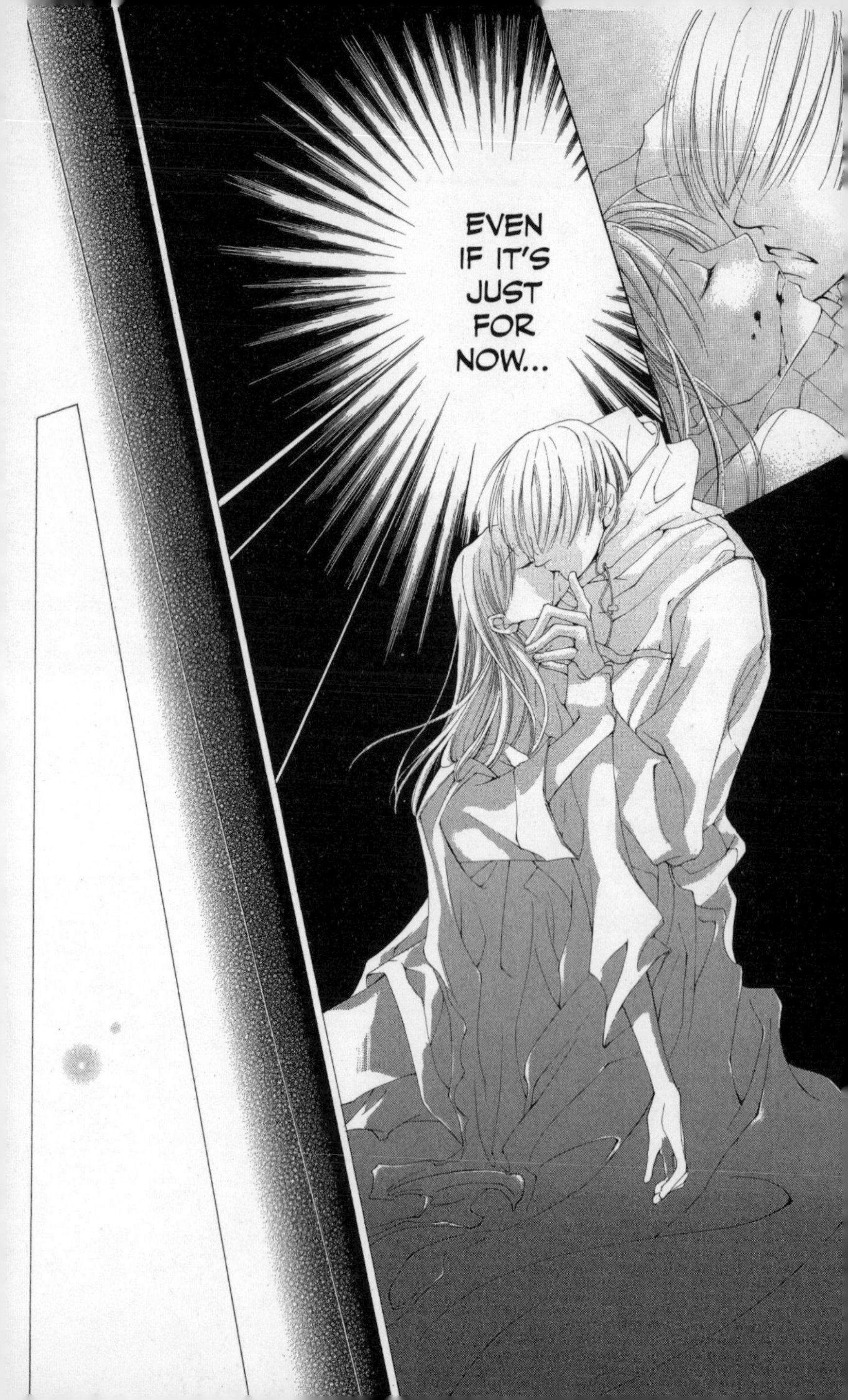
EVEN IF IT'S JUST FOR NOW...

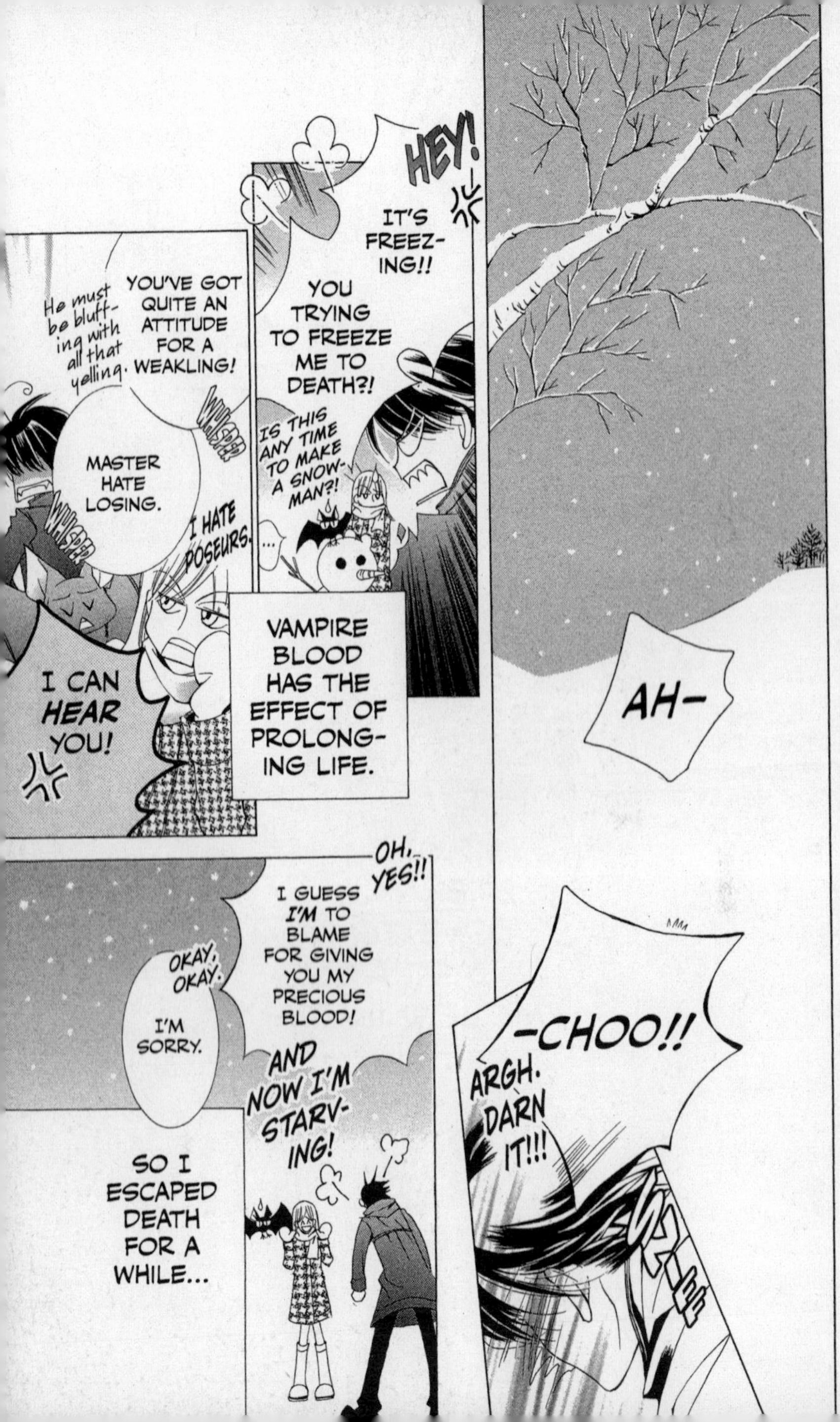
AH-
-CHOO!!
ARGH. DARN IT!!!
HEY!
IT'S FREEZ-ING!!
YOU TRYING TO FREEZE ME TO DEATH?!
IS THIS ANY TIME TO MAKE A SNOW-MAN?!
...
YOU'VE GOT QUITE AN ATTITUDE FOR A WEAKLING!
He must be bluff-ing with all that yelling.
WHISPER
MASTER HATE LOSING.
WHISPER
I HATE POSEURS.
I CAN HEAR YOU!
VAMPIRE BLOOD HAS THE EFFECT OF PROLONG-ING LIFE.
OH, YES!!
I GUESS I'M TO BLAME FOR GIVING YOU MY PRECIOUS BLOOD!
OKAY, OKAY.
I'M SORRY.
AND NOW I'M STARV-ING!
SO I ESCAPED DEATH FOR A WHILE...

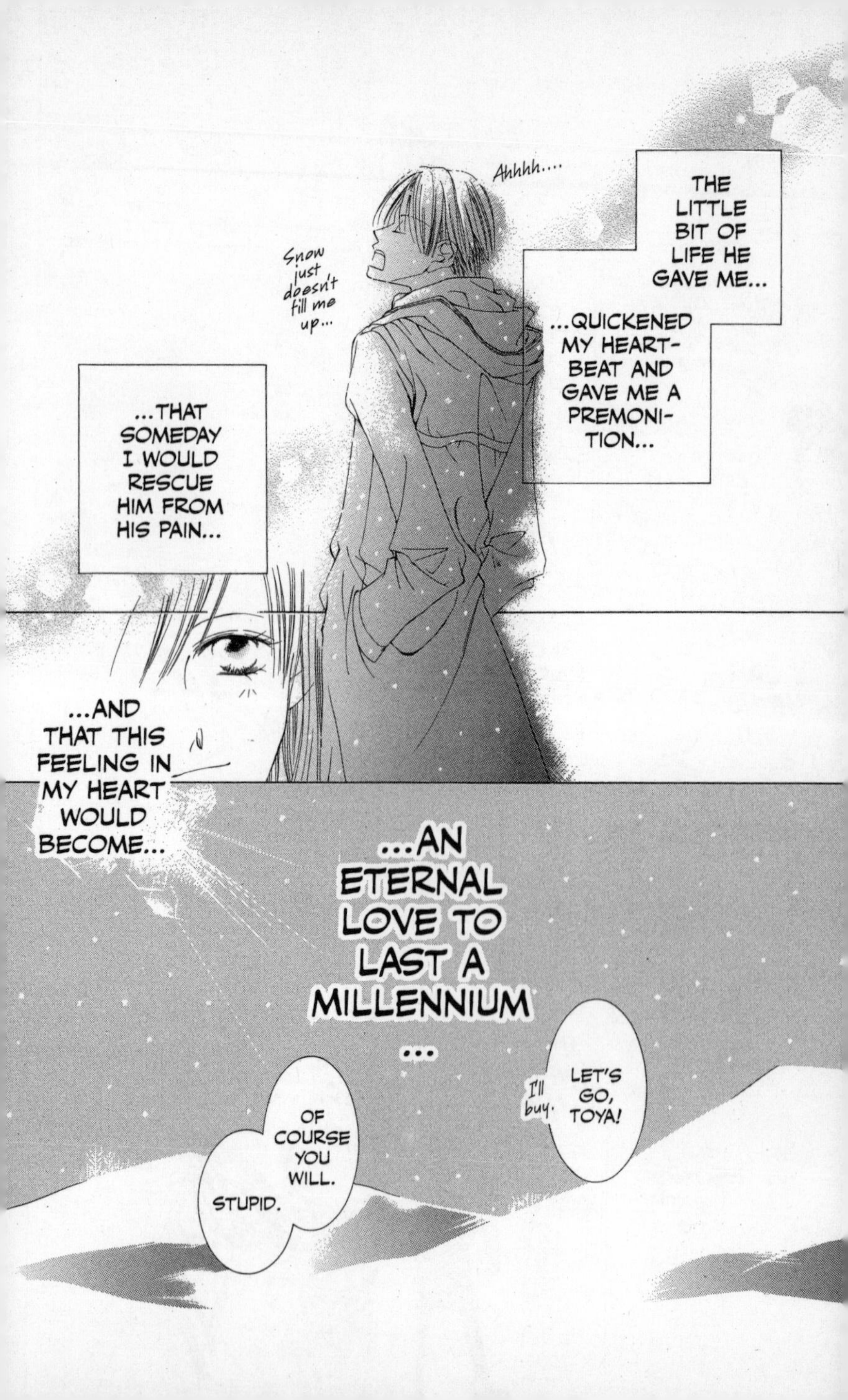
THE LITTLE BIT OF LIFE HE GAVE ME...
...QUICKENED MY HEART-BEAT AND GAVE ME A PREMONITION...
Ahhhh....
Snow just doesn't fill me up...
...THAT SOMEDAY I WOULD RESCUE HIM FROM HIS PAIN...
...AND THAT THIS FEELING IN MY HEART WOULD BECOME...
...AN ETERNAL LOVE TO LAST A MILLENNIUM ...
LET'S GO, TOYA!
I'll buy.
OF COURSE YOU WILL.
STUPID.

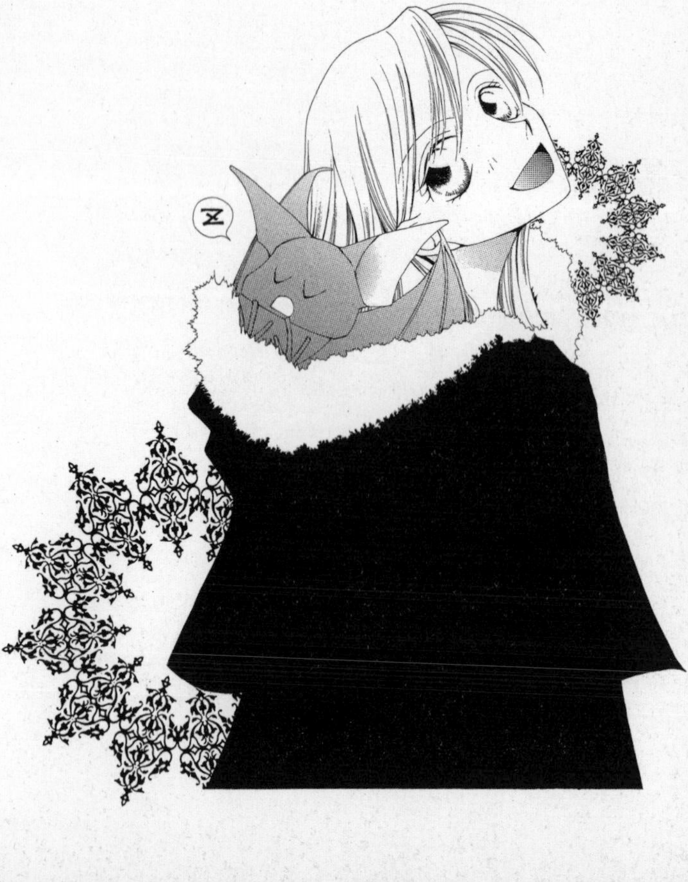
Z

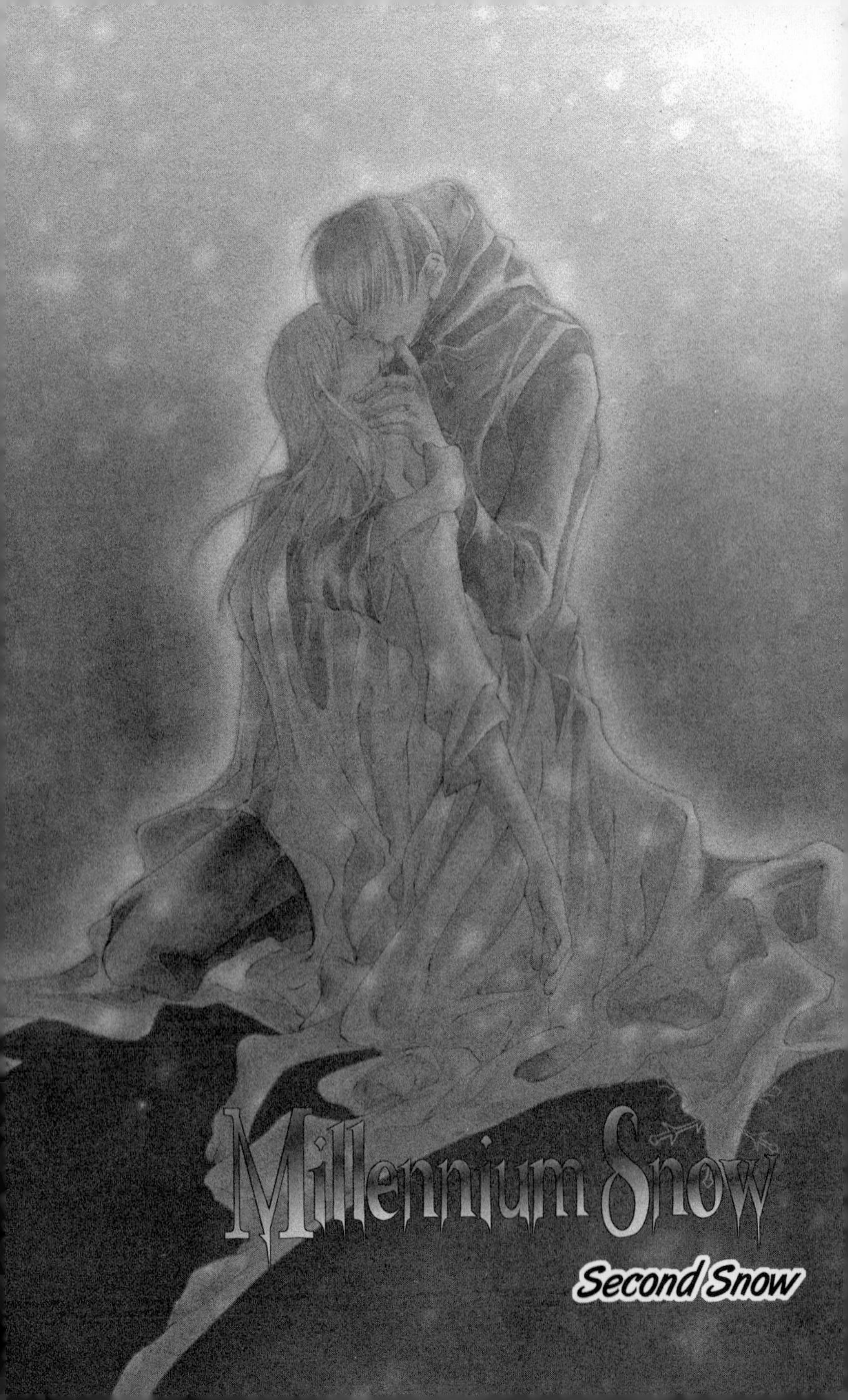
Millennium Snow
Second Snow

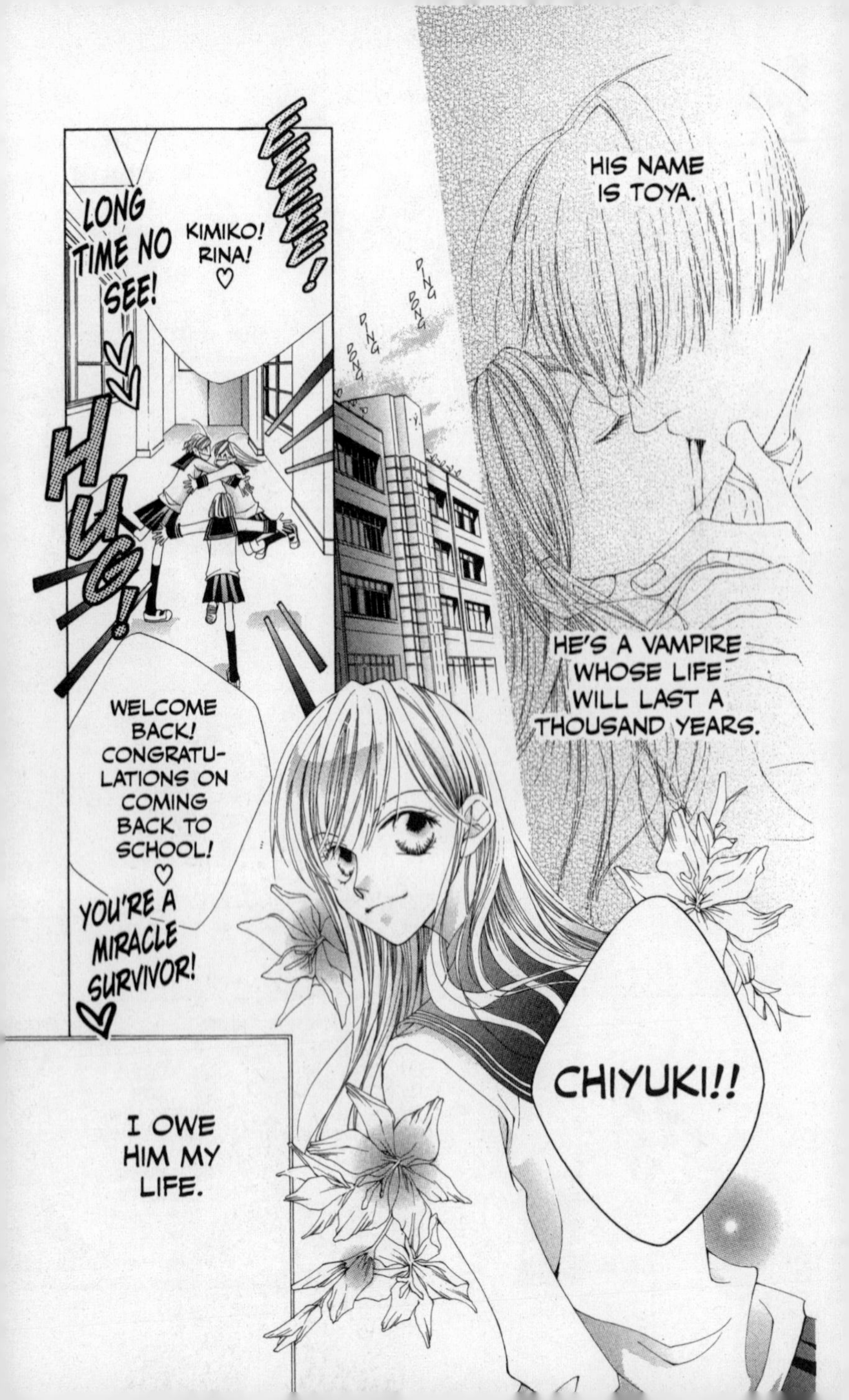
HIS NAME IS TOYA.
HE'S A VAMPIRE WHOSE LIFE WILL LAST A THOUSAND YEARS.
DING DONG DING DONG
KIMIKO! RINA! ♡
LONG TIME NO SEE!
HUG!
WELCOME BACK! CONGRATU-LATIONS ON COMING BACK TO SCHOOL! ♡
YOU'RE A MIRACLE SURVIVOR! ♡
CHIYUKI!!
I OWE HIM MY LIFE.

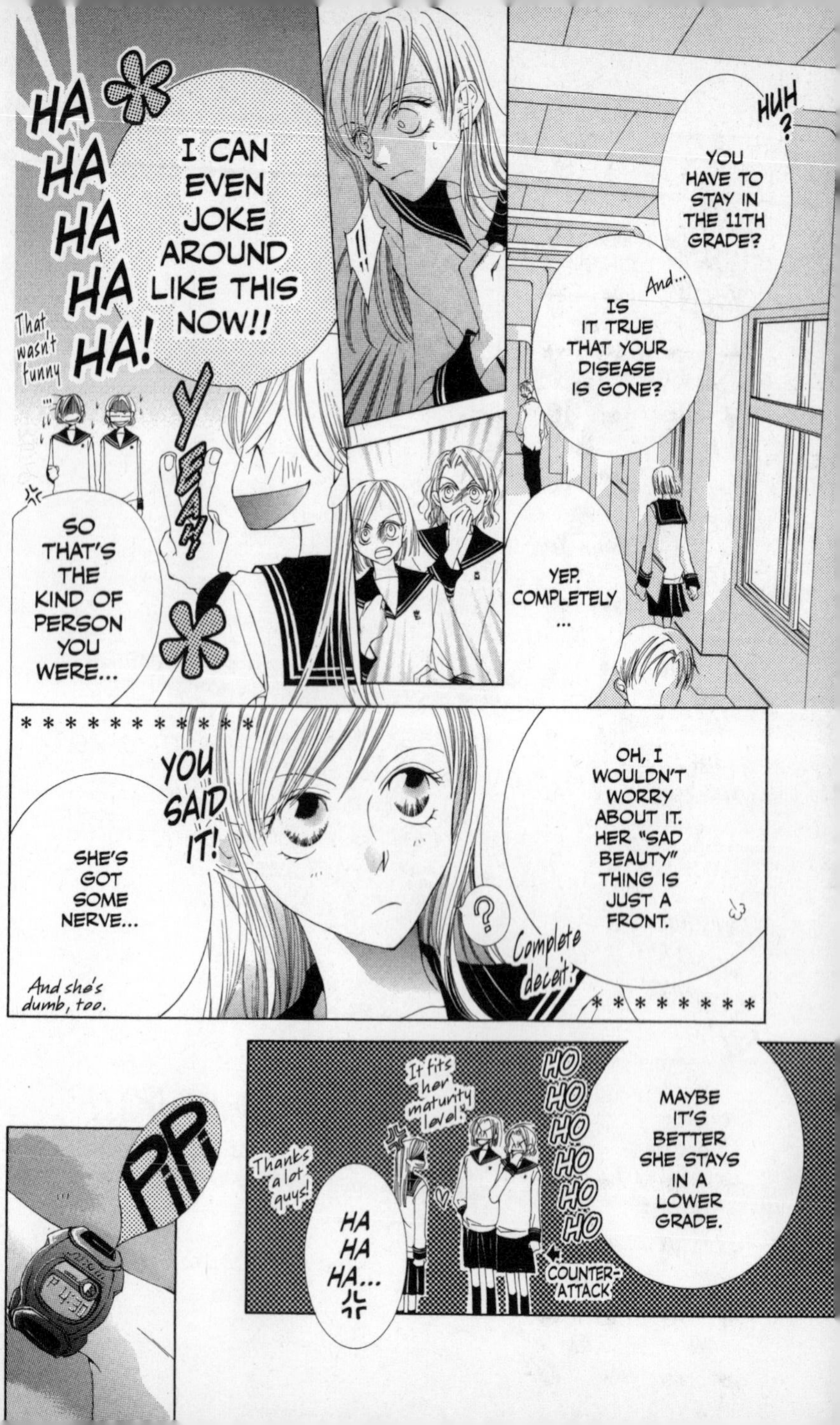
HUH?
YOU HAVE TO STAY IN THE 11TH GRADE?
And...
IS IT TRUE THAT YOUR DISEASE IS GONE?
YEP. COMPLETELY ...
I CAN EVEN JOKE AROUND LIKE THIS NOW!!
HA HA HA HA HA!
YEAH
That wasn't funny
SO THAT'S THE KIND OF PERSON YOU WERE...
OH, I WOULDN'T WORRY ABOUT IT. HER "SAD BEAUTY" THING IS JUST A FRONT.
Complete deceit!
?
YOU SAID IT!
SHE'S GOT SOME NERVE...
And she's dumb, too.
MAYBE IT'S BETTER SHE STAYS IN A LOWER GRADE.
HO HO HO HO HO HO
COUNTER-ATTACK
It fits her maturity level!
Thanks a lot guys!
HA HA HA...
PiPi

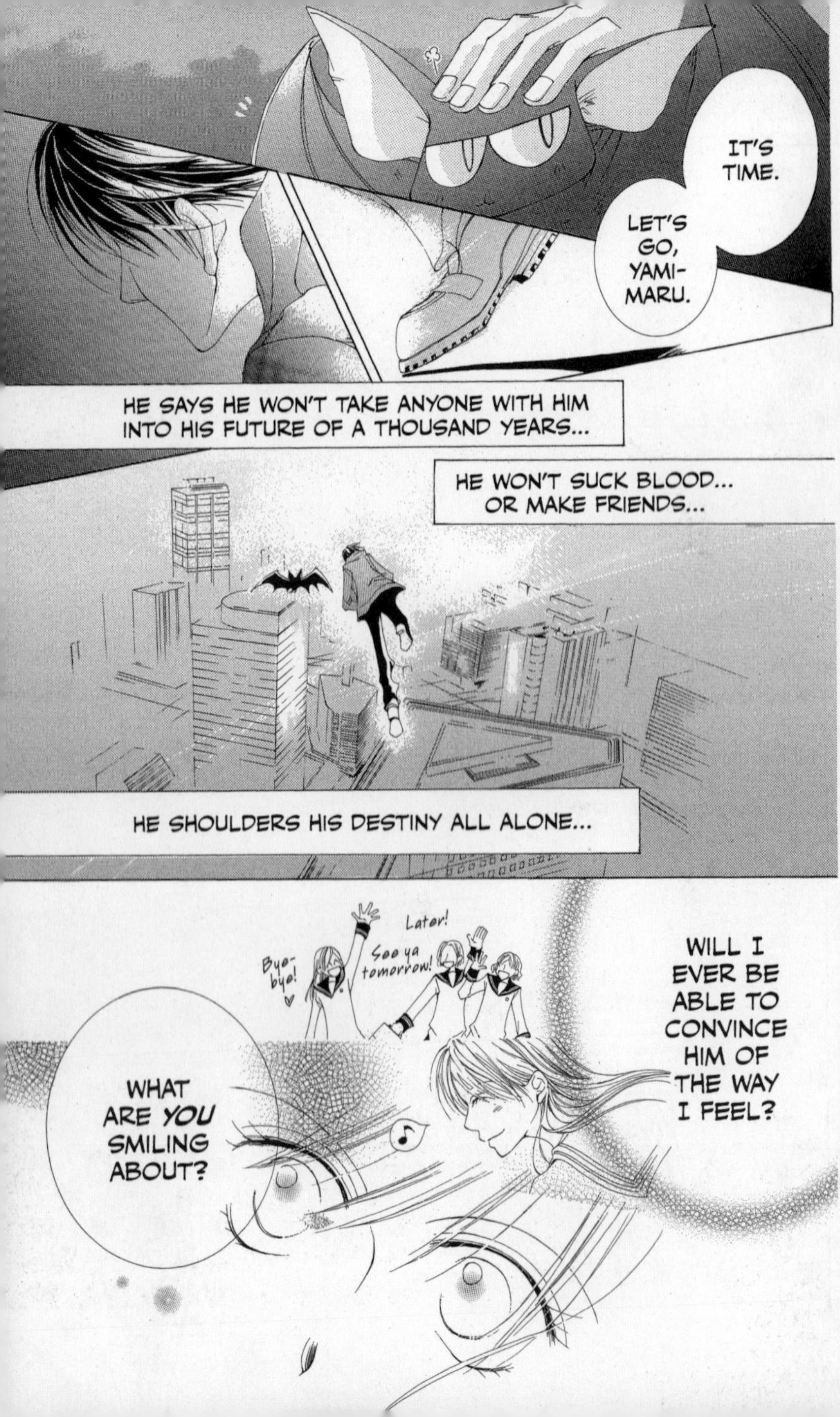
IT'S TIME.
LET'S GO, YAMI-MARU.
HE SAYS HE WON'T TAKE ANYONE WITH HIM INTO HIS FUTURE OF A THOUSAND YEARS...
HE WON'T SUCK BLOOD... OR MAKE FRIENDS...
HE SHOULDERS HIS DESTINY ALL ALONE...
WILL I EVER BE ABLE TO CONVINCE HIM OF THE WAY I FEEL?
Later!
See ya tomorrow!
Bye-bye!
WHAT ARE *YOU* SMILING ABOUT?

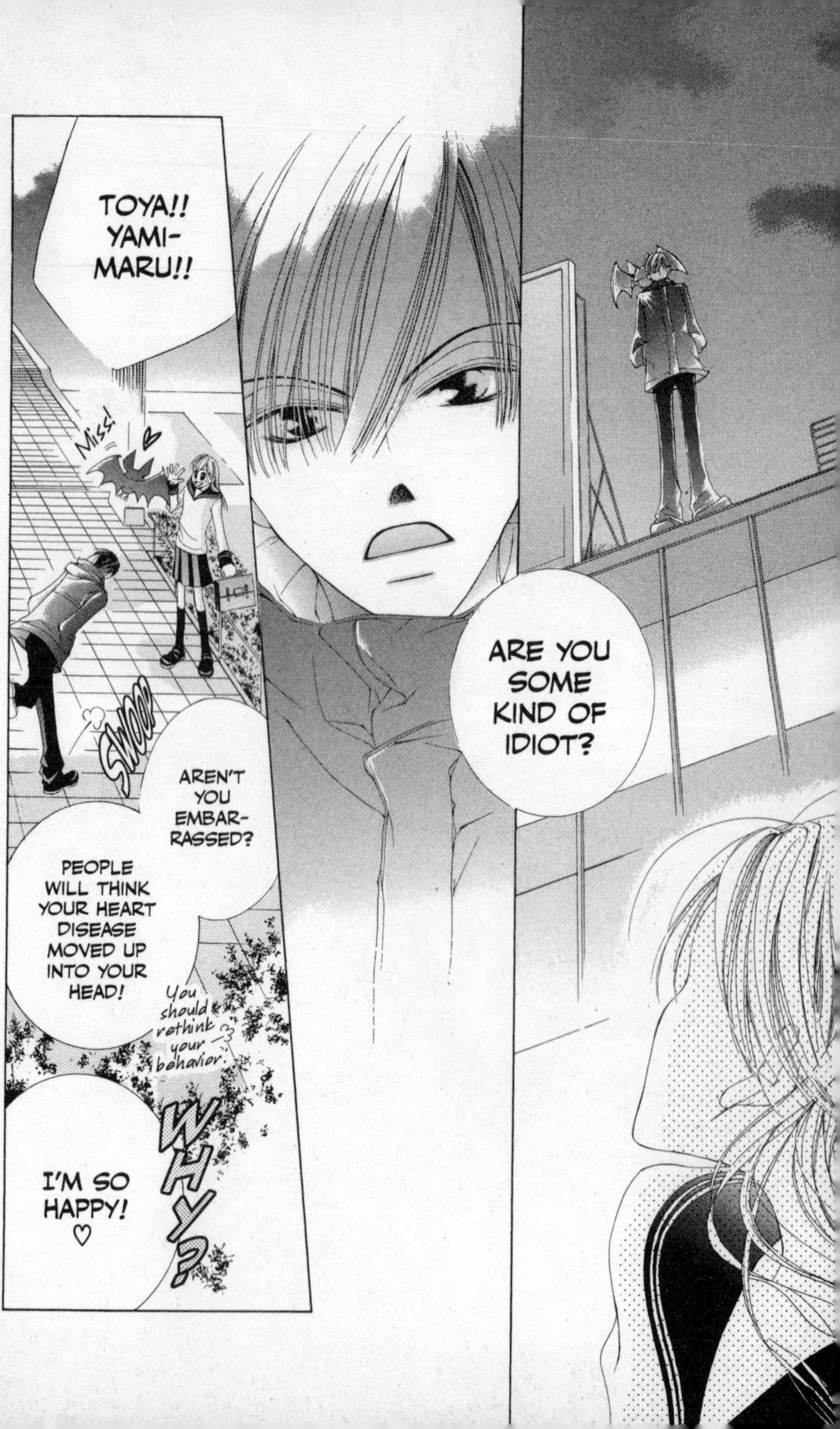
ARE YOU SOME KIND OF IDIOT?
TOYA!! YAMI-MARU!!
Miss!
SWOOP
AREN'T YOU EMBARRASSED?
PEOPLE WILL THINK YOUR HEART DISEASE MOVED UP INTO YOUR HEAD!
You should rethink your behavior.
I'M SO HAPPY! ♡
WHY?

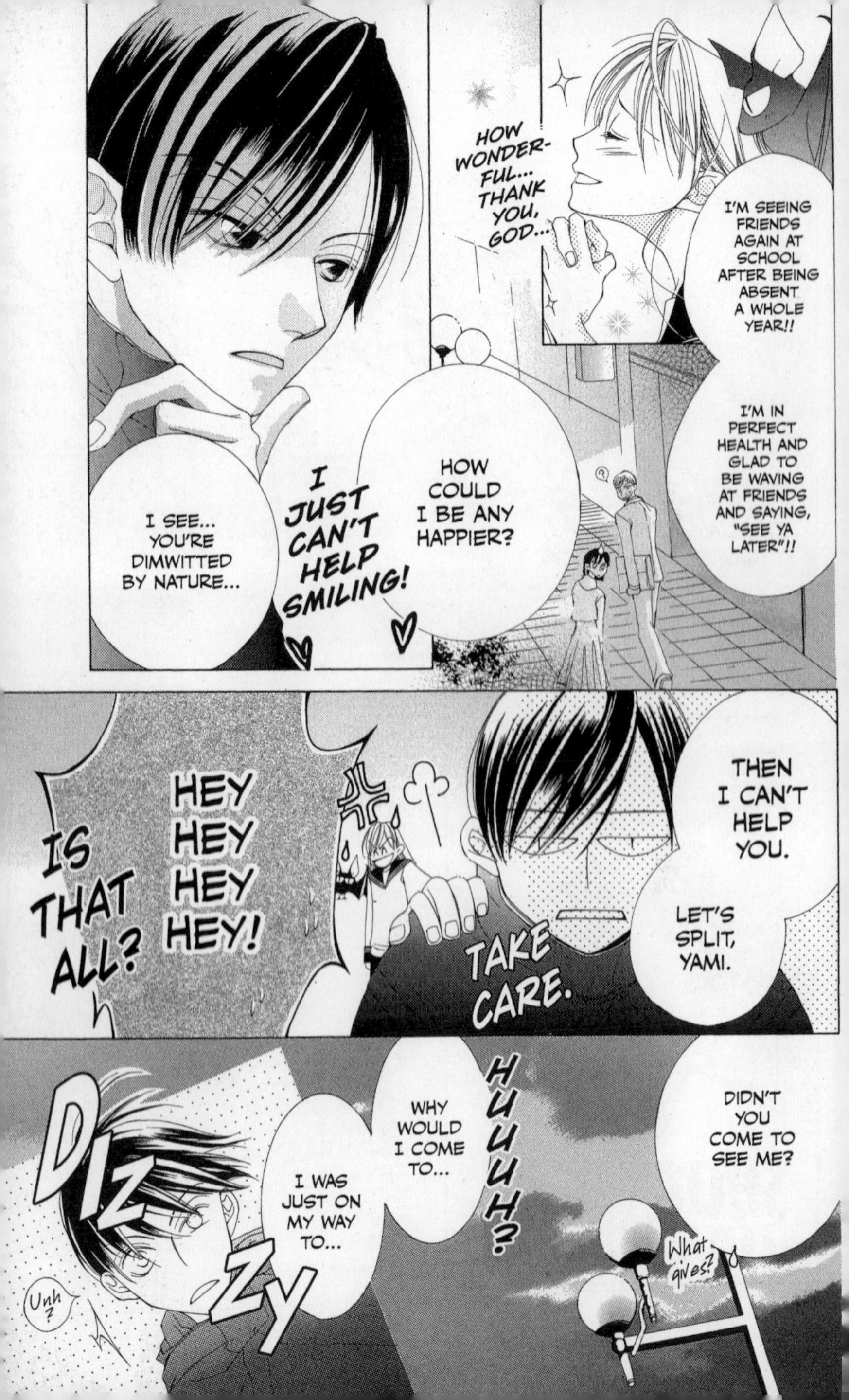
HOW WONDERFUL... THANK YOU, GOD...
I'M SEEING FRIENDS AGAIN AT SCHOOL AFTER BEING ABSENT A WHOLE YEAR!!
I'M IN PERFECT HEALTH AND GLAD TO BE WAVING AT FRIENDS AND SAYING, "SEE YA LATER"!!
HOW COULD I BE ANY HAPPIER?
I JUST CAN'T HELP SMILING!
I SEE... YOU'RE DIMWITTED BY NATURE...
THEN I CAN'T HELP YOU.
LET'S SPLIT, YAMI.
TAKE CARE.
HEY HEY HEY HEY!
IS THAT ALL?
DIDN'T YOU COME TO SEE ME?
What gives?
HUUUH?
WHY WOULD I COME TO...
I WAS JUST ON MY WAY TO...
DIZZY
Unh?

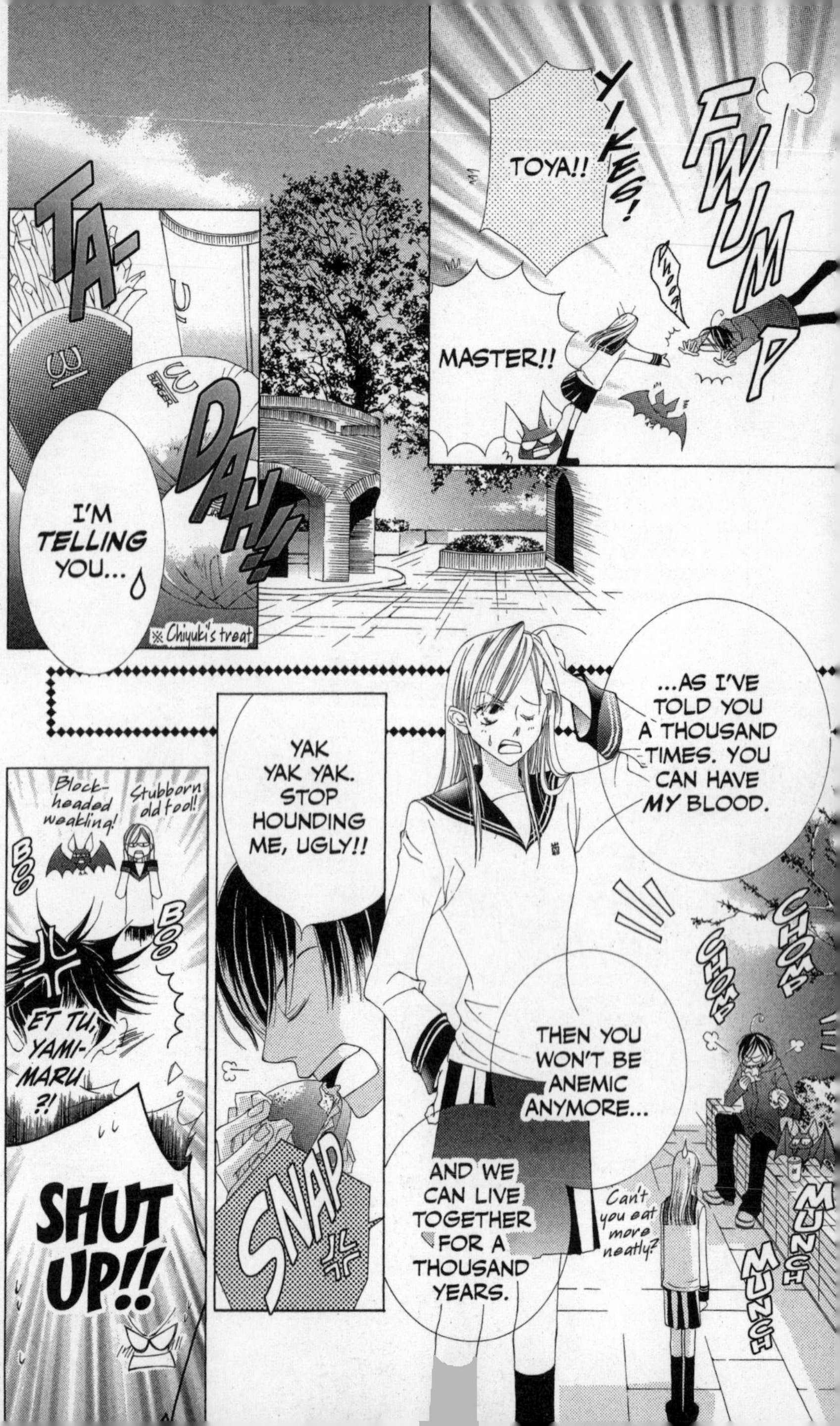
FWUMP
WHOA
YIKES!
TOYA!!
MASTER!!
TA-DAH!!
I'M TELLING YOU...
※Chiyuki's treat
...AS I'VE TOLD YOU A THOUSAND TIMES. YOU CAN HAVE MY BLOOD.
THEN YOU WON'T BE ANEMIC ANYMORE...
AND WE CAN LIVE TOGETHER FOR A THOUSAND YEARS.
CHOMP CHOMP
MUNCH MUNCH
Can't you eat more neatly?
YAK YAK YAK. STOP HOUNDING ME, UGLY!!
SNAP
Block-headed weakling!
Stubborn old fool!
BOO BOO
ET TU, YAMI-MARU ?!
SHUT UP!!

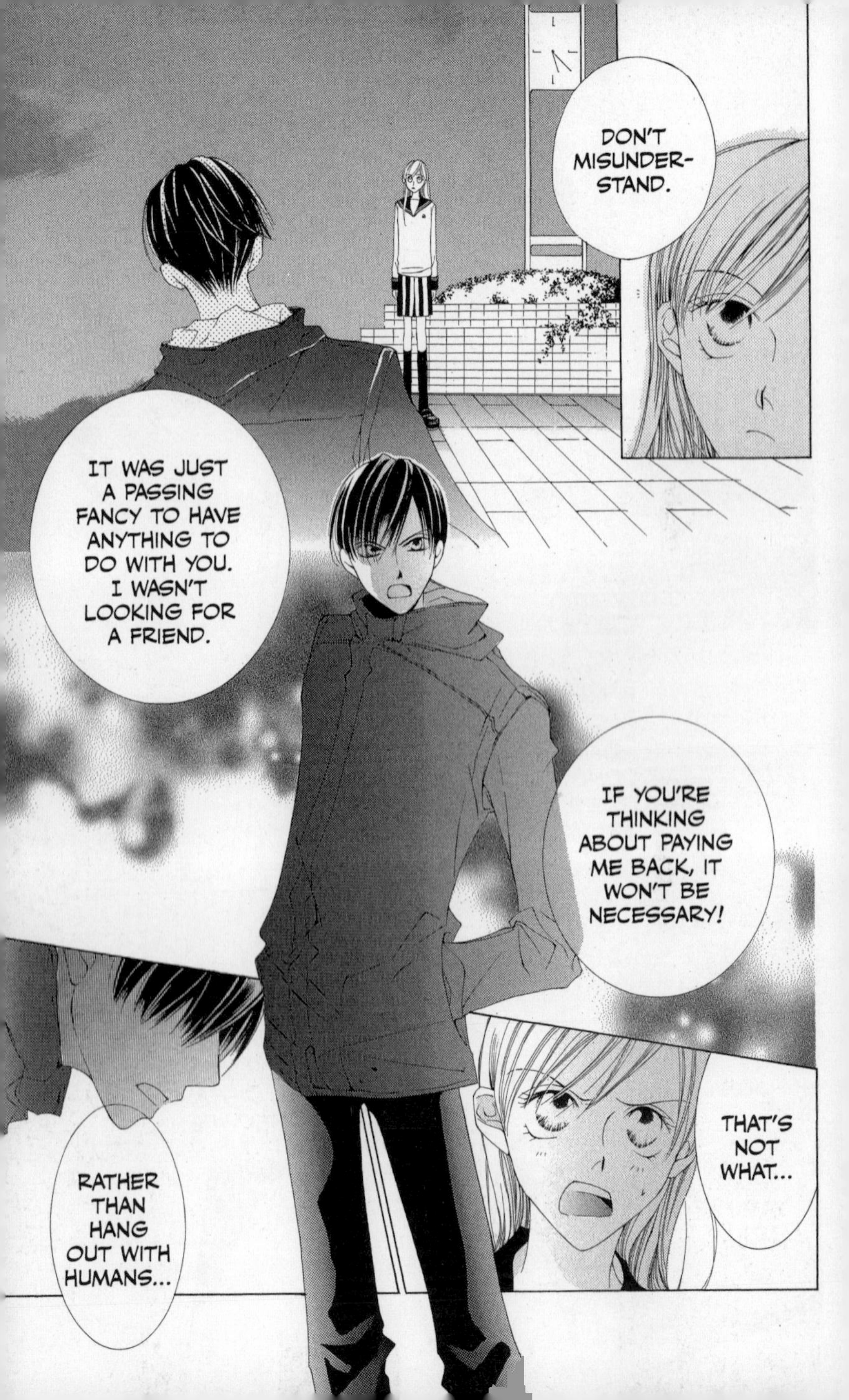
DON'T MISUNDER-STAND.
IT WAS JUST A PASSING FANCY TO HAVE ANYTHING TO DO WITH YOU. I WASN'T LOOKING FOR A FRIEND.
IF YOU'RE THINKING ABOUT PAYING ME BACK, IT WON'T BE NECESSARY!
THAT'S NOT WHAT...
RATHER THAN HANG OUT WITH HUMANS...

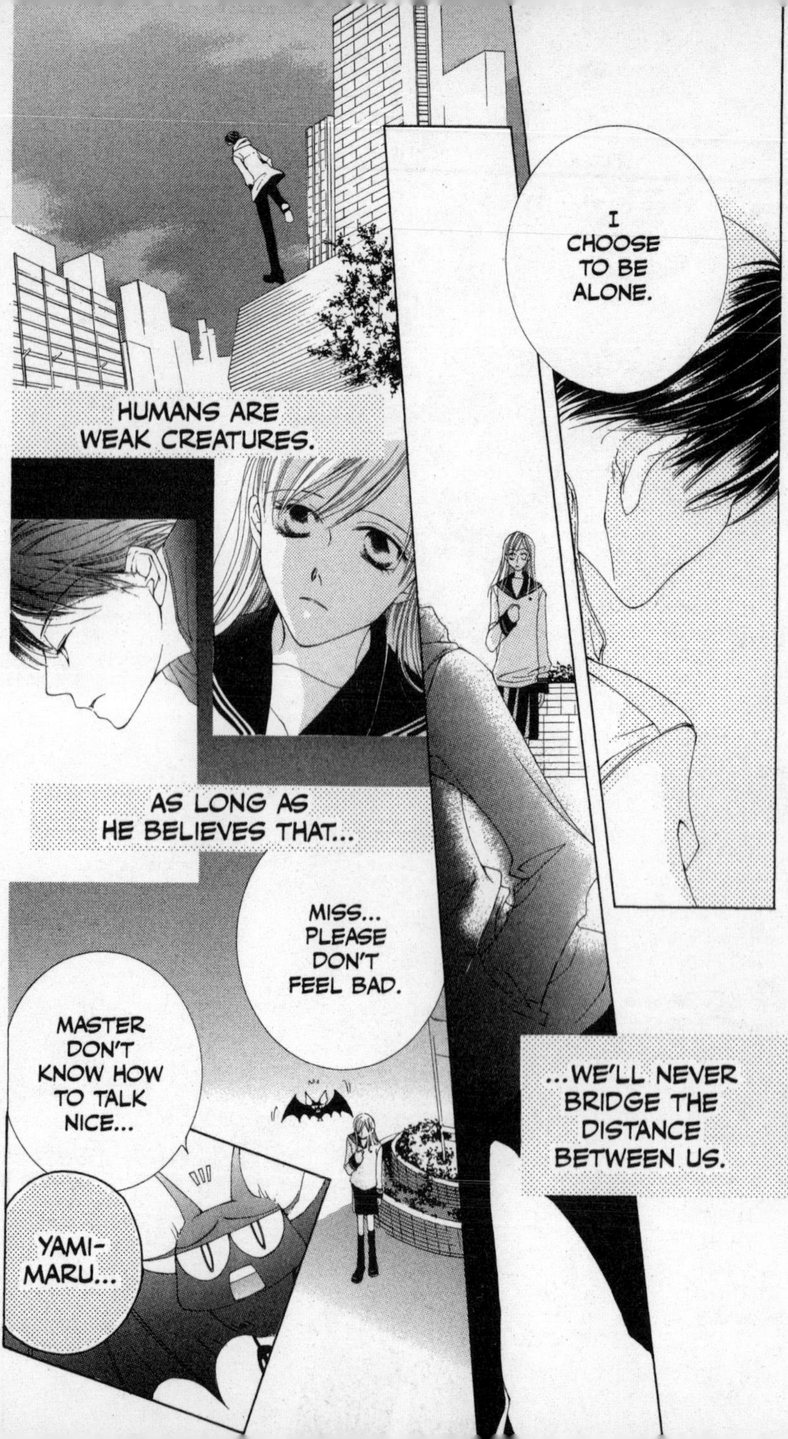
I CHOOSE TO BE ALONE.
HUMANS ARE WEAK CREATURES.
AS LONG AS HE BELIEVES THAT...
MISS... PLEASE DON'T FEEL BAD.
MASTER DON'T KNOW HOW TO TALK NICE...
YAMI-MARU...
...WE'LL NEVER BRIDGE THE DISTANCE BETWEEN US.

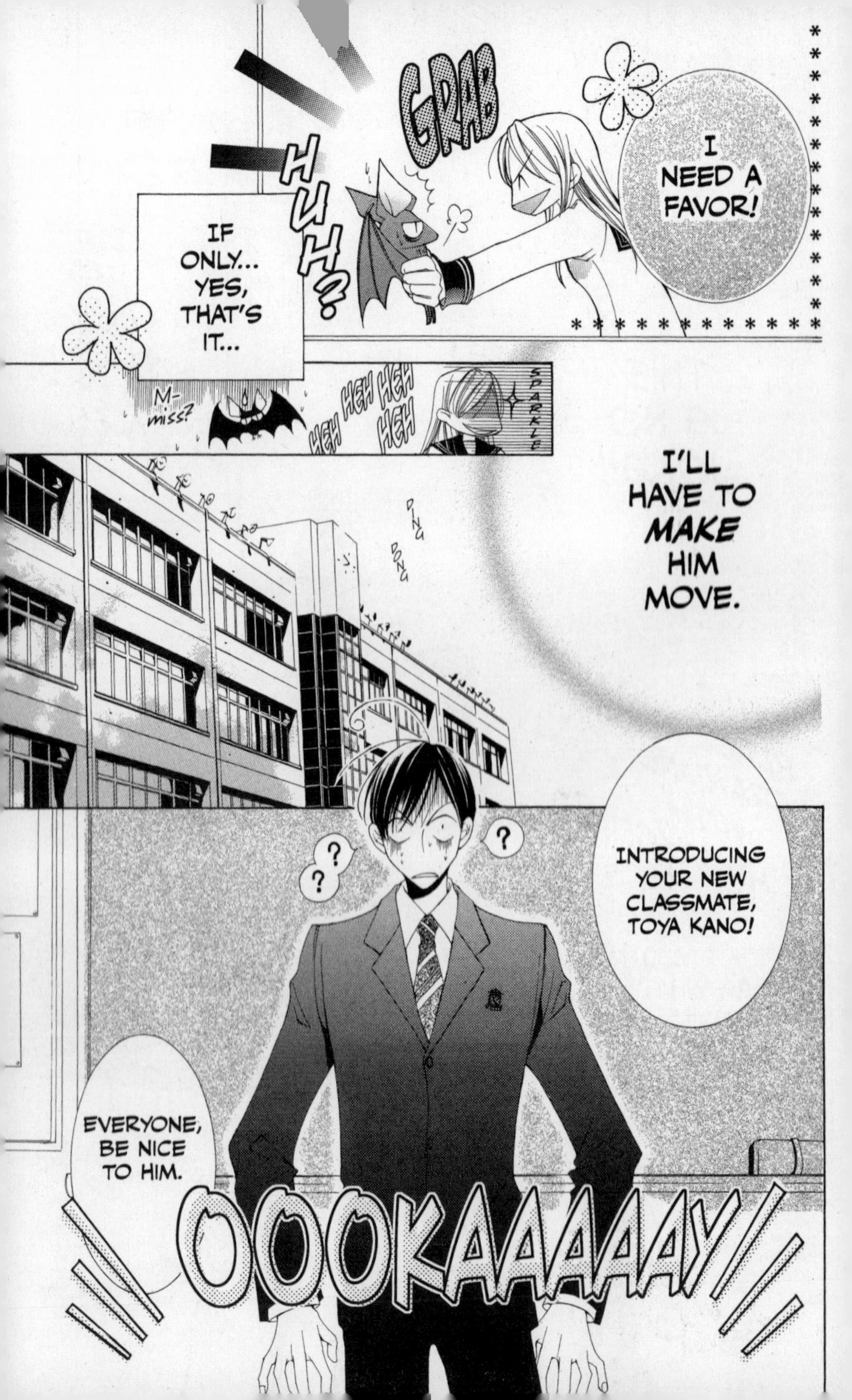
I NEED A FAVOR!
GRAB
HUH?
IF ONLY... YES, THAT'S IT...
SPARKLE
HEH HEH HEH HEH
M-MISS?
I'LL HAVE TO *MAKE* HIM MOVE.
DING DONG
INTRODUCING YOUR NEW CLASSMATE, TOYA KANO!
EVERYONE, BE NICE TO HIM.
OOOKAAAAAY!

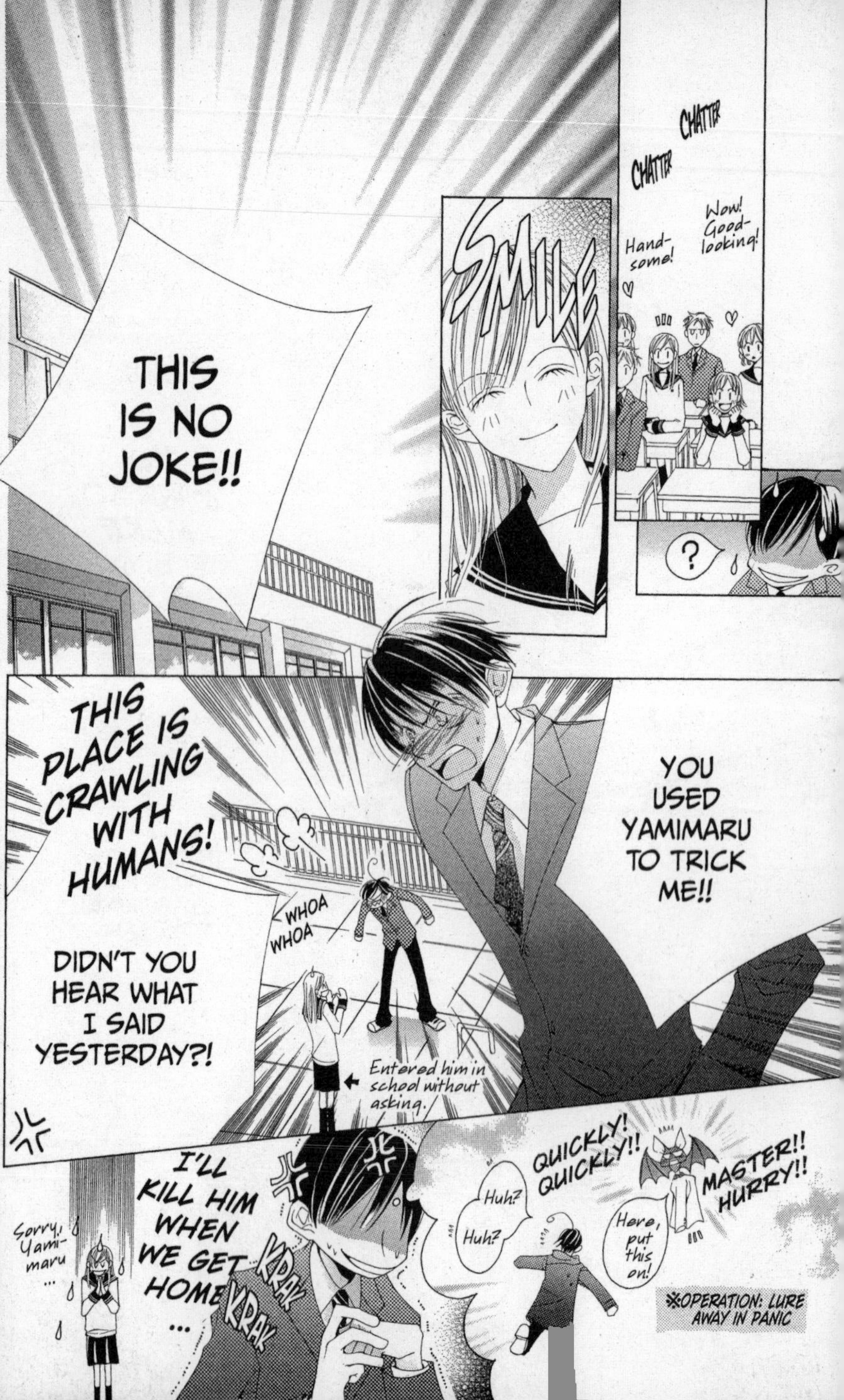
CHATTER
CHATTER
Wow! Good-looking!
Hand-some!
SMILE
?
THIS IS NO JOKE!!
YOU USED YAMIMARU TO TRICK ME!!
THIS PLACE IS CRAWLING WITH HUMANS!
WHOA WHOA
DIDN'T YOU HEAR WHAT I SAID YESTERDAY?!
Entered him in school without asking.
MASTER!! HURRY!!
Here, put this on!
QUICKLY! QUICKLY!!
Huh?
Huh?
※OPERATION: LURE AWAY IN PANIC
I'LL KILL HIM WHEN WE GET HOME...
KRAK
KRAK
Sorry, Yamimaru...

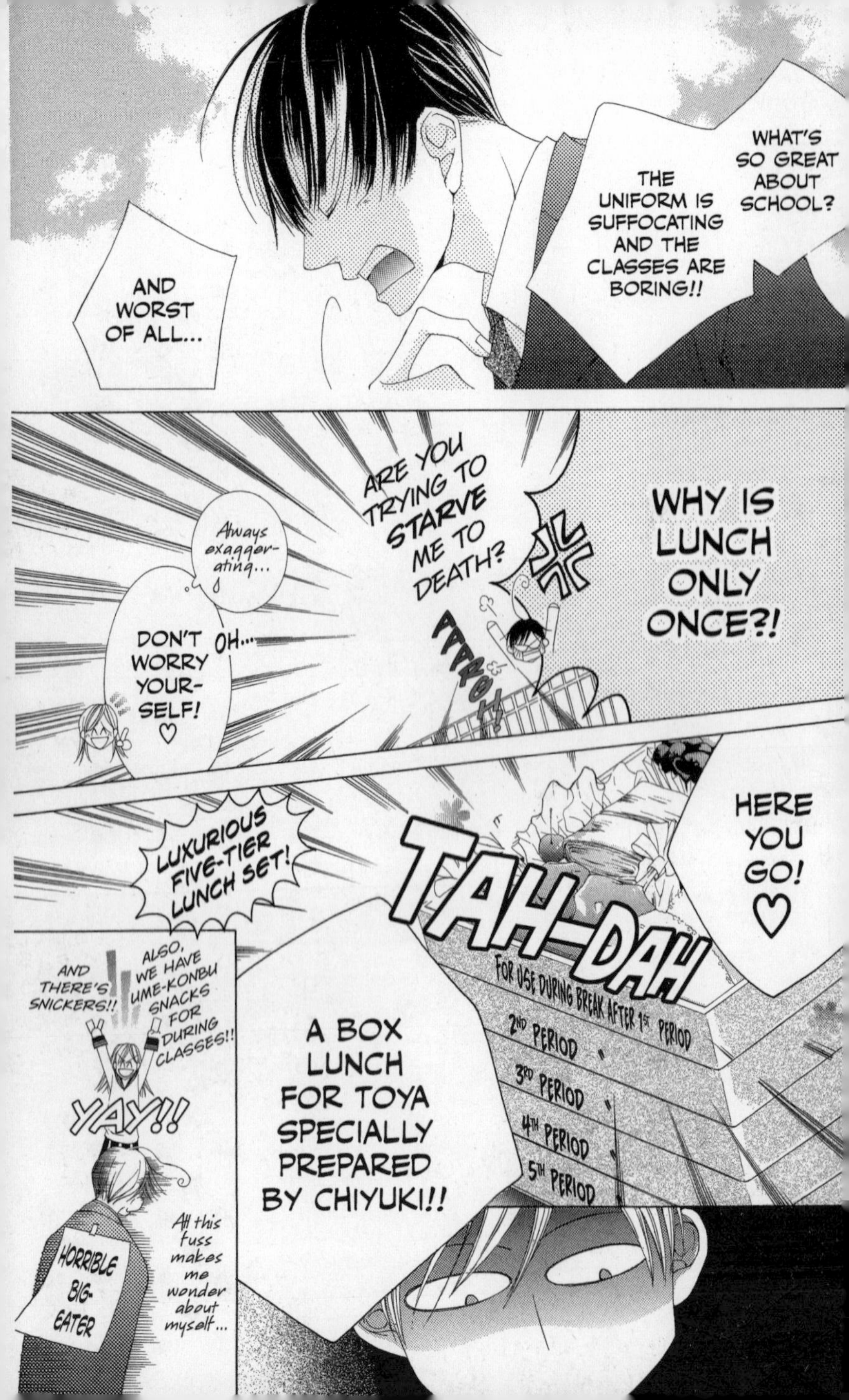
WHAT'S SO GREAT ABOUT SCHOOL?
THE UNIFORM IS SUFFOCATING AND THE CLASSES ARE BORING!!
AND WORST OF ALL...
WHY IS LUNCH ONLY ONCE?!
ARE YOU TRYING TO STARVE ME TO DEATH?
Always exaggerating...
OH...
DON'T WORRY YOURSELF! ♡
HERE YOU GO! ♡
TAH-DAH
LUXURIOUS FIVE-TIER LUNCH SET!
FOR USE DURING BREAK AFTER 1ST PERIOD
2ND PERIOD
3RD PERIOD
4TH PERIOD
5TH PERIOD
A BOX LUNCH FOR TOYA SPECIALLY PREPARED BY CHIYUKI!!
ALSO, WE HAVE UME-KONBU SNACKS FOR DURING CLASSES!!
AND THERE'S SNICKERS!!
YAY!!
HORRIBLE BIG-EATER
All this fuss makes me wonder about myself...

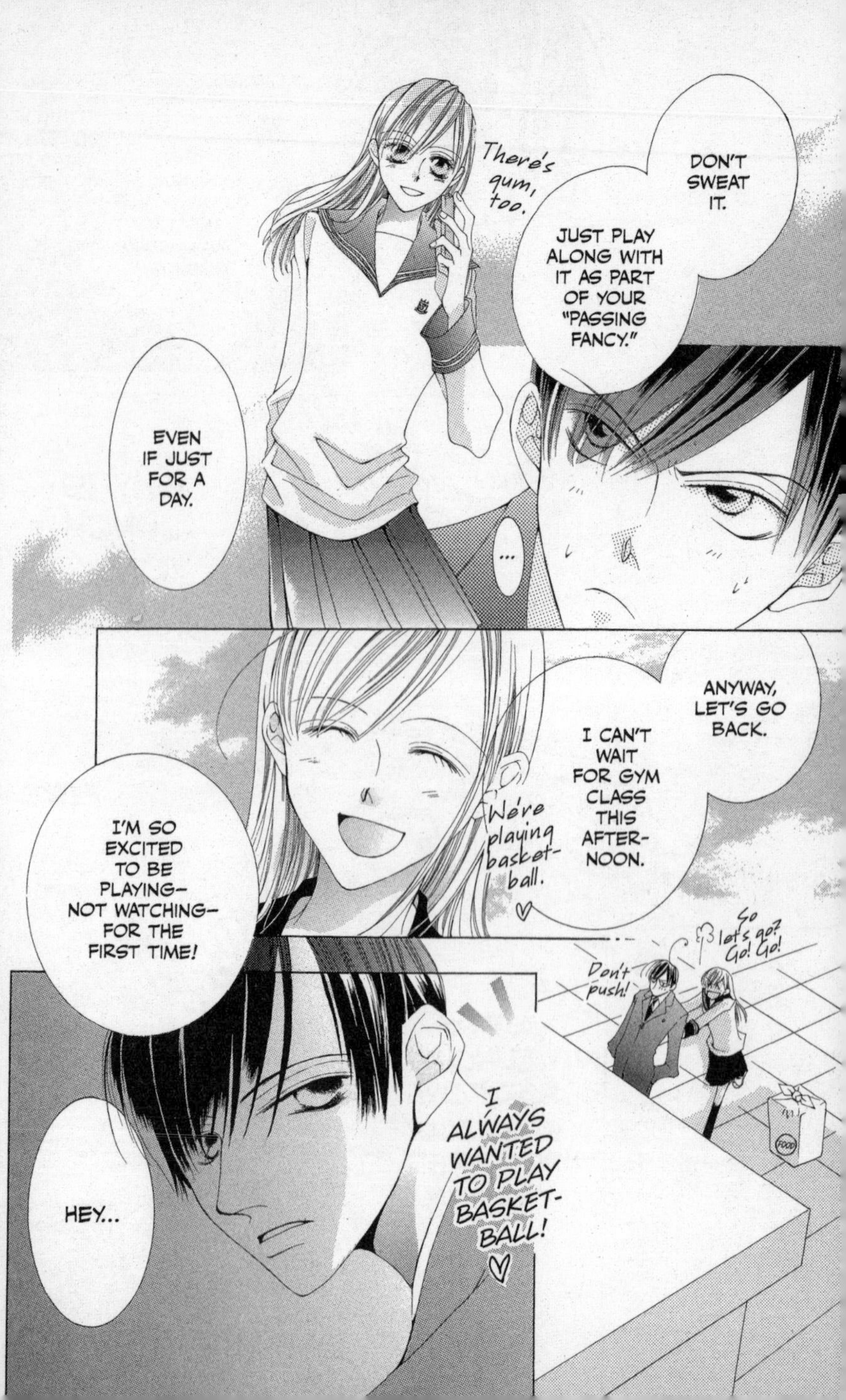
DON'T SWEAT IT.
JUST PLAY ALONG WITH IT AS PART OF YOUR "PASSING FANCY."
There's gum, too.
EVEN IF JUST FOR A DAY.
...
ANYWAY, LET'S GO BACK.
I CAN'T WAIT FOR GYM CLASS THIS AFTERNOON.
We're playing basketball. ♥
I'M SO EXCITED TO BE PLAYING—NOT WATCHING—FOR THE FIRST TIME!
So let's go? Go! Go!
Don't push!
I ALWAYS WANTED TO PLAY BASKETBALL! ♥
HEY...

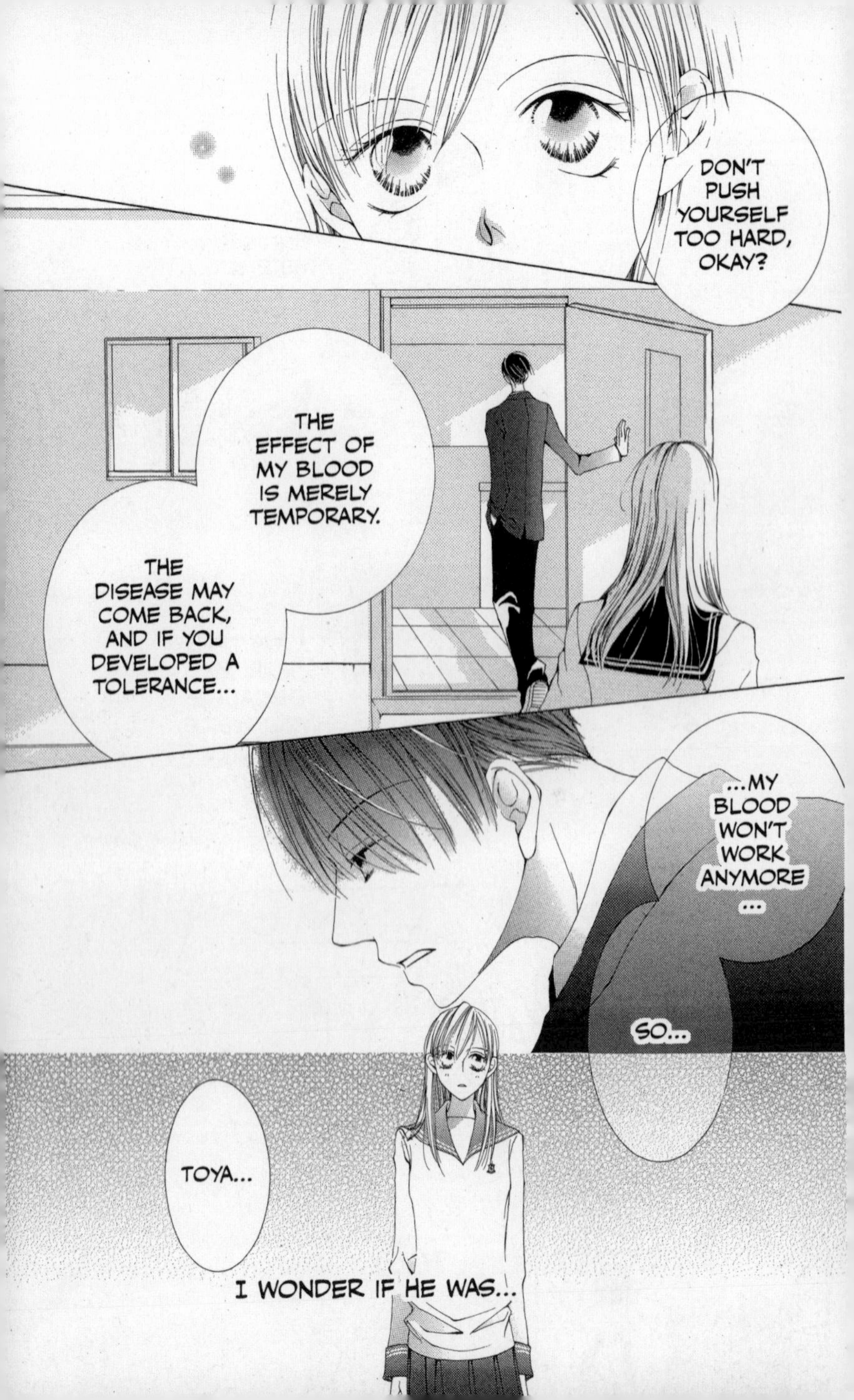
DON'T PUSH YOURSELF TOO HARD, OKAY?
THE EFFECT OF MY BLOOD IS MERELY TEMPORARY.
THE DISEASE MAY COME BACK, AND IF YOU DEVELOPED A TOLERANCE...
...MY BLOOD WON'T WORK ANYMORE...
SO...
TOYA...
I WONDER IF HE WAS...

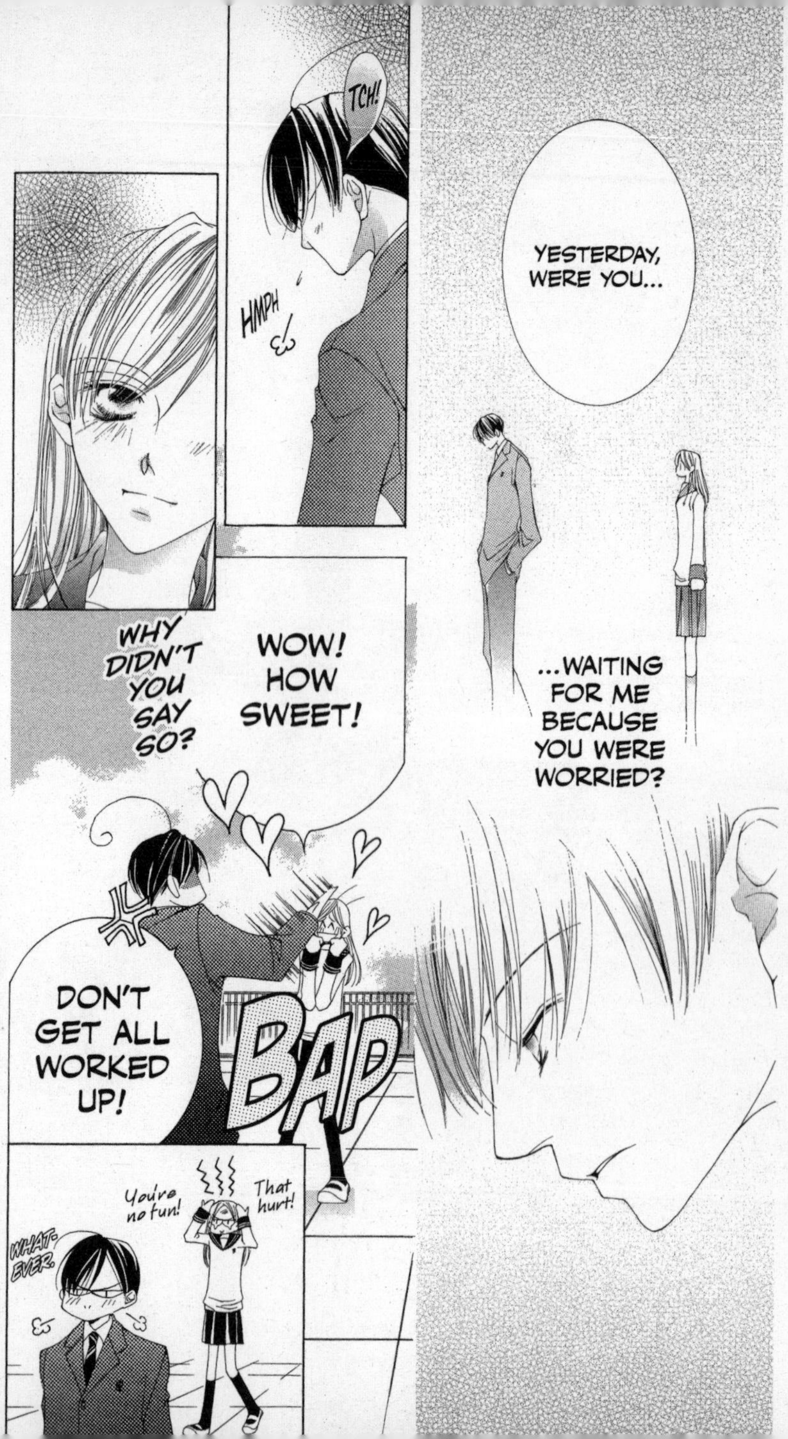
YESTERDAY, WERE YOU...
...WAITING FOR ME BECAUSE YOU WERE WORRIED?
TCH!
HMPH
WOW! HOW SWEET!
WHY DIDN'T YOU SAY SO?
DON'T GET ALL WORKED UP!
BAP
That hurt!
You're no fun!
WHAT-EVER.

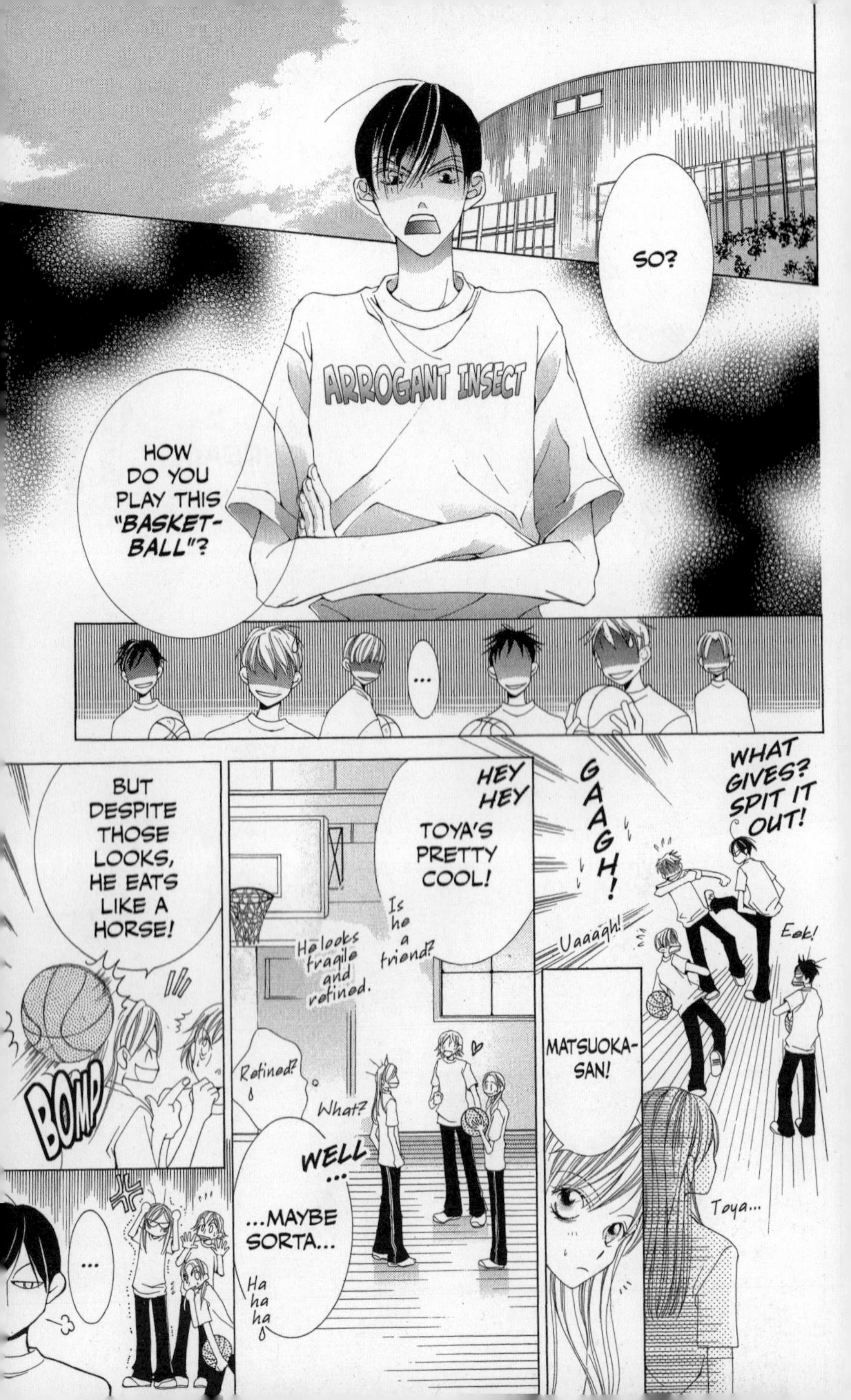
SO?
ARROGANT INSECT
HOW DO YOU PLAY THIS "BASKETBALL"?
...
WHAT GIVES? SPIT IT OUT!
GAAGH!
Uaaagh!
Eek!
MATSUOKA-SAN!
Toya...
HEY HEY
TOYA'S PRETTY COOL!
Is he a friend?
He looks fragile and refined.
Refined?
What?
WELL...
...MAYBE SORTA...
Ha ha ha
BUT DESPITE THOSE LOOKS, HE EATS LIKE A HORSE!
BOMP
...

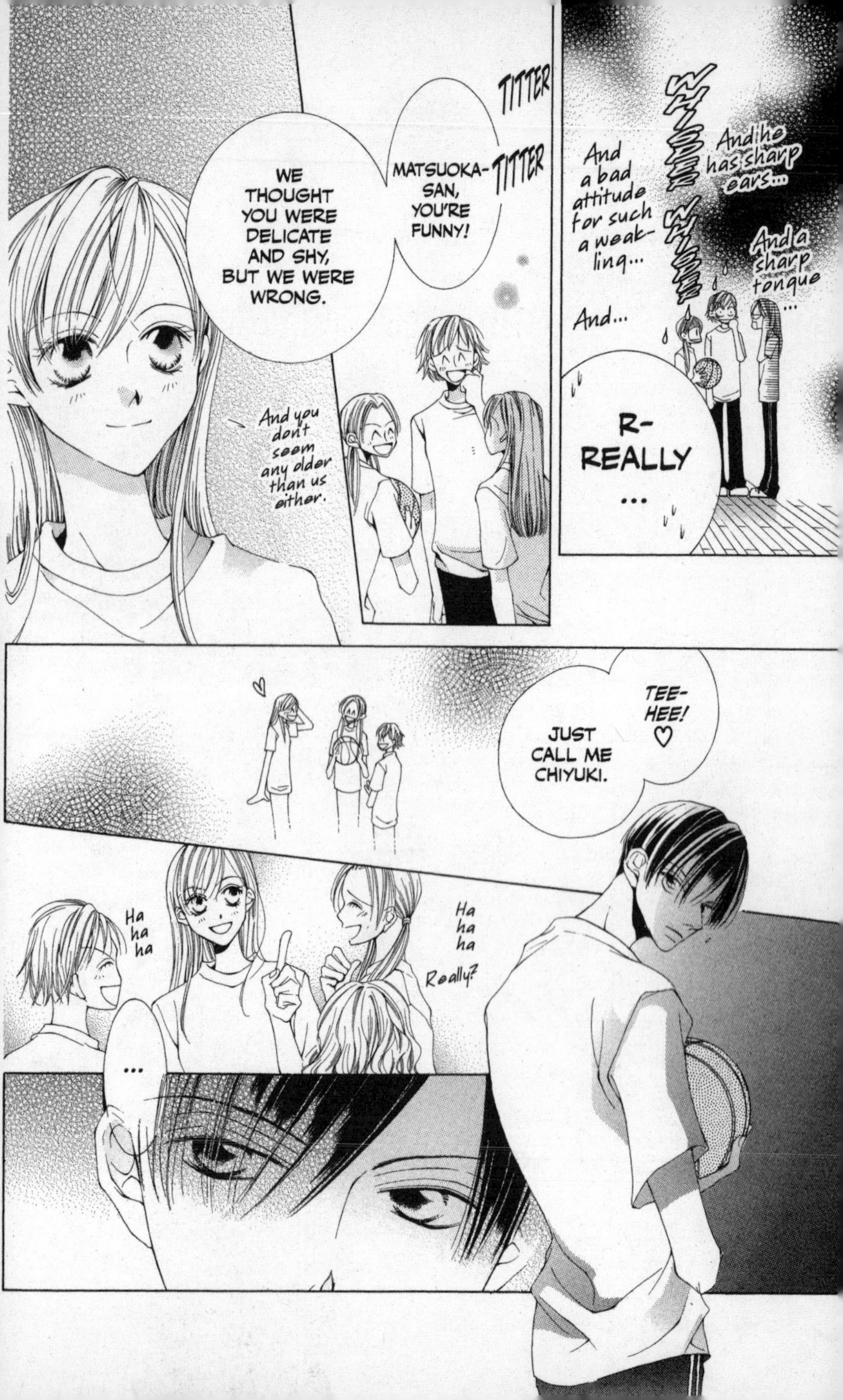

And he has sharp ears...
And a sharp tongue...
And a bad attitude for such a weakling...
And...
R-REALLY...
TITTER
TITTER
MATSUOKA-SAN, YOU'RE FUNNY!
And you don't seem any older than us either.
WE THOUGHT YOU WERE DELICATE AND SHY, BUT WE WERE WRONG.
TEE-HEE! ♡
JUST CALL ME CHIYUKI.
Ha ha ha
Really?
Ha ha ha
...

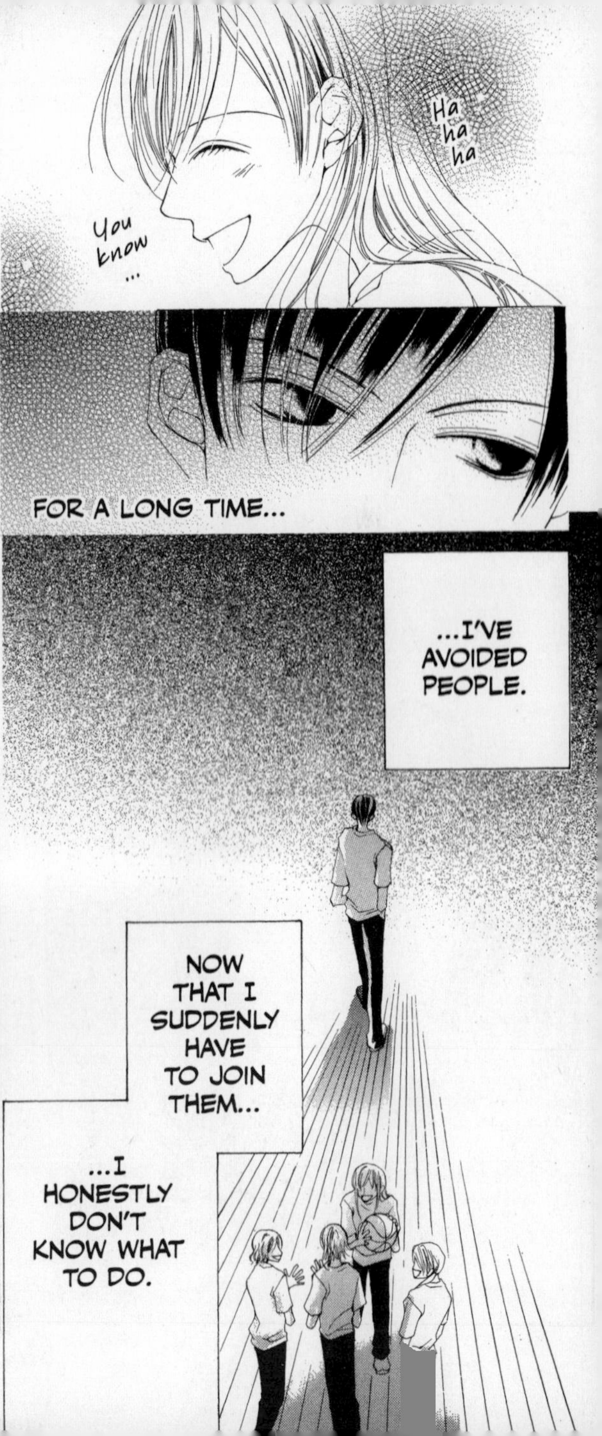
Ha ha ha
You know...
FOR A LONG TIME...
...I'VE AVOIDED PEOPLE.
NOW THAT I SUDDENLY HAVE TO JOIN THEM...
...I HONESTLY DON'T KNOW WHAT TO DO.

02

MANY PEOPLE ASK ME ABOUT MY PEN NAME, SO HERE I GO...

WITH "HATORI," I WANTED TO USE A JAPANESE CHARACTER FROM MY REAL NAME AND AT THE SAME TIME INCLUDE THE SOUND "HATO."

THE "BIS" OF "BISCO" SIGNIFIES A SCREW. I HAVE A WEAK SPOT FOR ITEMS REPRESENTATIVE OF THE PAST, LIKE SPRING-WOUND DEVICES.

AT FIRST I THOUGHT ABOUT "NEJIKO," BUT "BISCO" SOUNDS LIKE "BISQUE DOLL" (OR DOES IT?) AND THE VOWEL SOUNDS ARE SIMILAR TO THOSE IN MY REAL NAME. MANY PEOPLE HAVE TOLD ME THAT IT'S AN EASY NAME TO REMEMBER, SO I'M PRETTY HAPPY WITH IT.

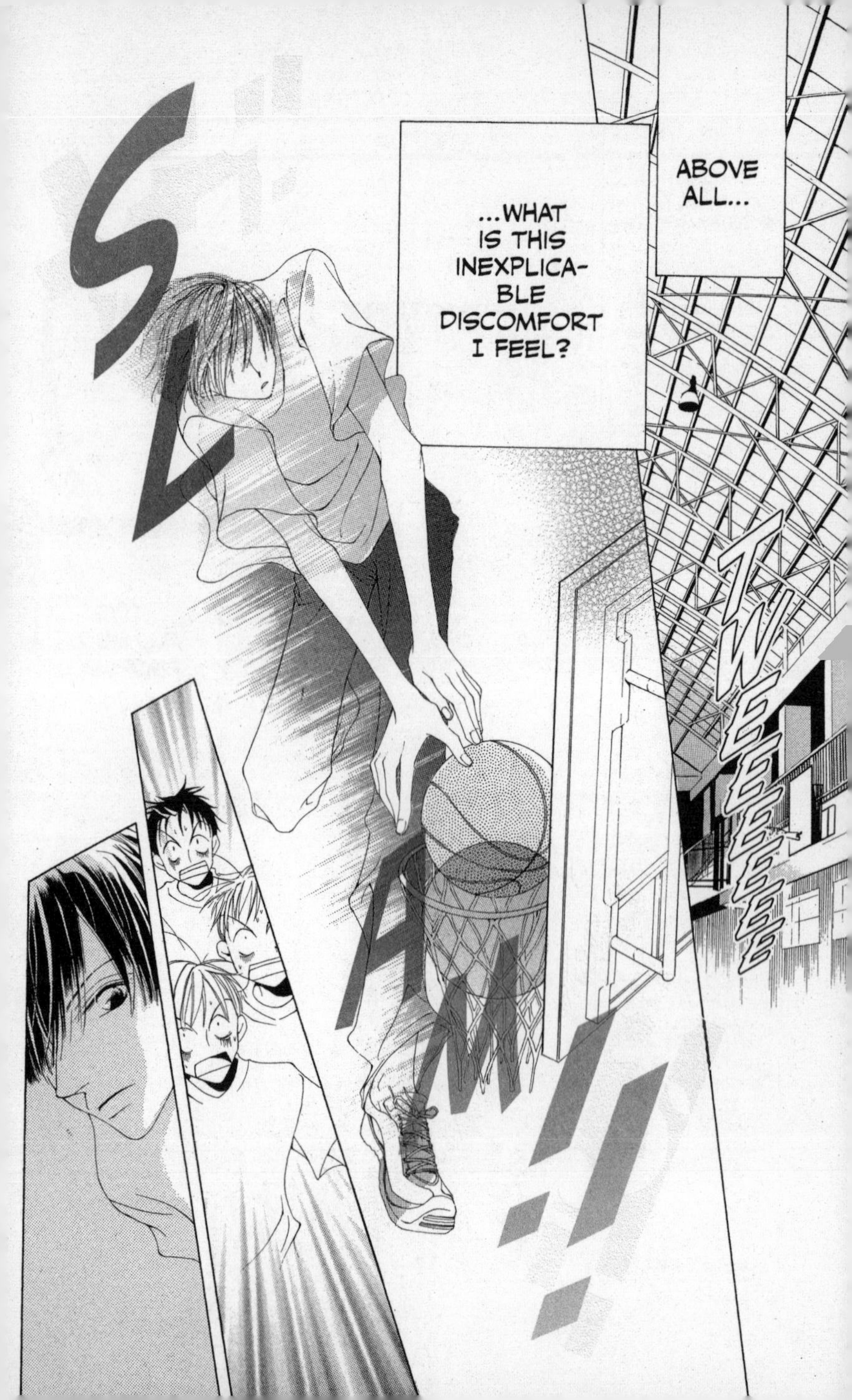
ABOVE ALL...
...WHAT IS THIS INEXPLICA-BLE DISCOMFORT I FEEL?
TWEEEEEE
SLAM!!

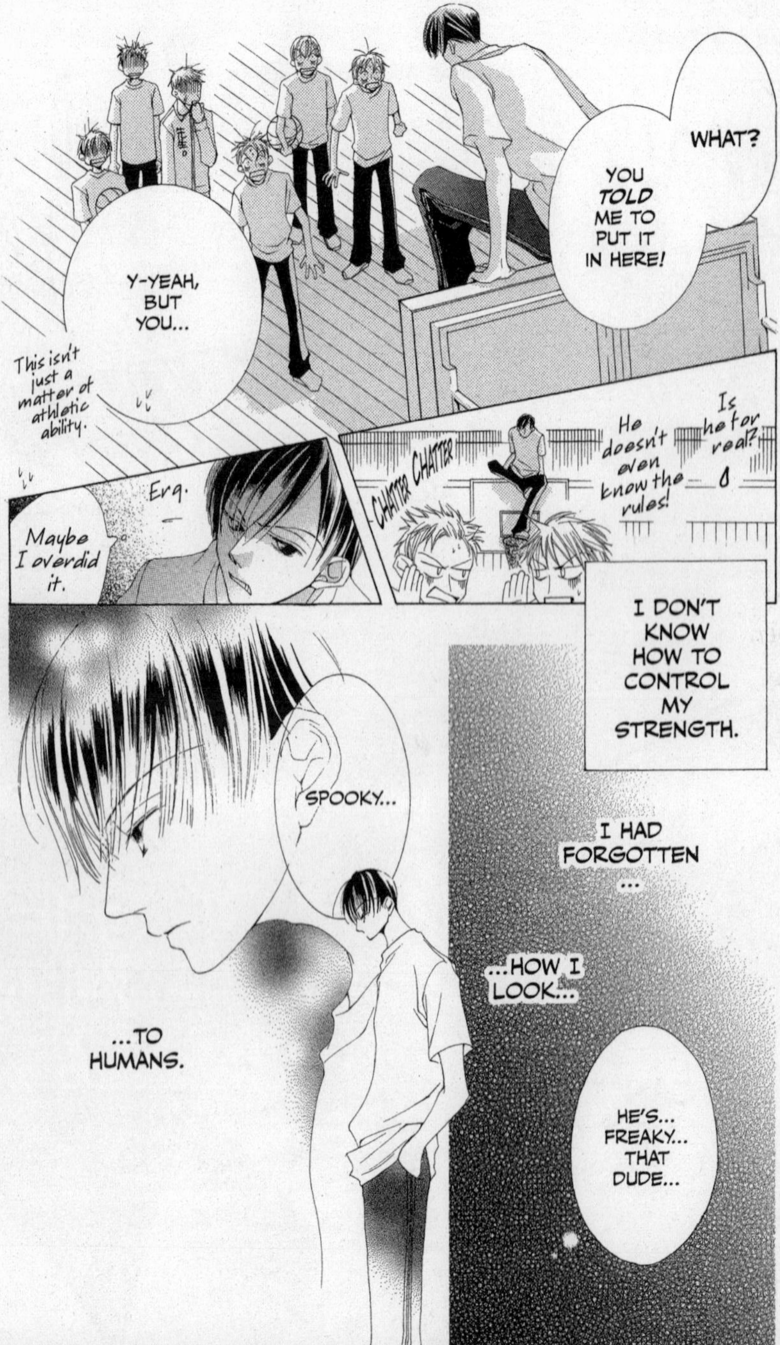
WHAT?
YOU *TOLD* ME TO PUT IT IN HERE!
Y-YEAH, BUT YOU...
This isn't just a matter of athletic ability.
Is he for real?
He doesn't even know the rules!
CHATTER CHATTER
Erg.
Maybe I overdid it.
I DON'T KNOW HOW TO CONTROL MY STRENGTH.
I HAD FORGOTTEN...
...HOW I LOOK...
HE'S... FREAKY... THAT DUDE...
SPOOKY...
...TO HUMANS.

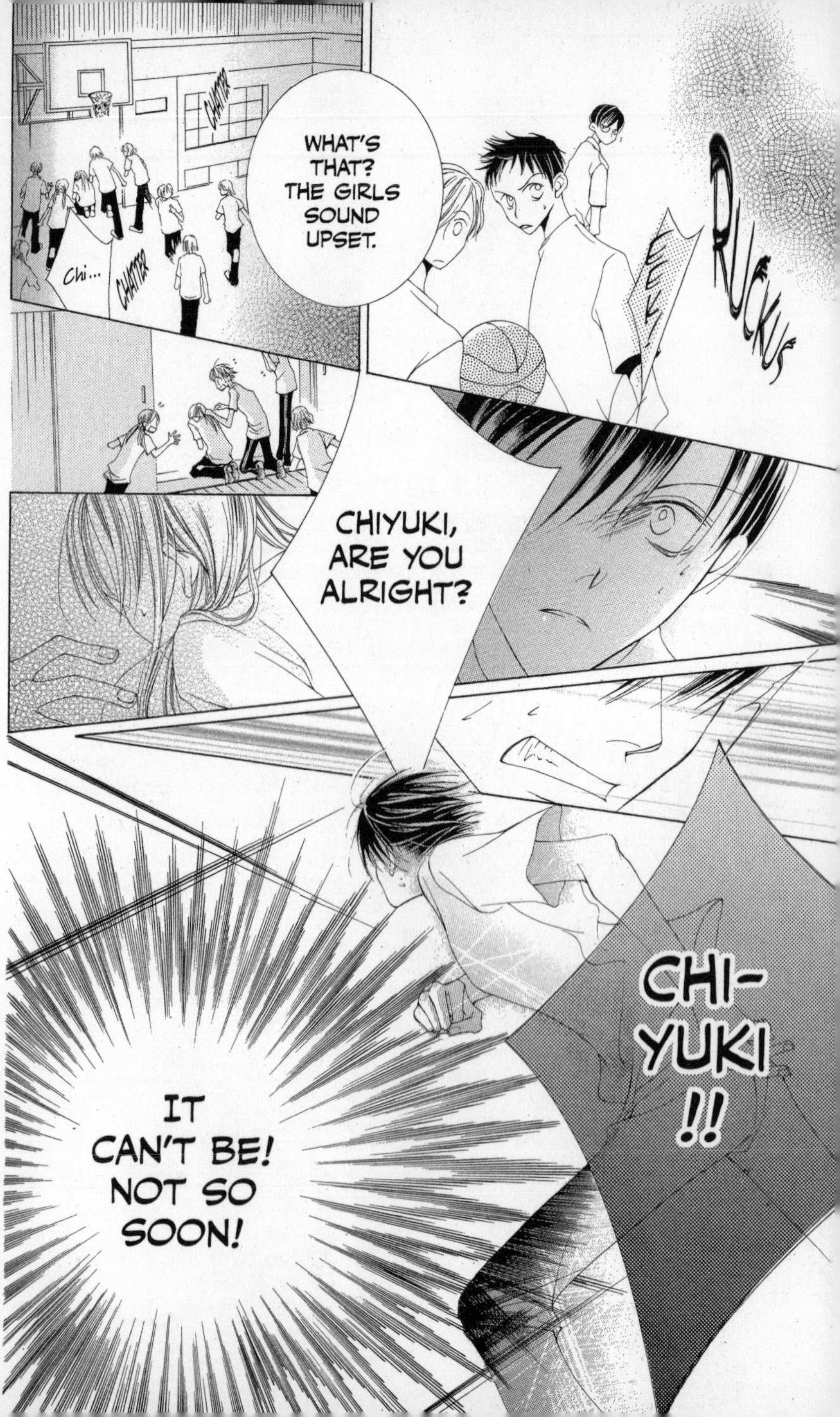
RUCKUS
EEK
WHAT'S THAT? THE GIRLS SOUND UPSET.
CHATTER
Chi...
CHATTER
CHIYUKI, ARE YOU ALRIGHT?
CHI-YUKI!!
IT CAN'T BE! NOT SO SOON!

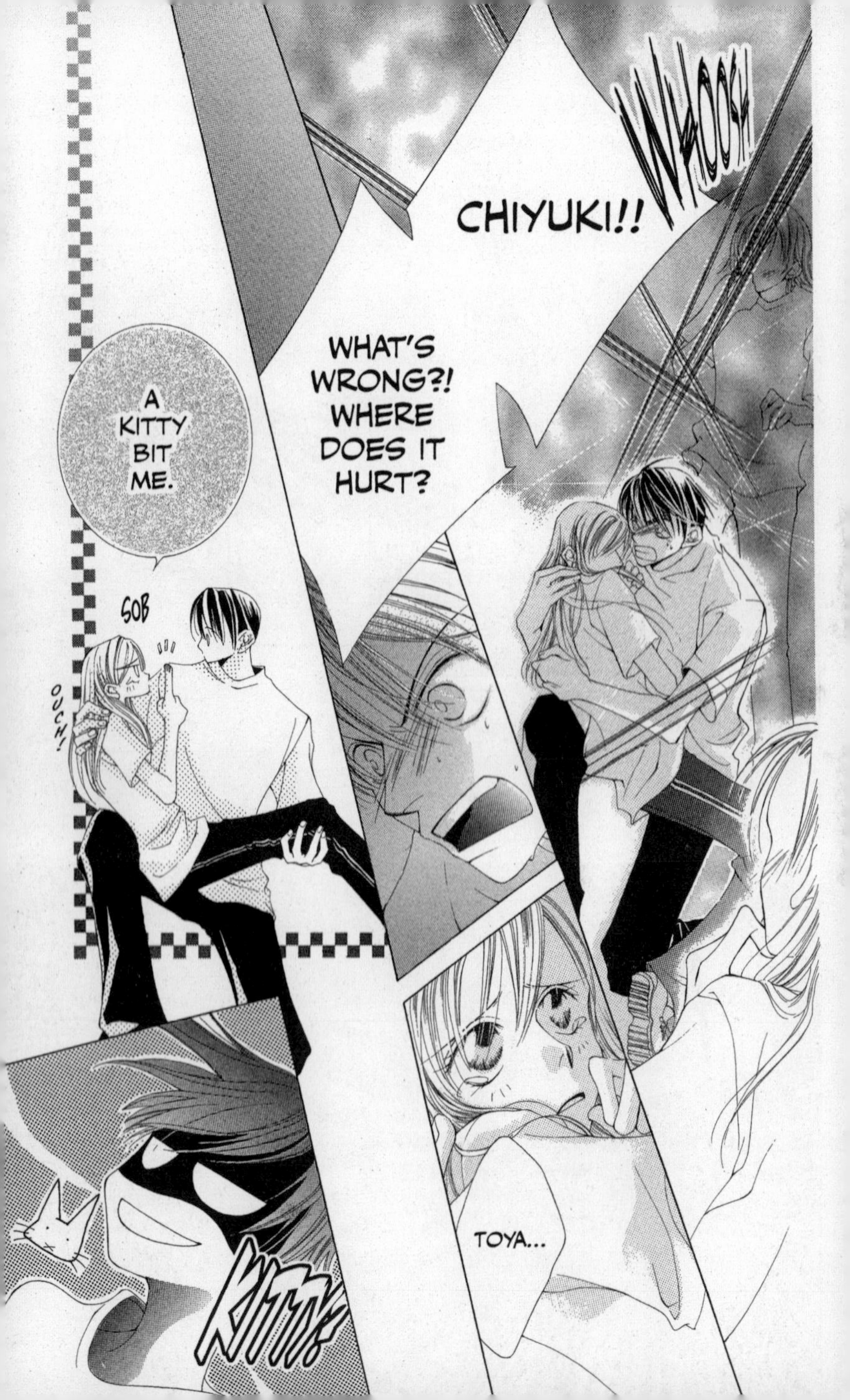
WHOOSH
CHIYUKI!!
WHAT'S WRONG?! WHERE DOES IT HURT?
A KITTY BIT ME.
SOB
OUCH!
TOYA...

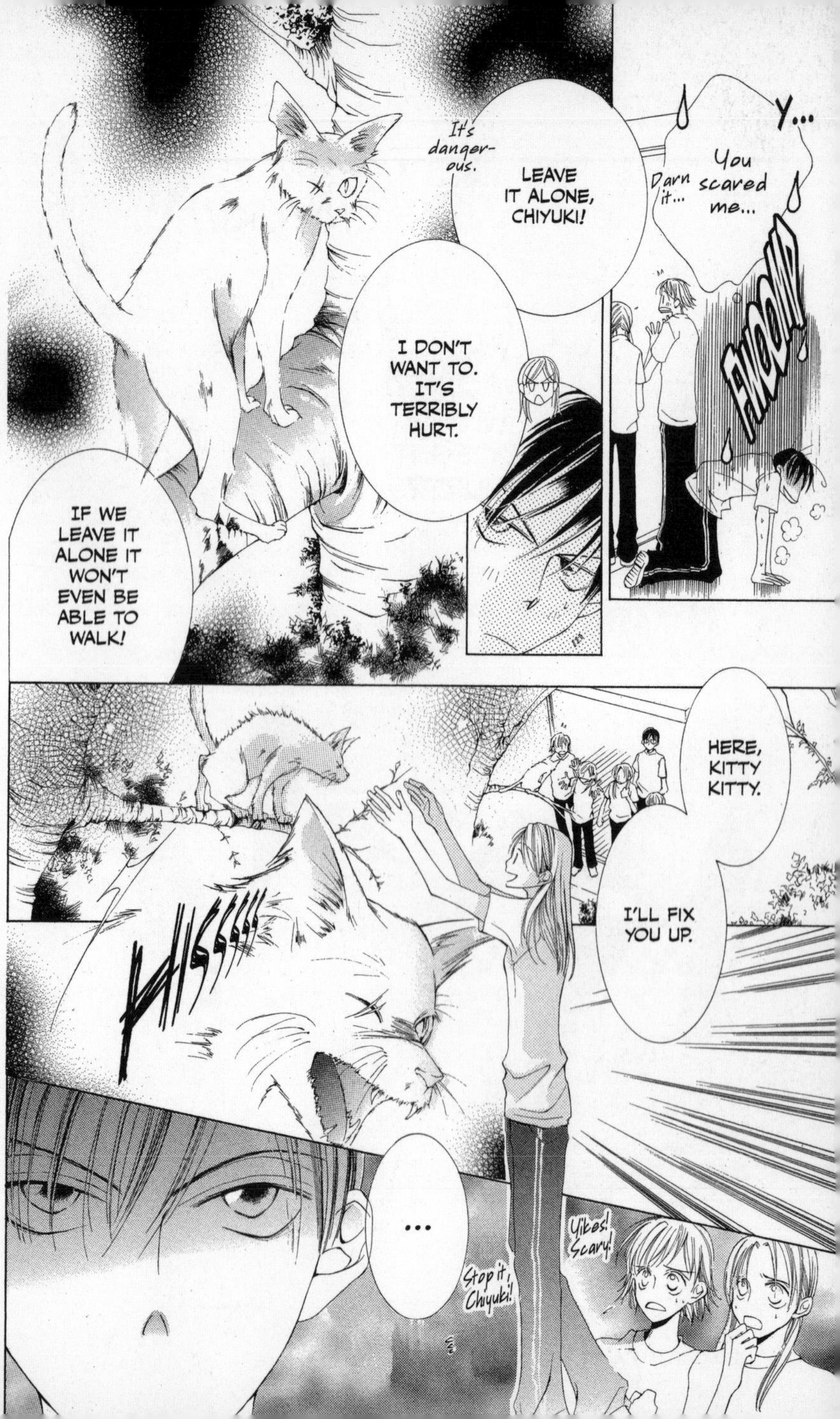
Y...
You scared me...
Darn it...
FWOOM!!
It's danger-ous.
LEAVE IT ALONE, CHIYUKI!
I DON'T WANT TO. IT'S TERRIBLY HURT.
IF WE LEAVE IT ALONE IT WON'T EVEN BE ABLE TO WALK!
HERE, KITTY KITTY.
I'LL FIX YOU UP.
HISSsss!!
...
Stop it, Chiyuki!
Yikes! Scary!

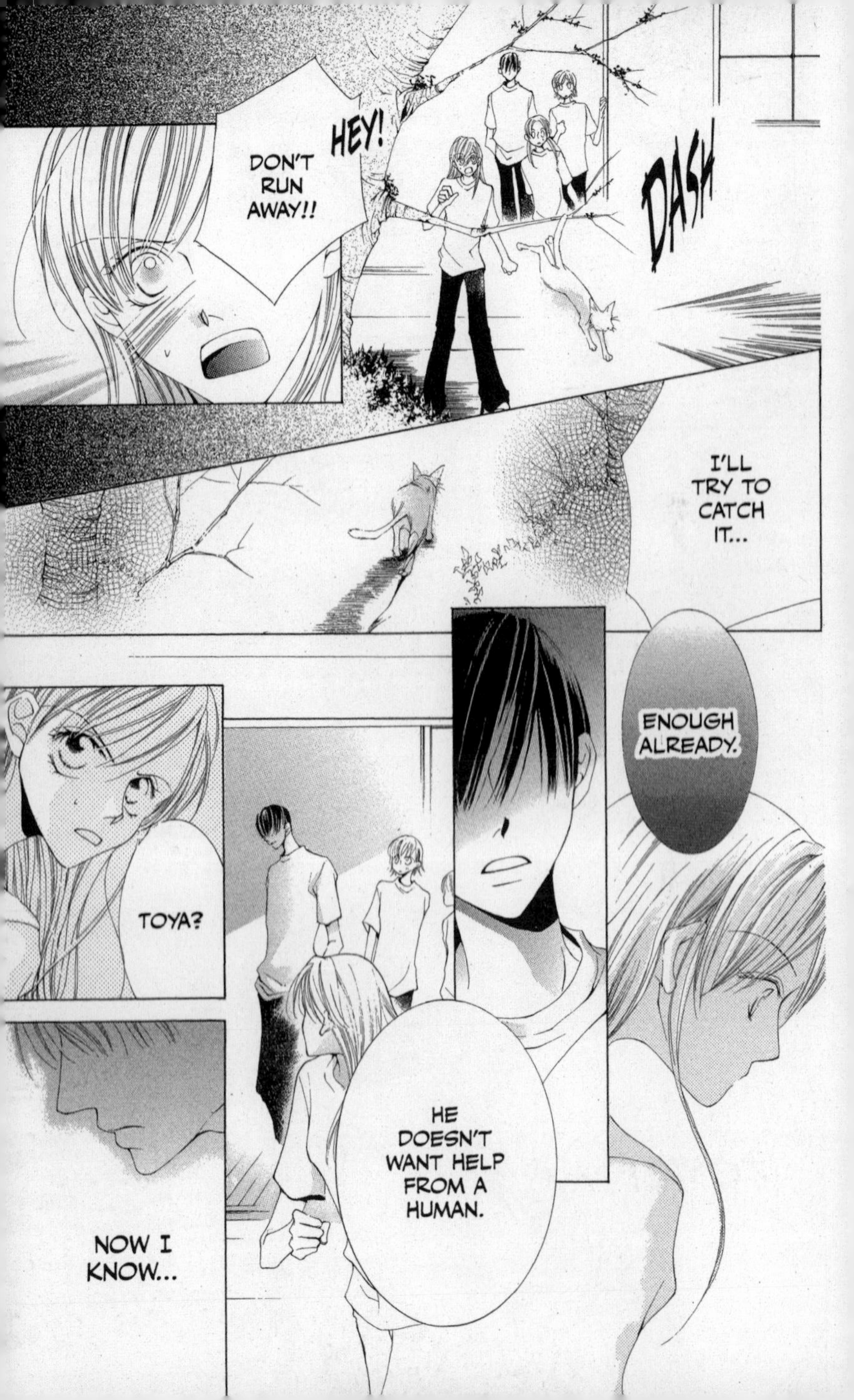
DASH
HEY!
DON'T RUN AWAY!!
I'LL TRY TO CATCH IT...
ENOUGH ALREADY.
TOYA?
HE DOESN'T WANT HELP FROM A HUMAN.
NOW I KNOW...

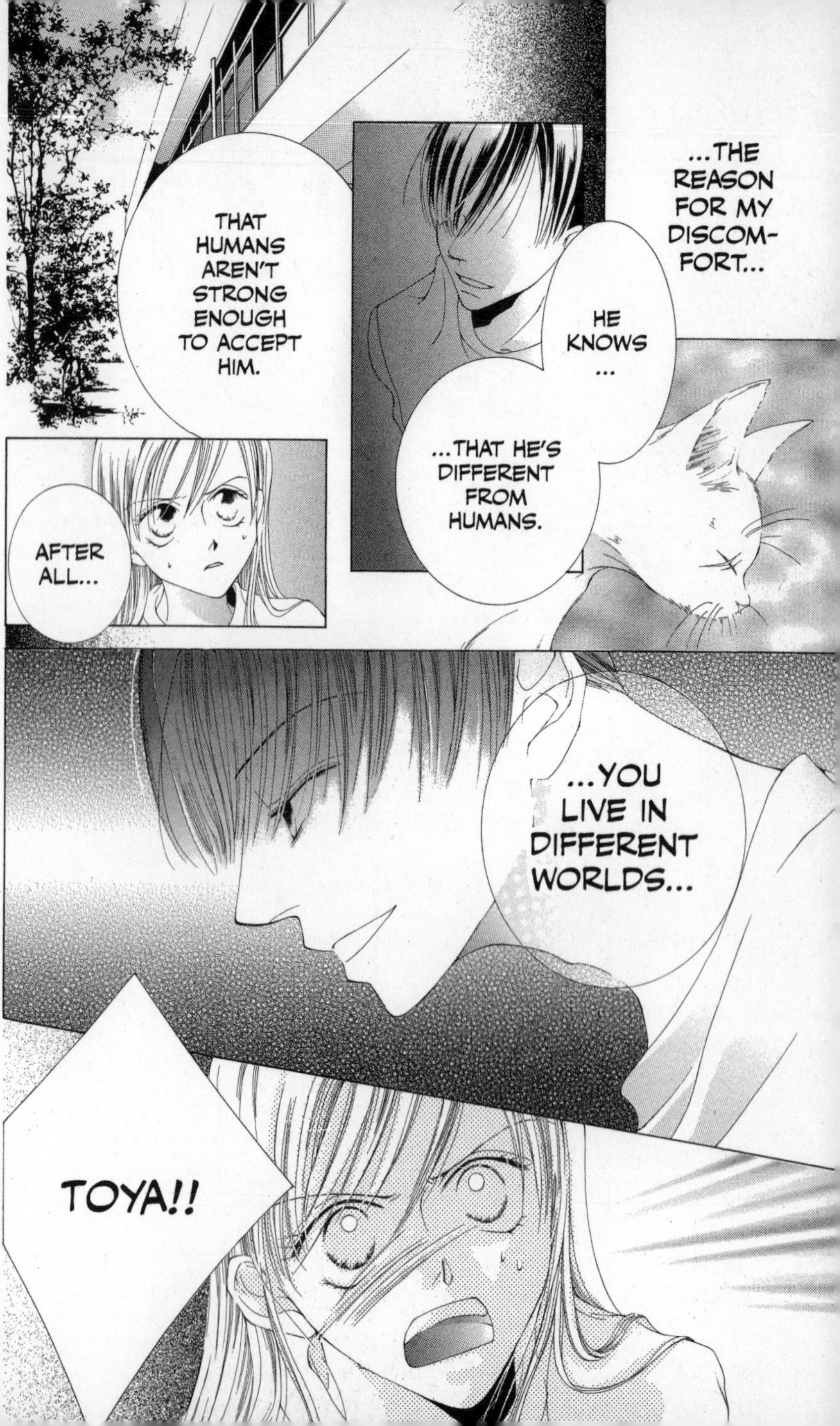
...THE REASON FOR MY DISCOMFORT...
HE KNOWS ...
...THAT HE'S DIFFERENT FROM HUMANS.
THAT HUMANS AREN'T STRONG ENOUGH TO ACCEPT HIM.
AFTER ALL...
...YOU LIVE IN DIFFERENT WORLDS...
TOYA!!

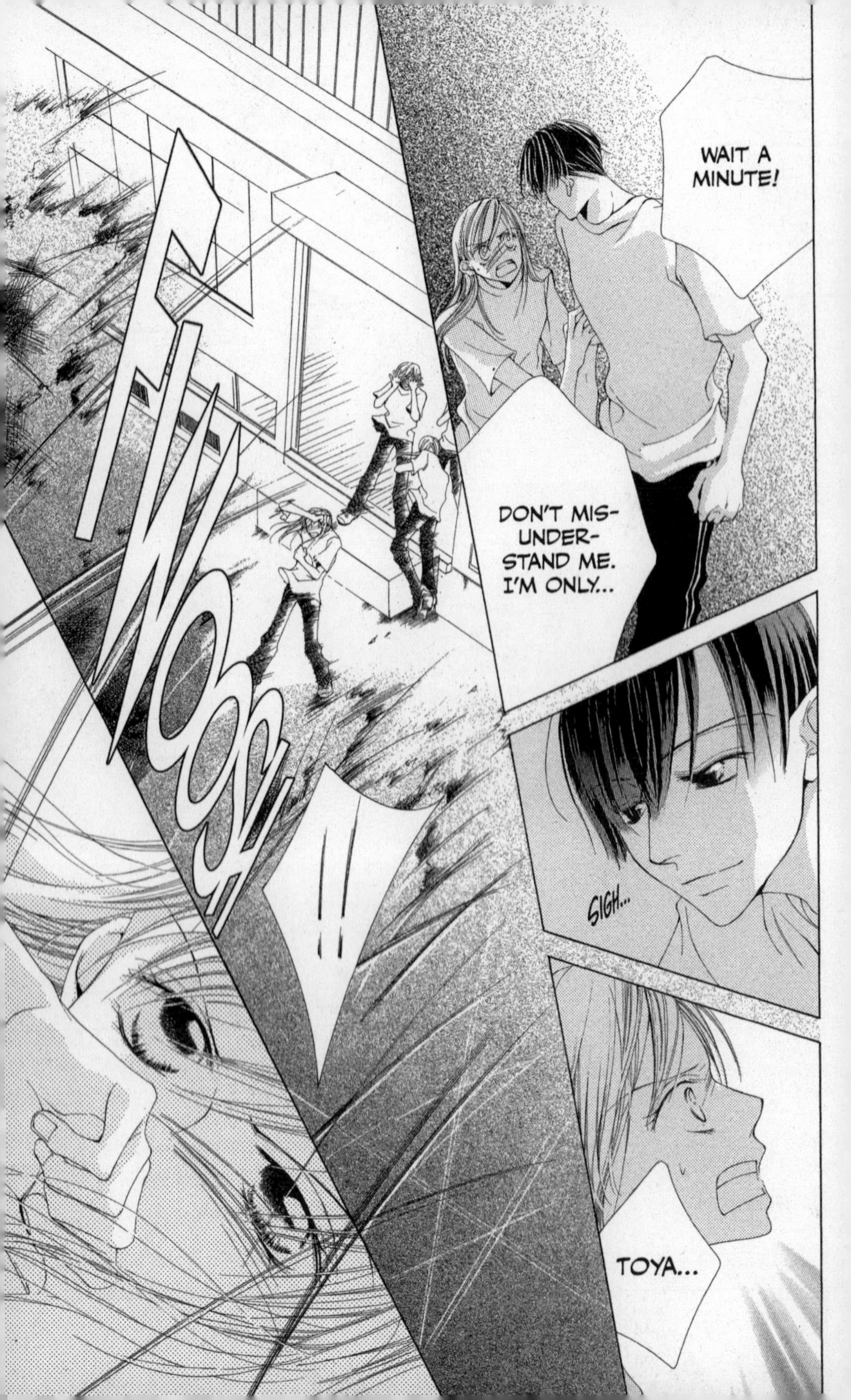
WAIT A MINUTE!
DON'T MIS-UNDER-STAND ME. I'M ONLY...
SIGH...
TOYA...
FWOOSH!
!!

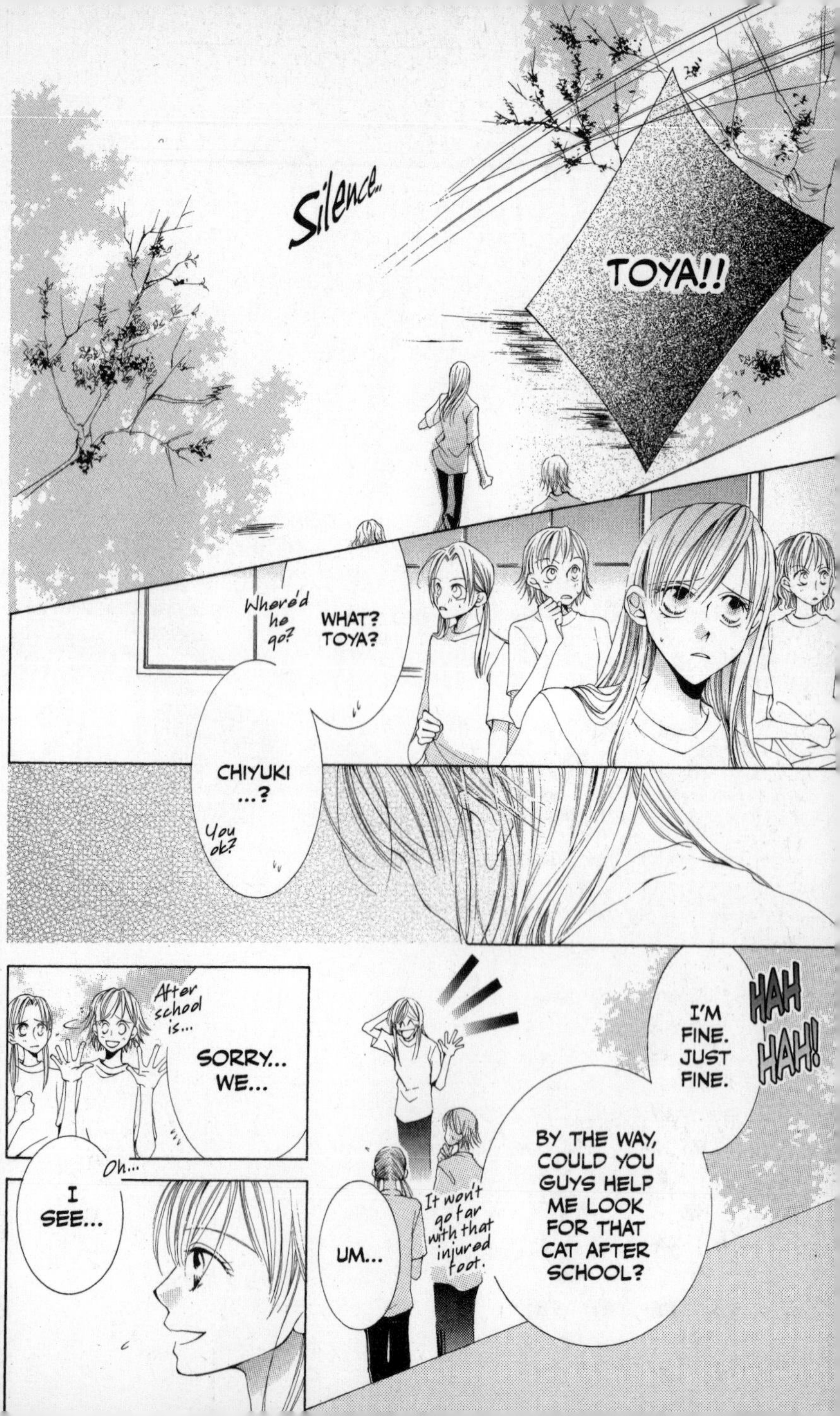
TOYA!!
Silence...
WHAT? TOYA?
Where'd he go?
CHIYUKI ...?
You ok?
HAH HAH!
I'M FINE. JUST FINE.
BY THE WAY, COULD YOU GUYS HELP ME LOOK FOR THAT CAT AFTER SCHOOL?
It won't go far with that injured foot.
UM...
SORRY... WE...
After school is...
Oh...
I SEE...

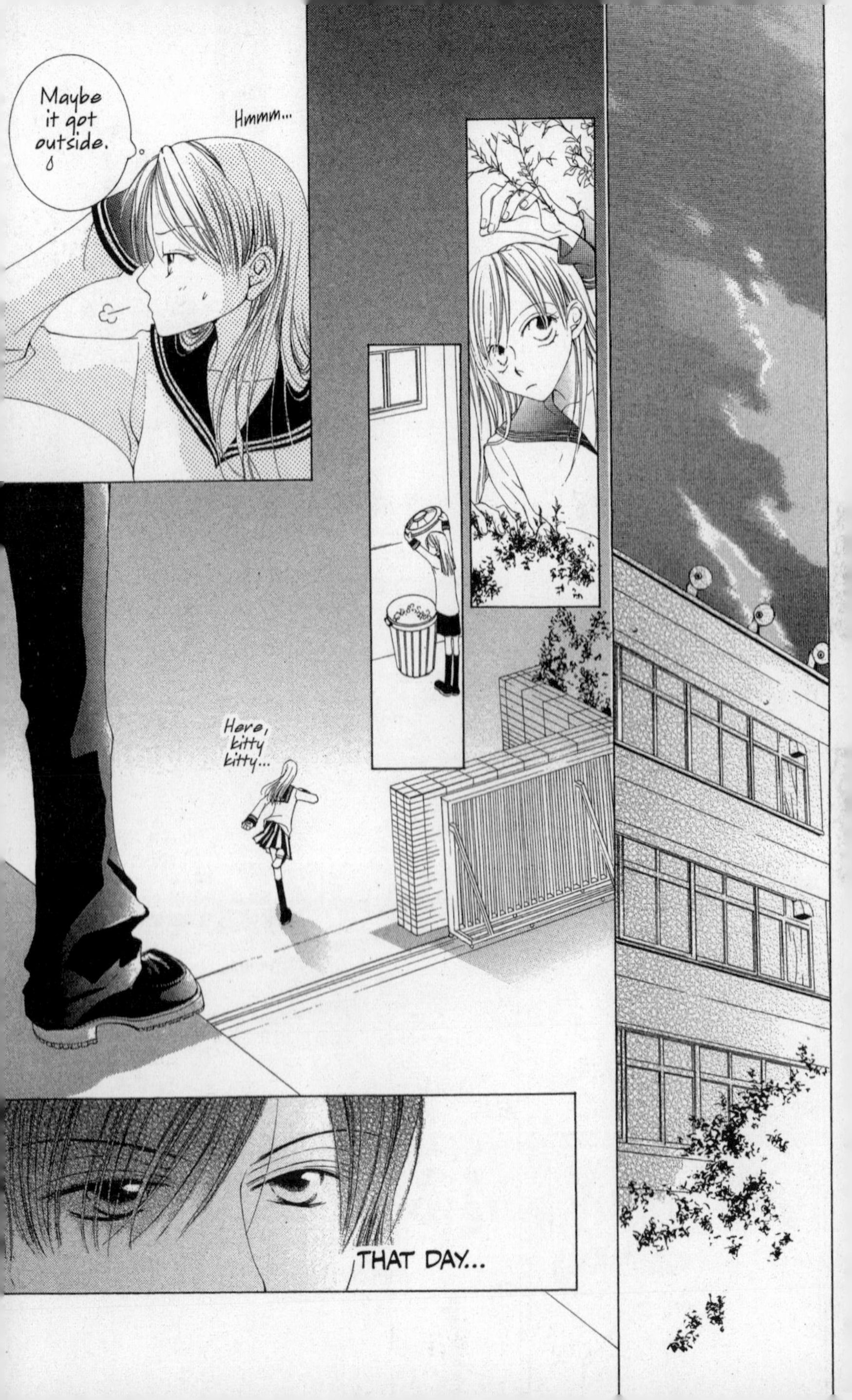
Hmmm...
Maybe it got outside.
Here, kitty kitty...
THAT DAY...

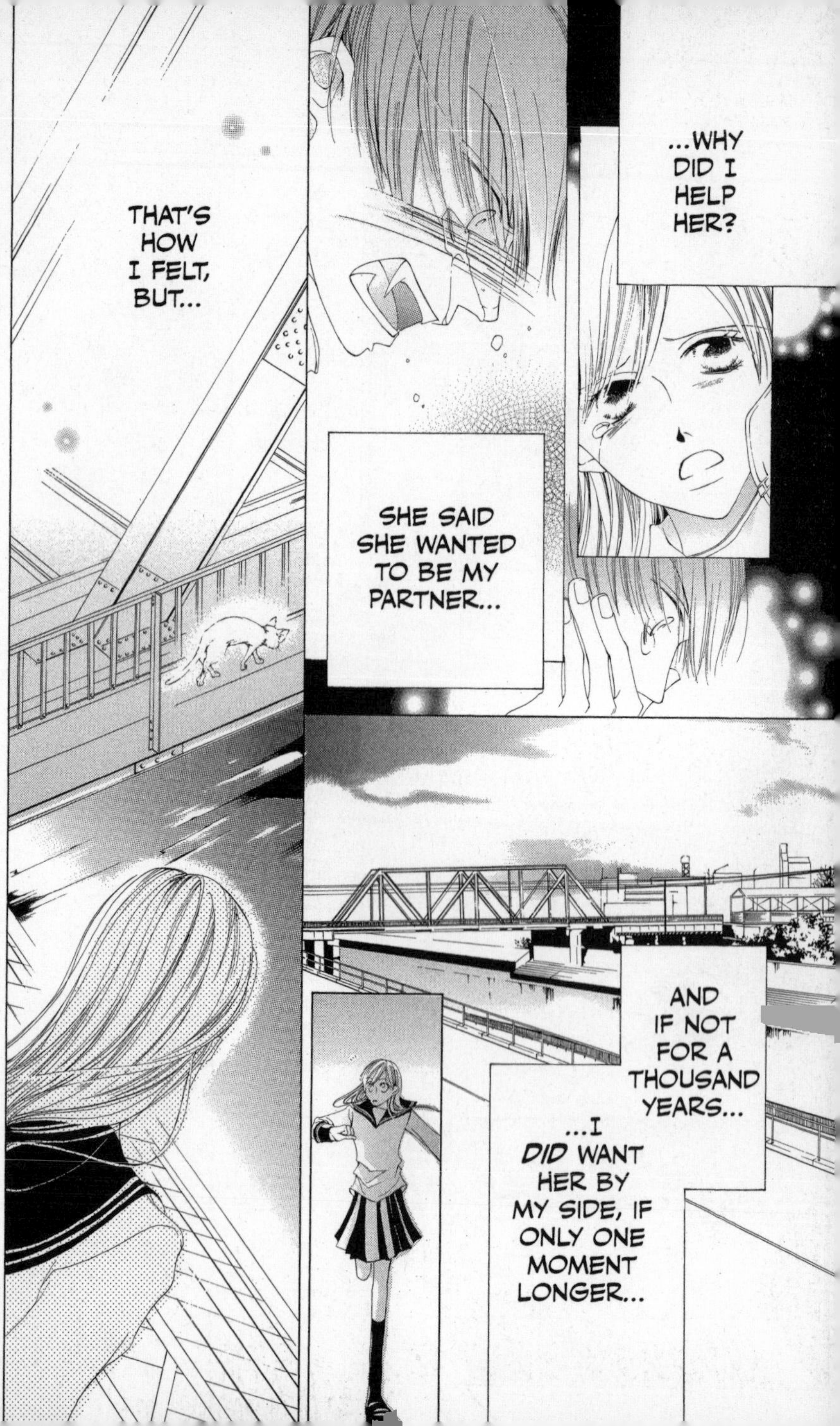
...WHY DID I HELP HER?
SHE SAID SHE WANTED TO BE MY PARTNER...
AND IF NOT FOR A THOUSAND YEARS...
...I *DID* WANT HER BY MY SIDE, IF ONLY ONE MOMENT LONGER...
THAT'S HOW I FELT, BUT...

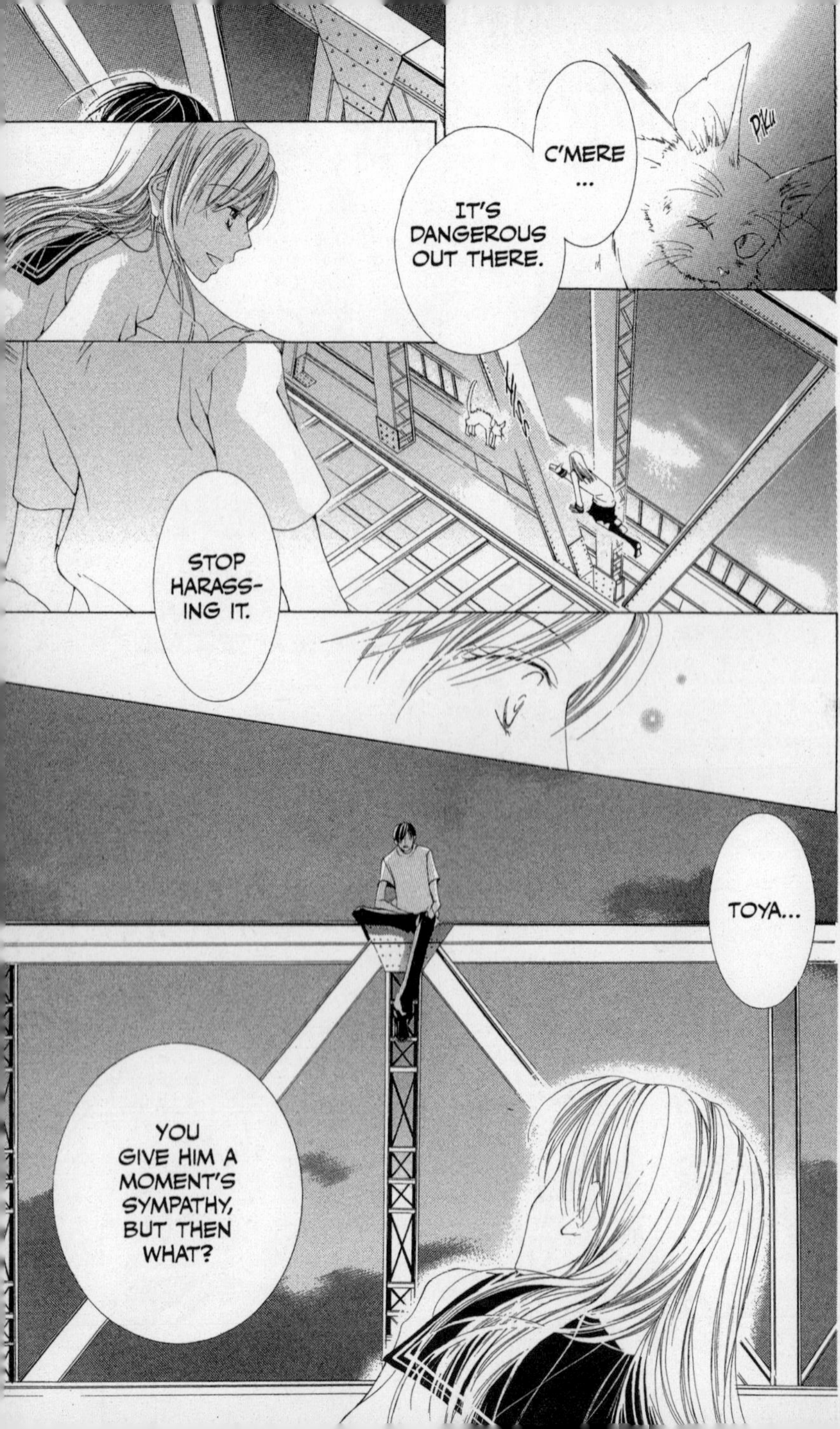

PIKU
C'MERE ...
IT'S DANGEROUS OUT THERE.
HISS
STOP HARASS-ING IT.
TOYA...
YOU GIVE HIM A MOMENT'S SYMPATHY, BUT THEN WHAT?

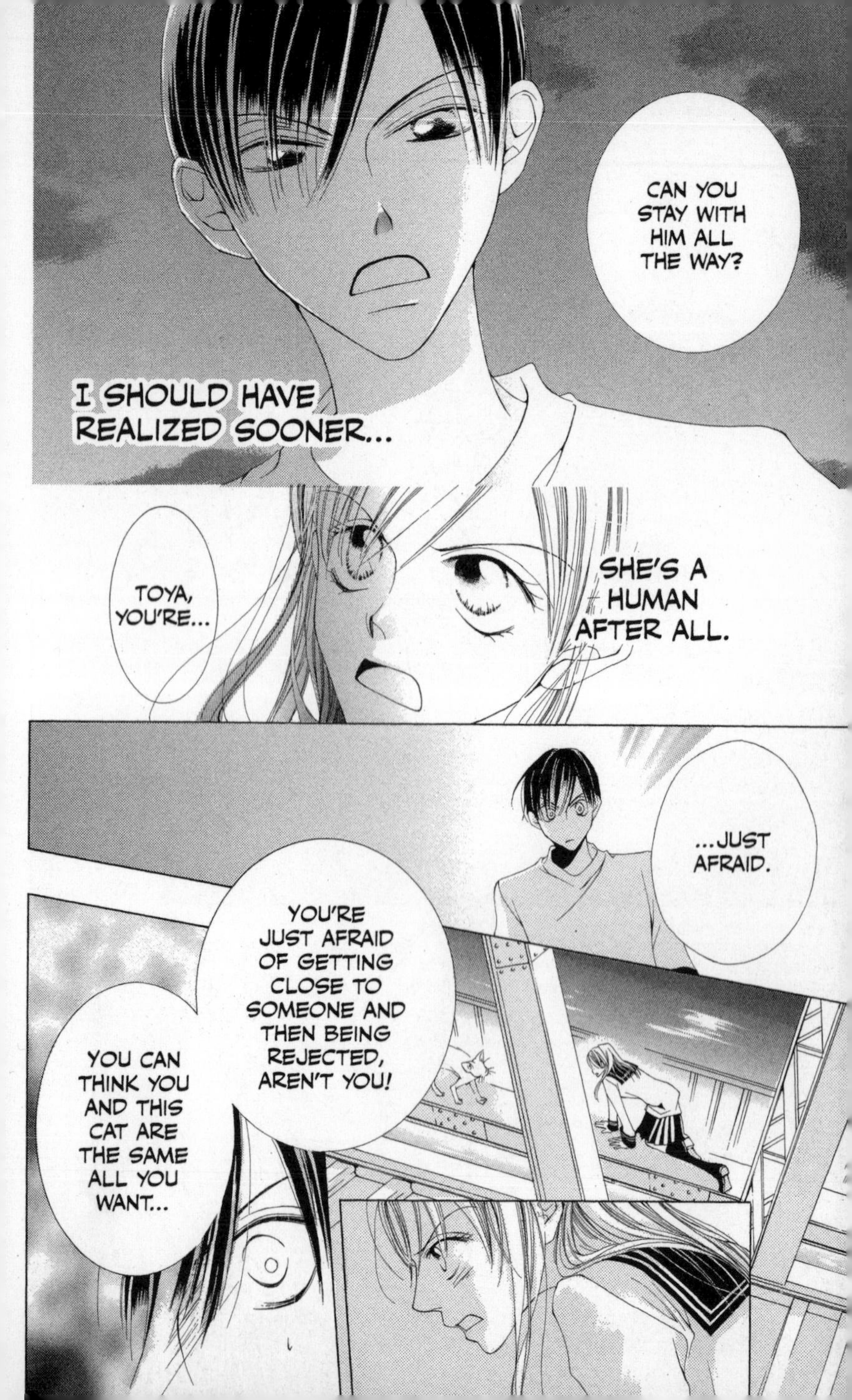
CAN YOU STAY WITH HIM ALL THE WAY?
I SHOULD HAVE REALIZED SOONER...
SHE'S A HUMAN AFTER ALL.
TOYA, YOU'RE...
...JUST AFRAID.
YOU'RE JUST AFRAID OF GETTING CLOSE TO SOMEONE AND THEN BEING REJECTED, AREN'T YOU!
YOU CAN THINK YOU AND THIS CAT ARE THE SAME ALL YOU WANT...

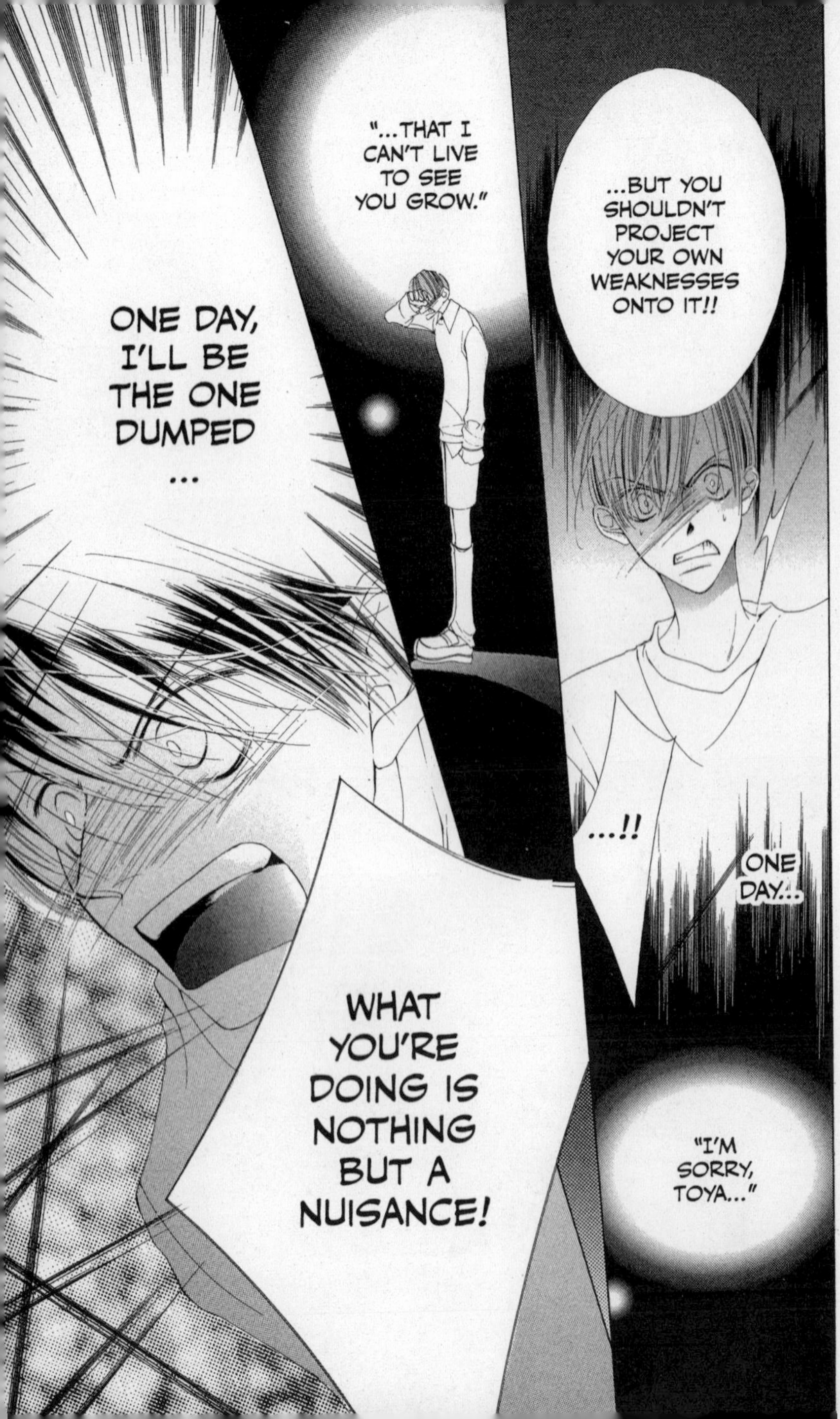
...BUT YOU SHOULDN'T PROJECT YOUR OWN WEAKNESSES ONTO IT!!
"...THAT I CAN'T LIVE TO SEE YOU GROW."
...!!
ONE DAY...
"I'M SORRY, TOYA..."
ONE DAY, I'LL BE THE ONE DUMPED ...
WHAT YOU'RE DOING IS NOTHING BUT A NUISANCE!

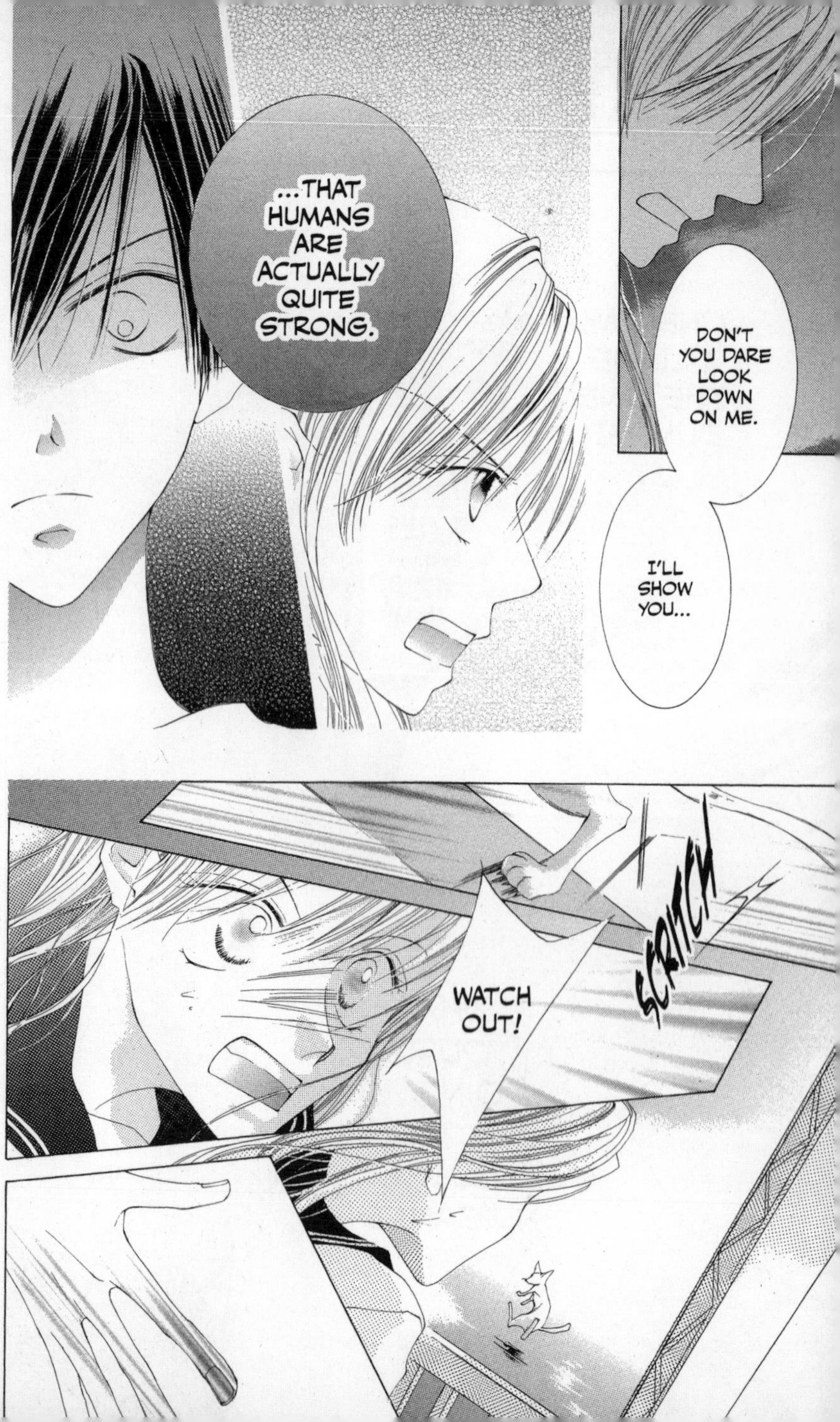
DON'T YOU DARE LOOK DOWN ON ME.
I'LL SHOW YOU...
...THAT HUMANS ARE ACTUALLY QUITE STRONG.
SCRITCH
WATCH OUT!

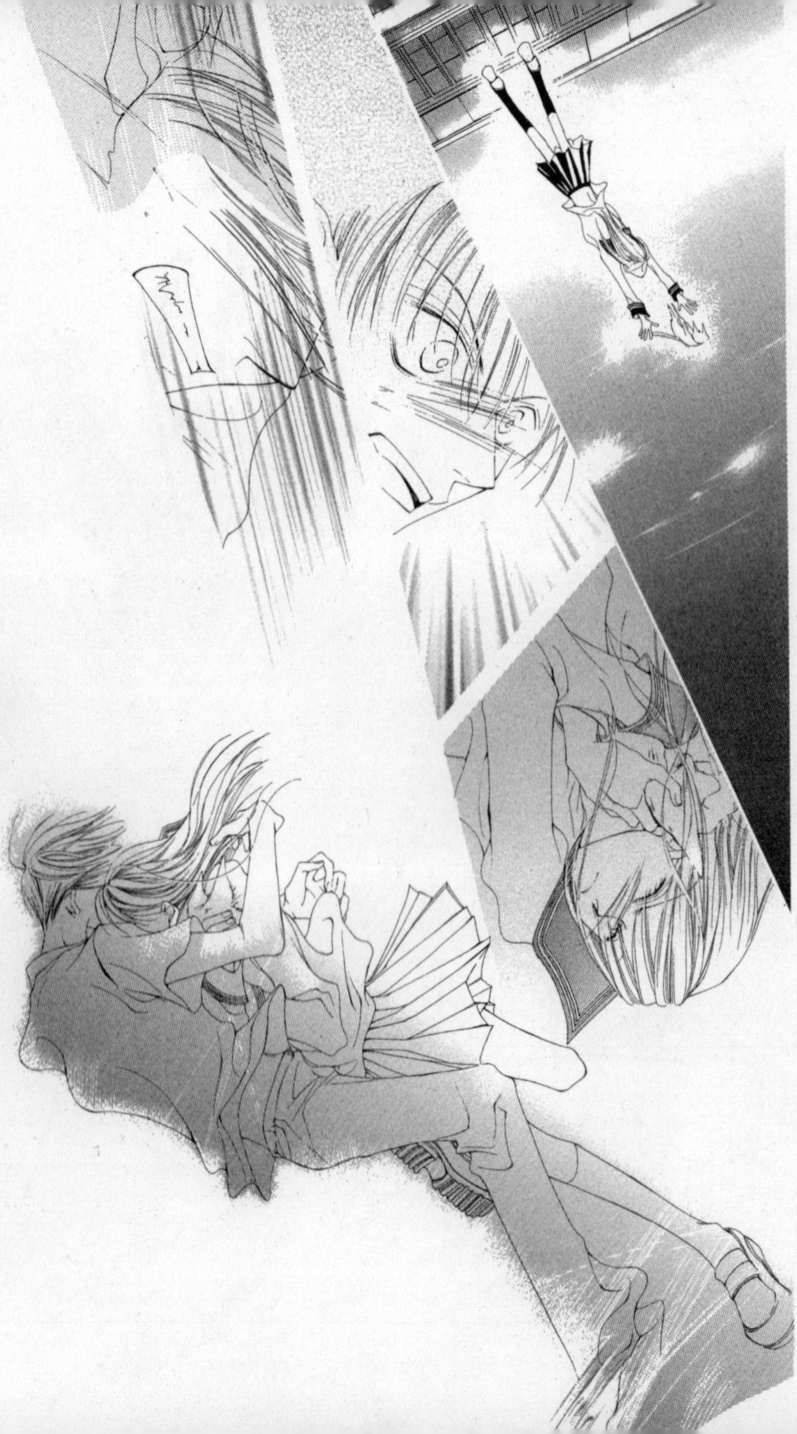

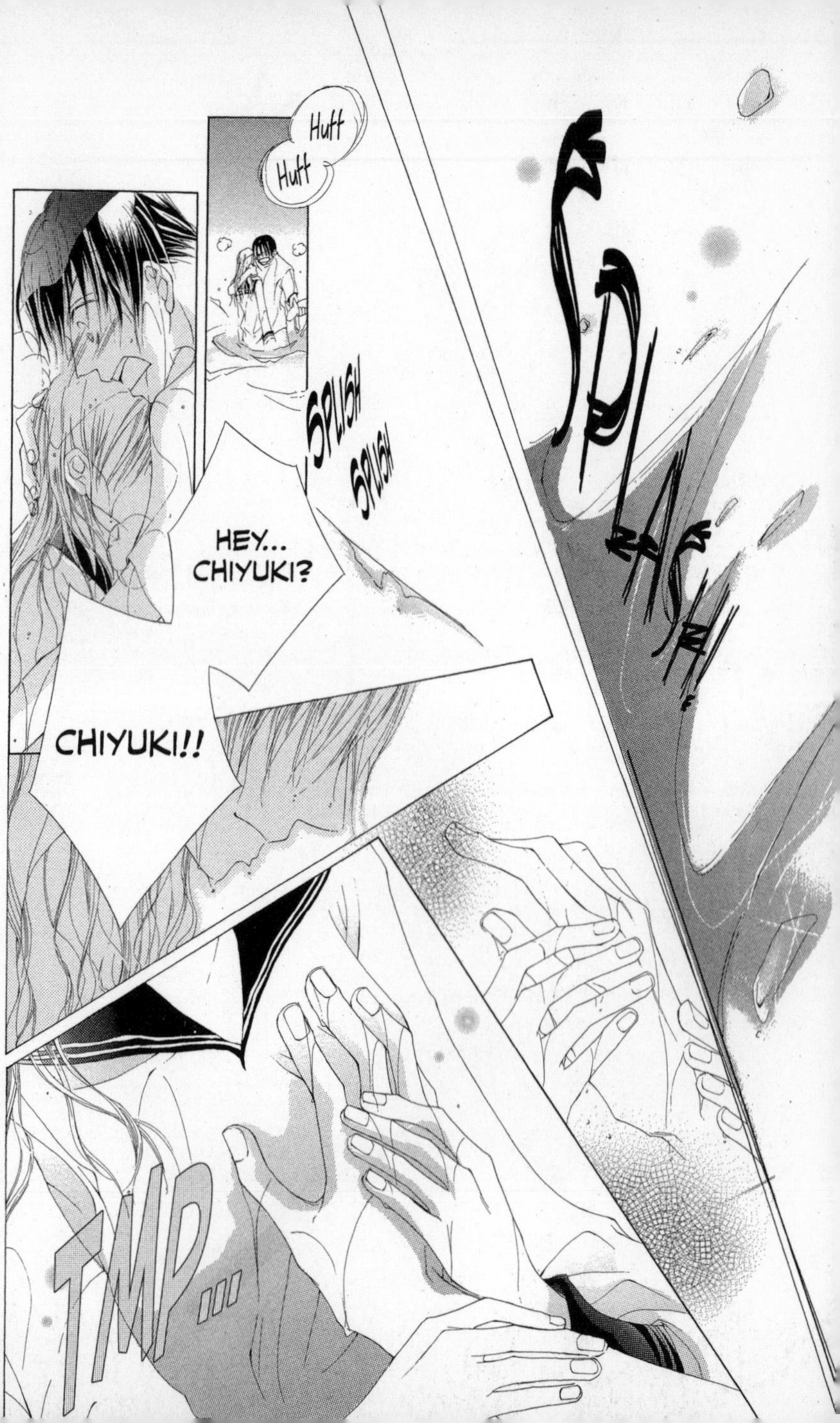
SPLASH
Huff
Huff
SPLISH
SPLISH
HEY... CHIYUKI?
CHIYUKI!!
TMP...

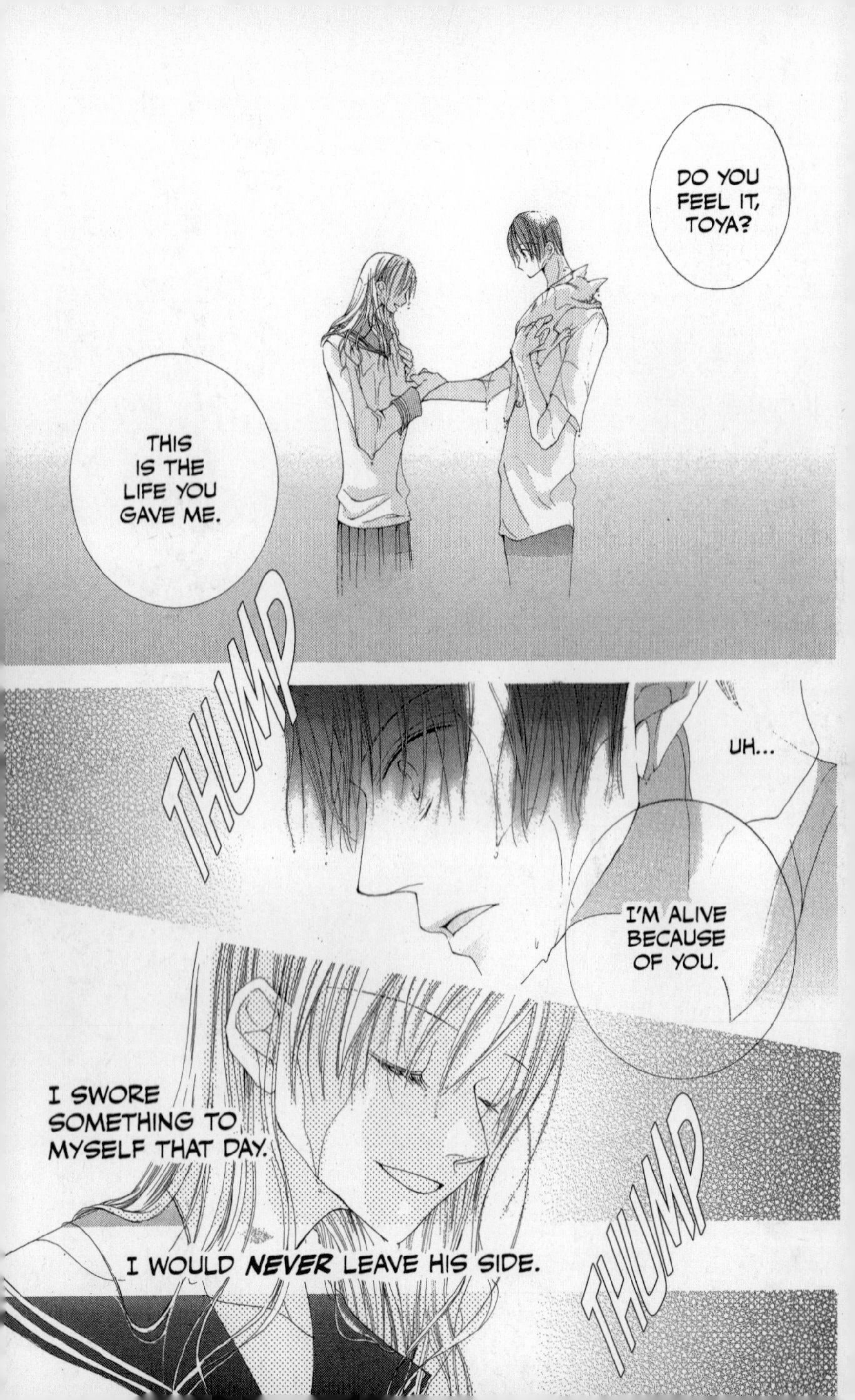
DO YOU FEEL IT, TOYA?
THIS IS THE LIFE YOU GAVE ME.
THUMP
UH...
I'M ALIVE BECAUSE OF YOU.
I SWORE SOMETHING TO MYSELF THAT DAY.
THUMP
I WOULD NEVER LEAVE HIS SIDE.

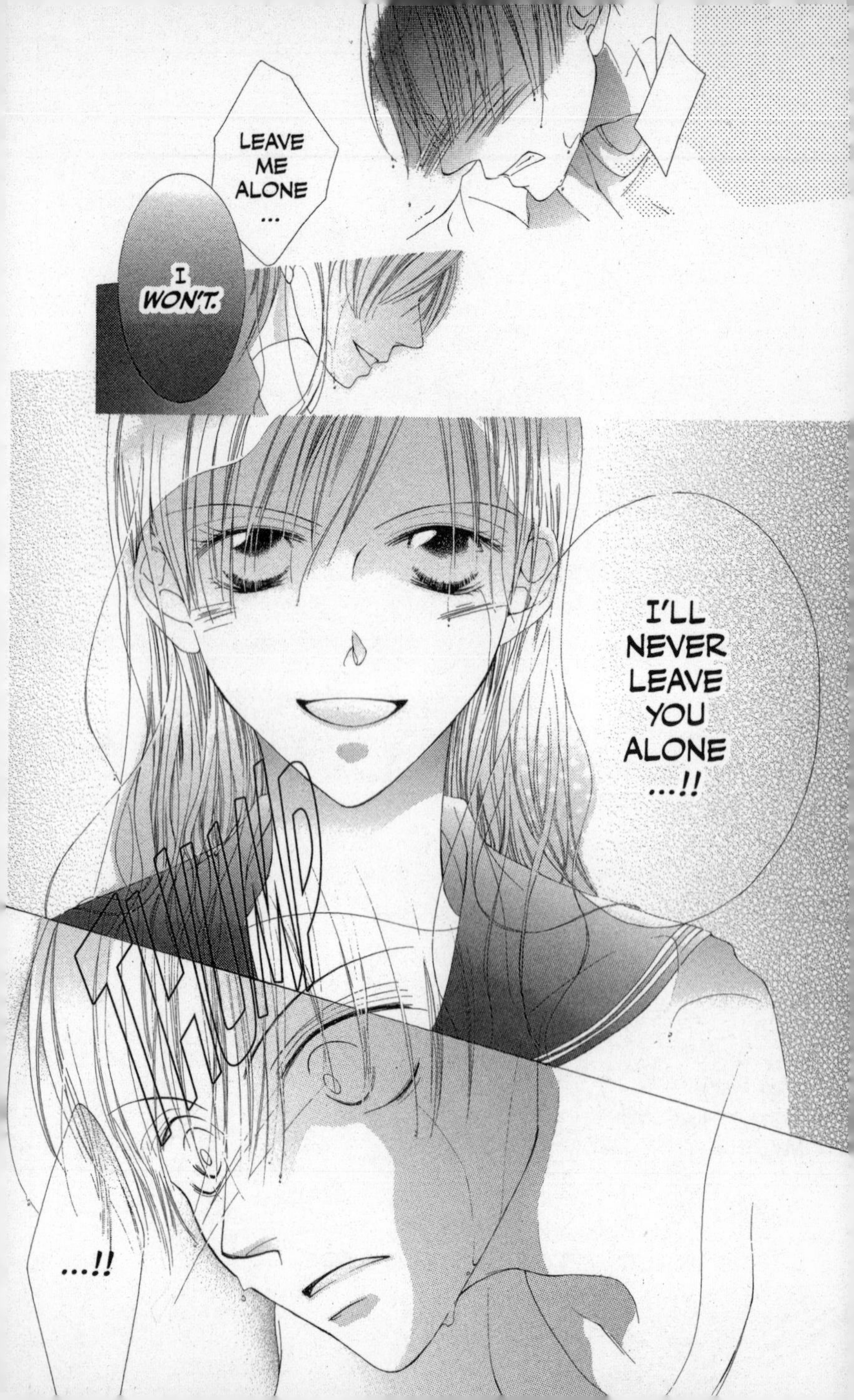
LEAVE ME ALONE ...
I WON'T.
I'LL NEVER LEAVE YOU ALONE ...!!
THUMP
...!!

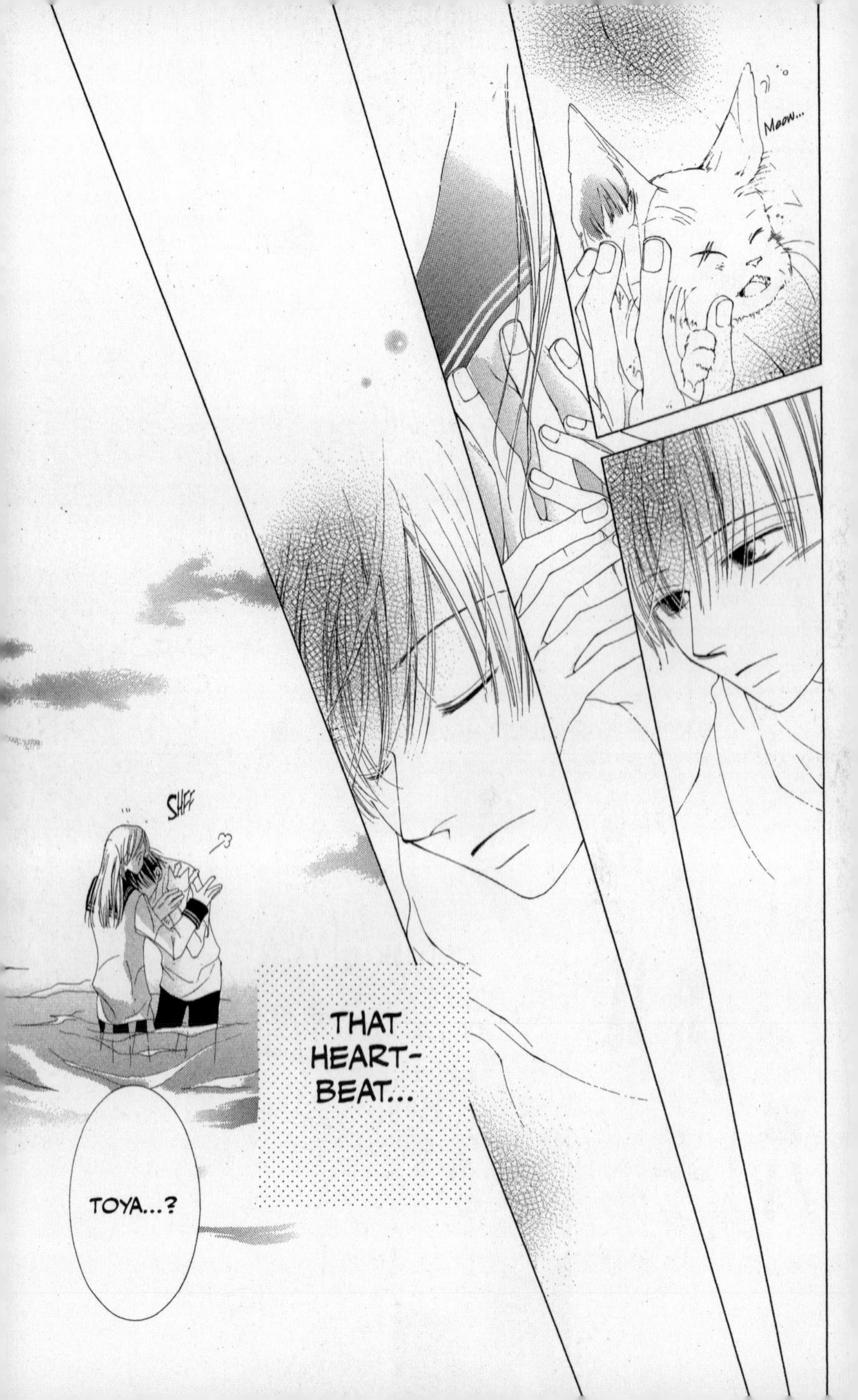
Meow...
THAT HEART-BEAT...
SHFF
TOYA...?

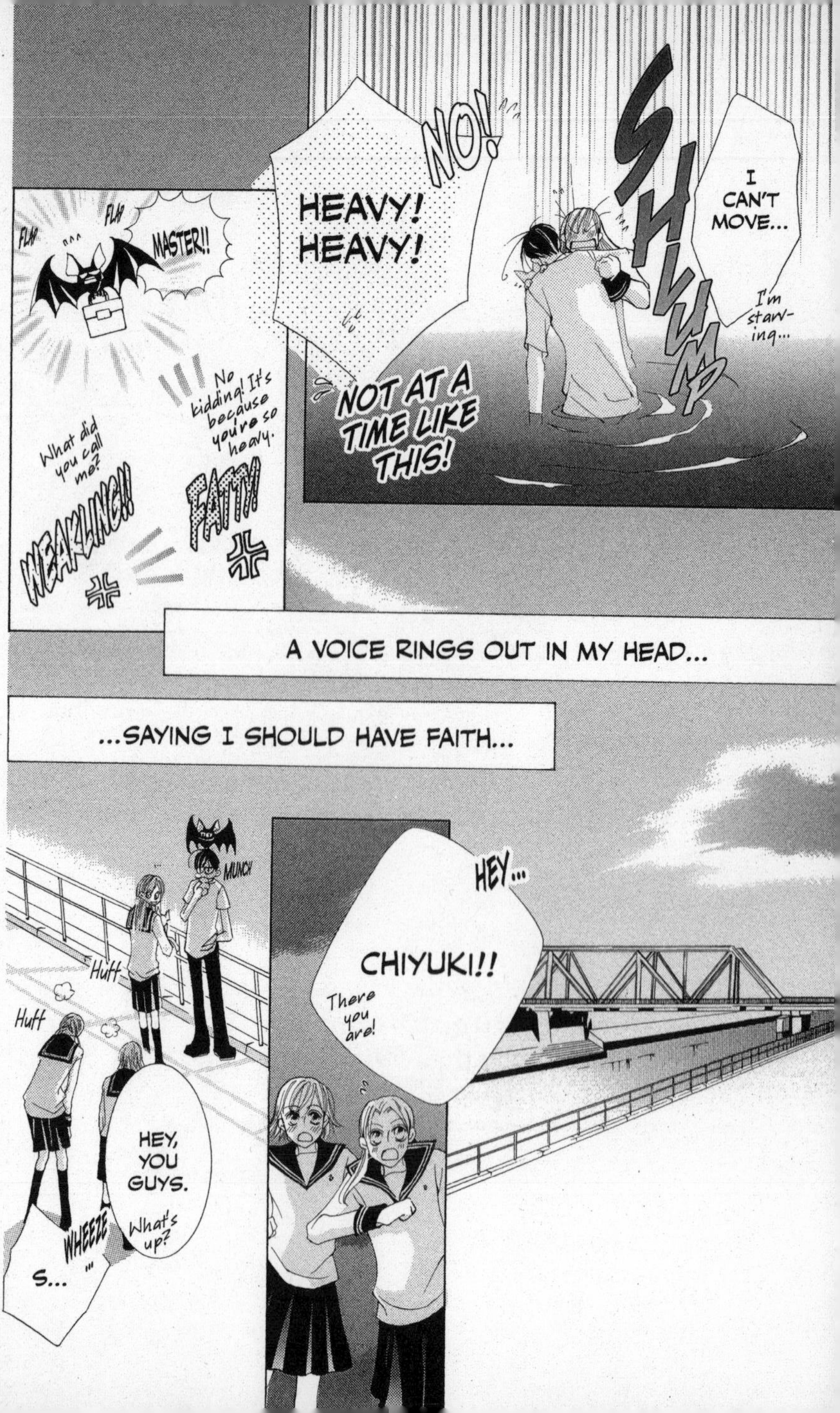
SHVUMP
I CAN'T MOVE...
I'm starving...
NO!
HEAVY! HEAVY!
NOT AT A TIME LIKE THIS!
FLAP FLAP
MASTER!!
No kidding! It's because you're so heavy.
FATTY!
What did you call me?
WEAKLING!!
A VOICE RINGS OUT IN MY HEAD...
...SAYING I SHOULD HAVE FAITH...
HEY...
CHIYUKI!!
There you are!
MUNCH
Huff
Huff
HEY, YOU GUYS.
What's up?
WHEEZE
S...

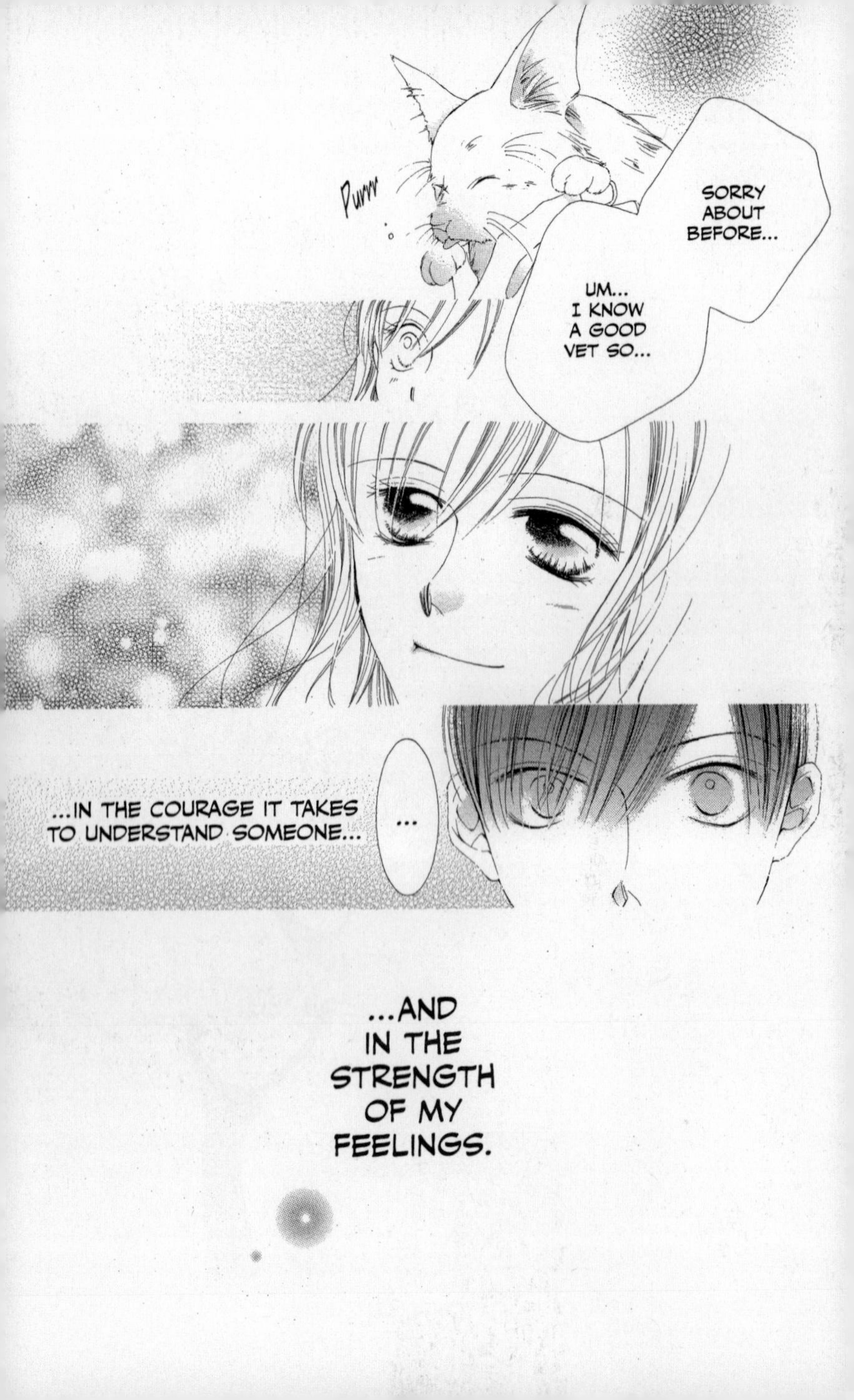
Purrr
SORRY ABOUT BEFORE...
UM... I KNOW A GOOD VET SO...
...
...IN THE COURAGE IT TAKES TO UNDERSTAND SOMEONE...
...AND IN THE STRENGTH OF MY FEELINGS.

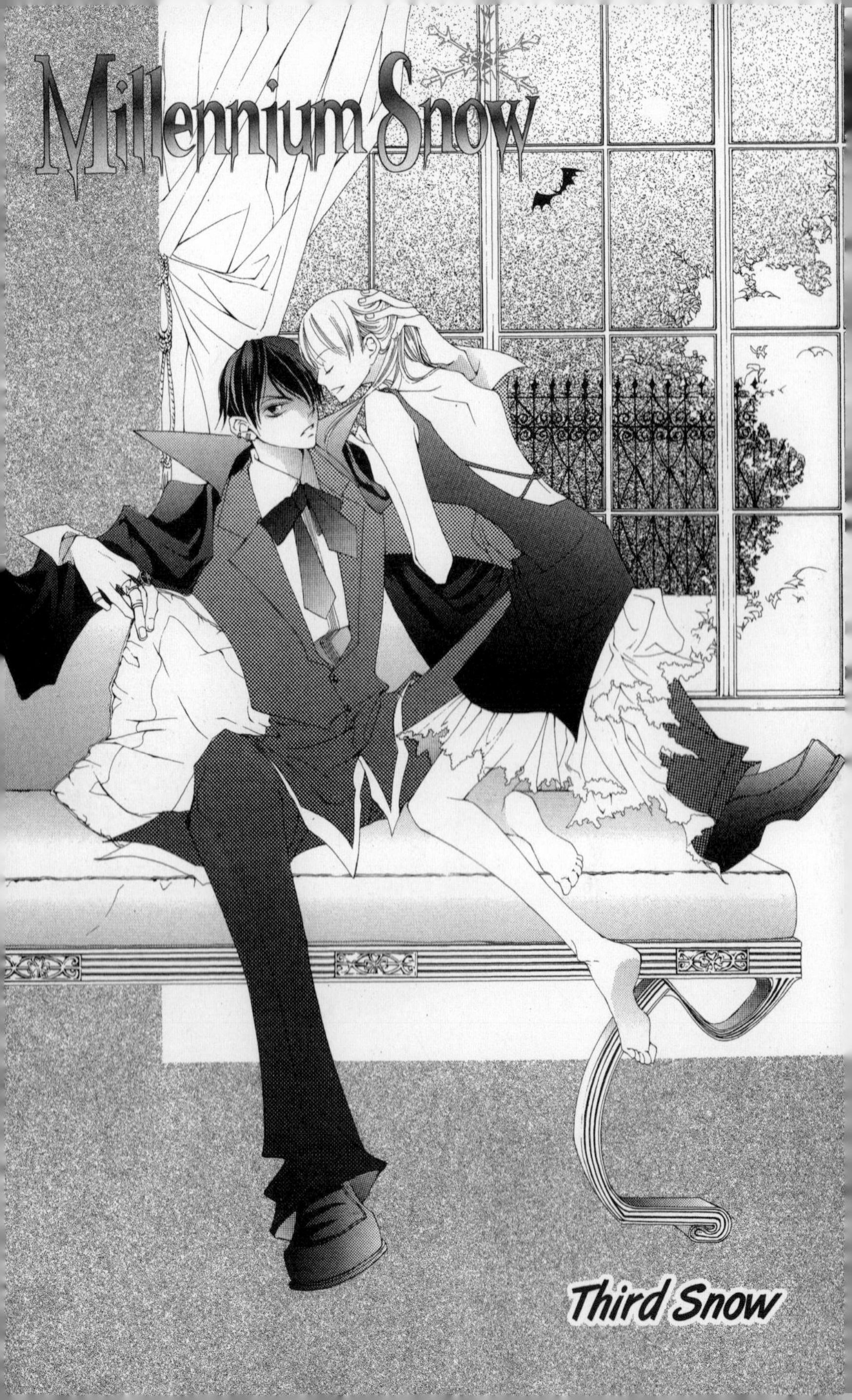
Millennium Snow
Third Snow

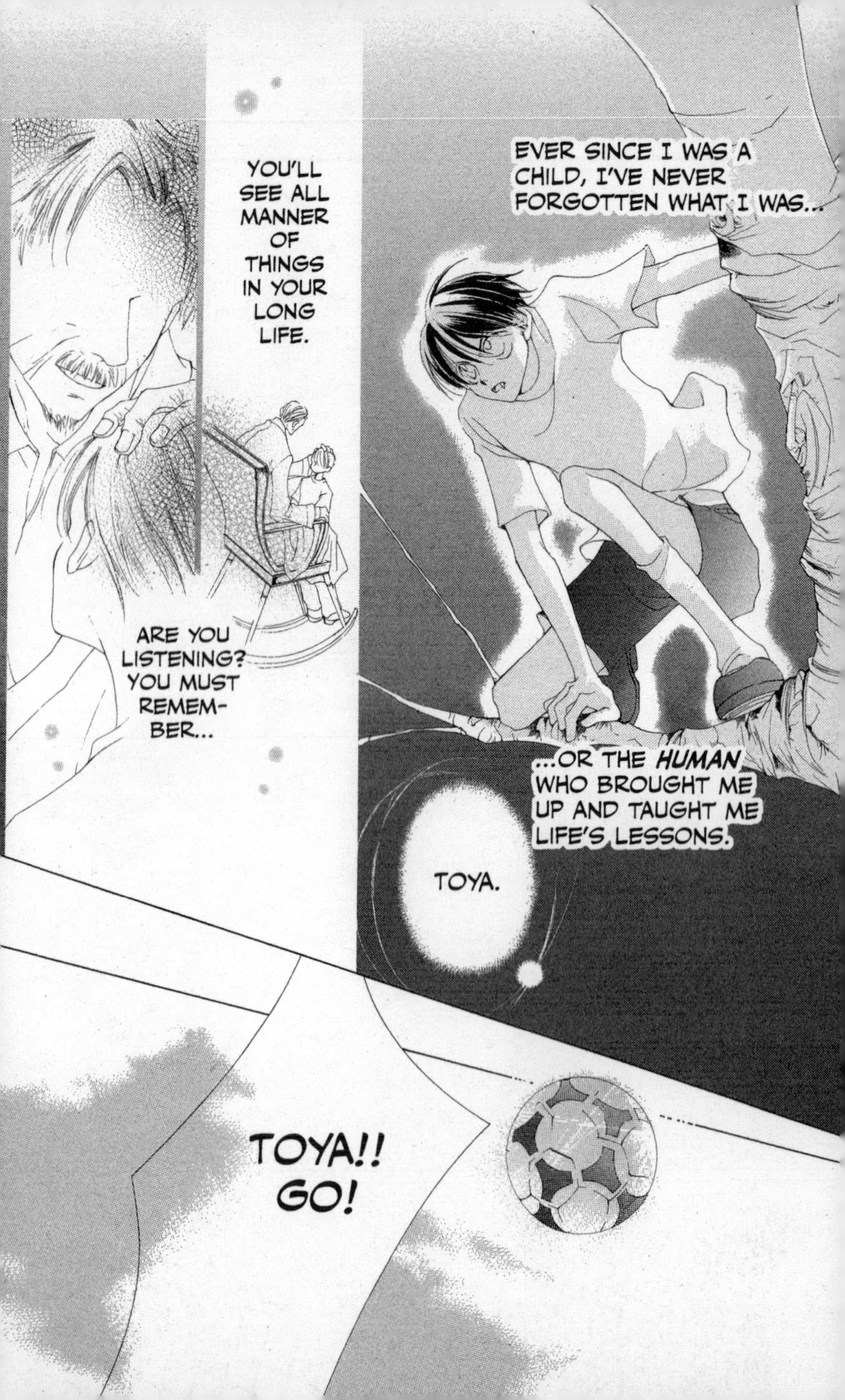
EVER SINCE I WAS A CHILD, I'VE NEVER FORGOTTEN WHAT I WAS...
...OR THE *HUMAN* WHO BROUGHT ME UP AND TAUGHT ME LIFE'S LESSONS.
TOYA.
YOU'LL SEE ALL MANNER OF THINGS IN YOUR LONG LIFE.
ARE YOU LISTENING? YOU MUST REMEMBER...
TOYA!! GO!

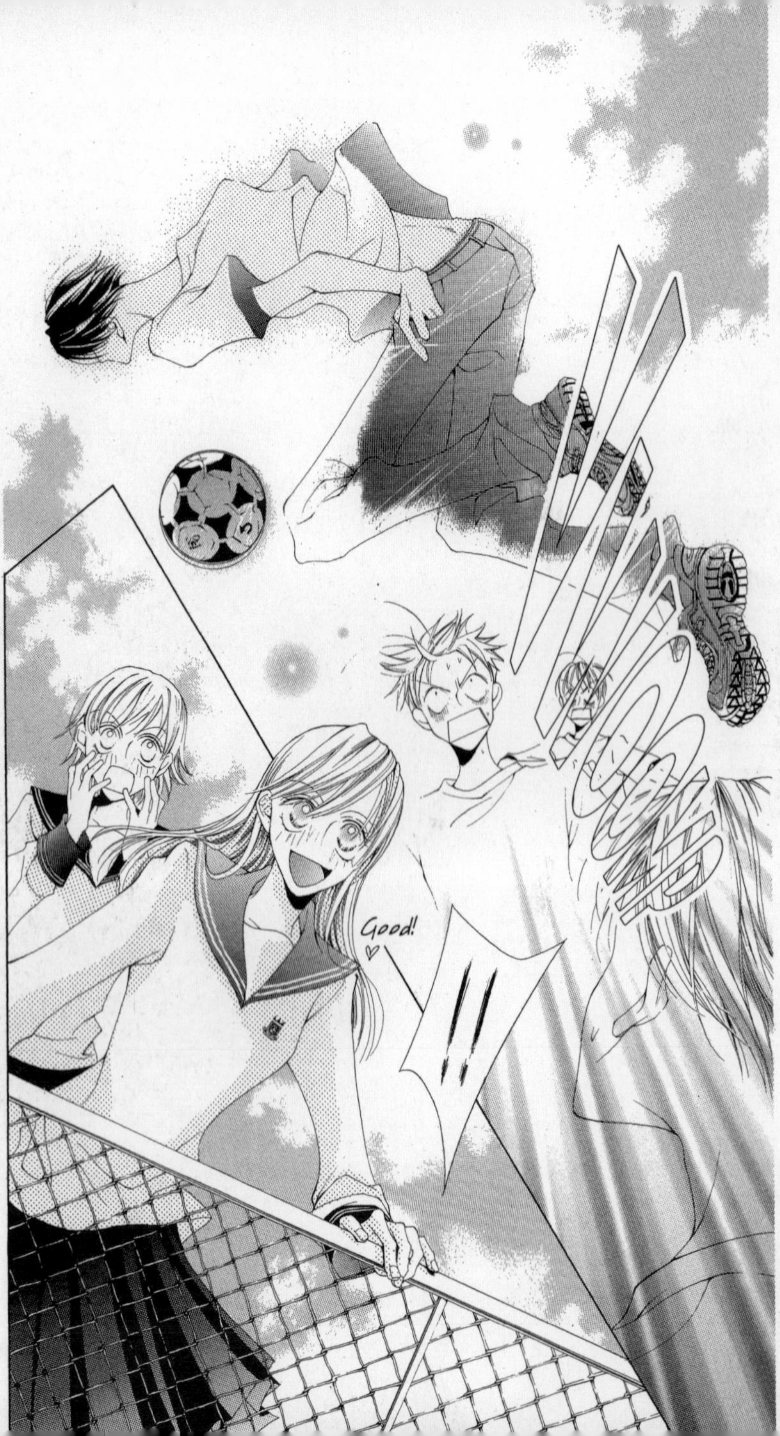
WHOOOMP!
Good! ♥
!!

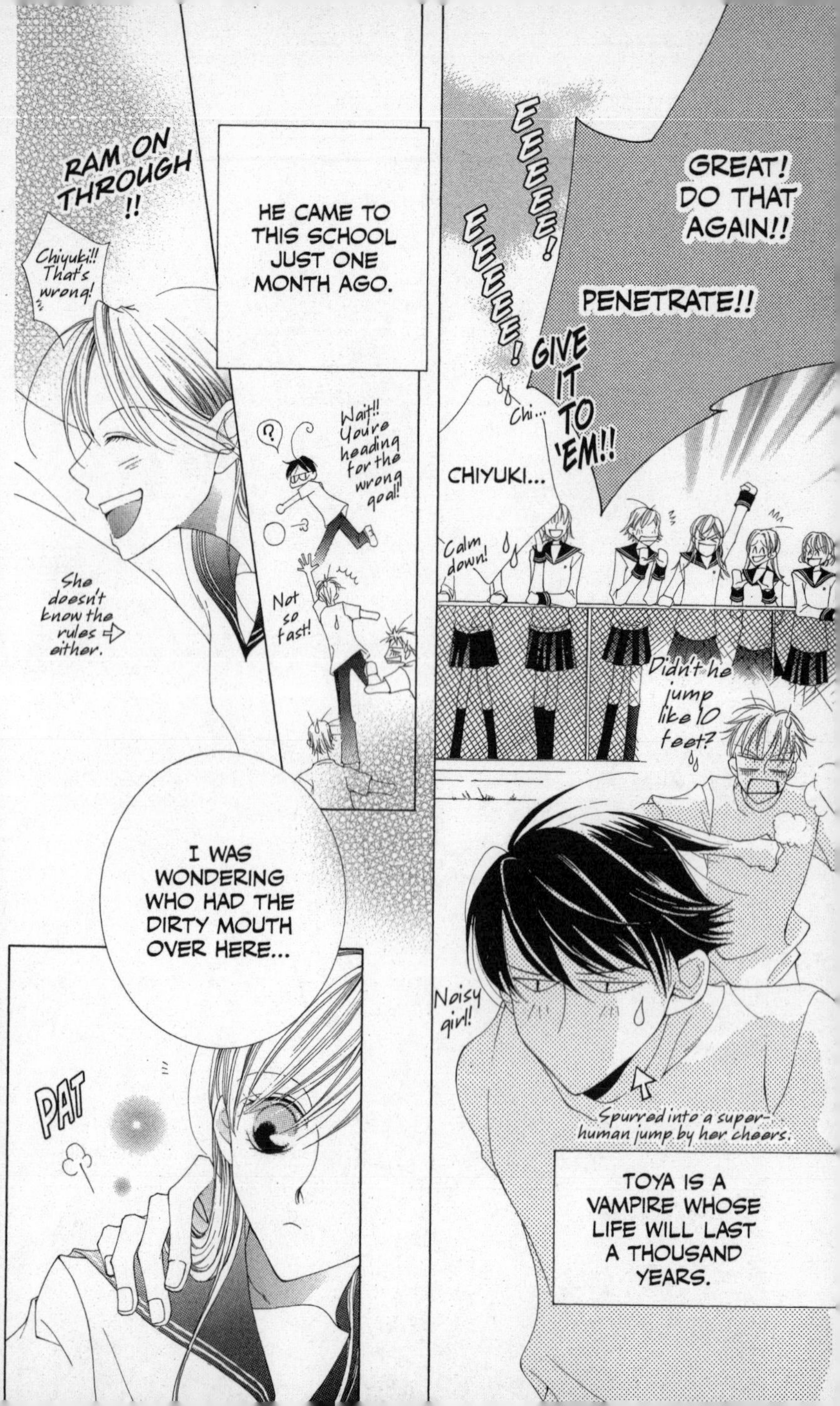
GREAT! DO THAT AGAIN!!
EEEEEE!
EEEEE!
PENETRATE!!
GIVE IT TO 'EM!!
Chi...
CHIYUKI...
Calm down!
Didn't he jump like 10 feet?
Noisy girl!
Spurred into a super-human jump by her cheers.
TOYA IS A VAMPIRE WHOSE LIFE WILL LAST A THOUSAND YEARS.
HE CAME TO THIS SCHOOL JUST ONE MONTH AGO.
RAM ON THROUGH!!
Chiyuki!! That's wrong!
She doesn't know the rules either.
Wait!! You're heading for the wrong goal!!
Not so fast!
I WAS WONDERING WHO HAD THE DIRTY MOUTH OVER HERE...
PAT

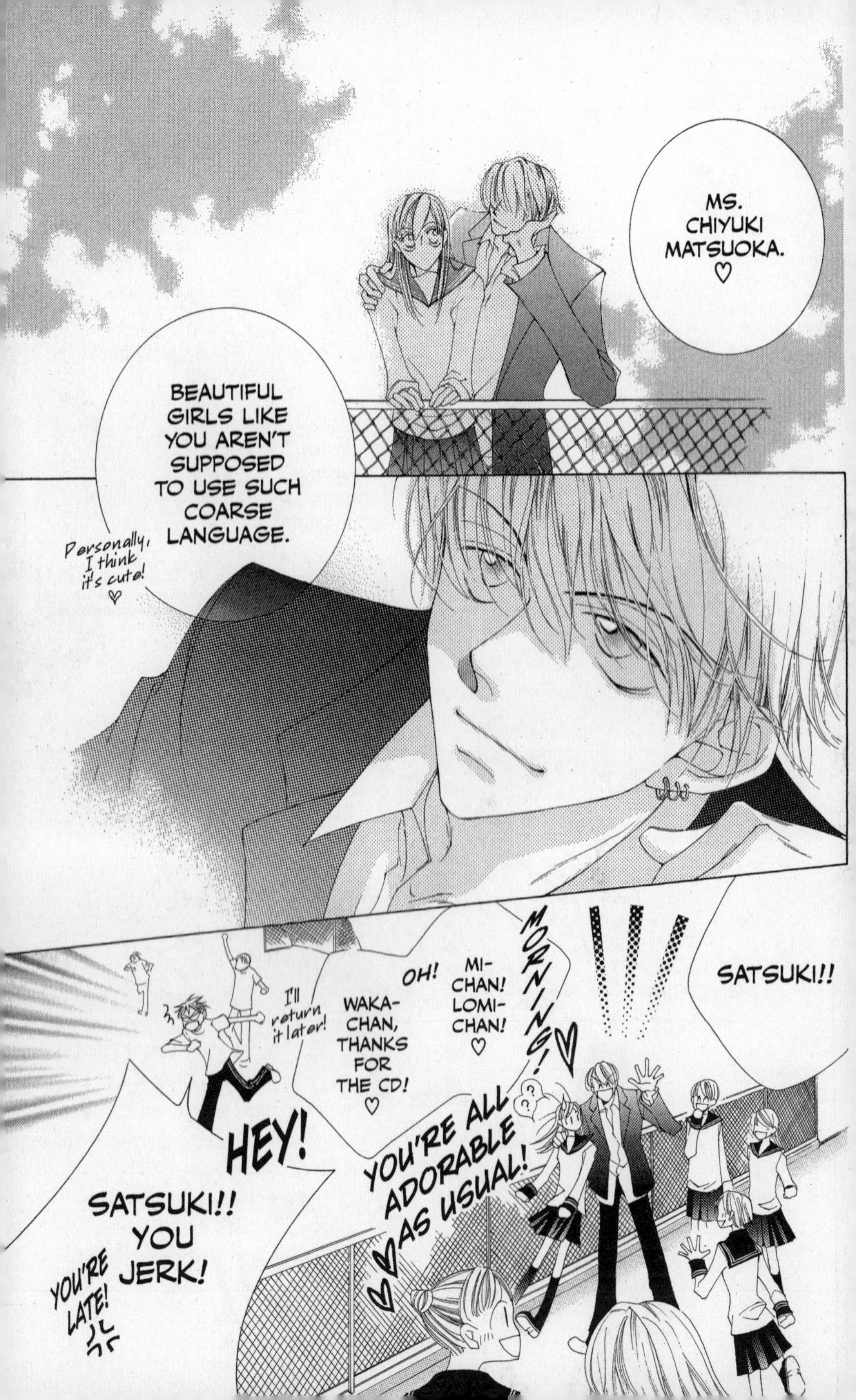
MS. CHIYUKI MATSUOKA. ♡
BEAUTIFUL GIRLS LIKE YOU AREN'T SUPPOSED TO USE SUCH COARSE LANGUAGE.
Personally, I think it's cute! ♡
SATSUKI!!
MORNING! ♡
MI-CHAN! LOMI-CHAN! ♡
OH!
WAKA-CHAN, THANKS FOR THE CD! ♡
I'll return it later!
YOU'RE ALL ADORABLE AS USUAL! ♡
HEY!
SATSUKI!! YOU JERK!
YOU'RE LATE!

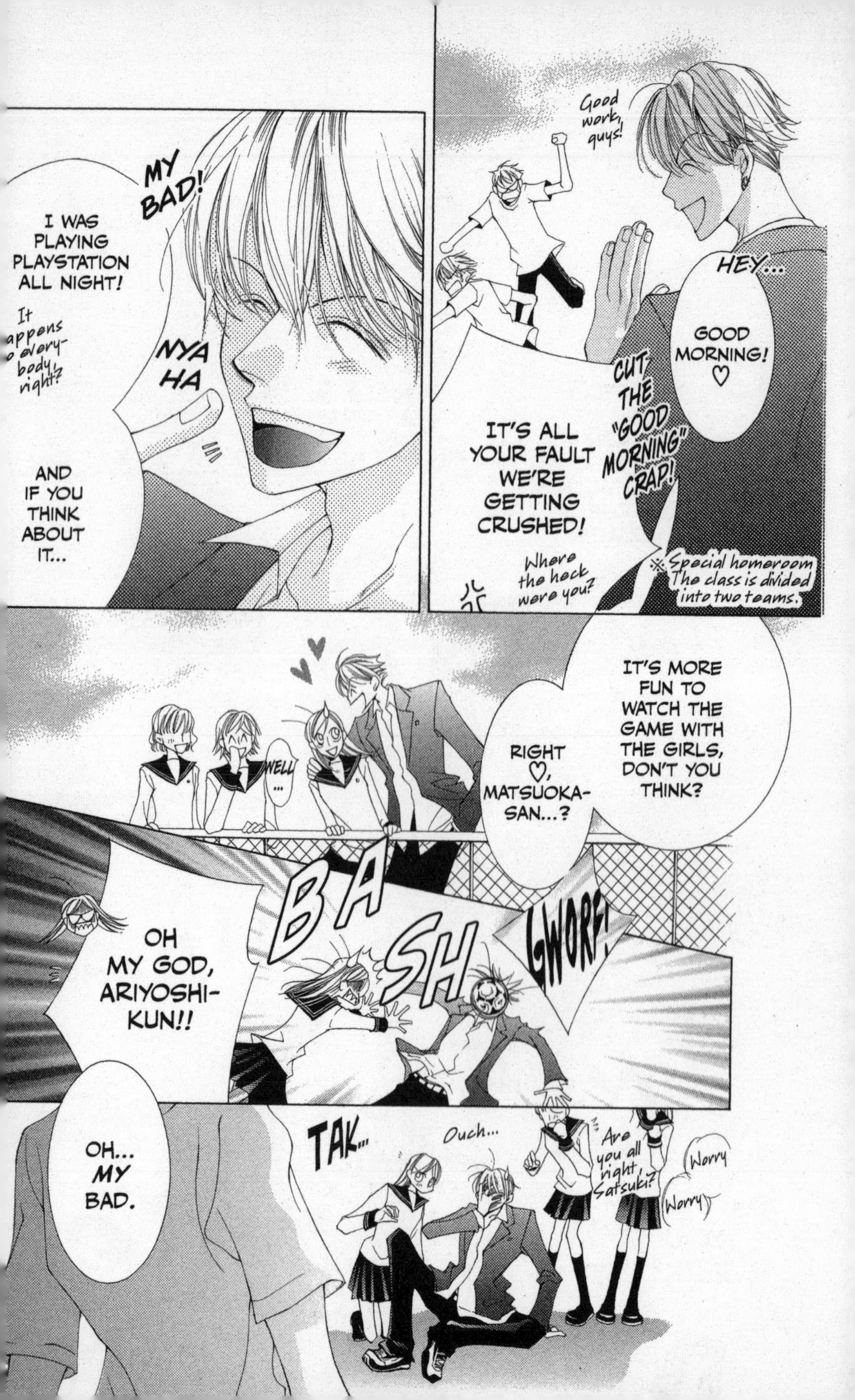
Good work, guys!
HEY...
GOOD MORNING! ♡
CUT THE "GOOD MORNING" CRAP!
IT'S ALL YOUR FAULT WE'RE GETTING CRUSHED!
Where the heck were you?
※Special homeroom The class is divided into two teams.
MY BAD!
I WAS PLAYING PLAYSTATION ALL NIGHT!
It appens o every-body, right?
NYA HA
AND IF YOU THINK ABOUT IT...
IT'S MORE FUN TO WATCH THE GAME WITH THE GIRLS, DON'T YOU THINK?
RIGHT ♡, MATSUOKA-SAN...?
WELL...
BASH
GWORF!
OH MY GOD, ARIYOSHI-KUN!!
Worry
Worry
Are you all right, Satsuki?
Ouch...
TAK...
OH... MY BAD.

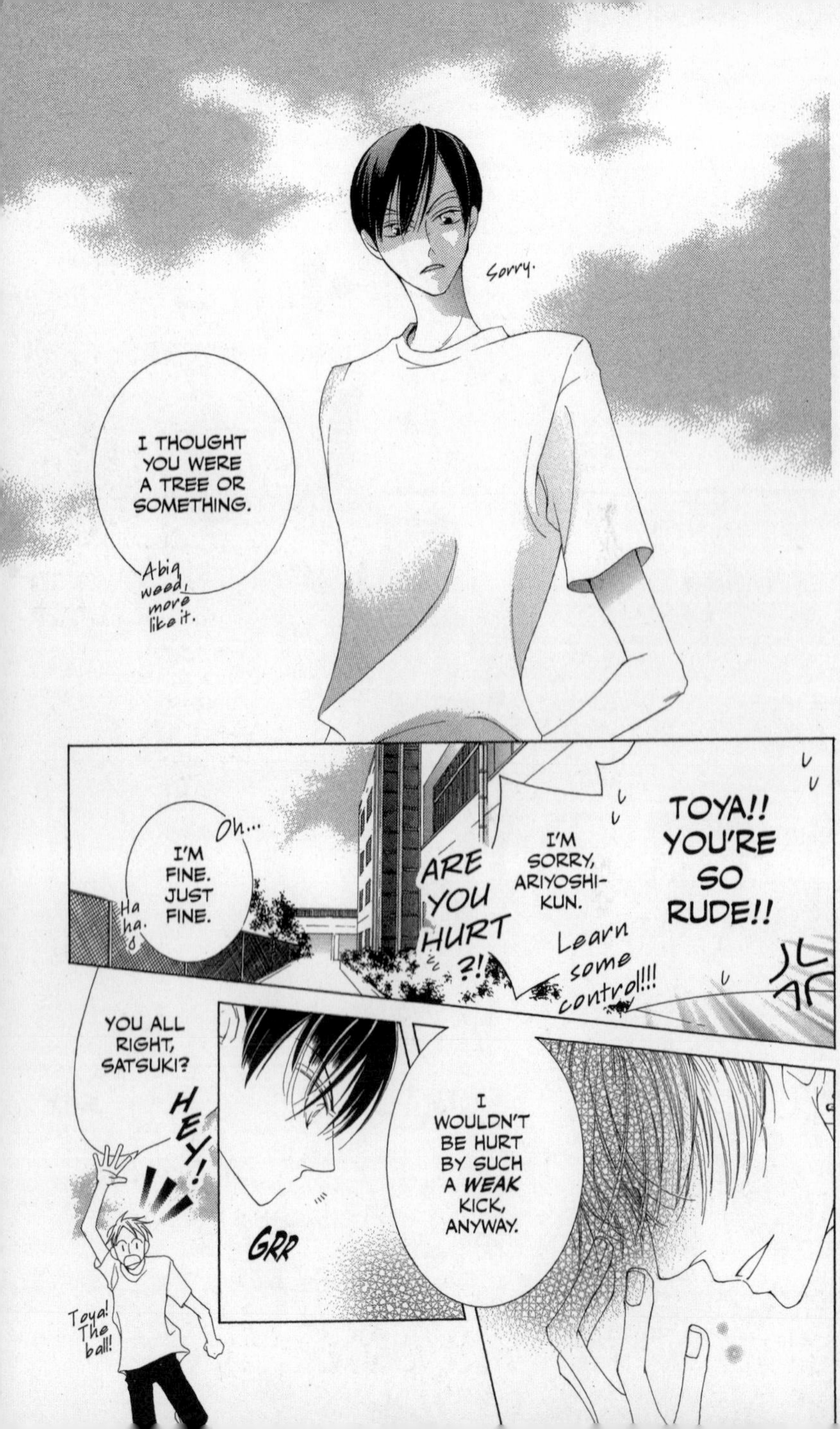
Sorry.
I THOUGHT YOU WERE A TREE OR SOMETHING.
A big weed, more like it.
TOYA!! YOU'RE SO RUDE!!
I'M SORRY, ARIYOSHI-KUN.
Learn some control!!!!
ARE YOU HURT?!
Oh...
I'M FINE. JUST FINE.
Ha ha.
I WOULDN'T BE HURT BY SUCH A WEAK KICK, ANYWAY.
GRR
YOU ALL RIGHT, SATSUKI?
HEY!
Toya! The ball!

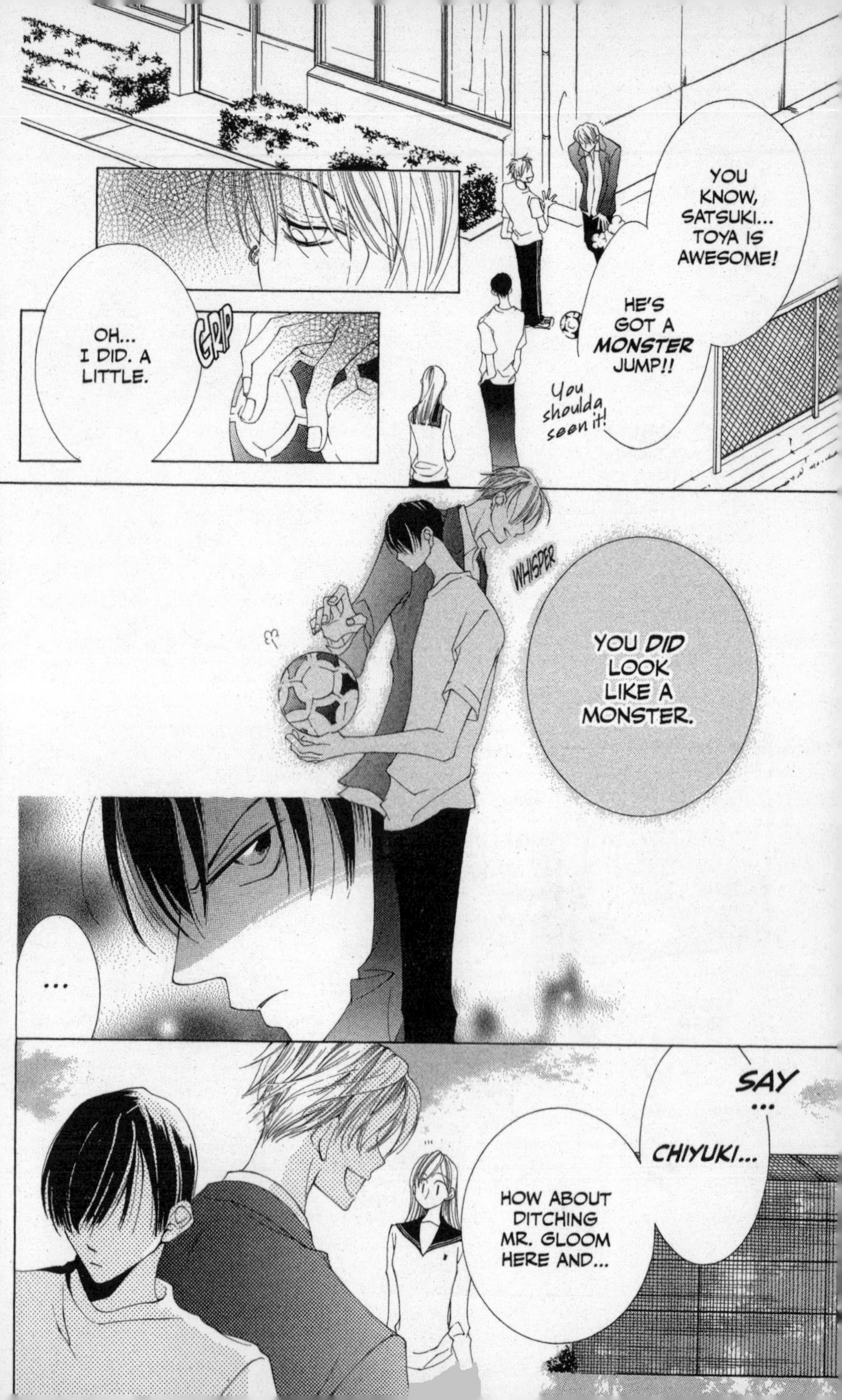
YOU KNOW, SATSUKI... TOYA IS AWESOME!
HE'S GOT A MONSTER JUMP!!
You shoulda seen it!
GRIP
OH... I DID. A LITTLE.
WHISPER
YOU DID LOOK LIKE A MONSTER.
...
SAY... CHIYUKI...
HOW ABOUT DITCHING MR. GLOOM HERE AND...

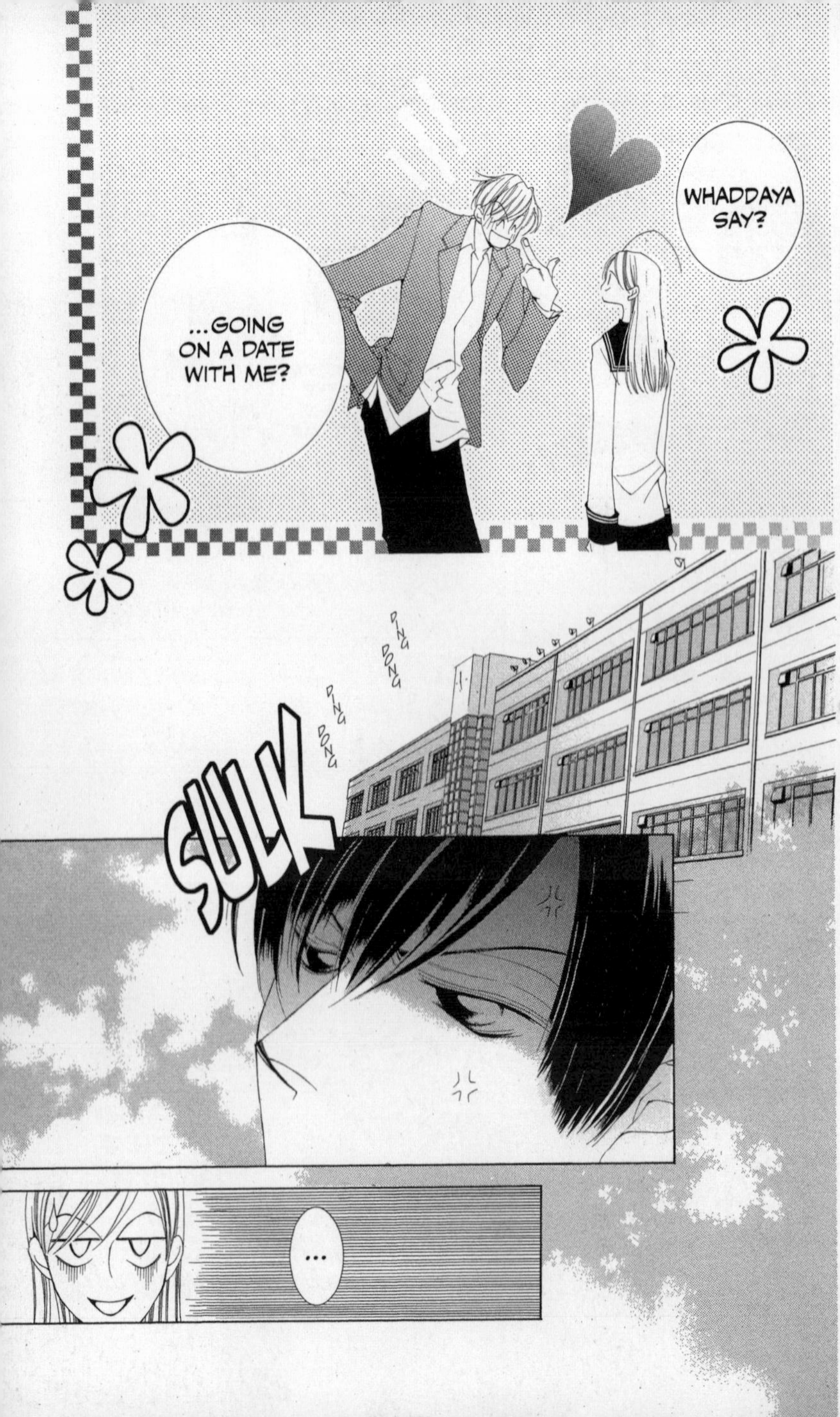
WHADDAYA SAY?
...GOING ON A DATE WITH ME?
DING DONG
DING DONG
SULK
...

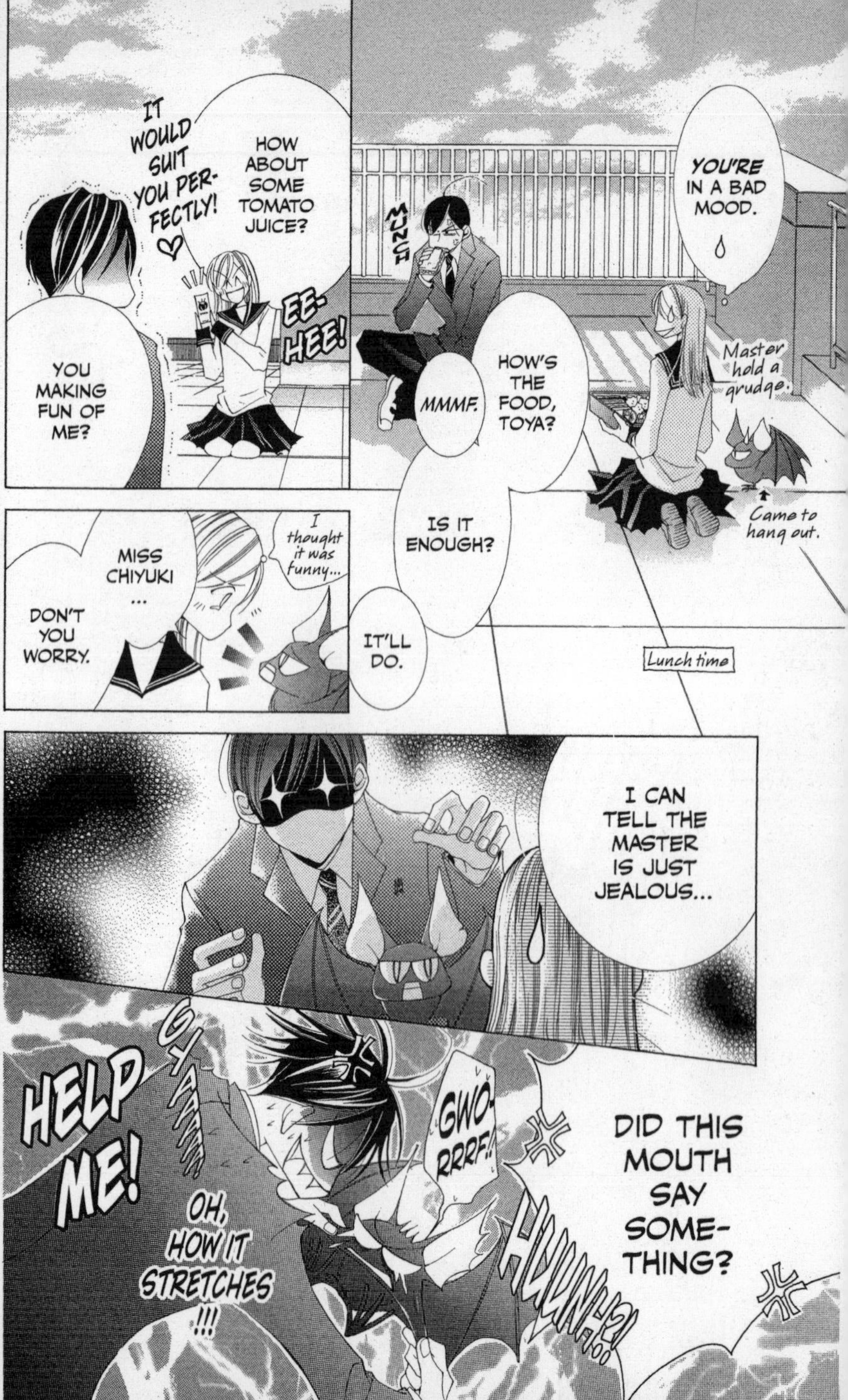
Lunch time
YOU'RE IN A BAD MOOD.
Master hold a grudge.
Came to hang out.
MUNCH
HOW'S THE FOOD, TOYA?
MMMF.
IS IT ENOUGH?
IT'LL DO.
HOW ABOUT SOME TOMATO JUICE?
IT WOULD SUIT YOU PERFECTLY! ♡
EE-HEE!
YOU MAKING FUN OF ME?
I thought it was funny...
MISS CHIYUKI...
DON'T YOU WORRY.
I CAN TELL THE MASTER IS JUST JEALOUS...
DID THIS MOUTH SAY SOMETHING?
HUUNH?!
GWO-RRRF!!
GYAAAAA
HELP ME!
OH, HOW IT STRETCHES!!!

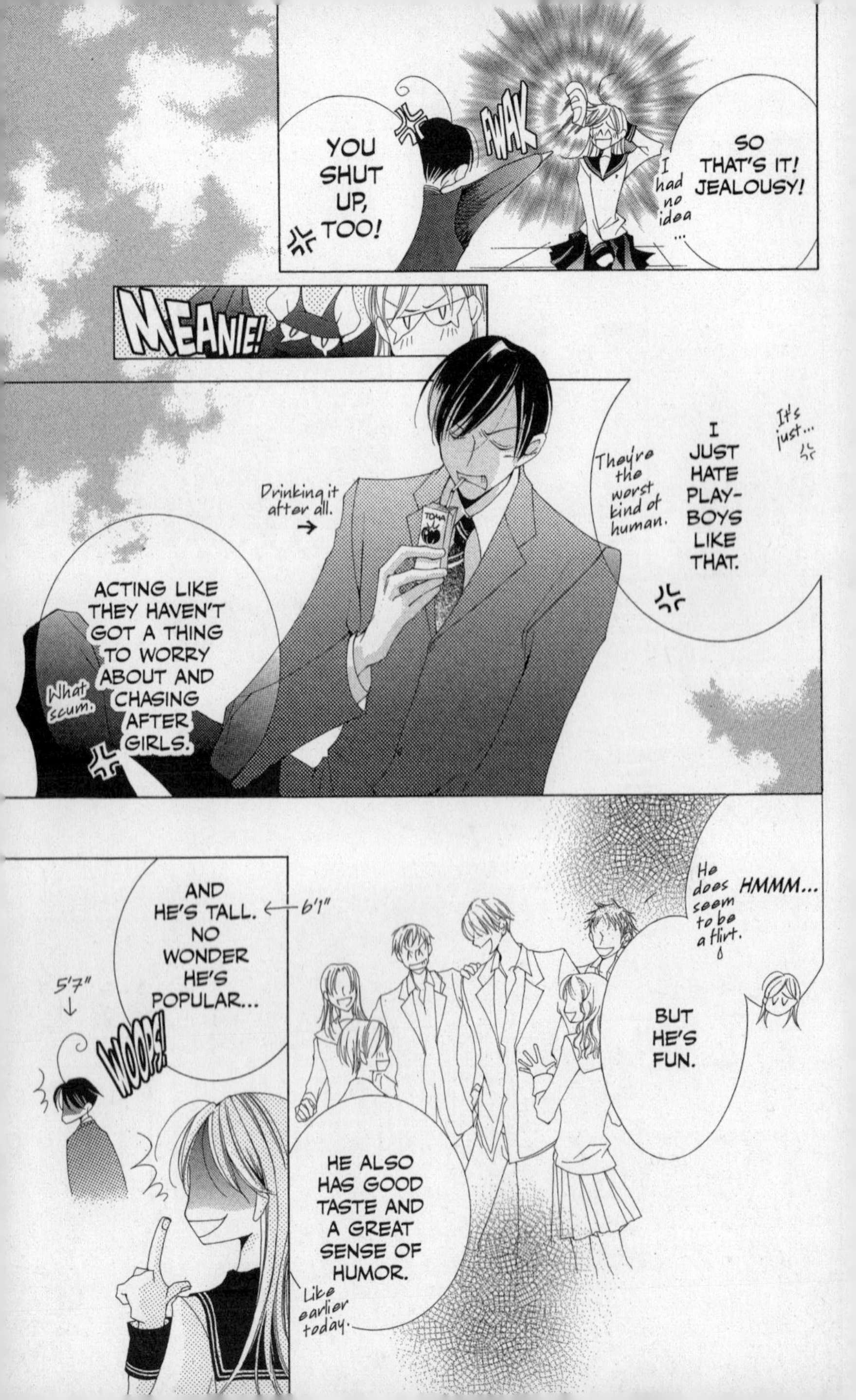
SO THAT'S IT! JEALOUSY!
I had no idea...
AWAK
YOU SHUT UP, TOO!
MEANIE!
It's just...
I JUST HATE PLAY-BOYS LIKE THAT.
They're the worst kind of human.
Drinking it after all. →
TOMA
ACTING LIKE THEY HAVEN'T GOT A THING TO WORRY ABOUT AND CHASING AFTER GIRLS.
What scum.
HMMM...
He does seem to be a flirt.
BUT HE'S FUN.
HE ALSO HAS GOOD TASTE AND A GREAT SENSE OF HUMOR.
Like earlier today.
AND HE'S TALL. ← 6'1"
NO WONDER HE'S POPULAR...
5'7" ↓
WOOPS!

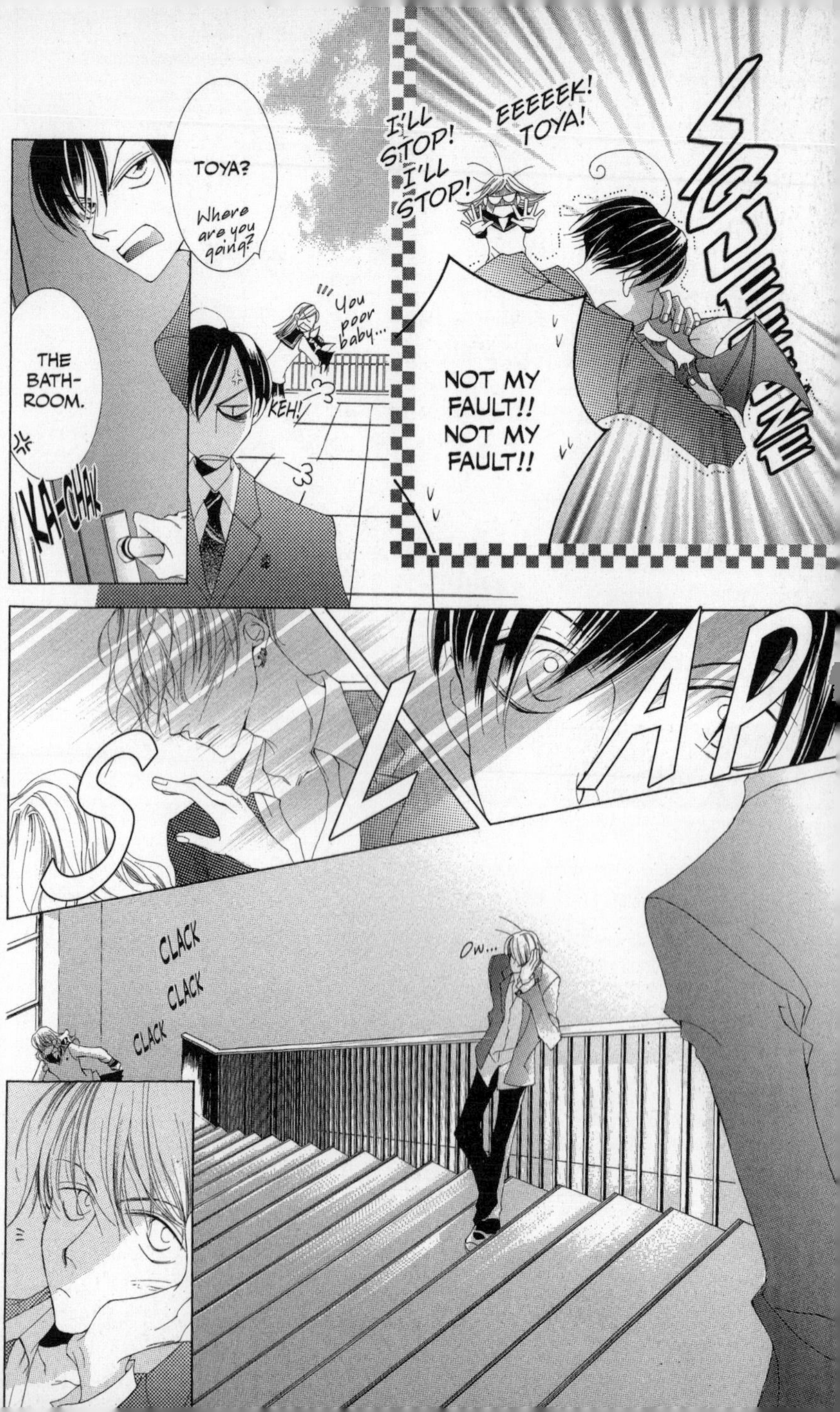
EEEEEK! TOYA!
I'LL STOP! I'LL STOP!
NOT MY FAULT!! NOT MY FAULT!!
TOYA?
Where are you going?
You poor baby...
KEH!
THE BATHROOM.
KA-CHAK
SLAP
Ow...
CLACK
CLACK
CLACK

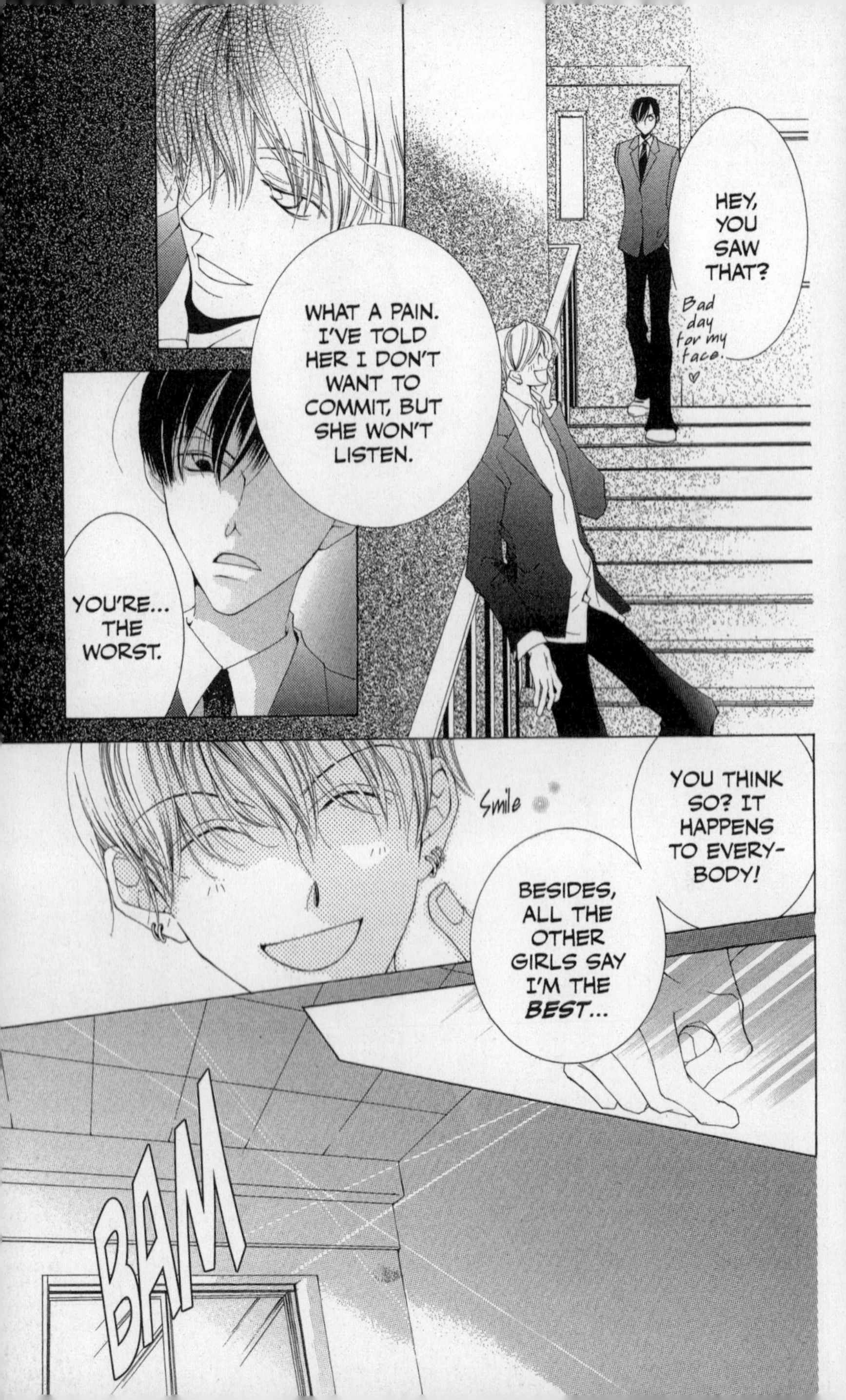

HEY, YOU SAW THAT?
Bad day for my face.
WHAT A PAIN. I'VE TOLD HER I DON'T WANT TO COMMIT, BUT SHE WON'T LISTEN.
YOU'RE... THE WORST.
YOU THINK SO? IT HAPPENS TO EVERY-BODY!
Smile
BESIDES, ALL THE OTHER GIRLS SAY I'M THE *BEST*...
BAM

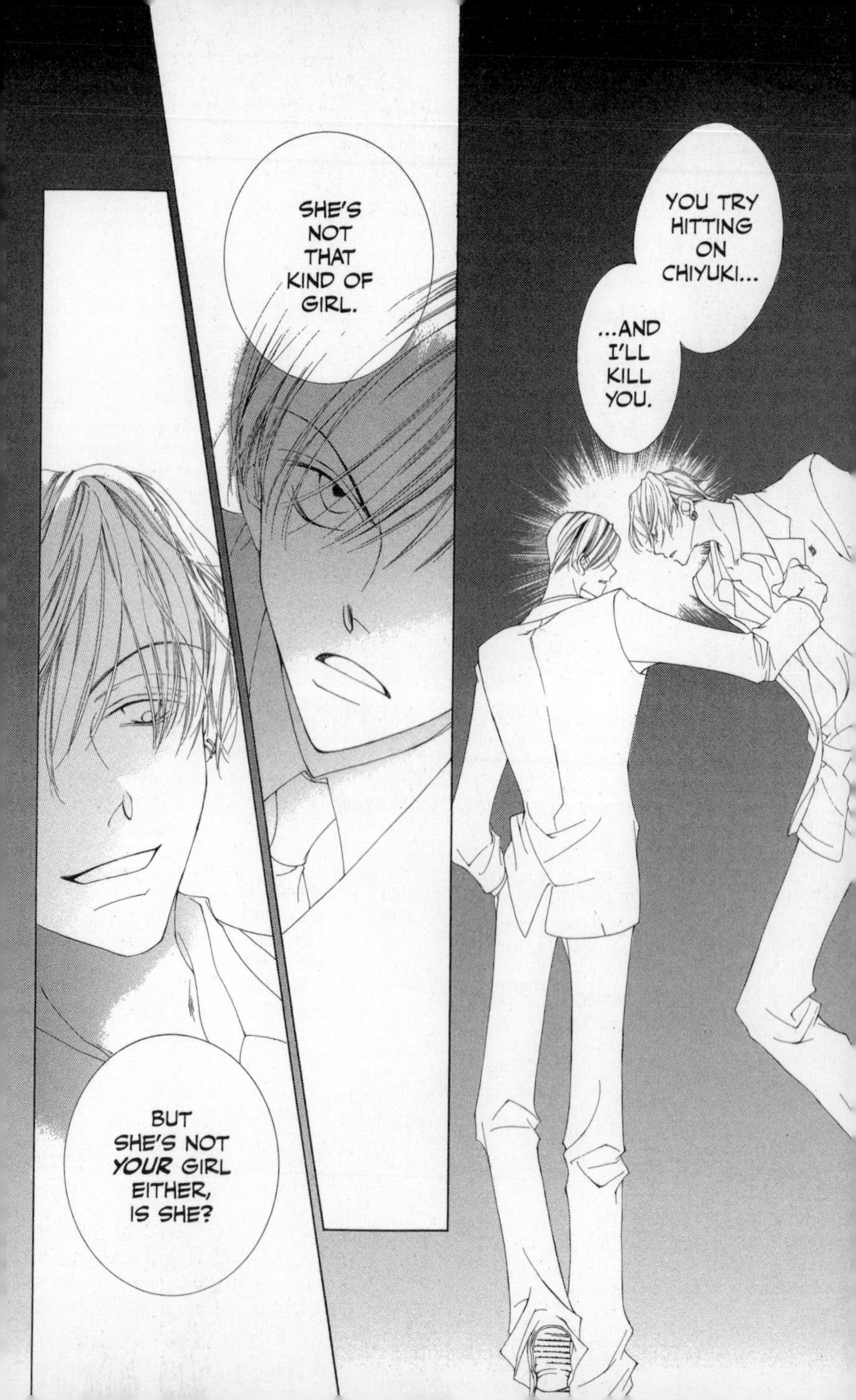
YOU TRY HITTING ON CHIYUKI...
...AND I'LL KILL YOU.
SHE'S NOT THAT KIND OF GIRL.
BUT SHE'S NOT *YOUR* GIRL EITHER, IS SHE?

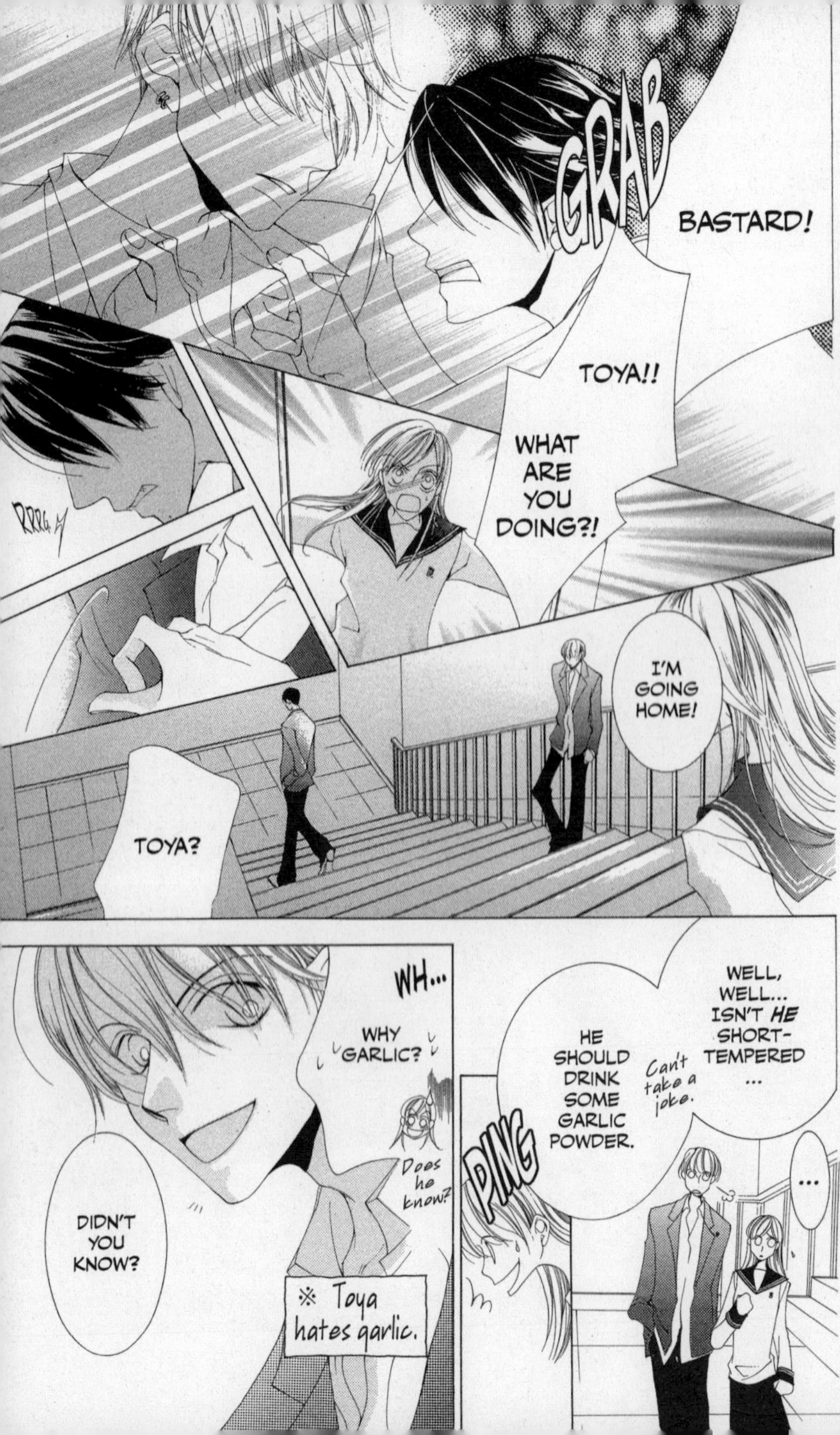
GRAB
BASTARD!
TOYA!!
WHAT ARE YOU DOING?!
RRRG
I'M GOING HOME!
TOYA?
WELL, WELL... ISN'T HE SHORT-TEMPERED...
Can't take a joke.
HE SHOULD DRINK SOME GARLIC POWDER.
PING
...
WH...
WHY GARLIC?
Does he know?
DIDN'T YOU KNOW?
※ Toya hates garlic.

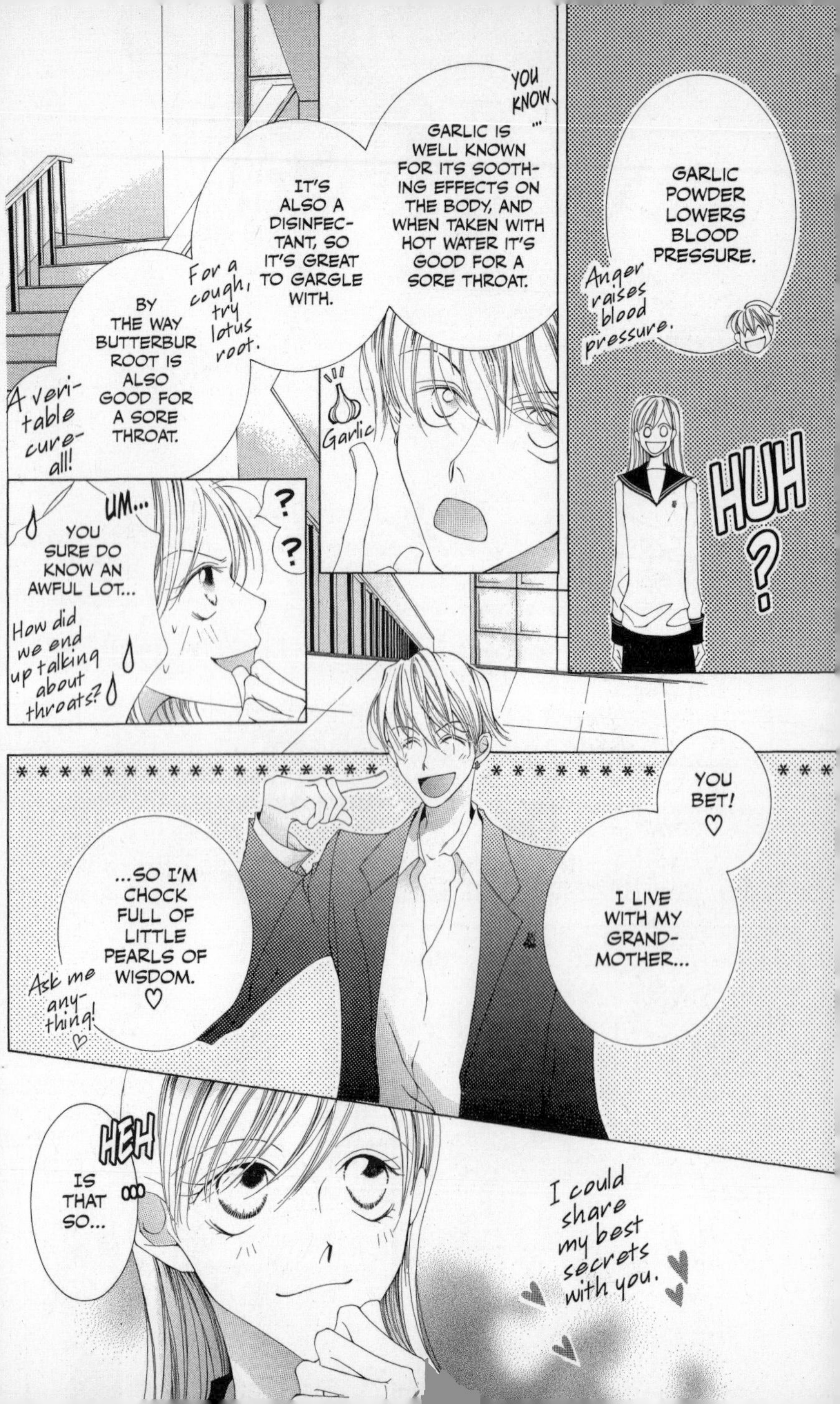
GARLIC POWDER LOWERS BLOOD PRESSURE.
Anger raises blood pressure.
HUH?
YOU KNOW...
GARLIC IS WELL KNOWN FOR ITS SOOTHING EFFECTS ON THE BODY, AND WHEN TAKEN WITH HOT WATER IT'S GOOD FOR A SORE THROAT.
Garlic
IT'S ALSO A DISINFECTANT, SO IT'S GREAT TO GARGLE WITH.
For a cough, try lotus root.
BY THE WAY BUTTERBUR ROOT IS ALSO GOOD FOR A SORE THROAT.
A veritable cure-all!
??
UM...
YOU SURE DO KNOW AN AWFUL LOT...
How did we end up talking about throats?
YOU BET! ♡
I LIVE WITH MY GRANDMOTHER...
...SO I'M CHOCK FULL OF LITTLE PEARLS OF WISDOM. ♡
Ask me anything! ♡
HEH
IS THAT SO...
I could share my best secrets with you.

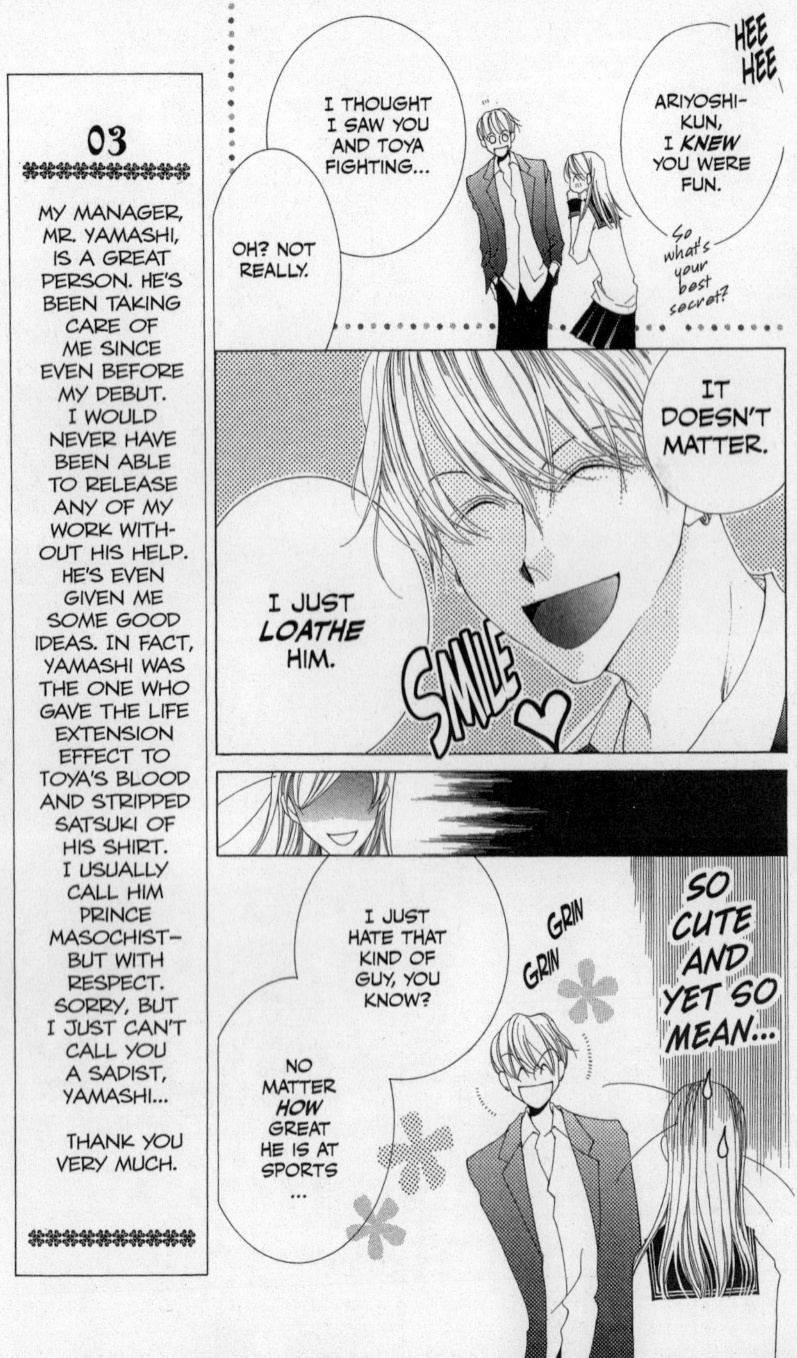
HEE HEE
ARIYOSHI-KUN, I *KNEW* YOU WERE FUN.
So what's your best secret?
I THOUGHT I SAW YOU AND TOYA FIGHTING...
OH? NOT REALLY.
IT DOESN'T MATTER.
I JUST *LOATHE* HIM.
SMILE
SO CUTE AND YET SO MEAN...
GRIN GRIN
I JUST HATE THAT KIND OF GUY, YOU KNOW?
NO MATTER *HOW* GREAT HE IS AT SPORTS ...

03

MY MANAGER, MR. YAMASHI, IS A GREAT PERSON. HE'S BEEN TAKING CARE OF ME SINCE EVEN BEFORE MY DEBUT. I WOULD NEVER HAVE BEEN ABLE TO RELEASE ANY OF MY WORK WITHOUT HIS HELP. HE'S EVEN GIVEN ME SOME GOOD IDEAS. IN FACT, YAMASHI WAS THE ONE WHO GAVE THE LIFE EXTENSION EFFECT TO TOYA'S BLOOD AND STRIPPED SATSUKI OF HIS SHIRT. I USUALLY CALL HIM PRINCE MASOCHIST–BUT WITH RESPECT. SORRY, BUT I JUST CAN'T CALL YOU A SADIST, YAMASHI...

THANK YOU VERY MUCH.

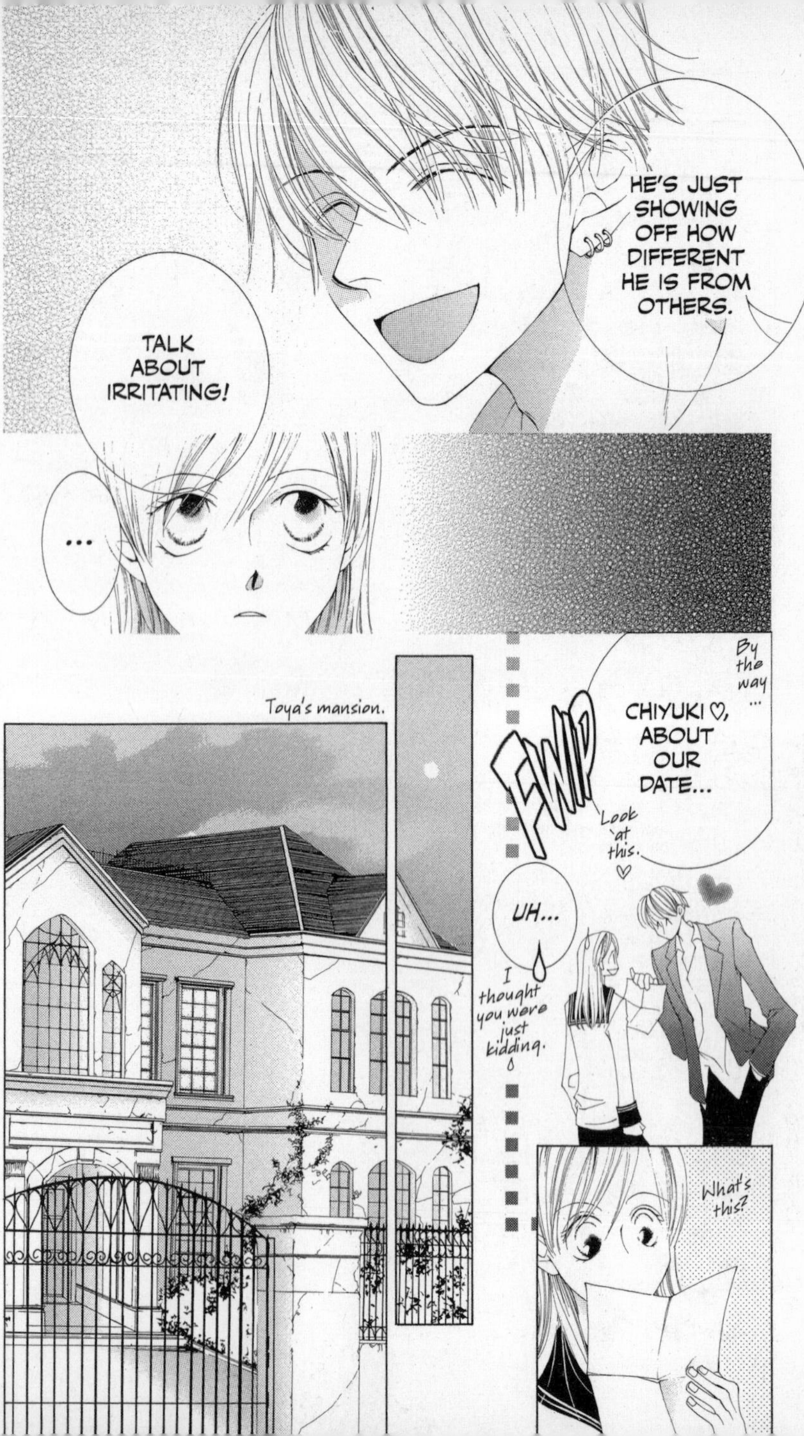
HE'S JUST SHOWING OFF HOW DIFFERENT HE IS FROM OTHERS.
TALK ABOUT IRRITATING!
...
By the way...
CHIYUKI ♡, ABOUT OUR DATE...
FWIP
Look at this. ♡
UH...
I thought you were just kidding.
What's this?
Toya's mansion.

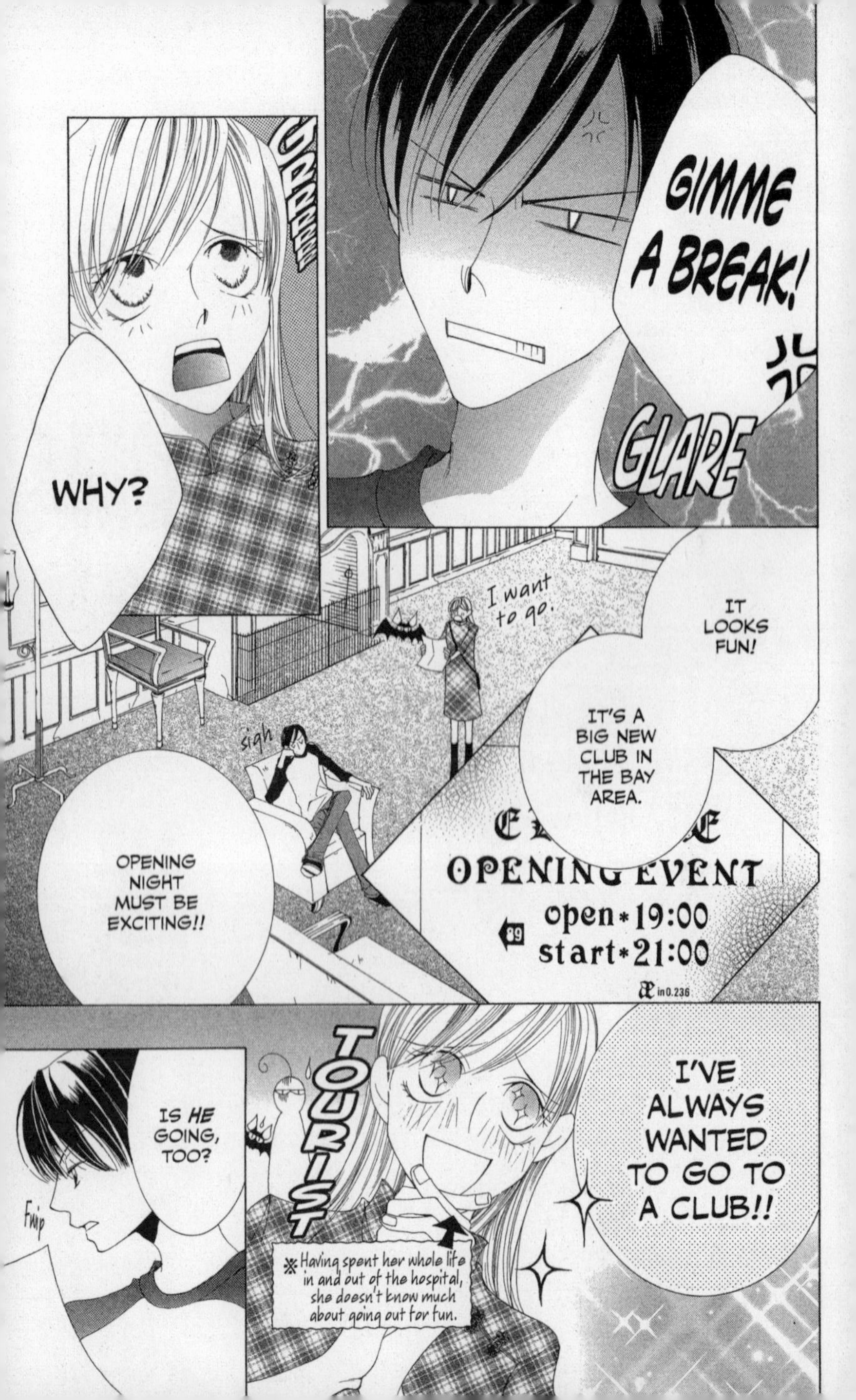
GIMME A BREAK!
GLARE
WHY?
IT LOOKS FUN!
I want to go.
IT'S A BIG NEW CLUB IN THE BAY AREA.
OPENING EVENT
open*19:00
start*21:00
sigh
OPENING NIGHT MUST BE EXCITING!!
I'VE ALWAYS WANTED TO GO TO A CLUB!!
TOURIST
※Having spent her whole life in and out of the hospital, she doesn't know much about going out for fun.
IS HE GOING, TOO?
Fwip

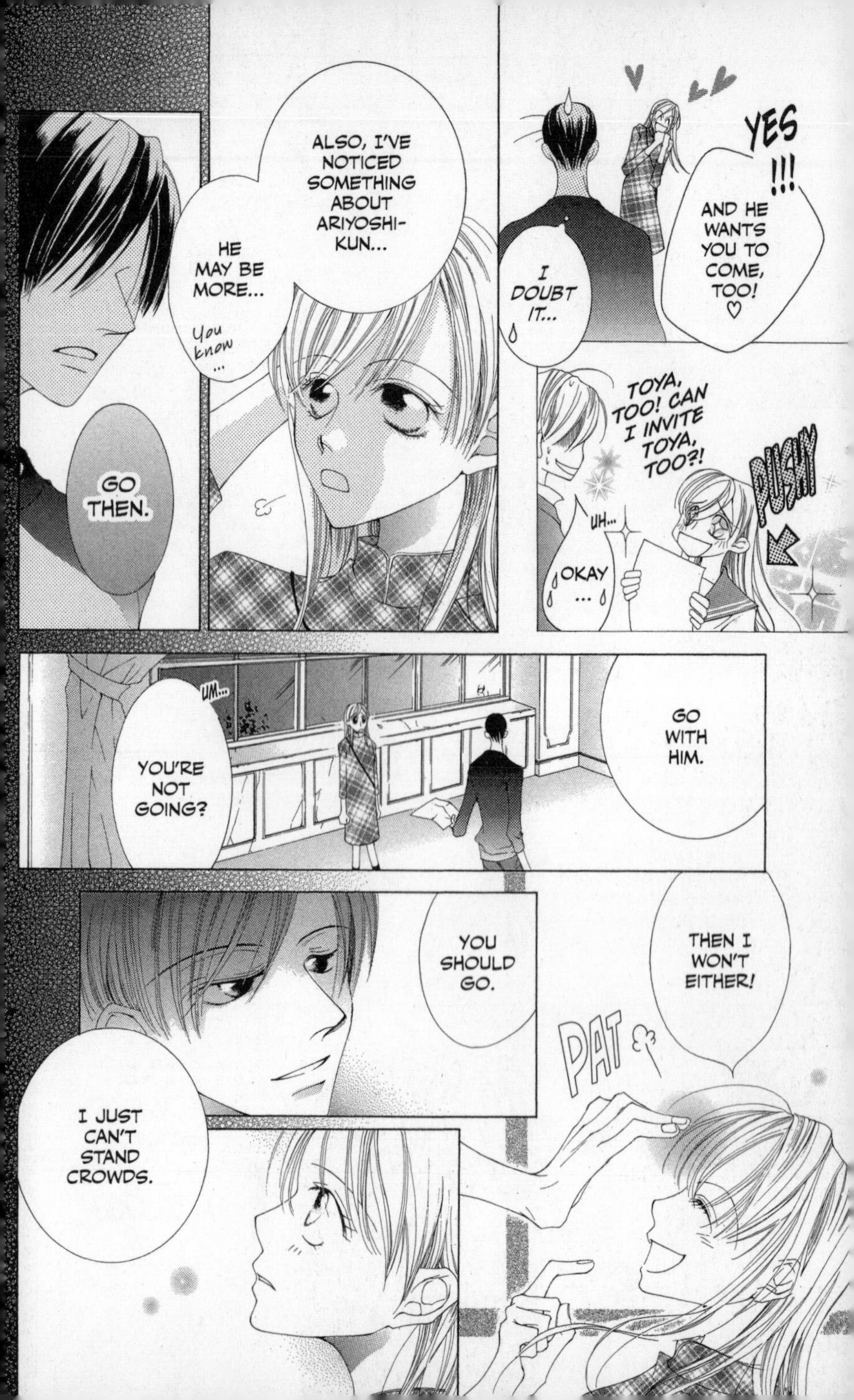
YES!!!
AND HE WANTS YOU TO COME, TOO! ♡
I DOUBT IT...
TOYA, TOO! CAN I INVITE TOYA, TOO?!
PUSHY
UH... OKAY...
ALSO, I'VE NOTICED SOMETHING ABOUT ARIYOSHI-KUN...
HE MAY BE MORE...
You know...
GO THEN.
GO WITH HIM.
UM...
YOU'RE NOT GOING?
THEN I WON'T EITHER!
PAT
YOU SHOULD GO.
I JUST CAN'T STAND CROWDS.

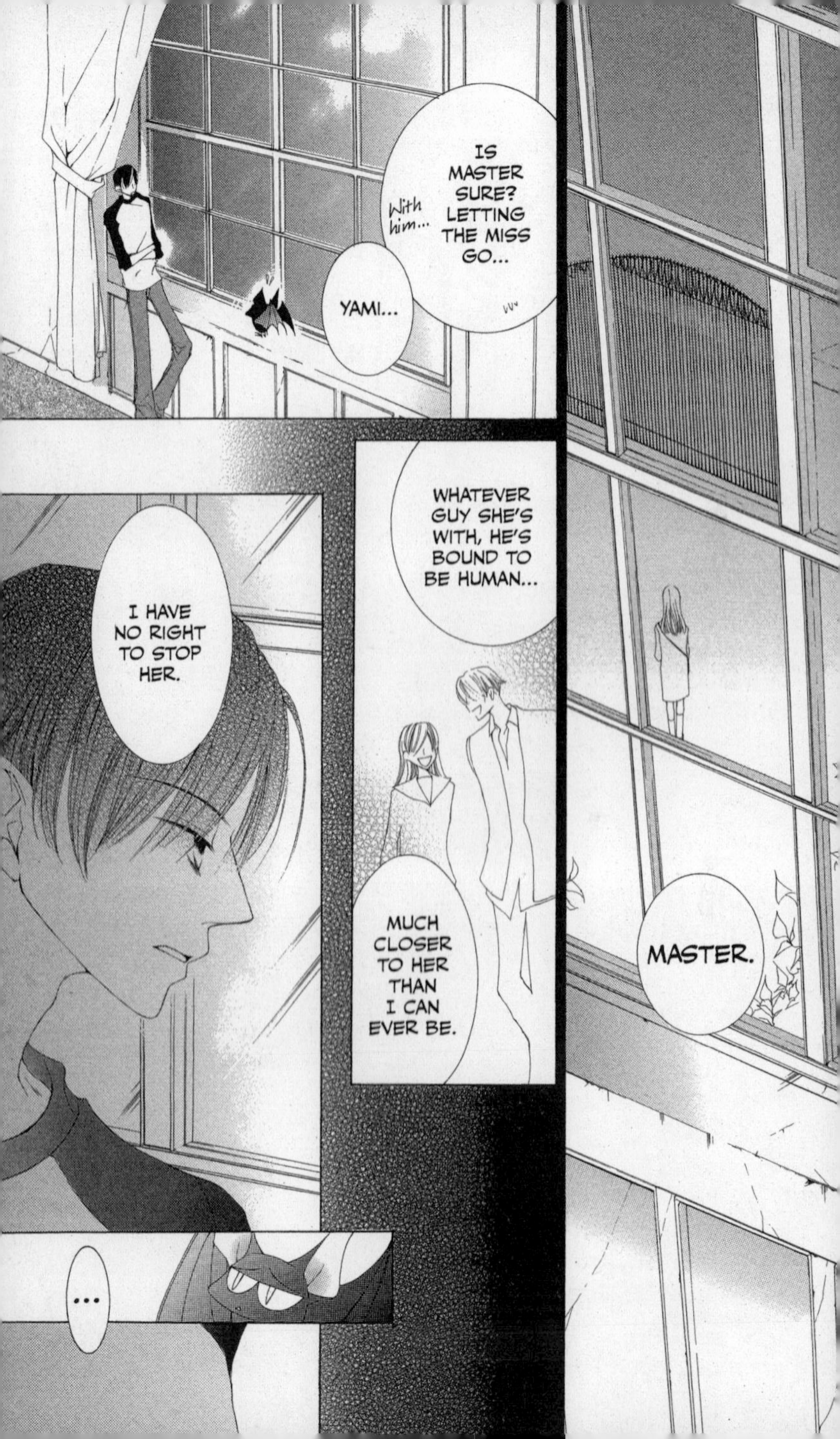
MASTER.
IS MASTER SURE? LETTING THE MISS GO...
With him...
YAMI...
WHATEVER GUY SHE'S WITH, HE'S BOUND TO BE HUMAN...
MUCH CLOSER TO HER THAN I CAN EVER BE.
I HAVE NO RIGHT TO STOP HER.
...

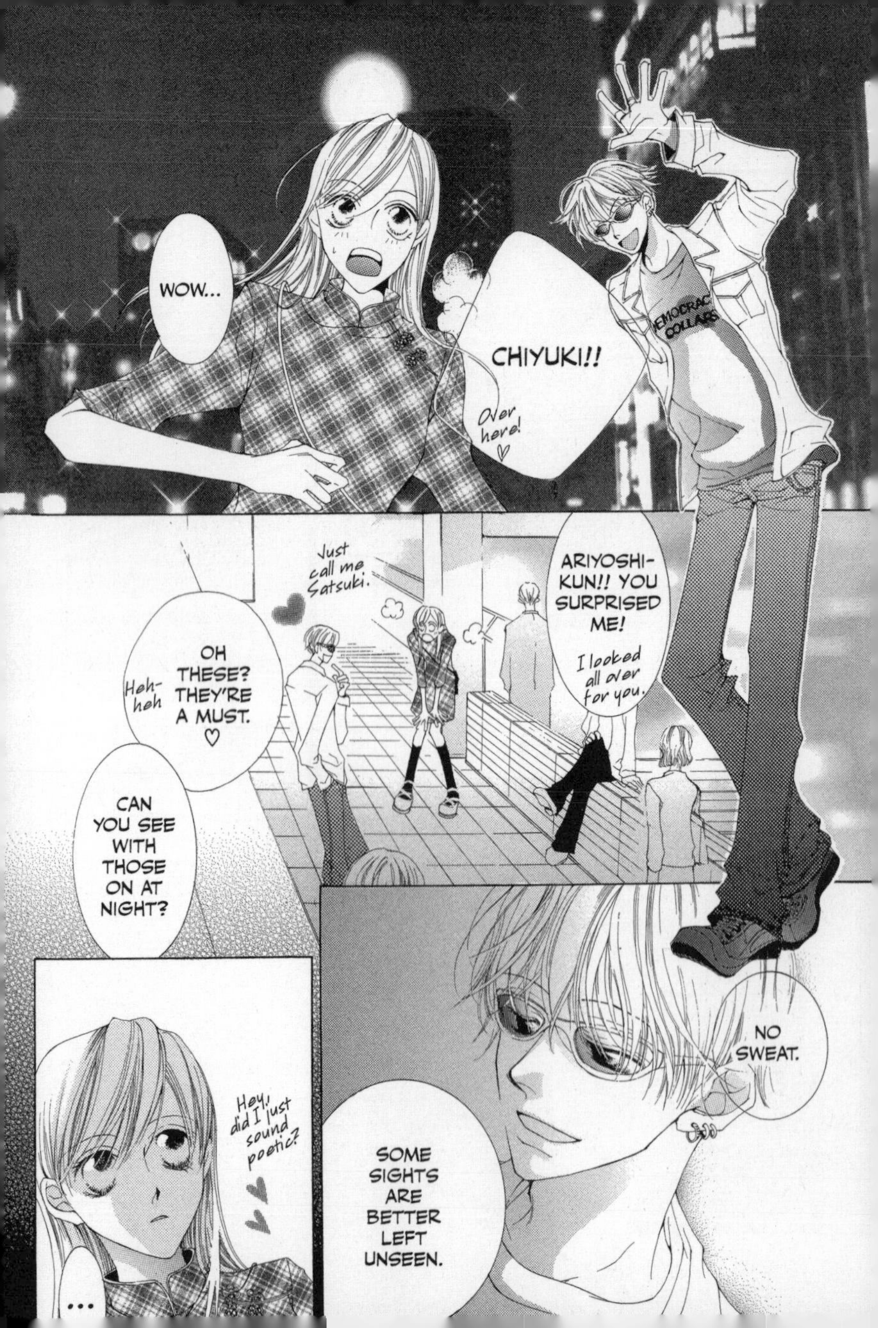
CHIYUKI!!
Over here! ♡
WOW...
ARIYOSHI-KUN!! YOU SURPRISED ME!
I looked all over for you.
Just call me Satsuki.
OH THESE? THEY'RE A MUST. ♡
Heh-heh
CAN YOU SEE WITH THOSE ON AT NIGHT?
NO SWEAT.
SOME SIGHTS ARE BETTER LEFT UNSEEN.
Hey, did I just sound poetic?
...

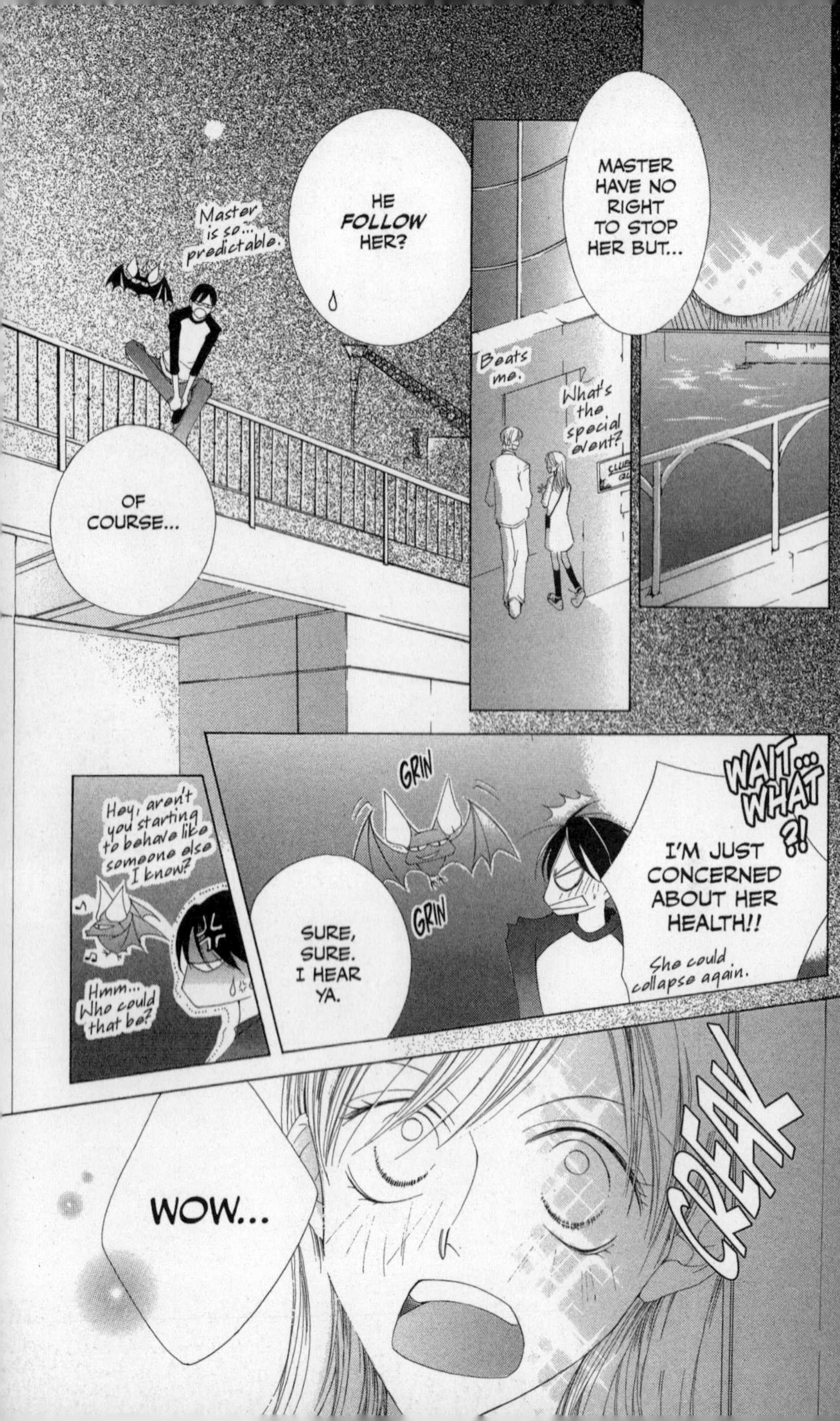
MASTER HAVE NO RIGHT TO STOP HER BUT...
What's the special event?
Beats me.
HE FOLLOW HER?
Master is so... predictable.
OF COURSE...
WAIT... WHAT?!
I'M JUST CONCERNED ABOUT HER HEALTH!!
She could collapse again.
GRIN
GRIN
SURE, SURE. I HEAR YA.
Hey, aren't you starting to behave like someone else I know?
Hmm... Who could that be?
CREAK
WOW...

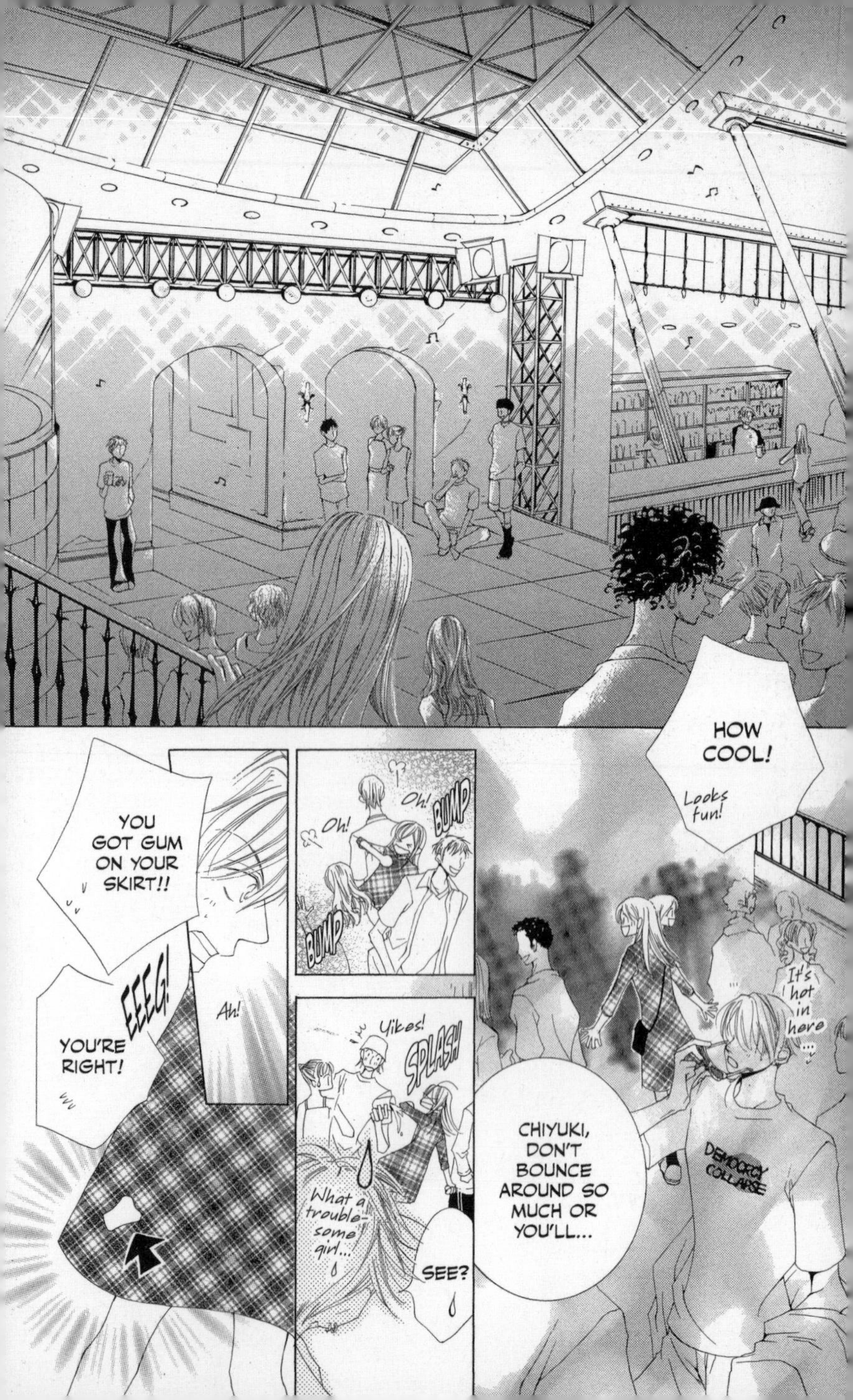
HOW COOL!
Looks fun!
It's hot in here...
CHIYUKI, DON'T BOUNCE AROUND SO MUCH OR YOU'LL...
Oh!
BUMP
Oh!
BUMP
Yikes!
SPLASH
What a trouble-some girl...
SEE?
YOU GOT GUM ON YOUR SKIRT!!
EEEG!
YOU'RE RIGHT!
Ah!

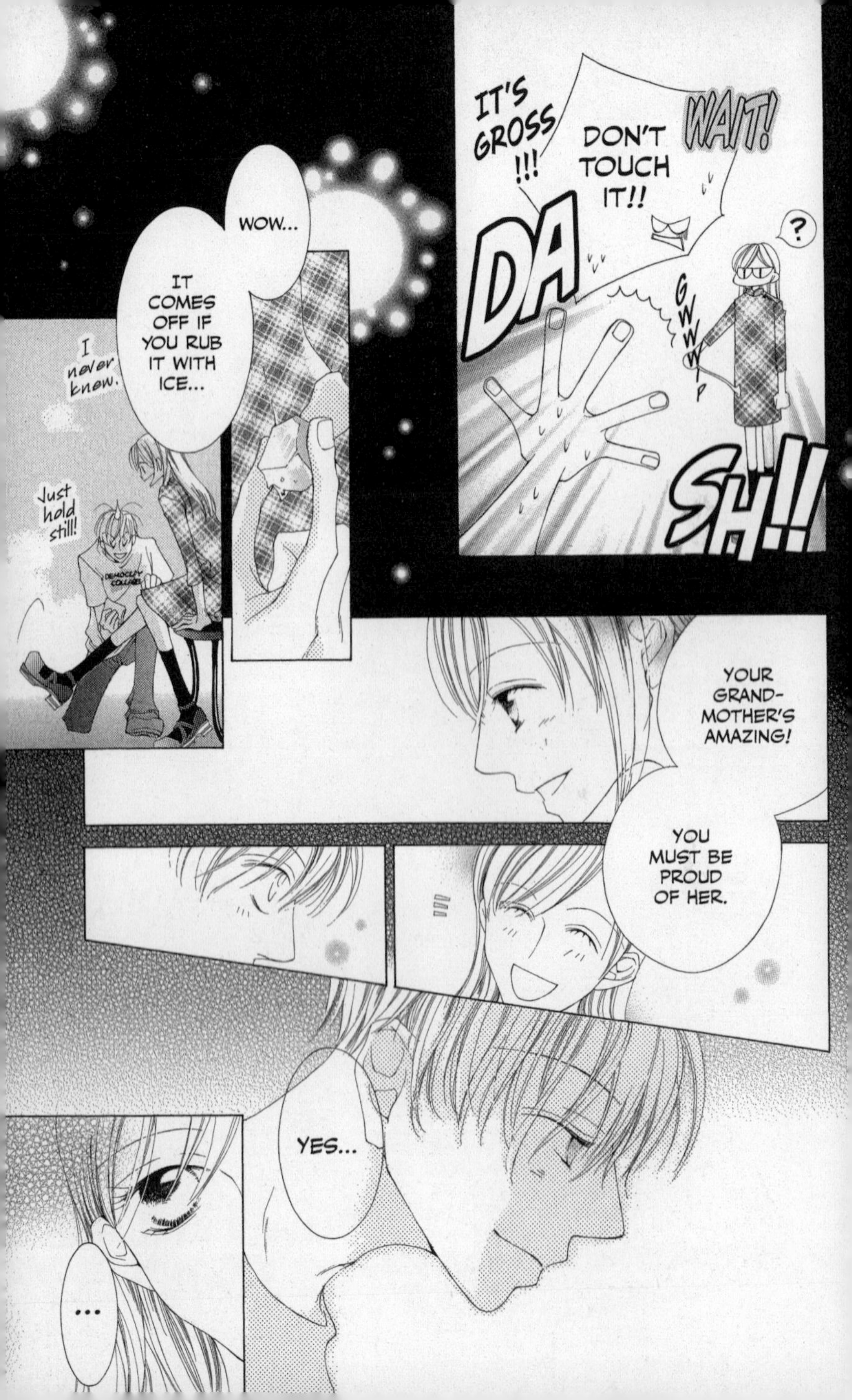
?
WAIT!
DON'T TOUCH IT!!
IT'S GROSS!!!
GWWWIP
DA
SH!!
WOW...
IT COMES OFF IF YOU RUB IT WITH ICE...
I never knew.
Just hold still!
YOUR GRAND-MOTHER'S AMAZING!
YOU MUST BE PROUD OF HER.
!!!
YES...
...

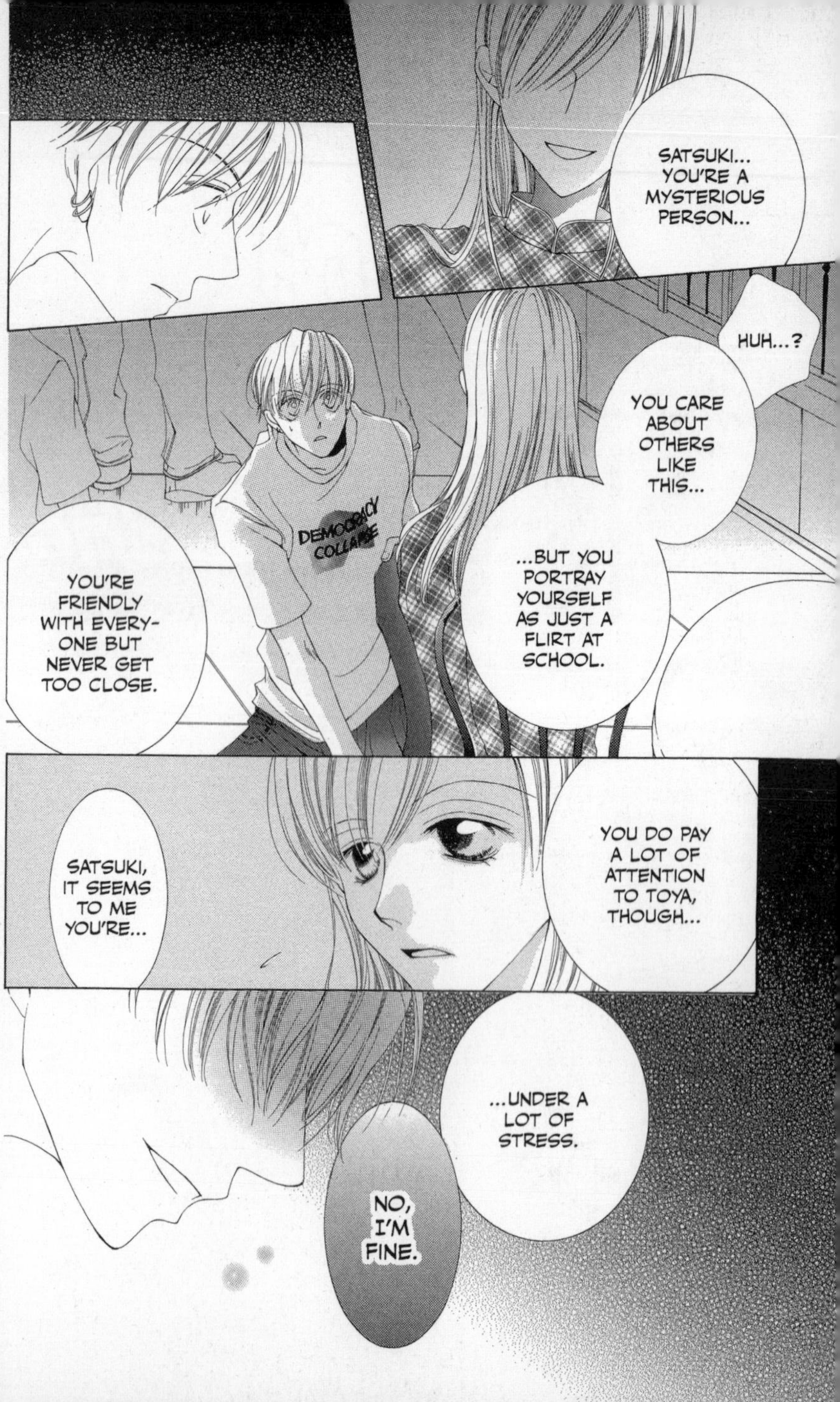
SATSUKI... YOU'RE A MYSTERIOUS PERSON...
HUH...?
YOU CARE ABOUT OTHERS LIKE THIS...
...BUT YOU PORTRAY YOURSELF AS JUST A FLIRT AT SCHOOL.
YOU'RE FRIENDLY WITH EVERY-ONE BUT NEVER GET TOO CLOSE.
YOU DO PAY A LOT OF ATTENTION TO TOYA, THOUGH...
SATSUKI, IT SEEMS TO ME YOU'RE...
...UNDER A LOT OF STRESS.
NO, I'M FINE.

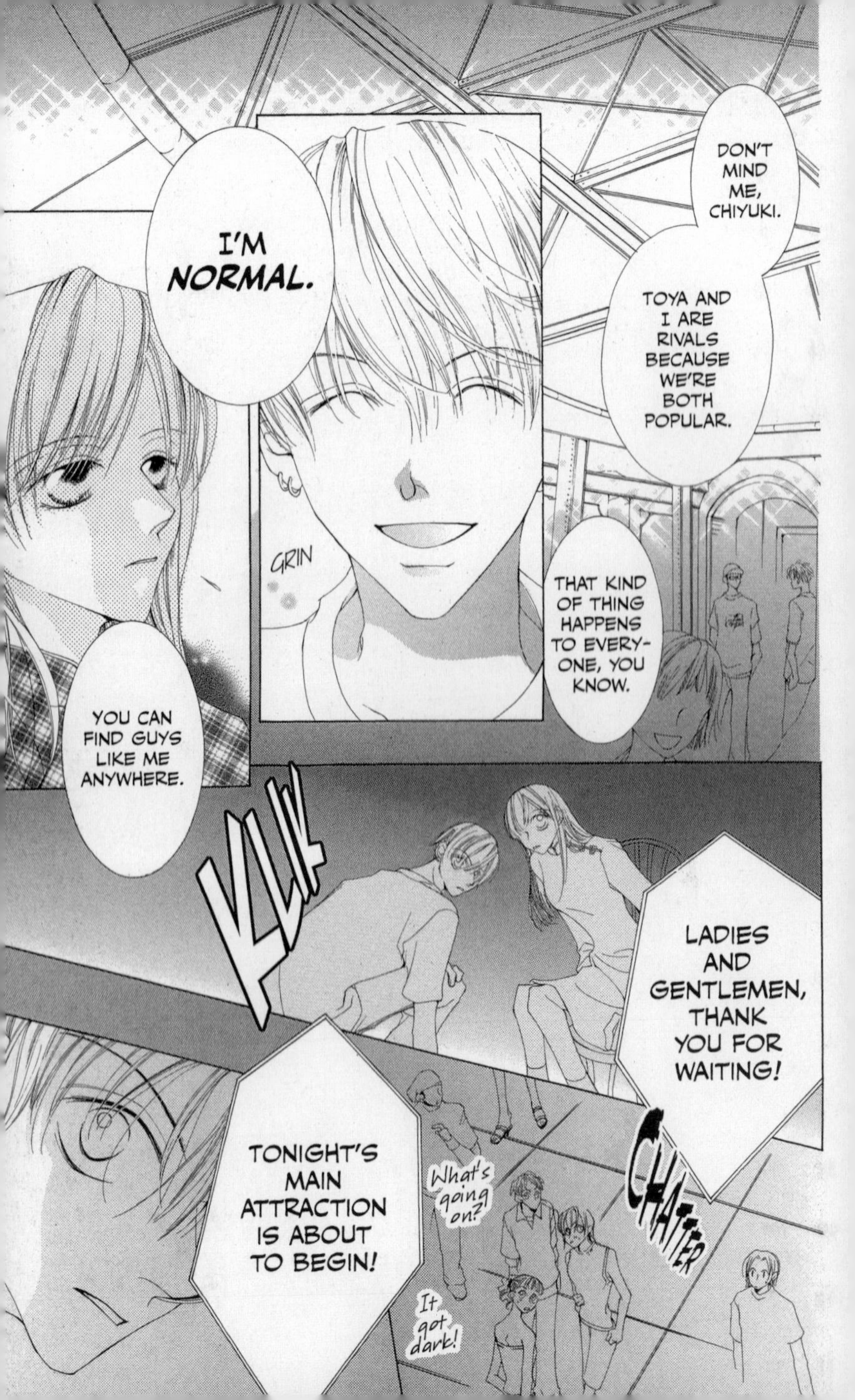

DON'T MIND ME, CHIYUKI.
TOYA AND I ARE RIVALS BECAUSE WE'RE BOTH POPULAR.
THAT KIND OF THING HAPPENS TO EVERY-ONE, YOU KNOW.
I'M **NORMAL.**
GRIN
YOU CAN FIND GUYS LIKE ME ANYWHERE.
KLIK
LADIES AND GENTLEMEN, THANK YOU FOR WAITING!
CHATTER
What's going on?
It got dark!
TONIGHT'S MAIN ATTRACTION IS ABOUT TO BEGIN!

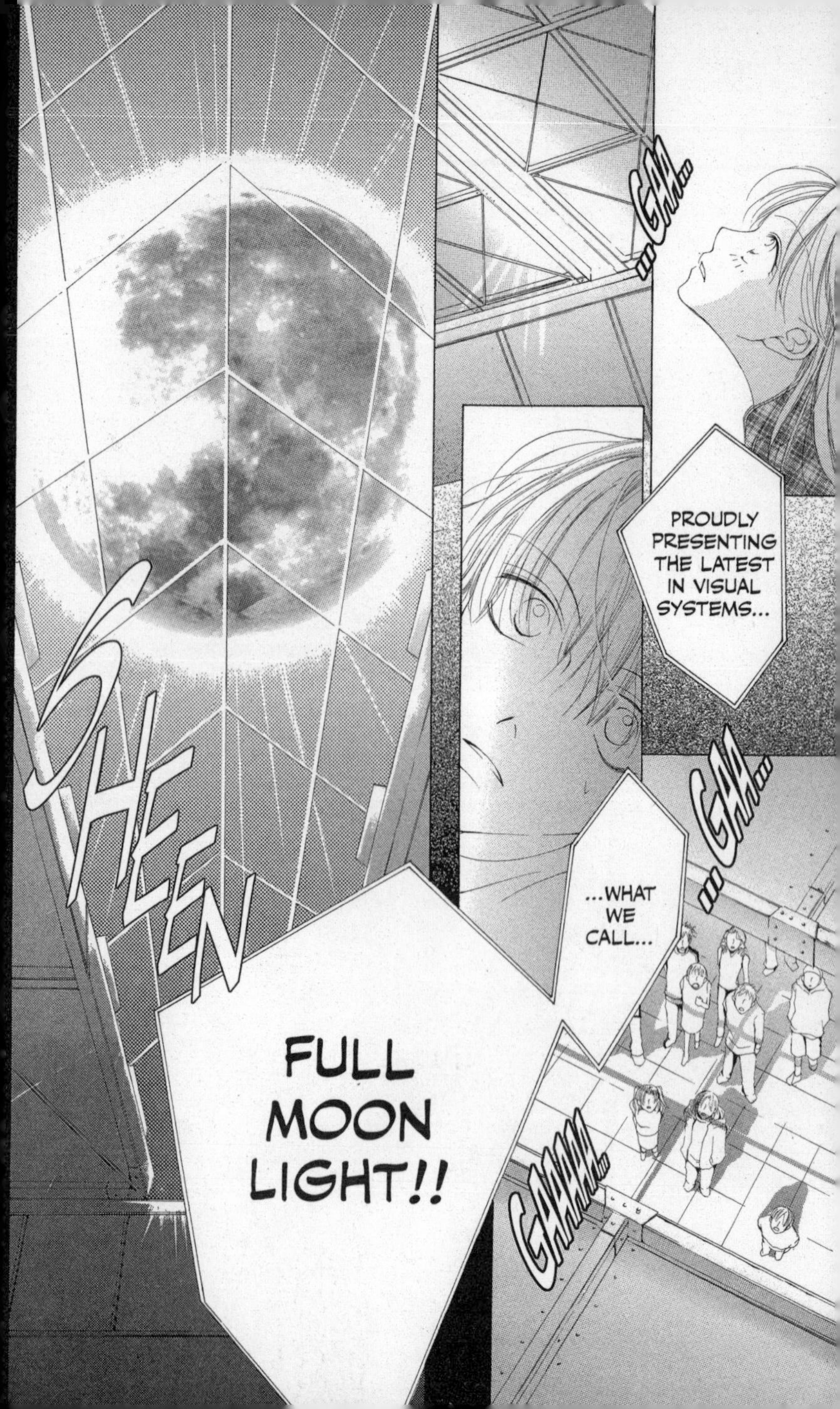
...GAA...
PROUDLY PRESENTING THE LATEST IN VISUAL SYSTEMS...
...GAA...
GAAAA...
...WHAT WE CALL...
SHEEN
FULL MOON LIGHT!!

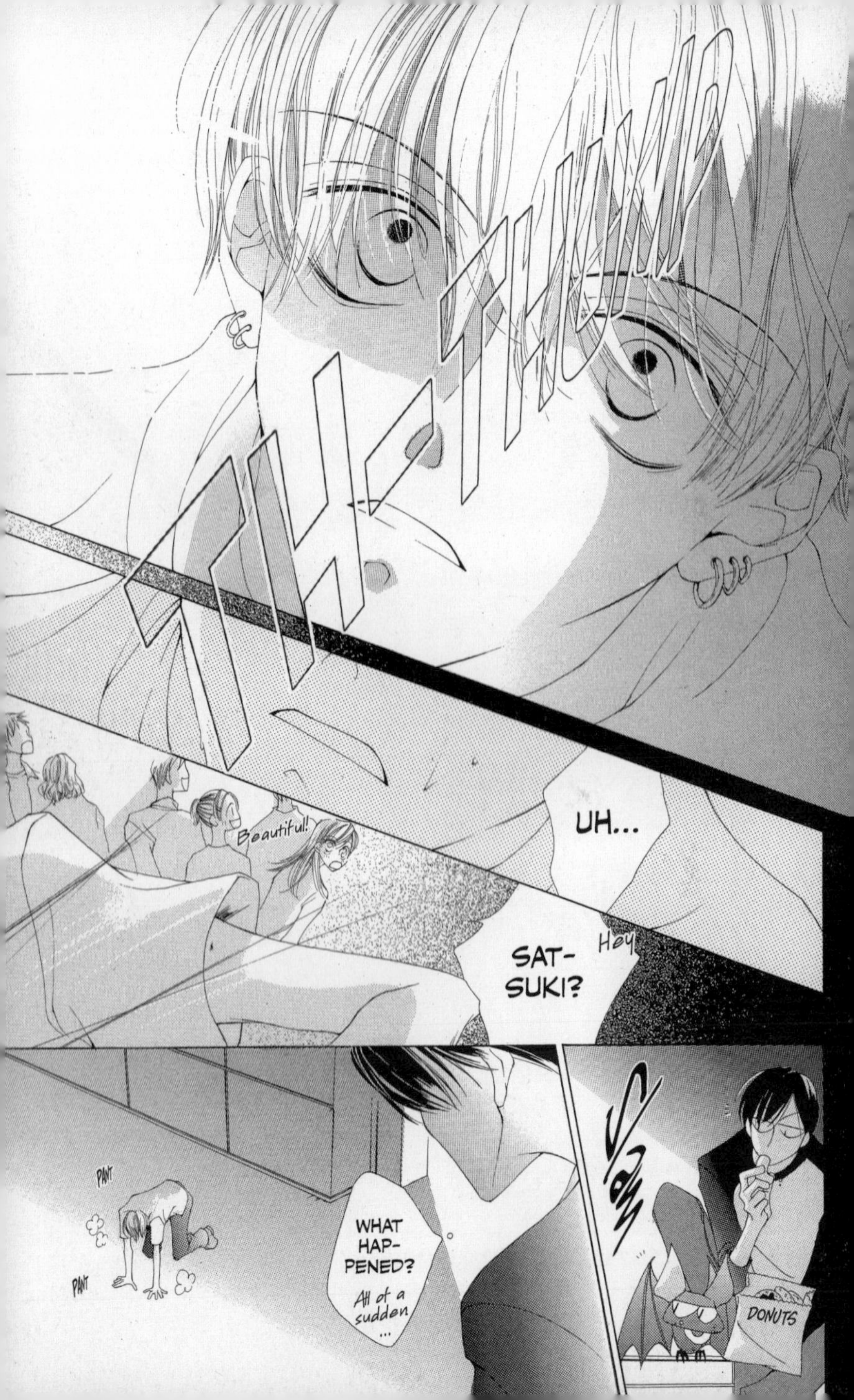
THUNK
Beautiful!
UH...
Hey
SAT-
SUKI?
SLAM
WHAT HAP-PENED?
All of a sudden ...
DONUTS
PANT
PANT

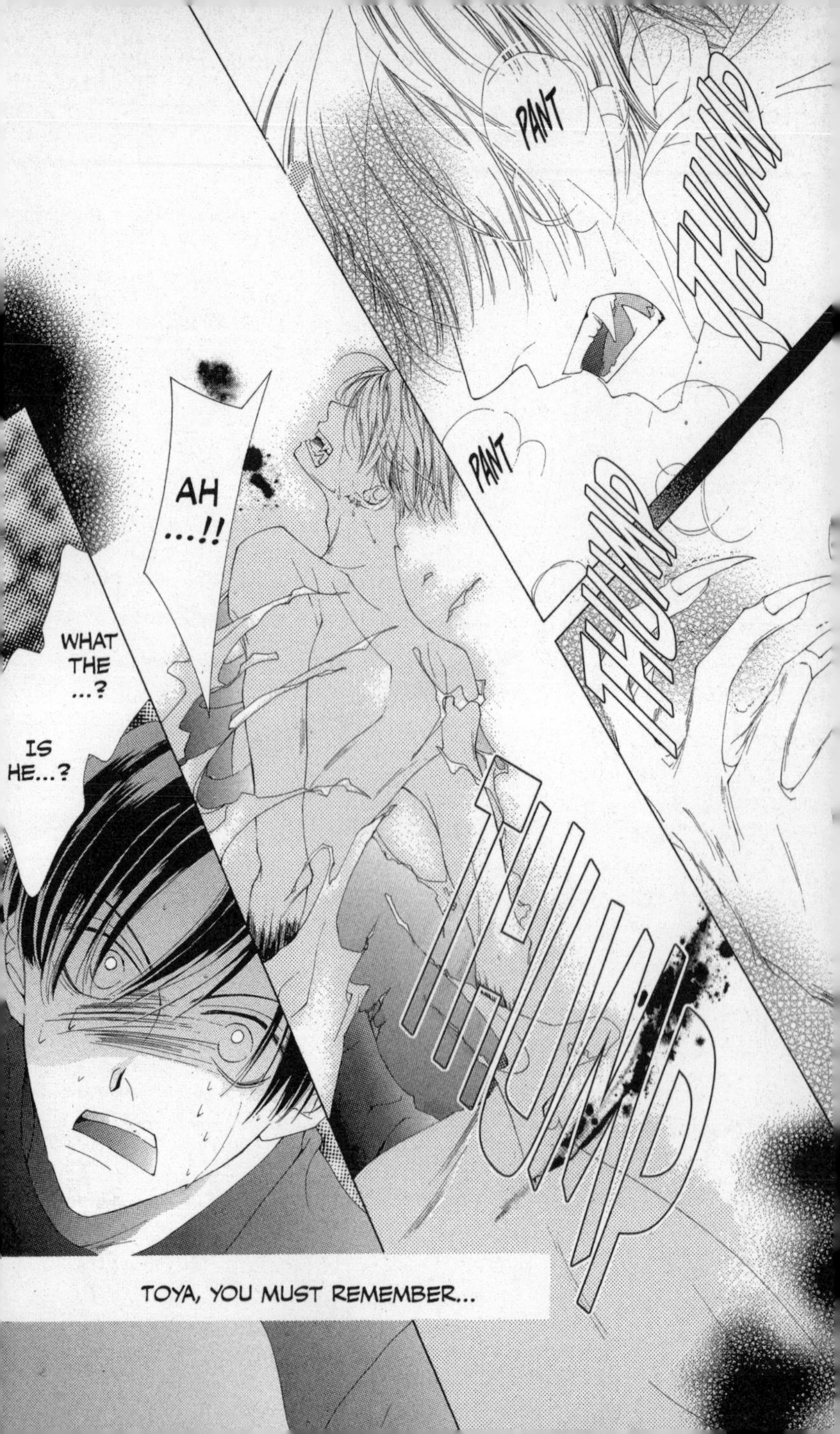
PANT
THUMP
PANT
THUMP
THUMP
AH ...!!
THUMP
WHAT THE ...?
IS HE...?
TOYA, YOU MUST REMEMBER...

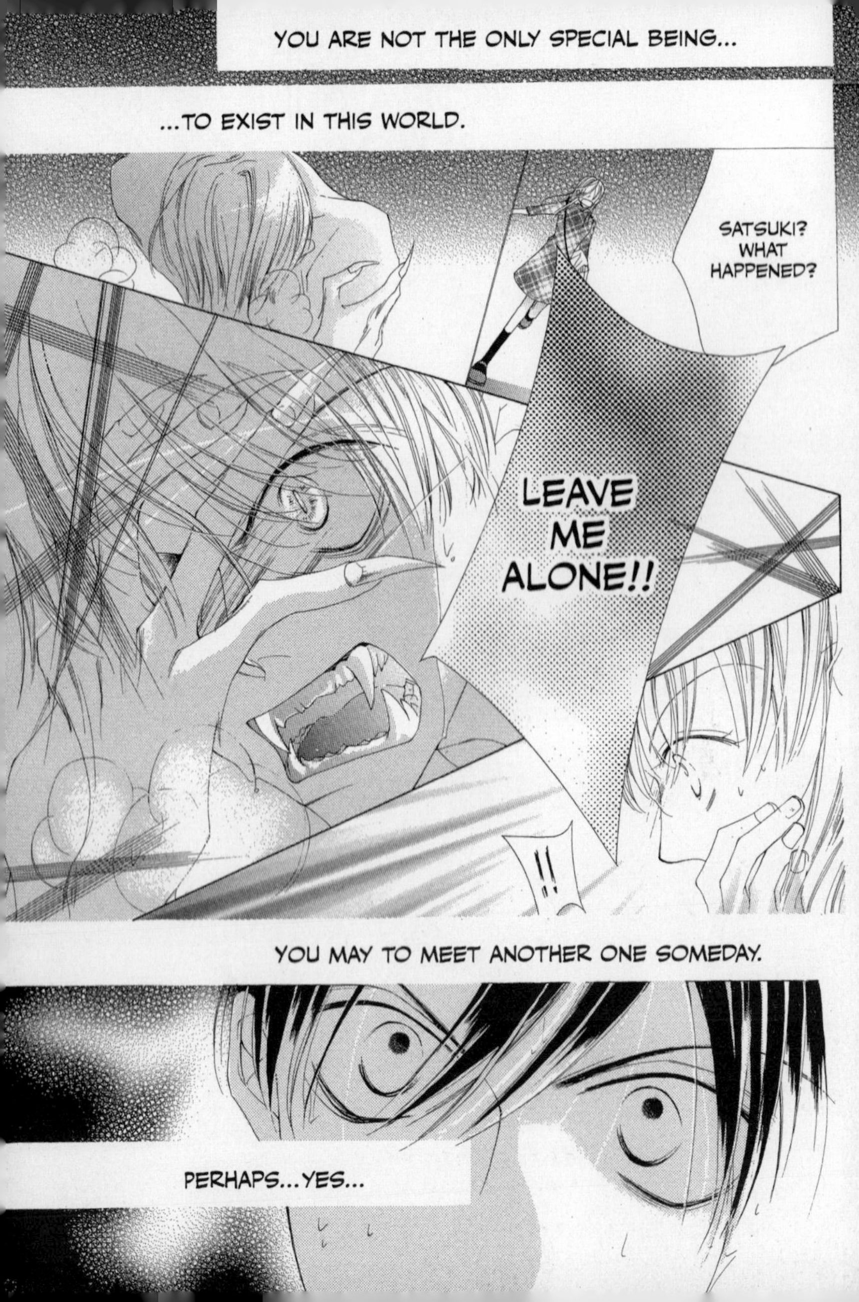
YOU ARE NOT THE ONLY SPECIAL BEING...
...TO EXIST IN THIS WORLD.
SATSUKI? WHAT HAPPENED?
LEAVE ME ALONE!!
!!
YOU MAY TO MEET ANOTHER ONE SOMEDAY.
PERHAPS...YES...

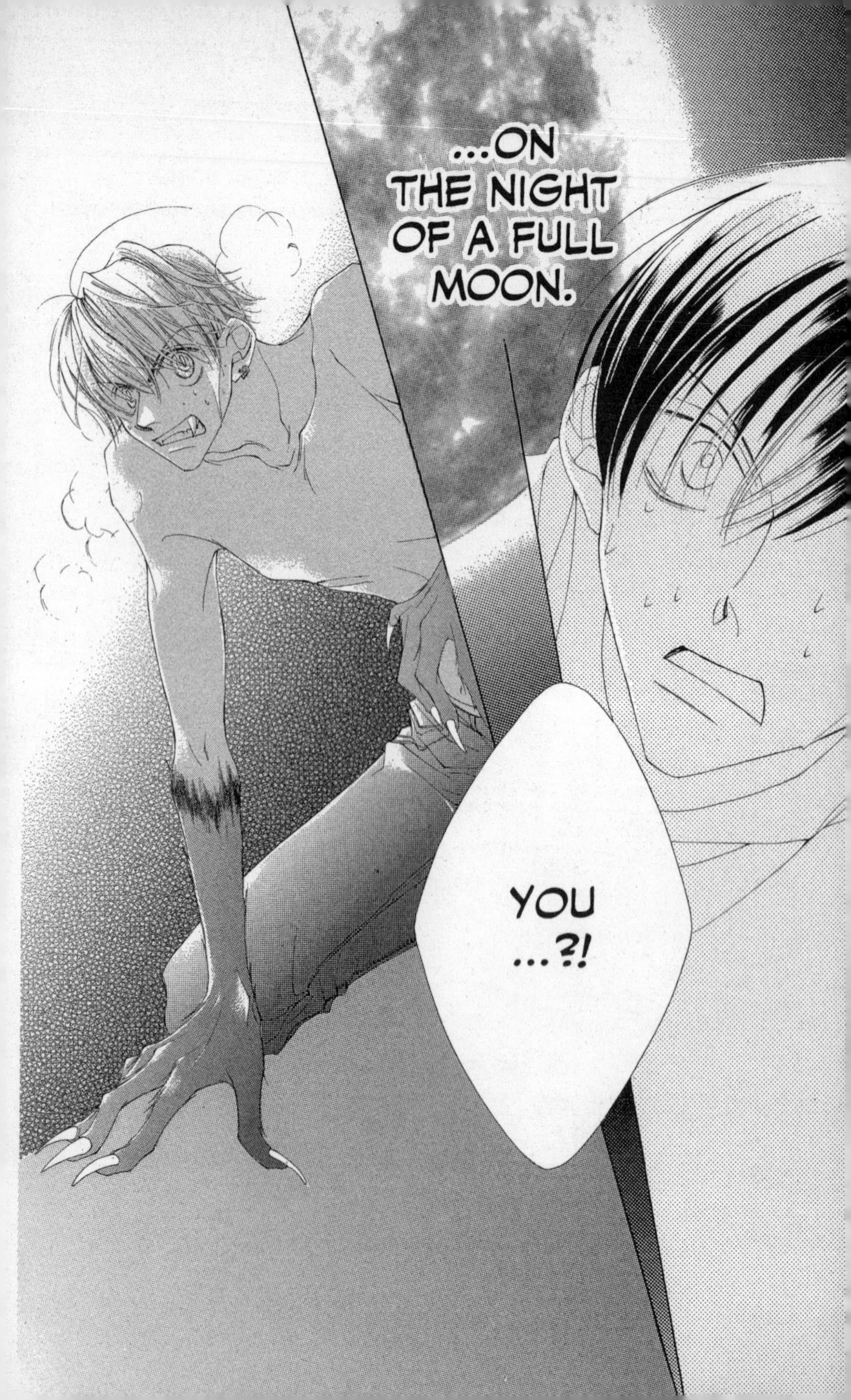
...ON THE NIGHT OF A FULL MOON.
YOU ...?!

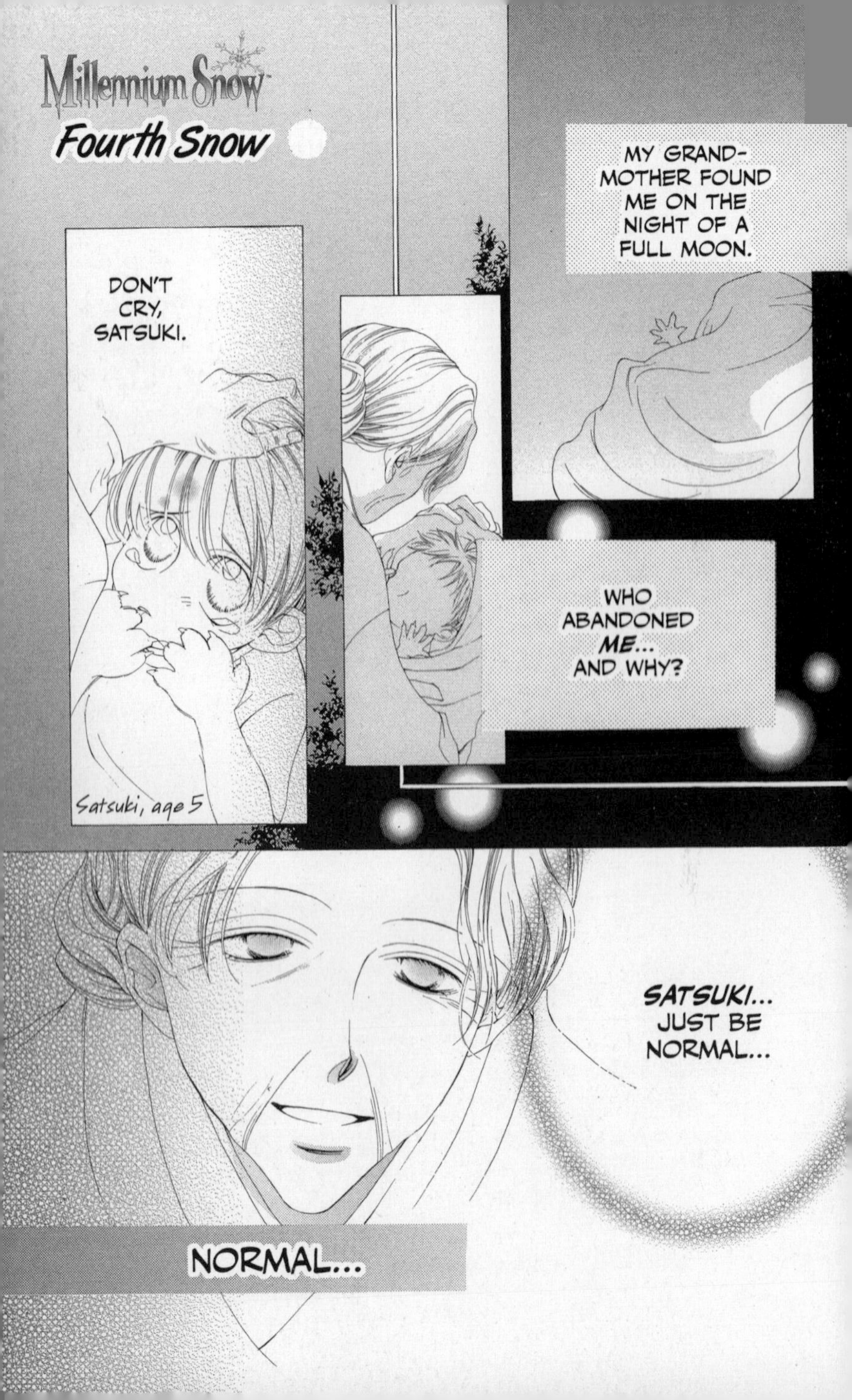
Millennium Snow
Fourth Snow
MY GRAND-MOTHER FOUND ME ON THE NIGHT OF A FULL MOON.
WHO ABANDONED ME... AND WHY?
DON'T CRY, SATSUKI.
Satsuki, age 5
SATSUKI... JUST BE NORMAL...
NORMAL...

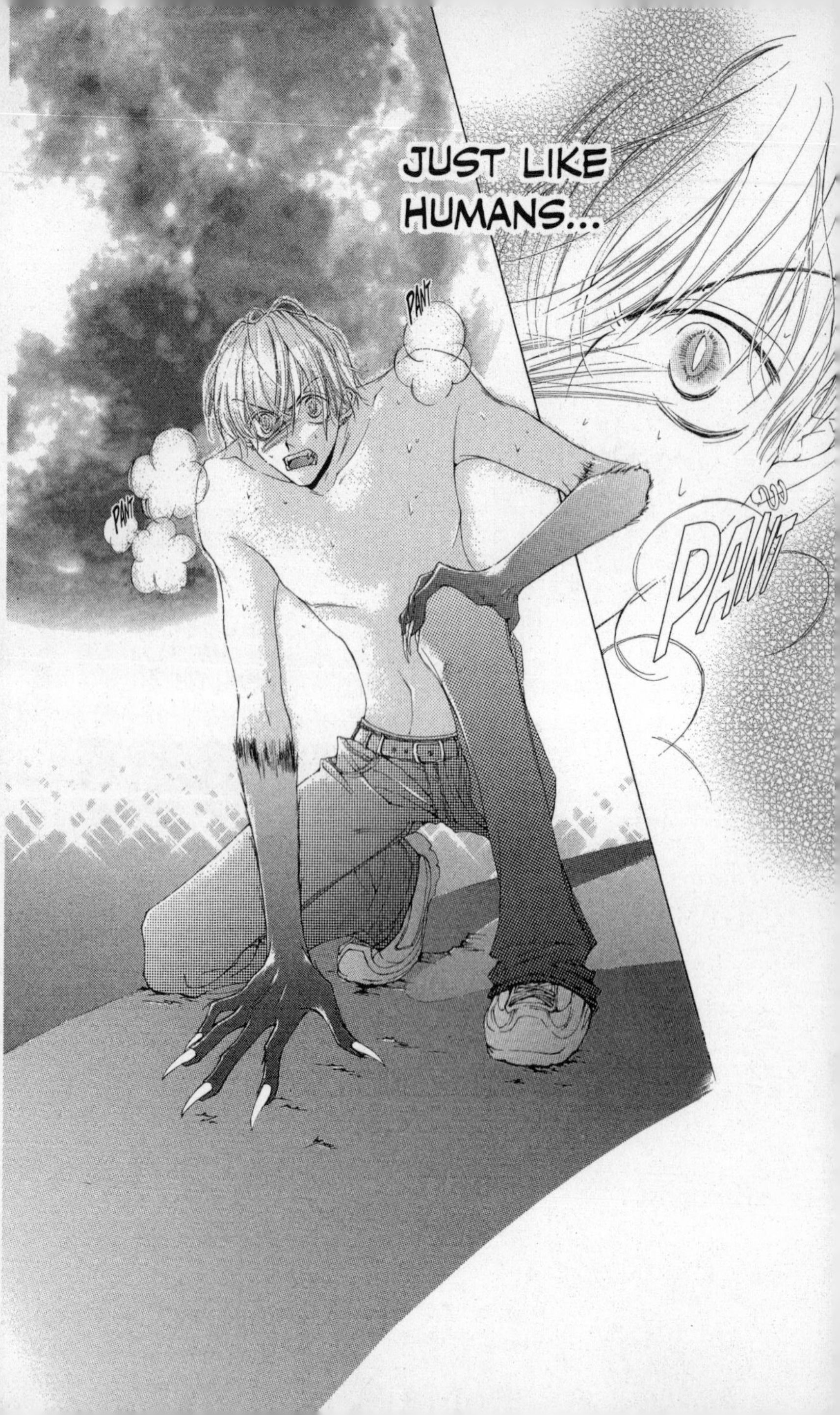
JUST LIKE HUMANS...
PANT
PANT
PANT

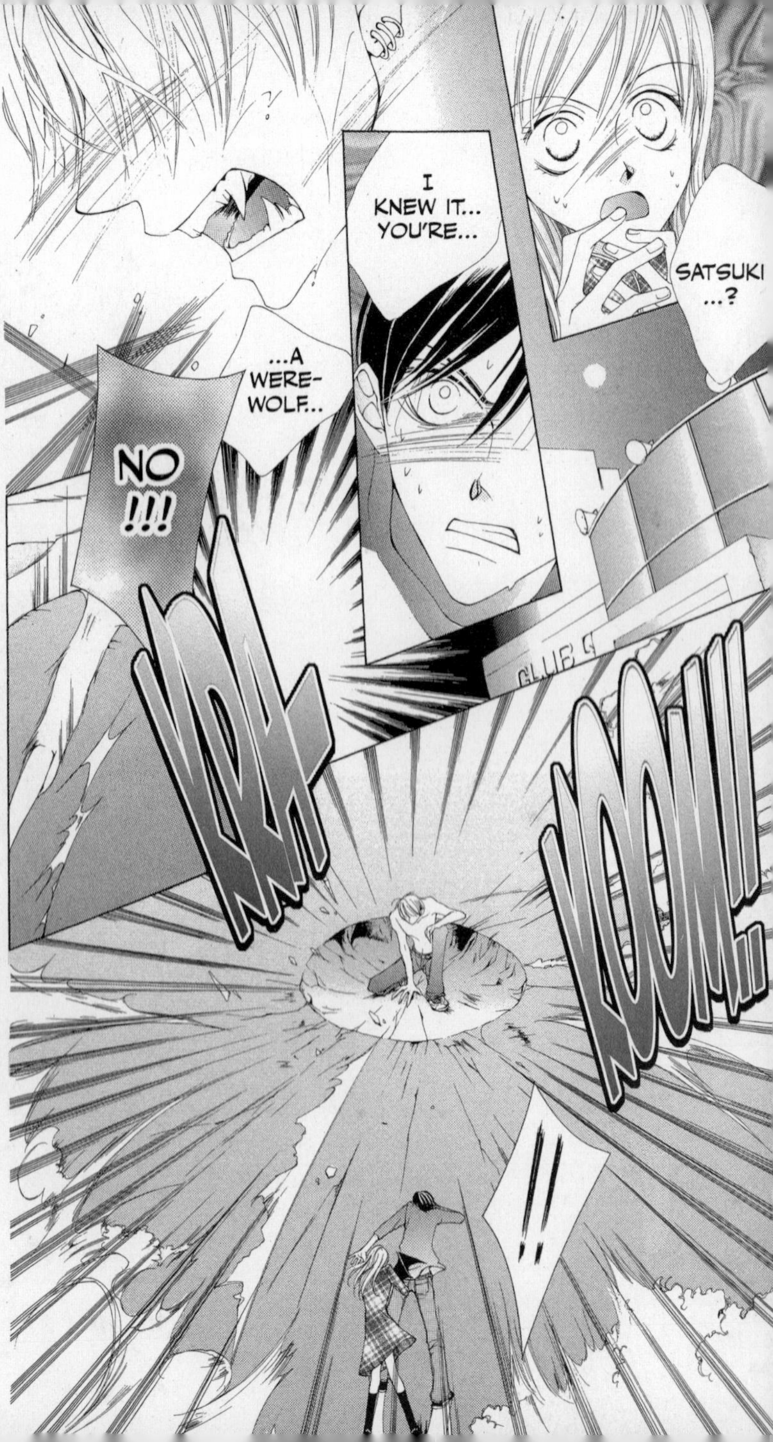
SATSUKI ...?
I KNEW IT... YOU'RE...
...A WERE-WOLF...
NO !!!
!!

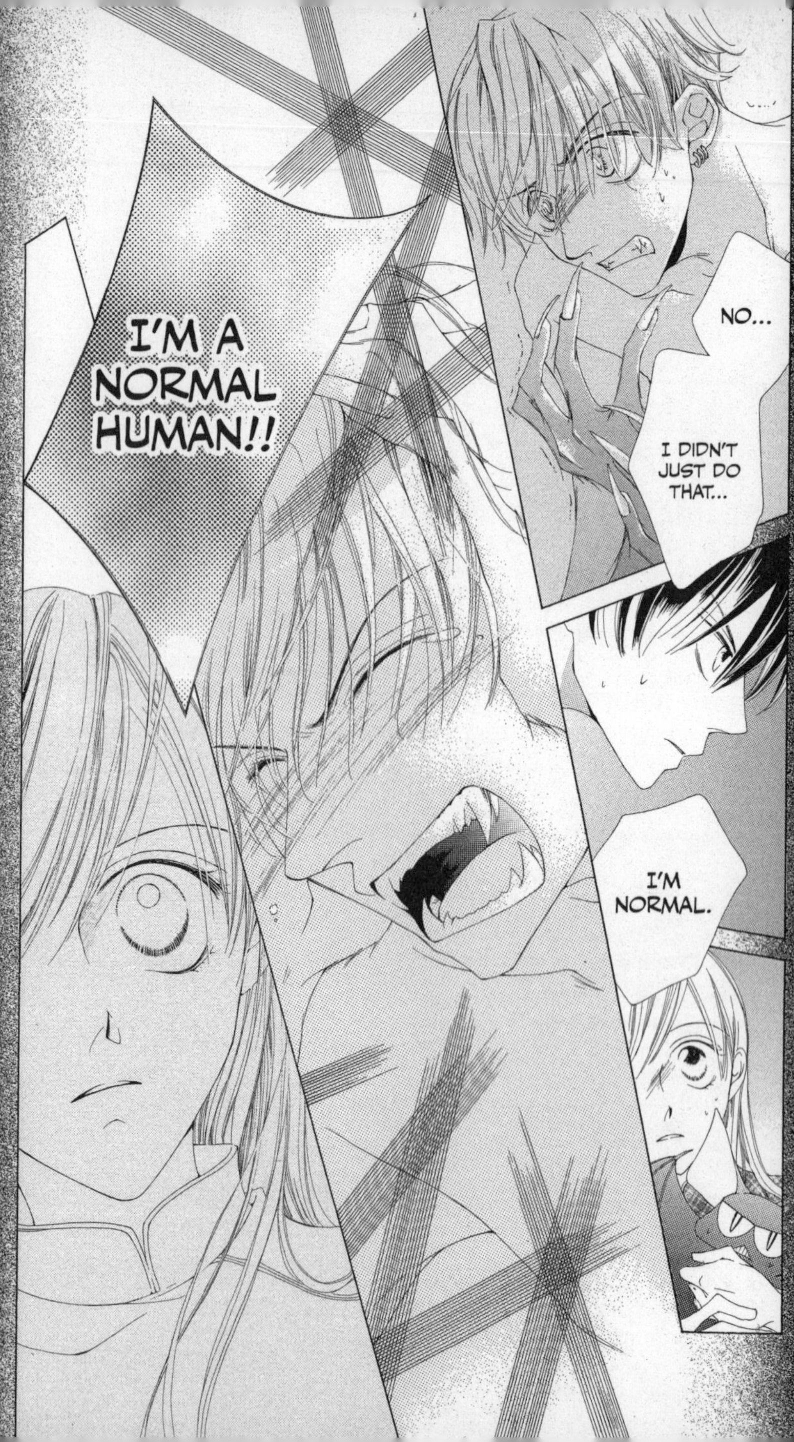
NO...
I DIDN'T JUST DO THAT...
I'M NORMAL.
I'M A NORMAL HUMAN!!

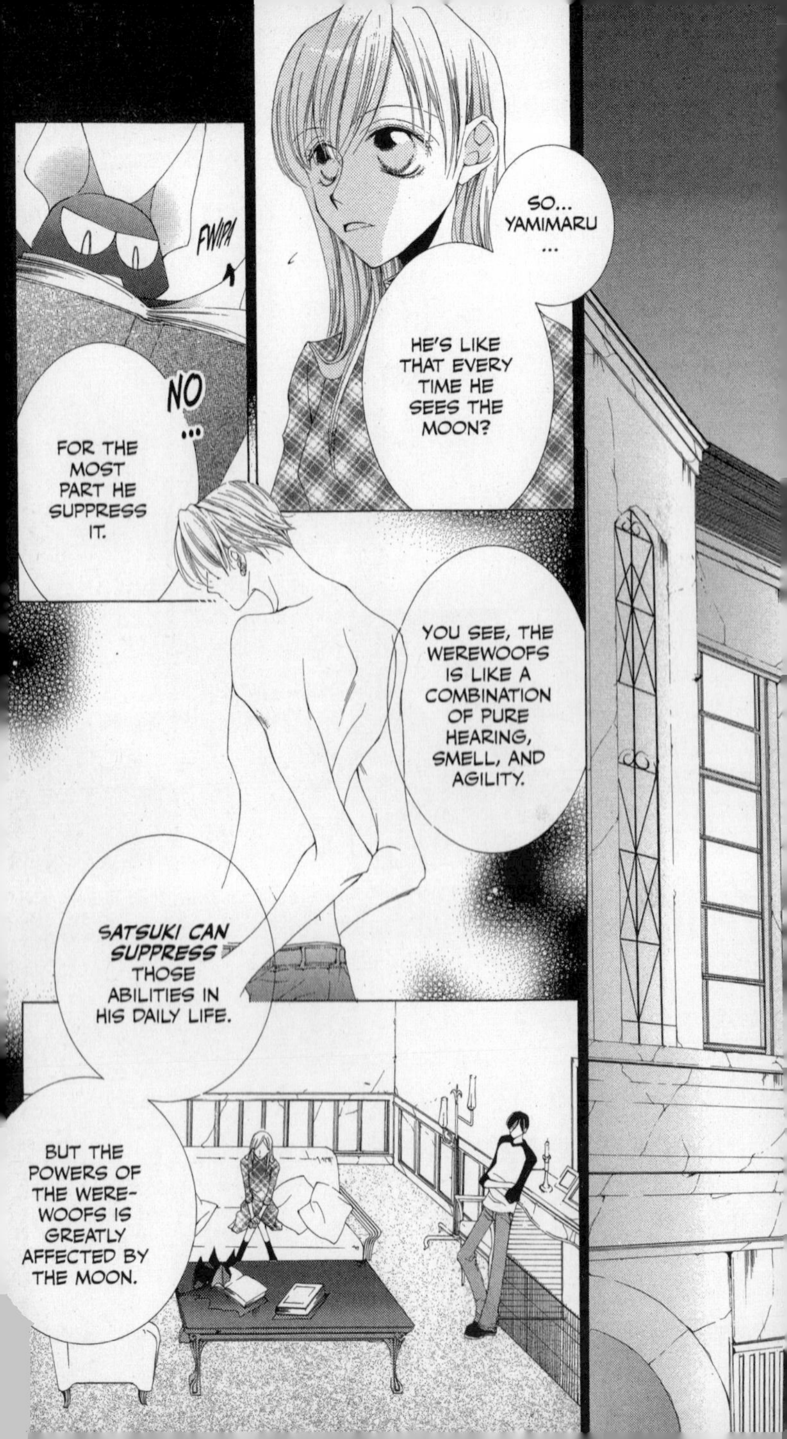
SO... YAMIMARU ...
HE'S LIKE THAT EVERY TIME HE SEES THE MOON?
FWIPA
NO ...
FOR THE MOST PART HE SUPPRESS IT.
YOU SEE, THE WEREWOOFS IS LIKE A COMBINATION OF PURE HEARING, SMELL, AND AGILITY.
SATSUKI CAN SUPPRESS THOSE ABILITIES IN HIS DAILY LIFE.
BUT THE POWERS OF THE WERE-WOOFS IS GREATLY AFFECTED BY THE MOON.

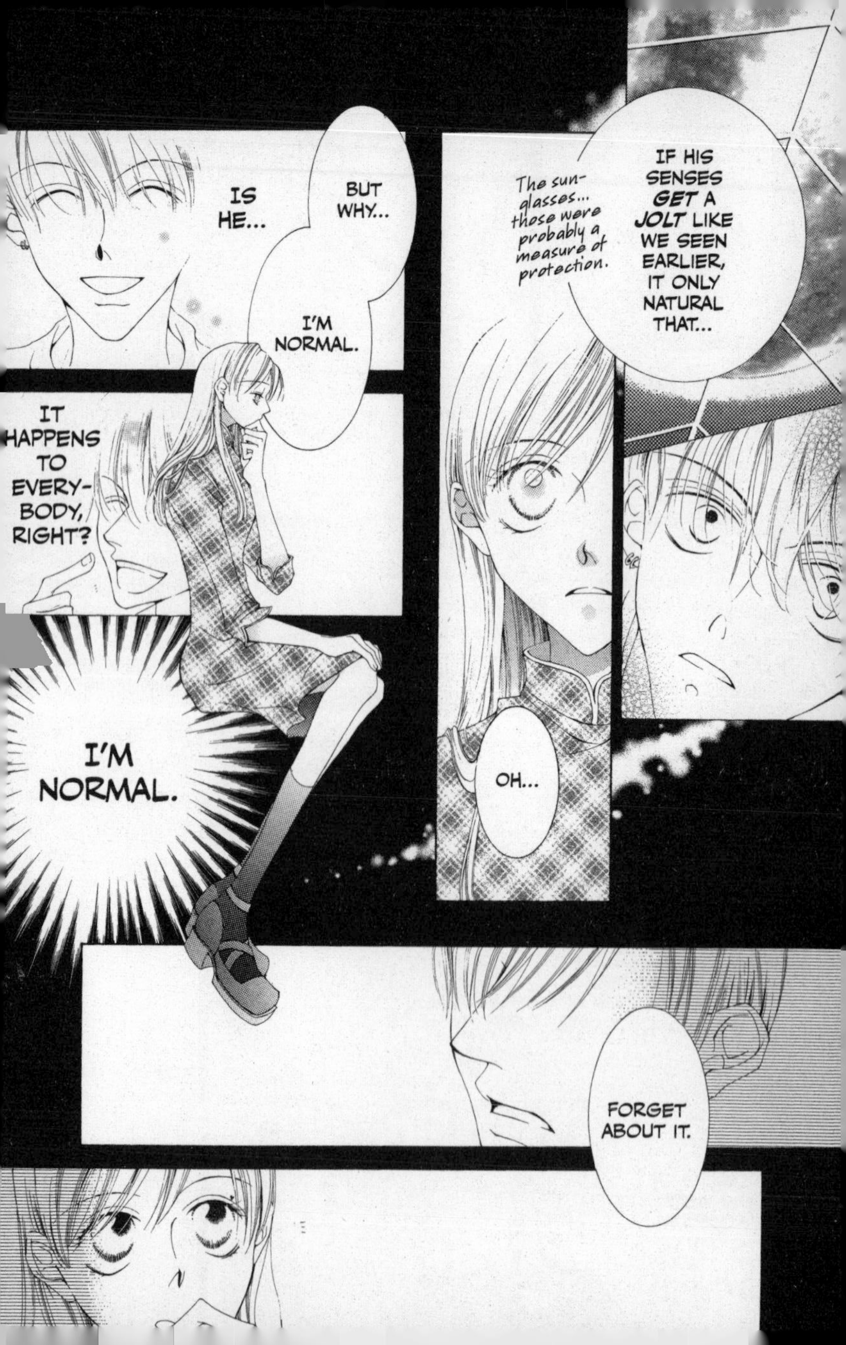
BUT WHY...
IS HE...
I'M NORMAL.
IT HAPPENS TO EVERY-BODY, RIGHT?
I'M NORMAL.
IF HIS SENSES GET A JOLT LIKE WE SEEN EARLIER, IT ONLY NATURAL THAT...
The sun-glasses... those were probably a measure of protection.
OH...
FORGET ABOUT IT.

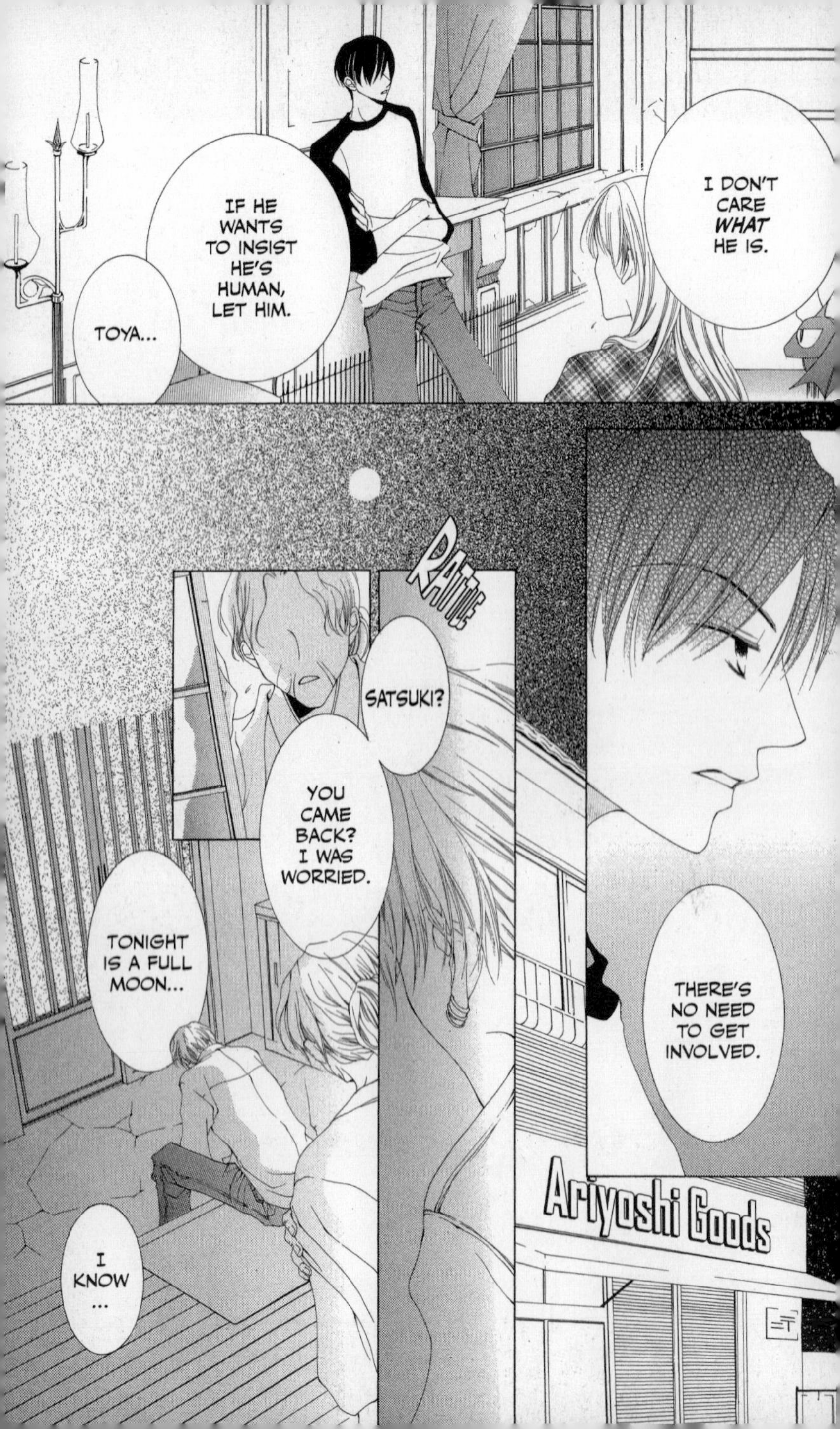
I DON'T CARE *WHAT* HE IS.
IF HE WANTS TO INSIST HE'S HUMAN, LET HIM.
TOYA...
THERE'S NO NEED TO GET INVOLVED.
Ariyoshi Goods
RATTLE
SATSUKI?
YOU CAME BACK? I WAS WORRIED.
TONIGHT IS A FULL MOON...
I KNOW...

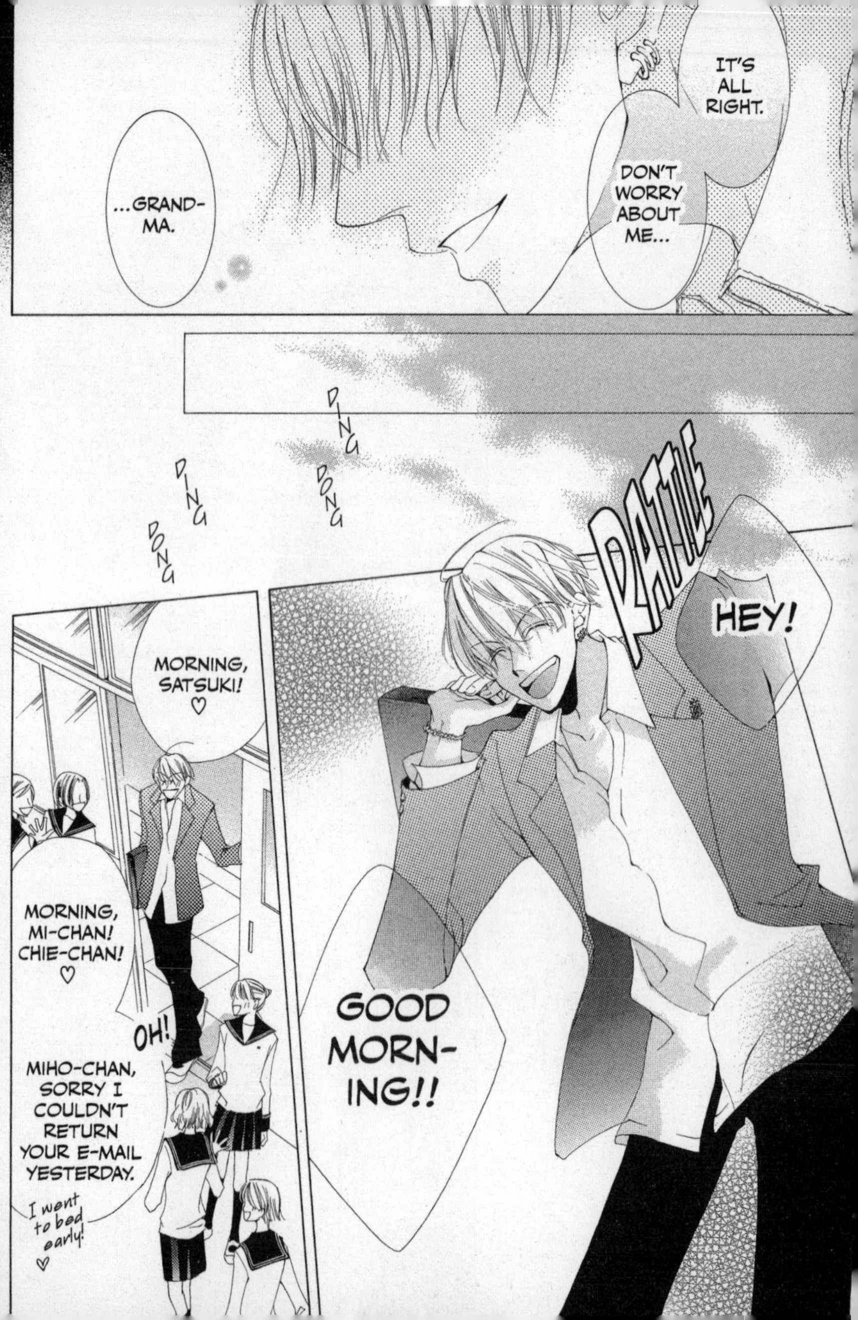
IT'S ALL RIGHT.
DON'T WORRY ABOUT ME...
...GRAND-MA.
DING DONG
DING DONG
RATTLE
HEY!
GOOD MORN-ING!!
MORNING, SATSUKI! ♡
MORNING, MI-CHAN! CHIE-CHAN! ♡
OH!
MIHO-CHAN, SORRY I COULDN'T RETURN YOUR E-MAIL YESTERDAY.
I went to bed early! ♡

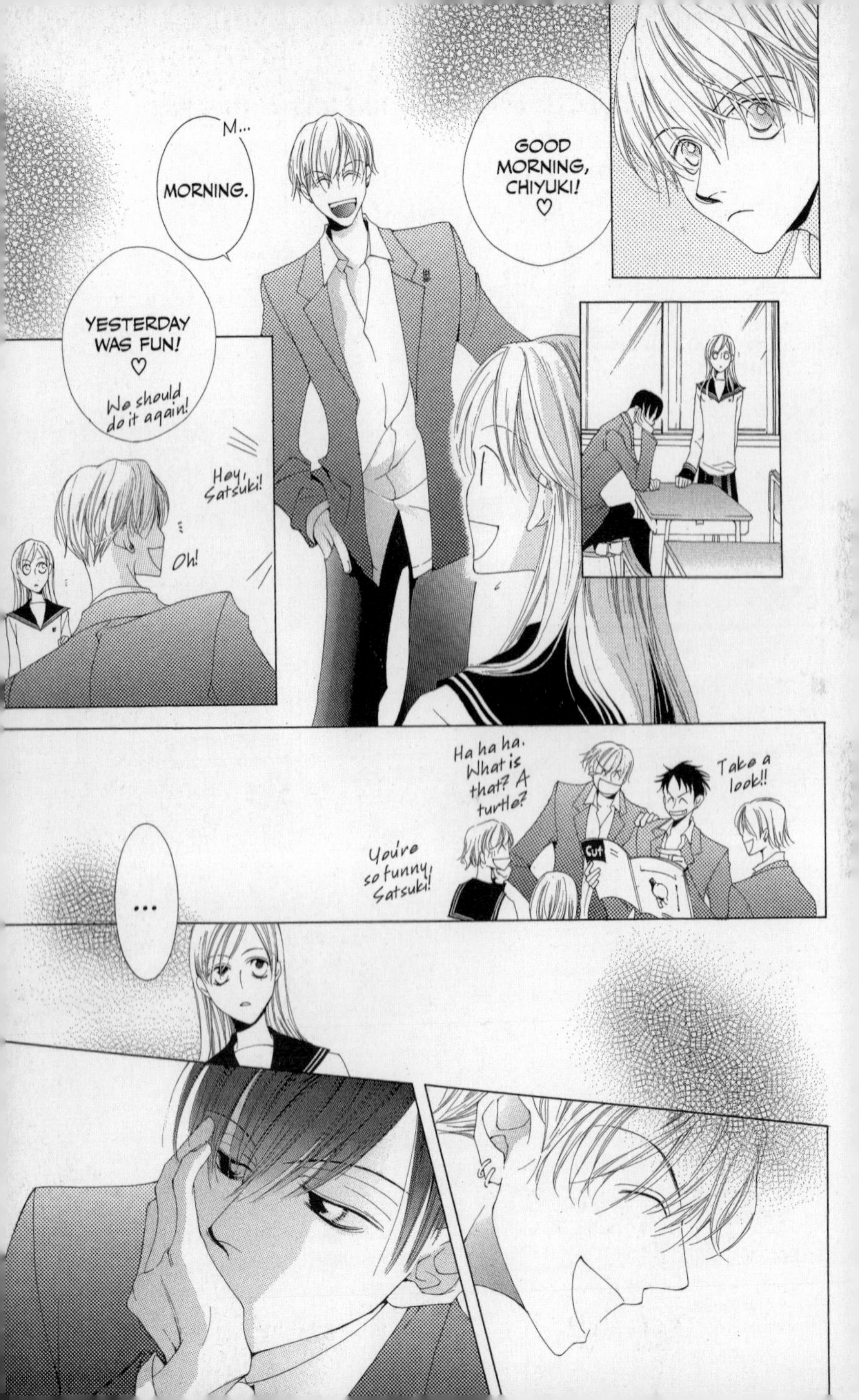
GOOD MORNING, CHIYUKI! ♡
M... MORNING.
YESTERDAY WAS FUN! ♡ We should do it again!
Hey, Satsuki!
Oh!
Take a look!!
Ha ha ha. What is that? A turtle?
Cut
You're so funny, Satsuki!
...

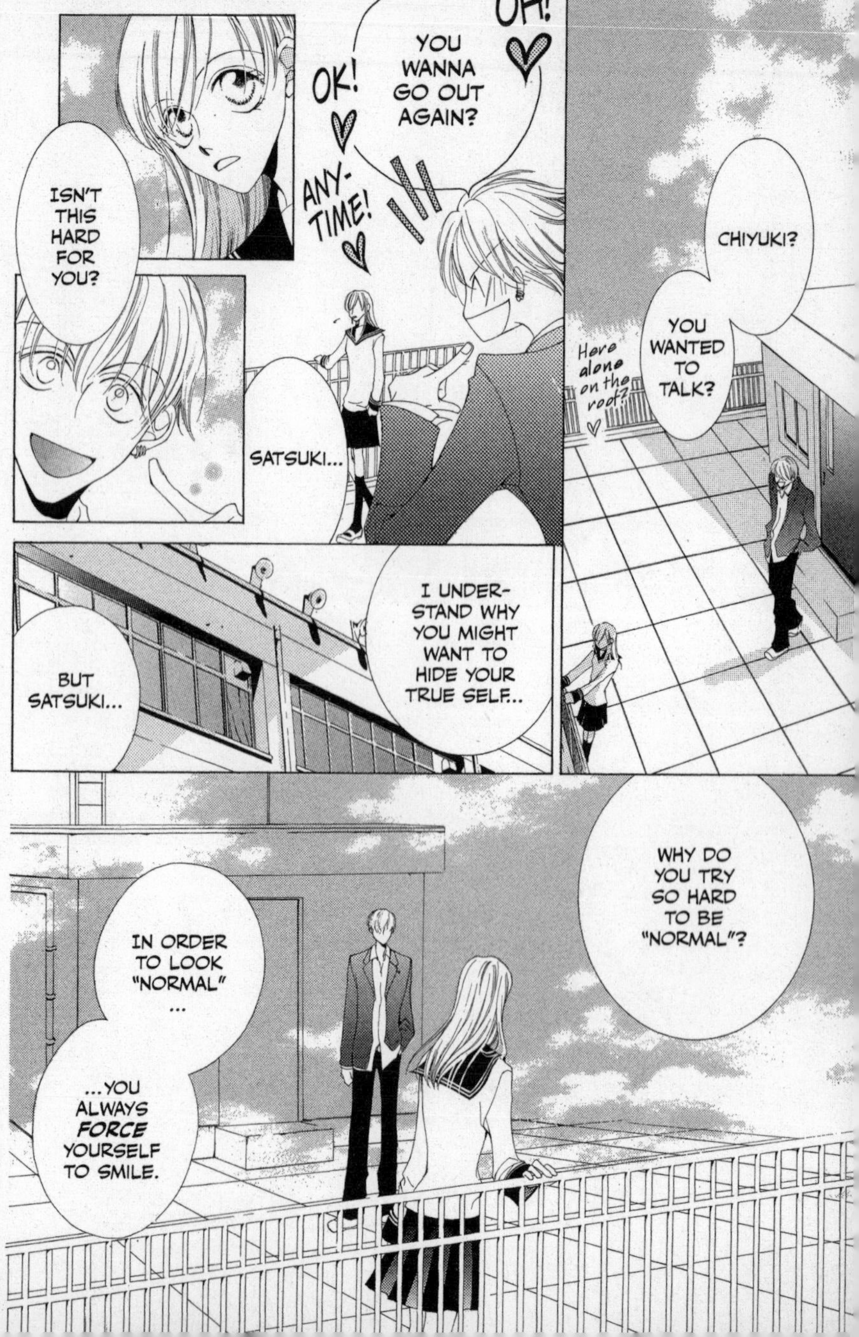
CHIYUKI?
YOU WANTED TO TALK?
Here alone on the roof?
OH!
YOU WANNA GO OUT AGAIN?
OK!
ANY-TIME!
SATSUKI...
ISN'T THIS HARD FOR YOU?
I UNDER-STAND WHY YOU MIGHT WANT TO HIDE YOUR TRUE SELF...
BUT SATSUKI...
WHY DO YOU TRY SO HARD TO BE "NORMAL"?
IN ORDER TO LOOK "NORMAL" ...
...YOU ALWAYS *FORCE* YOURSELF TO SMILE.

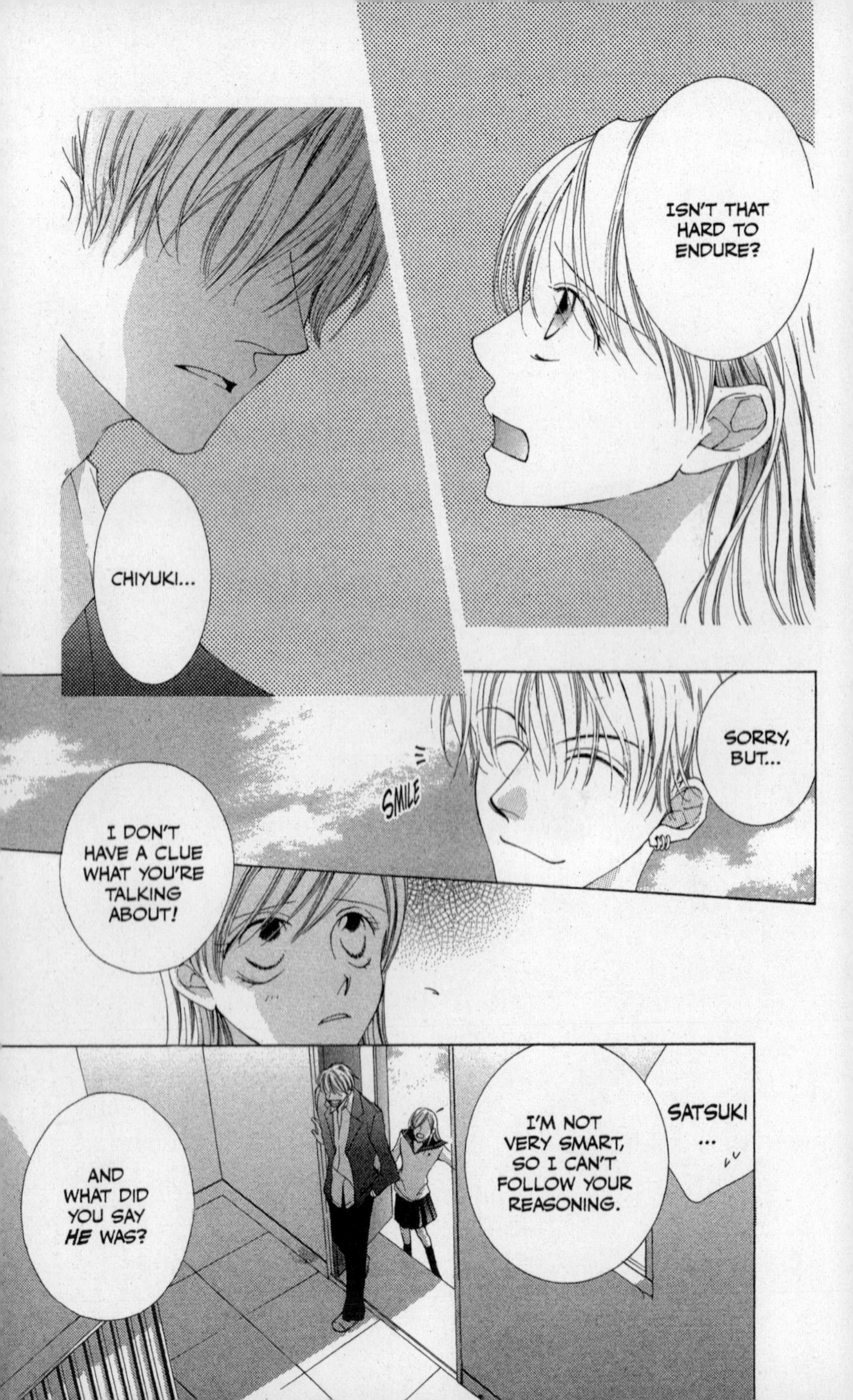
ISN'T THAT HARD TO ENDURE?
CHIYUKI...
SORRY, BUT...
SMILE
I DON'T HAVE A CLUE WHAT YOU'RE TALKING ABOUT!
SATSUKI ...
I'M NOT VERY SMART, SO I CAN'T FOLLOW YOUR REASONING.
AND WHAT DID YOU SAY *HE* WAS?

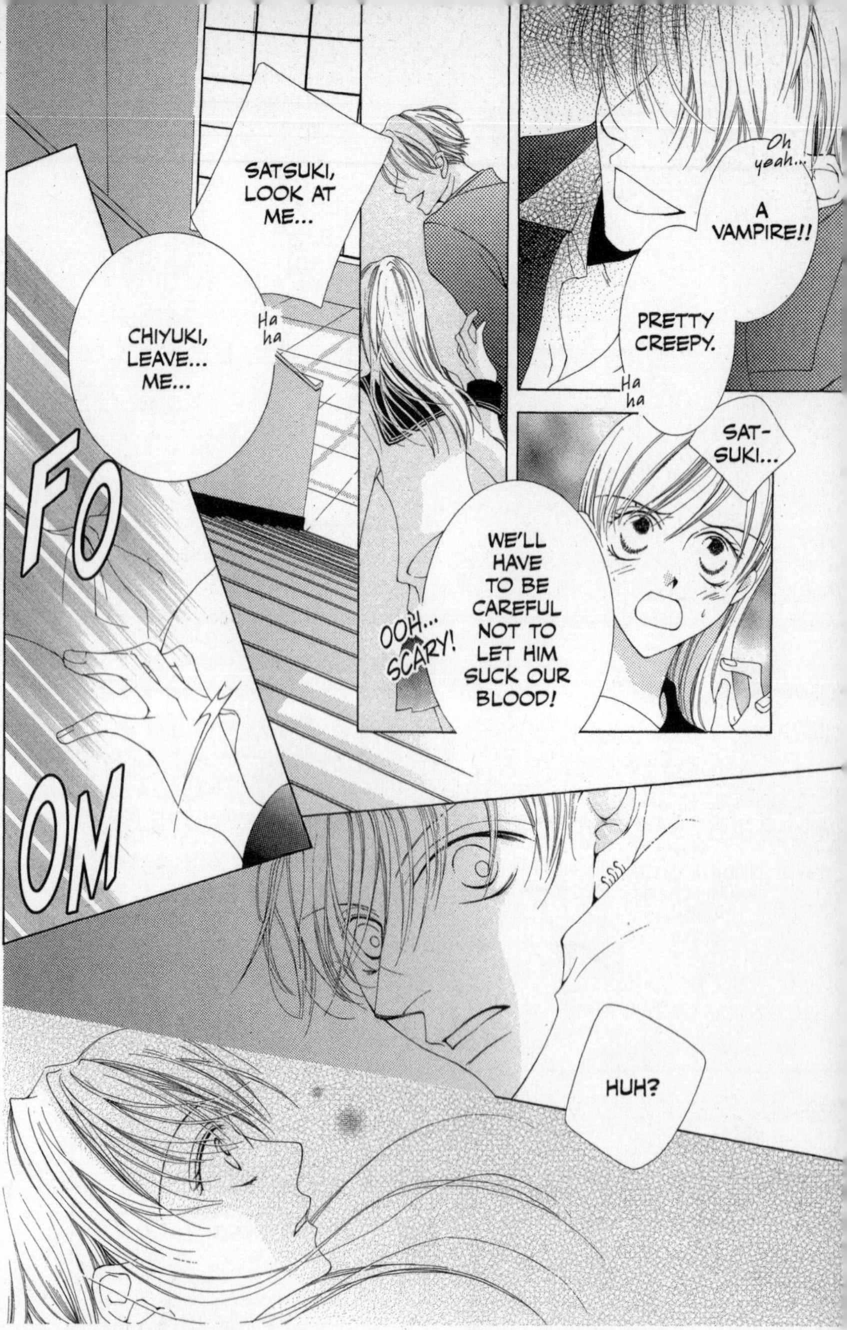
Oh yeah...
A VAMPIRE!!
PRETTY CREEPY.
Ha ha
SAT-SUKI...
WE'LL HAVE TO BE CAREFUL NOT TO LET HIM SUCK OUR BLOOD!
OOH... SCARY!
SATSUKI, LOOK AT ME...
Ha ha
CHIYUKI, LEAVE... ME...
FO OM
HUH?

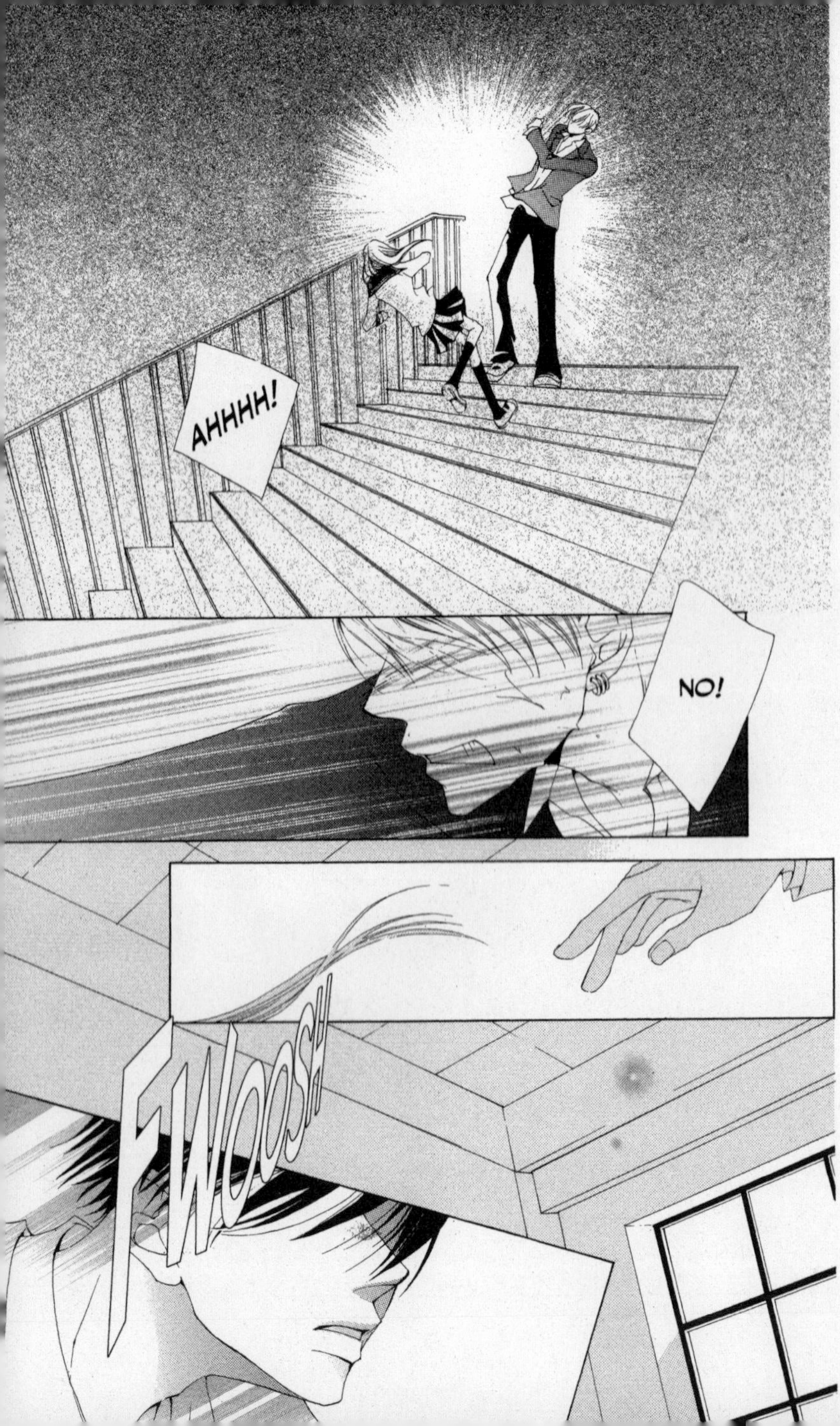
AHHHH!
NO!
FWOOSH

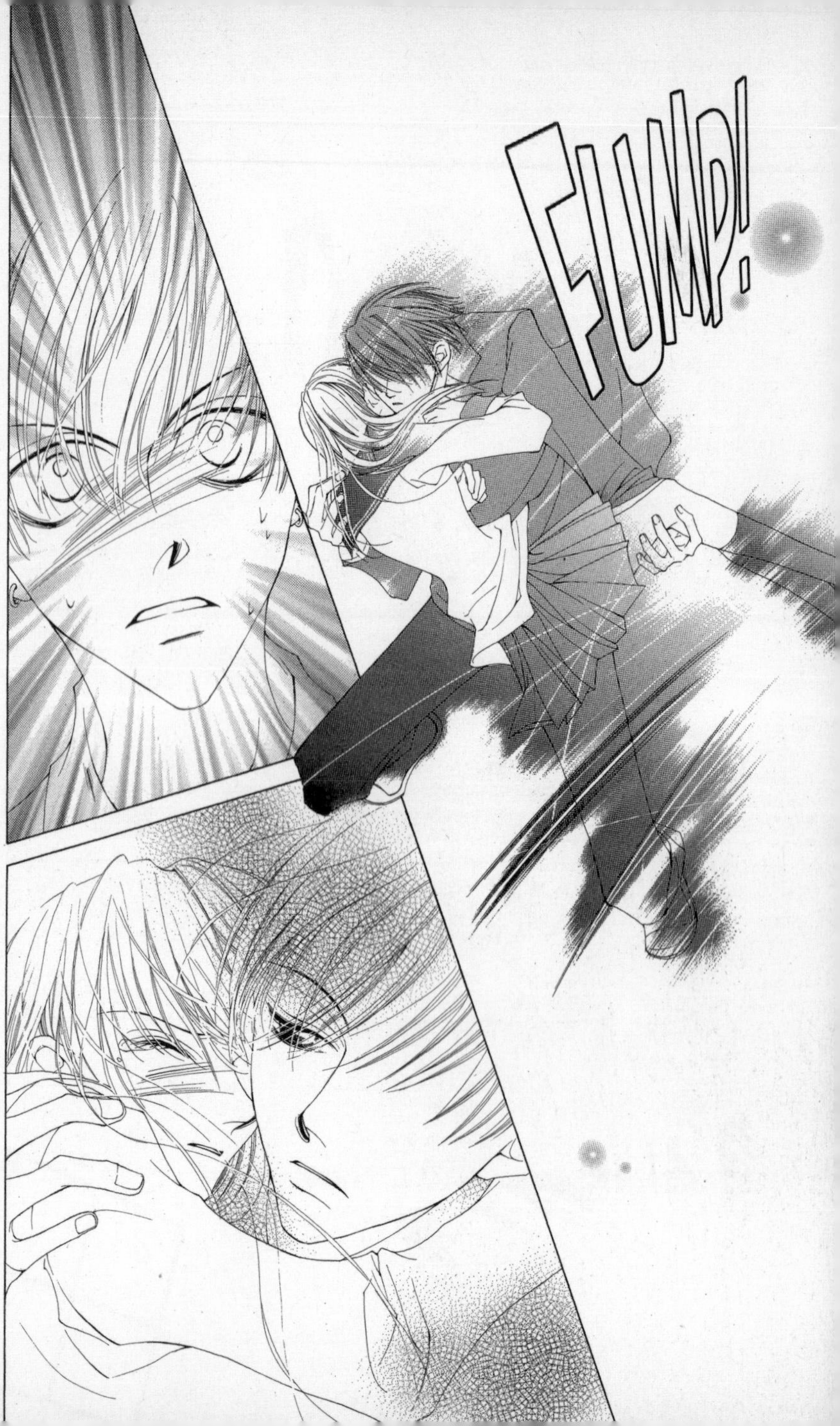
FUMP!!

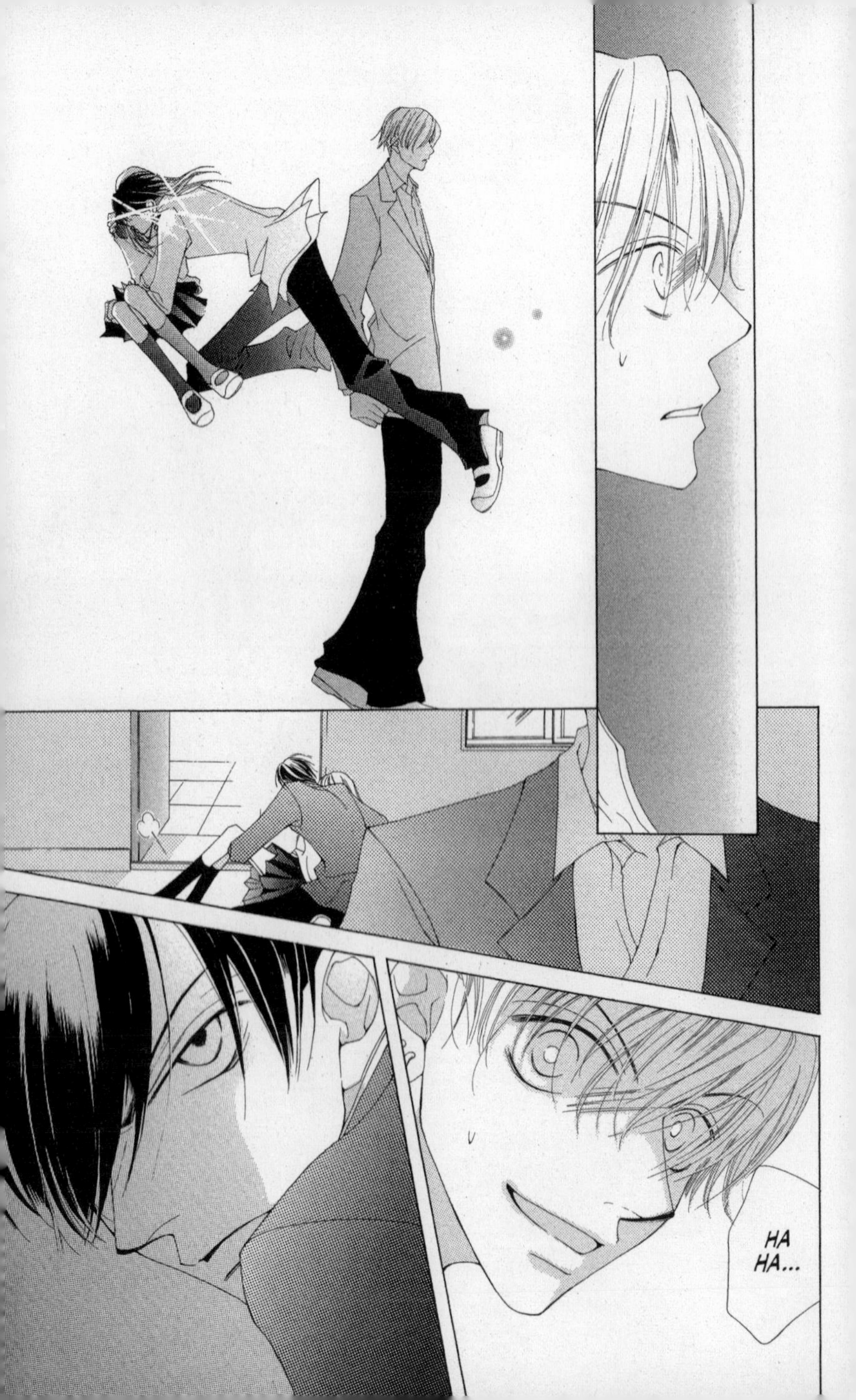
HA
HA...

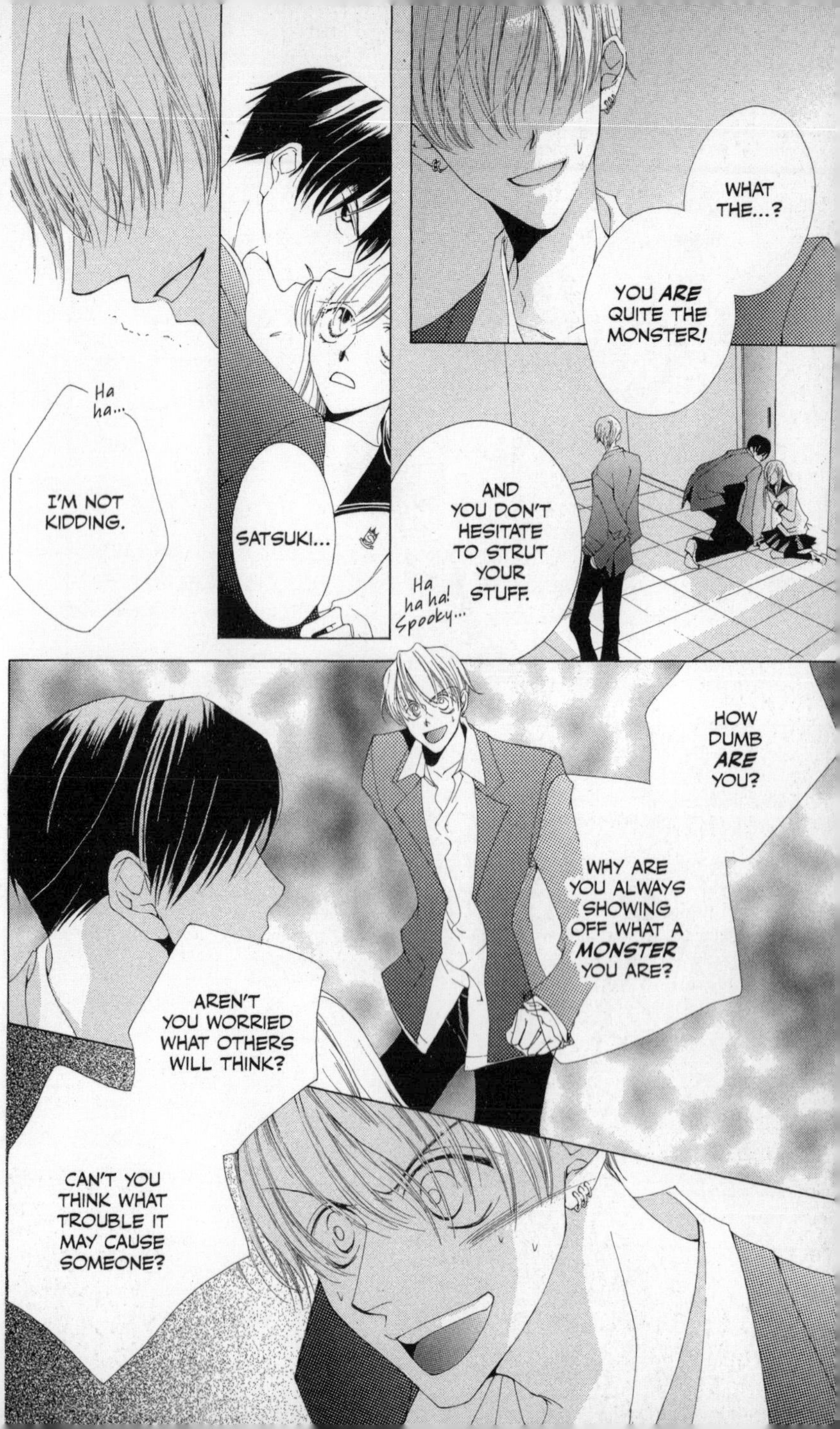
WHAT THE...?
YOU *ARE* QUITE THE MONSTER!
AND YOU DON'T HESITATE TO STRUT YOUR STUFF.
Ha ha ha! Spooky...
SATSUKI...
Ha ha...
I'M NOT KIDDING.
HOW DUMB *ARE* YOU?
WHY ARE YOU ALWAYS SHOWING OFF WHAT A *MONSTER* YOU ARE?
AREN'T YOU WORRIED WHAT OTHERS WILL THINK?
CAN'T YOU THINK WHAT TROUBLE IT MAY CAUSE SOMEONE?

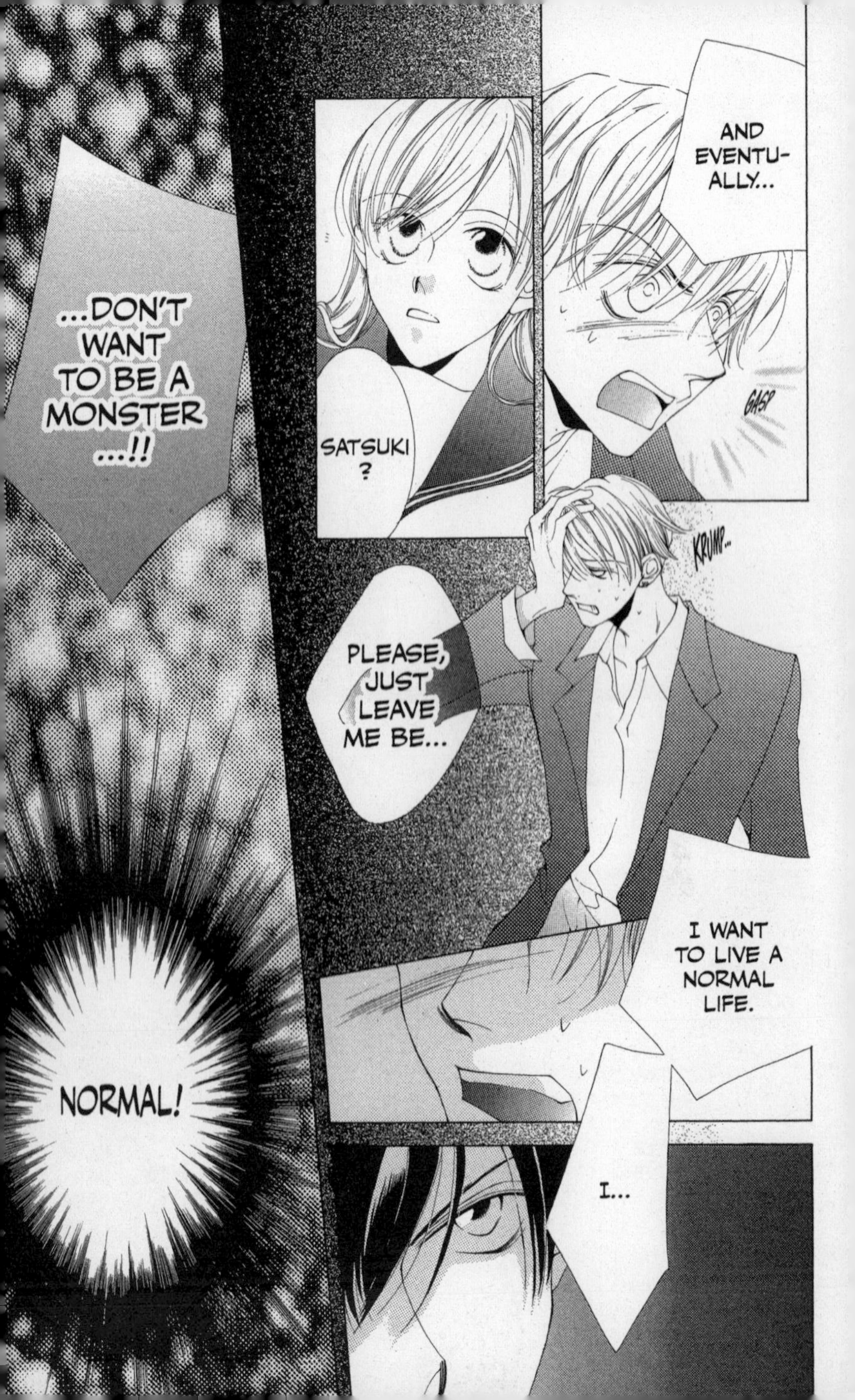
AND EVENTU-ALLY...
GASP
SATSUKI ?
KRUMP...
PLEASE, JUST LEAVE ME BE...
I WANT TO LIVE A NORMAL LIFE.
I...
...DON'T WANT TO BE A MONSTER ...!!
NORMAL!

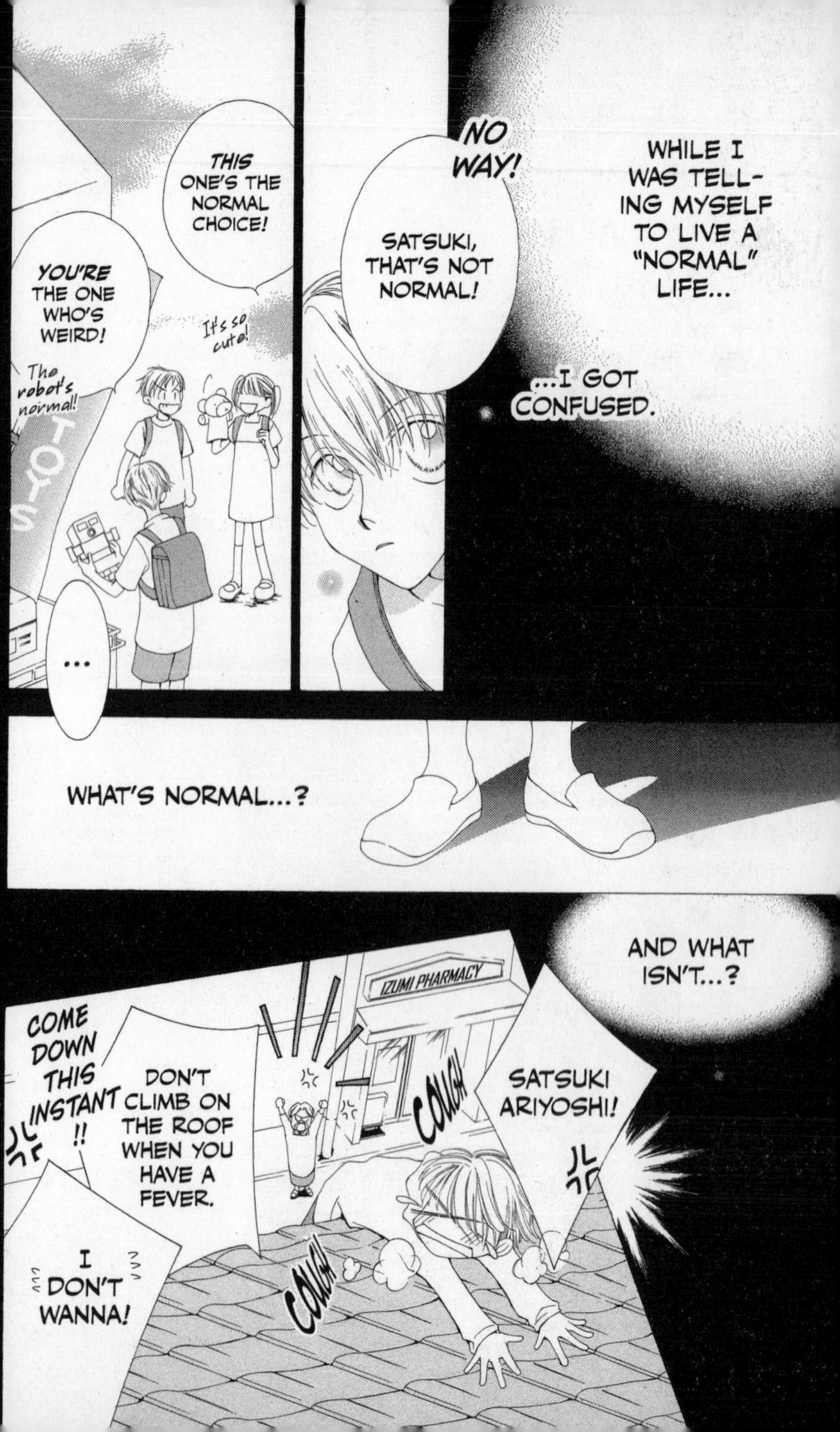
WHILE I WAS TELLING MYSELF TO LIVE A "NORMAL" LIFE...
...I GOT CONFUSED.
NO WAY!
SATSUKI, THAT'S NOT NORMAL!
THIS ONE'S THE NORMAL CHOICE!
YOU'RE THE ONE WHO'S WEIRD!
It's so cute!
The robot's normal!
TOYS
...
WHAT'S NORMAL...?
AND WHAT ISN'T...?
IZUMI PHARMACY
SATSUKI ARIYOSHI!
COUGH
DON'T CLIMB ON THE ROOF WHEN YOU HAVE A FEVER.
COME DOWN THIS INSTANT!!
COUGH
I DON'T WANNA!

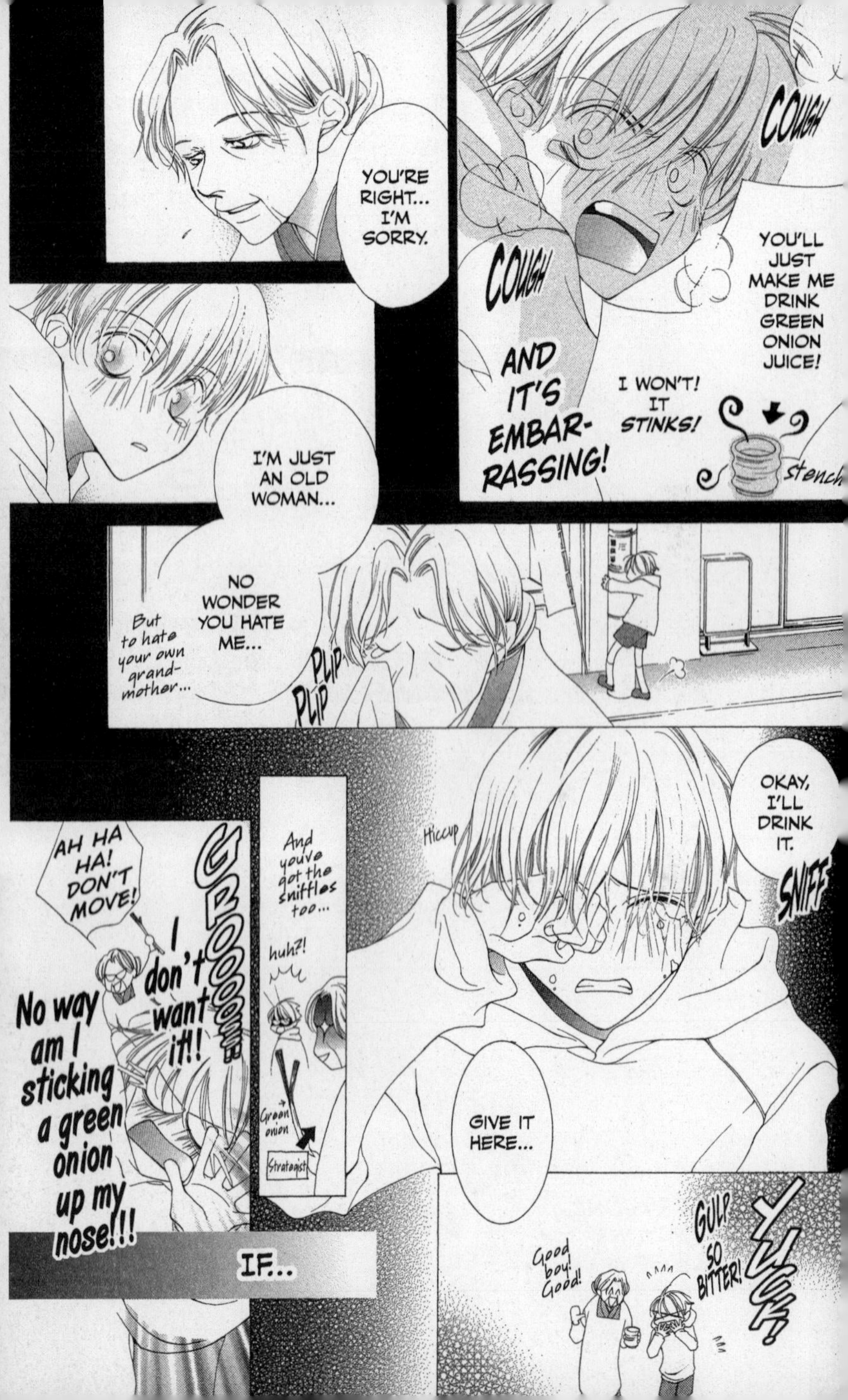
COUGH
YOU'LL JUST MAKE ME DRINK GREEN ONION JUICE!
COUGH
I WON'T! IT STINKS!
stench
AND IT'S EMBAR-RASSING!
YOU'RE RIGHT... I'M SORRY.
I'M JUST AN OLD WOMAN...
NO WONDER YOU HATE ME...
But to hate your own grand-mother...
PLIP PLIP
OKAY, I'LL DRINK IT.
SNIFF
Hiccup
GIVE IT HERE...
And you've got the sniffles too...
huh?!
Green onion
Strategist
AH HA HA! DON'T MOVE!
GROOOOW!!
I don't want it!!
No way am I sticking a green onion up my nose!!!
IF...
YUCK!
GULP SO BITTER!
Good boy! Good!

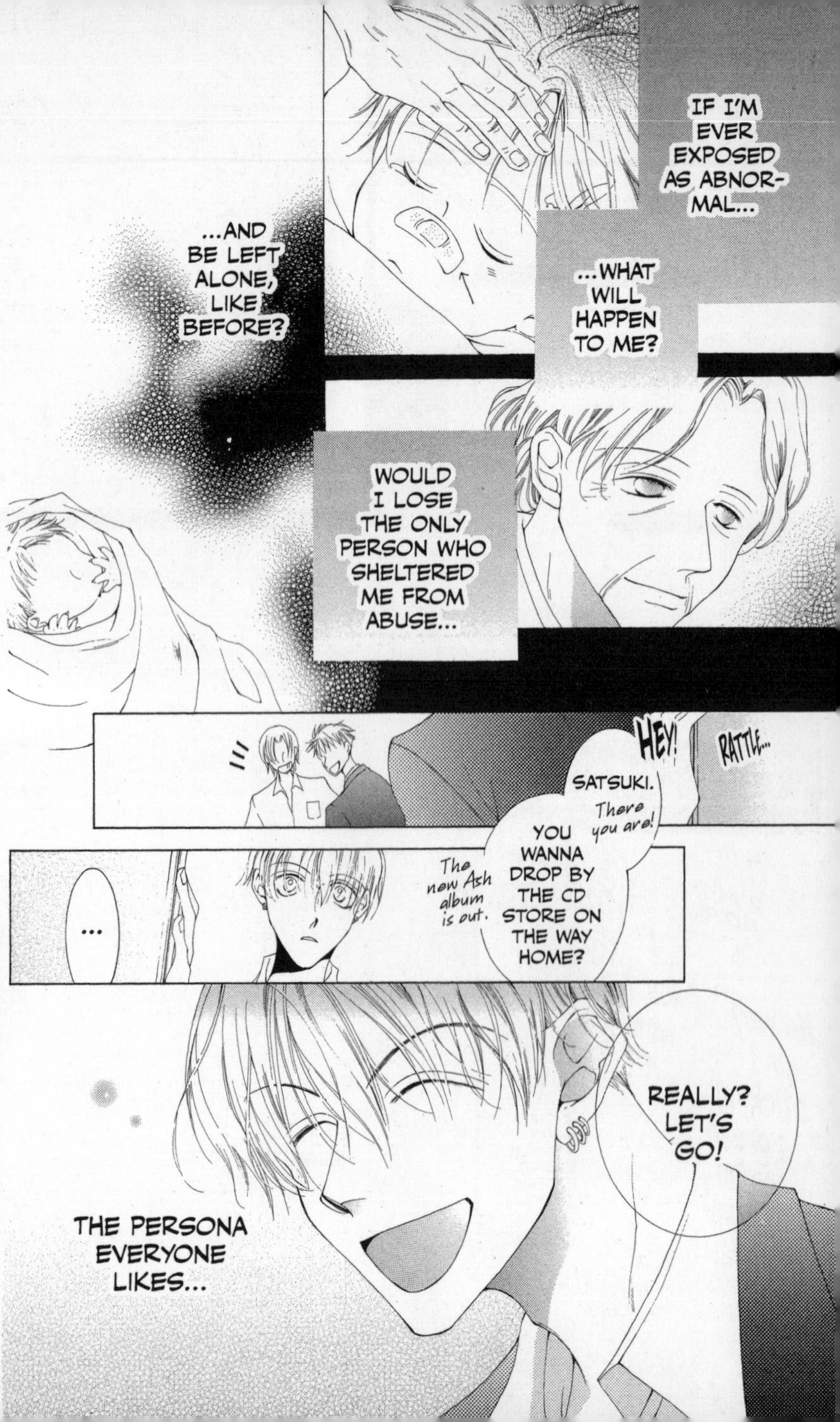
IF I'M EVER EXPOSED AS ABNOR-MAL...
...WHAT WILL HAPPEN TO ME?
WOULD I LOSE THE ONLY PERSON WHO SHELTERED ME FROM ABUSE...
...AND BE LEFT ALONE, LIKE BEFORE?
RATTLE...
HEY!
SATSUKI.
There you are!
YOU WANNA DROP BY THE CD STORE ON THE WAY HOME?
The new Ash album is out.
...
REALLY? LET'S GO!
THE PERSONA EVERYONE LIKES...

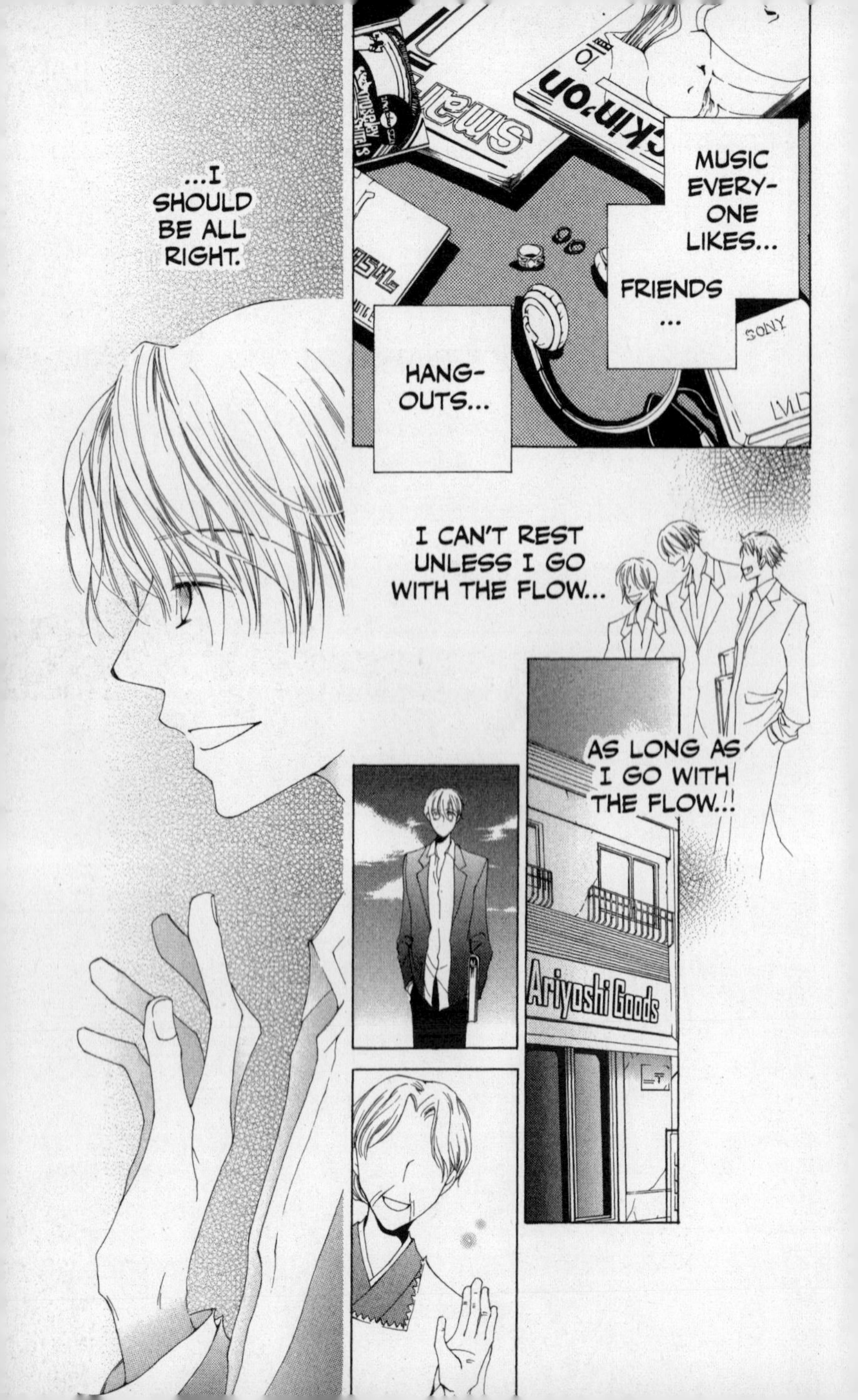
MUSIC EVERY-ONE LIKES...
FRIENDS ...
SONY
HANG-OUTS...
I CAN'T REST UNLESS I GO WITH THE FLOW...
AS LONG AS I GO WITH THE FLOW..!!
Ariyoshi Goods
...I SHOULD BE ALL RIGHT.

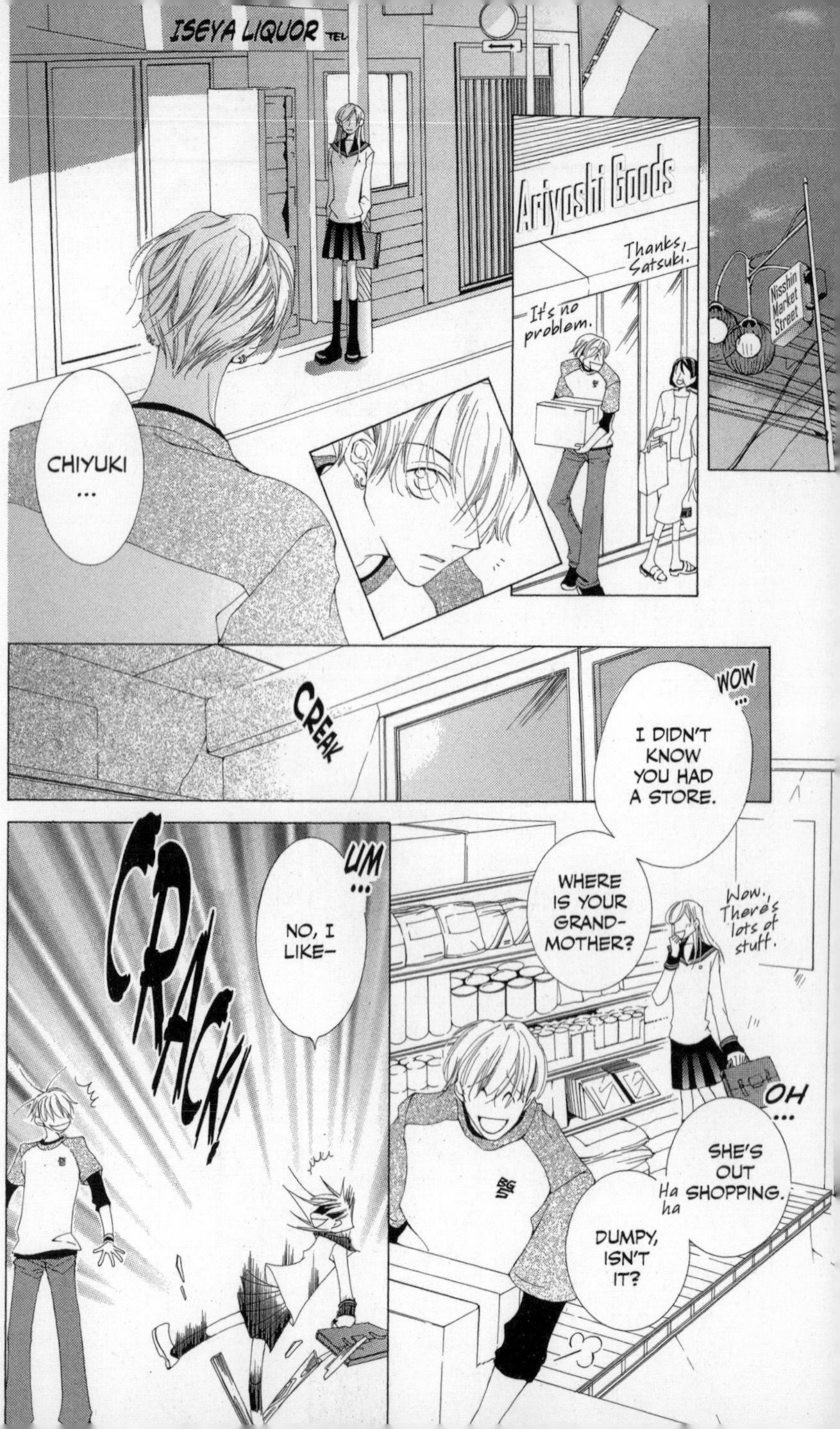
Nisshin Market Street
Ariyoshi Goods
Thanks, Satsuki.
It's no problem.
ISEYA LIQUOR TEL
CHIYUKI ...
WOW...
I DIDN'T KNOW YOU HAD A STORE.
CREAK
WHERE IS YOUR GRAND-MOTHER?
Wow. There's lots of stuff.
OH...
SHE'S OUT SHOPPING.
Ha ha
DUMPY, ISN'T IT?
UM...
NO, I LIKE—
CRACK!

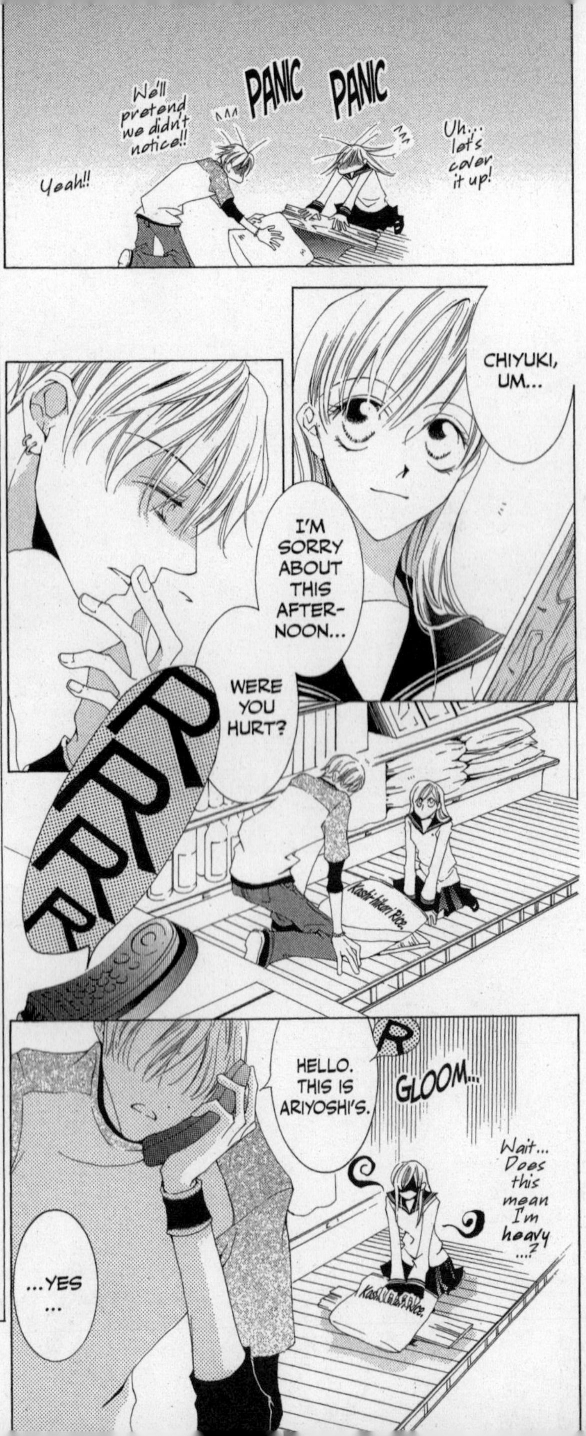
Uh... let's cover it up!
PANIC
PANIC
We'll pretend we didn't notice!!
Yeah!!
CHIYUKI, UM...
I'M SORRY ABOUT THIS AFTERNOON...
WERE YOU HURT?
RRRR
Koshi-hikari Rice
R
GLOOM...
Wait... Does this mean I'm heavy...?
HELLO. THIS IS ARIYOSHI'S.
...YES ...

04

I WROTE THAT I'M ATTRACTED TO THINGS REPRESENTATIVE OF THE PAST. I LIKE ANYTHING ANTIQUE, WHETHER IT'S JAPANESE OR WESTERN. THE MOST IMPRESSIVE ARCHITECTURE I'VE EVER SEEN WAS ST. PETER'S BASILICA IN ROME. I WOULD LOVE TO GO THERE AGAIN SOMETIME.

HOWEVER, I ALSO LIKE POP AND ROCK STUFF. I LIKE TO LISTEN TO BANDS (BRITISH) AND POP IDOLS. I'M PRETTY MUCH A TRUE FANATIC. BUT WHAT I LIKE MOST OF ALL IS DRAWING MANGA. THAT'S JUST HOW I AM!

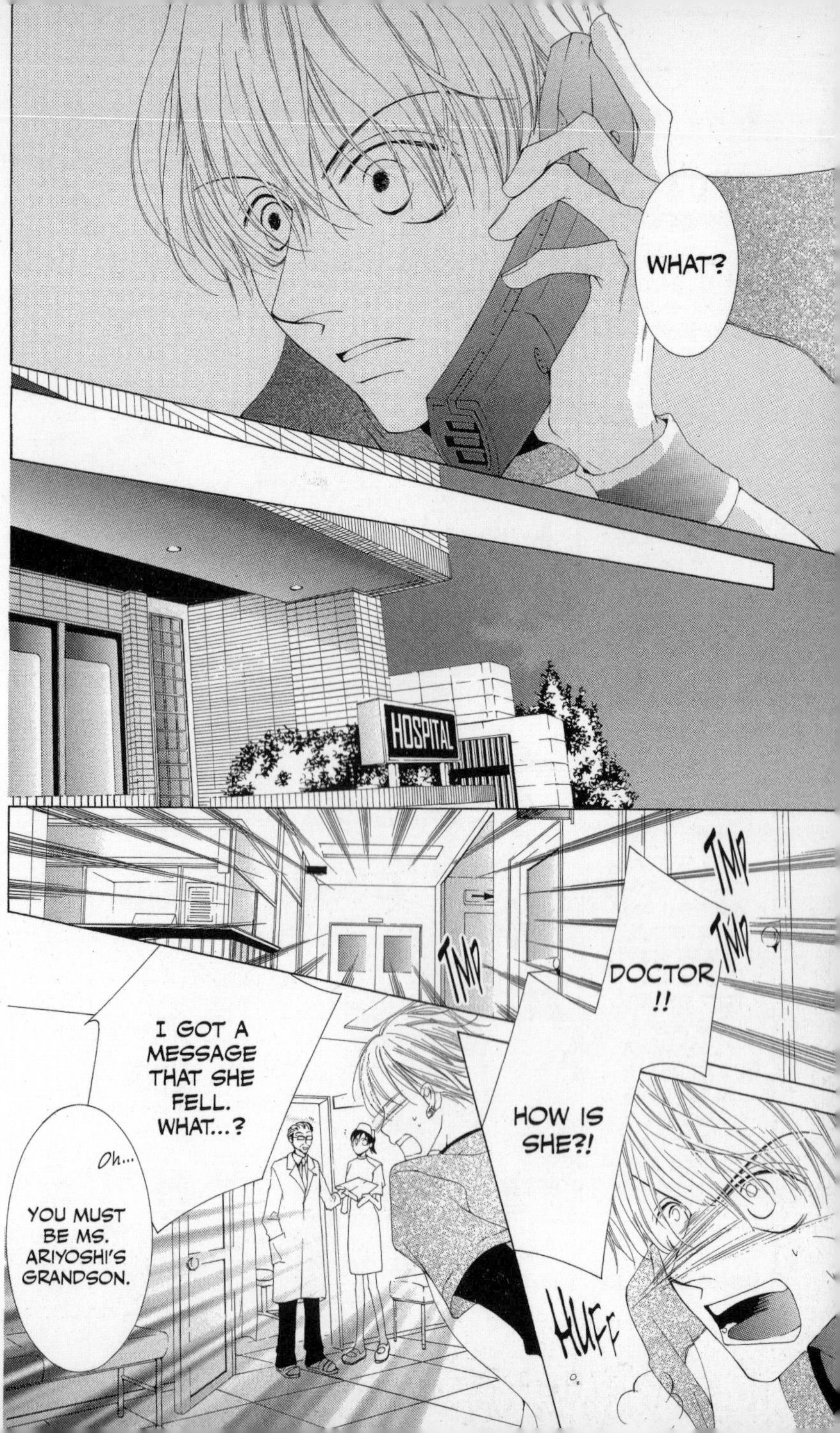
WHAT?
HOSPITAL
TMP
TMP
DOCTOR!!
HOW IS SHE?!
TMP
HUFF
I GOT A MESSAGE THAT SHE FELL. WHAT...?
Oh...
YOU MUST BE MS. ARIYOSHI'S GRANDSON.

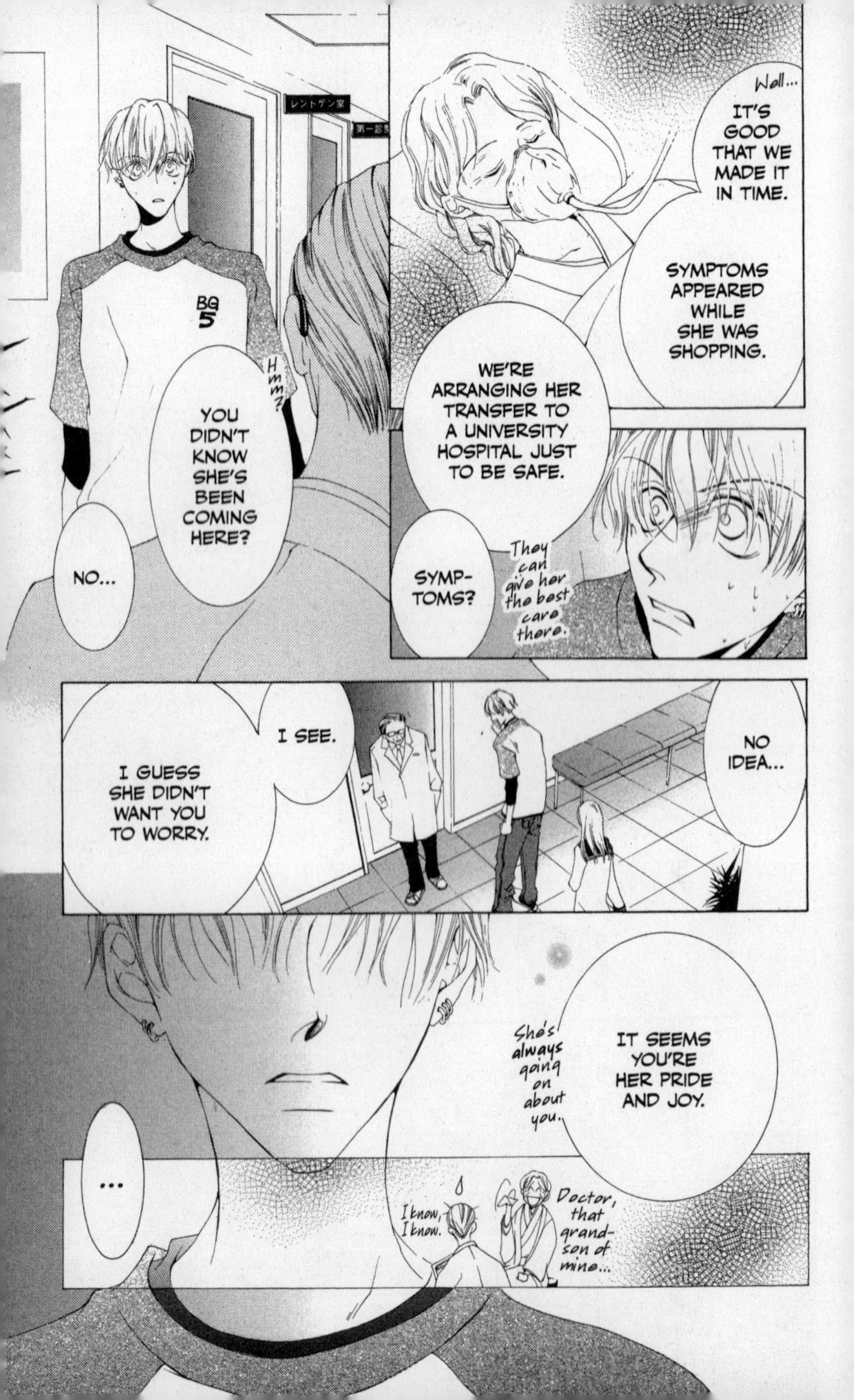
Well...
IT'S GOOD THAT WE MADE IT IN TIME.
SYMPTOMS APPEARED WHILE SHE WAS SHOPPING.
WE'RE ARRANGING HER TRANSFER TO A UNIVERSITY HOSPITAL JUST TO BE SAFE.
They can give her the best care there.
SYMP-TOMS?
レントゲン室
BG 5
Hmm?
YOU DIDN'T KNOW SHE'S BEEN COMING HERE?
NO...
NO IDEA...
I SEE.
I GUESS SHE DIDN'T WANT YOU TO WORRY.
IT SEEMS YOU'RE HER PRIDE AND JOY.
She's always going on about you.
Doctor, that grand-son of mine...
I know, I know.
...

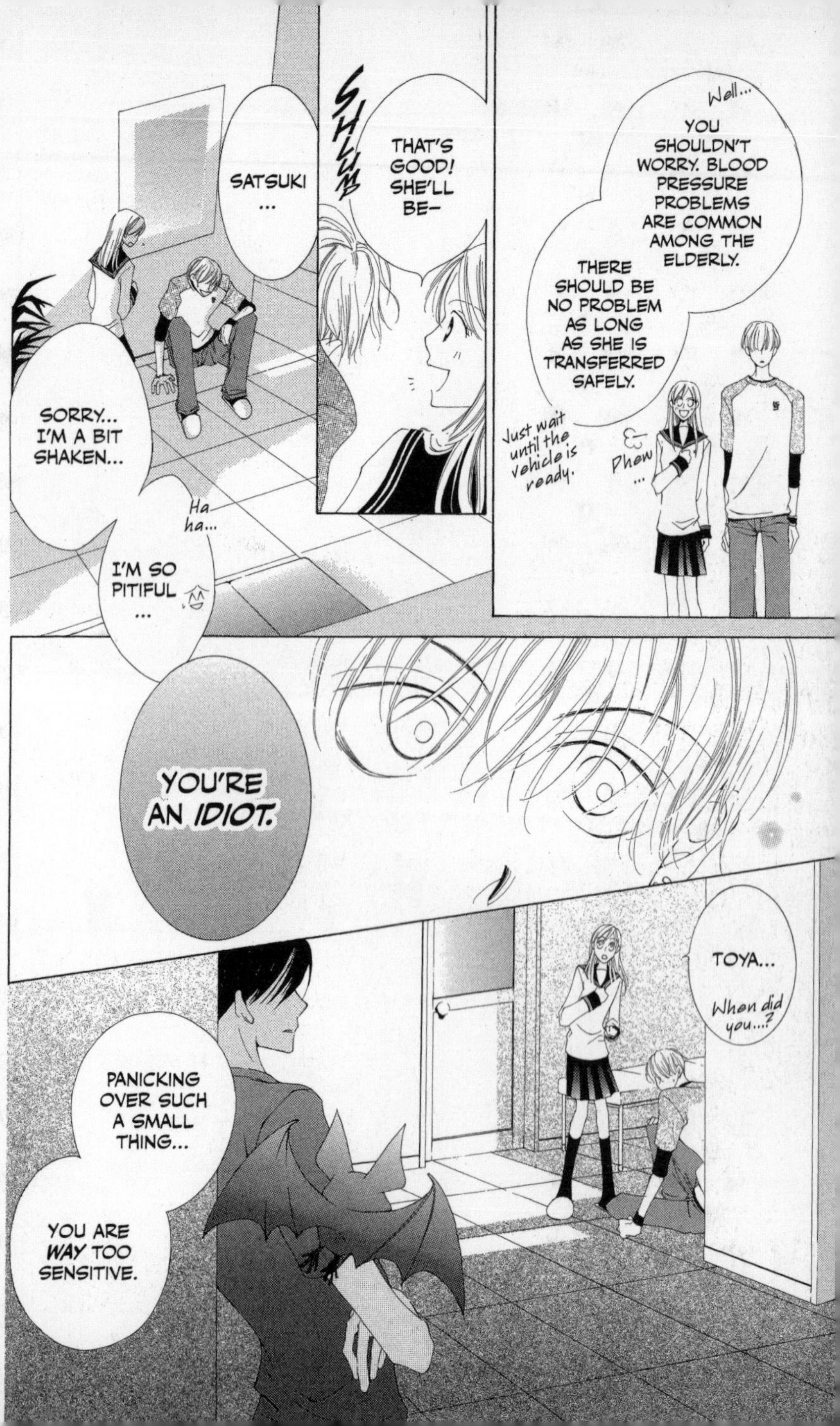
Well...
YOU SHOULDN'T WORRY. BLOOD PRESSURE PROBLEMS ARE COMMON AMONG THE ELDERLY.
THERE SHOULD BE NO PROBLEM AS LONG AS SHE IS TRANSFERRED SAFELY.
Just wait until the vehicle is ready.
Phew...
SHLUMP
THAT'S GOOD! SHE'LL BE—
SATSUKI...
SORRY... I'M A BIT SHAKEN...
Ha ha...
I'M SO PITIFUL...
YOU'RE AN *IDIOT.*
TOYA...
When did you...?
PANICKING OVER SUCH A SMALL THING...
YOU ARE *WAY* TOO SENSITIVE.

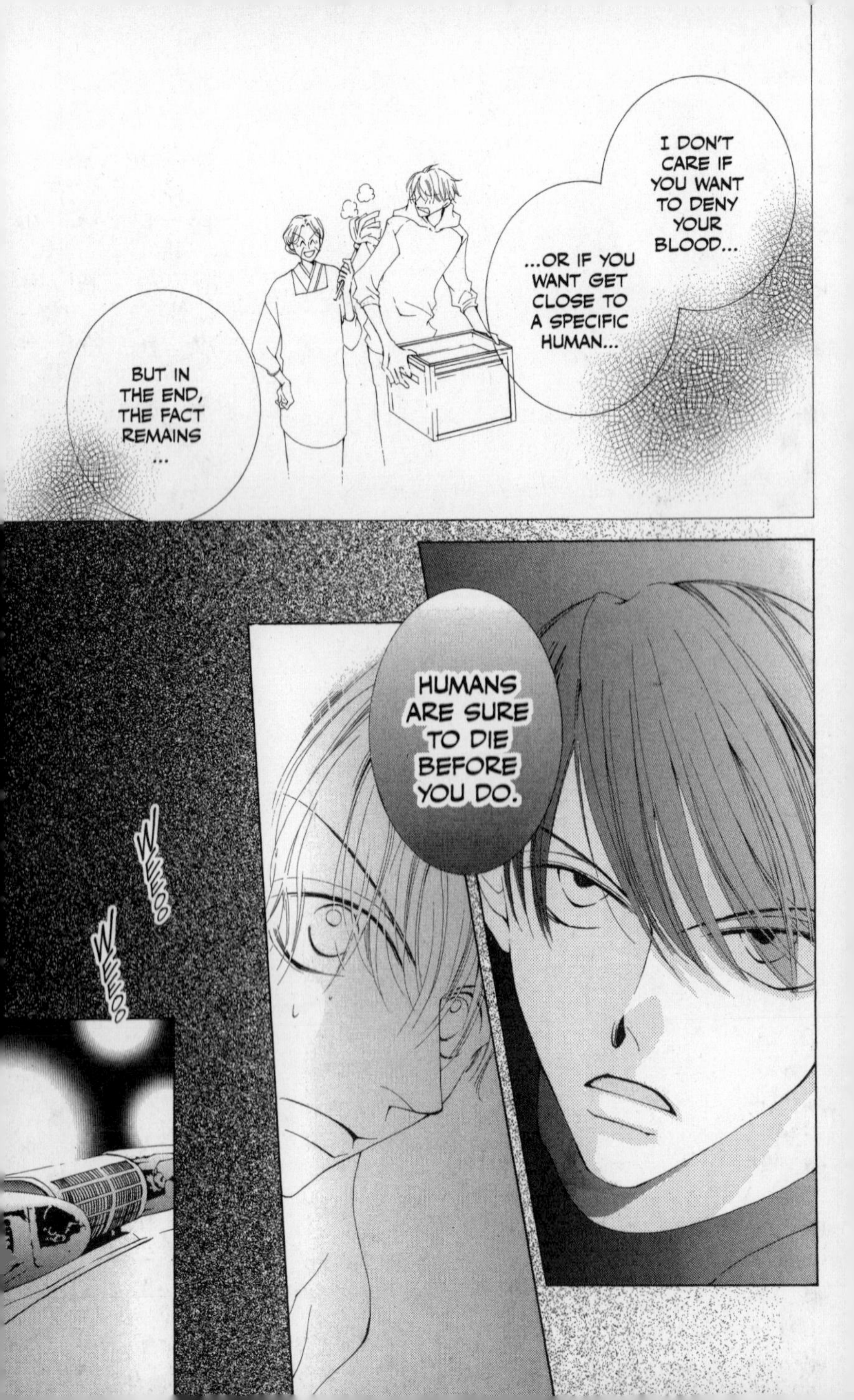
I DON'T CARE IF YOU WANT TO DENY YOUR BLOOD...
...OR IF YOU WANT GET CLOSE TO A SPECIFIC HUMAN...
BUT IN THE END, THE FACT REMAINS ...
HUMANS ARE SURE TO DIE BEFORE YOU DO.

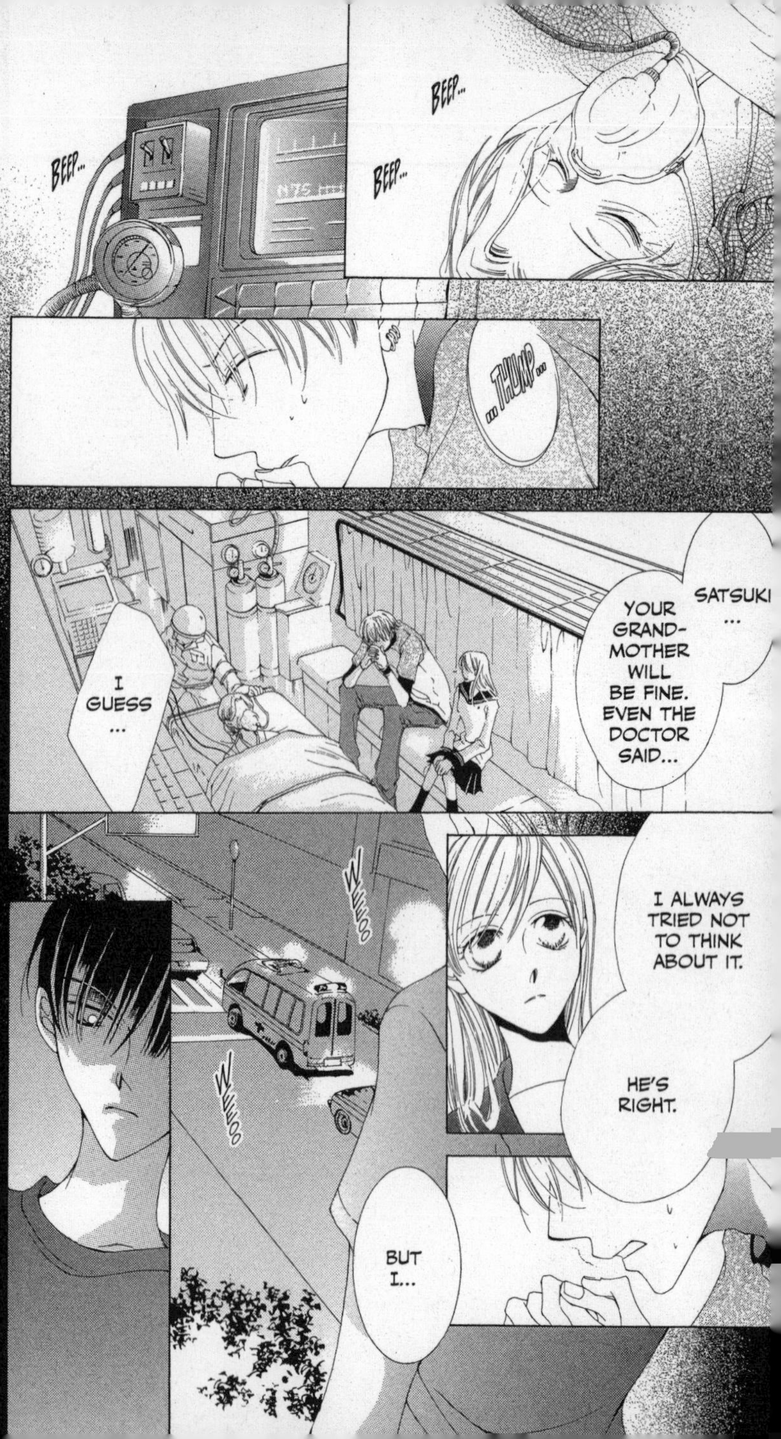
BEEP...
BEEP...
BEEP...
...THUMP...
SATSUKI...
YOUR GRANDMOTHER WILL BE FINE. EVEN THE DOCTOR SAID...
I GUESS...
WEEOO
WEEOO
I ALWAYS TRIED NOT TO THINK ABOUT IT.
HE'S RIGHT.
BUT I...

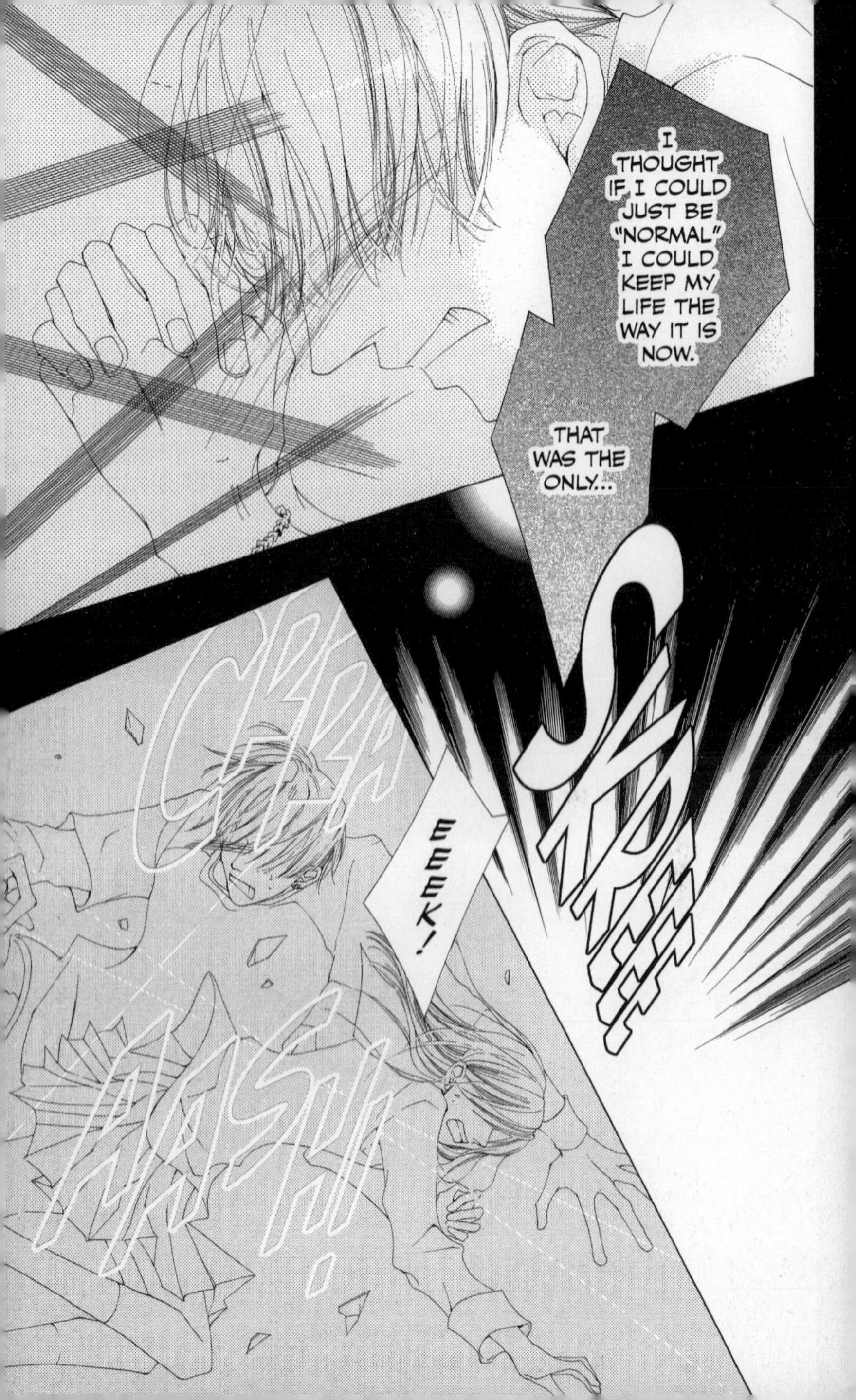
I THOUGHT IF I COULD JUST BE "NORMAL" I COULD KEEP MY LIFE THE WAY IT IS NOW.
THAT WAS THE ONLY...
EEEEK!

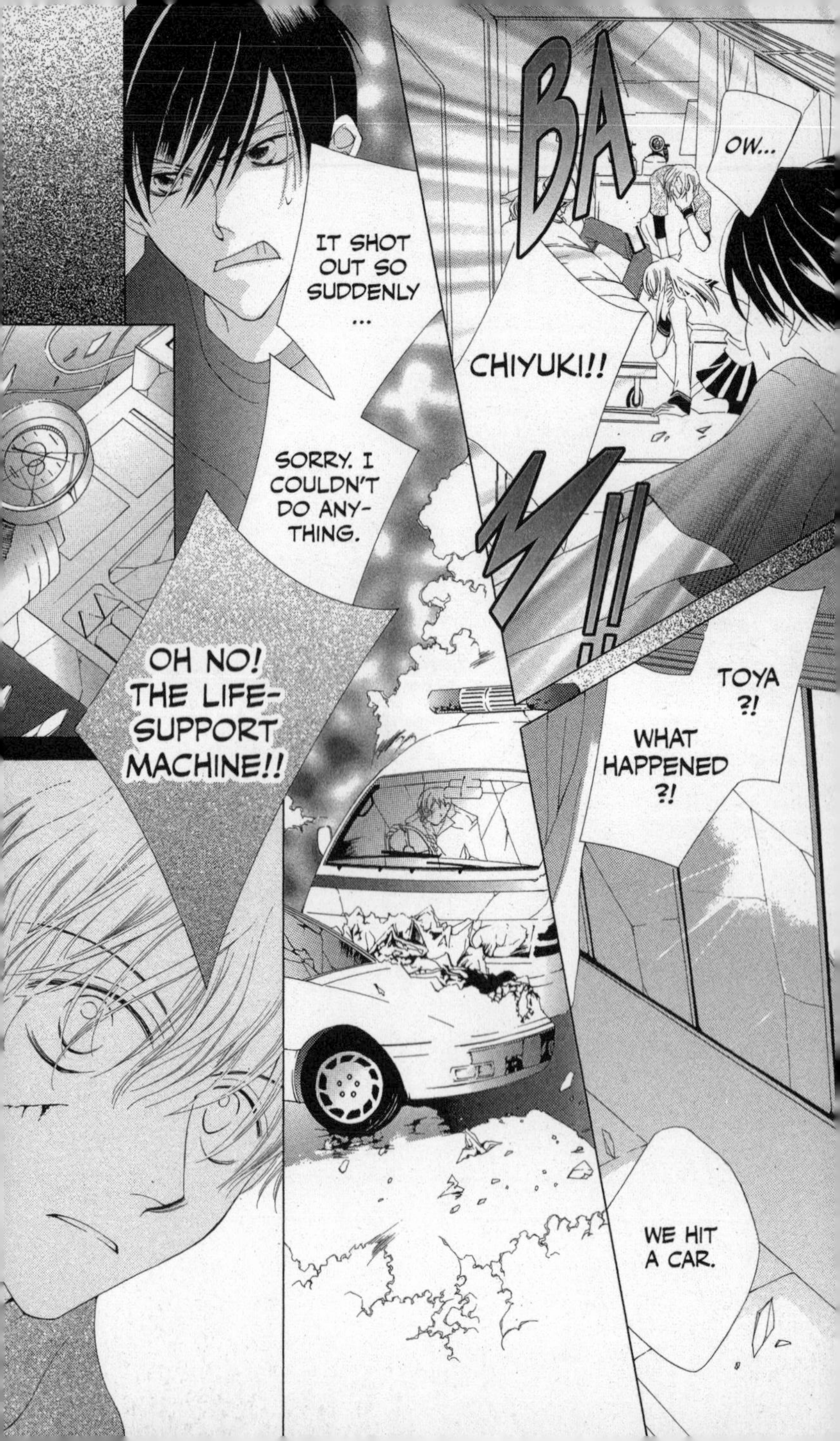
BAM!!
OW...
CHIYUKI!!
TOYA?!
WHAT HAPPENED?!
WE HIT A CAR.
IT SHOT OUT SO SUDDENLY...
SORRY. I COULDN'T DO ANYTHING.
OH NO! THE LIFE-SUPPORT MACHINE!!

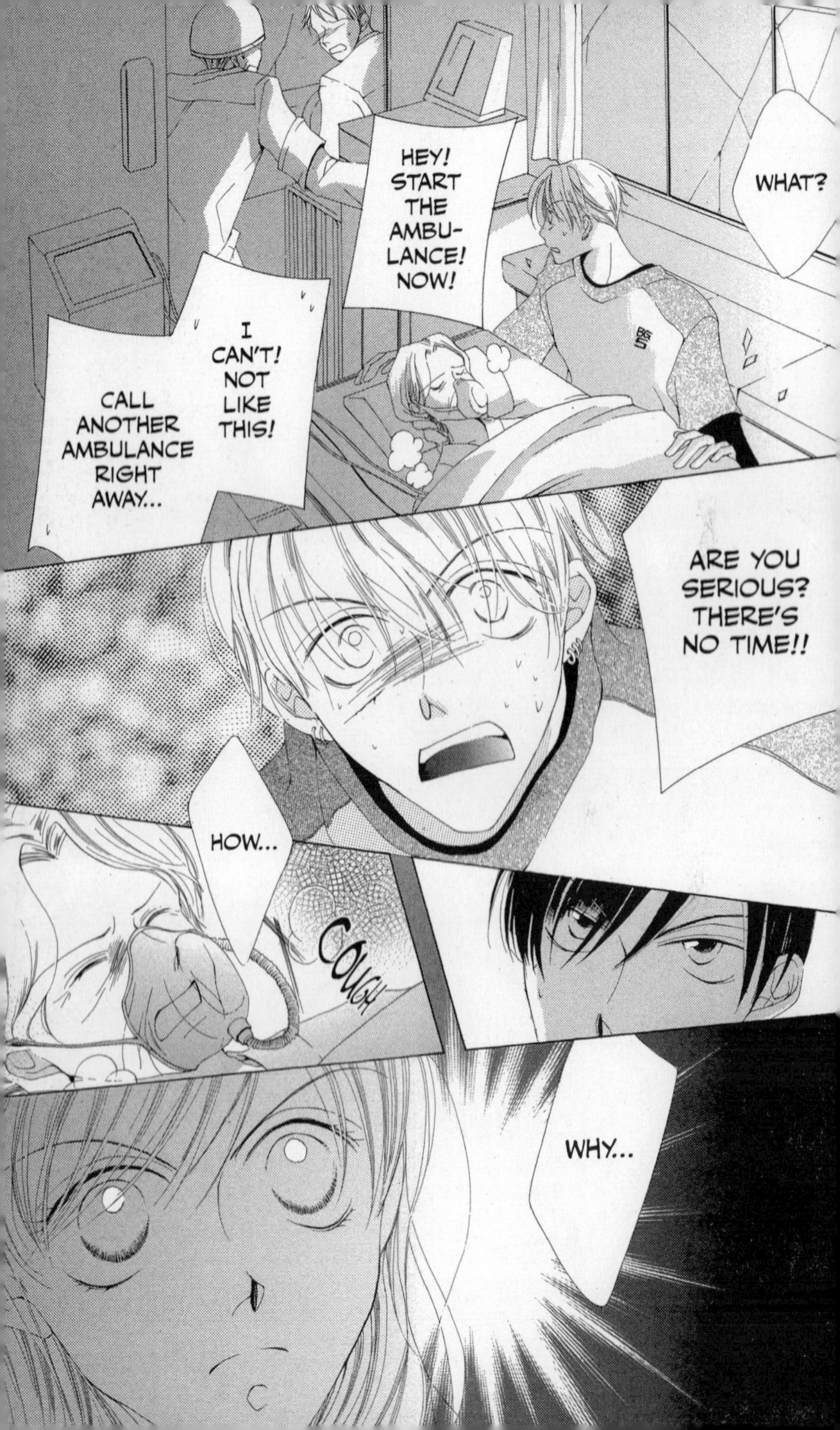
WHAT?
HEY! START THE AMBULANCE! NOW!
I CAN'T! NOT LIKE THIS!
CALL ANOTHER AMBULANCE RIGHT AWAY...
ARE YOU SERIOUS? THERE'S NO TIME!!
HOW...
COUGH
WHY...

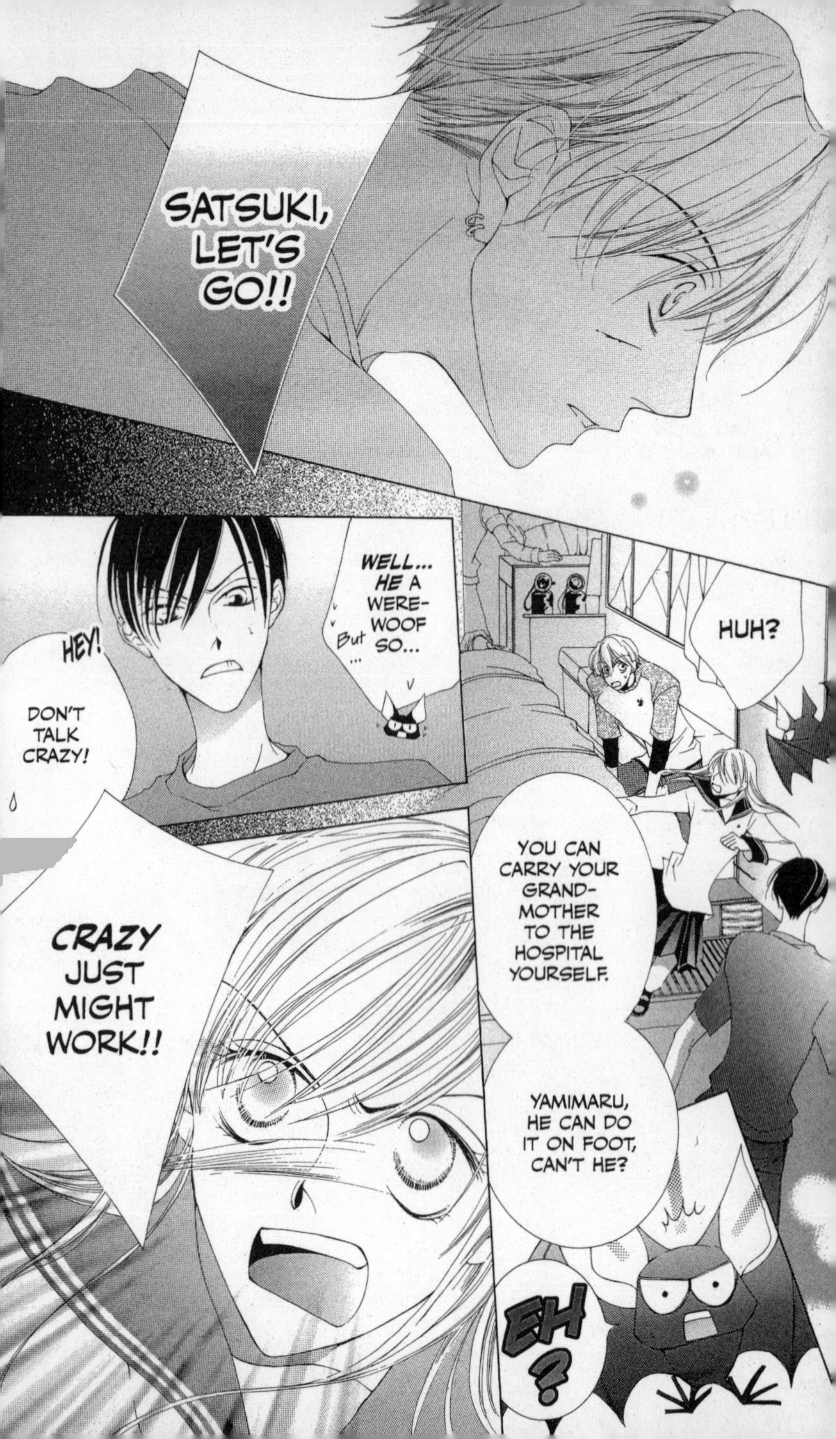
SATSUKI, LET'S GO!!
HUH?
WELL... HE A WERE-WOOF SO...
But ...
HEY!
DON'T TALK CRAZY!
CRAZY JUST MIGHT WORK!!
YOU CAN CARRY YOUR GRAND-MOTHER TO THE HOSPITAL YOURSELF.
YAMIMARU, HE CAN DO IT ON FOOT, CAN'T HE?
EH?

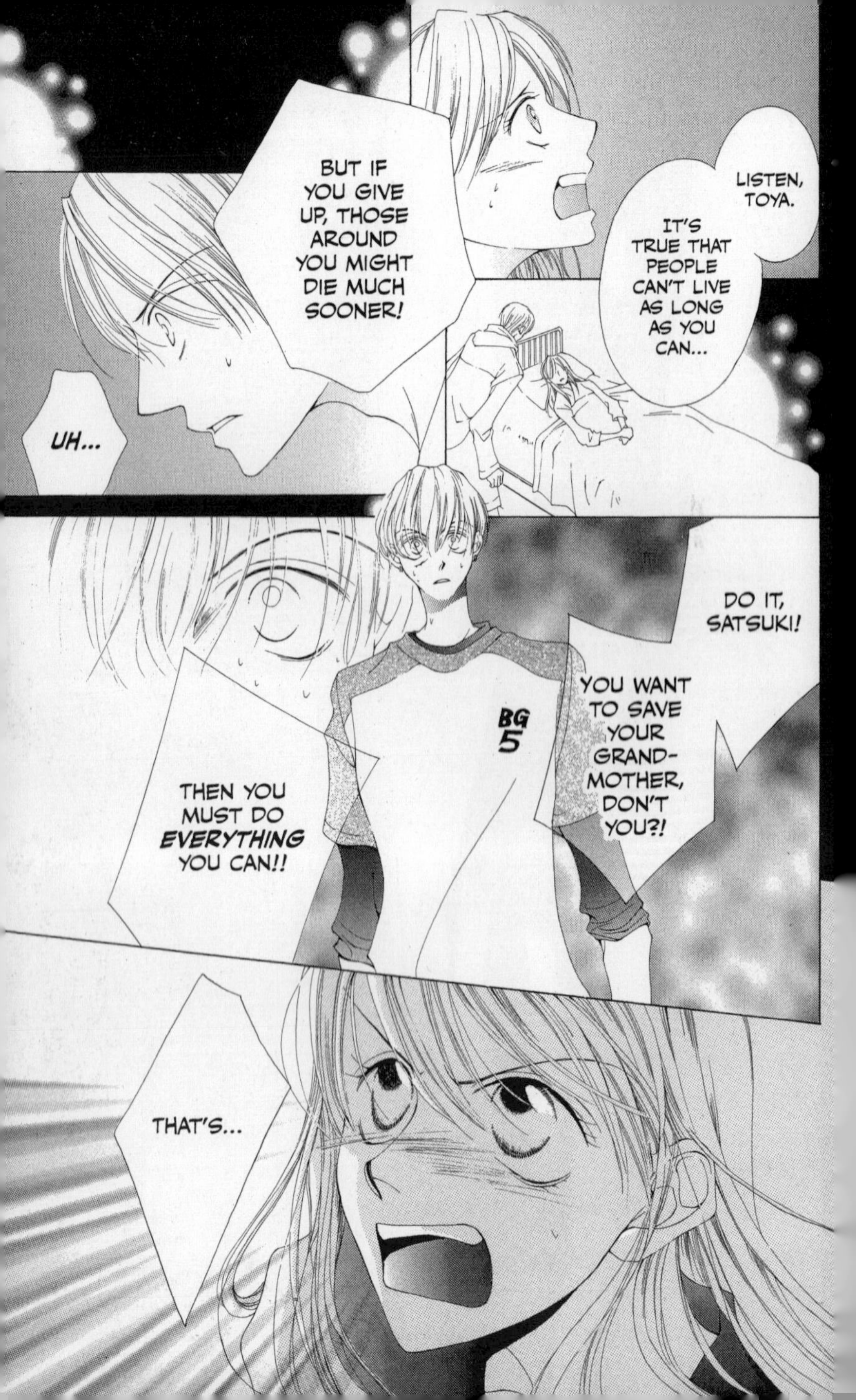
LISTEN, TOYA.
IT'S TRUE THAT PEOPLE CAN'T LIVE AS LONG AS YOU CAN...
BUT IF YOU GIVE UP, THOSE AROUND YOU MIGHT DIE MUCH SOONER!
UH...
DO IT, SATSUKI!
YOU WANT TO SAVE YOUR GRAND-MOTHER, DON'T YOU?!
THEN YOU MUST DO EVERYTHING YOU CAN!!
THAT'S...

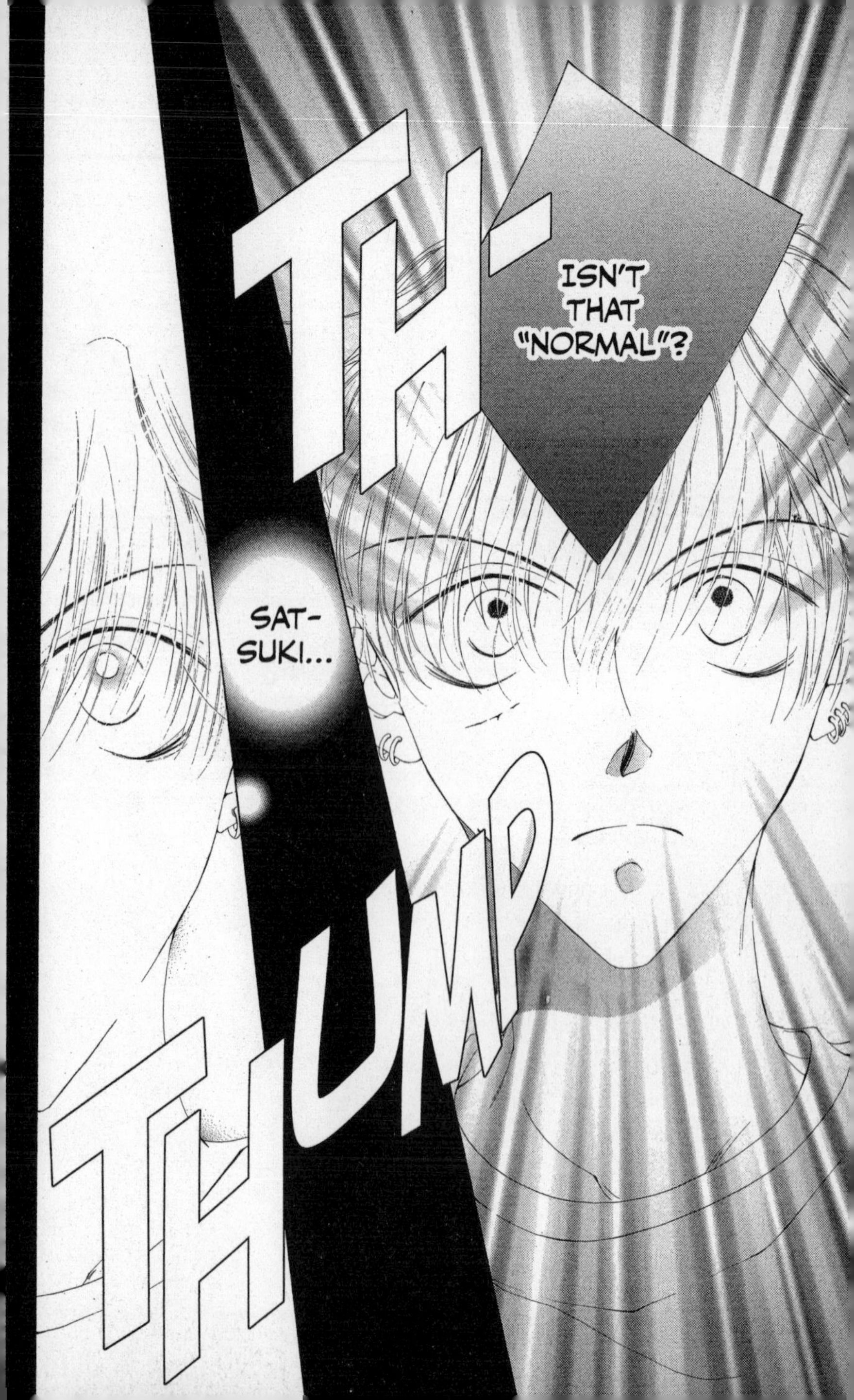
ISN'T THAT "NORMAL"?
TH-
SAT-SUKI...
THUMP
TH-

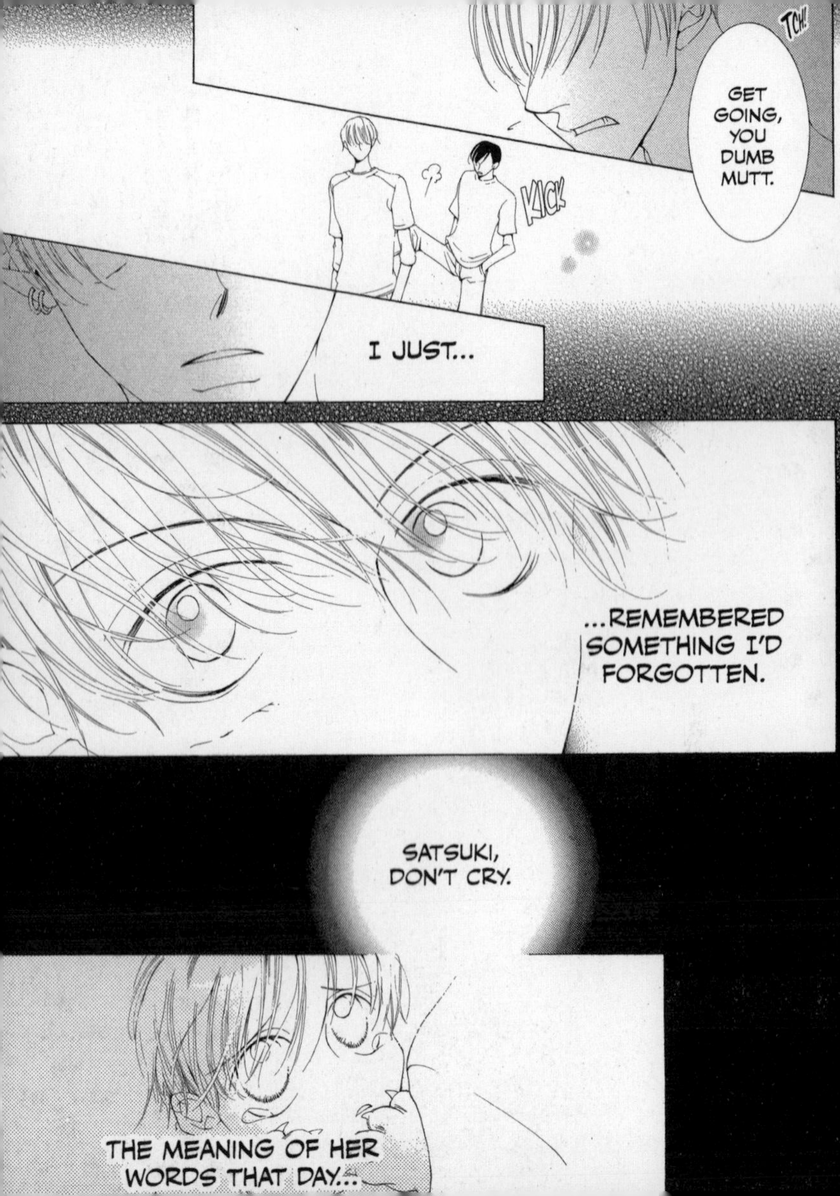
TCH!
GET GOING, YOU DUMB MUTT.
KICK
I JUST...
...REMEMBERED SOMETHING I'D FORGOTTEN.
SATSUKI, DON'T CRY.
THE MEANING OF HER WORDS THAT DAY...

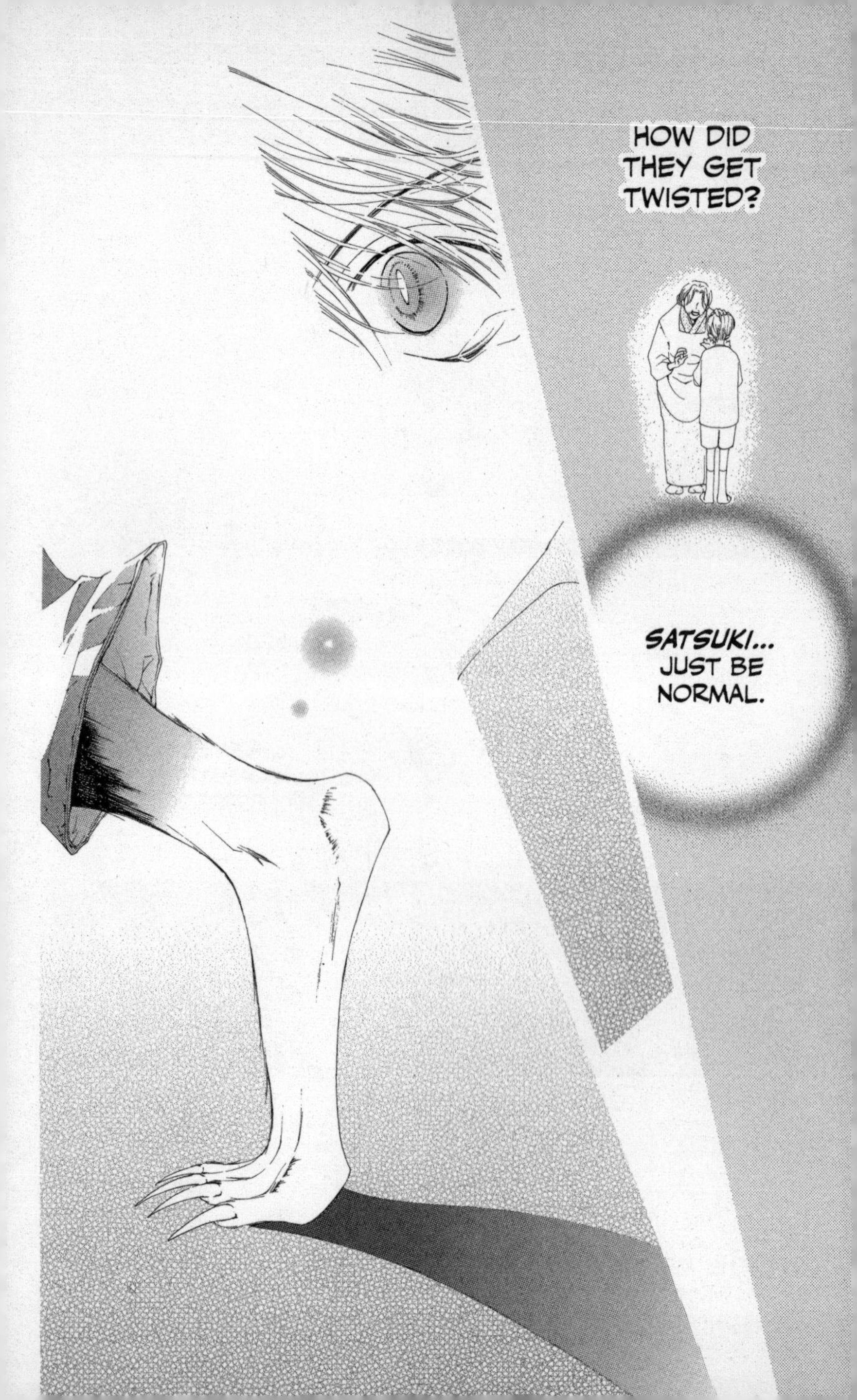
HOW DID THEY GET TWISTED?
SATSUKI... JUST BE NORMAL.

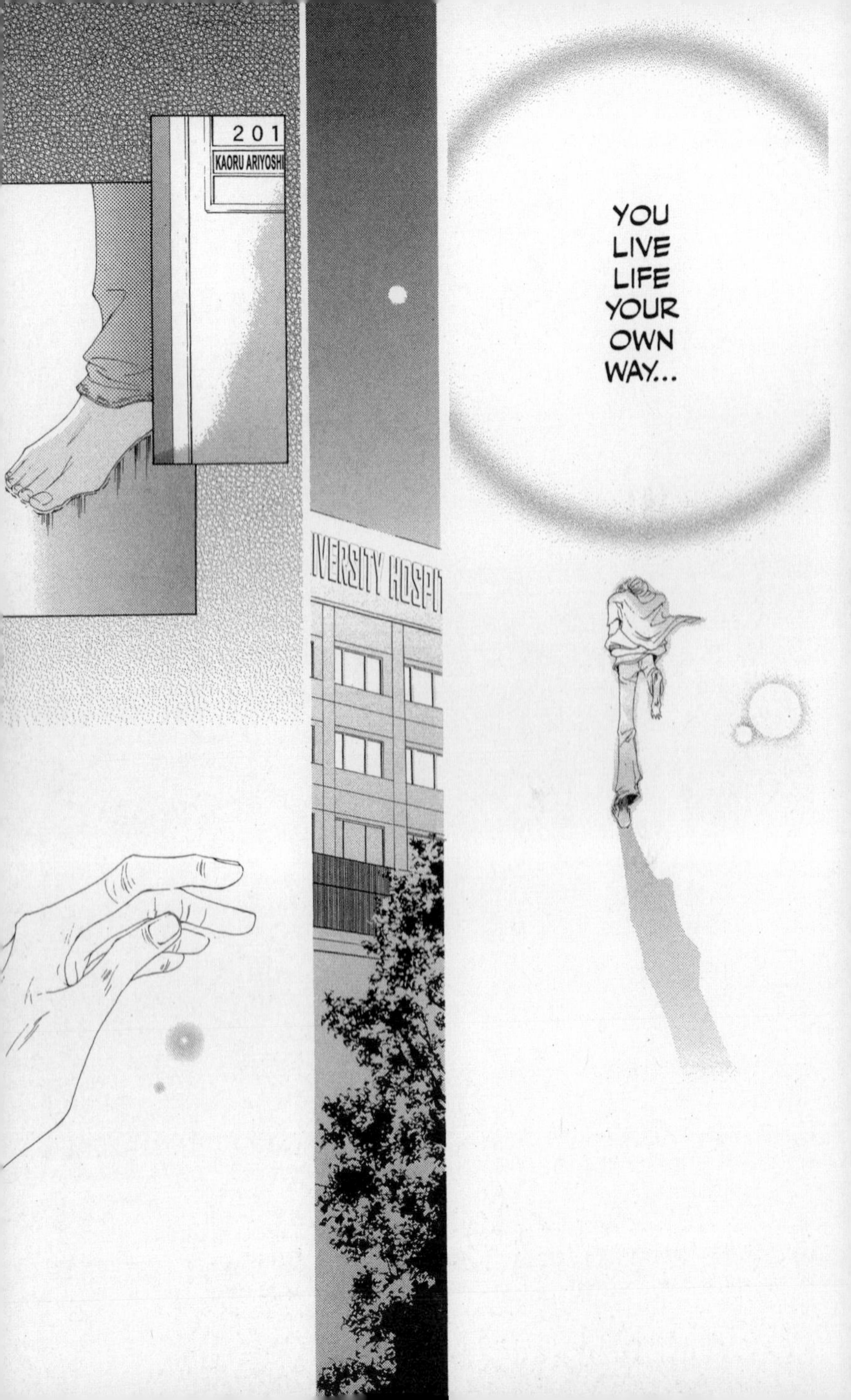
YOU LIVE LIFE YOUR OWN WAY...
IVERSITY HOSPIT
201
KAORU ARIYOSHI

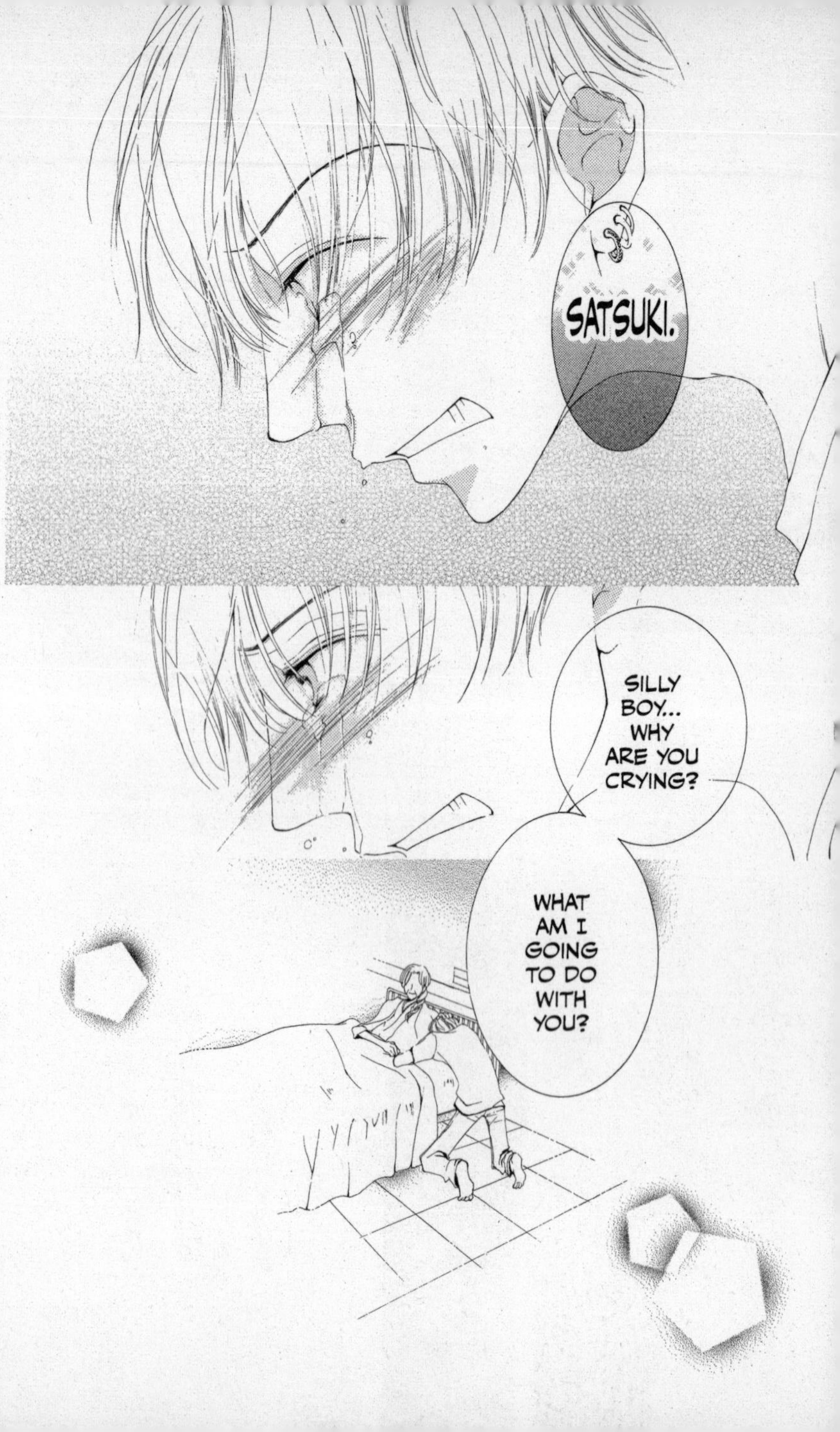
SATSUKI.
SILLY BOY... WHY ARE YOU CRYING?
WHAT AM I GOING TO DO WITH YOU?

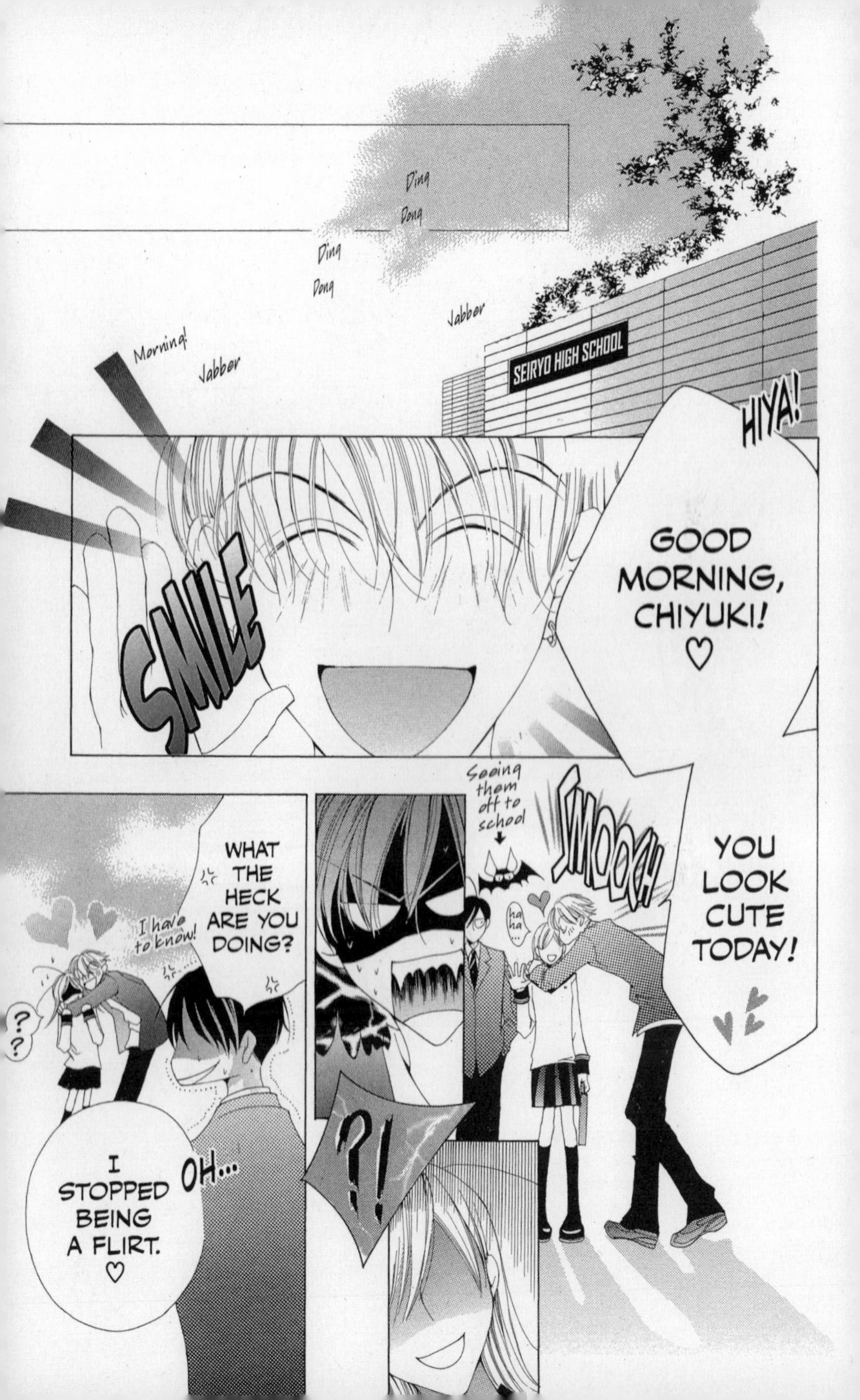
Ding
Dong
Ding
Dong
Jabber
SEIRYO HIGH SCHOOL
Morning!
Jabber
HIYA!
GOOD MORNING, CHIYUKI! ♡
SMILE
YOU LOOK CUTE TODAY!
SMOOCH
Seeing them off to school
ha ha...
WHAT THE HECK ARE YOU DOING?
I have to know!
??
?!
OH...
I STOPPED BEING A FLIRT. ♡

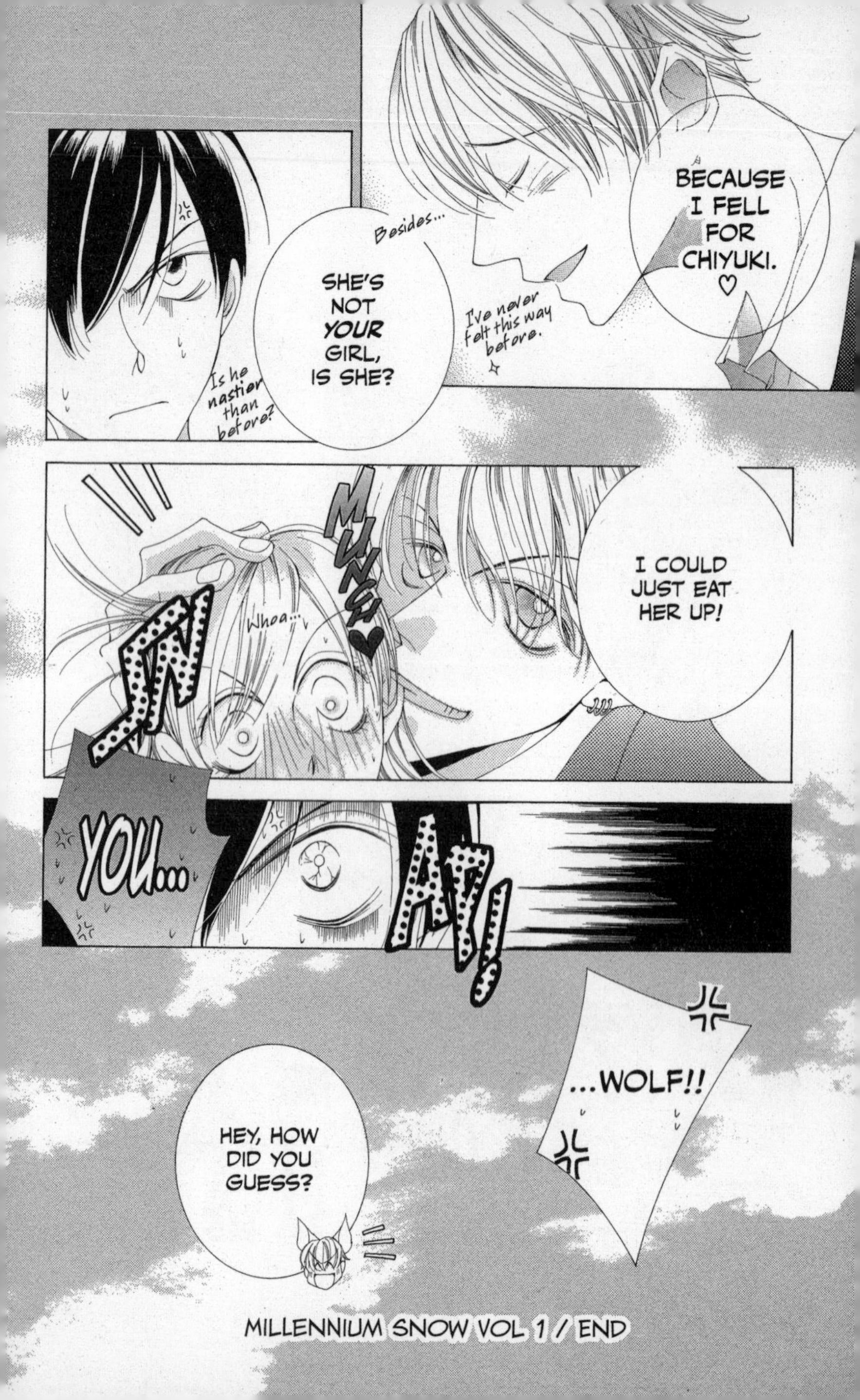
BECAUSE I FELL FOR CHIYUKI. ♡
I've never felt this way before.
Besides...
SHE'S NOT YOUR GIRL, IS SHE?
Is he nastier than before?
I COULD JUST EAT HER UP!
MUNCH! ♥
Whoa...
YOU...
...WOLF!!
HEY, HOW DID YOU GUESS?
MILLENNIUM SNOW VOL 1 / END

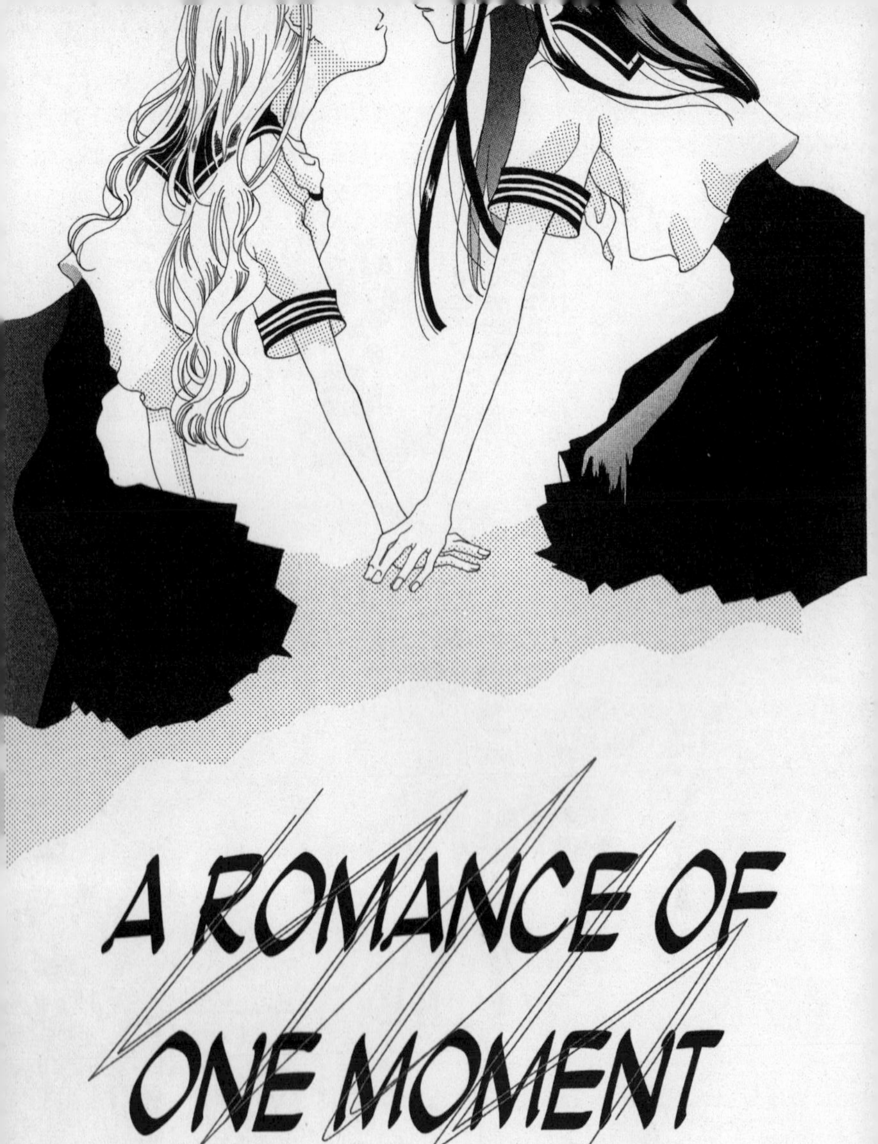

A ROMANCE OF ONE MOMENT

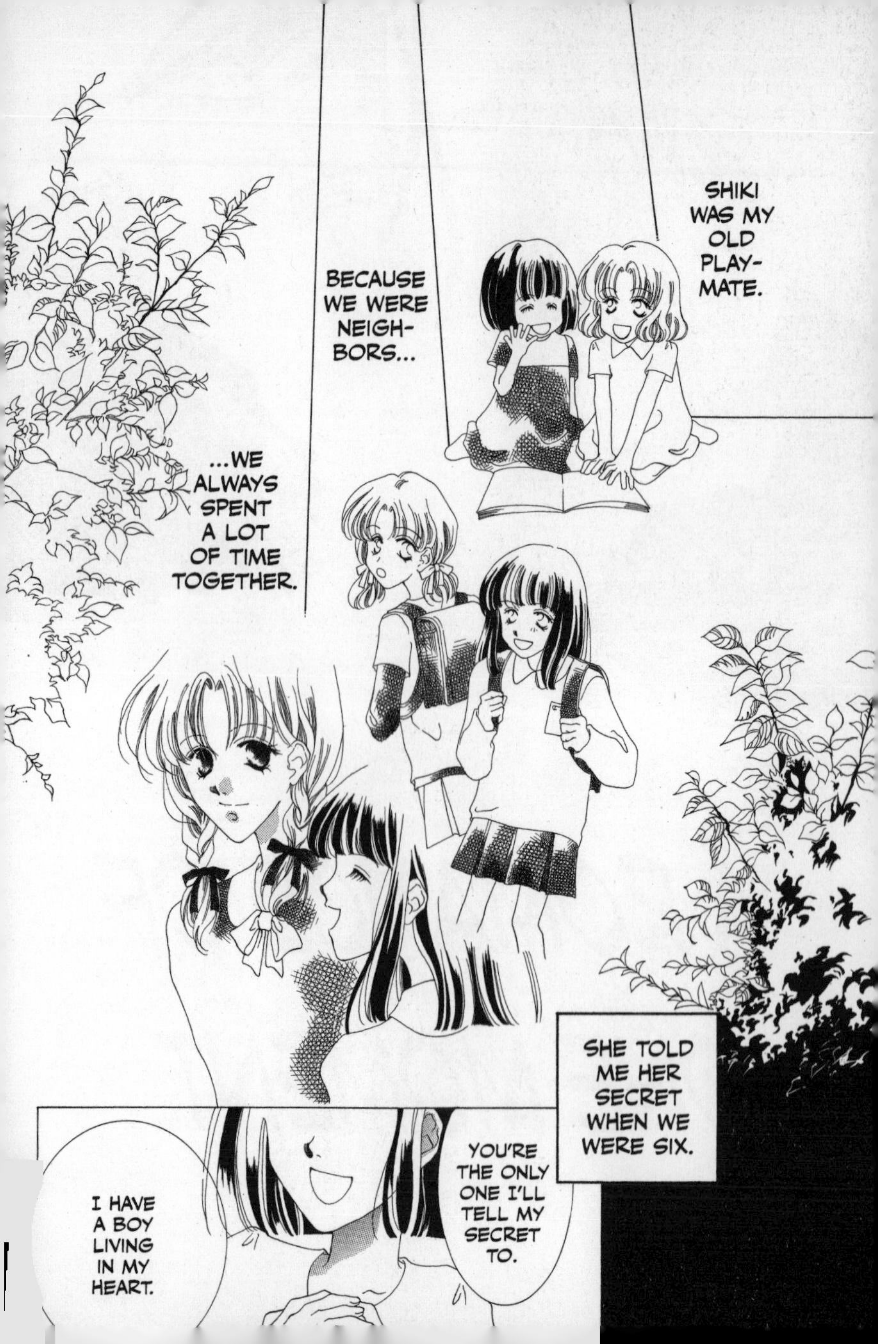
SHIKI WAS MY OLD PLAY-MATE.
BECAUSE WE WERE NEIGH-BORS...
...WE ALWAYS SPENT A LOT OF TIME TOGETHER.
SHE TOLD ME HER SECRET WHEN WE WERE SIX.
YOU'RE THE ONLY ONE I'LL TELL MY SECRET TO.
I HAVE A BOY LIVING IN MY HEART.

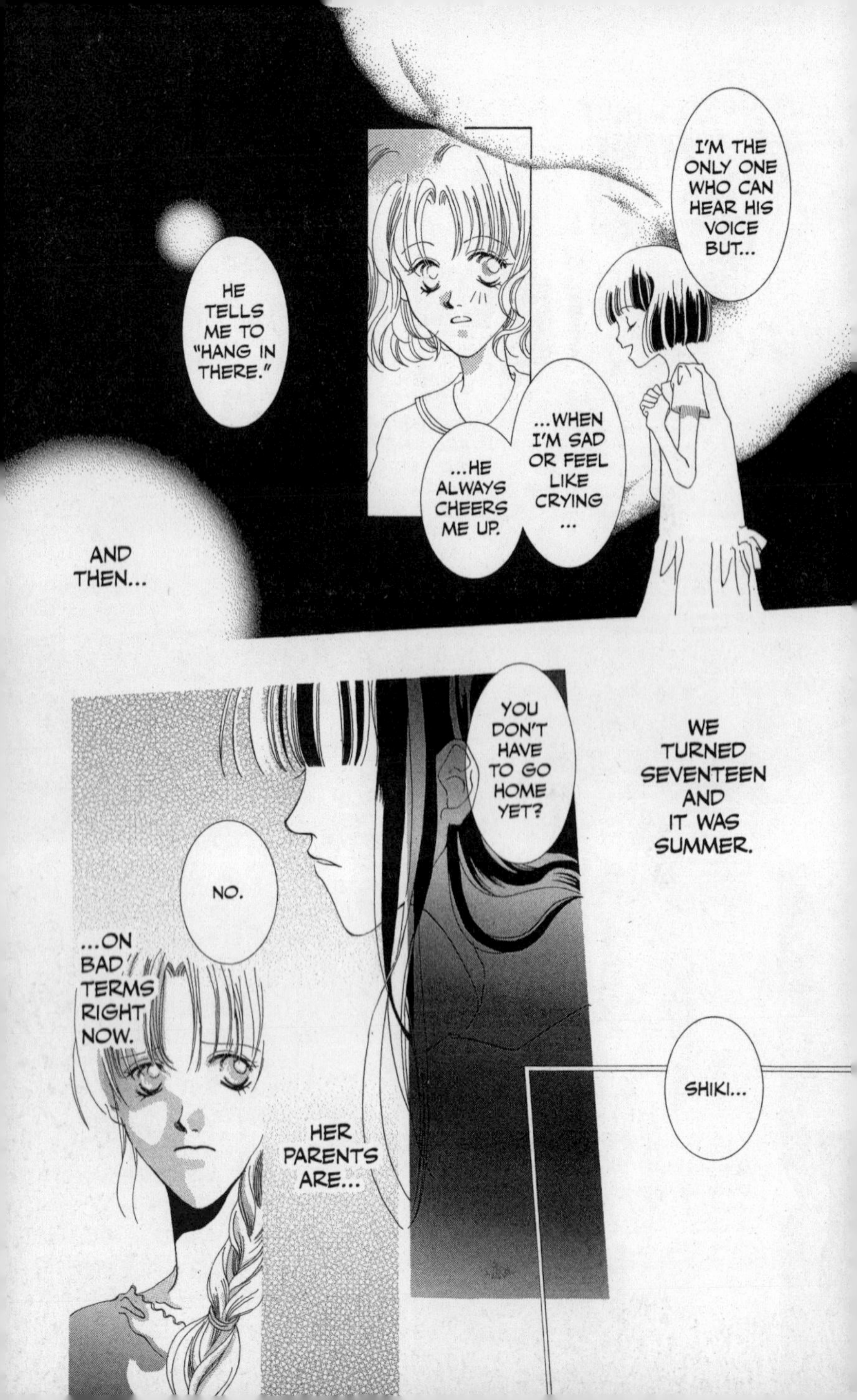
I'M THE ONLY ONE WHO CAN HEAR HIS VOICE BUT...
...WHEN I'M SAD OR FEEL LIKE CRYING...
...HE ALWAYS CHEERS ME UP.
HE TELLS ME TO "HANG IN THERE."
AND THEN...
WE TURNED SEVENTEEN AND IT WAS SUMMER.
YOU DON'T HAVE TO GO HOME YET?
NO.
SHIKI...
HER PARENTS ARE...
...ON BAD TERMS RIGHT NOW.

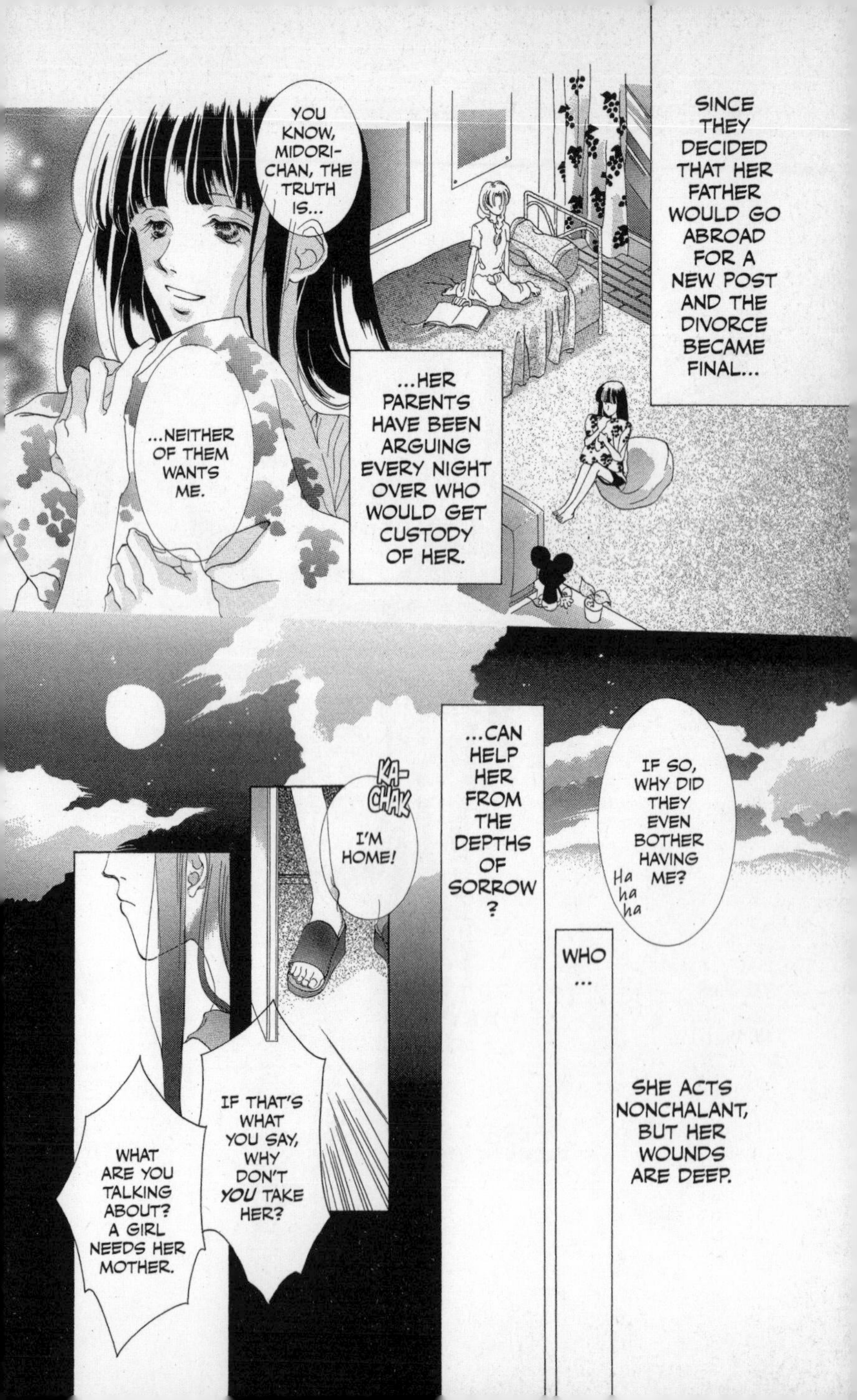
SINCE THEY DECIDED THAT HER FATHER WOULD GO ABROAD FOR A NEW POST AND THE DIVORCE BECAME FINAL...
...HER PARENTS HAVE BEEN ARGUING EVERY NIGHT OVER WHO WOULD GET CUSTODY OF HER.
YOU KNOW, MIDORI-CHAN, THE TRUTH IS...
...NEITHER OF THEM WANTS ME.
IF SO, WHY DID THEY EVEN BOTHER HAVING ME?
Ha ha ha
WHO...
...CAN HELP HER FROM THE DEPTHS OF SORROW?
SHE ACTS NONCHALANT, BUT HER WOUNDS ARE DEEP.
KA-CHAK
I'M HOME!
IF THAT'S WHAT YOU SAY, WHY DON'T *YOU* TAKE HER?
WHAT ARE YOU TALKING ABOUT? A GIRL NEEDS HER MOTHER.

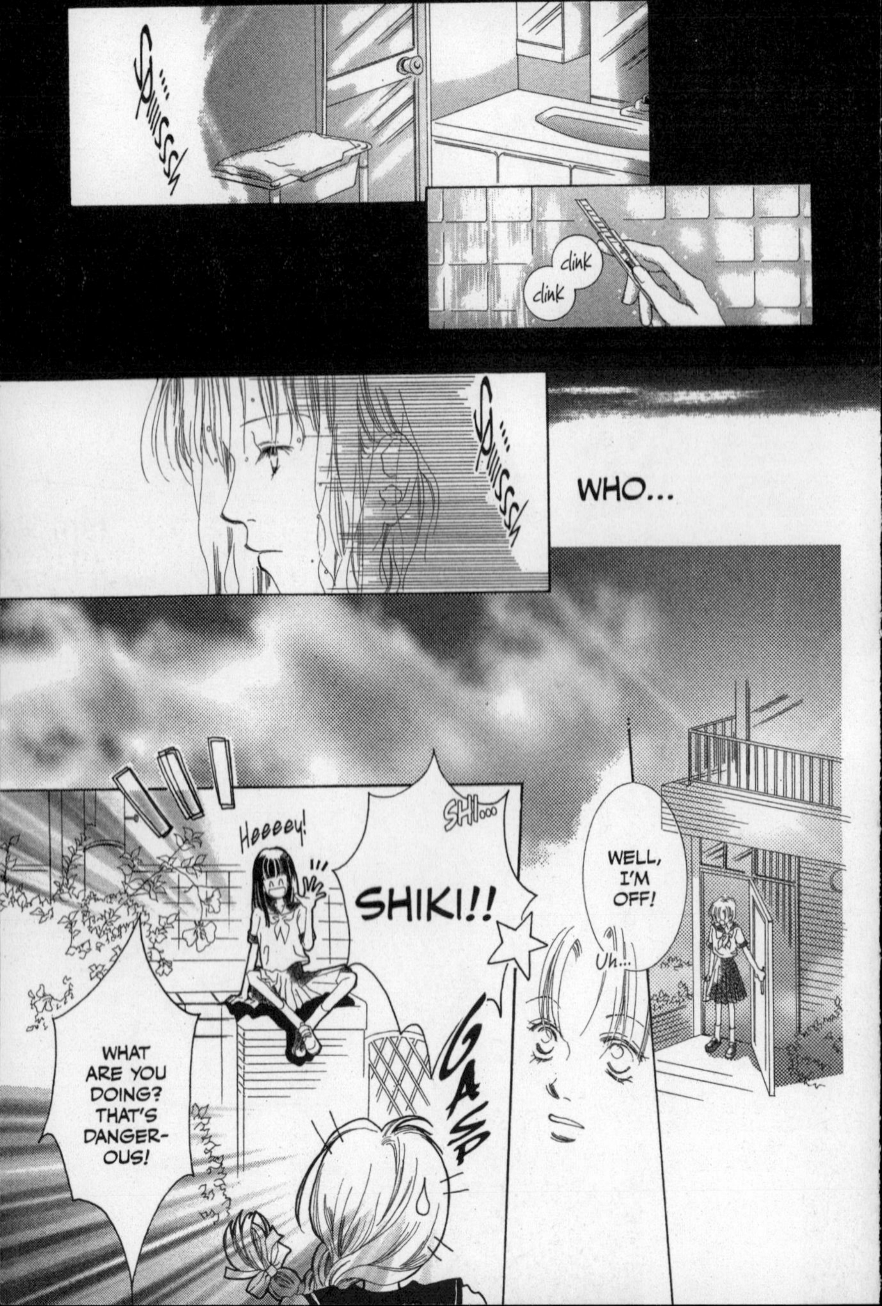
Spiiissssh...
clink
clink
WHO...
Spiiissssh...
WELL, I'M OFF!
Uh...
SHH...
SHIKI!!
Heeeey!
GASP
WHAT ARE YOU DOING? THAT'S DANGER-OUS!

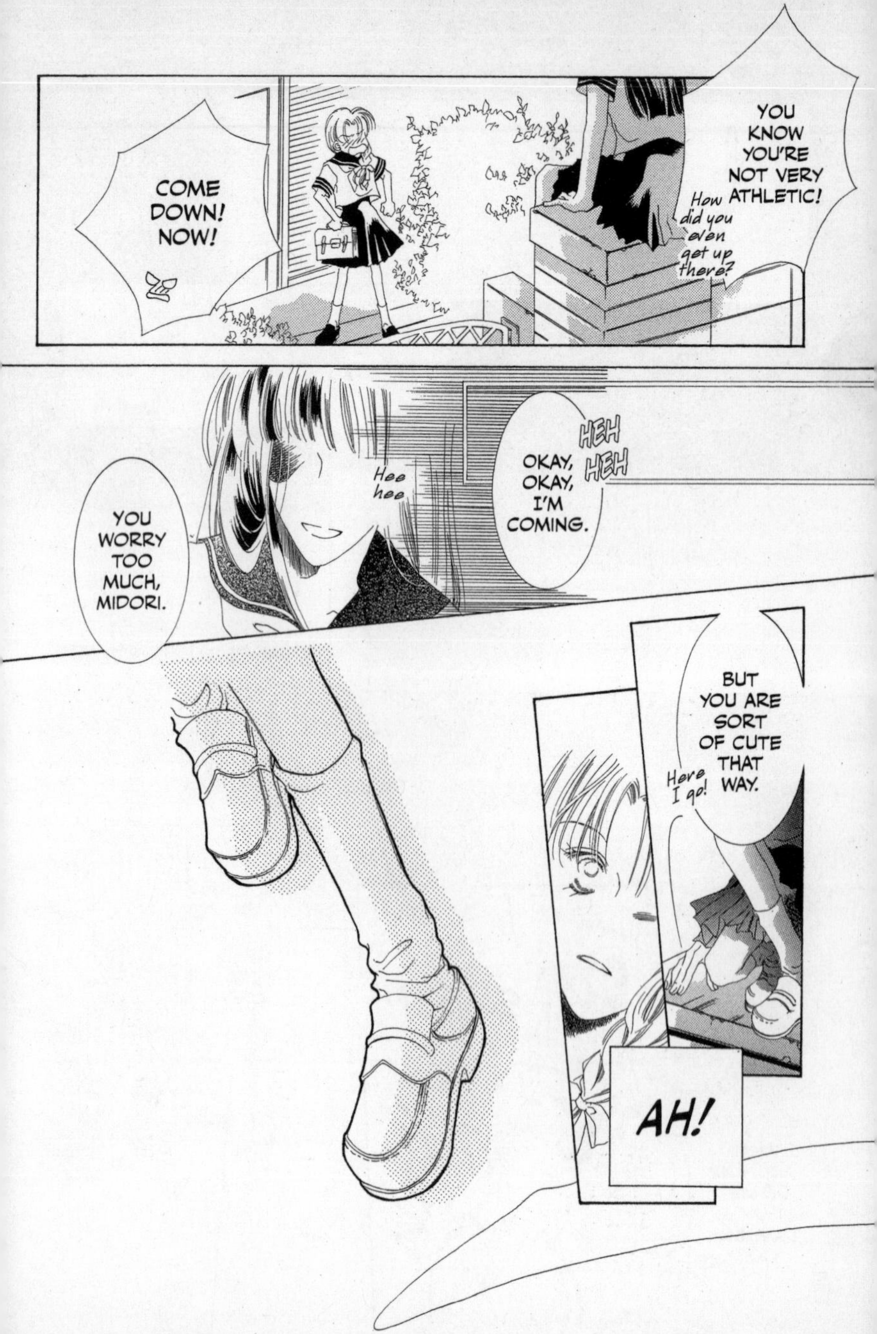
YOU KNOW YOU'RE NOT VERY ATHLETIC!
How did you even get up there?
COME DOWN! NOW!
HEH HEH
OKAY, OKAY, I'M COMING.
Hee hee
YOU WORRY TOO MUCH, MIDORI.
BUT YOU ARE SORT OF CUTE THAT WAY.
Here I go!
AH!

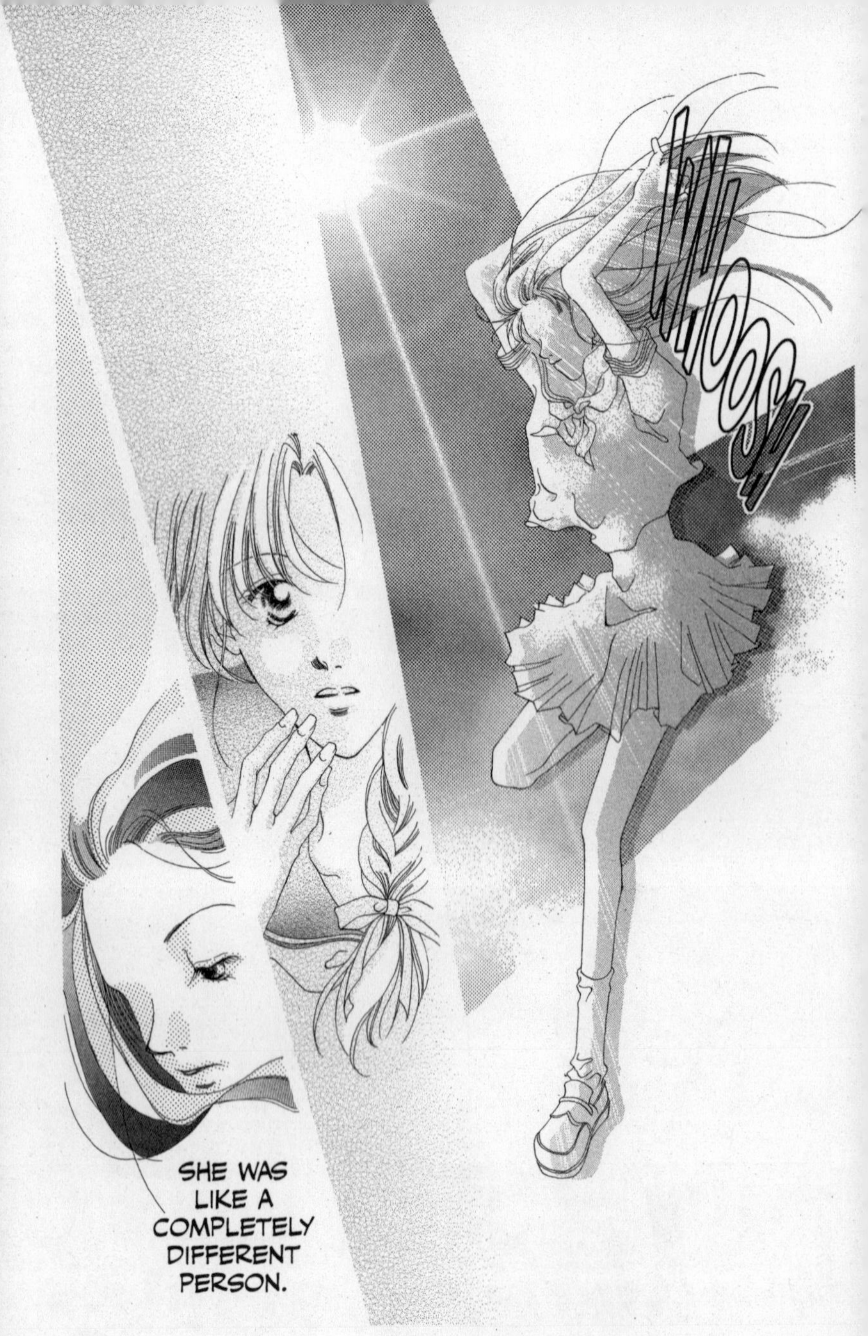
WHOOSH
SHE WAS LIKE A COMPLETELY DIFFERENT PERSON.

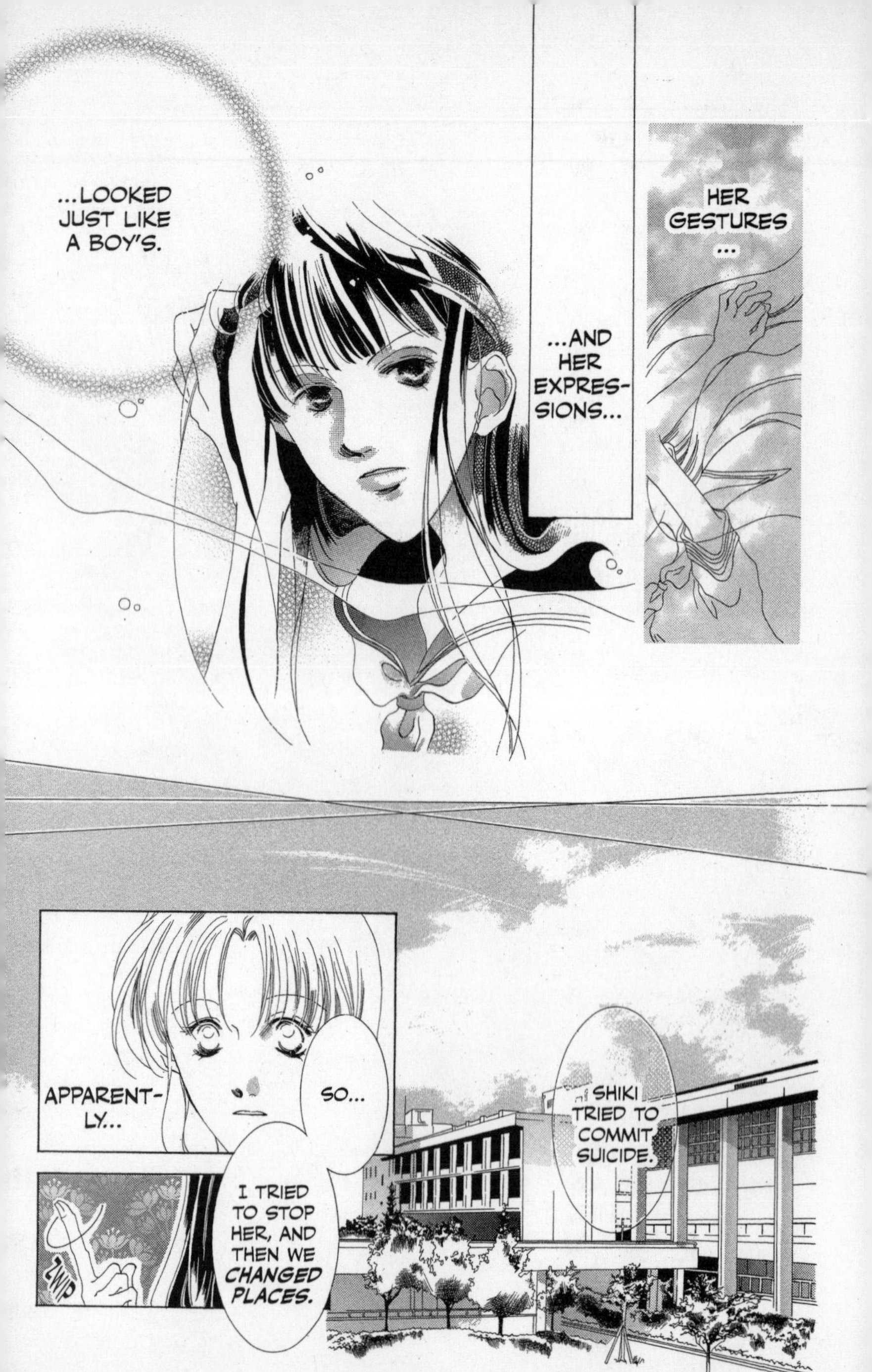
HER GESTURES...
...AND HER EXPRESSIONS...
...LOOKED JUST LIKE A BOY'S.
APPARENTLY...
SHIKI TRIED TO COMMIT SUICIDE.
SO...
I TRIED TO STOP HER, AND THEN WE *CHANGED PLACES.*
ZWIP

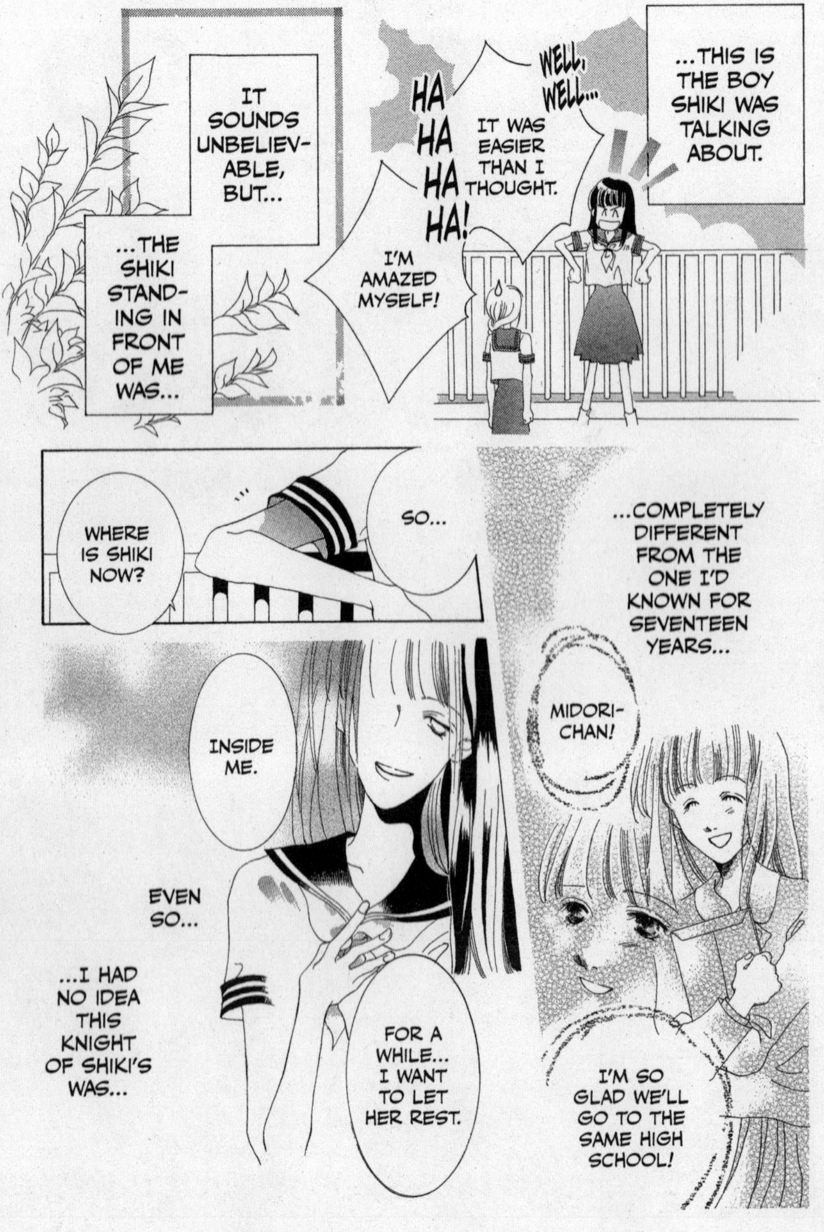
...THIS IS THE BOY SHIKI WAS TALKING ABOUT.
WELL, WELL...
HA HA HA HA!
IT WAS EASIER THAN I THOUGHT.
I'M AMAZED MYSELF!
IT SOUNDS UNBELIEVABLE, BUT...
...THE SHIKI STANDING IN FRONT OF ME WAS...
...COMPLETELY DIFFERENT FROM THE ONE I'D KNOWN FOR SEVENTEEN YEARS...
MIDORI-CHAN!
I'M SO GLAD WE'LL GO TO THE SAME HIGH SCHOOL!
SO...
WHERE IS SHIKI NOW?
INSIDE ME.
FOR A WHILE... I WANT TO LET HER REST.
EVEN SO...
...I HAD NO IDEA THIS KNIGHT OF SHIKI'S WAS...

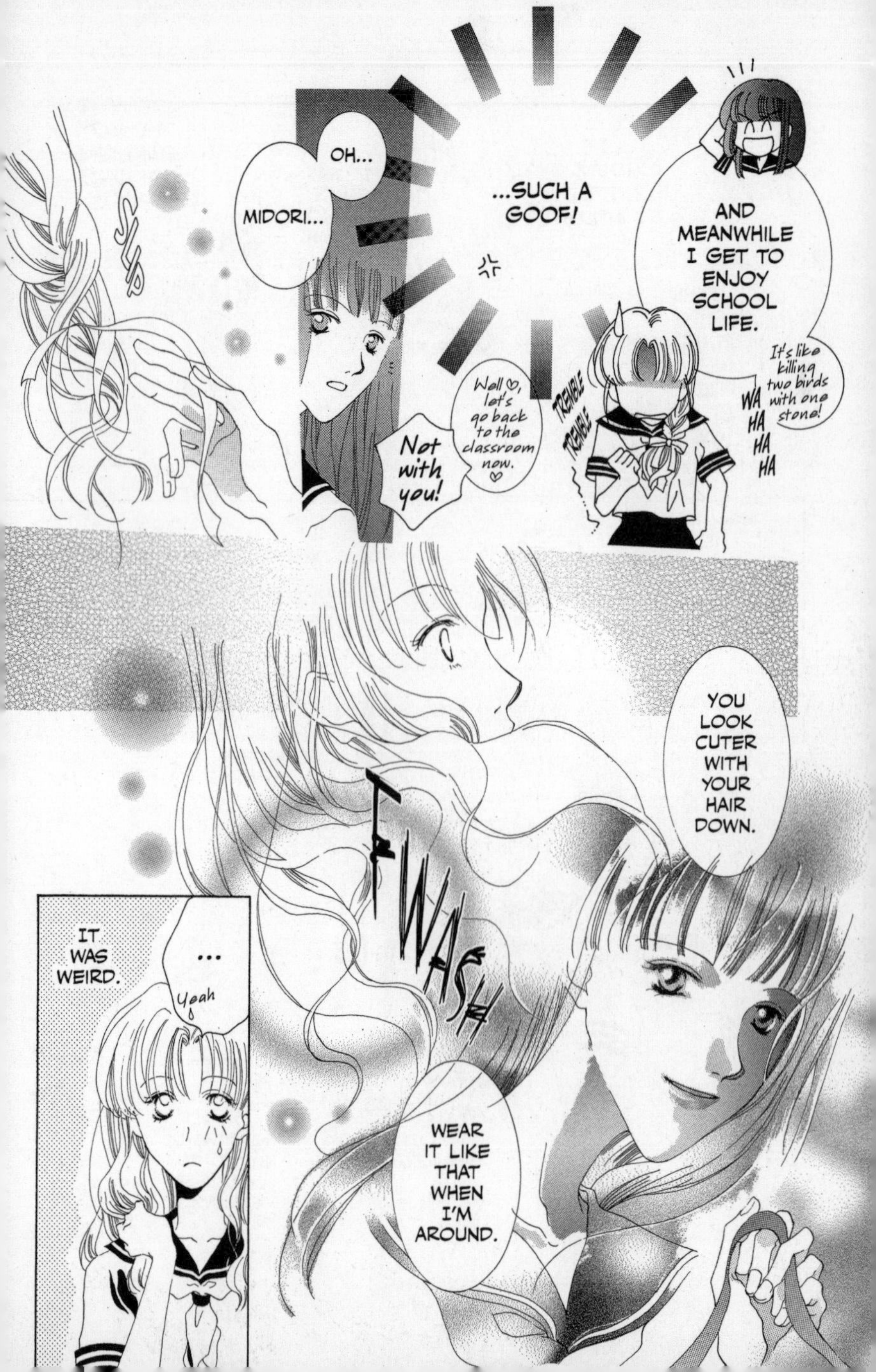
AND MEANWHILE I GET TO ENJOY SCHOOL LIFE.
It's like killing two birds with one stone!
WA HA HA HA
TREMBLE TREMBLE
...SUCH A GOOF!
Well♡, let's go back to the classroom now. ♡
Not with you!
OH...
MIDORI...
SLIP
YOU LOOK CUTER WITH YOUR HAIR DOWN.
FWASH
WEAR IT LIKE THAT WHEN I'M AROUND.
IT WAS WEIRD.
...
Yeah

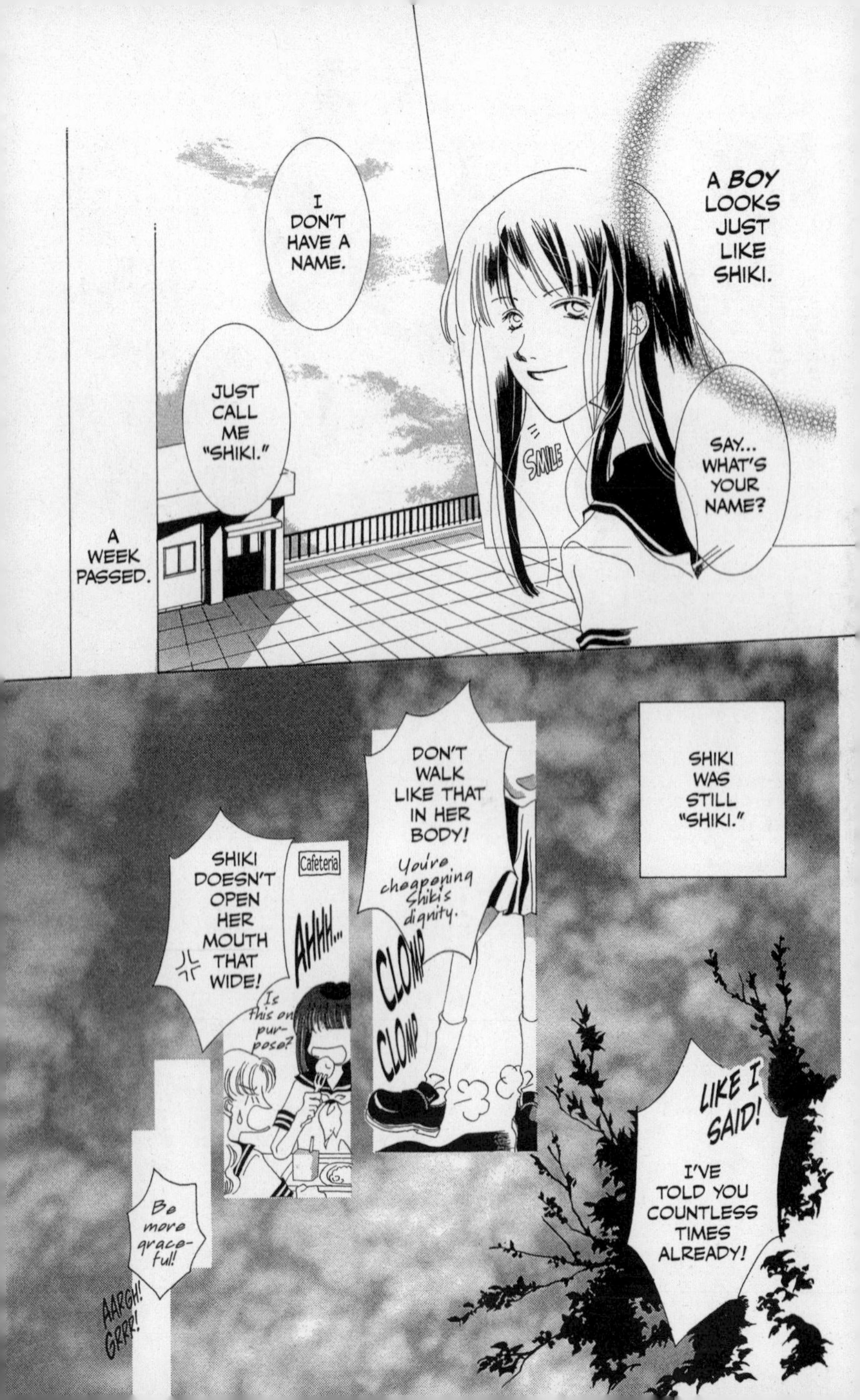
A BOY LOOKS JUST LIKE SHIKI.
SAY... WHAT'S YOUR NAME?
SMILE
I DON'T HAVE A NAME.
JUST CALL ME "SHIKI."
A WEEK PASSED.
SHIKI WAS STILL "SHIKI."
DON'T WALK LIKE THAT IN HER BODY!
You're cheapening Shiki's dignity.
CLOMP
CLOMP
SHIKI DOESN'T OPEN HER MOUTH THAT WIDE!
Cafeteria
AHHH...
Is this on pur-pose?
LIKE I SAID!
I'VE TOLD YOU COUNTLESS TIMES ALREADY!
Be more grace-ful!
AARGH! GRRR!

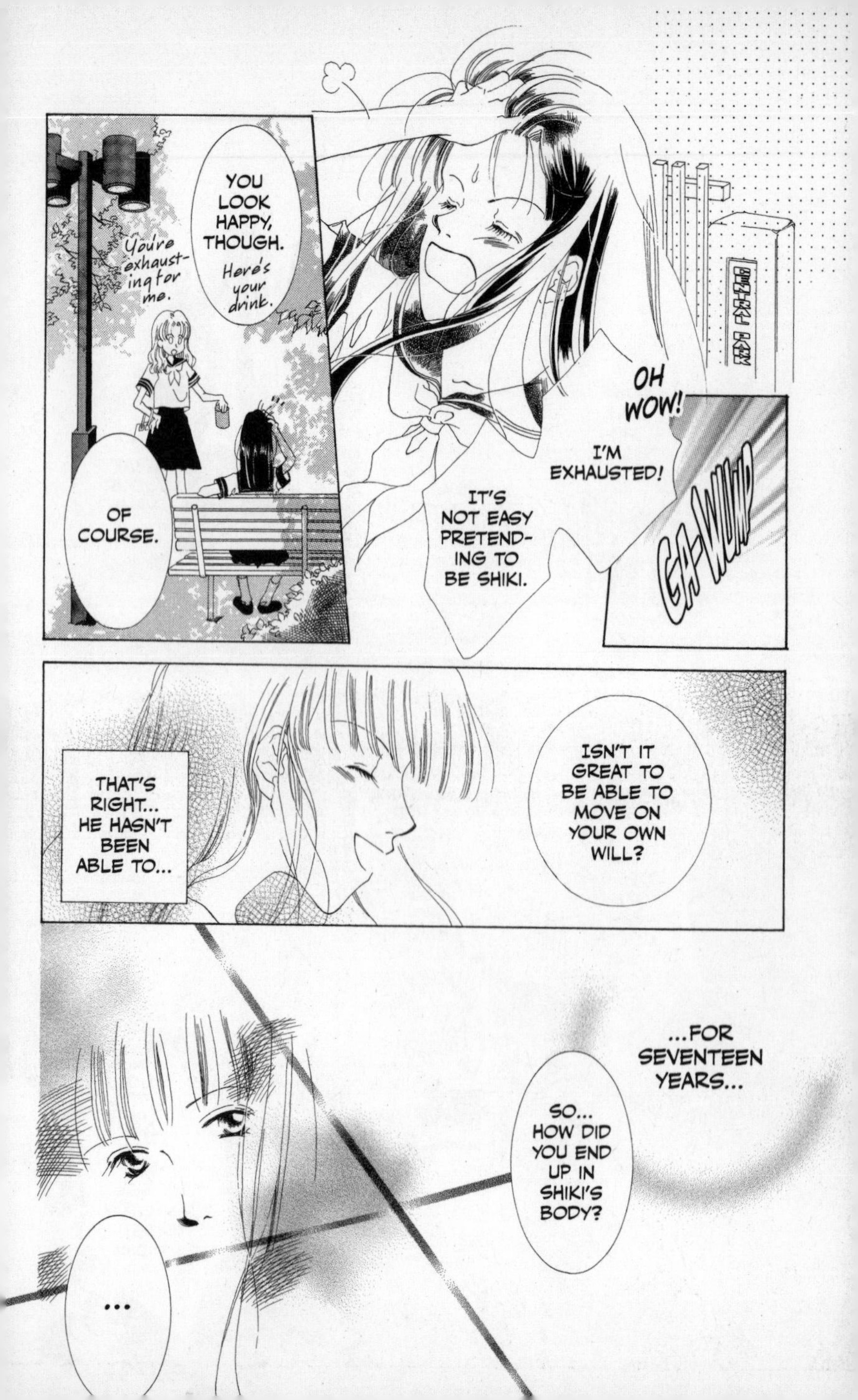
CENTRAL PARK
OH WOW!
I'M EXHAUSTED!
GA-WUMP
IT'S NOT EASY PRETENDING TO BE SHIKI.
YOU LOOK HAPPY, THOUGH.
Here's your drink.
You're exhausting for me.
OF COURSE.
ISN'T IT GREAT TO BE ABLE TO MOVE ON YOUR OWN WILL?
THAT'S RIGHT... HE HASN'T BEEN ABLE TO...
...FOR SEVENTEEN YEARS...
SO... HOW DID YOU END UP IN SHIKI'S BODY?
...

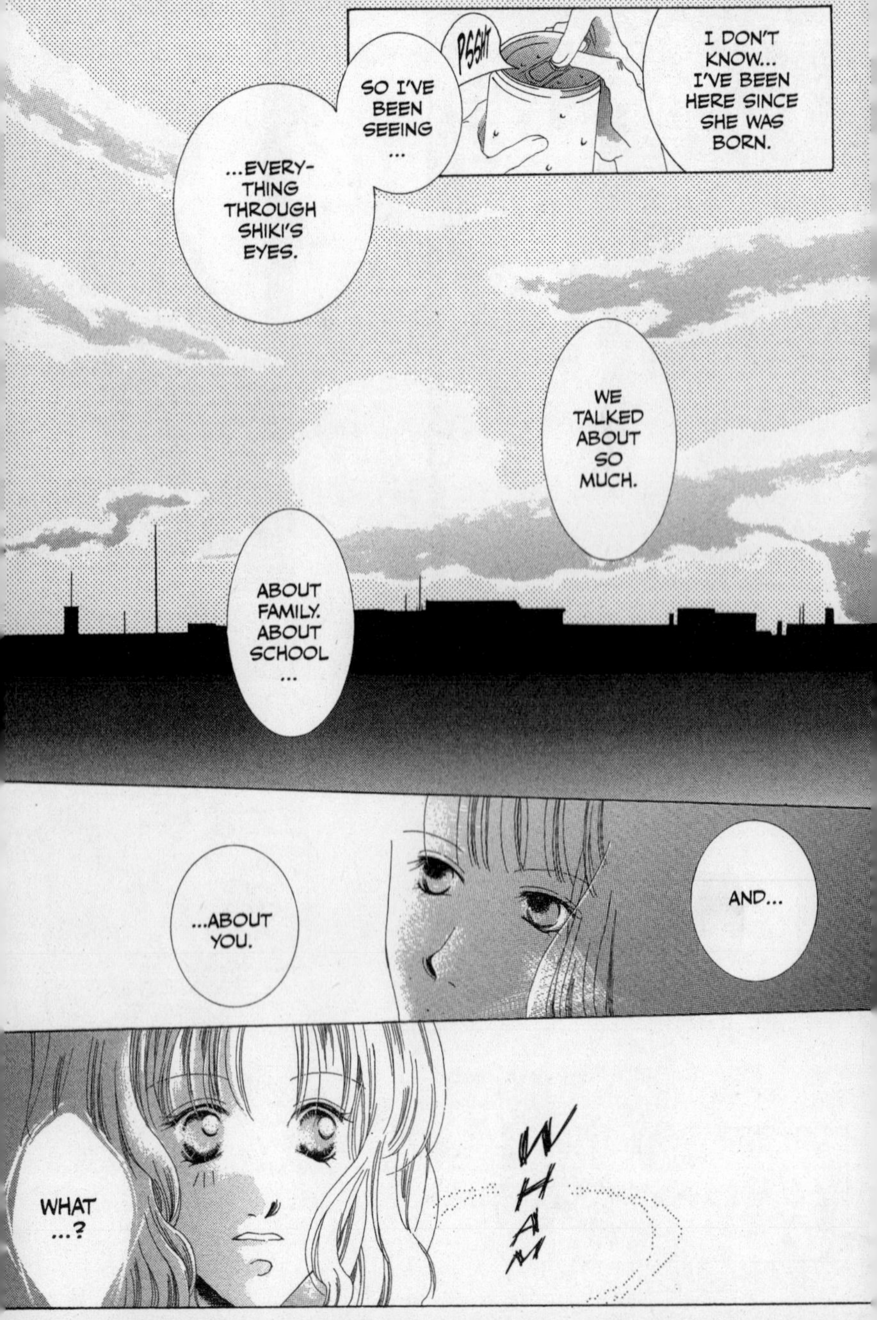
I DON'T KNOW... I'VE BEEN HERE SINCE SHE WAS BORN.
PSSHT
SO I'VE BEEN SEEING ...
...EVERY-THING THROUGH SHIKI'S EYES.
WE TALKED ABOUT SO MUCH.
ABOUT FAMILY. ABOUT SCHOOL ...
AND...
...ABOUT YOU.
WHAM
WHAT ...?

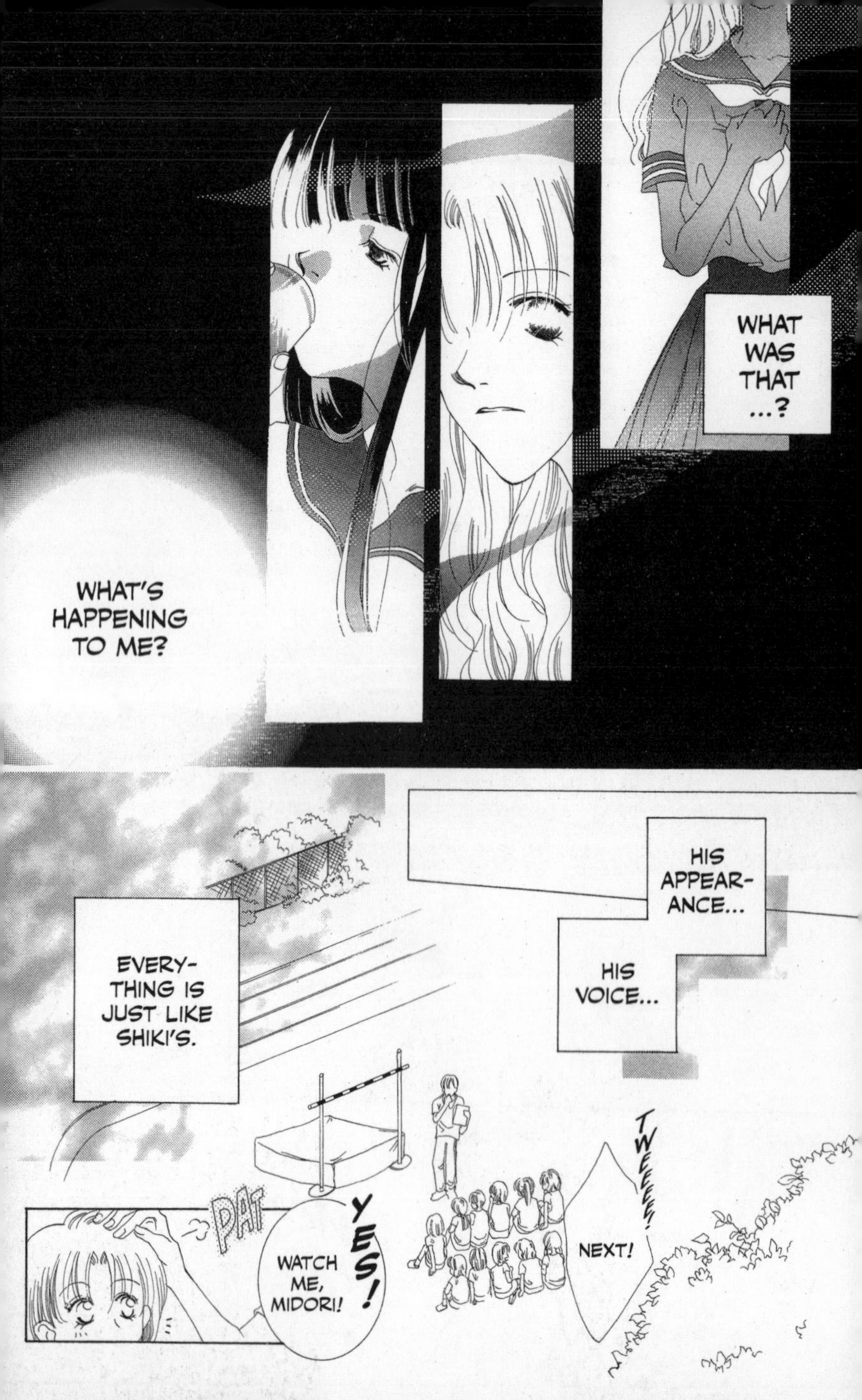
WHAT WAS THAT ...?
WHAT'S HAPPENING TO ME?
HIS APPEAR-ANCE...
HIS VOICE...
EVERY-THING IS JUST LIKE SHIKI'S.
TWEEEE!
NEXT!
YES!
WATCH ME, MIDORI!
PAT

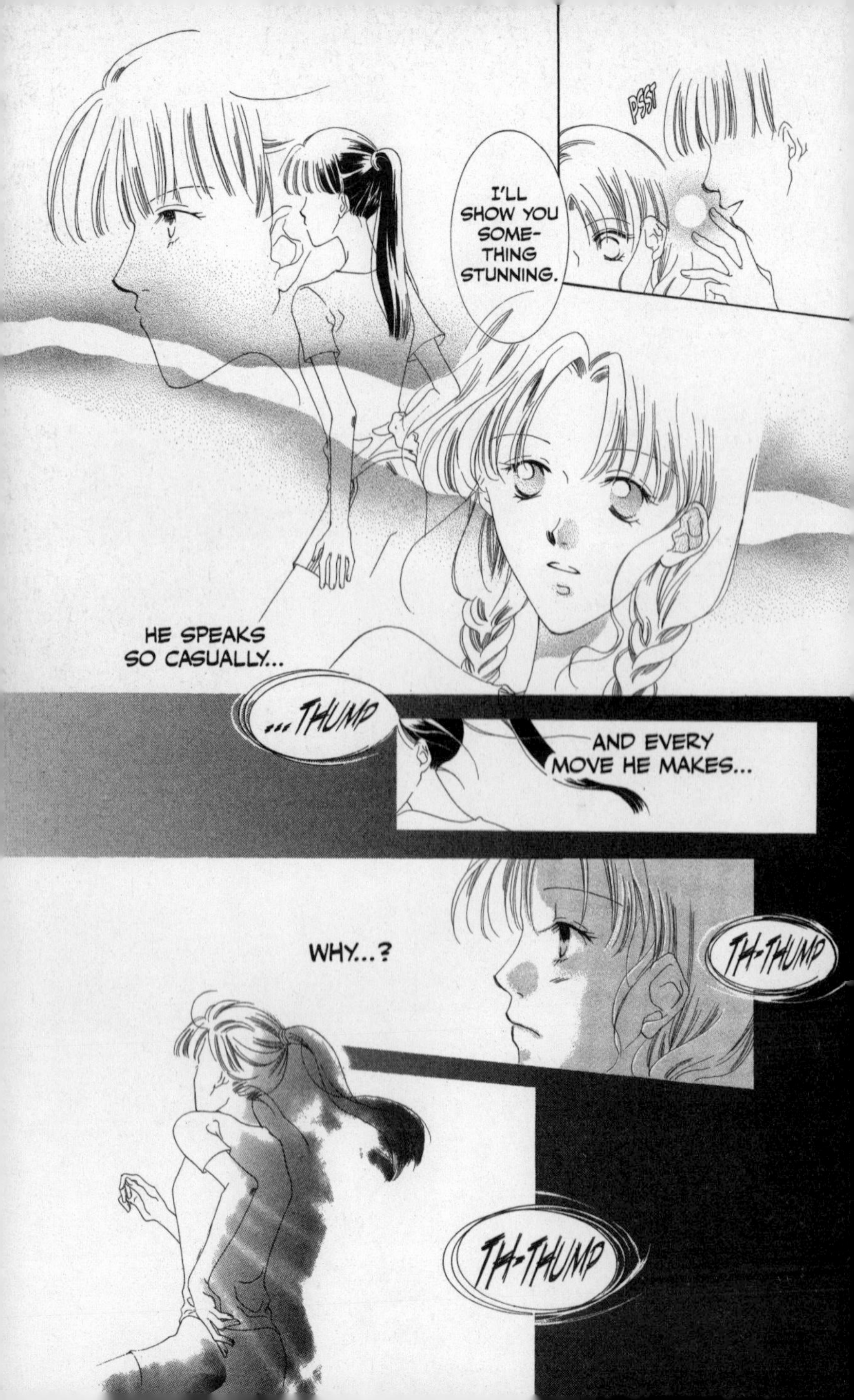
PSST
I'LL SHOW YOU SOME-THING STUNNING.
HE SPEAKS SO CASUALLY...
...THUMP
AND EVERY MOVE HE MAKES...
TH-THUMP
WHY...?
TH-THUMP

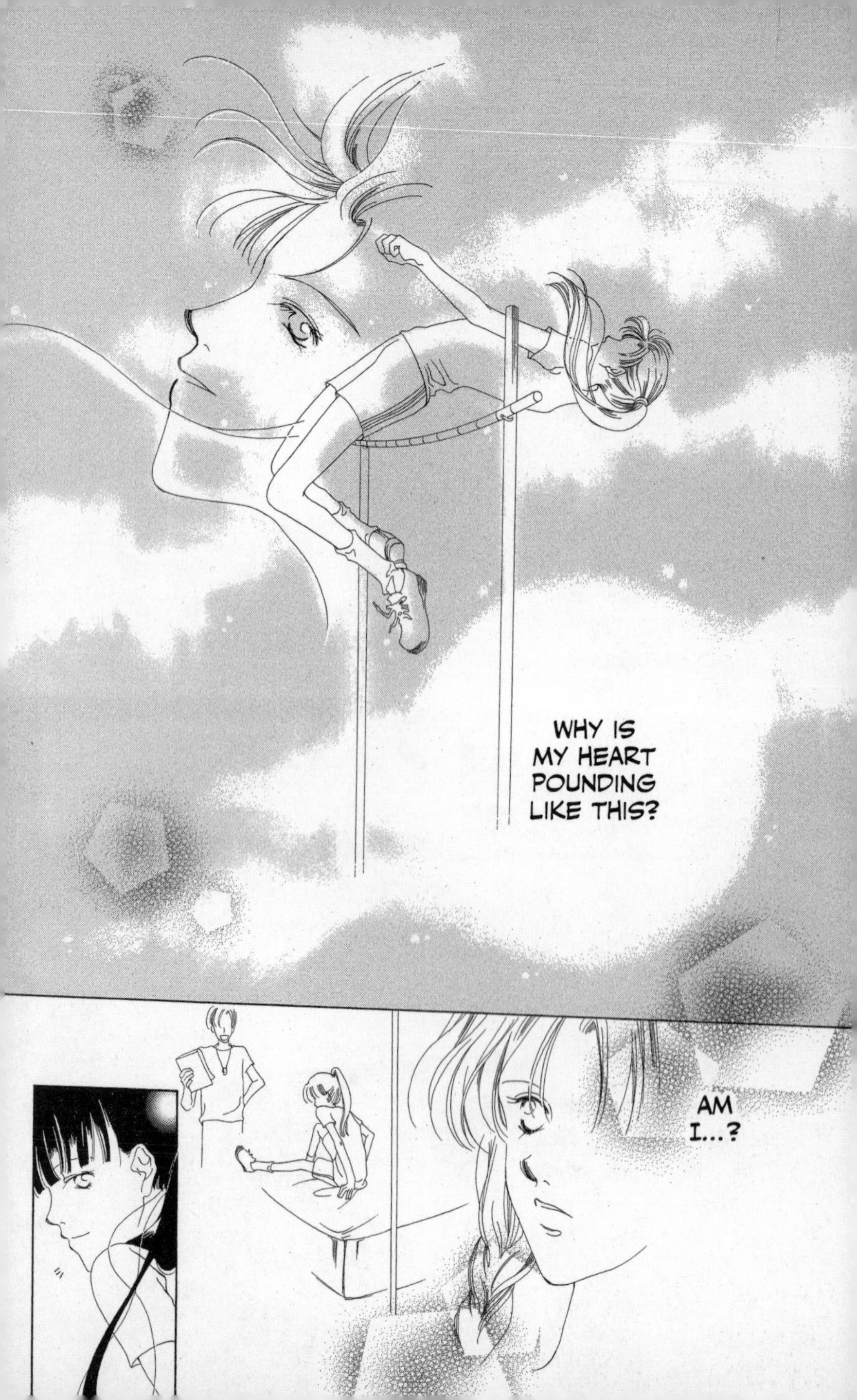
WHY IS MY HEART POUNDING LIKE THIS?
AM I...?

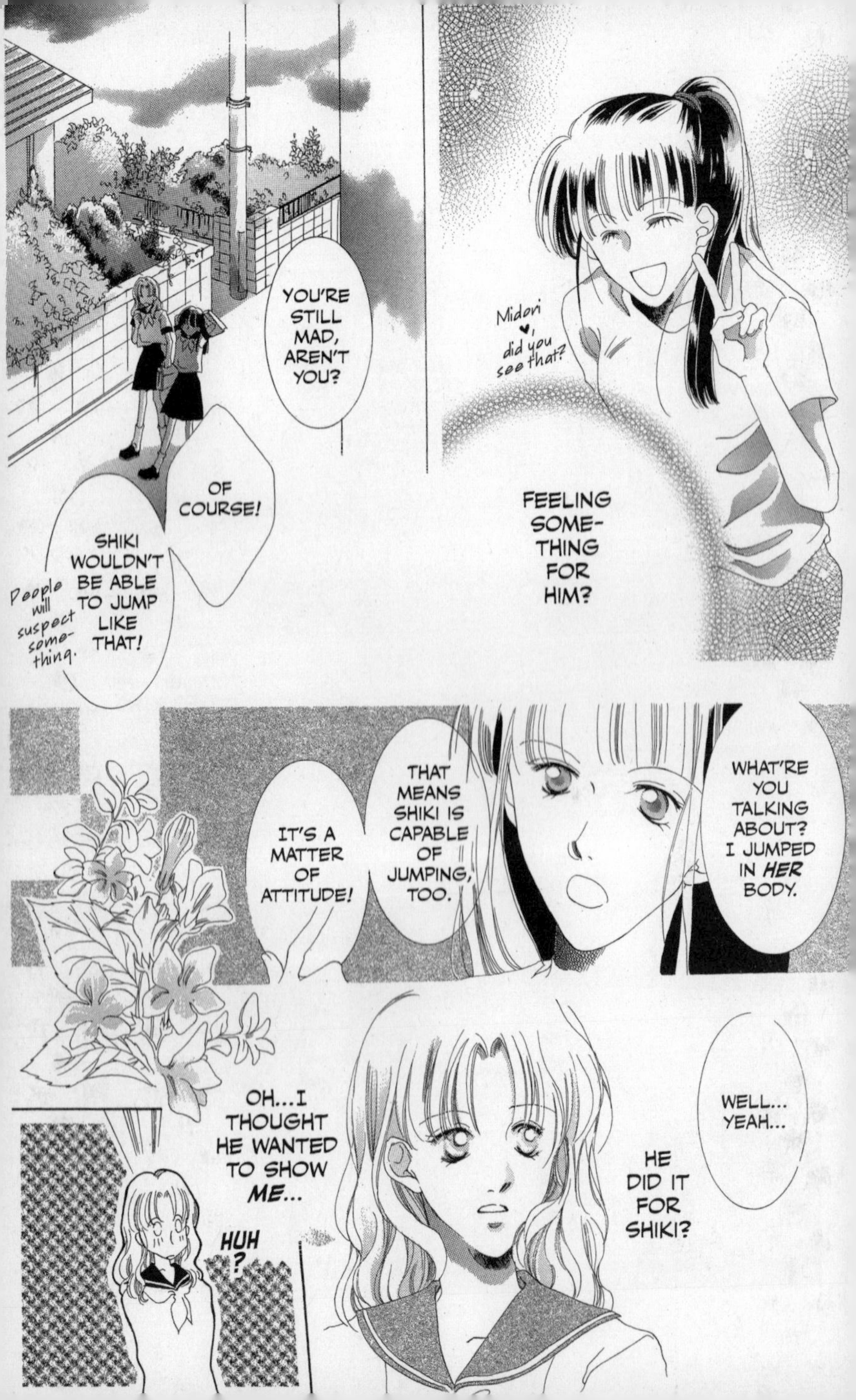
Midori ♥, did you see that?
FEELING SOME-THING FOR HIM?
YOU'RE STILL MAD, AREN'T YOU?
OF COURSE!
SHIKI WOULDN'T BE ABLE TO JUMP LIKE THAT!
People will suspect some-thing.
WHAT'RE YOU TALKING ABOUT? I JUMPED IN *HER* BODY.
THAT MEANS SHIKI IS CAPABLE OF JUMPING, TOO.
IT'S A MATTER OF ATTITUDE!
WELL... YEAH...
HE DID IT FOR SHIKI?
OH...I THOUGHT HE WANTED TO SHOW *ME*...
HUH?

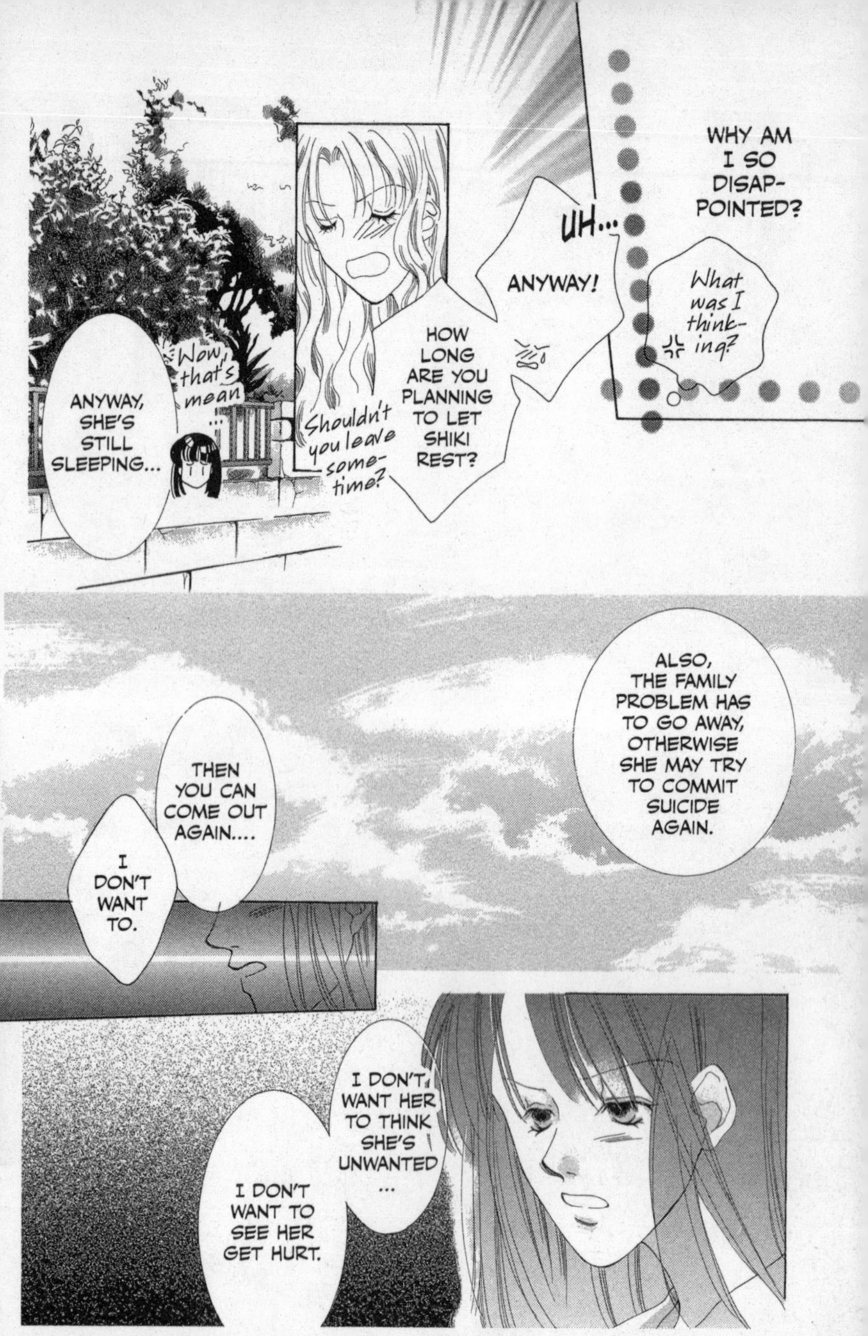
WHY AM I SO DISAPPOINTED?
What was I thinking?
UH...
ANYWAY!
HOW LONG ARE YOU PLANNING TO LET SHIKI REST?
Shouldn't you leave sometime?
ANYWAY, SHE'S STILL SLEEPING...
Wow, that's mean...
ALSO, THE FAMILY PROBLEM HAS TO GO AWAY, OTHERWISE SHE MAY TRY TO COMMIT SUICIDE AGAIN.
THEN YOU CAN COME OUT AGAIN....
I DON'T WANT TO.
I DON'T WANT HER TO THINK SHE'S UNWANTED...
I DON'T WANT TO SEE HER GET HURT.

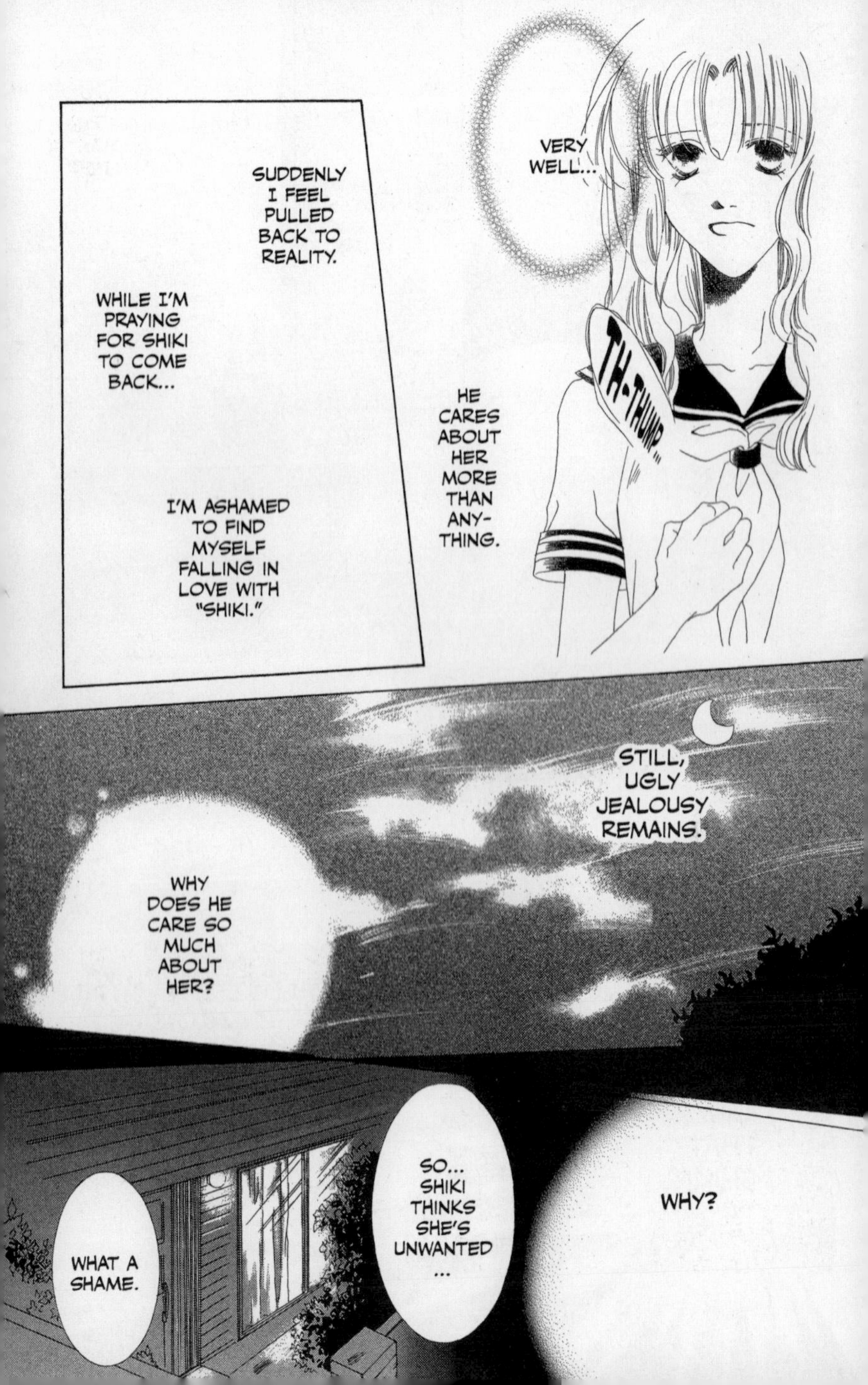
VERY WELL...
TH-THUMP...
HE CARES ABOUT HER MORE THAN ANYTHING.
SUDDENLY I FEEL PULLED BACK TO REALITY.
WHILE I'M PRAYING FOR SHIKI TO COME BACK...
I'M ASHAMED TO FIND MYSELF FALLING IN LOVE WITH "SHIKI."
STILL, UGLY JEALOUSY REMAINS.
WHY DOES HE CARE SO MUCH ABOUT HER?
WHY?
SO... SHIKI THINKS SHE'S UNWANTED...
WHAT A SHAME.

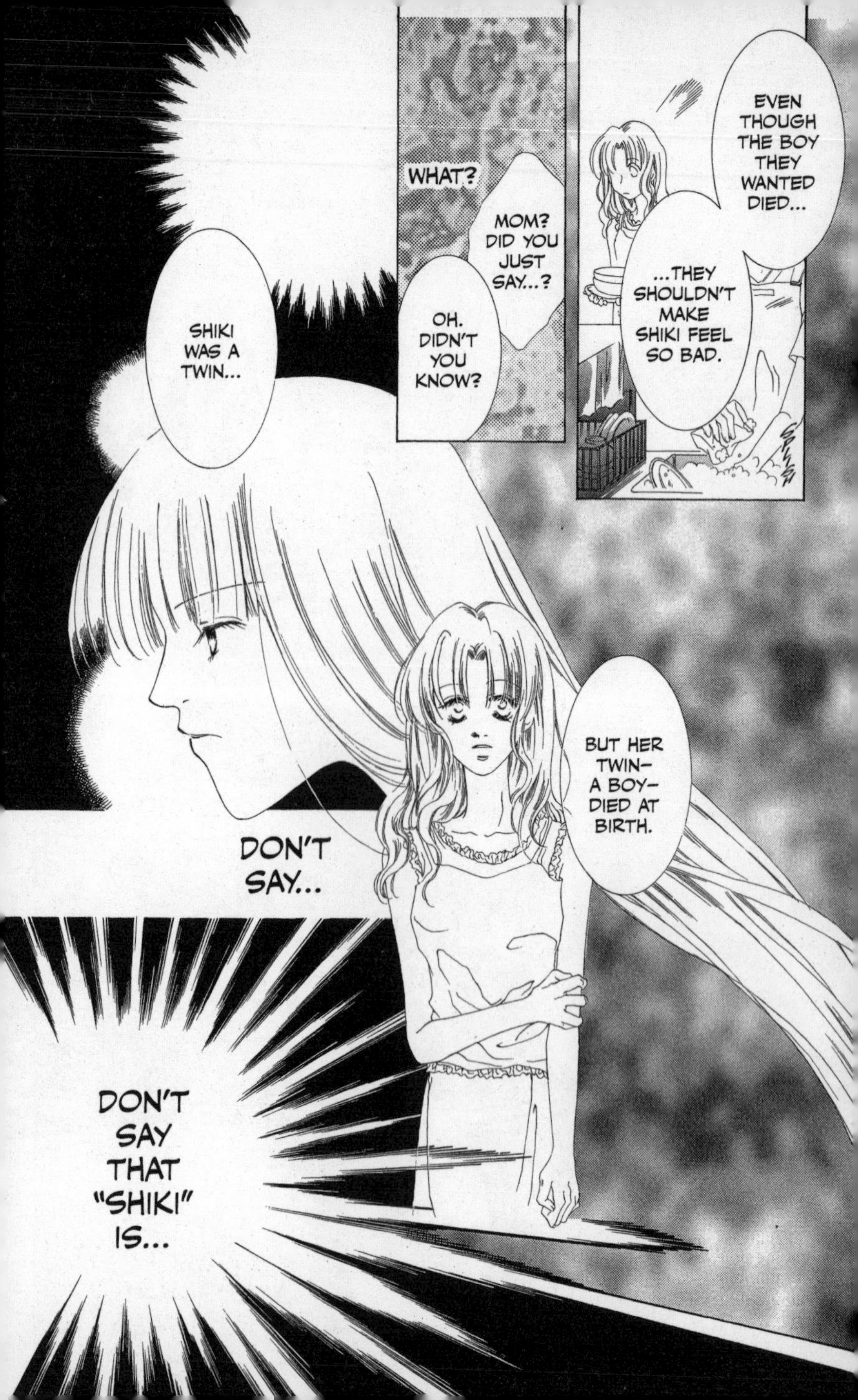
EVEN THOUGH THE BOY THEY WANTED DIED...
...THEY SHOULDN'T MAKE SHIKI FEEL SO BAD.
SPLISH
WHAT?
MOM? DID YOU JUST SAY...?
OH. DIDN'T YOU KNOW?
SHIKI WAS A TWIN...
BUT HER TWIN— A BOY— DIED AT BIRTH.
DON'T SAY...
DON'T SAY THAT "SHIKI" IS...

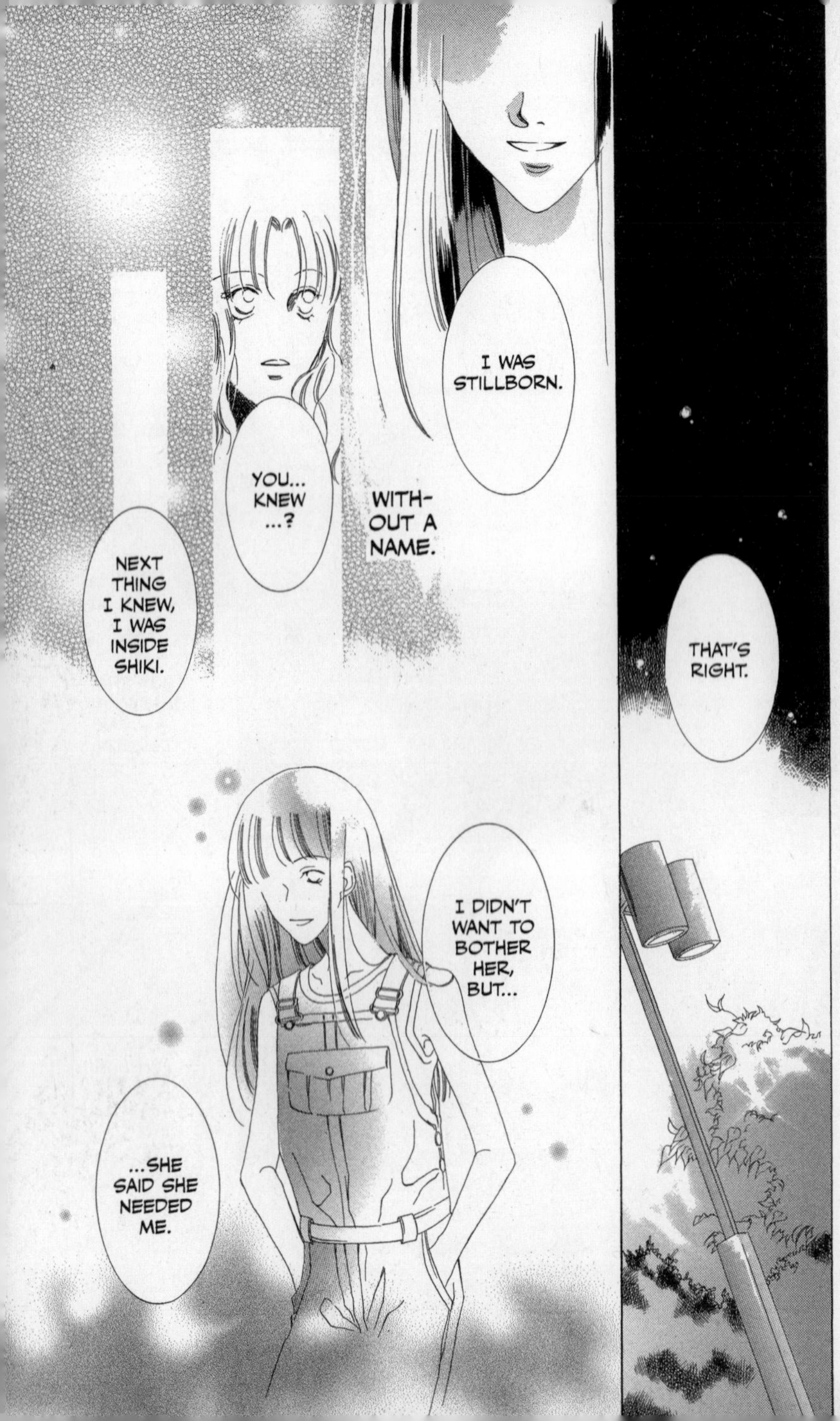
THAT'S RIGHT.
I WAS STILLBORN.
WITH-OUT A NAME.
YOU... KNEW ...?
NEXT THING I KNEW, I WAS INSIDE SHIKI.
I DIDN'T WANT TO BOTHER HER, BUT...
...SHE SAID SHE NEEDED ME.

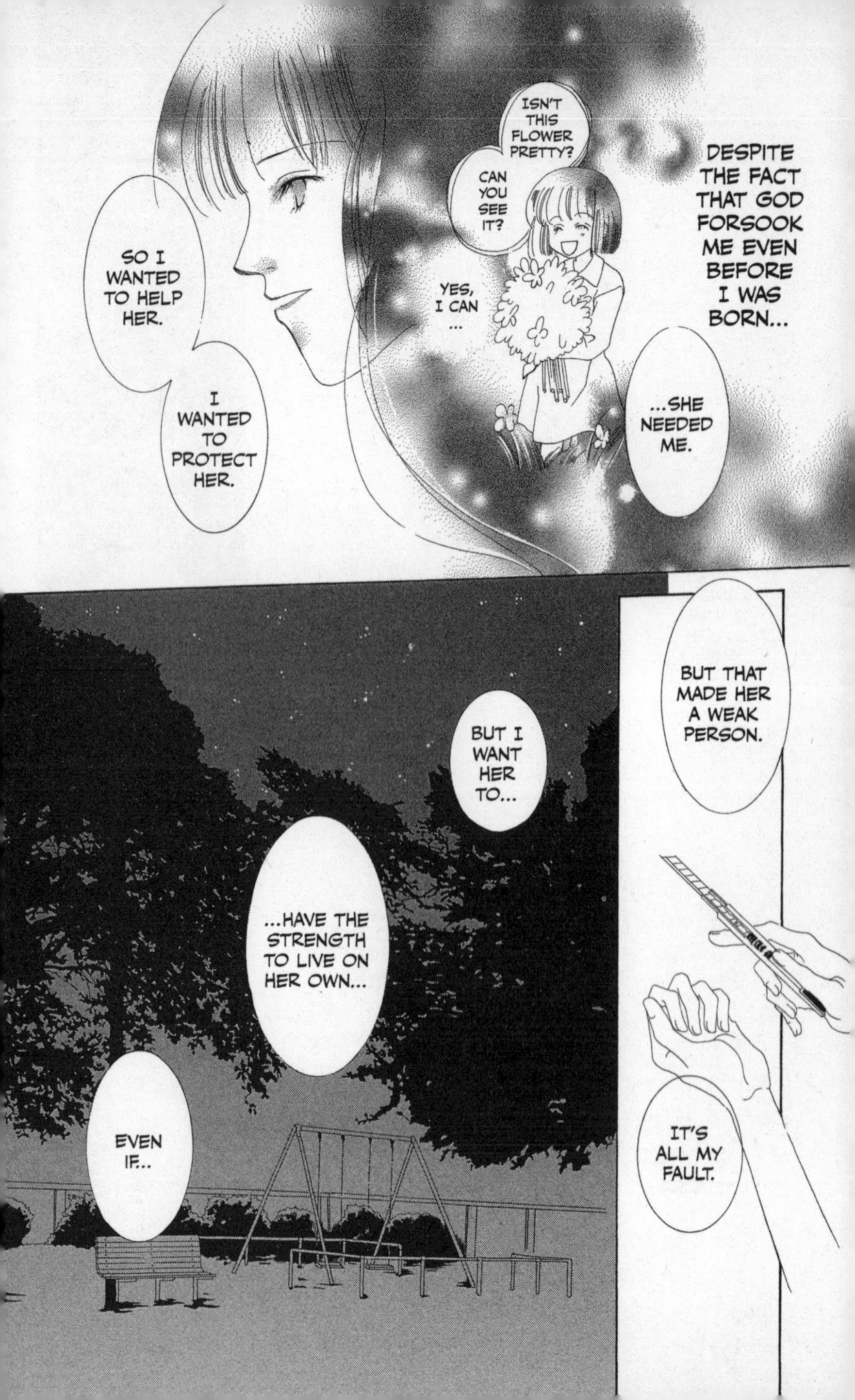
DESPITE THE FACT THAT GOD FORSOOK ME EVEN BEFORE I WAS BORN...
ISN'T THIS FLOWER PRETTY?
CAN YOU SEE IT?
YES, I CAN ...
...SHE NEEDED ME.
SO I WANTED TO HELP HER.
I WANTED TO PROTECT HER.
BUT THAT MADE HER A WEAK PERSON.
IT'S ALL MY FAULT.
BUT I WANT HER TO...
...HAVE THE STRENGTH TO LIVE ON HER OWN...
EVEN IF...

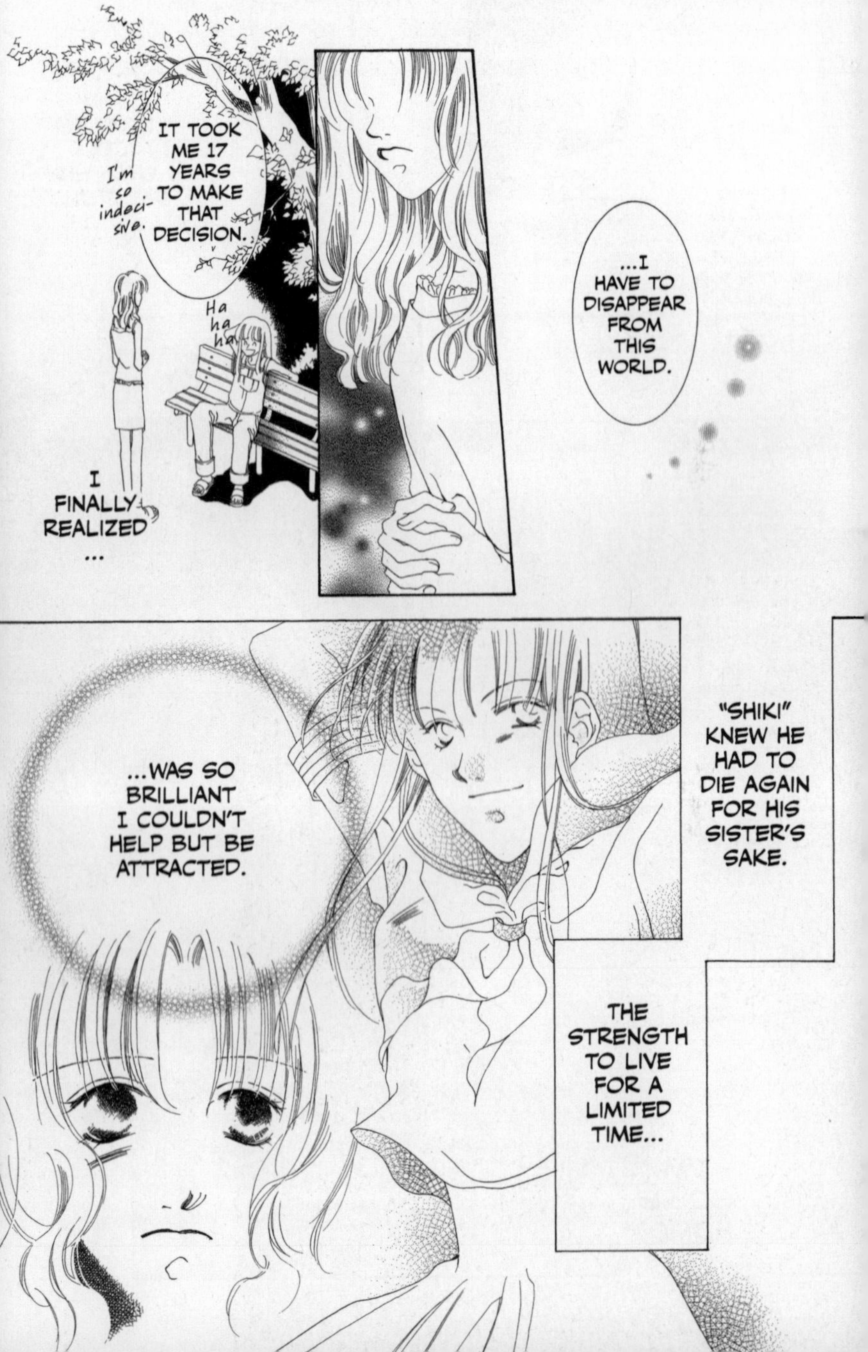
...I HAVE TO DISAPPEAR FROM THIS WORLD.
IT TOOK ME 17 YEARS TO MAKE THAT DECISION.
I'm so indecisive.
Ha ha ha
I FINALLY REALIZED ...
"SHIKI" KNEW HE HAD TO DIE AGAIN FOR HIS SISTER'S SAKE.
THE STRENGTH TO LIVE FOR A LIMITED TIME...
...WAS SO BRILLIANT I COULDN'T HELP BUT BE ATTRACTED.

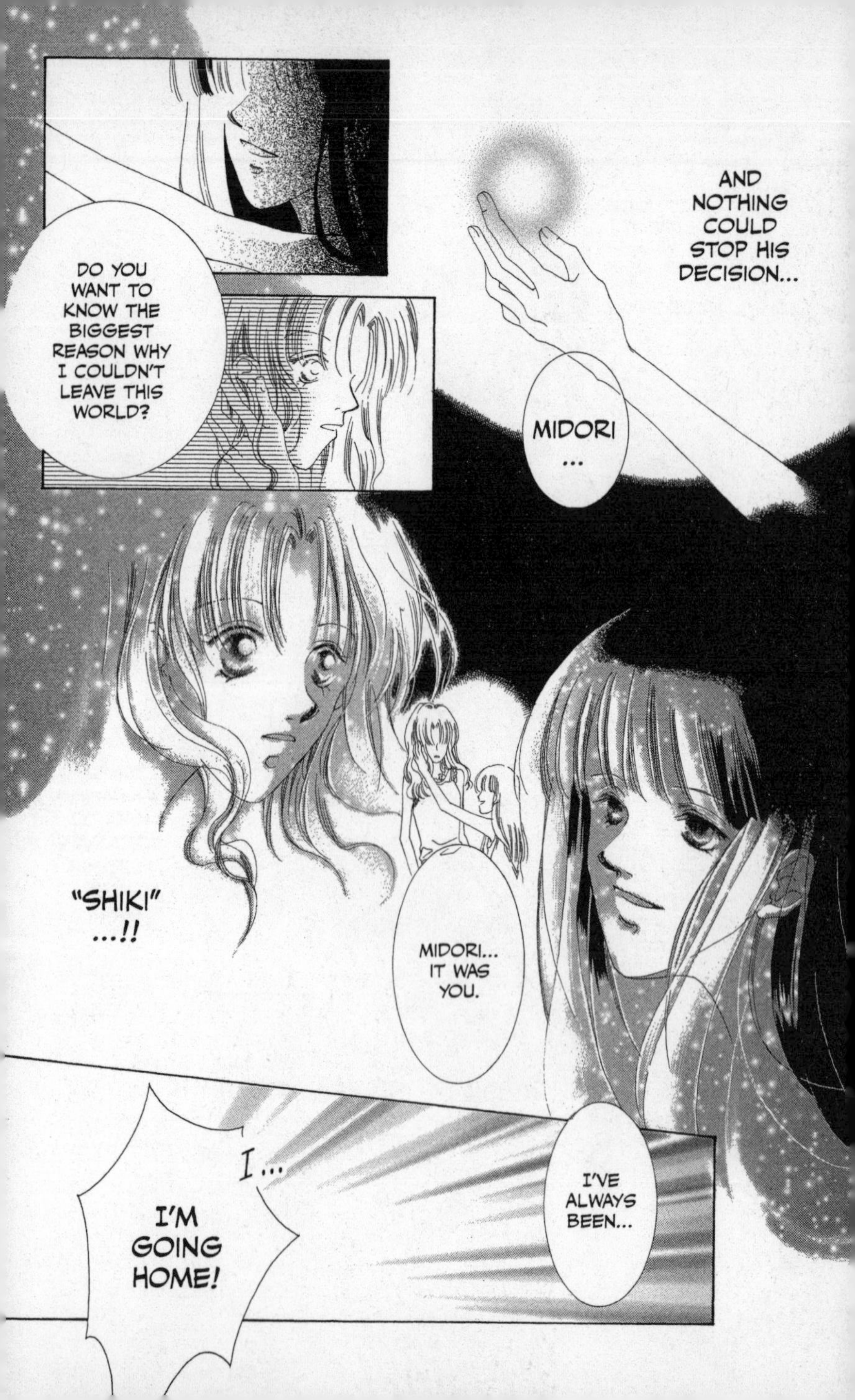
AND NOTHING COULD STOP HIS DECISION...
MIDORI ...
DO YOU WANT TO KNOW THE BIGGEST REASON WHY I COULDN'T LEAVE THIS WORLD?
MIDORI... IT WAS YOU.
"SHIKI" ...!!
I'VE ALWAYS BEEN...
I...
I'M GOING HOME!

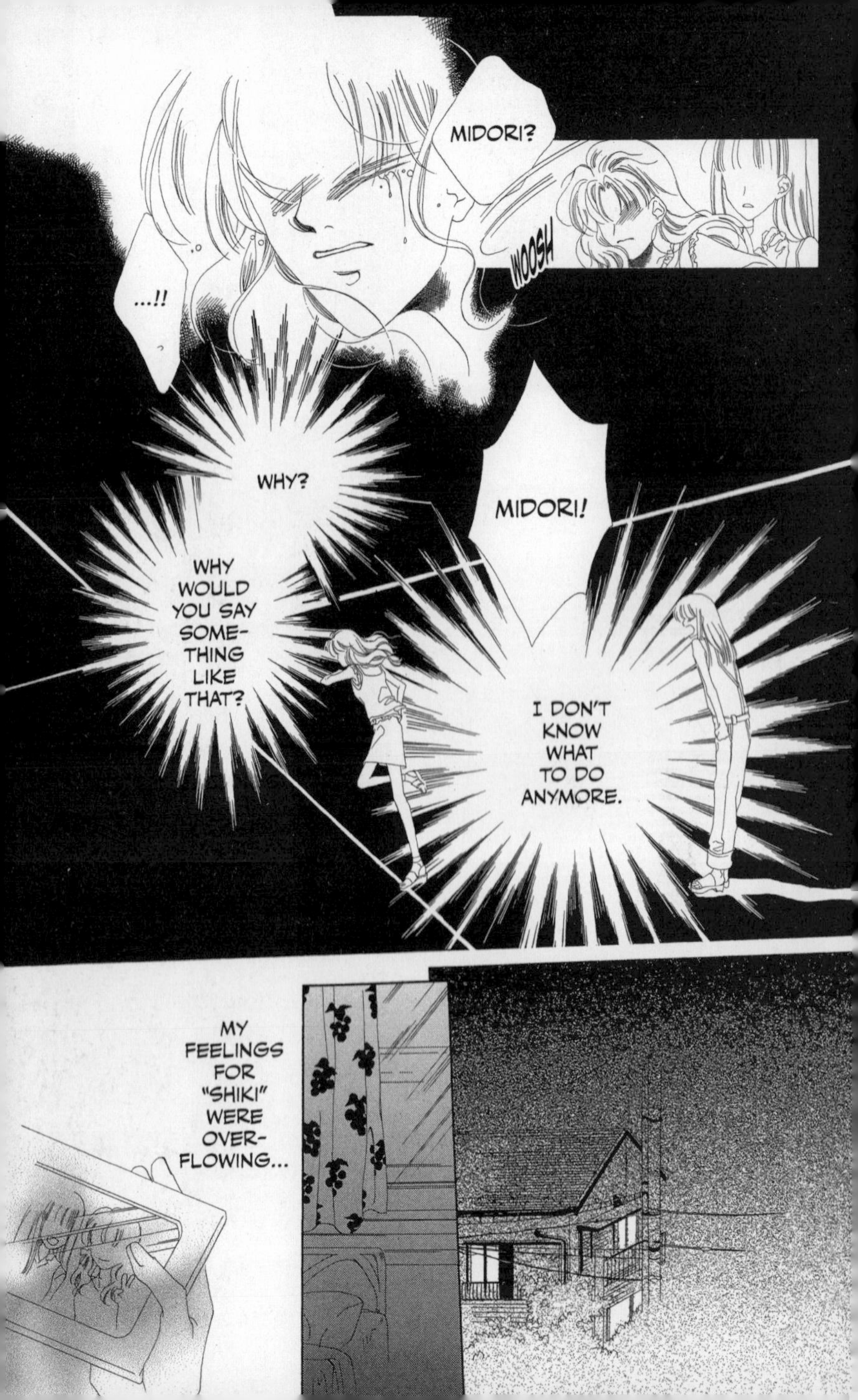
MIDORI?
WOOSH
...!!
MIDORI!
WHY?
WHY WOULD YOU SAY SOME-THING LIKE THAT?
I DON'T KNOW WHAT TO DO ANYMORE.
MY FEELINGS FOR "SHIKI" WERE OVER-FLOWING...

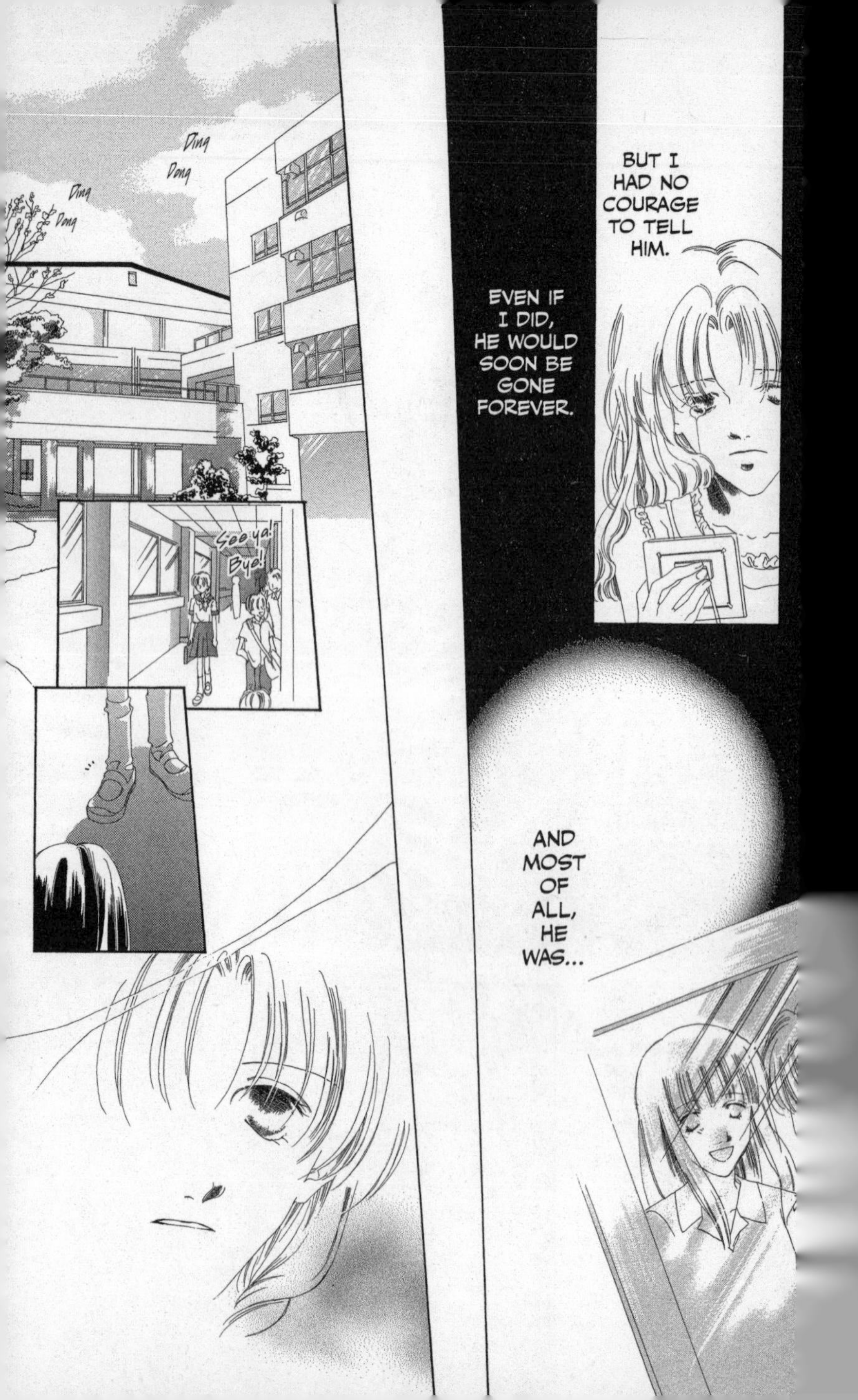
BUT I HAD NO COURAGE TO TELL HIM.
EVEN IF I DID, HE WOULD SOON BE GONE FOREVER.
AND MOST OF ALL, HE WAS...
Ding Dong
Ding Dong
See ya!
Bye!
...

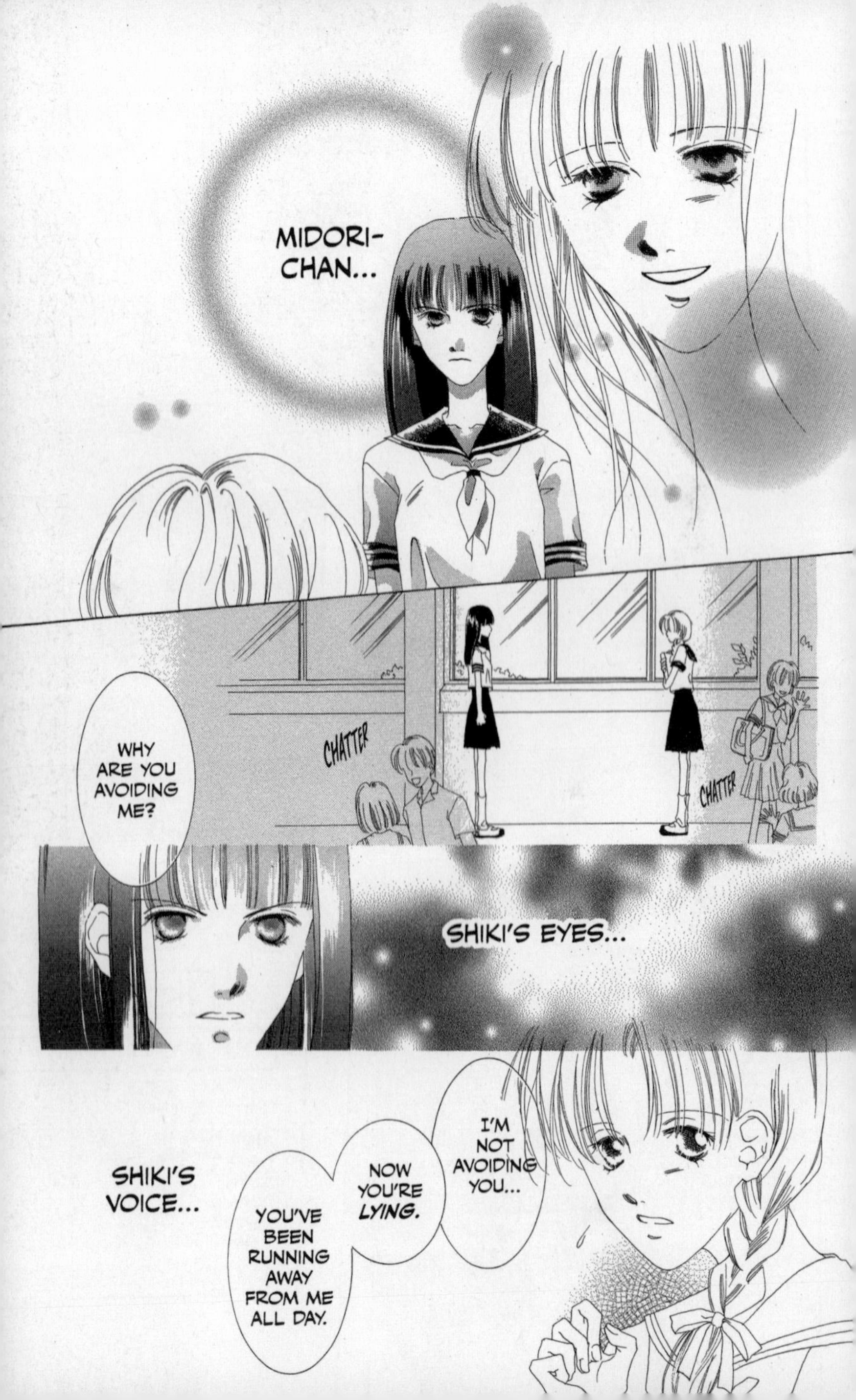
MIDORI-CHAN...
CHATTER
CHATTER
WHY ARE YOU AVOIDING ME?
SHIKI'S EYES...
I'M NOT AVOIDING YOU...
NOW YOU'RE *LYING.*
YOU'VE BEEN RUNNING AWAY FROM ME ALL DAY.
SHIKI'S VOICE...

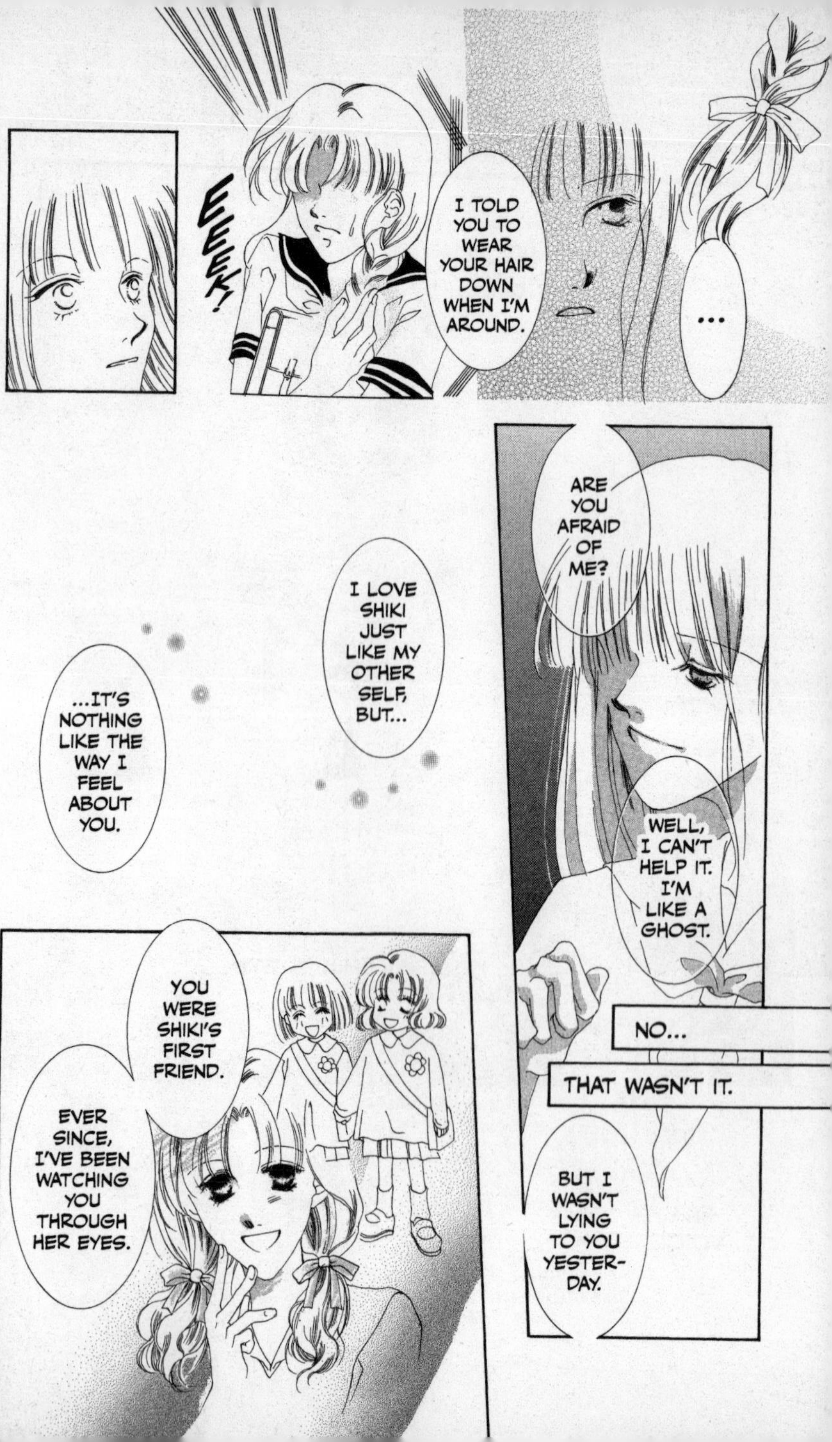
...
I TOLD YOU TO WEAR YOUR HAIR DOWN WHEN I'M AROUND.
EEEK!
ARE YOU AFRAID OF ME?
WELL, I CAN'T HELP IT. I'M LIKE A GHOST.
NO...
THAT WASN'T IT.
BUT I WASN'T LYING TO YOU YESTER-DAY.
I LOVE SHIKI JUST LIKE MY OTHER SELF, BUT...
...IT'S NOTHING LIKE THE WAY I FEEL ABOUT YOU.
YOU WERE SHIKI'S FIRST FRIEND.
EVER SINCE, I'VE BEEN WATCHING YOU THROUGH HER EYES.

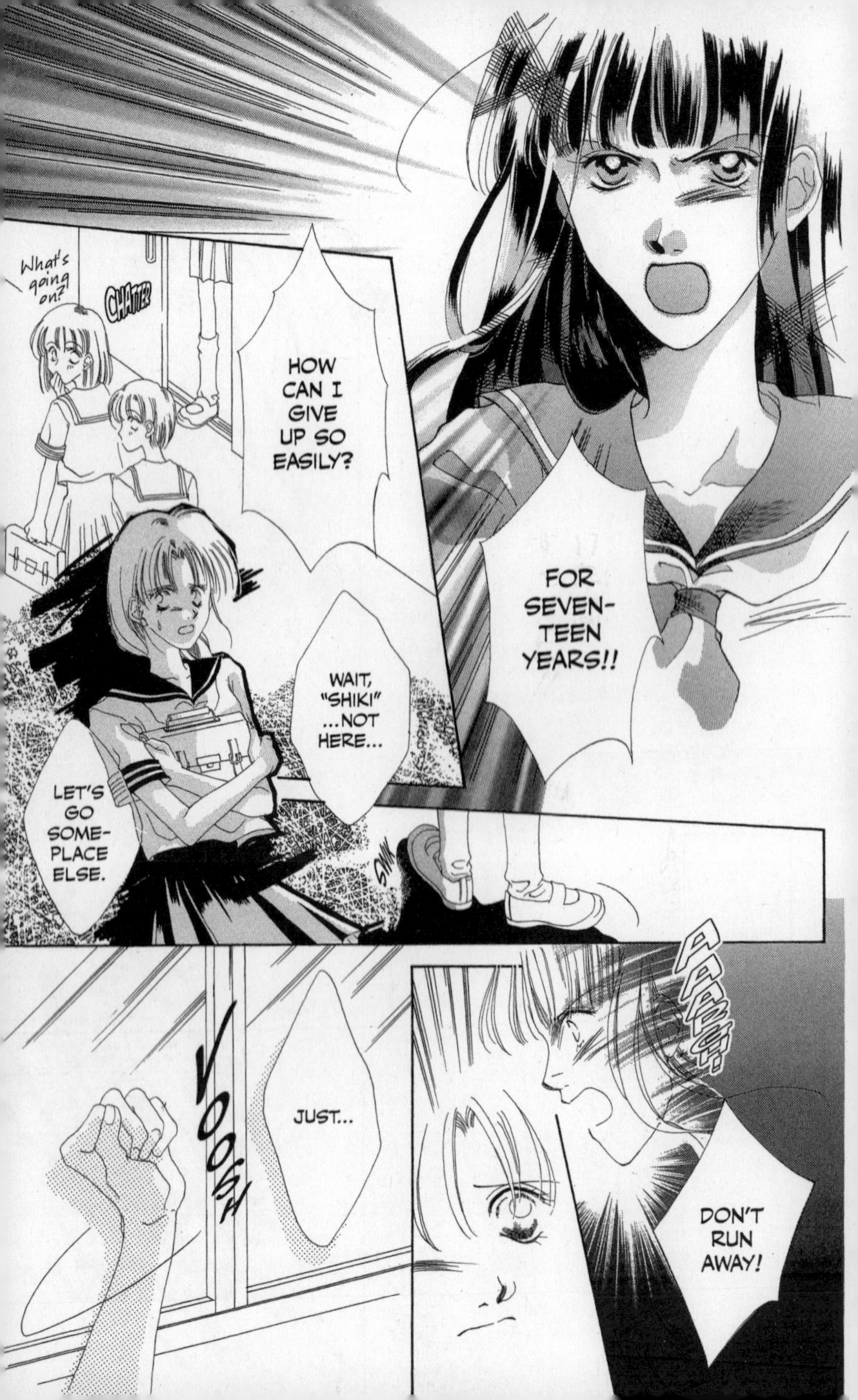
HOW CAN I GIVE UP SO EASILY?
FOR SEVEN-TEEN YEARS!!
What's going on?
CHATTER
WAIT, "SHIKI" ...NOT HERE...
LET'S GO SOME-PLACE ELSE.
SNIK
AAACK!
DON'T RUN AWAY!
JUST...
VOOSH

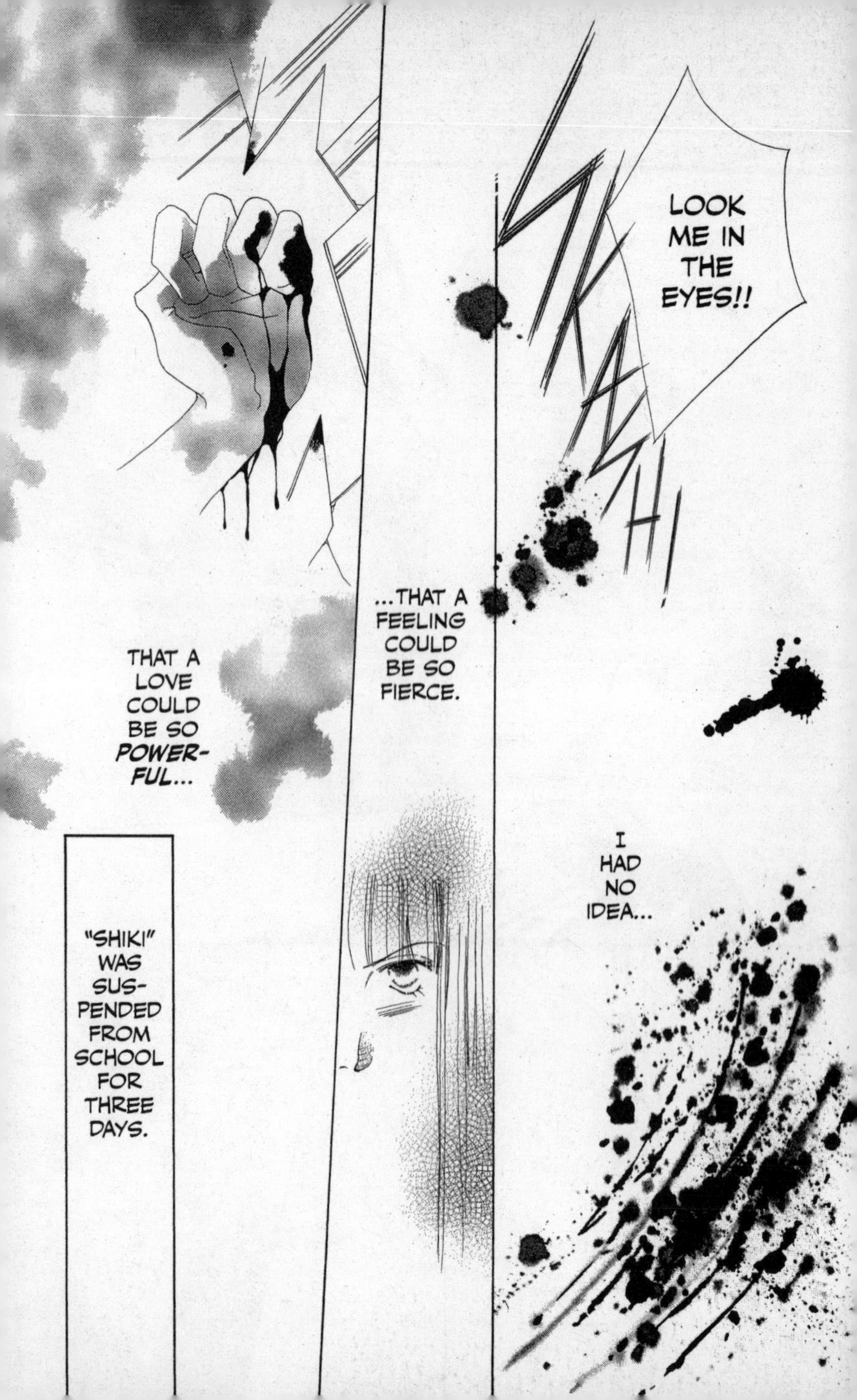
LOOK ME IN THE EYES!!
SKRASH!
I HAD NO IDEA...
THAT A LOVE COULD BE SO *POWERFUL...*
...THAT A FEELING COULD BE SO FIERCE.
"SHIKI" WAS SUSPENDED FROM SCHOOL FOR THREE DAYS.

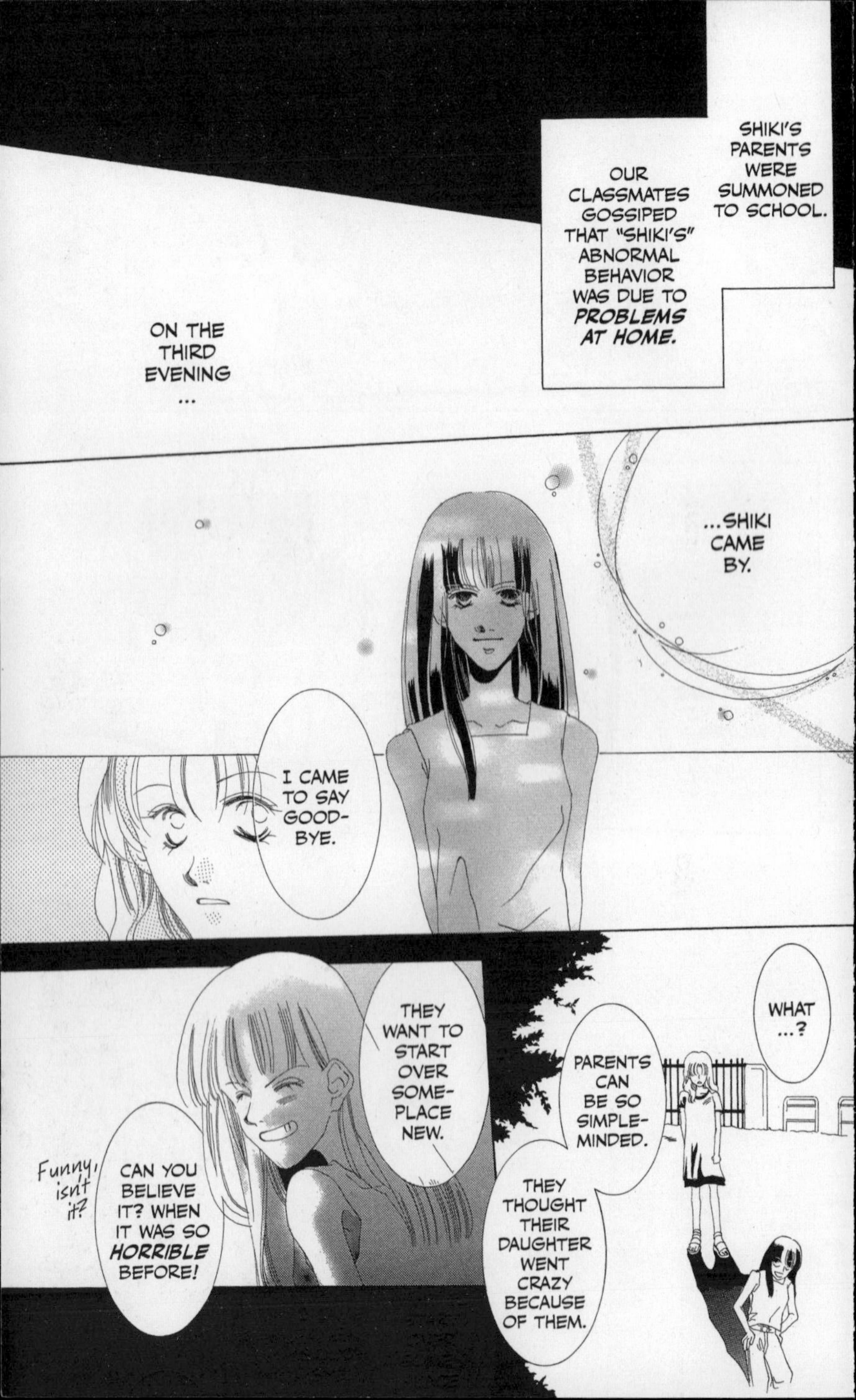
SHIKI'S PARENTS WERE SUMMONED TO SCHOOL.
OUR CLASSMATES GOSSIPED THAT "SHIKI'S" ABNORMAL BEHAVIOR WAS DUE TO *PROBLEMS AT HOME.*
ON THE THIRD EVENING ...
...SHIKI CAME BY.
I CAME TO SAY GOOD-BYE.
WHAT ...?
PARENTS CAN BE SO SIMPLE-MINDED.
THEY THOUGHT THEIR DAUGHTER WENT CRAZY BECAUSE OF THEM.
THEY WANT TO START OVER SOME-PLACE NEW.
CAN YOU BELIEVE IT? WHEN IT WAS SO *HORRIBLE* BEFORE!
Funny, isn't it?

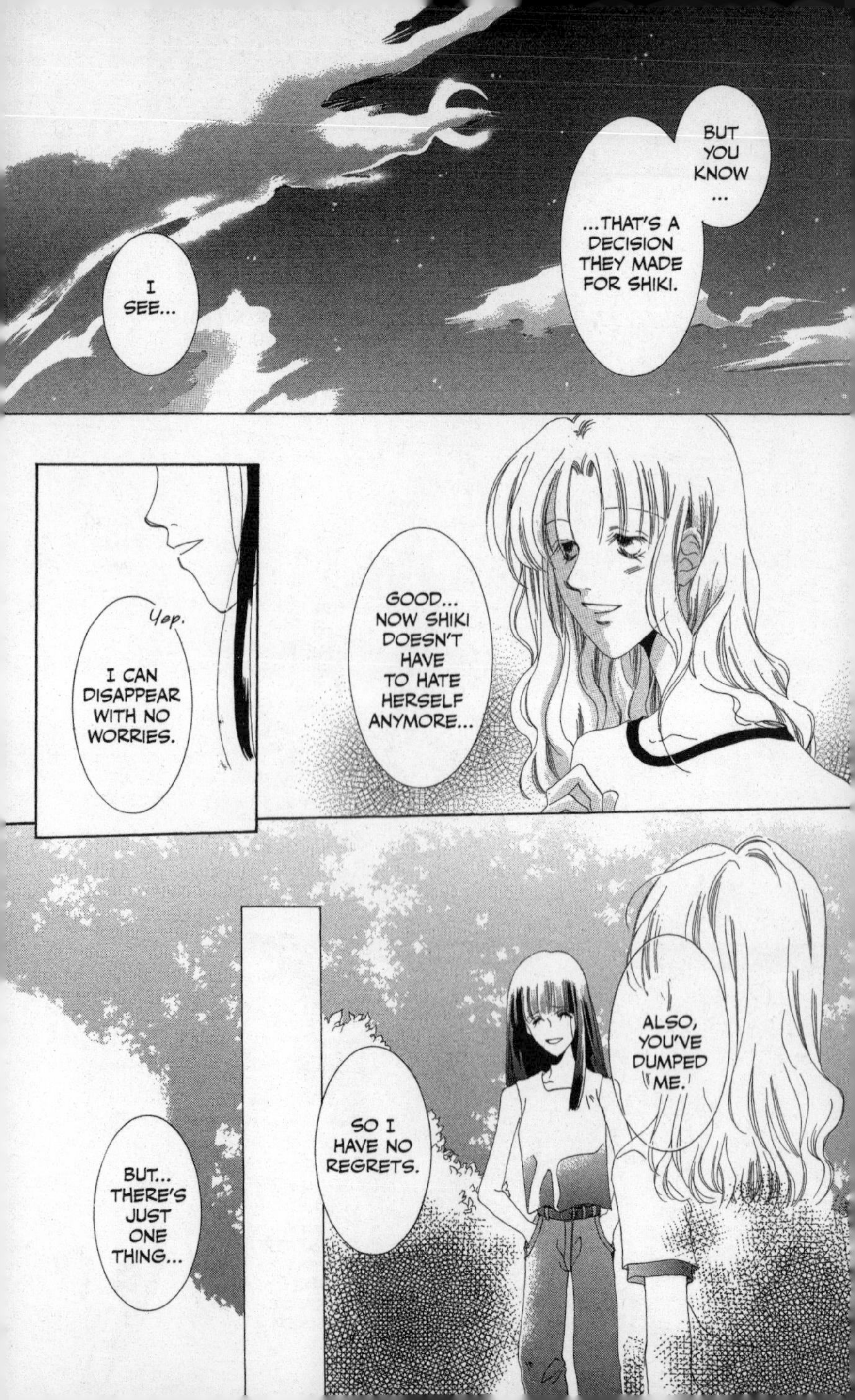
BUT YOU KNOW ...
...THAT'S A DECISION THEY MADE FOR SHIKI.
I SEE...
GOOD... NOW SHIKI DOESN'T HAVE TO HATE HERSELF ANYMORE...
Yep.
I CAN DISAPPEAR WITH NO WORRIES.
ALSO, YOU'VE DUMPED ME.
SO I HAVE NO REGRETS.
BUT... THERE'S JUST ONE THING...

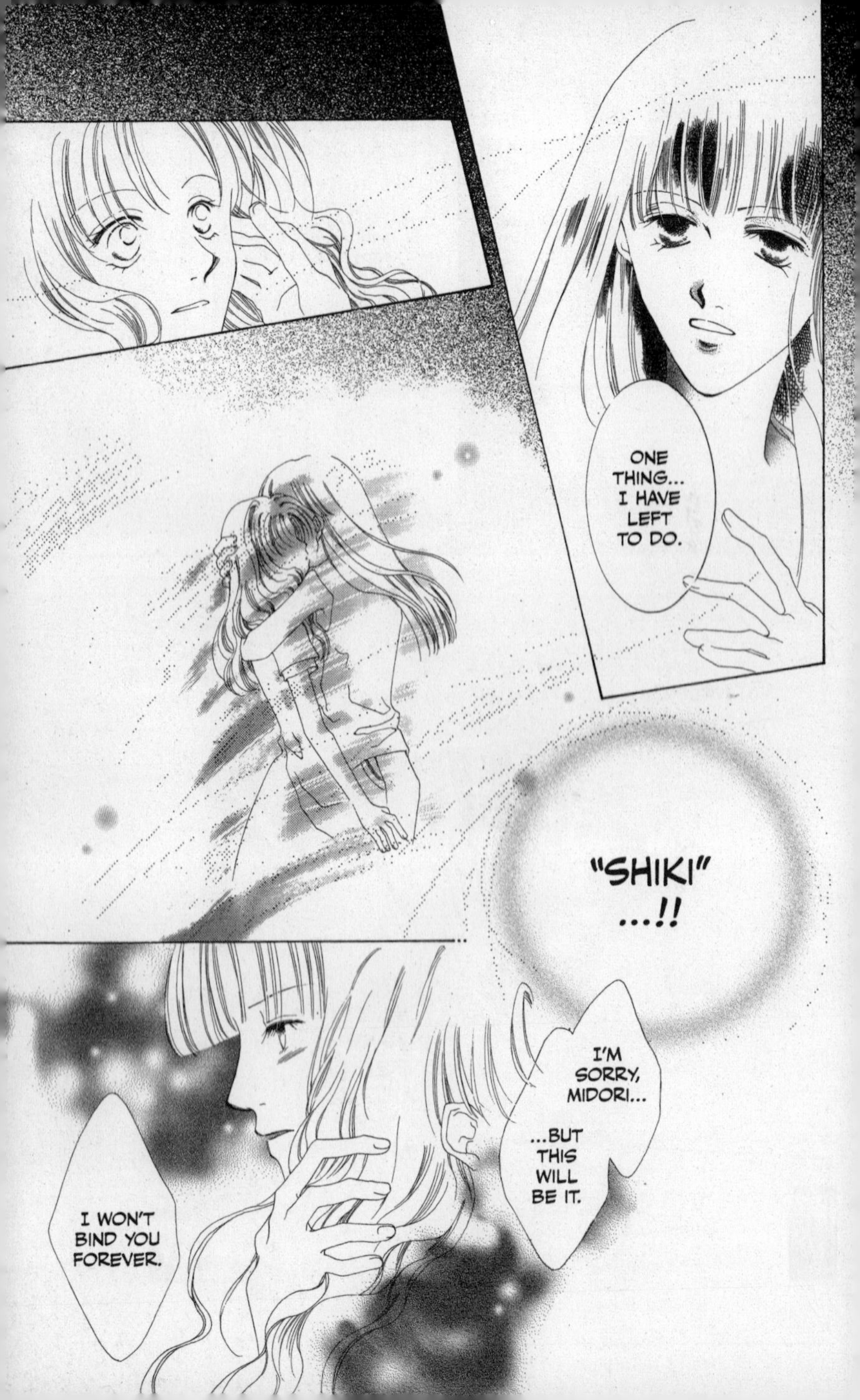
ONE THING... I HAVE LEFT TO DO.
"SHIKI" ...!!
I'M SORRY, MIDORI...
...BUT THIS WILL BE IT.
I WON'T BIND YOU FOREVER.

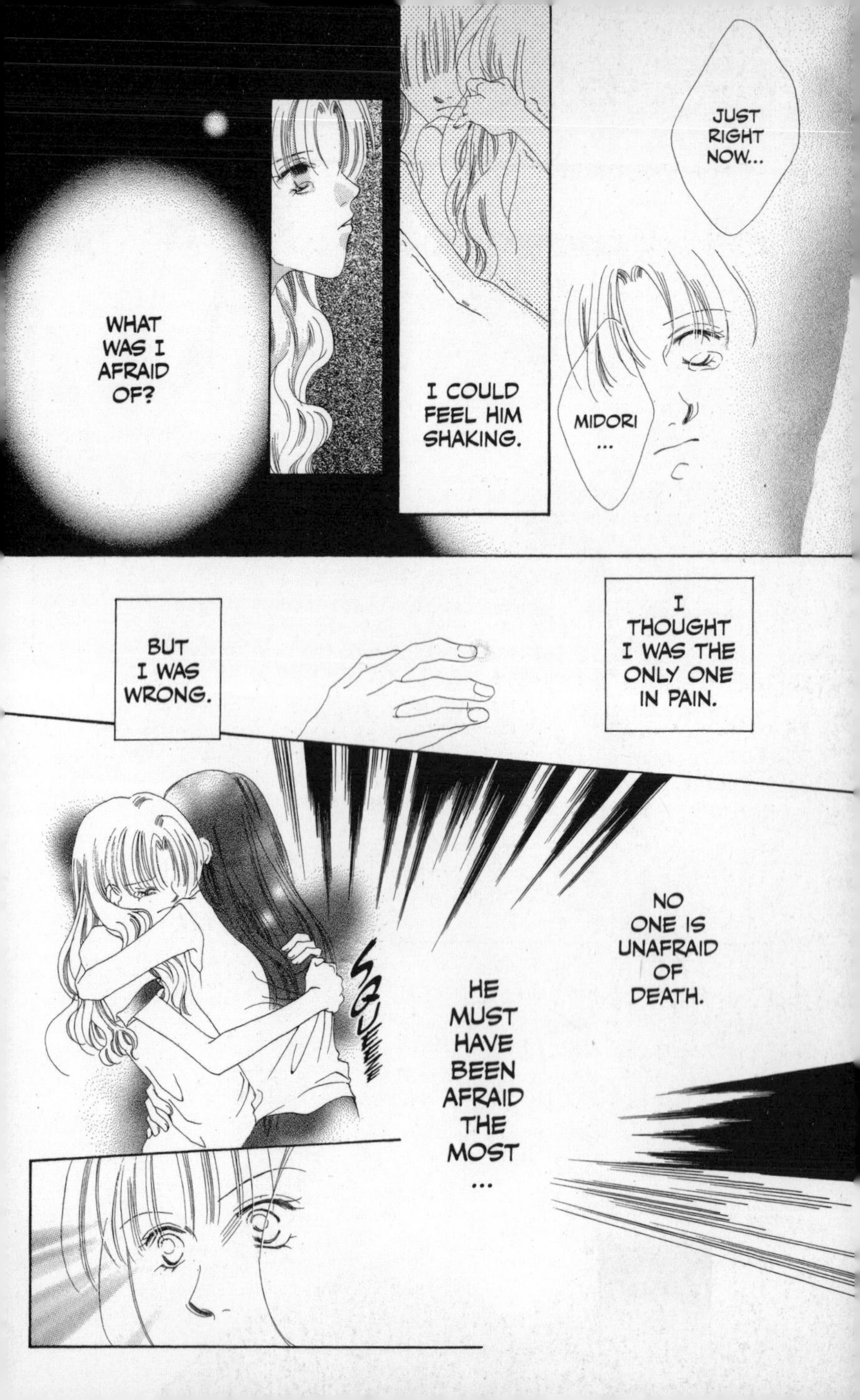
JUST RIGHT NOW...
MIDORI ...
I COULD FEEL HIM SHAKING.
WHAT WAS I AFRAID OF?
I THOUGHT I WAS THE ONLY ONE IN PAIN.
BUT I WAS WRONG.
NO ONE IS UNAFRAID OF DEATH.
HE MUST HAVE BEEN AFRAID THE MOST ...

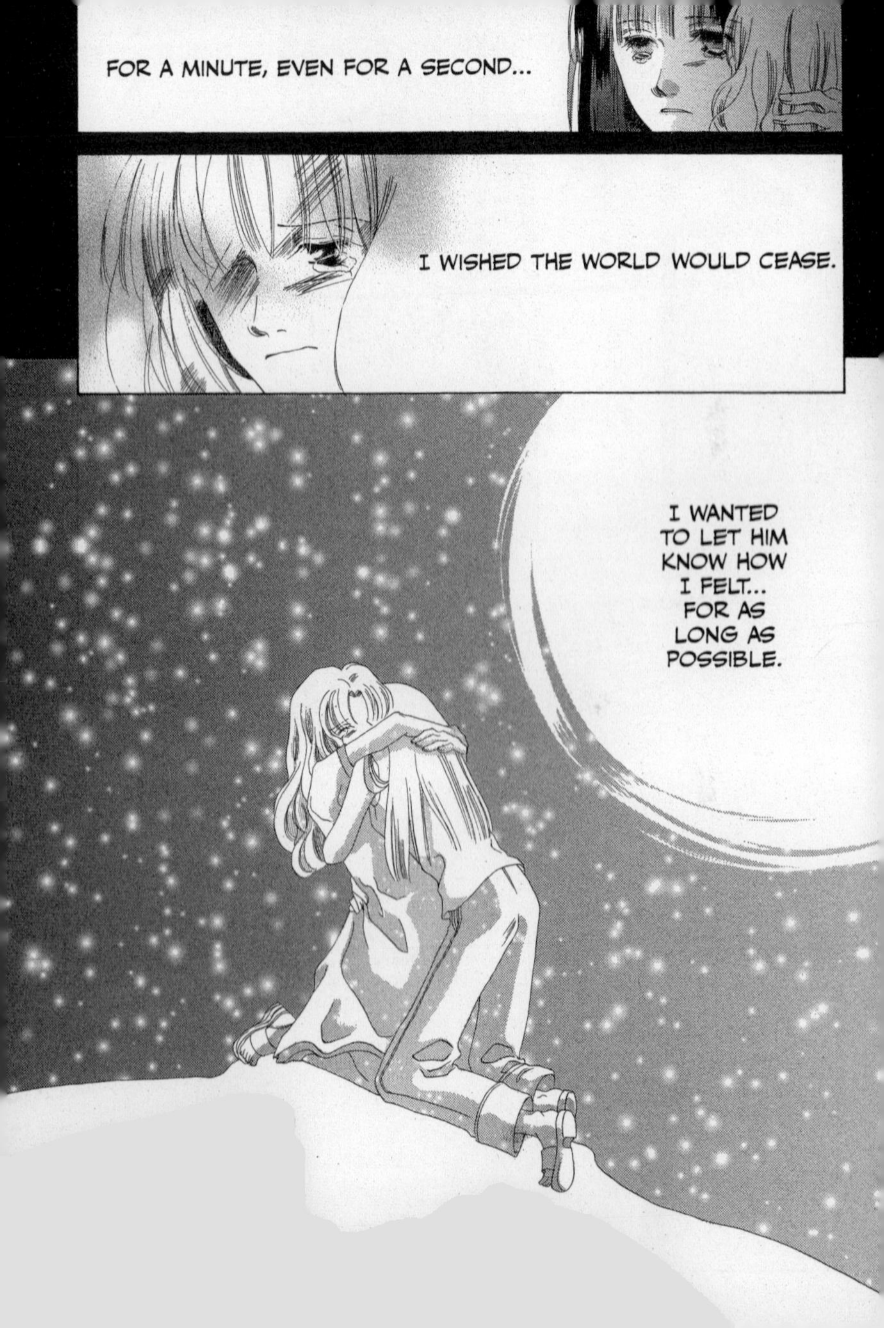
FOR A MINUTE, EVEN FOR A SECOND...
I WISHED THE WORLD WOULD CEASE.
I WANTED TO LET HIM KNOW HOW I FELT... FOR AS LONG AS POSSIBLE.

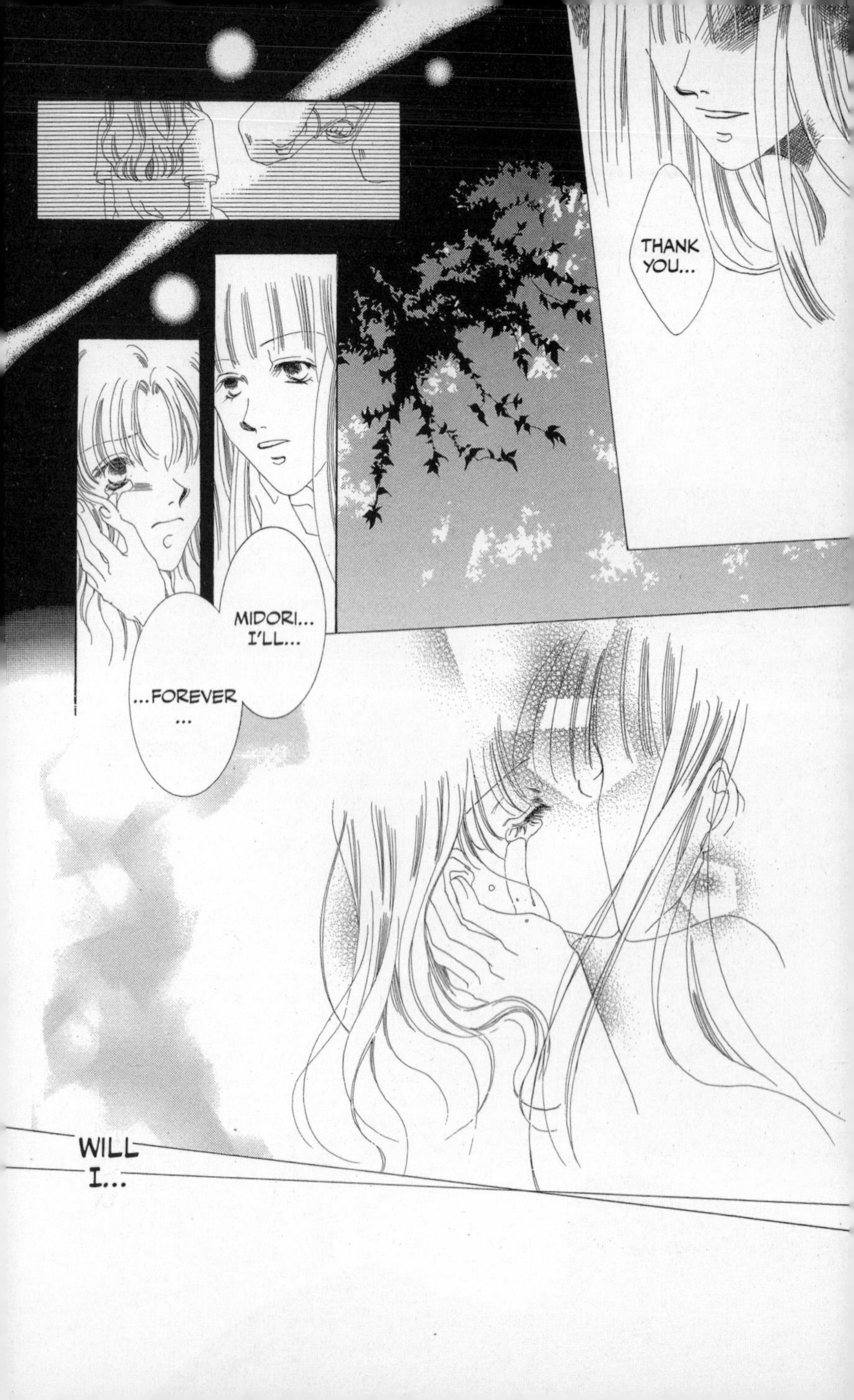
THANK YOU...
MIDORI... I'LL...
...FOREVER ...
WILL I...

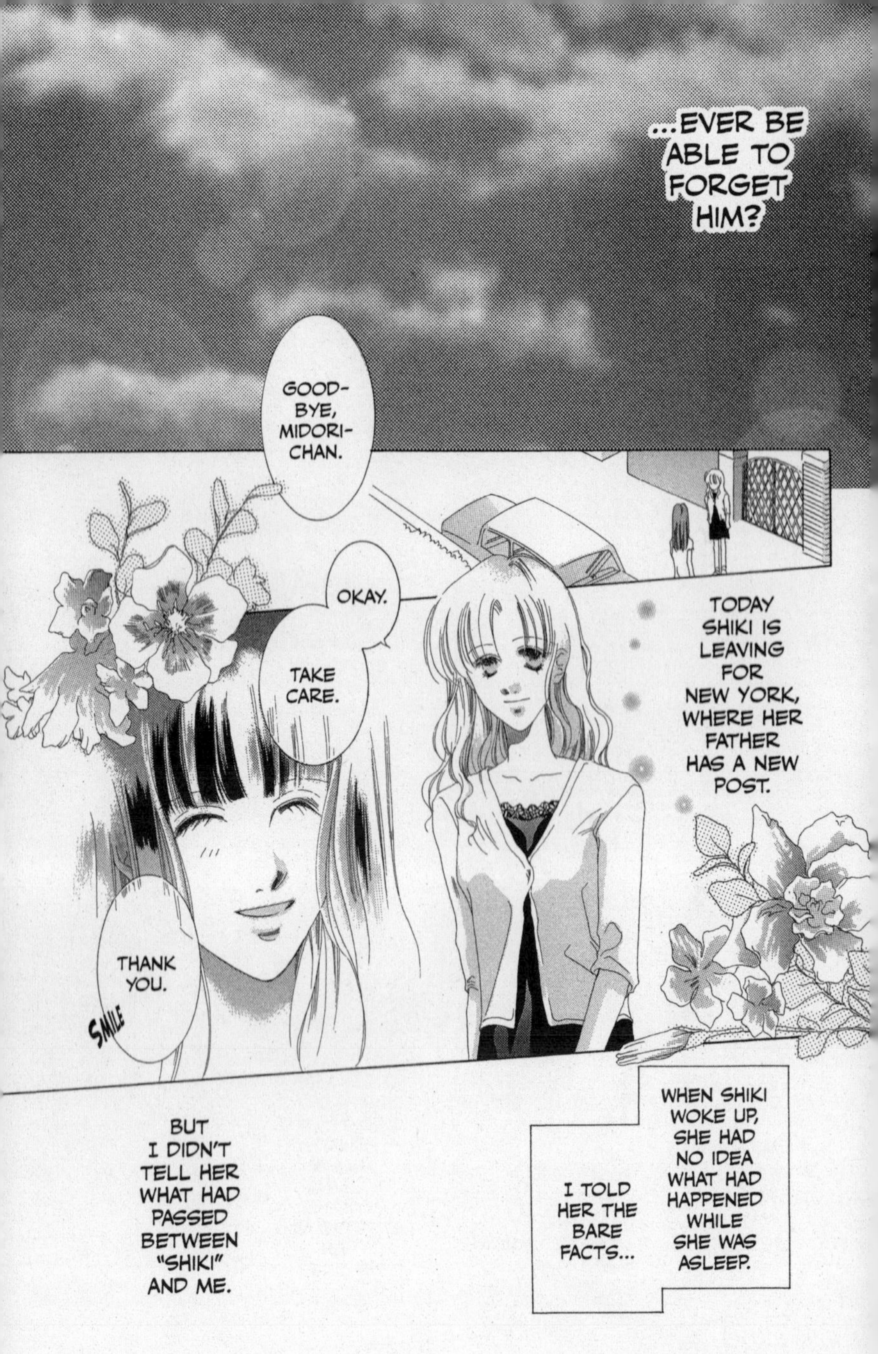
...EVER BE ABLE TO FORGET HIM?
GOOD-BYE, MIDORI-CHAN.
TODAY SHIKI IS LEAVING FOR NEW YORK, WHERE HER FATHER HAS A NEW POST.
OKAY.
TAKE CARE.
THANK YOU.
SMILE
WHEN SHIKI WOKE UP, SHE HAD NO IDEA WHAT HAD HAPPENED WHILE SHE WAS ASLEEP.
I TOLD HER THE BARE FACTS...
BUT I DIDN'T TELL HER WHAT HAD PASSED BETWEEN "SHIKI" AND ME.

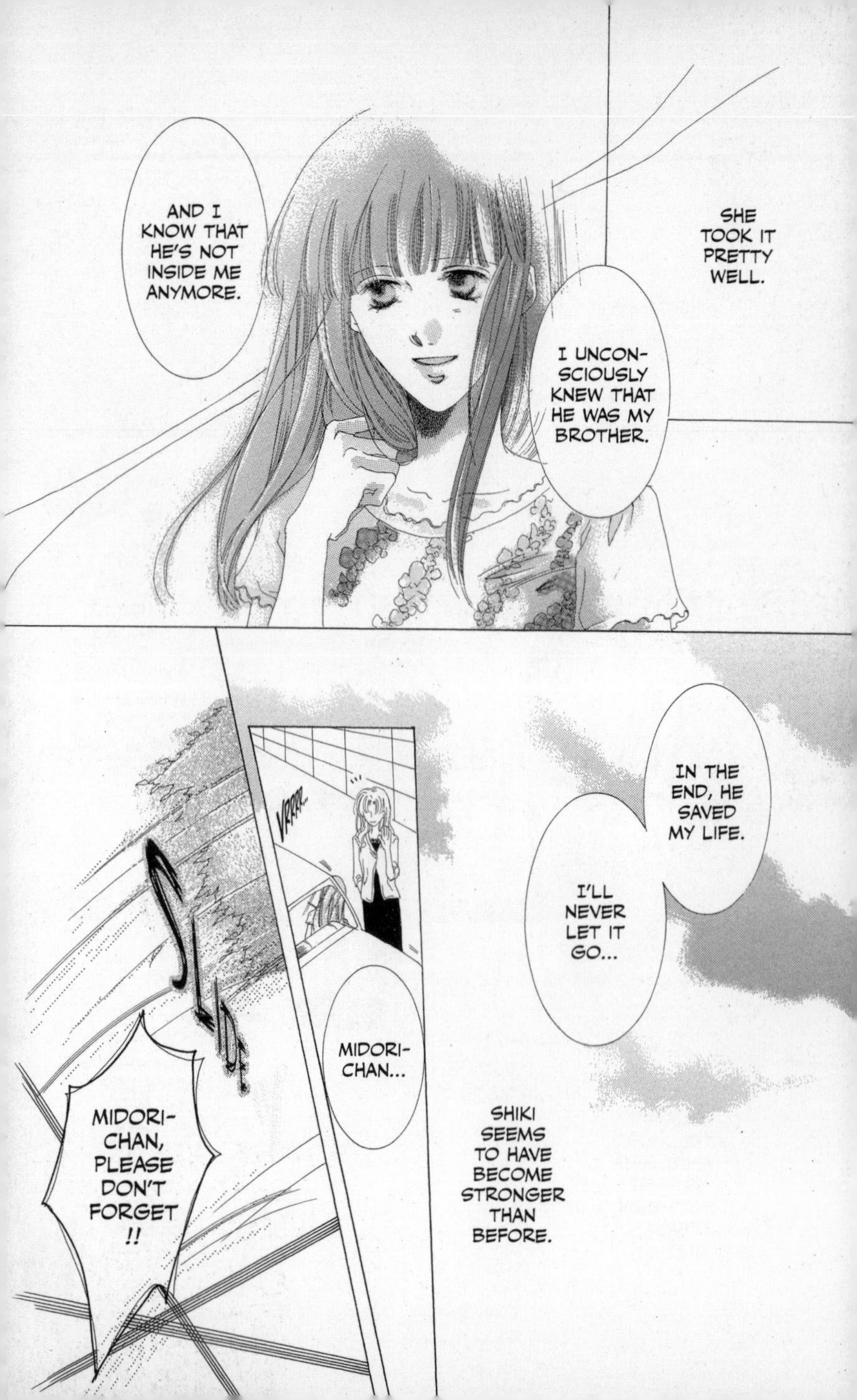
SHE TOOK IT PRETTY WELL.
I UNCON-SCIOUSLY KNEW THAT HE WAS MY BROTHER.
AND I KNOW THAT HE'S NOT INSIDE ME ANYMORE.
IN THE END, HE SAVED MY LIFE.
I'LL NEVER LET IT GO...
SHIKI SEEMS TO HAVE BECOME STRONGER THAN BEFORE.
MIDORI-CHAN...
VRRRR...
MIDORI-CHAN, PLEASE DON'T FORGET !!

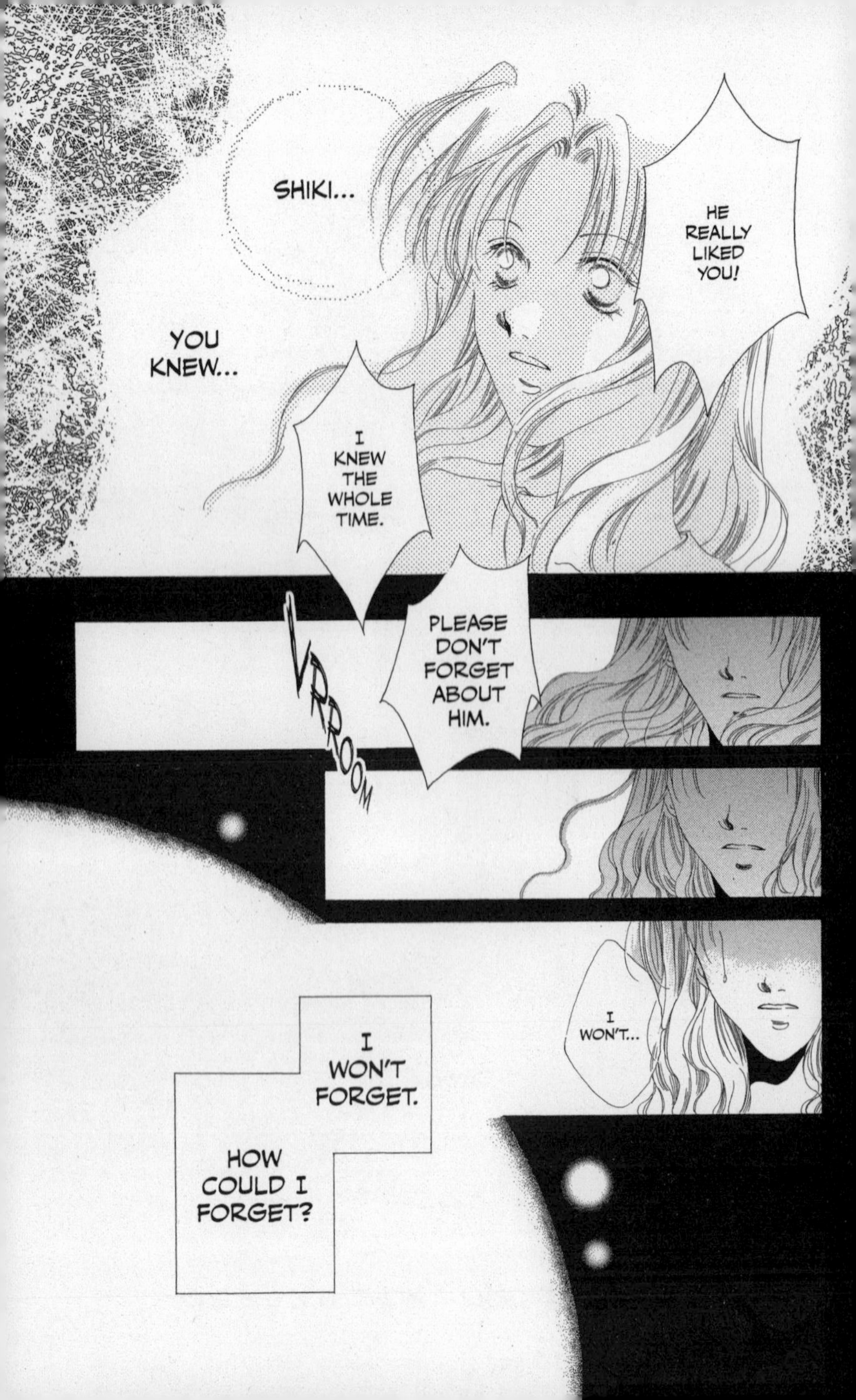
HE REALLY LIKED YOU!
SHIKI...
YOU KNEW...
I KNEW THE WHOLE TIME.
PLEASE DON'T FORGET ABOUT HIM.
VRROOM
I WON'T...
I WON'T FORGET.
HOW COULD I FORGET?

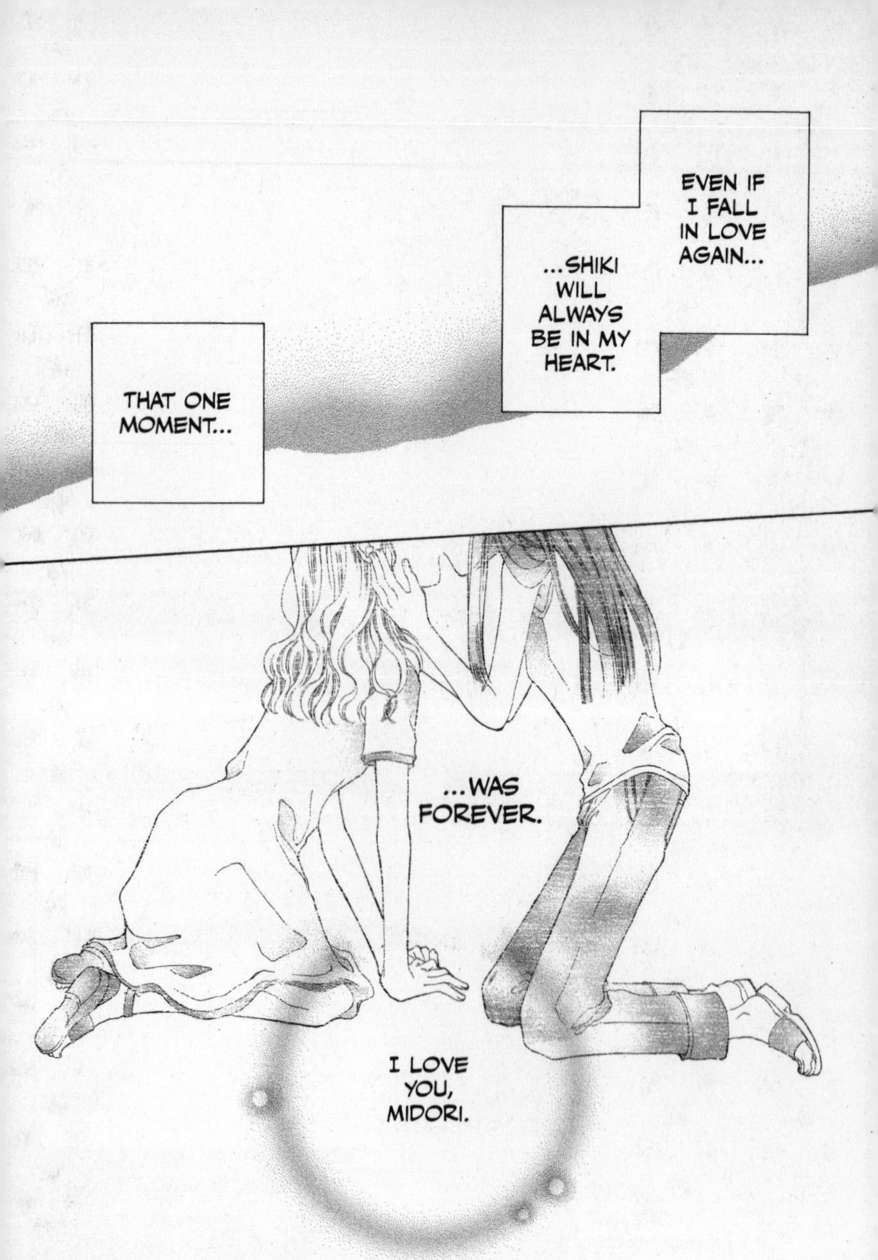
EVEN IF I FALL IN LOVE AGAIN...
...SHIKI WILL ALWAYS BE IN MY HEART.
THAT ONE MOMENT...
...WAS FOREVER.
I LOVE YOU, MIDORI.

A ROMANCE OF ONE MOMENT / THE END

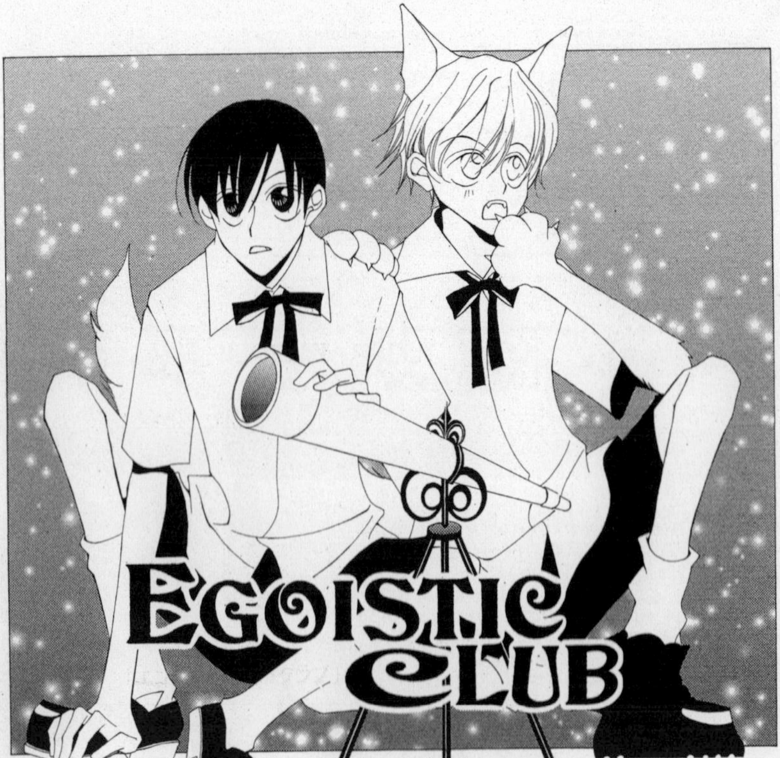
EGOISTIC CLUB

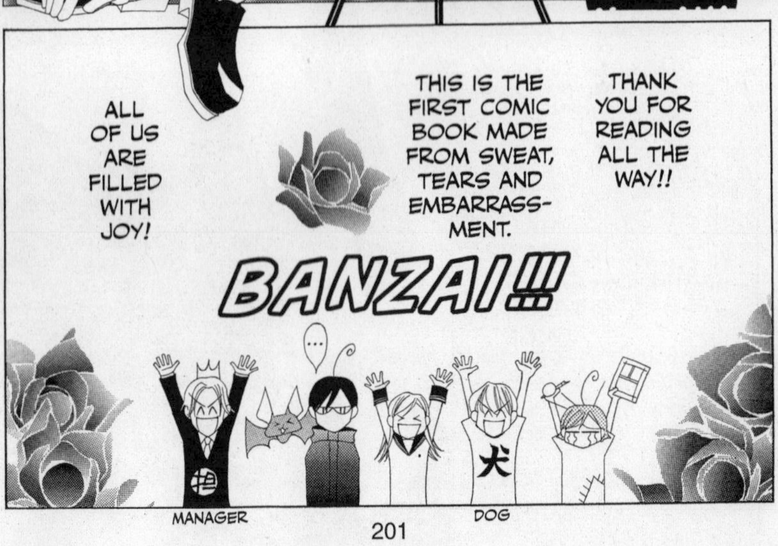
THANK YOU FOR READING ALL THE WAY!!
THIS IS THE FIRST COMIC BOOK MADE FROM SWEAT, TEARS AND EMBARRASS-MENT.
ALL OF US ARE FILLED WITH JOY!
BANZAI!!!
...
MANAGER
DOG

THE SUMMER OF 2000, HATORI HAD AN IDEA.

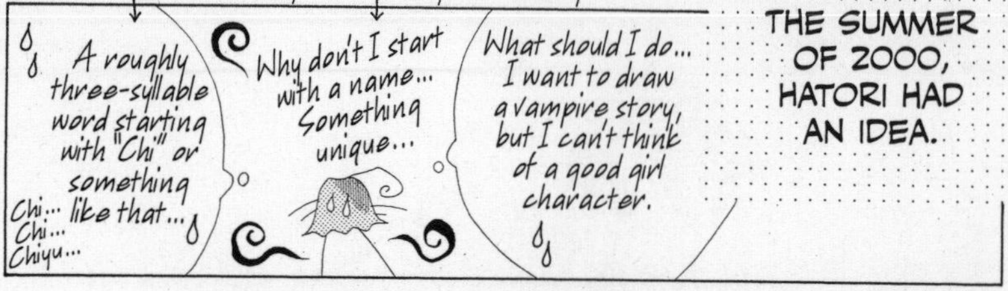

Negative thinking
What should I do... I want to draw a vampire story, but I can't think of a good girl character.
Why don't I start with a name... Something unique...
Bad thinking
A roughly three-syllable word starting with "Chi" or something like that...
Chi... Chi... Chiyu...

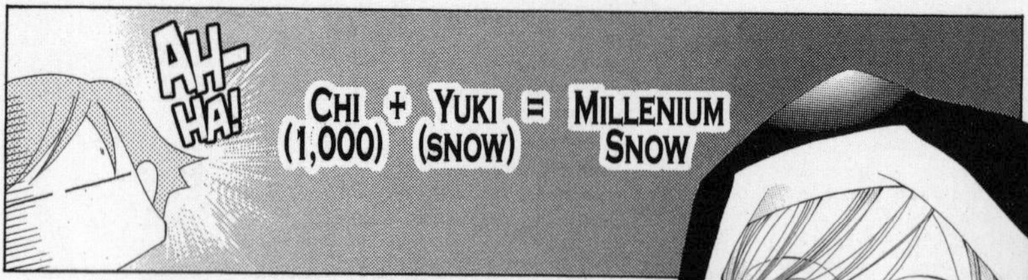

AH-HA!
CHI (1,000) + YUKI (SNOW) = MILLENIUM SNOW

THAT'S RIGHT! THIS STORY WAS BORN OF HER NAME.

SORRY IF I CONFUSED ANY OF YOU BY HAVING CHIYUKI BE SO ENERGETIC AFTER SHE WAS DISCHARGED FROM THE HOSPITAL, BUT IT WAS STILL THE SAME CHARACTER FROM MY POINT OF VIEW.

I tried to think of how her character would act after getting well.

I heard that some people actually have the name Chiyuki, and that surprised me. Personally, it's my favorite name.

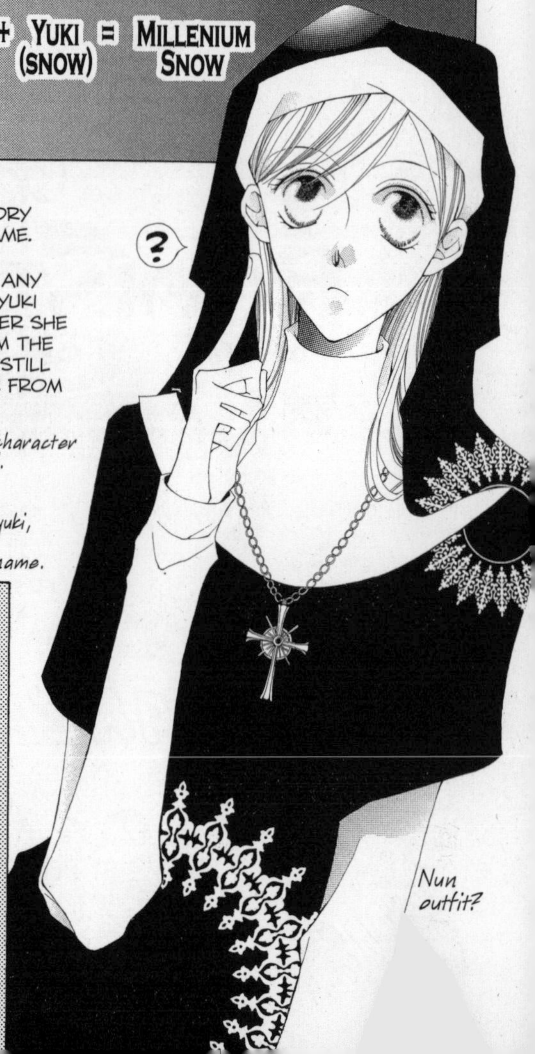

?
Nun outfit?

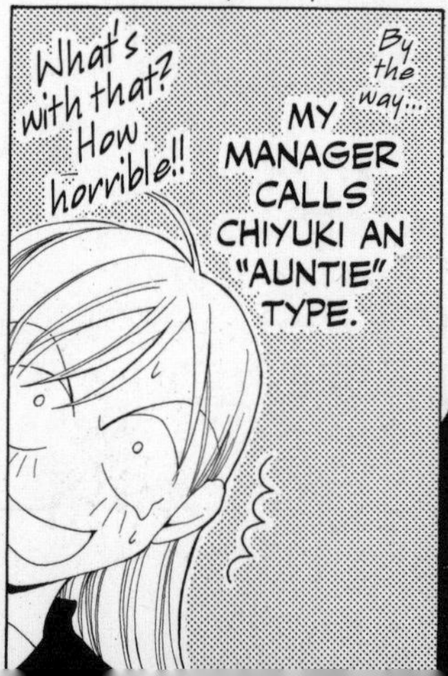

By the way...
MY MANAGER CALLS CHIYUKI AN "AUNTIE" TYPE.
What's with that? How horrible!!

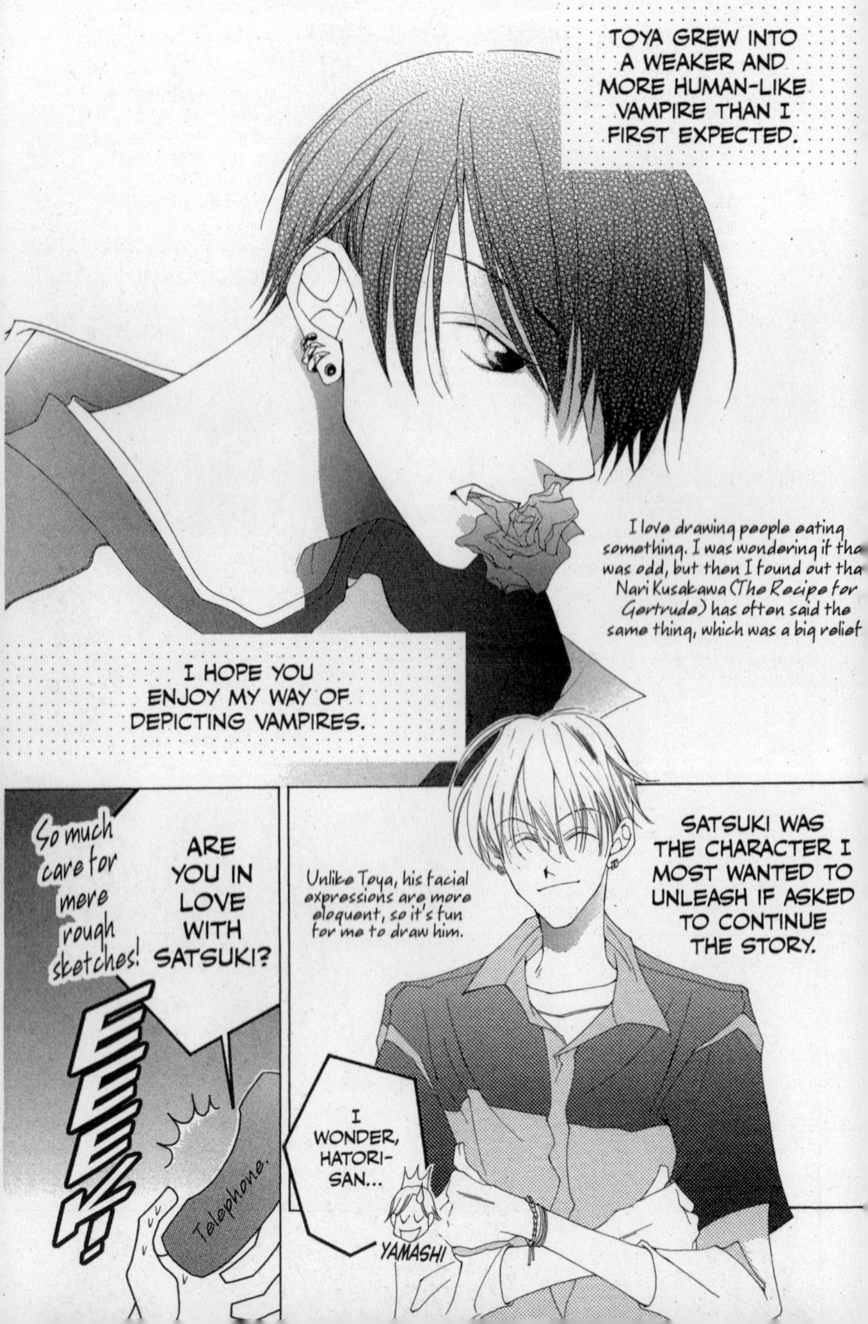
TOYA GREW INTO A WEAKER AND MORE HUMAN-LIKE VAMPIRE THAN I FIRST EXPECTED.
I love drawing people eating something. I was wondering if tha was odd, but then I found out tha Nari Kusakawa (The Recipe for Gertrude) has often said the same thing, which was a big relief
I HOPE YOU ENJOY MY WAY OF DEPICTING VAMPIRES.
SATSUKI WAS THE CHARACTER I MOST WANTED TO UNLEASH IF ASKED TO CONTINUE THE STORY.
Unlike Toya, his facial expressions are more eloquent, so it's fun for me to draw him.
I WONDER, HATORI-SAN...
YAMASHI
ARE YOU IN LOVE WITH SATSUKI?
So much care for mere rough sketches!
EEEK!
Telephone.

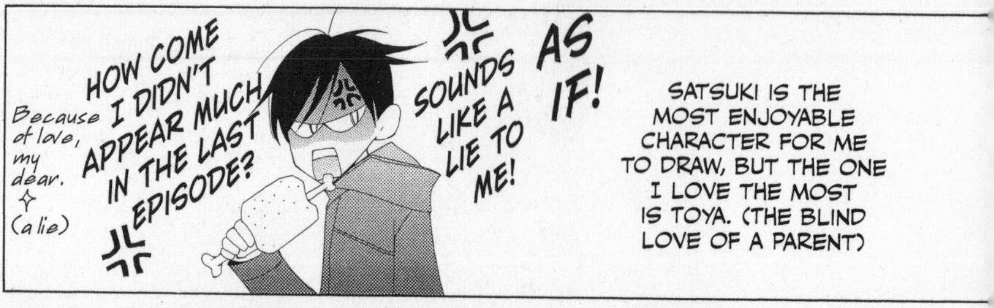
SATSUKI IS THE MOST ENJOYABLE CHARACTER FOR ME TO DRAW, BUT THE ONE I LOVE THE MOST IS TOYA. (THE BLIND LOVE OF A PARENT)
AS IF!
SOUNDS LIKE A LIE TO ME!
HOW COME I DIDN'T APPEAR MUCH IN THE LAST EPISODE?
Because of love, my dear. ✧ (a lie)

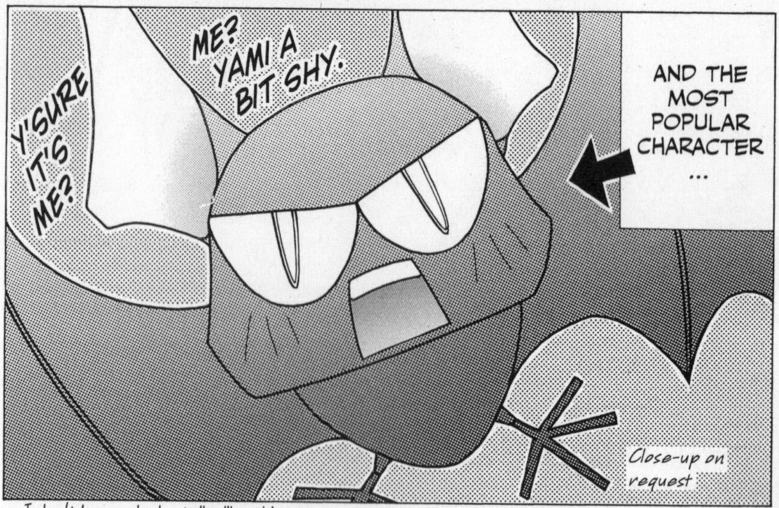
AND THE MOST POPULAR CHARACTER ...
ME? YAMI A BIT SHY.
Y'SURE IT'S ME?
Close-up on request

I don't know why he talks like this.

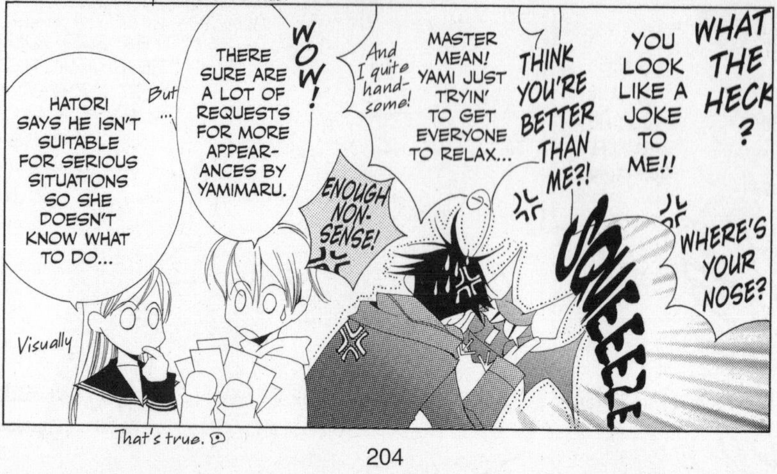
WHAT THE HECK?
YOU LOOK LIKE A JOKE TO ME!!
WHERE'S YOUR NOSE?
THINK YOU'RE BETTER THAN ME?!
SQUEEEEE
MASTER MEAN! YAMI JUST TRYIN' TO GET EVERYONE TO RELAX...
And I quite handsome!
ENOUGH NON-SENSE!
WOW!
THERE SURE ARE A LOT OF REQUESTS FOR MORE APPEAR-ANCES BY YAMIMARU.
But ...
HATORI SAYS HE ISN'T SUITABLE FOR SERIOUS SITUATIONS SO SHE DOESN'T KNOW WHAT TO DO...
Visually

That's true.

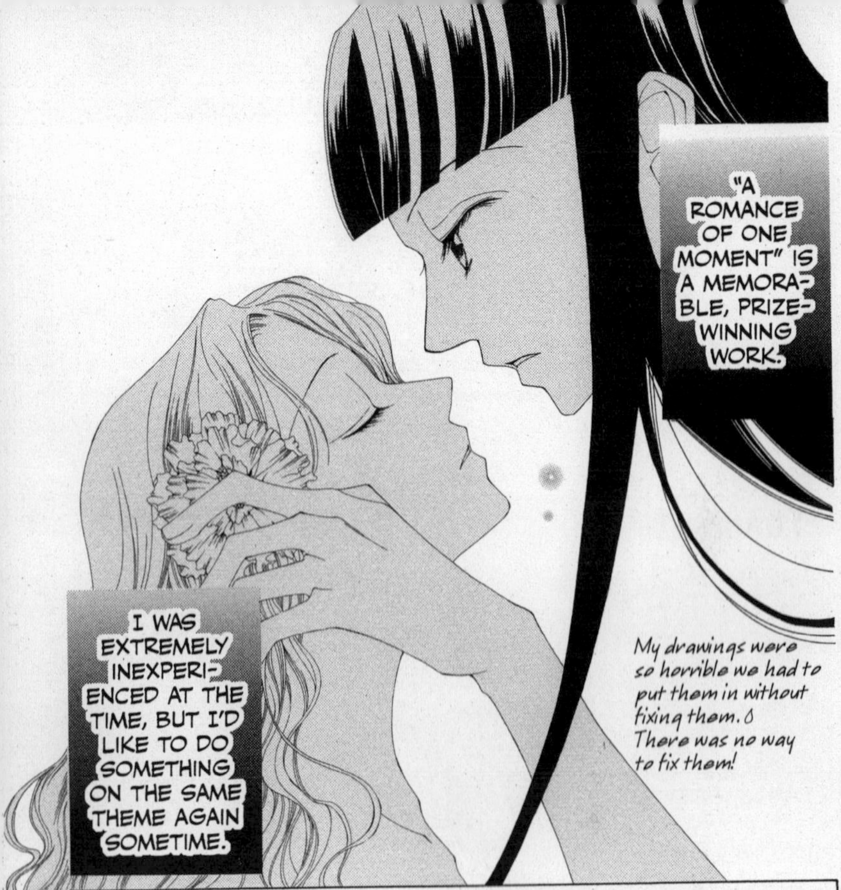
"A ROMANCE OF ONE MOMENT" IS A MEMORABLE, PRIZE-WINNING WORK.
My drawings were so horrible we had to put them in without fixing them. ◊ There was no way to fix them!
I WAS EXTREMELY INEXPERIENCED AT THE TIME, BUT I'D LIKE TO DO SOMETHING ON THE SAME THEME AGAIN SOMETIME.

EVERY DAY I THINK ABOUT HOW TO CREATE INTERESTING STORIES.

THERE IS A LOT TO DO, BUT I'M THANKFUL FOR HAVING A GOAL AND FOR BEING GIVEN A PLACE TO COMMENT UPON IT.

I'LL DO MY BEST TO MAKE YOU WANT TO READ MY WORK AGAIN! ♡

I READ ALL YOUR LETTERS WITH CARE.
PLEASE SEND ME YOUR COMMENTS ON THIS MANGA.

BISCO HATORI C/O SHOJO BEAT
VIZ MEDIA
P.O. BOX 77010
SAN FRANCISCO, CA 94107

Special Thanks!!

YAMASHITA
ALL THE EDITORS
*
EVERYONE
INVOLVED IN
PUBLISHING
THIS BOOK
*
FAMILY, FRIENDS
*
HIROMI KAMIYA
AZUMA SHIMAMURA
AYA AOMURA
RINA HASEGAWA
*
MECA TANAKA
*
NORIKO NAGAHAMA
*
AND ALL YOU
READERS!

2001. Nov.

BISCO.H

Glossary

While the appeal of the vampire needs no help to cross the language barrier, here are a few terms that could use a little extra explaining.

Chiyuki Matsuoka 千雪 松岡
The kanji in her first name mean "one thousand" and "snow."

Toya Kano トウヤ (冬哉) 叶
The first kanji in his last name means "winter."

Yamimaru 闇丸
The first kanji in his name means "dark" and the second is a common ending for boys' names.

Page 5, panel 1: Eika General Hospital
Eika means glory, prosperity, and other good things. It's a name of hope for a place often equated with despair.

Page 25, panel 7: Odaiba
An artificial island in Tokyo Bay that began as part of six fortresses built in 1853 to protect Tokyo from attack by sea. In the 1980s and early '90s Odaiba was rebuilt to be a showcase of futuristic living, but was largely abandoned when the economy collapsed. Today the district is a popular destination for tourists and Tokyo residents, with many shopping malls, a hot springs, a beach, a science museum, a giant Ferris wheel, and more.

Page 57, panel 5: Ume-konbu
Literally "plum-kelp," these are popular plum—and kelp—flavored Japanese snacks.

Page 93, panel 1: A big weed
Refers to the Japanese *udoka* (*Aralia cordata*), a large leafy tree that is more like an overgrown weed. It is sometimes used in Japan as a symbol for big idiots.

Page 138, panel 5: Ash
An indie Japanese band.

Page 141, panel 4: Koshi-hikari rice
A very popular, expensive brand of Japanese rice. *Koshi* means "surpass" and *hikari* means "bright."

Page 171, panel 2: "Shiki"
In the original Japanese, Shiki is spelled with kanji and "Shiki" is spelled with katakana.

Shojo Beat

Millennium Snow

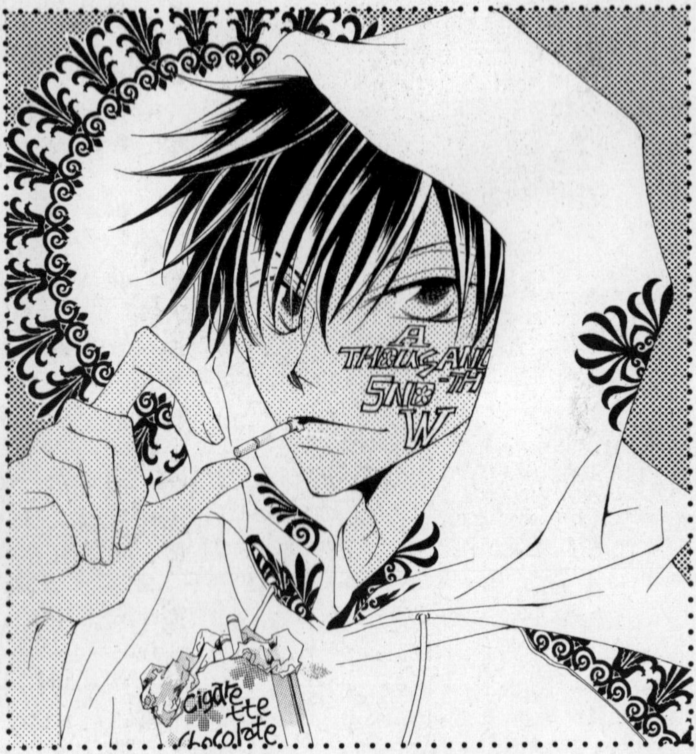
A THOUSAND-TH SNOW
Cigarette chocolate

Vol. 2 Story & Art by **Bisco Hatori**

Table of Contents

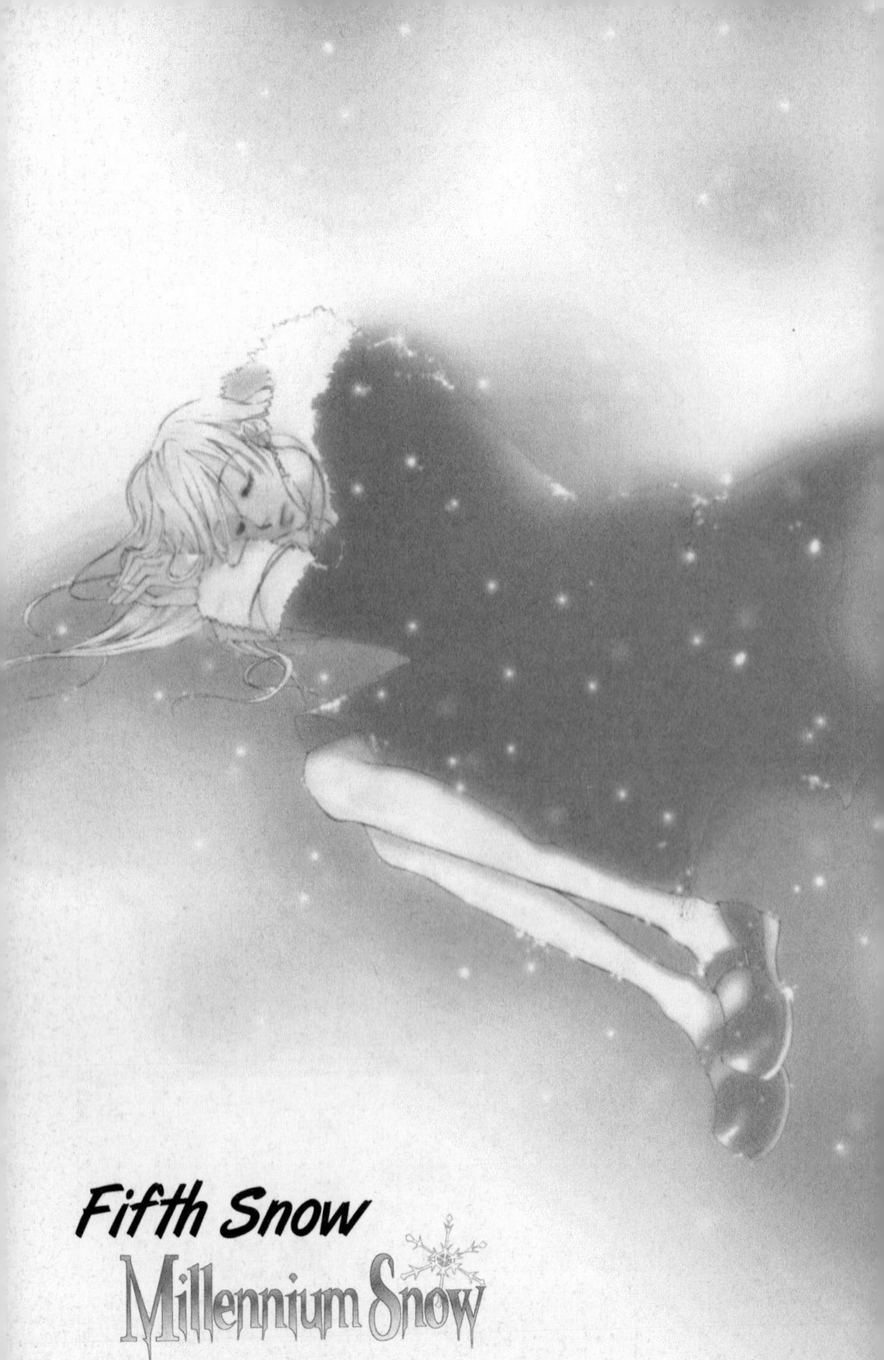

Fifth Snow

Millennium Snow

The Night Before Departure

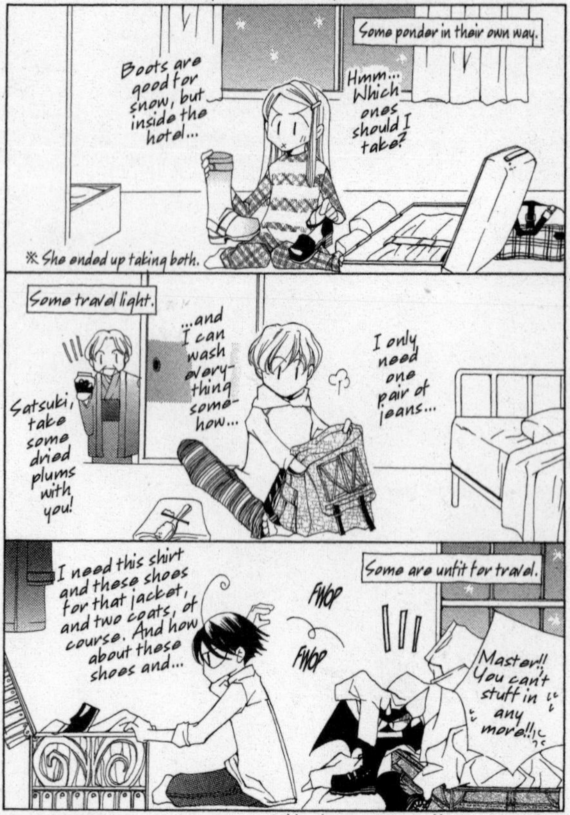
Some ponder in their own way.
Hmm... Which ones should I take?
Boots are good for snow, but inside the hotel...
※ She ended up taking both.
Some travel light.
I only need one pair of jeans...
...and I can wash everything somehow...
Satsuki, take some dried plums with you!
Some are unfit for travel.
Master!! You can't stuff in any more!!
FWOP
FWOP
I need this shirt and these shoes for that jacket, and two coats, of course. And how about these shoes and...

※ Yamimaru went stuffed in a handbag.

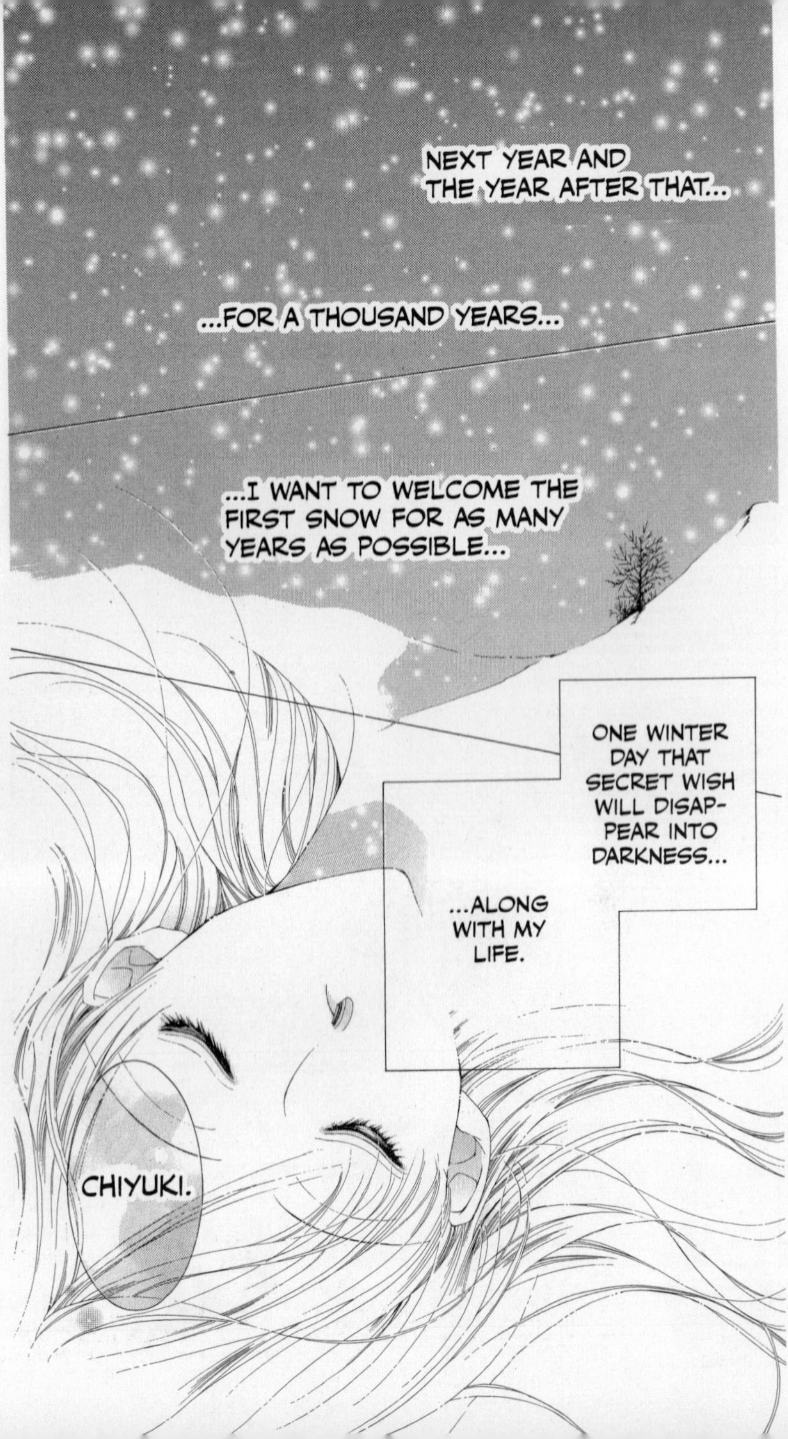
NEXT YEAR AND THE YEAR AFTER THAT...
...FOR A THOUSAND YEARS...
...I WANT TO WELCOME THE FIRST SNOW FOR AS MANY YEARS AS POSSIBLE...
ONE WINTER DAY THAT SECRET WISH WILL DISAPPEAR INTO DARKNESS...
...ALONG WITH MY LIFE.
CHIYUKI.

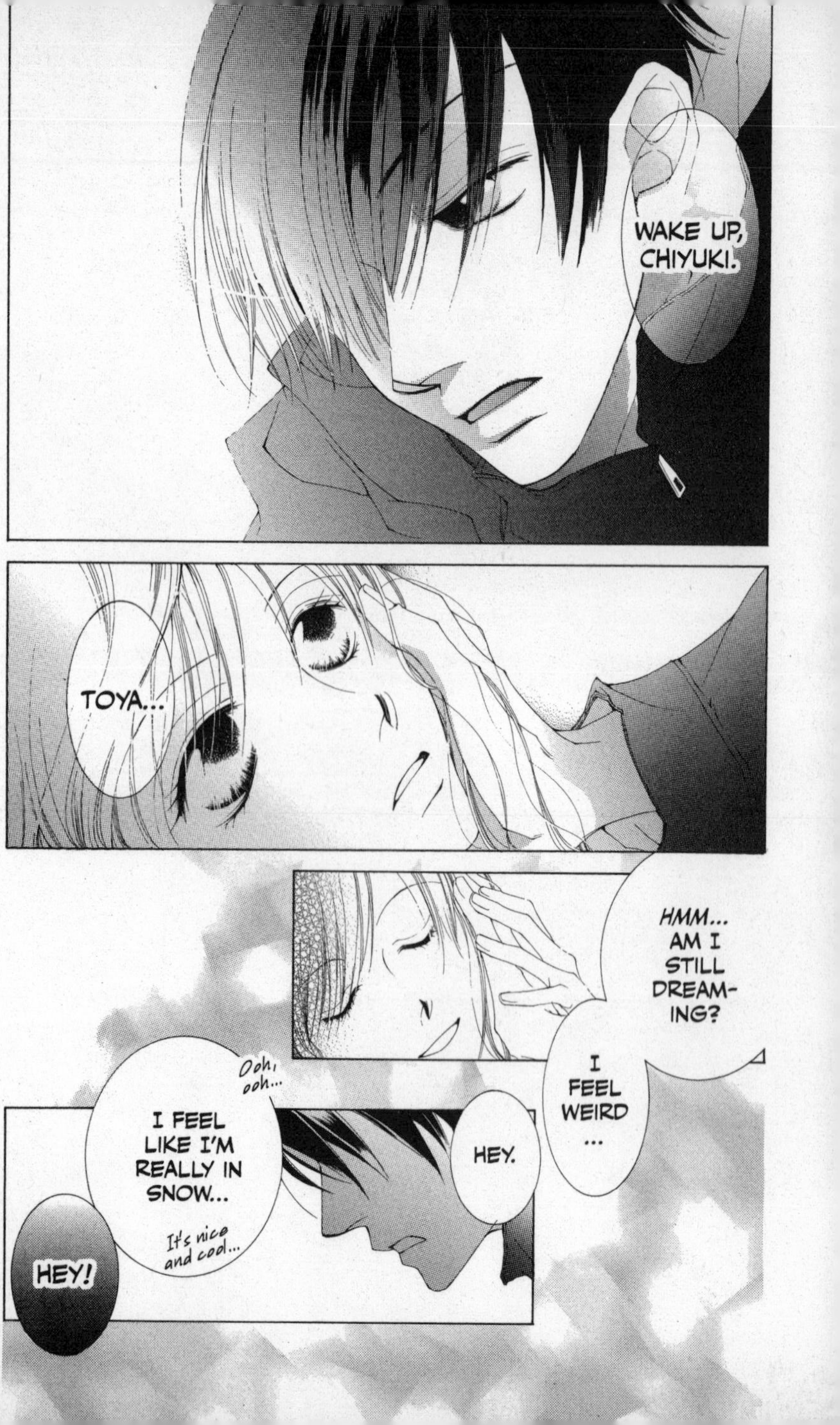
WAKE UP, CHIYUKI.
TOYA...
HMM... AM I STILL DREAMING?
I FEEL WEIRD...
Ooh, ooh...
I FEEL LIKE I'M REALLY IN SNOW...
It's nice and cool...
HEY.
HEY!

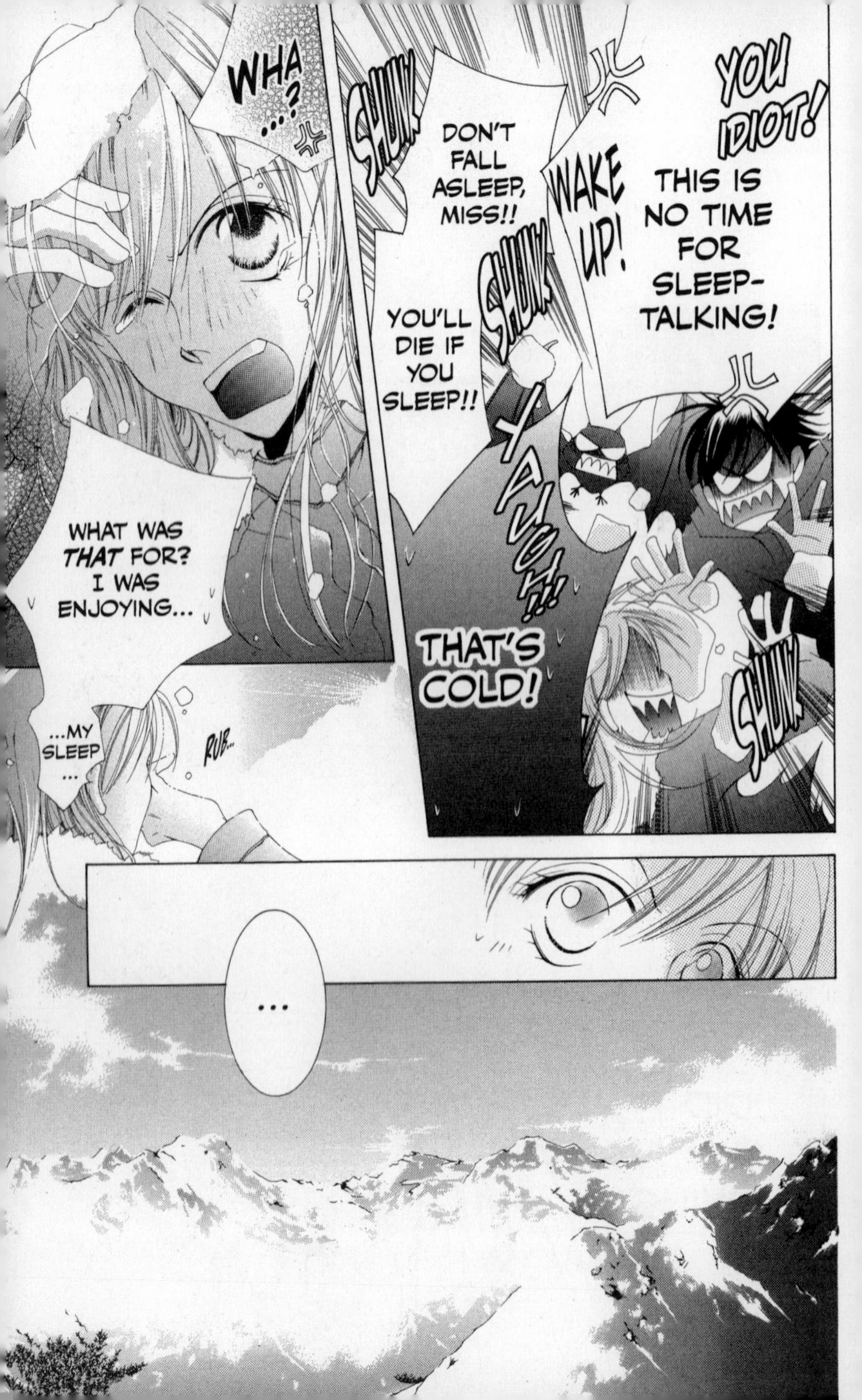
YOU IDIOT!
THIS IS NO TIME FOR SLEEP-TALKING!
WAKE UP!
SHUNK
DON'T FALL ASLEEP, MISS!!
SHUNK
YOU'LL DIE IF YOU SLEEP!!
SHUNK
YAOUCH!!
THAT'S COLD!
WHA...?
WHAT WAS *THAT* FOR? I WAS ENJOYING...
...MY SLEEP...
RUB...
...

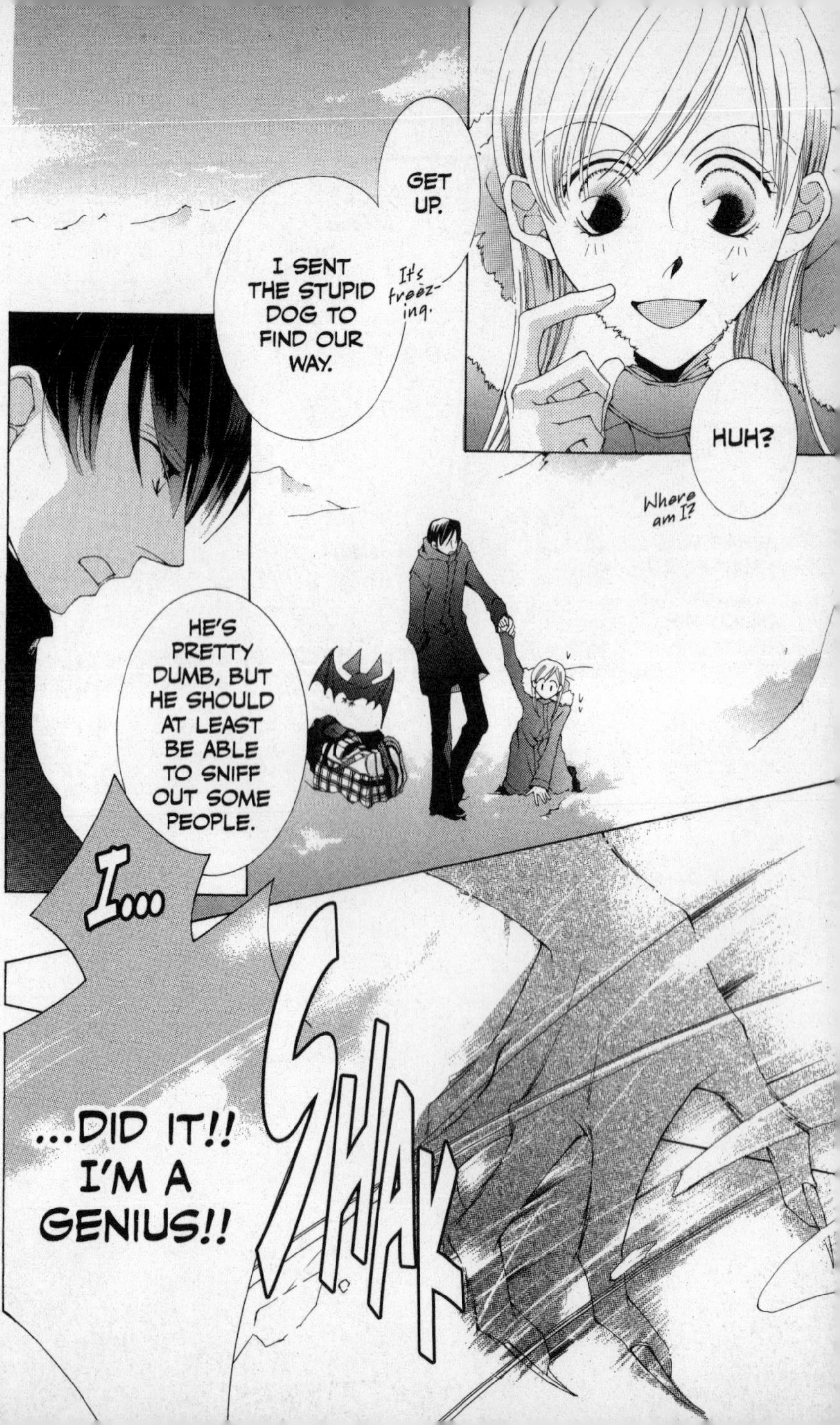
HUH?
Where am I?
GET UP.
It's freezing.
I SENT THE STUPID DOG TO FIND OUR WAY.
HE'S PRETTY DUMB, BUT HE SHOULD AT LEAST BE ABLE TO SNIFF OUT SOME PEOPLE.
I...
SHAK
...DID IT!! I'M A GENIUS!!

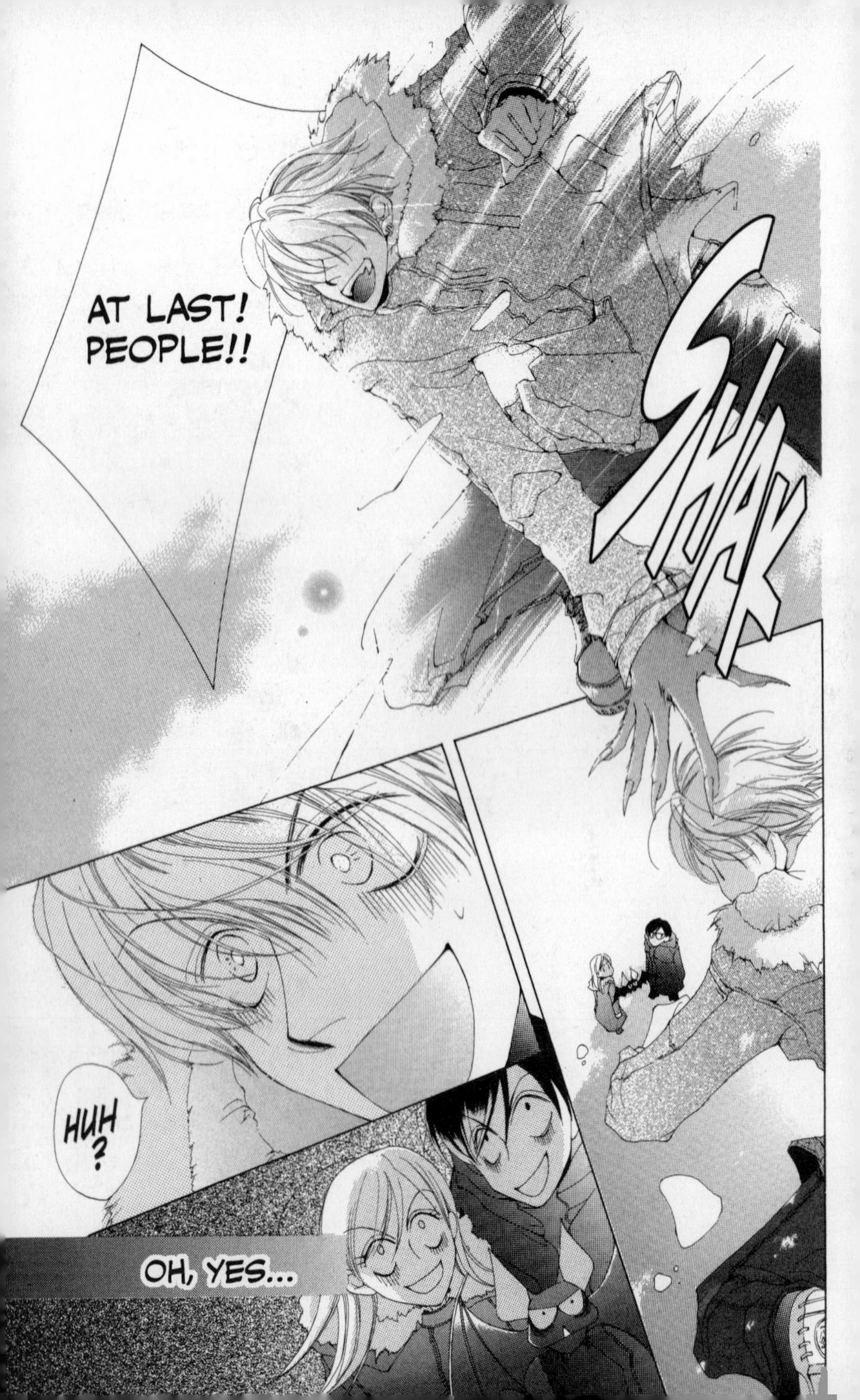
AT LAST! PEOPLE!!
SHAAK
HUH?
OH, YES...

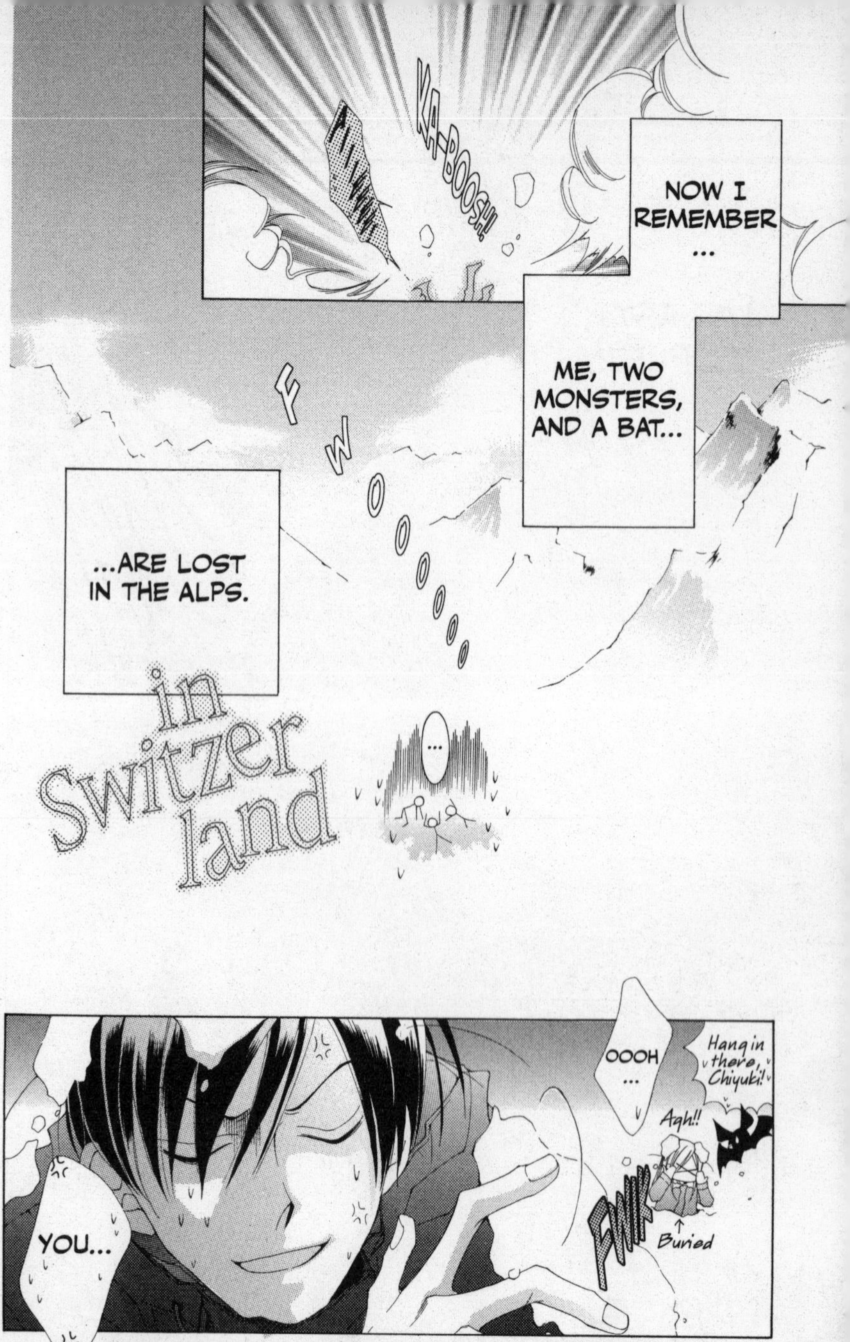
KA-BOOSH!!
NOW I REMEMBER ...
ME, TWO MONSTERS, AND A BAT...
FWOOOOOOO
...ARE LOST IN THE ALPS.
in Switzerland
...
Hang in there, Chiyuki!
OOOH ...
Agh!!
Buried
FWIK
YOU...

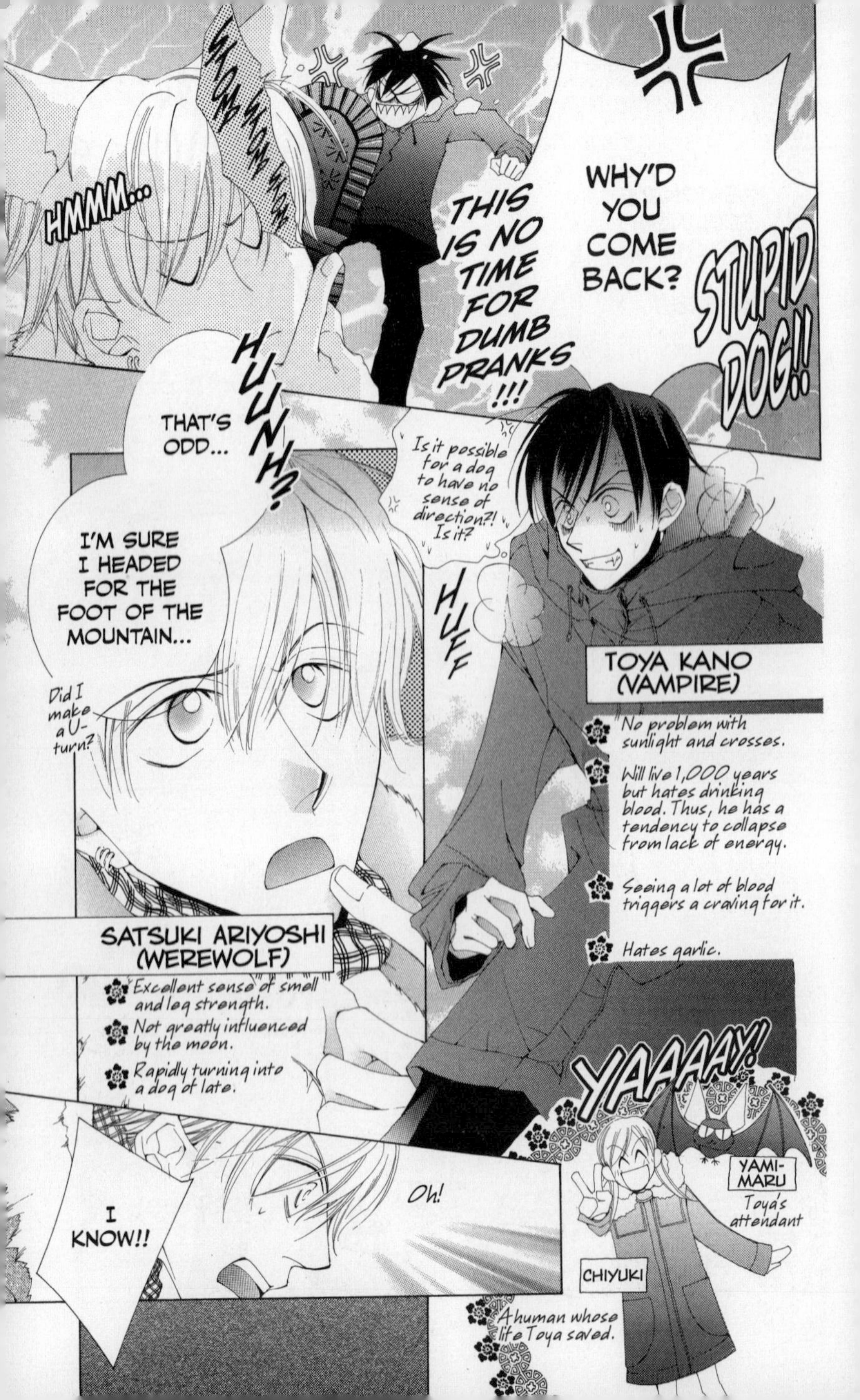
WHY'D YOU COME BACK?
STUPID DOG!!
THIS IS NO TIME FOR DUMB PRANKS!!!
HMMM...
Is it possible for a dog to have no sense of direction?! Is it?
HUFF
TOYA KANO (VAMPIRE)
No problem with sunlight and crosses.
Will live 1,000 years but hates drinking blood. Thus, he has a tendency to collapse from lack of energy.
Seeing a lot of blood triggers a craving for it.
Hates garlic.
HUUNH?
THAT'S ODD...
I'M SURE I HEADED FOR THE FOOT OF THE MOUNTAIN...
Did I make a U-turn?
SATSUKI ARIYOSHI (WEREWOLF)
Excellent sense of smell and leg strength.
Not greatly influenced by the moon.
Rapidly turning into a dog of late.
YAAAAY!
YAMI-MARU
Toya's attendant
CHIYUKI
A human whose life Toya saved.
Oh!
I KNOW!!

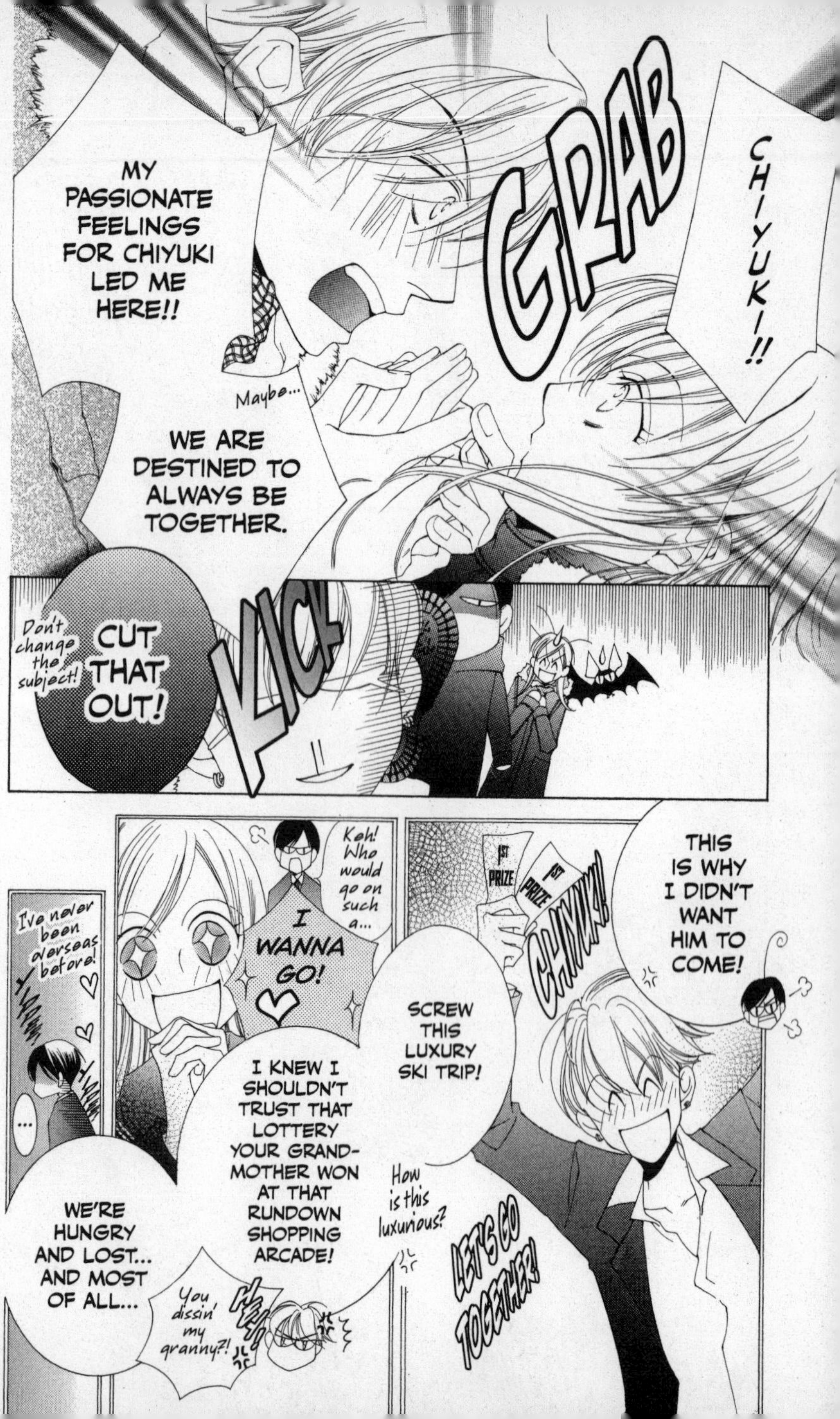
CHIYUKI!!
GRAB
MY PASSIONATE FEELINGS FOR CHIYUKI LED ME HERE!!
Maybe...
WE ARE DESTINED TO ALWAYS BE TOGETHER.
KICK
CUT THAT OUT!
Don't change the subject!
THIS IS WHY I DIDN'T WANT HIM TO COME!
1ST PRIZE
1ST PRIZE
CHIYUKI!
LET'S GO TOGETHER!
SCREW THIS LUXURY SKI TRIP!
How is this luxurious?
Keh! Who would go on such a...
I WANNA GO!
I KNEW I SHOULDN'T TRUST THAT LOTTERY YOUR GRAND-MOTHER WON AT THAT RUNDOWN SHOPPING ARCADE!
I've never been overseas before!
...
WE'RE HUNGRY AND LOST... AND MOST OF ALL...
You dissin' my granny?!

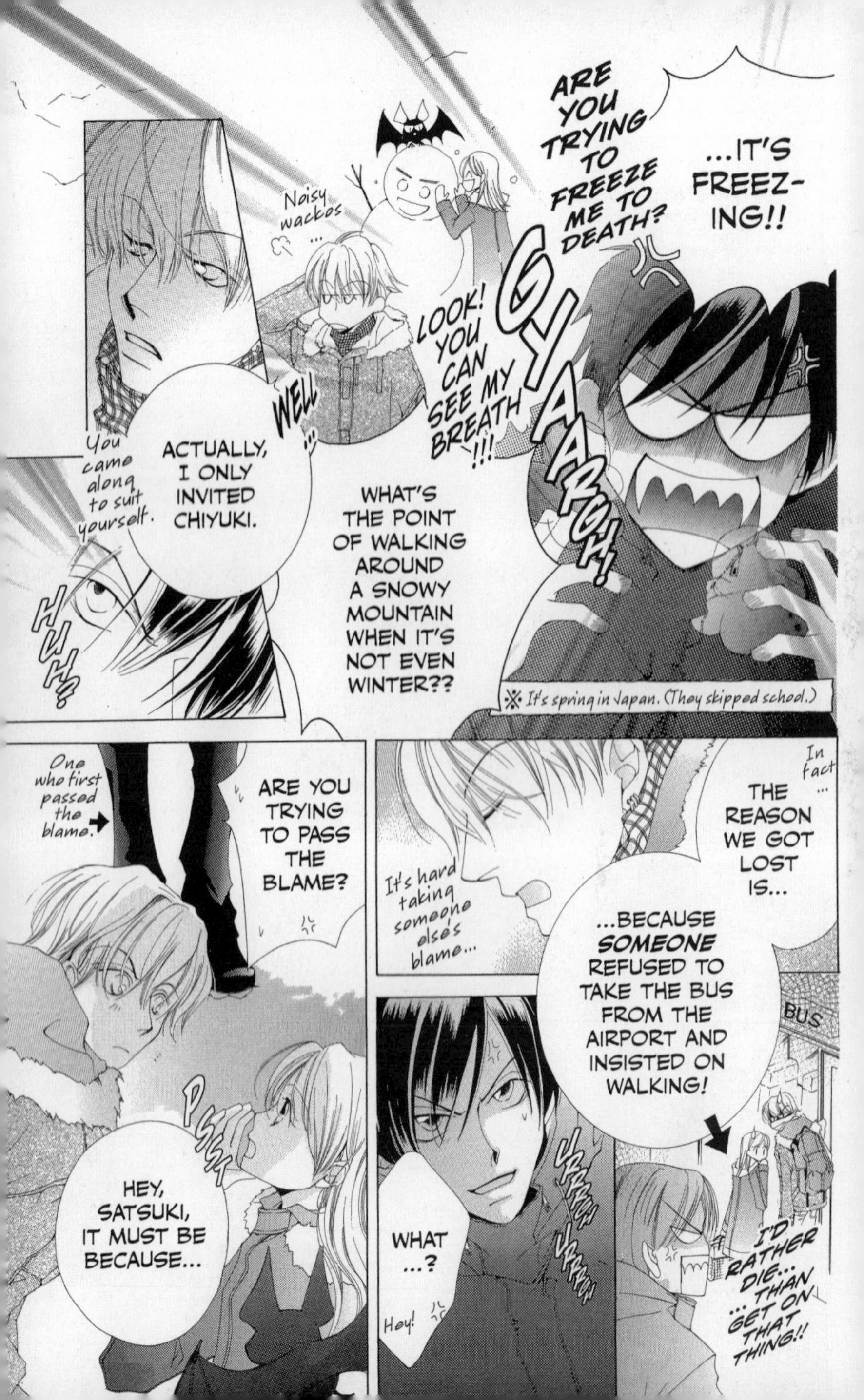
...IT'S FREEZ-ING!!
ARE YOU TRYING TO FREEZE ME TO DEATH?
GYAARGH!
LOOK! YOU CAN SEE MY BREATH!!!
Noisy wackos...
WELL...
ACTUALLY, I ONLY INVITED CHIYUKI.
You came along to suit yourself.
HUH?
WHAT'S THE POINT OF WALKING AROUND A SNOWY MOUNTAIN WHEN IT'S NOT EVEN WINTER??
※ It's spring in Japan. (They skipped school.)
In fact...
THE REASON WE GOT LOST IS...
It's hard taking someone else's blame...
ARE YOU TRYING TO PASS THE BLAME?
One who first passed the blame.
...BECAUSE SOMEONE REFUSED TO TAKE THE BUS FROM THE AIRPORT AND INSISTED ON WALKING!
BUS
I'D RATHER DIE... THAN GET ON THAT THING!!
WHAT...?
Hey!
PSST
HEY, SATSUKI, IT MUST BE BECAUSE...

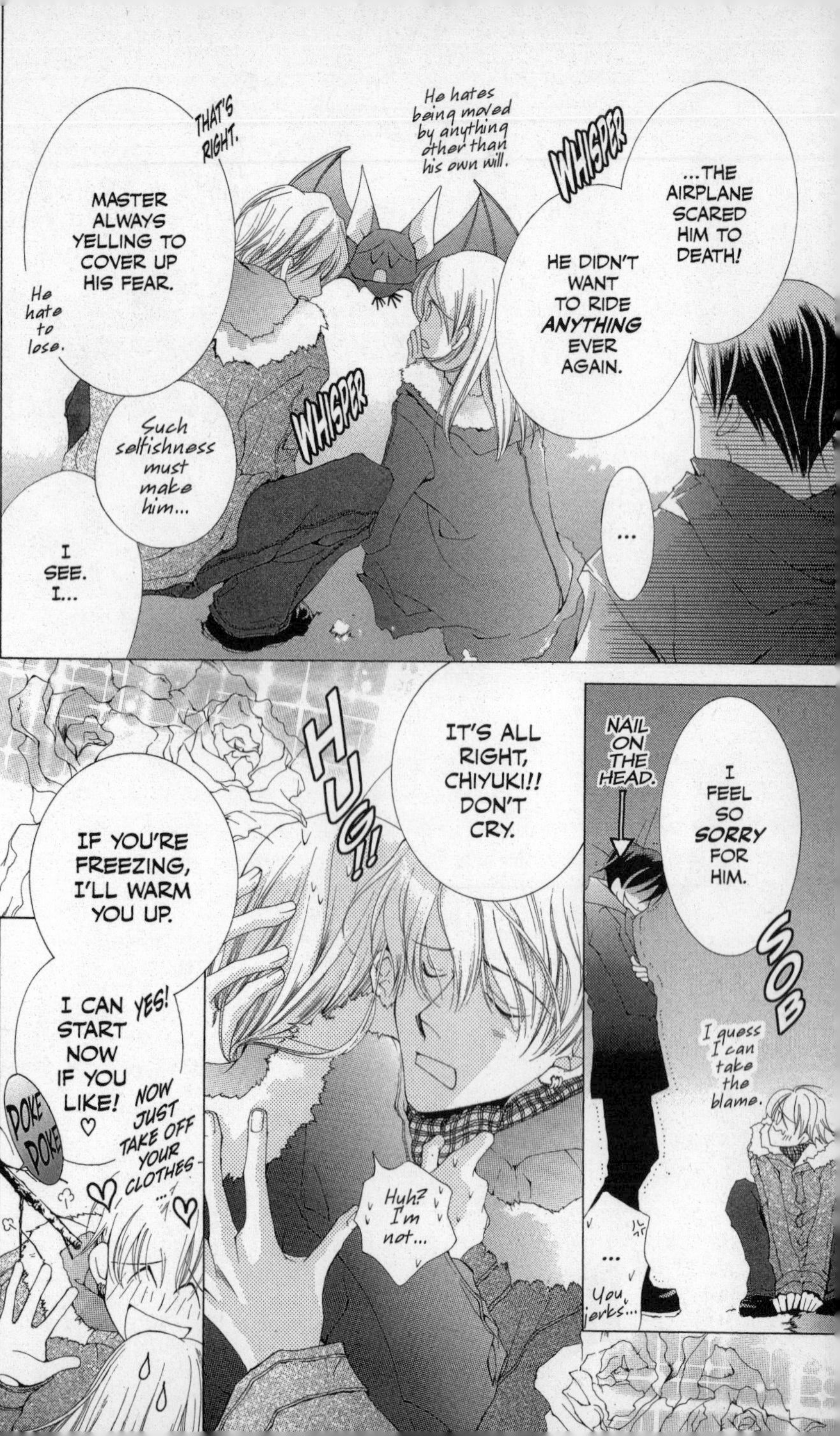
...THE AIRPLANE SCARED HIM TO DEATH!
WHISPER
HE DIDN'T WANT TO RIDE ANYTHING EVER AGAIN.
He hates being moved by anything other than his own will.
THAT'S RIGHT.
MASTER ALWAYS YELLING TO COVER UP HIS FEAR.
He hate to lose.
WHISPER
...
Such selfishness must make him...
I SEE. I...
NAIL ON THE HEAD.
I FEEL SO SORRY FOR HIM.
SOB
I guess I can take the blame.
...
You jerks...
HUG!!
IT'S ALL RIGHT, CHIYUKI!! DON'T CRY.
IF YOU'RE FREEZING, I'LL WARM YOU UP.
YES!
I CAN START NOW IF YOU LIKE! ♡
NOW JUST TAKE OFF YOUR CLOTHES...
POKE POKE
Huh? I'm not...

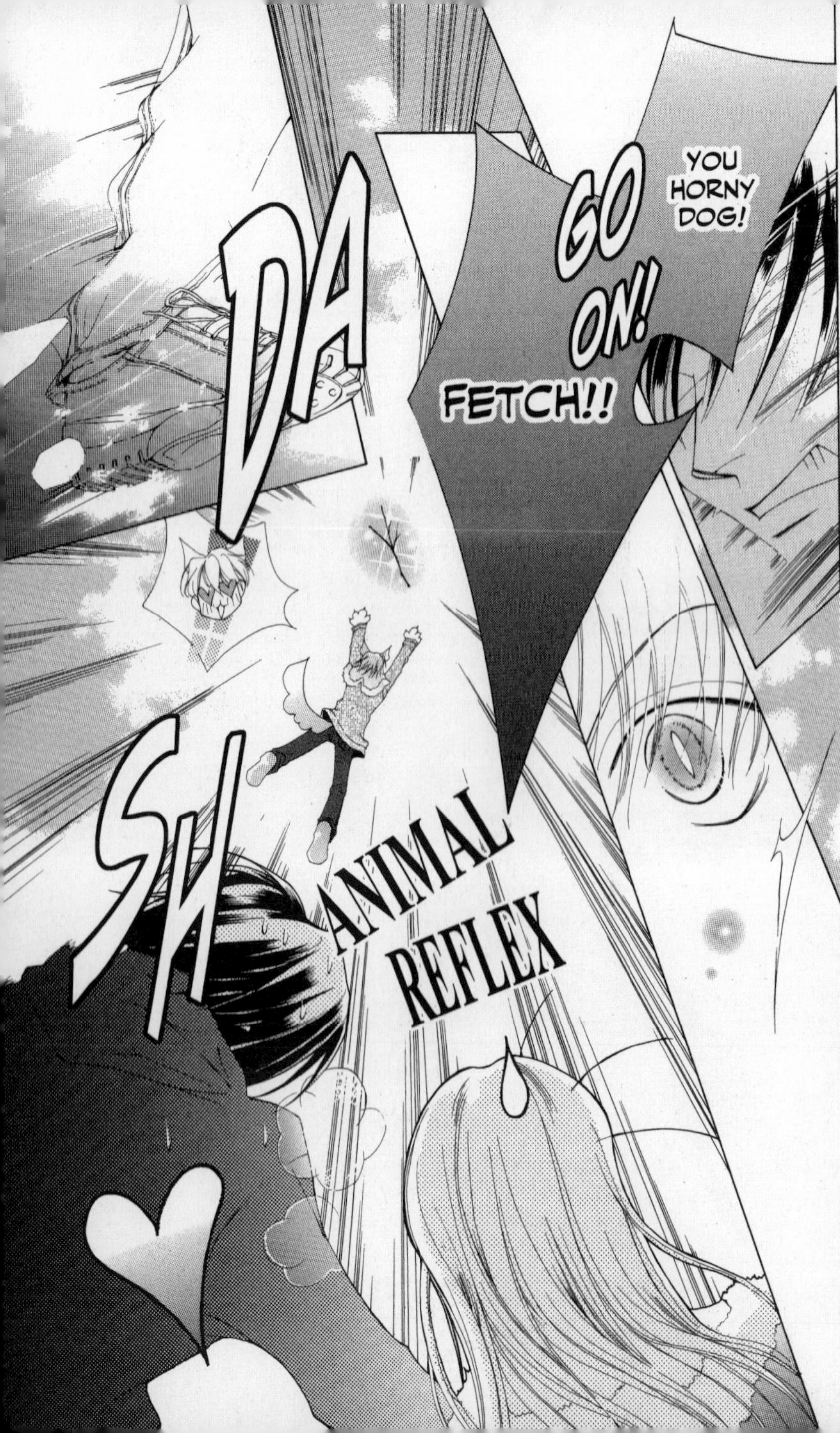
YOU HORNY DOG!
GO ON!
FETCH!!
DA
SH
ANIMAL REFLEX

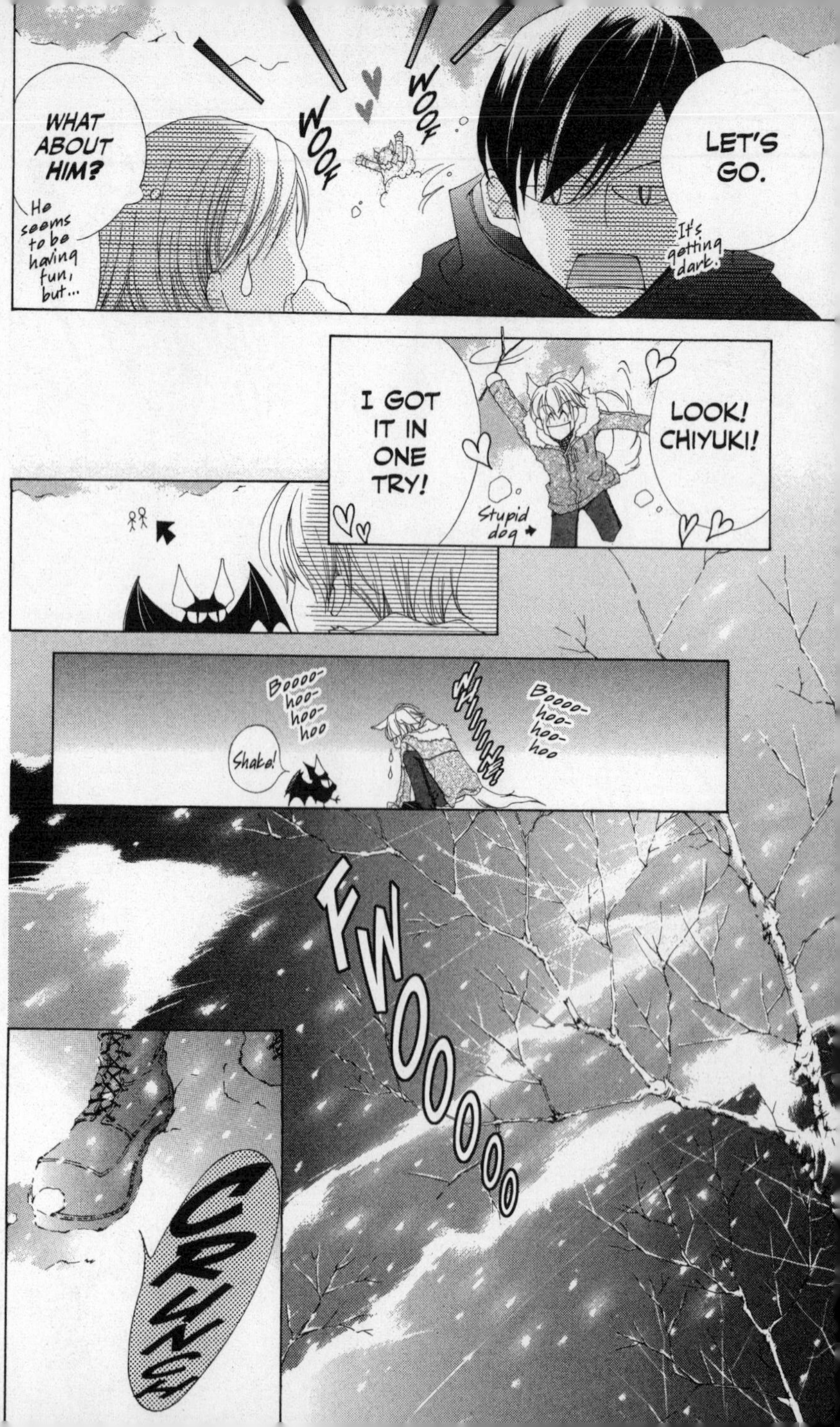

LET'S GO.
It's getting dark.
WOOF
WOOF
WHAT ABOUT HIM?
He seems to be having fun, but...
LOOK! CHIYUKI!
I GOT IT IN ONE TRY!
Stupid dog
Boooo-hoo-hoo-hoo
Boooo-hoo-hoo-hoo
Shake!
FWOOOOOO
CRUNCH

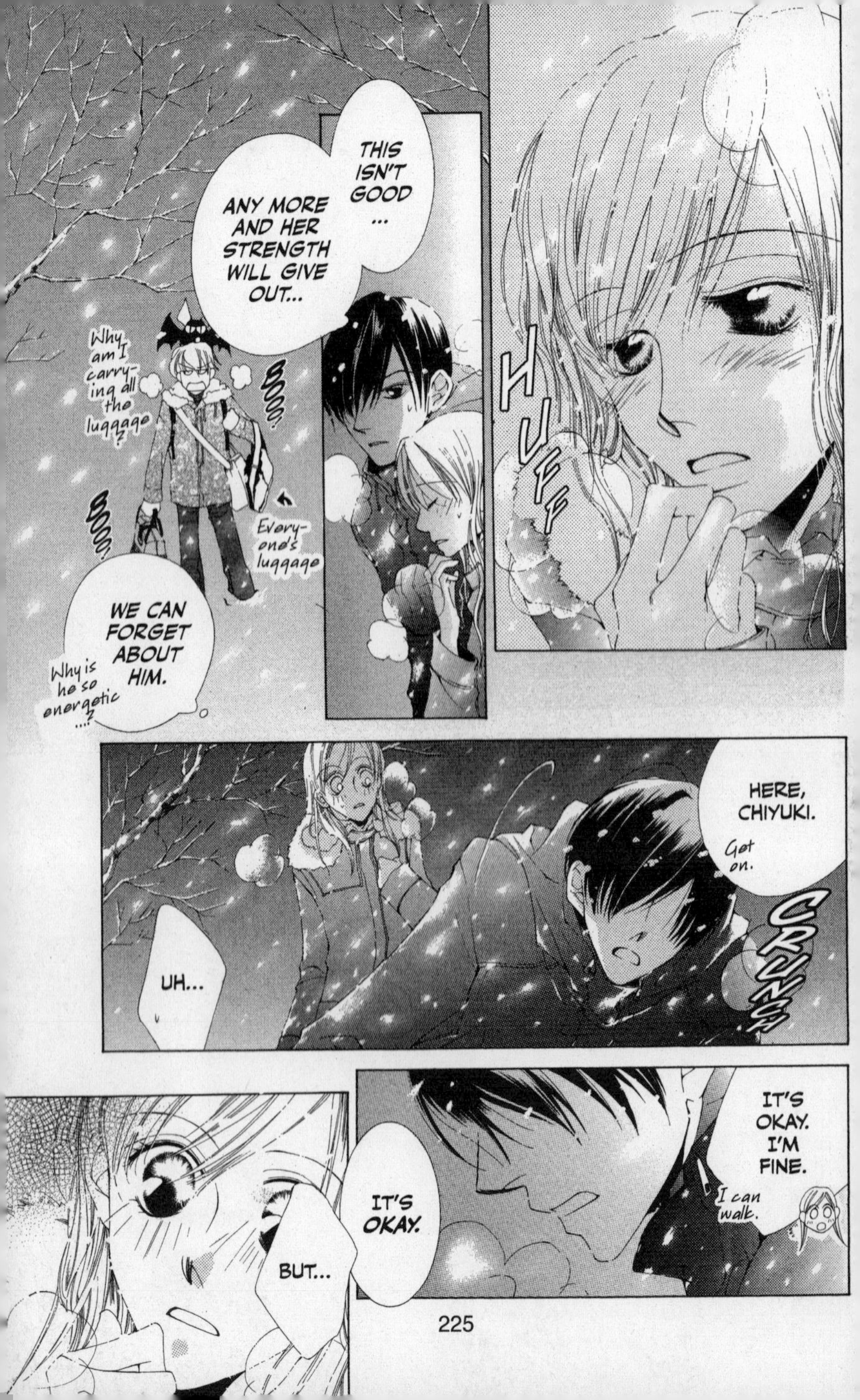
HUFF
THIS ISN'T GOOD...
ANY MORE AND HER STRENGTH WILL GIVE OUT...
Why am I carrying all the luggage?
Everyone's luggage
WE CAN FORGET ABOUT HIM.
Why is he so energetic...?
HERE, CHIYUKI.
Get on.
CRUNCH
UH...
IT'S OKAY. I'M FINE.
I can walk.
IT'S OKAY.
BUT...

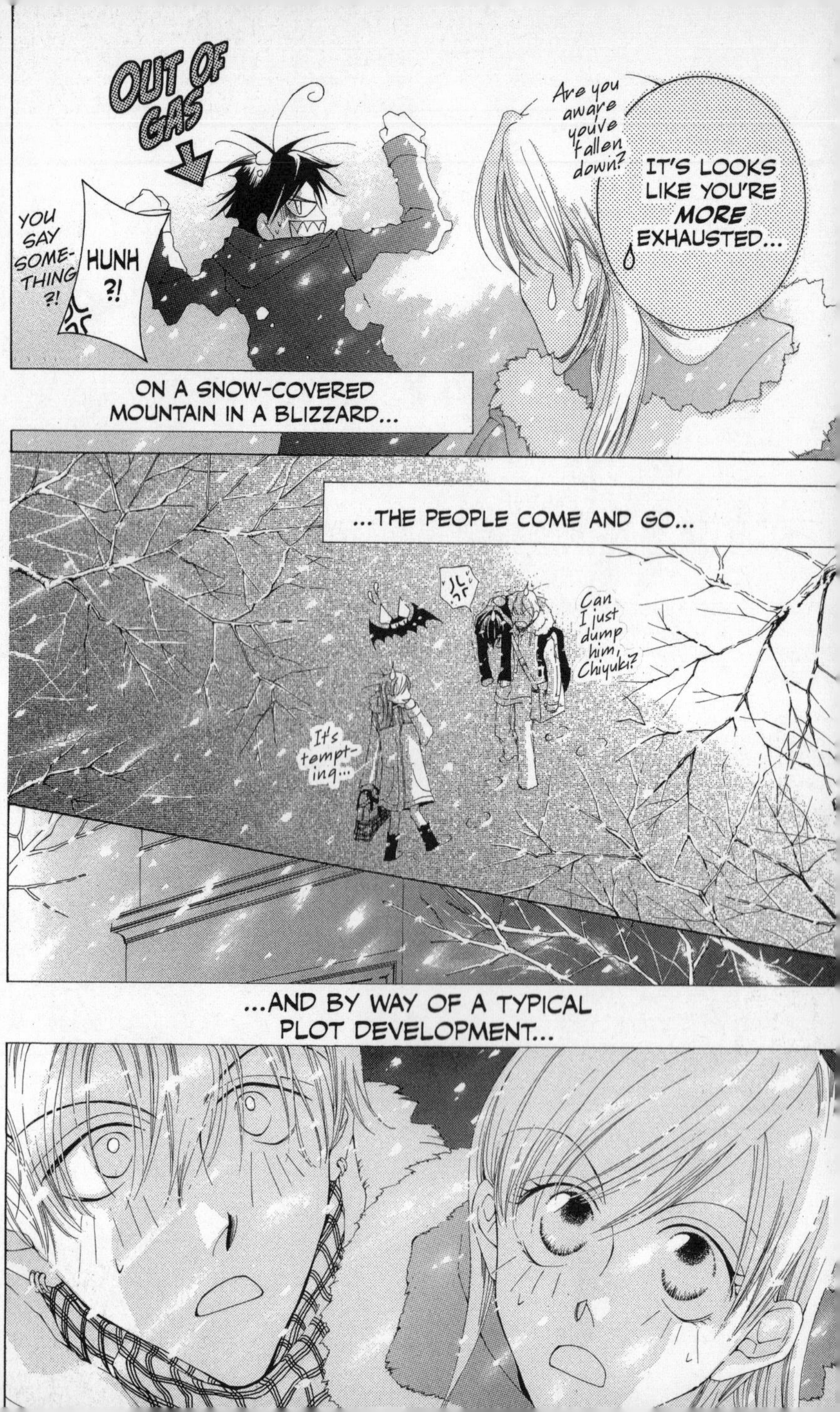

Are you aware you've fallen down?
IT'S LOOKS LIKE YOU'RE MORE EXHAUSTED...
OUT OF GAS
HUNH ?!
YOU SAY SOMETHING ?!
ON A SNOW-COVERED MOUNTAIN IN A BLIZZARD...
...THE PEOPLE COME AND GO...
Can I just dump him, Chiyuki?
It's tempting...
...AND BY WAY OF A TYPICAL PLOT DEVELOPMENT...

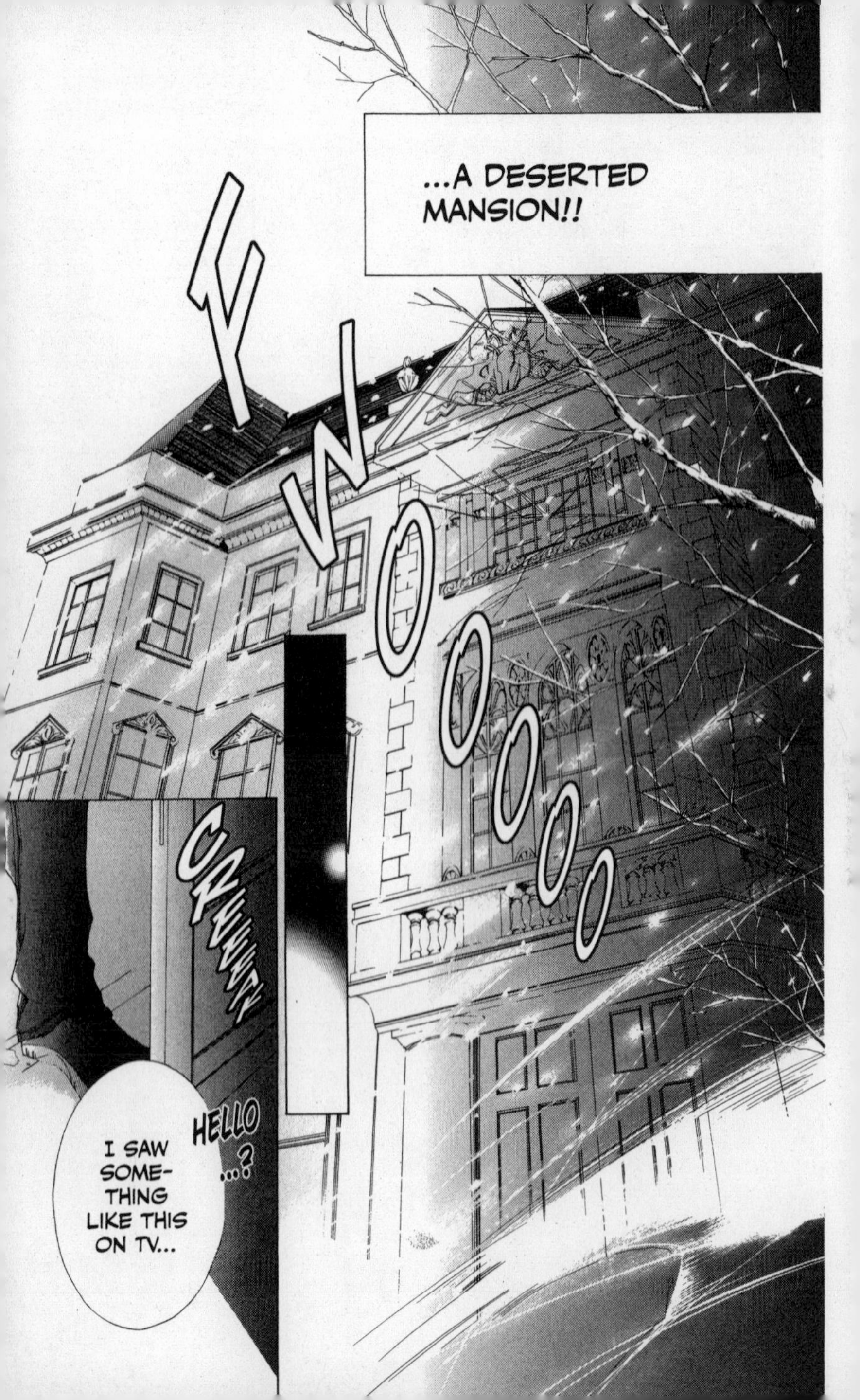
...A DESERTED MANSION!!
FWOOOOOOO
CRNNNCH
HELLO ...?
I SAW SOME-THING LIKE THIS ON TV...

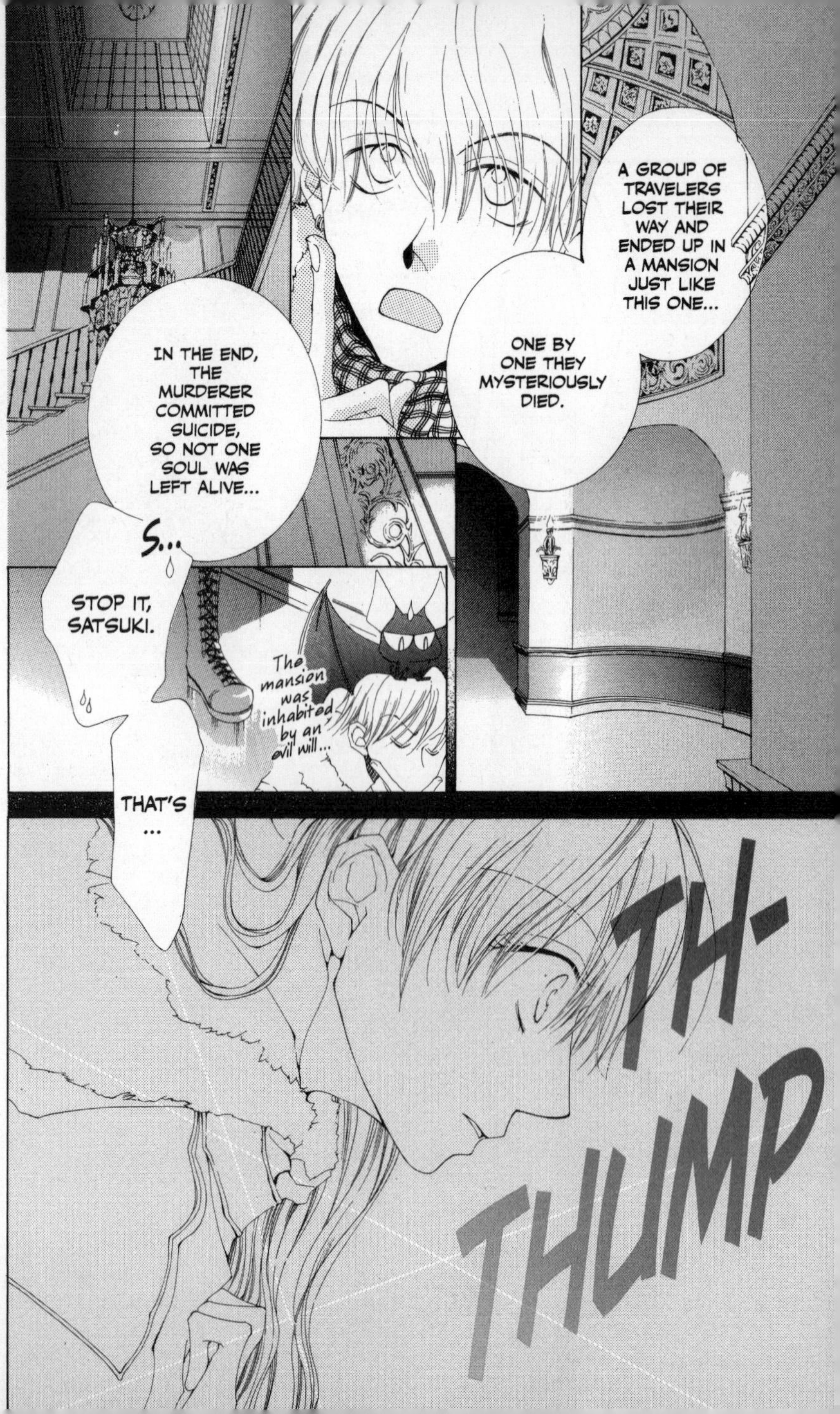
A GROUP OF TRAVELERS LOST THEIR WAY AND ENDED UP IN A MANSION JUST LIKE THIS ONE...
ONE BY ONE THEY MYSTERIOUSLY DIED.
IN THE END, THE MURDERER COMMITTED SUICIDE, SO NOT ONE SOUL WAS LEFT ALIVE...
The mansion was inhabited by an evil will...
S...
STOP IT, SATSUKI.
THAT'S ...
TH-THUMP

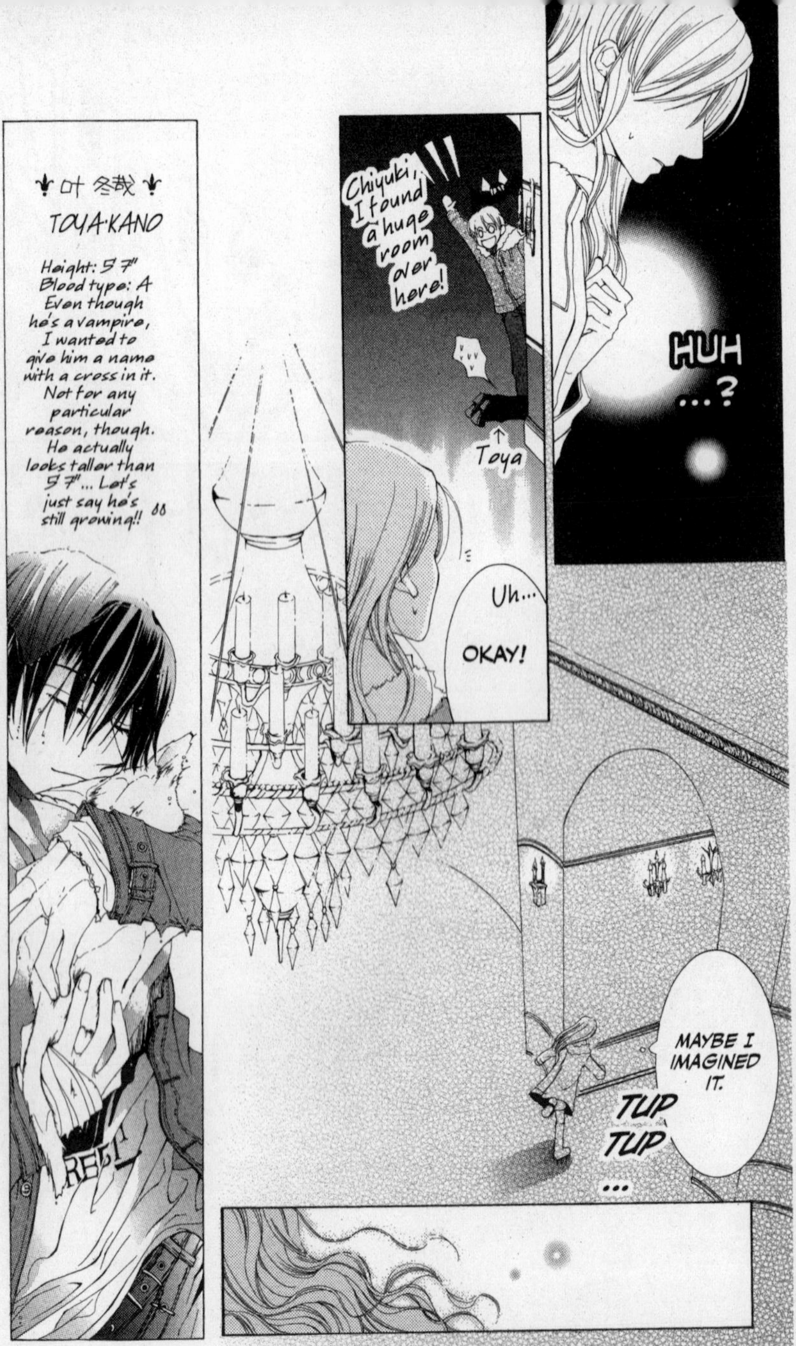
HUH ...?
Chiyuki, I found a huge room over here!
↑ Toya
Uh...
OKAY!
MAYBE I IMAGINED IT.
TUP TUP ...
叶 冬哉
TOYA·KANO
Height: 5'7"
Blood type: A
Even though he's a vampire, I wanted to give him a name with a cross in it. Not for any particular reason, though. He actually looks taller than 5'7"... Let's just say he's still growing!!

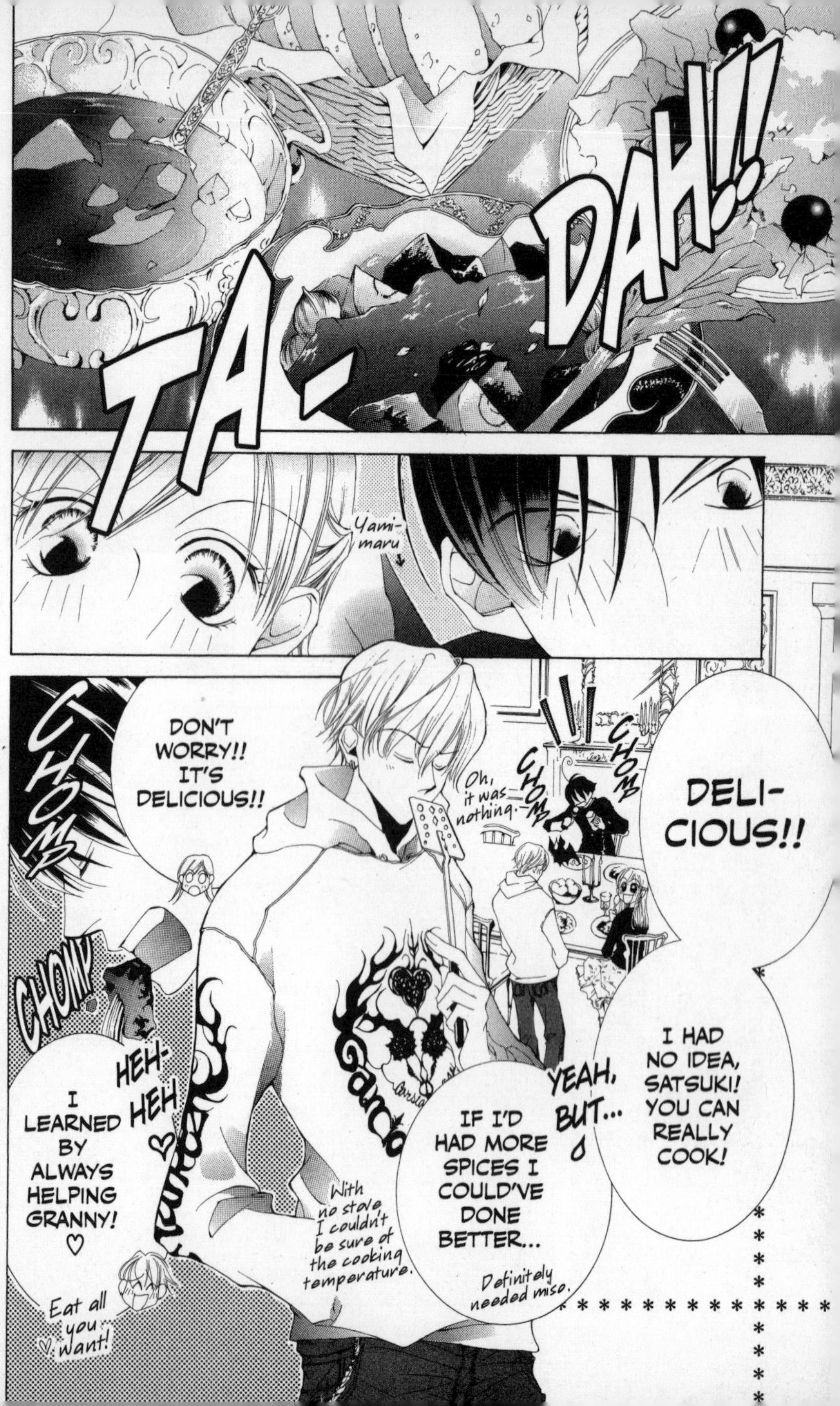
TA-DAH!!
Yami-maru
DELI-CIOUS!!
CHOMP CHOMP
Oh, it was nothing.
DON'T WORRY!! IT'S DELICIOUS!!
CHOMP CHOMP
I HAD NO IDEA, SATSUKI! YOU CAN REALLY COOK!
YEAH, BUT...
IF I'D HAD MORE SPICES I COULD'VE DONE BETTER...
Definitely needed miso.
With no stove I couldn't be sure of the cooking temperature.
HEH-HEH
I LEARNED BY ALWAYS HELPING GRANNY! ♡
Eat all you want! ♡

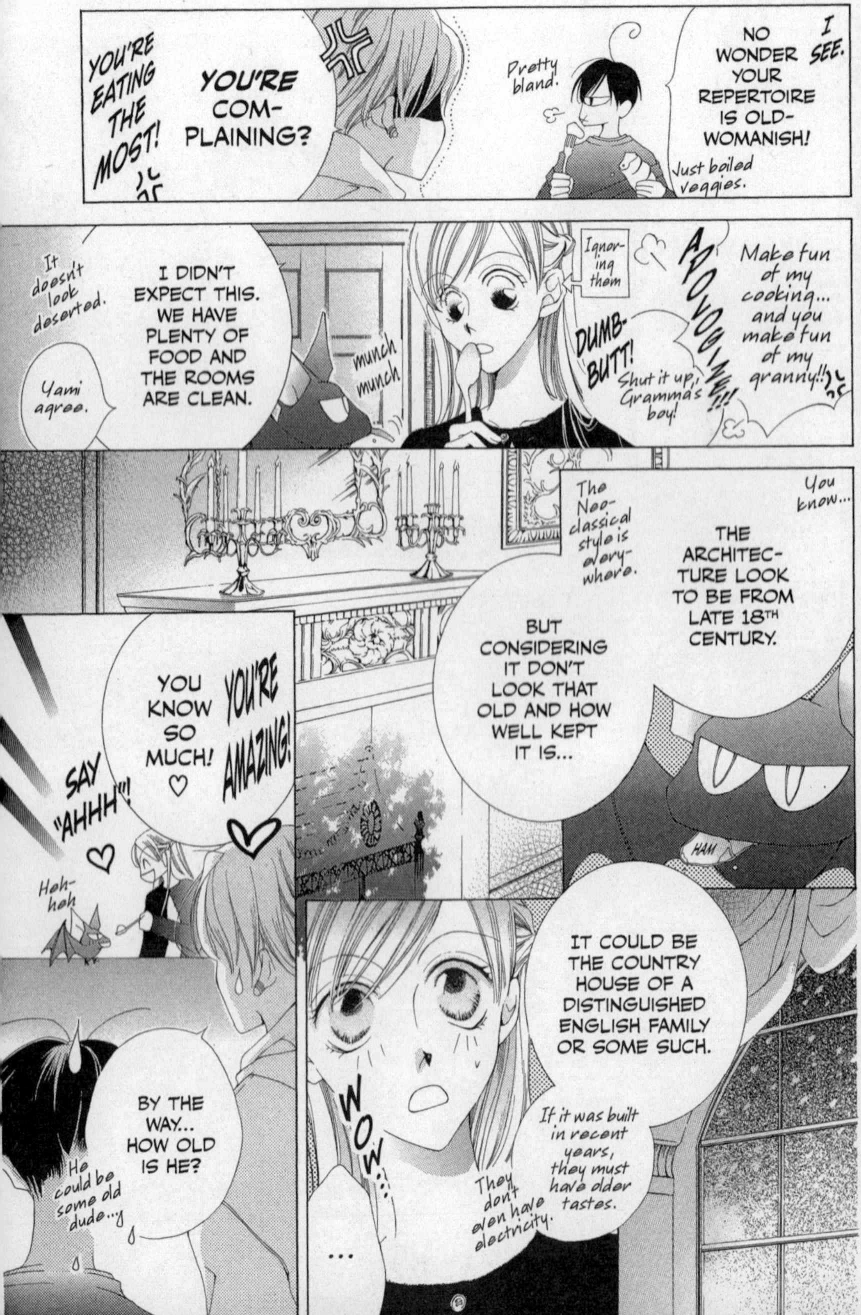
I SEE.
NO WONDER YOUR REPERTOIRE IS OLD-WOMANISH!
Just boiled veggies.
Pretty bland.
YOU'RE COM-PLAINING?
YOU'RE EATING THE MOST!
Make fun of my cooking... and you make fun of my granny!!
Shut it up, Gramma's boy!
DUMB-BUTT!
Ignor-ing them
munch munch
I DIDN'T EXPECT THIS. WE HAVE PLENTY OF FOOD AND THE ROOMS ARE CLEAN.
It doesn't look deserted.
Yami agree.
You know...
THE ARCHITEC-TURE LOOK TO BE FROM LATE 18TH CENTURY.
The Neo-classical style is every-where.
BUT CONSIDERING IT DON'T LOOK THAT OLD AND HOW WELL KEPT IT IS...
HAM
YOU'RE AMAZING!
YOU KNOW SO MUCH! ♡
SAY "AHHH"!
Heh-heh
IT COULD BE THE COUNTRY HOUSE OF A DISTINGUISHED ENGLISH FAMILY OR SOME SUCH.
If it was built in recent years, they must have older tastes.
They don't even have electricity.
WOW...
...
BY THE WAY... HOW OLD IS HE?
He could be some old dude...

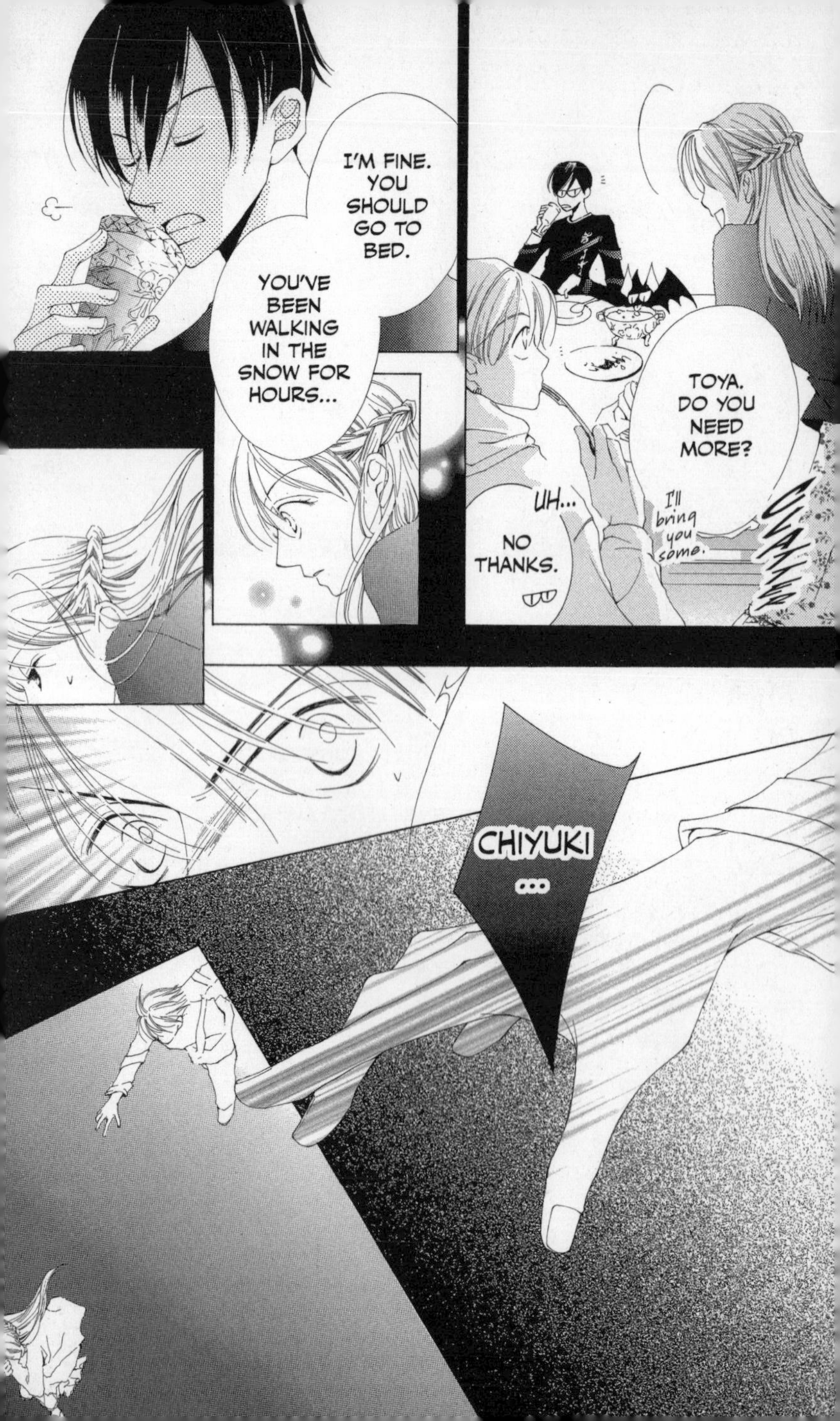
TOYA. DO YOU NEED MORE?
UH...
NO THANKS.
I'll bring you some.
YOU'VE BEEN WALKING IN THE SNOW FOR HOURS...
I'M FINE. YOU SHOULD GO TO BED.
CHIYUKI ...

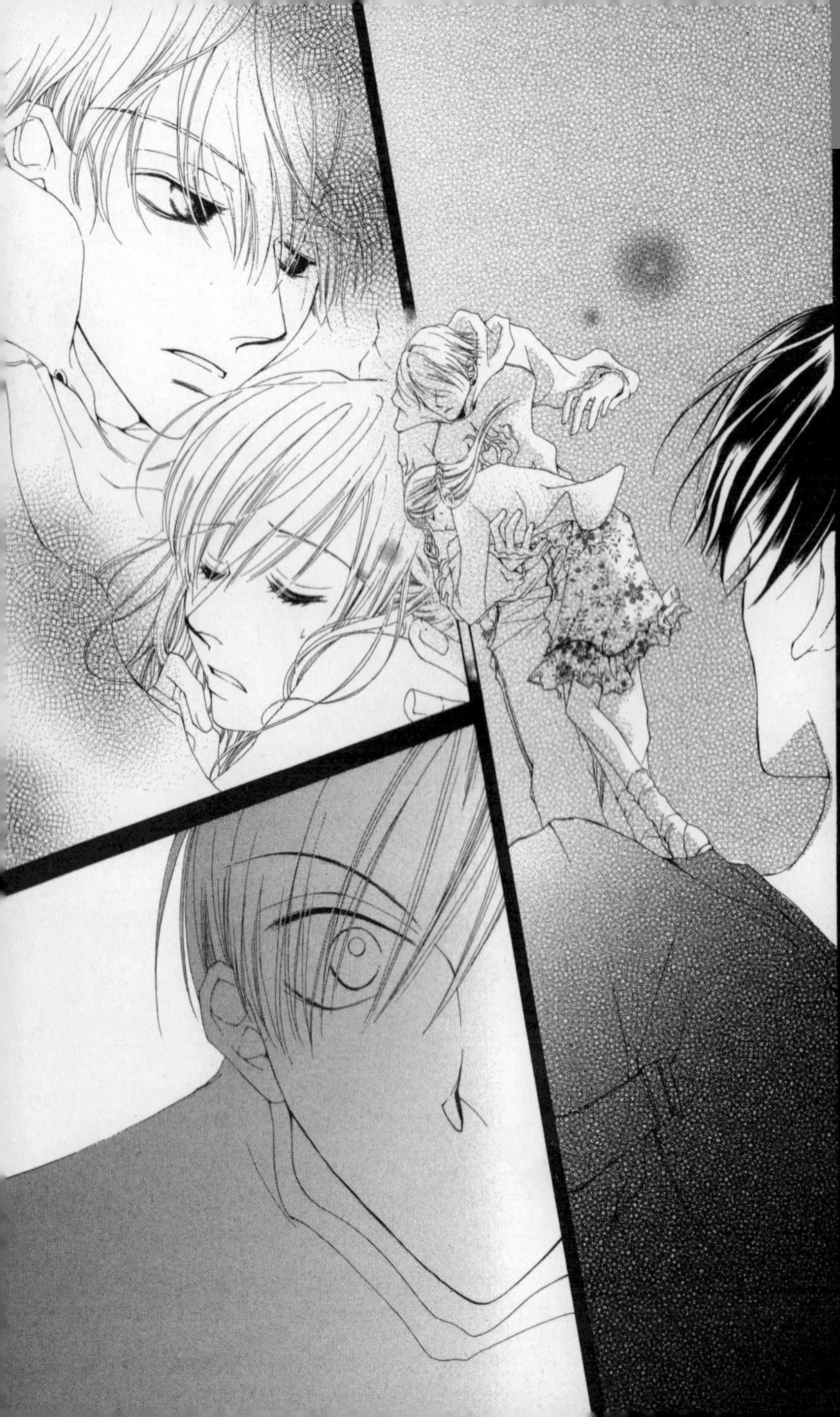

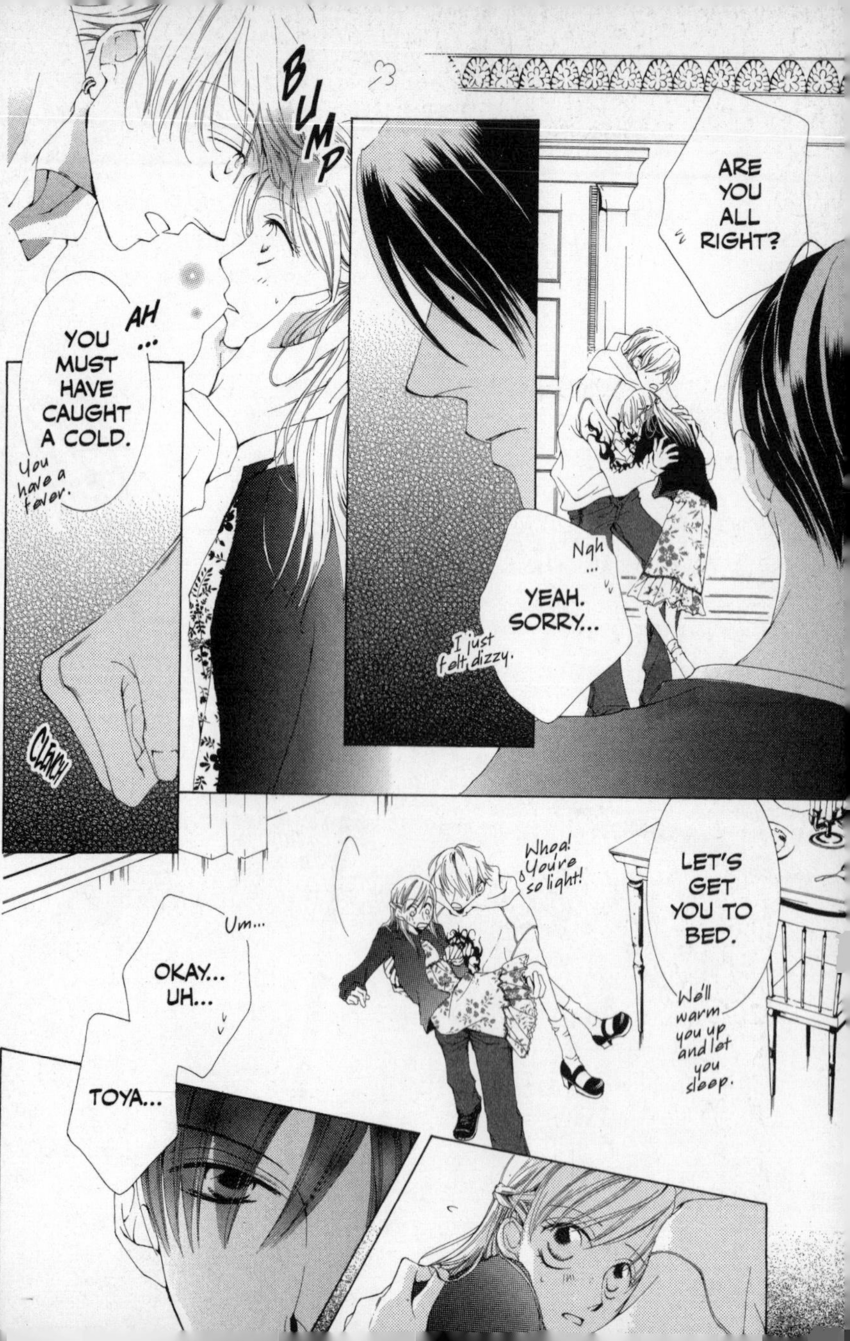
ARE YOU ALL RIGHT?
Ngh...
YEAH. SORRY...
I just felt dizzy.
BUMP
AH...
YOU MUST HAVE CAUGHT A COLD.
You have a fever.
CLENCH
LET'S GET YOU TO BED.
We'll warm you up and let you sleep.
Whoa! You're so light!
Um...
OKAY... UH...
TOYA...

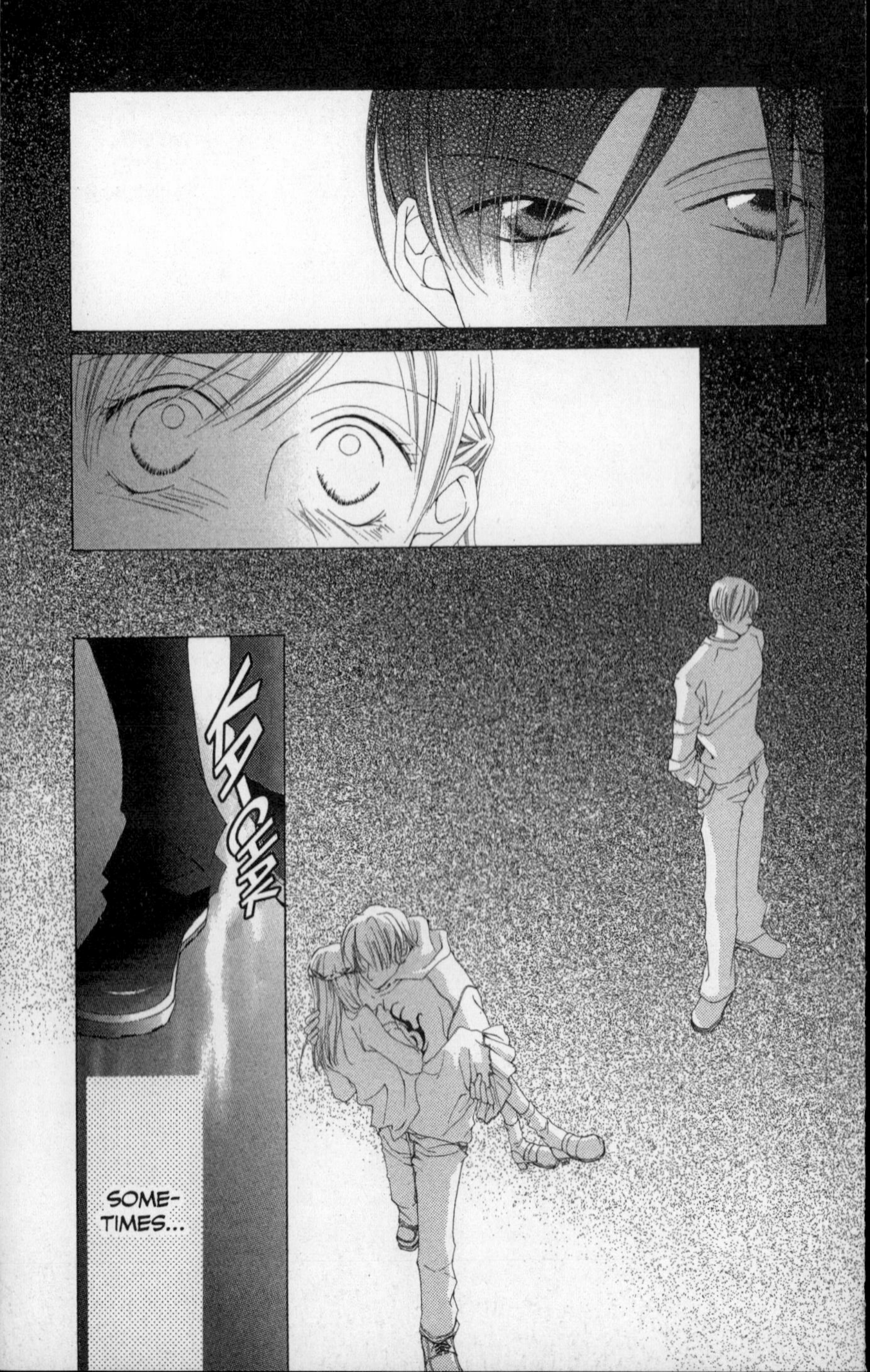
KA-CHAK
SOME-
TIMES...

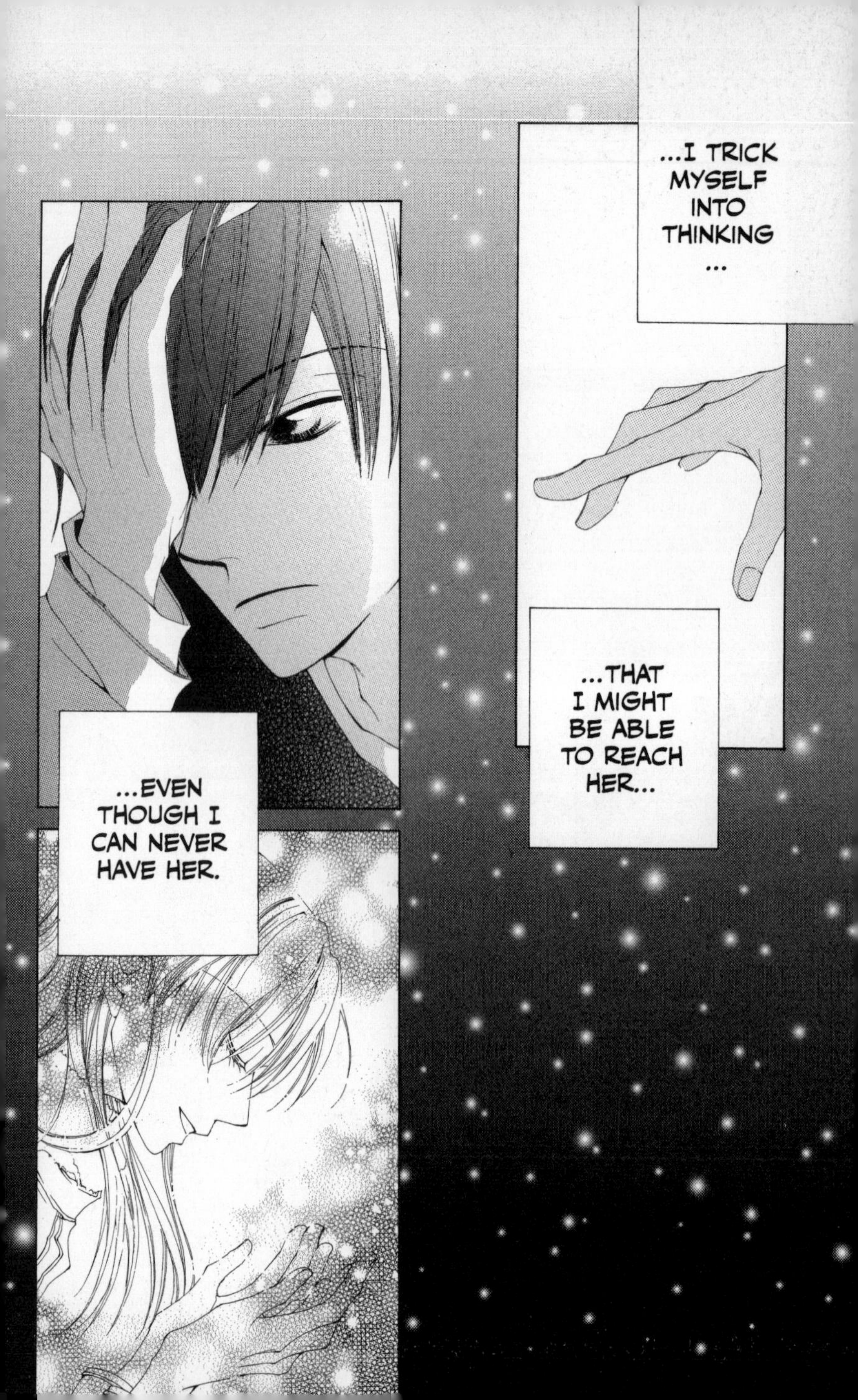
...I TRICK MYSELF INTO THINKING ...
...THAT I MIGHT BE ABLE TO REACH HER...
...EVEN THOUGH I CAN NEVER HAVE HER.

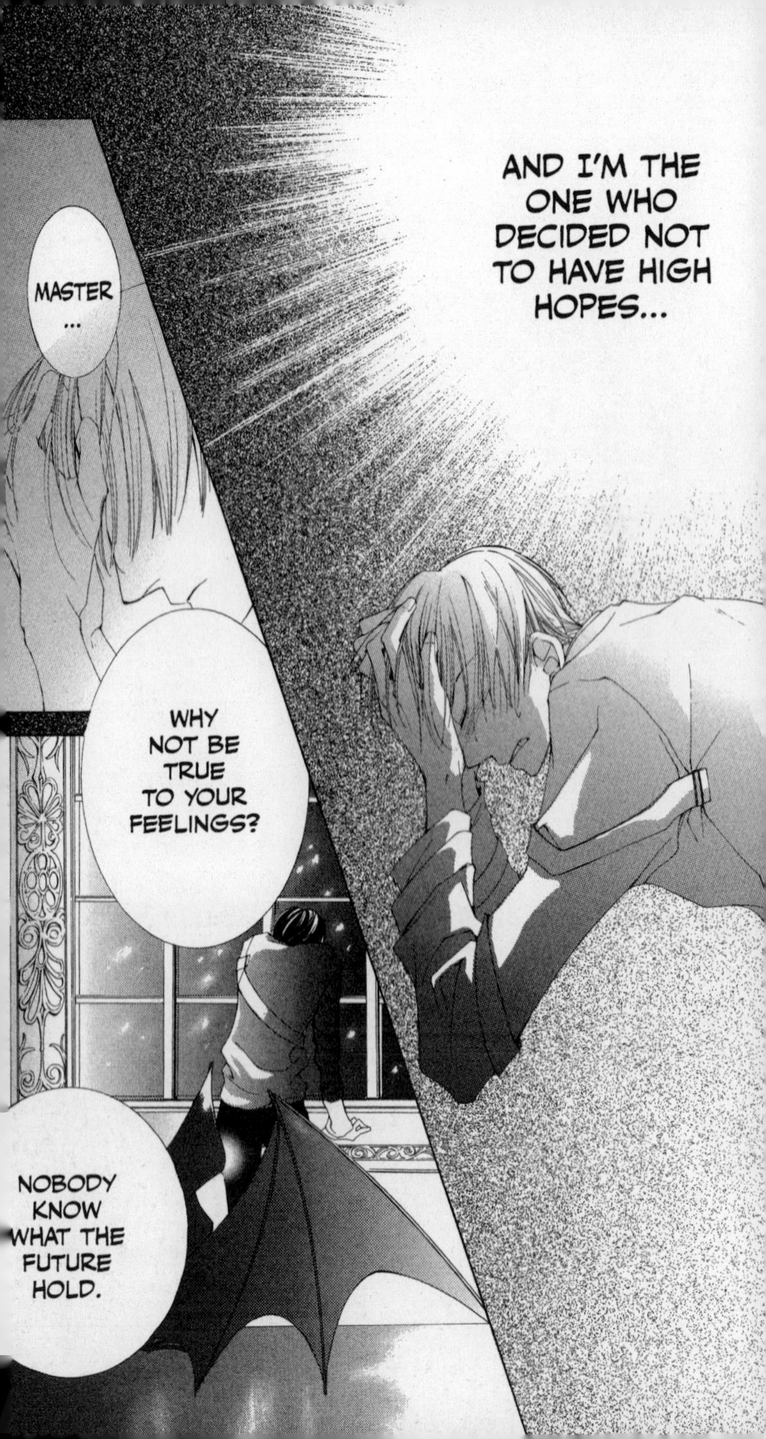
AND I'M THE ONE WHO DECIDED NOT TO HAVE HIGH HOPES...
MASTER ...
WHY NOT BE TRUE TO YOUR FEELINGS?
NOBODY KNOW WHAT THE FUTURE HOLD.

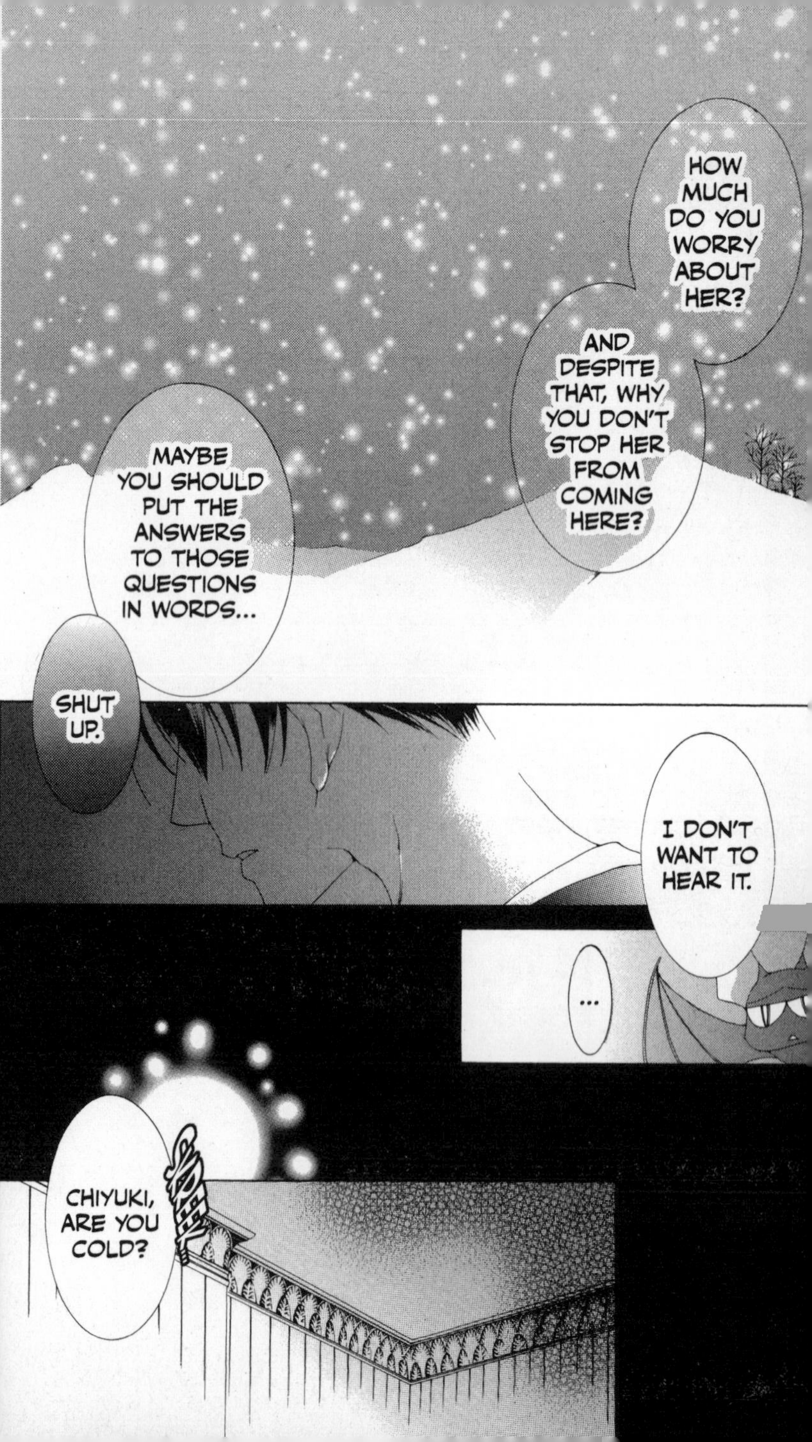
HOW MUCH DO YOU WORRY ABOUT HER?
AND DESPITE THAT, WHY YOU DON'T STOP HER FROM COMING HERE?
MAYBE YOU SHOULD PUT THE ANSWERS TO THOSE QUESTIONS IN WORDS...
SHUT UP.
I DON'T WANT TO HEAR IT.
...
CHIYUKI, ARE YOU COLD?

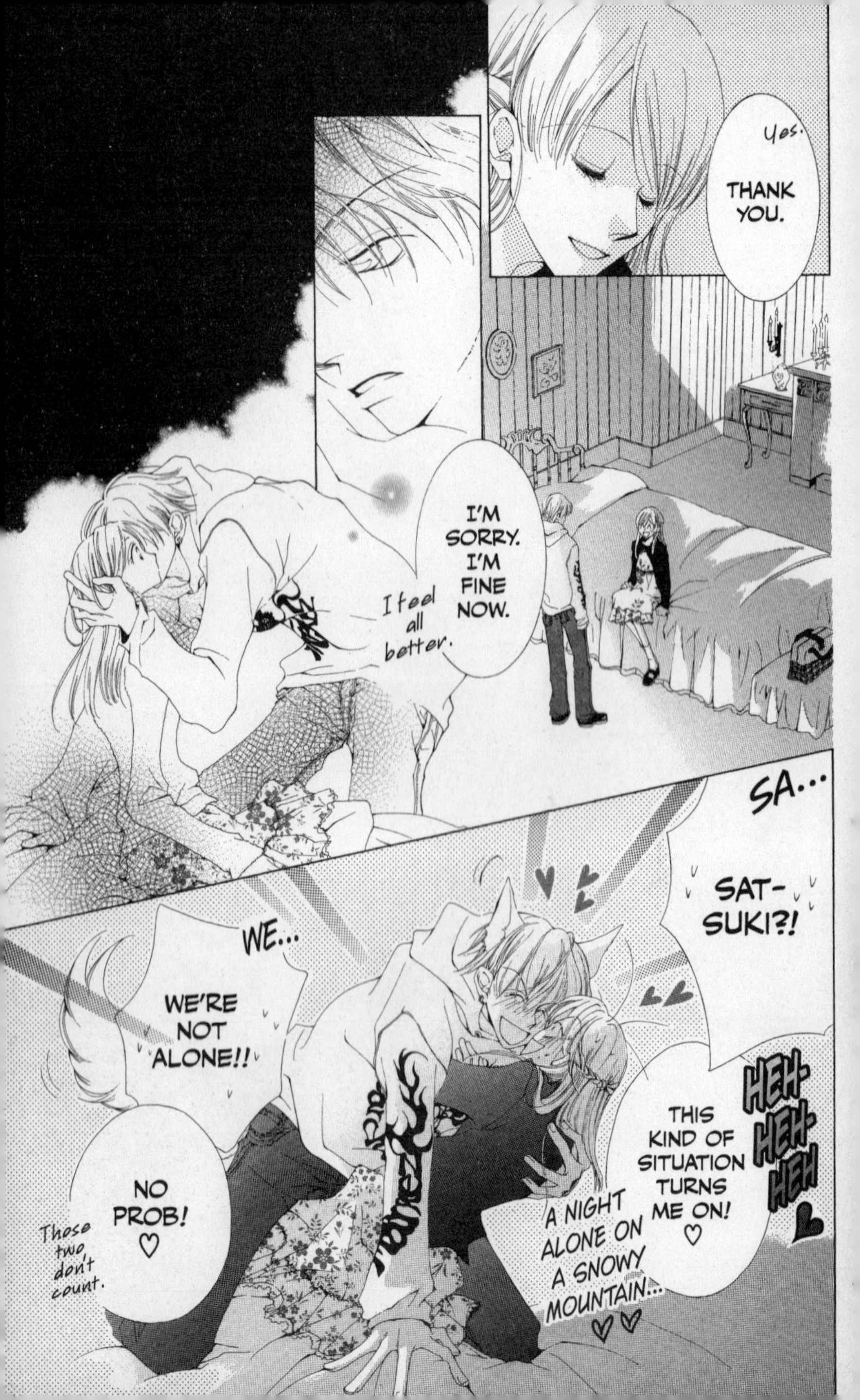
Yes.
THANK YOU.
I'M SORRY. I'M FINE NOW.
I feel all better.
SA...
SAT-SUKI?!
HEH HEH HEH
THIS KIND OF SITUATION TURNS ME ON! ♡
A NIGHT ALONE ON A SNOWY MOUNTAIN... ♡ ♡
WE...
WE'RE NOT ALONE!!
NO PROB! ♡
Those two don't count.

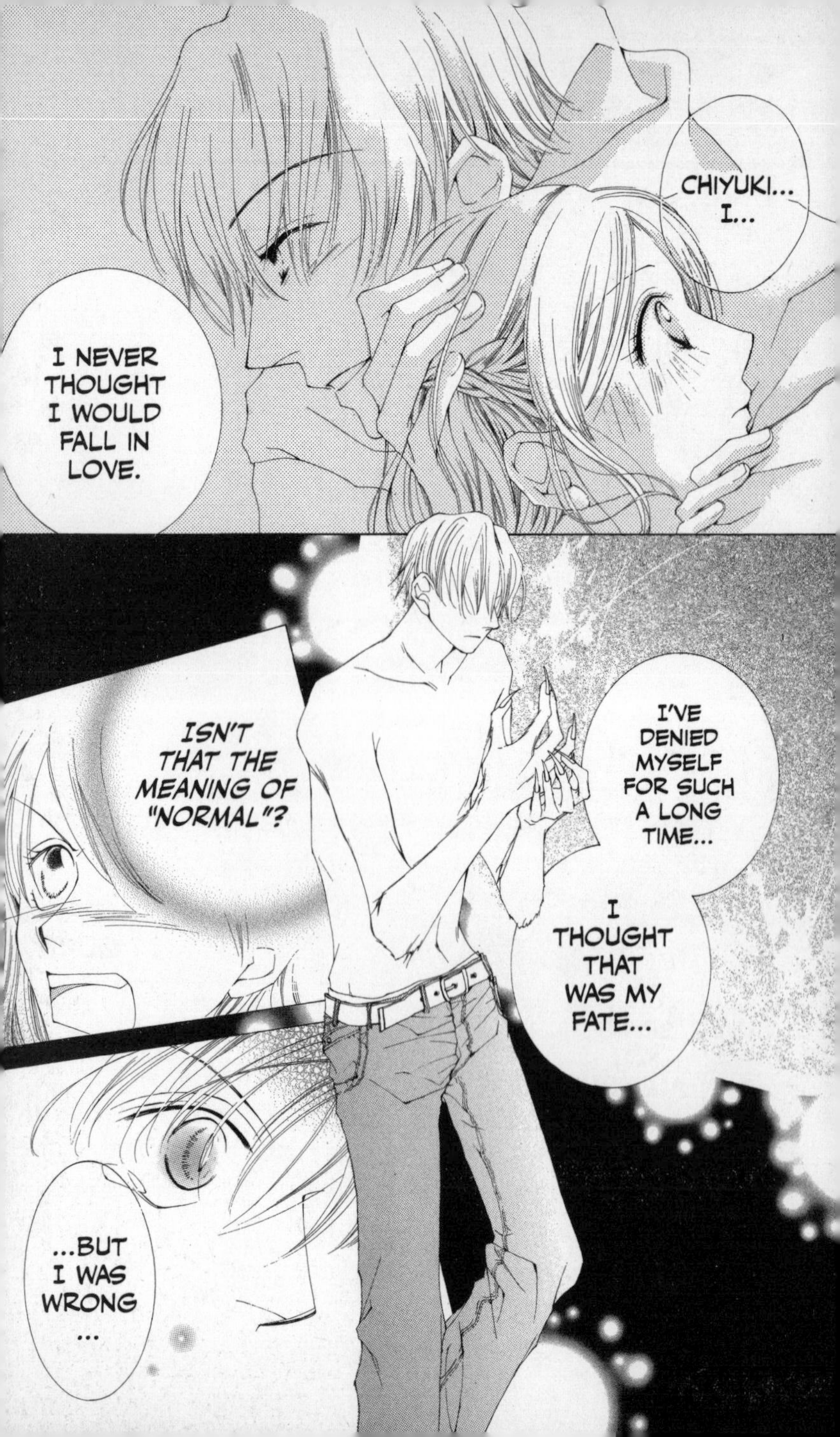
CHIYUKI... I...
I NEVER THOUGHT I WOULD FALL IN LOVE.
I'VE DENIED MYSELF FOR SUCH A LONG TIME...
I THOUGHT THAT WAS MY FATE...
ISN'T THAT THE MEANING OF "NORMAL"?
...BUT I WAS WRONG...

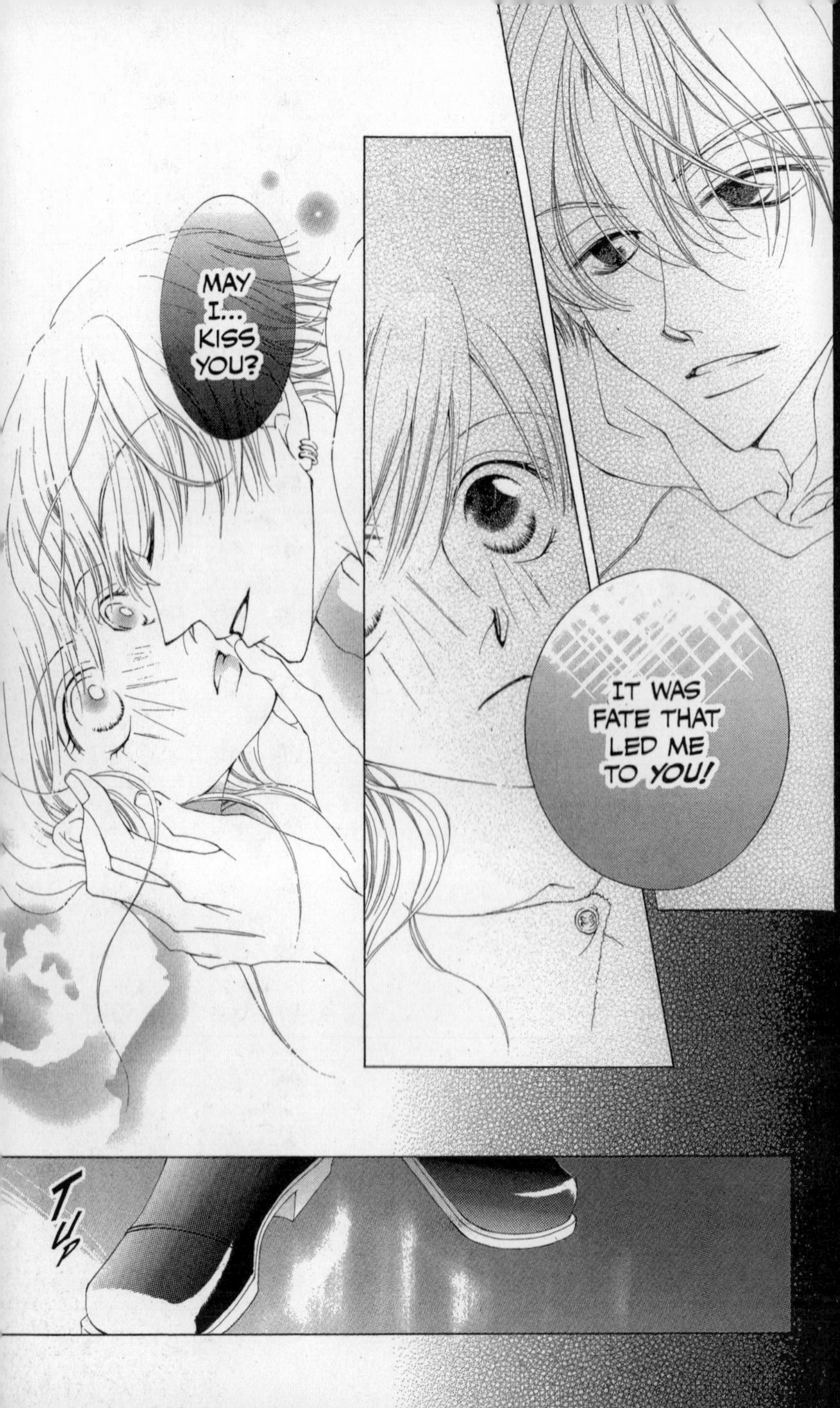
IT WAS FATE THAT LED ME TO *YOU!*
MAY I... KISS YOU?
TUP

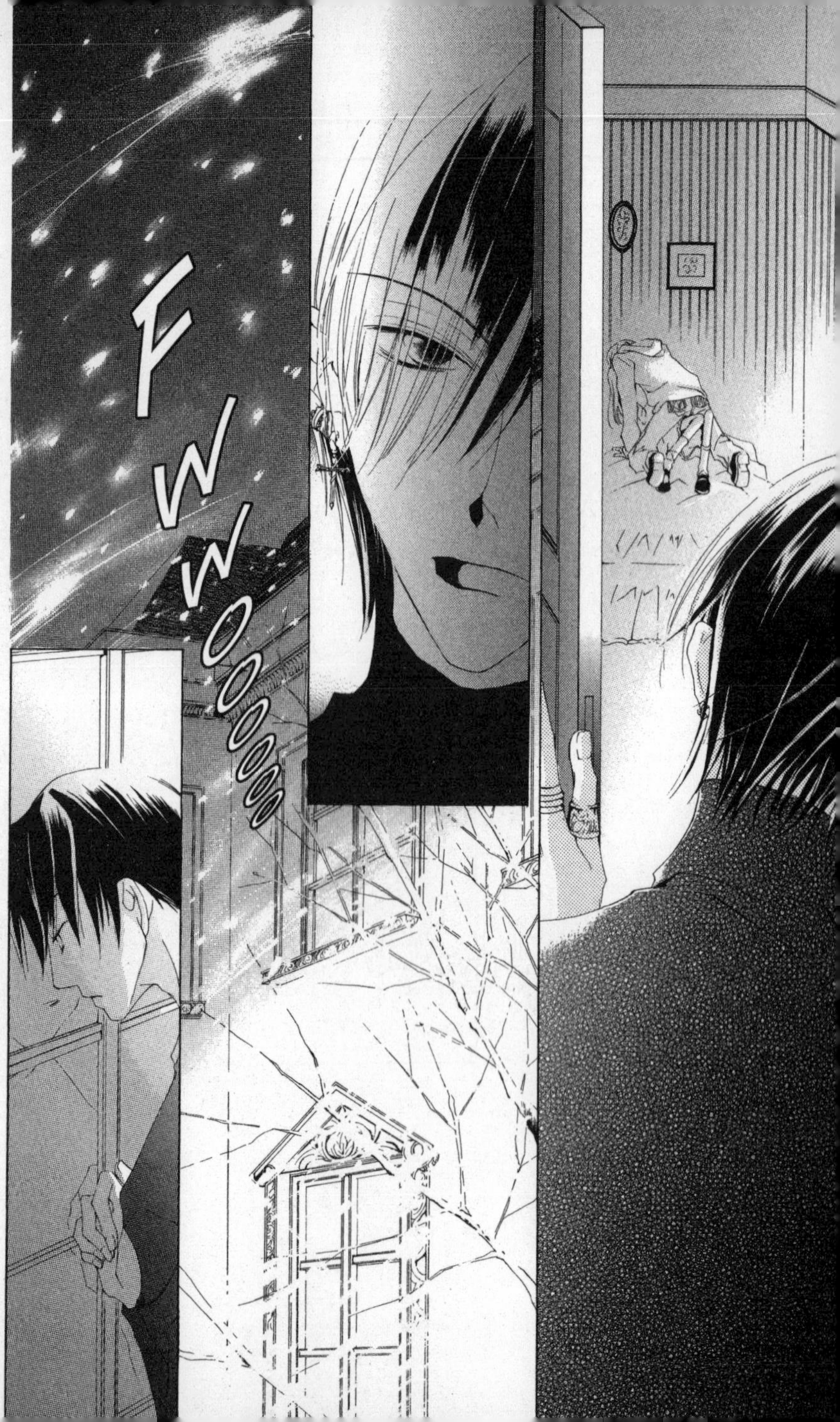
FWOOOOOO

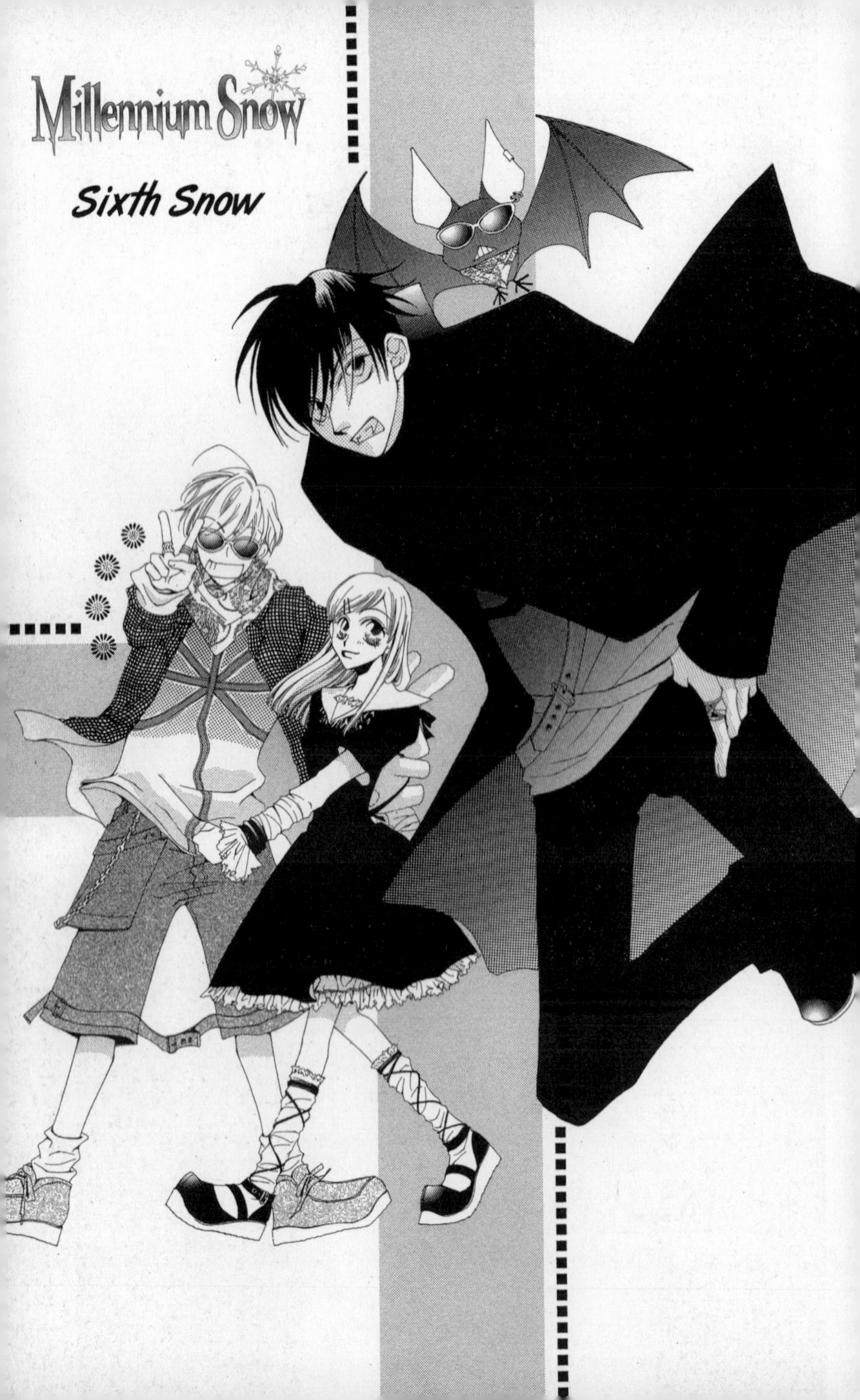
Millennium Snow
Sixth Snow

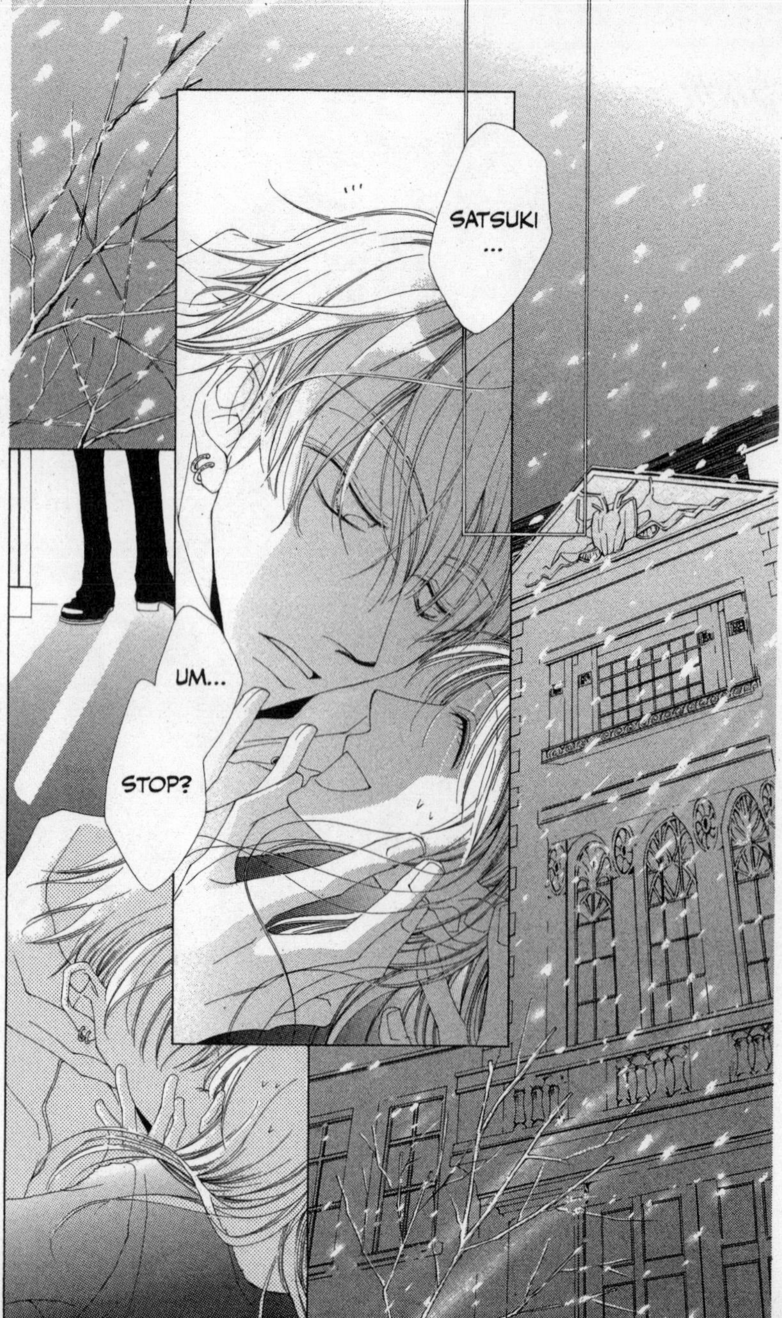
SATSUKI ...
UM...
STOP?

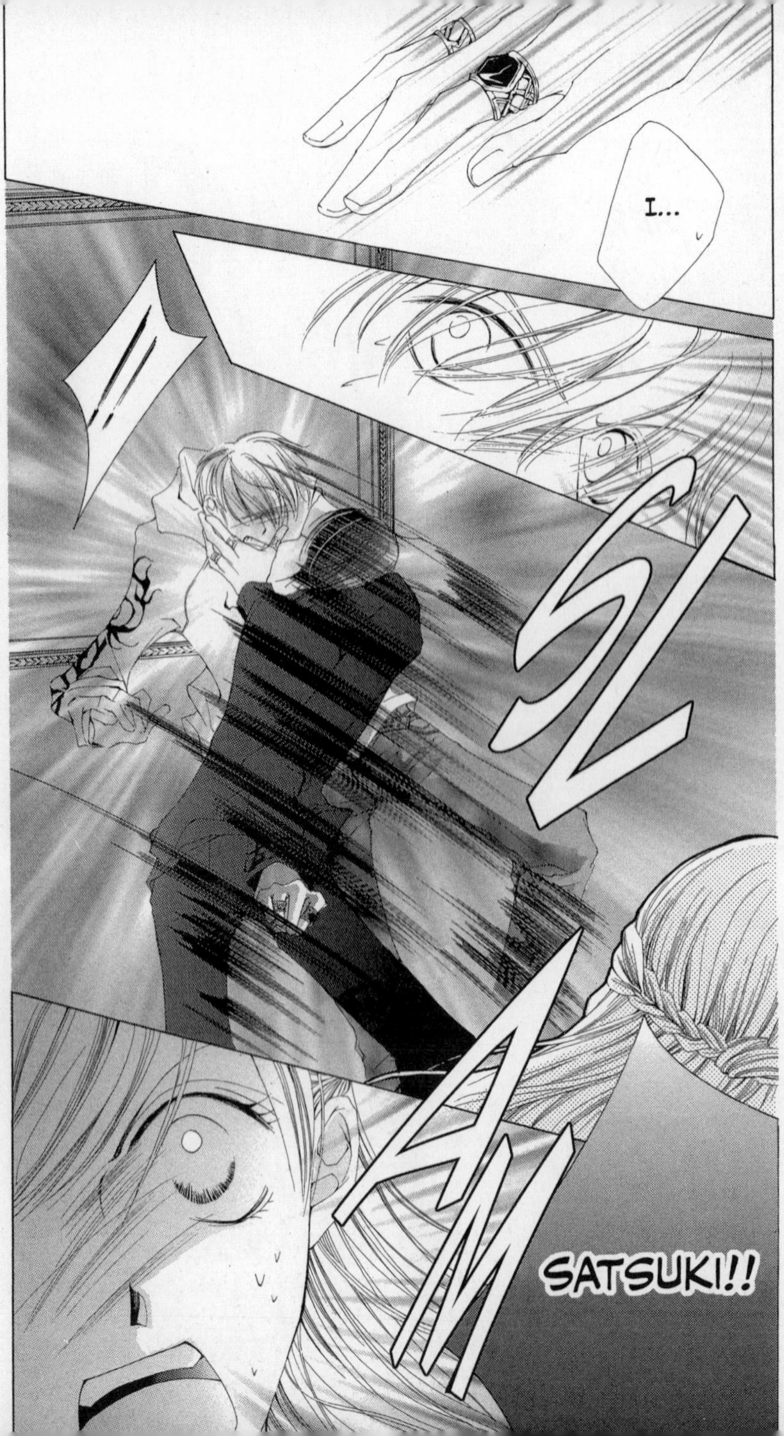
I...
SATSUKI!!

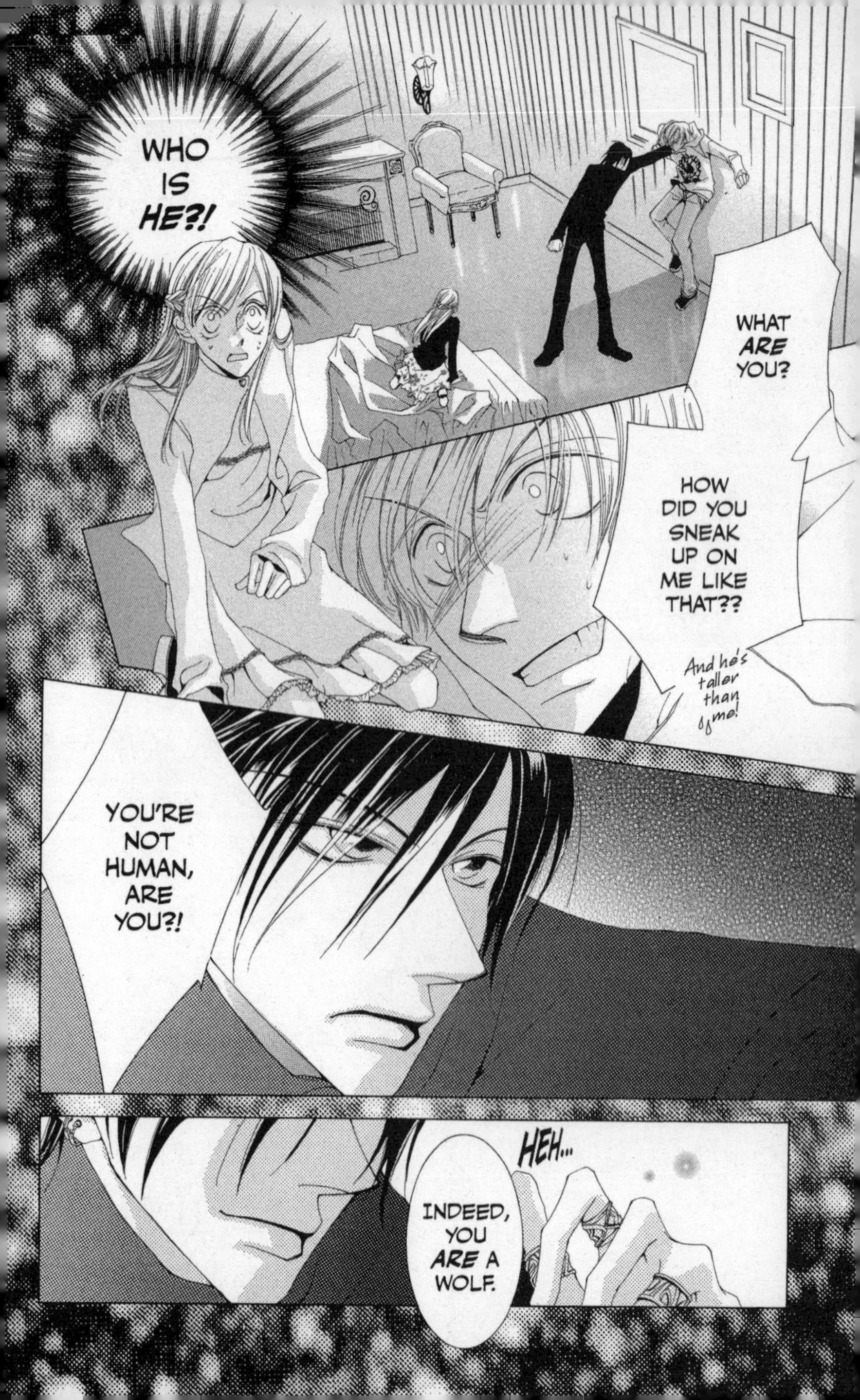
WHO IS HE?!
WHAT ARE YOU?
HOW DID YOU SNEAK UP ON ME LIKE THAT??
And he's taller than me!
YOU'RE NOT HUMAN, ARE YOU?!
HEH...
INDEED, YOU ARE A WOLF.

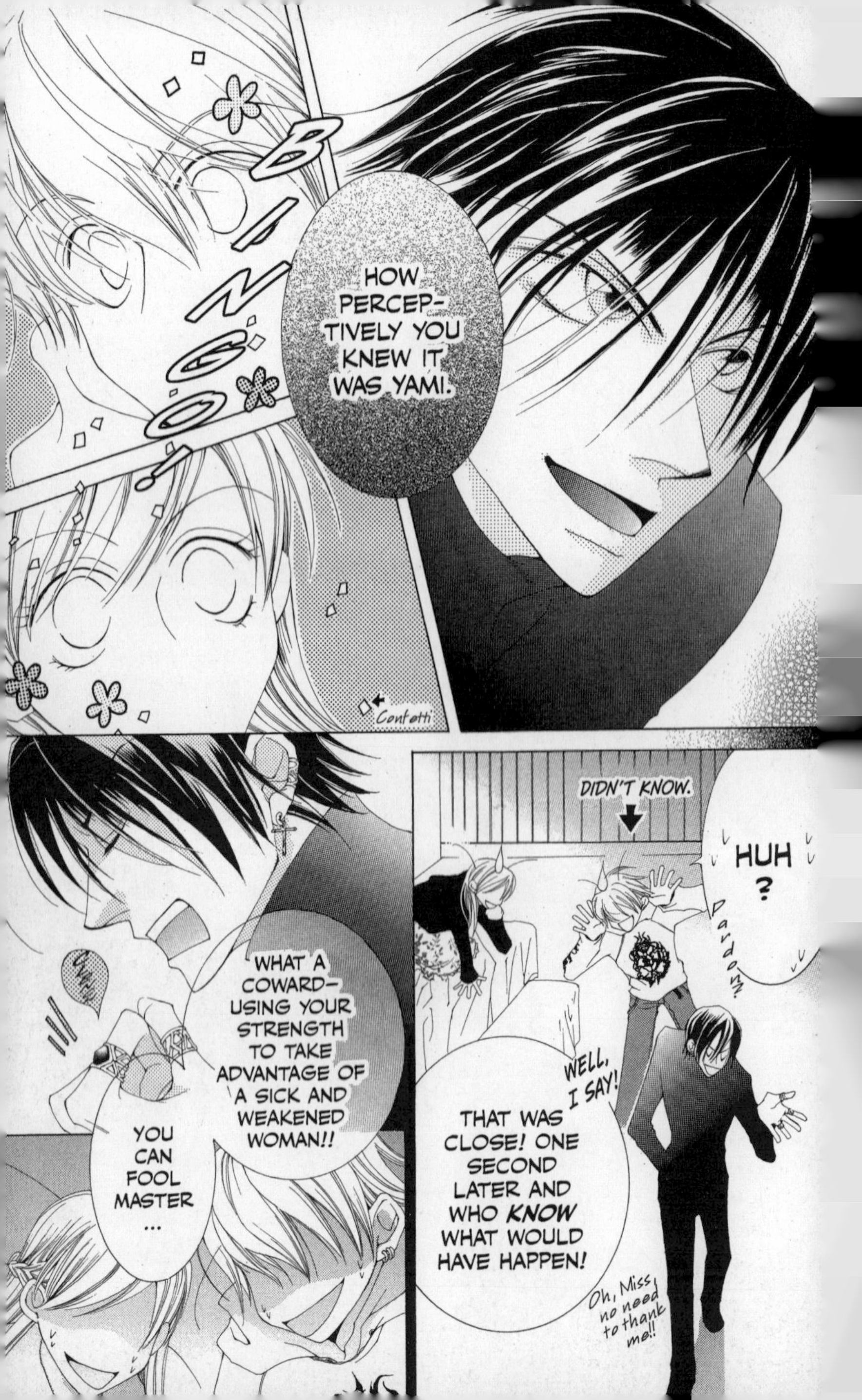

BINGO!
HOW PERCEPTIVELY YOU KNEW IT WAS YAMI.
Confetti
HUH?
Pardon?
DIDN'T KNOW.
WELL, I SAY!
THAT WAS CLOSE! ONE SECOND LATER AND WHO KNOW WHAT WOULD HAVE HAPPEN!
Oh, Miss, no need to thank me!!
WHAT A COWARD–USING YOUR STRENGTH TO TAKE ADVANTAGE OF A SICK AND WEAKENED WOMAN!!
YOU CAN FOOL MASTER...

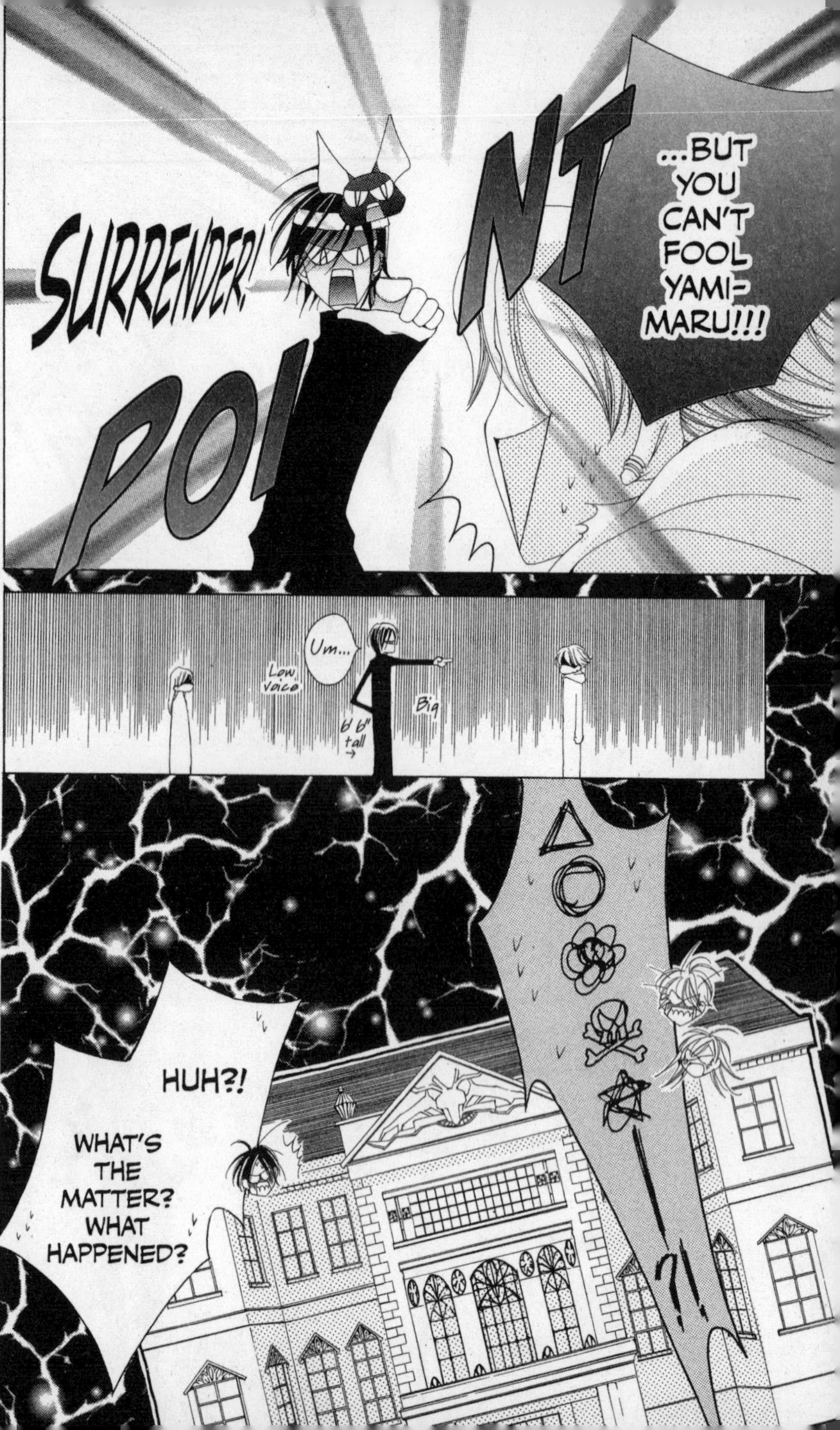
...BUT YOU CAN'T FOOL YAMI-MARU!!!
SURRENDER!
POINT
Um...
Low voice
Big
6' 6" tall
?!
HUH?!
WHAT'S THE MATTER? WHAT HAPPENED?

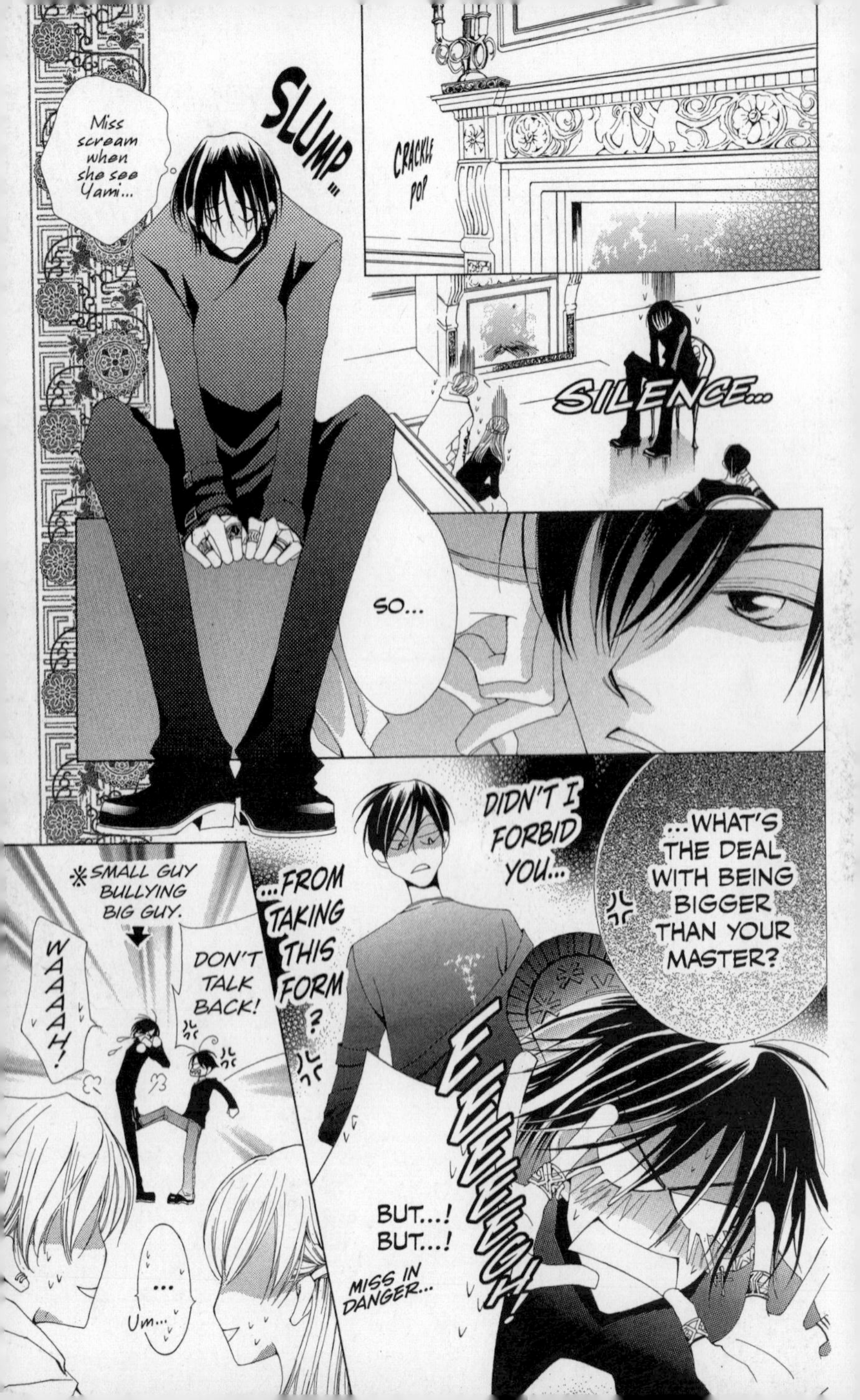
CRACKLE POP
SILENCE...
SO...
SLUMP...
Miss scream when she see Yami...
...WHAT'S THE DEAL WITH BEING BIGGER THAN YOUR MASTER?
DIDN'T I FORBID YOU...
...FROM TAKING THIS FORM?
BUT...! BUT...!
MISS IN DANGER...
※SMALL GUY BULLYING BIG GUY.
DON'T TALK BACK!
WAAAAH!
...
Um...

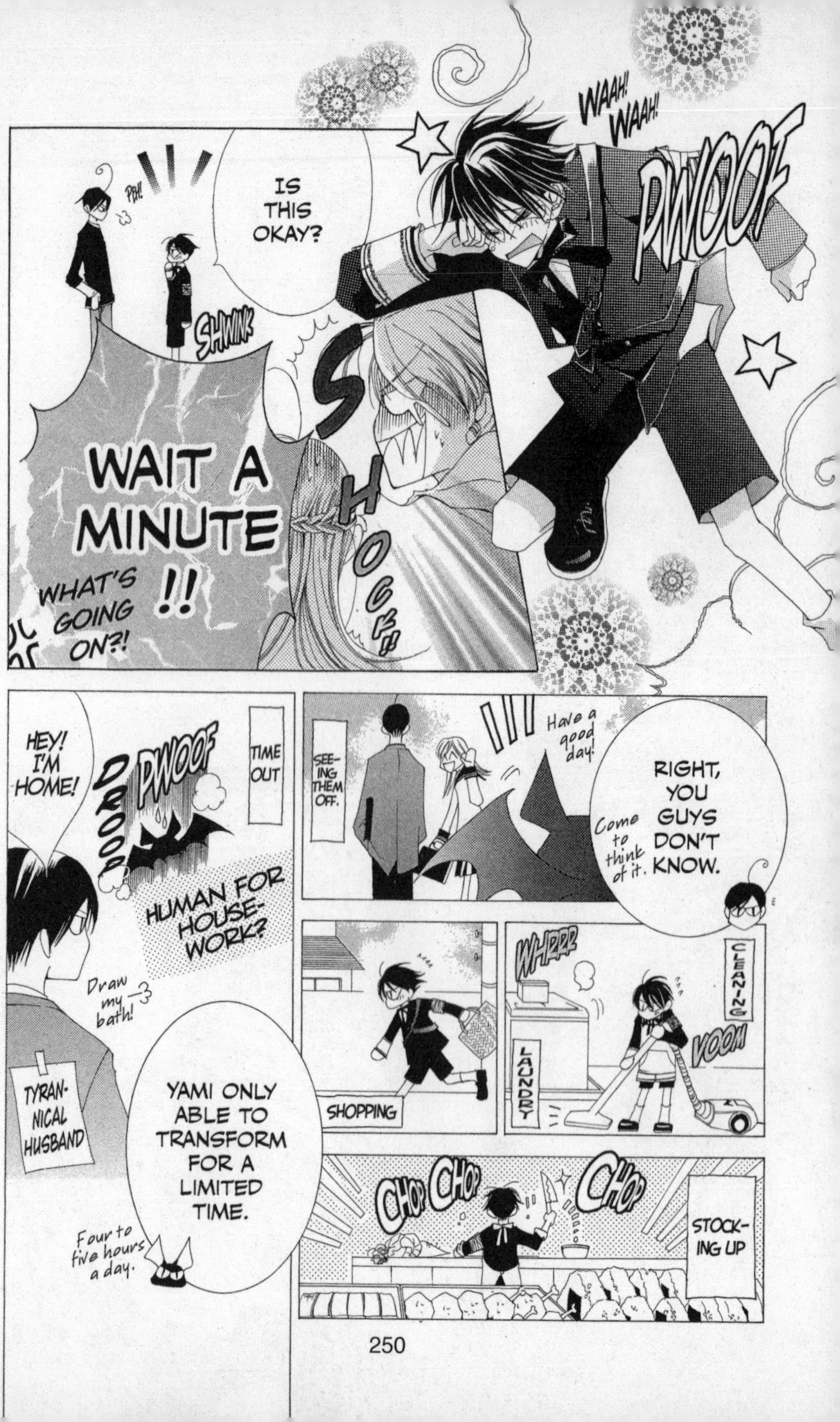
WAAH! WAAH!
PWOOF
IS THIS OKAY?
PBH!
SHWINK
SHOCK!!
WAIT A MINUTE !!
WHAT'S GOING ON?!
RIGHT, YOU GUYS DON'T KNOW.
Come to think of it.
Have a good day!
SEEING THEM OFF.
CLEANING
WHRRR
VOOM
LAUNDRY
SHOPPING
STOCKING UP
CHOP CHOP
CHOP
TIME OUT
HEY! I'M HOME!
DROOP
PWOOF
HUMAN FOR HOUSEWORK?
Draw my bath!
TYRANNICAL HUSBAND
YAMI ONLY ABLE TO TRANSFORM FOR A LIMITED TIME.
Four to five hours a day.

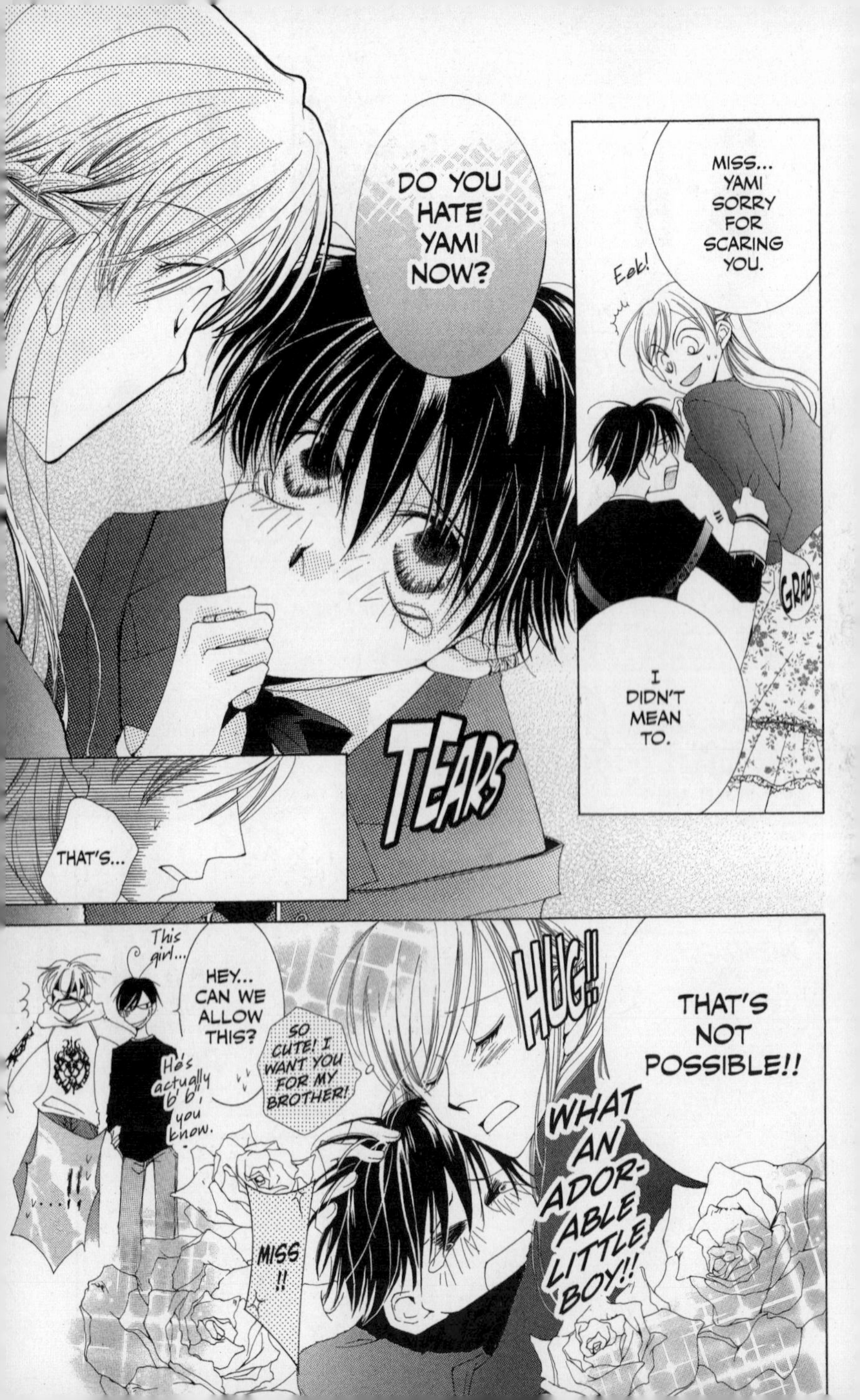
MISS... YAMI SORRY FOR SCARING YOU.
Eek!
GRAB
I DIDN'T MEAN TO.
DO YOU HATE YAMI NOW?
TEARS
THAT'S...
THAT'S NOT POSSIBLE!!
HUG!!
WHAT AN ADOR-ABLE LITTLE BOY!!
MISS!!
SO CUTE! I WANT YOU FOR MY BROTHER!
HEY... CAN WE ALLOW THIS?
This girl...
He's actually 'b' 'b' you know.
...!!

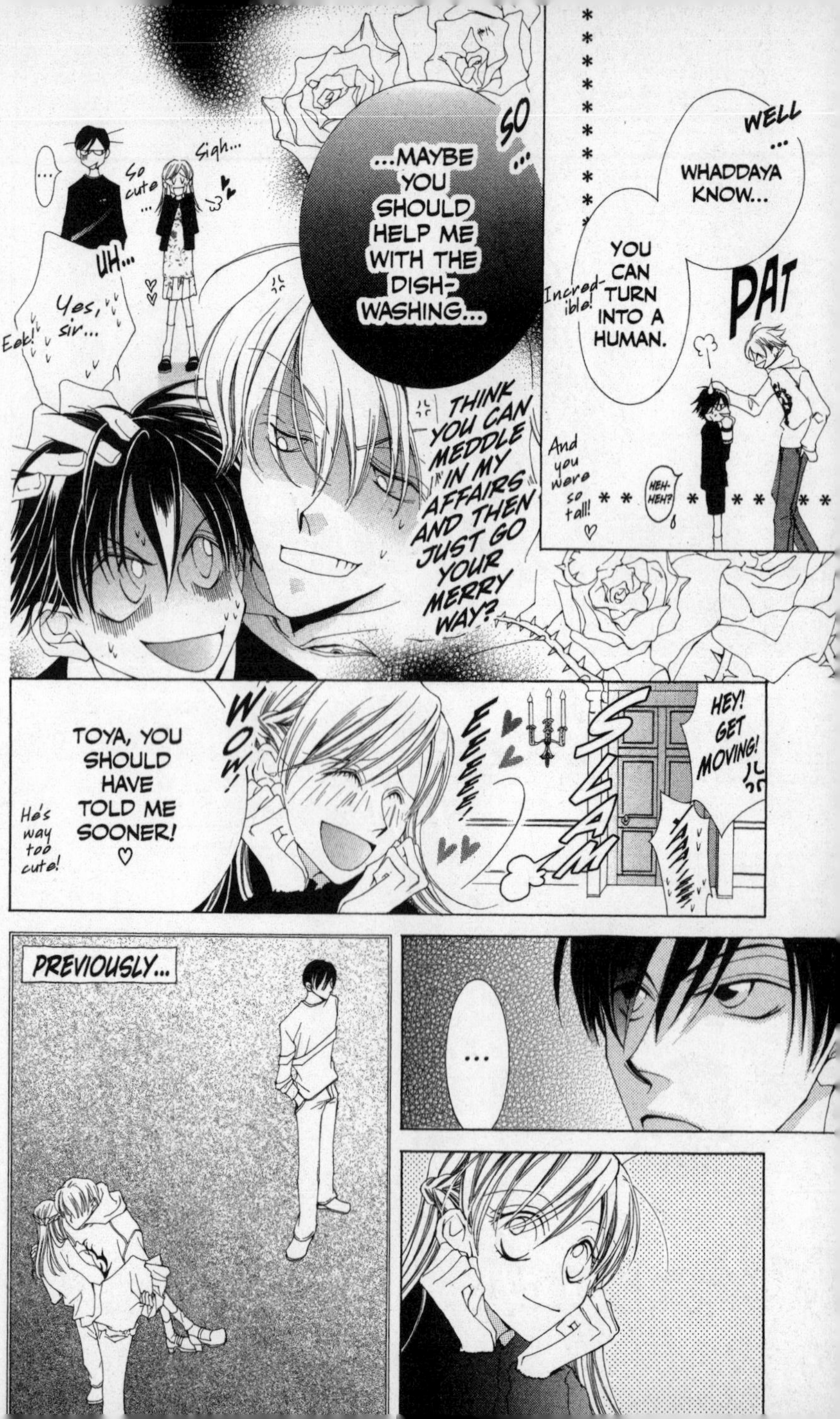
WELL ...
WHADDAYA KNOW...
YOU CAN TURN INTO A HUMAN.
Incredible!
PAT
And you were so tall! ♡
HEH-HEH?
SO ...
...MAYBE YOU SHOULD HELP ME WITH THE DISH-WASHING...
THINK YOU CAN MEDDLE IN MY AFFAIRS AND THEN JUST GO YOUR MERRY WAY?
UH...
Yes, sir...
Eek!
Sigh...
So cute...
...
HEY! GET MOVING!
SLAM
EEEEE!
WOW!
TOYA, YOU SHOULD HAVE TOLD ME SOONER! ♡
He's way too cute!
...
PREVIOUSLY...

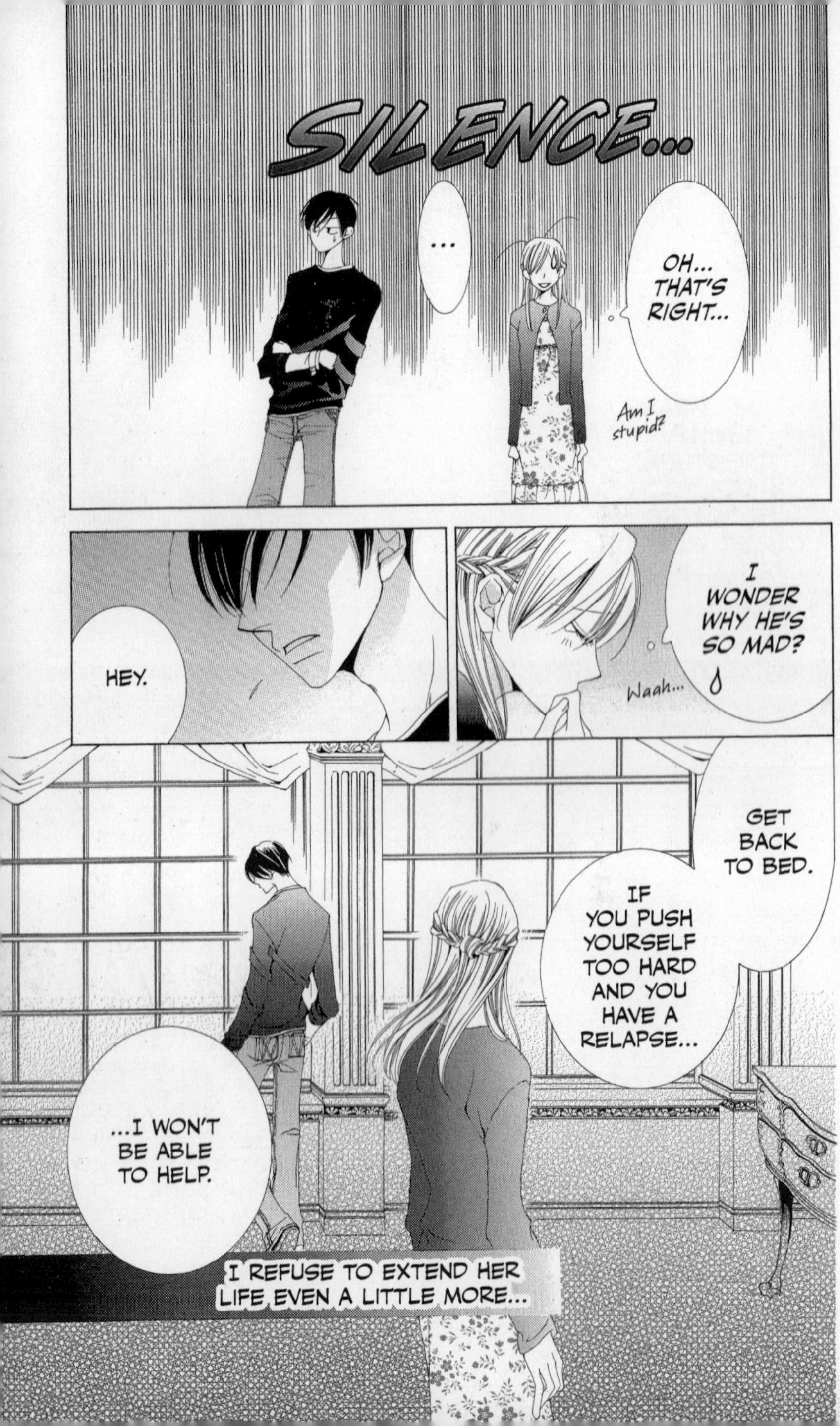
SILENCE...
OH... THAT'S RIGHT...
Am I stupid?
...
I WONDER WHY HE'S SO MAD?
Waah...
HEY.
GET BACK TO BED.
IF YOU PUSH YOURSELF TOO HARD AND YOU HAVE A RELAPSE...
...I WON'T BE ABLE TO HELP.
I REFUSE TO EXTEND HER LIFE EVEN A LITTLE MORE...

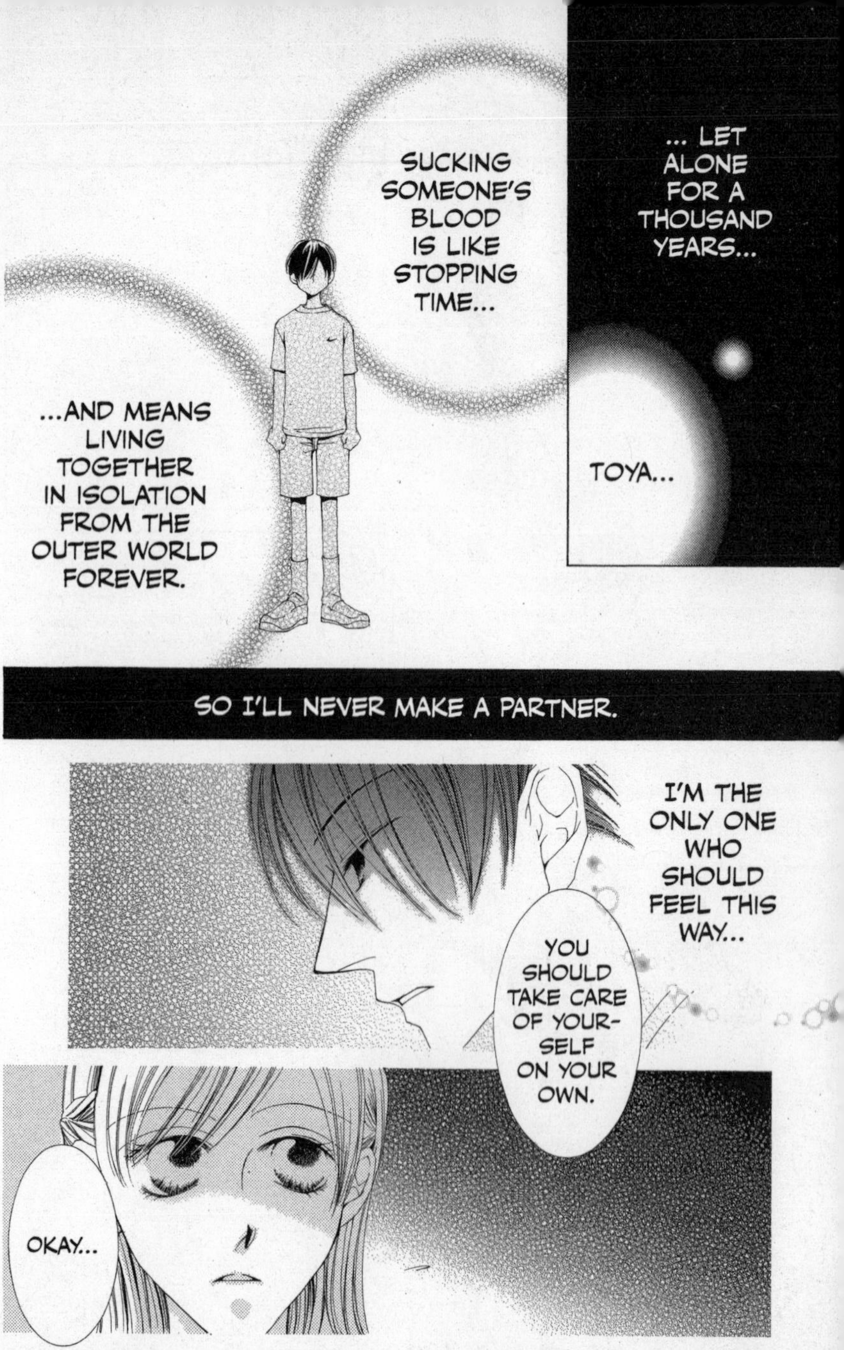
... LET ALONE FOR A THOUSAND YEARS...
TOYA...
SUCKING SOMEONE'S BLOOD IS LIKE STOPPING TIME...
...AND MEANS LIVING TOGETHER IN ISOLATION FROM THE OUTER WORLD FOREVER.
SO I'LL NEVER MAKE A PARTNER.
I'M THE ONLY ONE WHO SHOULD FEEL THIS WAY...
YOU SHOULD TAKE CARE OF YOUR-SELF ON YOUR OWN.
OKAY...

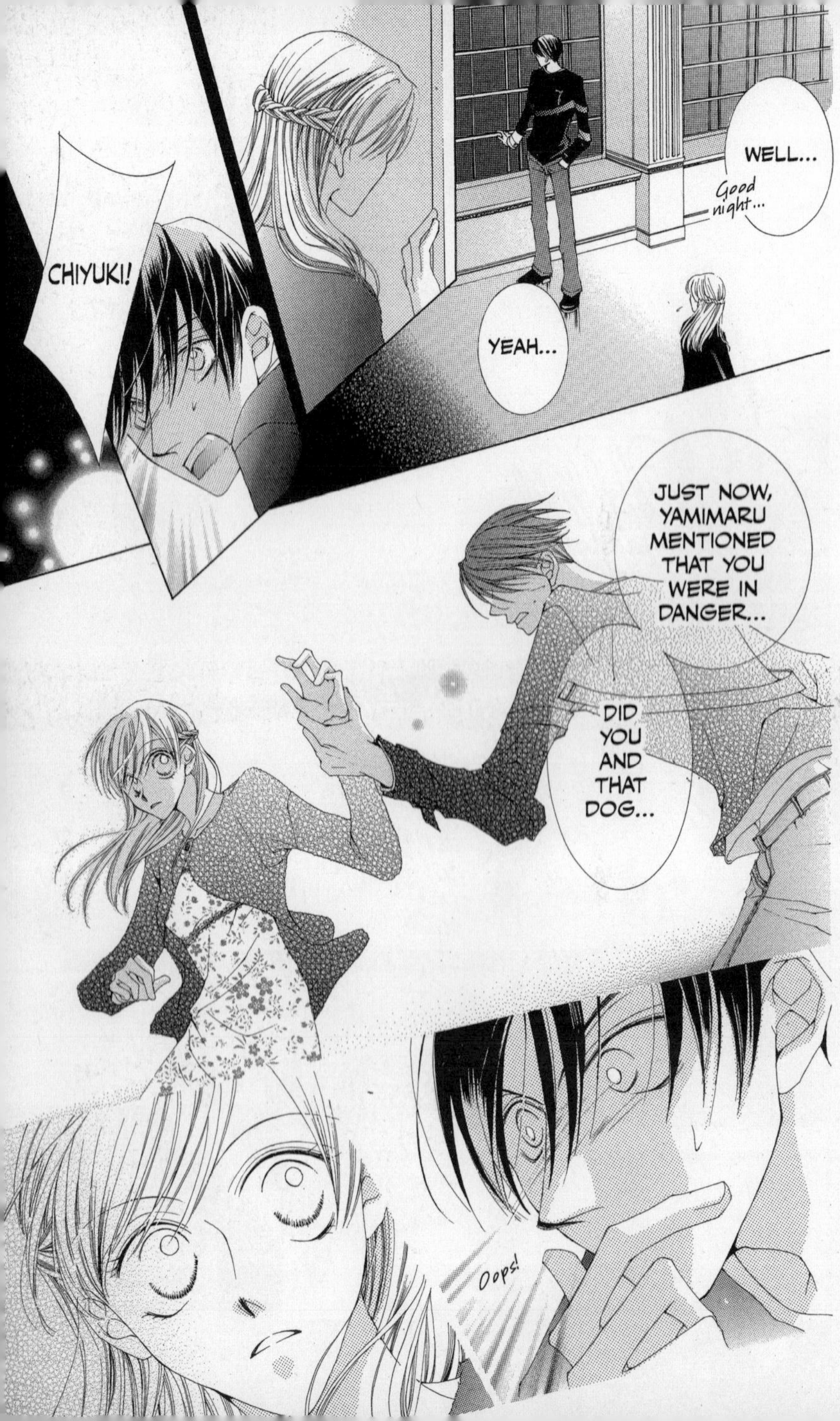
WELL...
Good night...
YEAH...
CHIYUKI!
JUST NOW, YAMIMARU MENTIONED THAT YOU WERE IN DANGER...
DID YOU AND THAT DOG...
Oops!

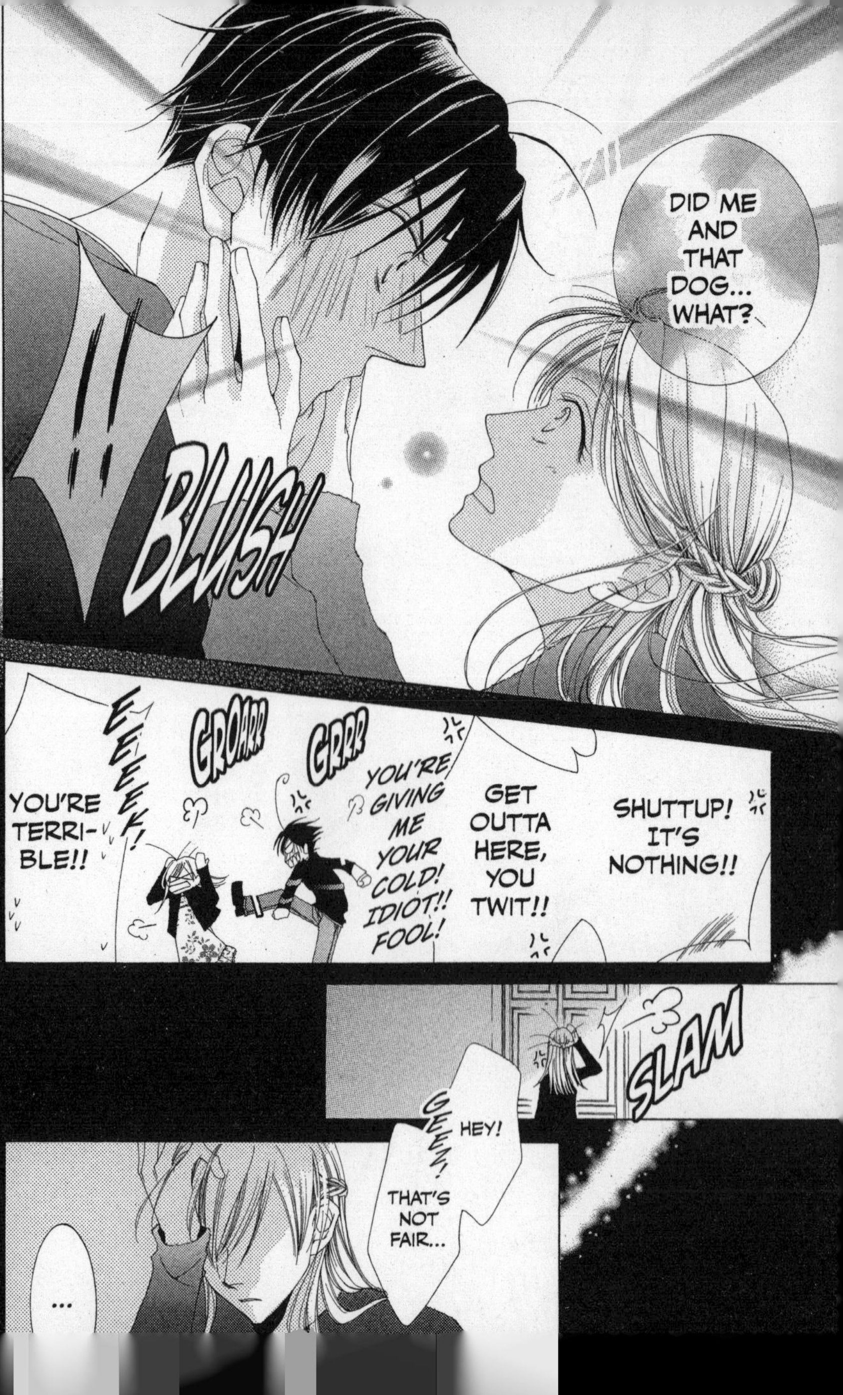
DID ME AND THAT DOG... WHAT?
BLUSH
!!
SHUTTUP! IT'S NOTHING!!
GET OUTTA HERE, YOU TWIT!!
YOU'RE GIVING ME YOUR COLD! IDIOT!! FOOL!
GRRR
GROARR
EEEEK!
YOU'RE TERRIBLE!!
SLAM
HEY!
GEEZ!
THAT'S NOT FAIR...
...

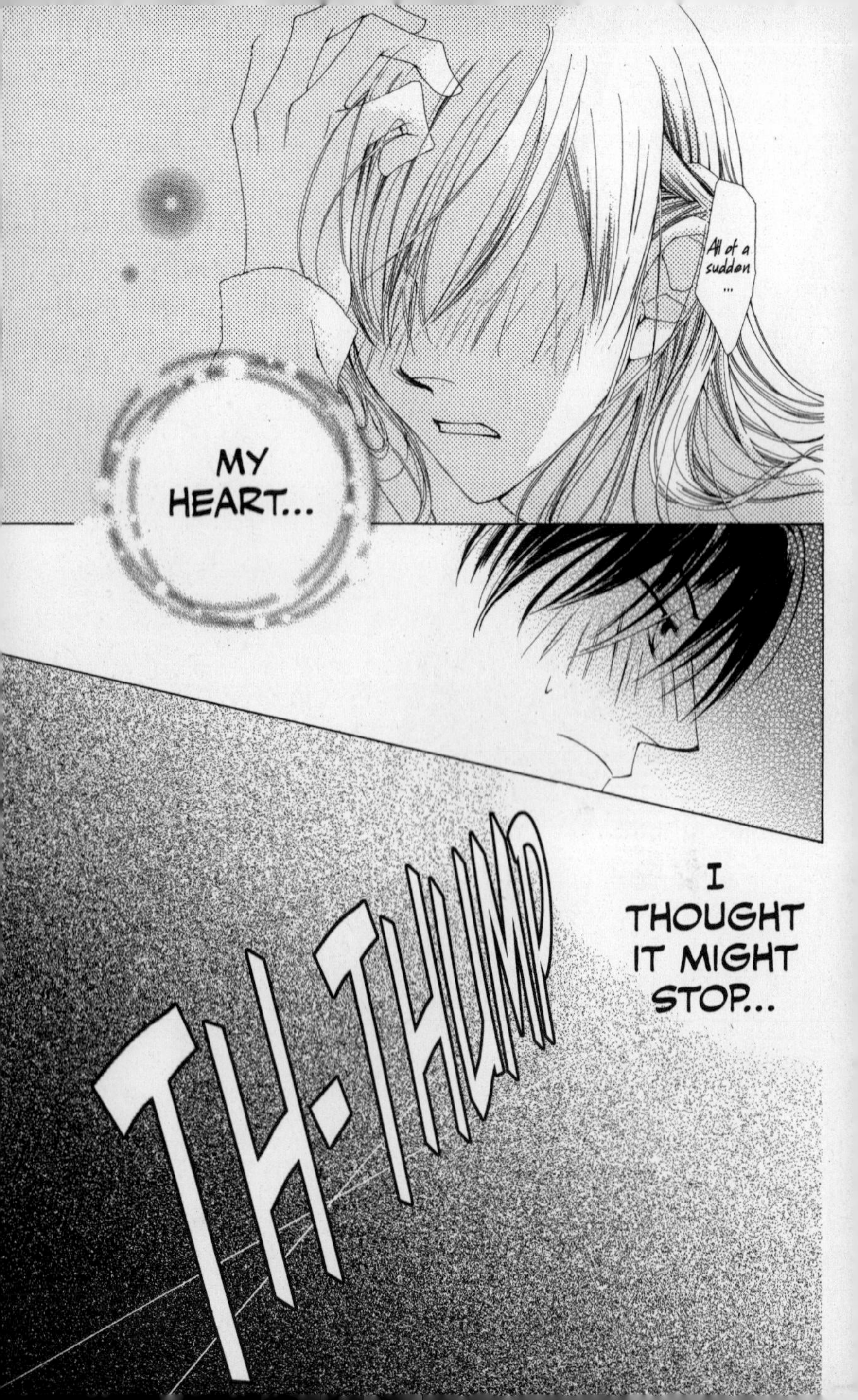
All of a sudden ...
MY HEART...
I THOUGHT IT MIGHT STOP...
TH-THUMP

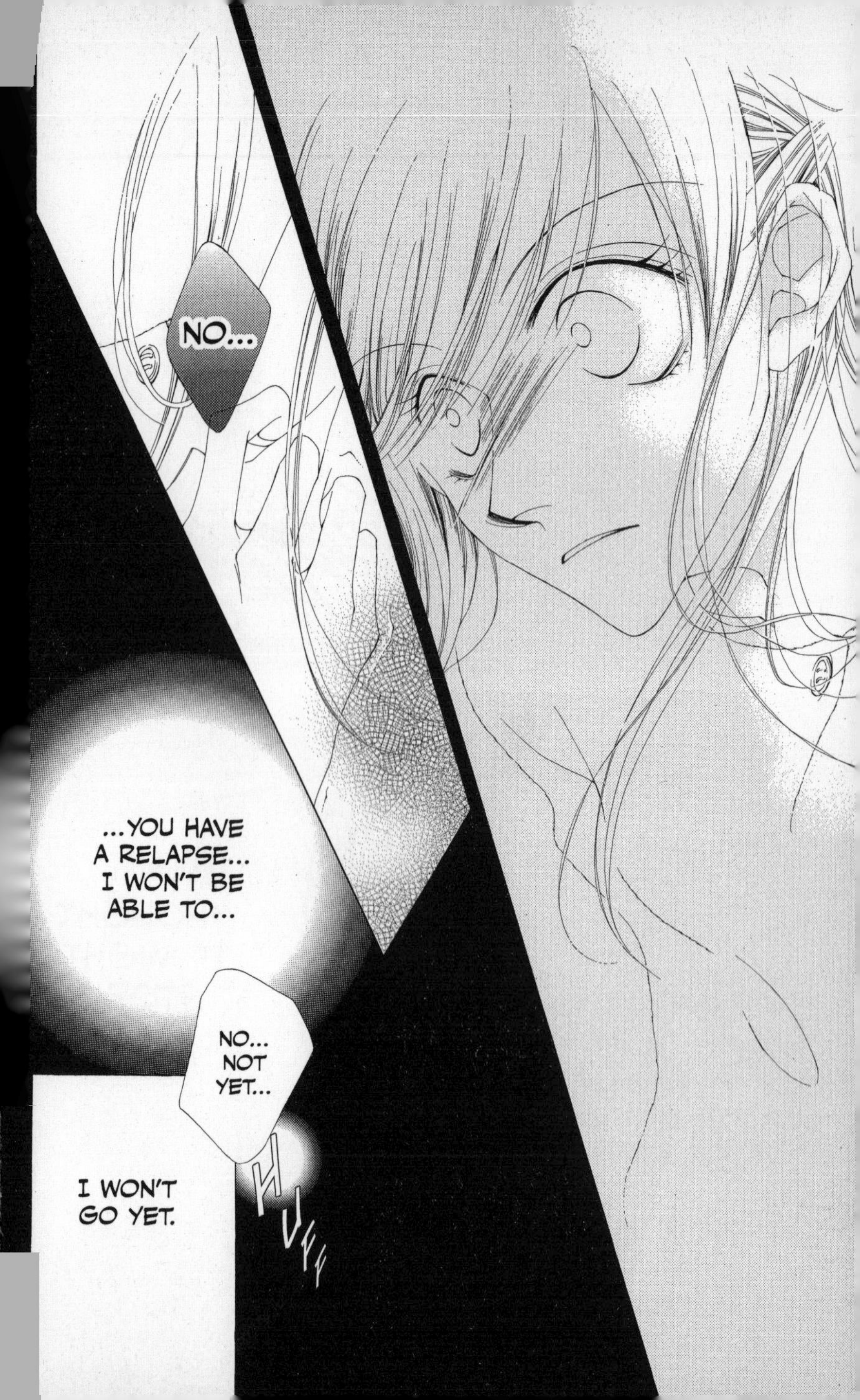
NO...
...YOU HAVE A RELAPSE... I WON'T BE ABLE TO...
NO... NOT YET...
HUFF
I WON'T GO YET.

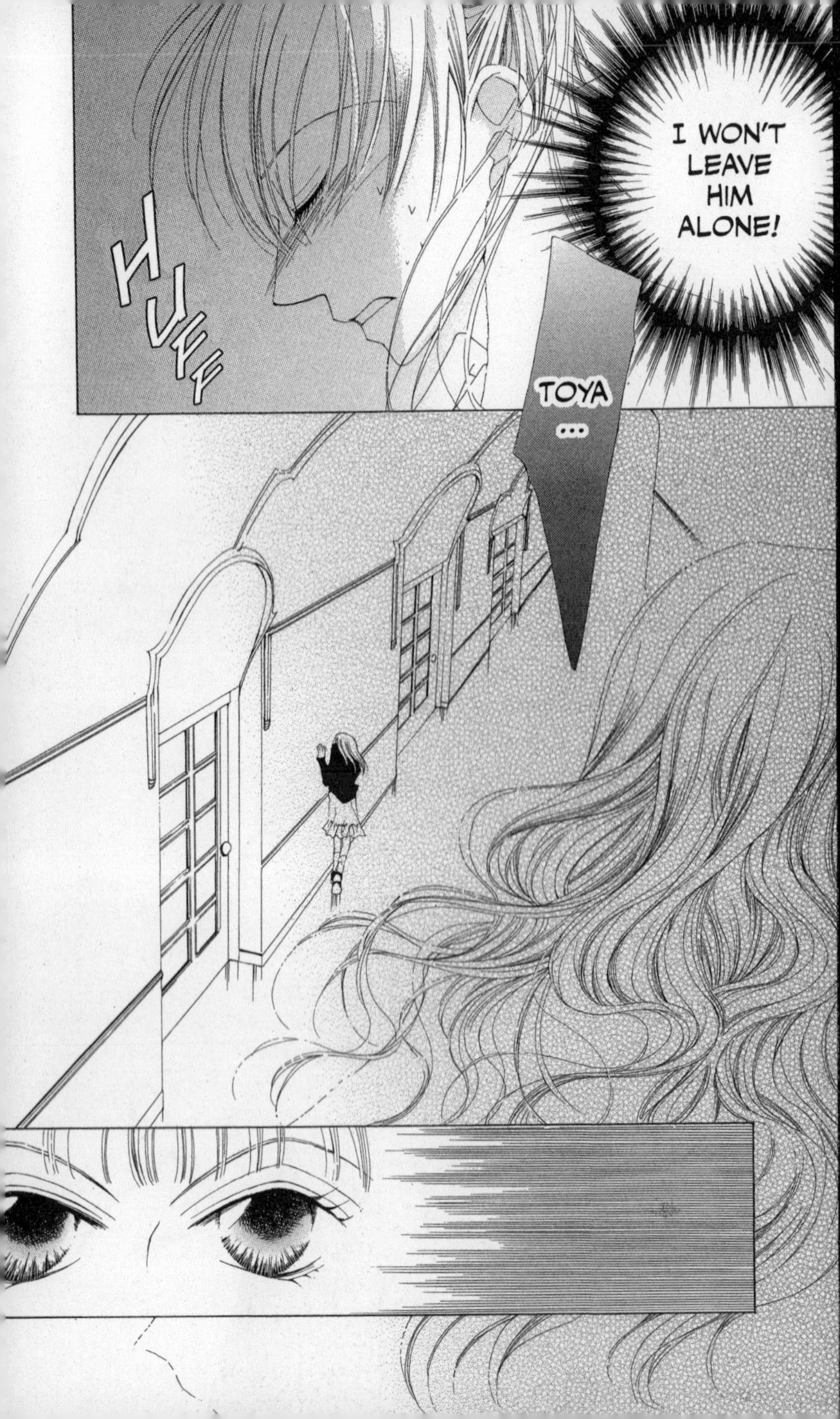
I WON'T LEAVE HIM ALONE!
HUFF
TOYA ...

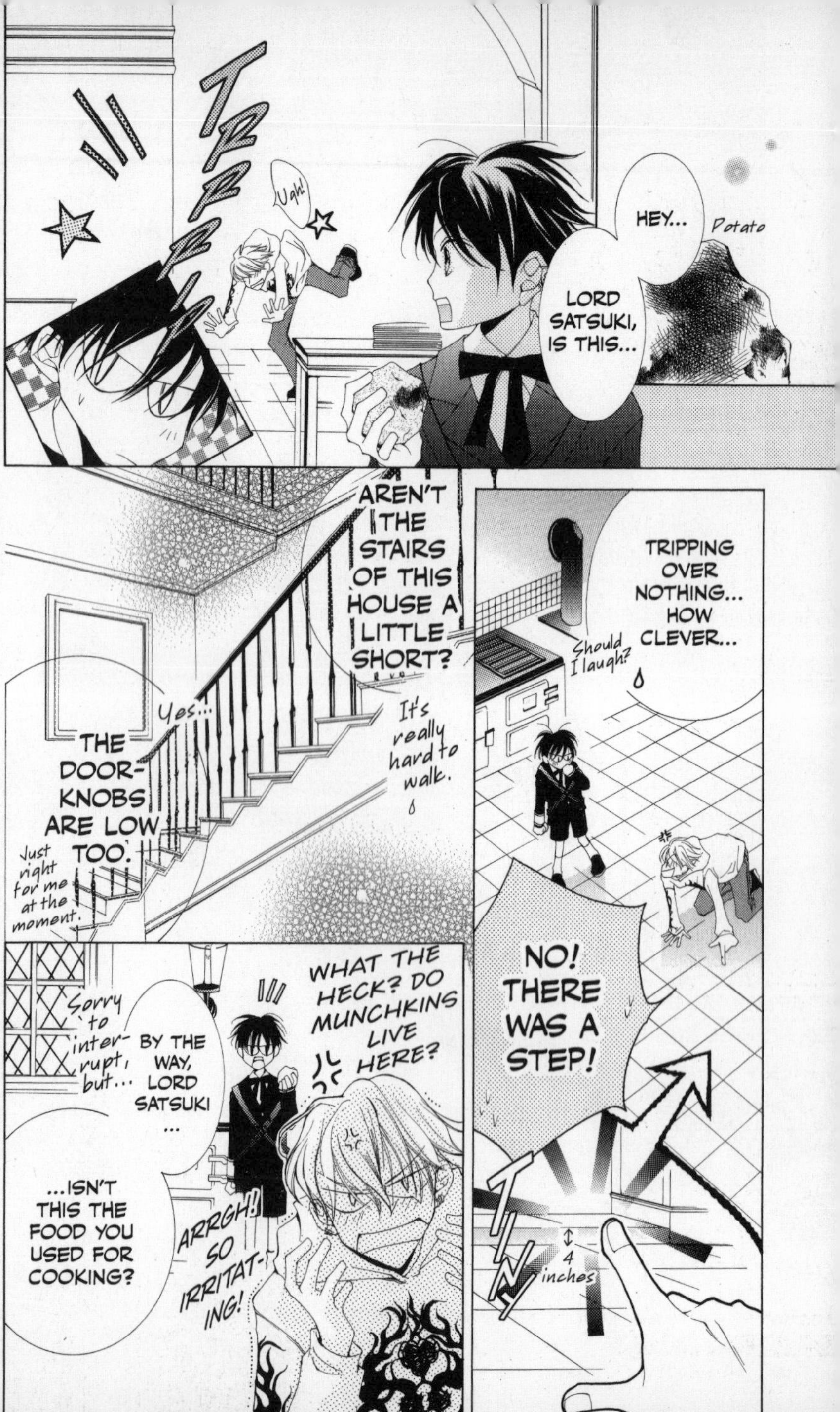
HEY...
Potato
LORD SATSUKI, IS THIS...
Ugh!
TRIPPING OVER NOTHING... HOW CLEVER...
Should I laugh?
AREN'T THE STAIRS OF THIS HOUSE A LITTLE SHORT?
It's really hard to walk.
Yes...
THE DOOR-KNOBS ARE LOW TOO.
Just right for me at the moment.
NO! THERE WAS A STEP!
4 inches
WHAT THE HECK? DO MUNCHKINS LIVE HERE?
BY THE WAY, LORD SATSUKI...
Sorry to interrupt, but...
...ISN'T THIS THE FOOD YOU USED FOR COOKING?
ARRGH! SO IRRITATING!

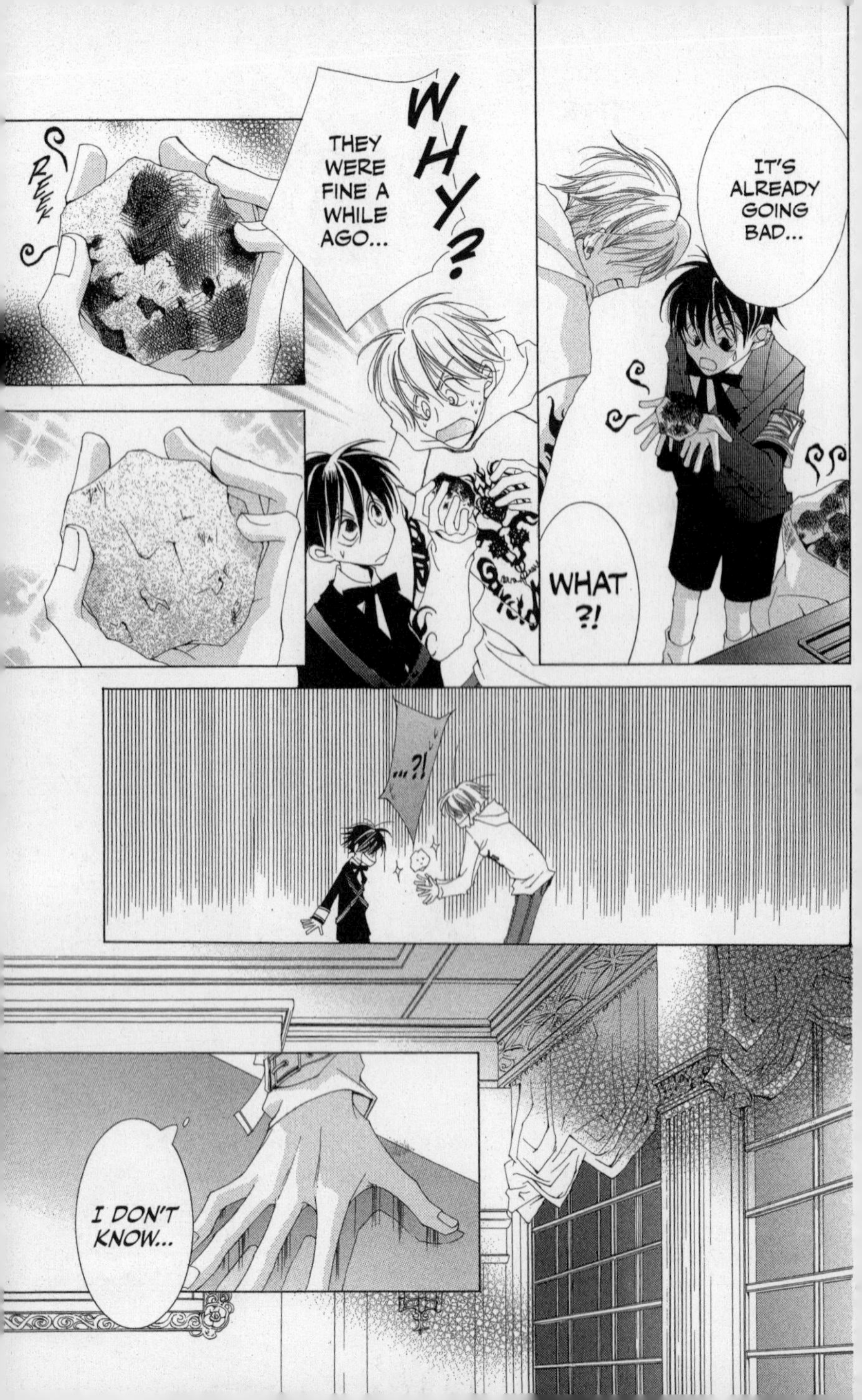
IT'S ALREADY GOING BAD...
WHAT?!
WHY?
THEY WERE FINE A WHILE AGO...
REEK
...?!
I DON'T KNOW...

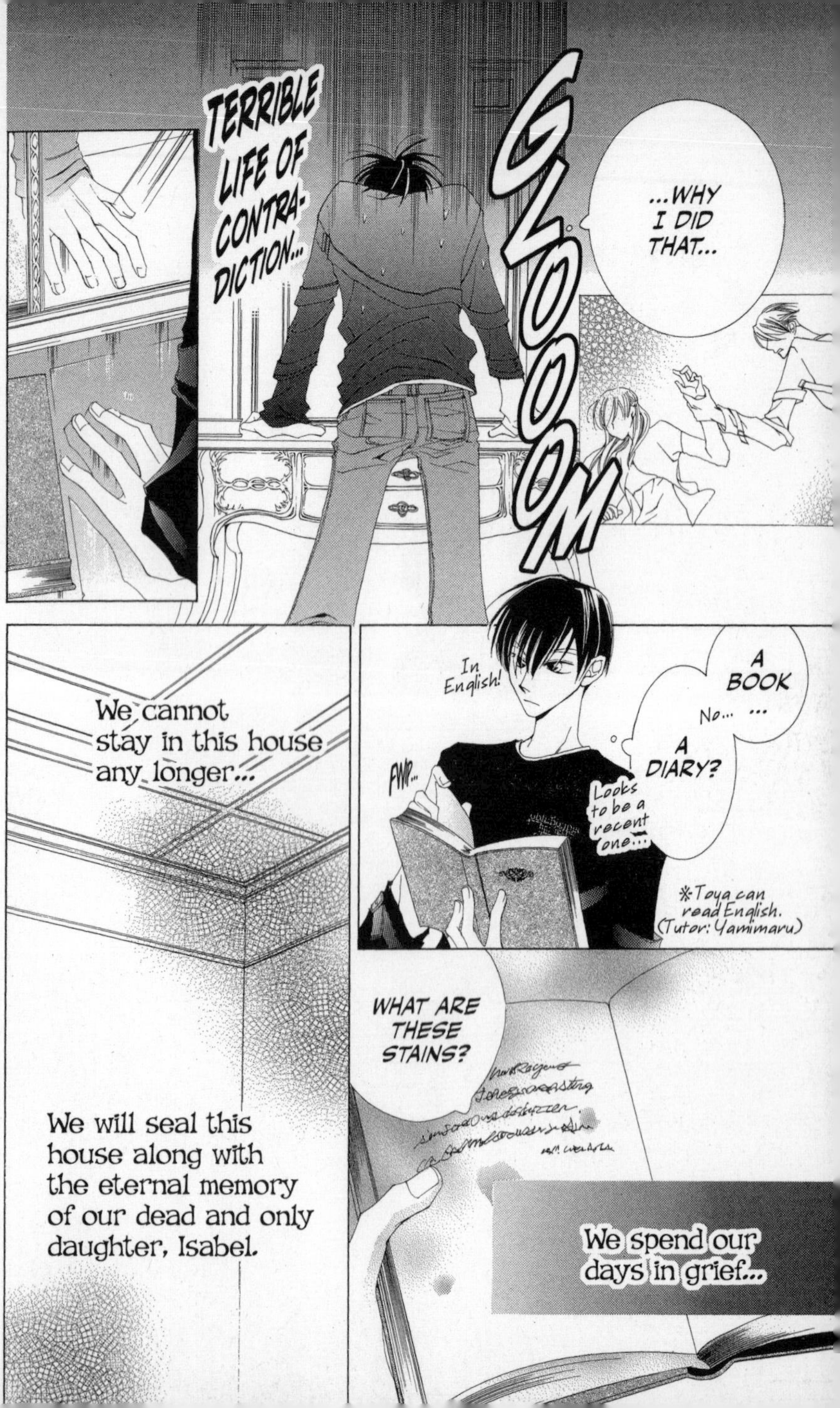
...WHY I DID THAT...
GLOOOOM
TERRIBLE LIFE OF CONTRA-DICTION...
A BOOK ... No... A DIARY?
In English!
FWIP...
Looks to be a recent one...
※Toya can read English. (Tutor: Yamimaru)
WHAT ARE THESE STAINS?
We spend our days in grief...
We cannot stay in this house any longer...
We will seal this house along with the eternal memory of our dead and only daughter, Isabel.

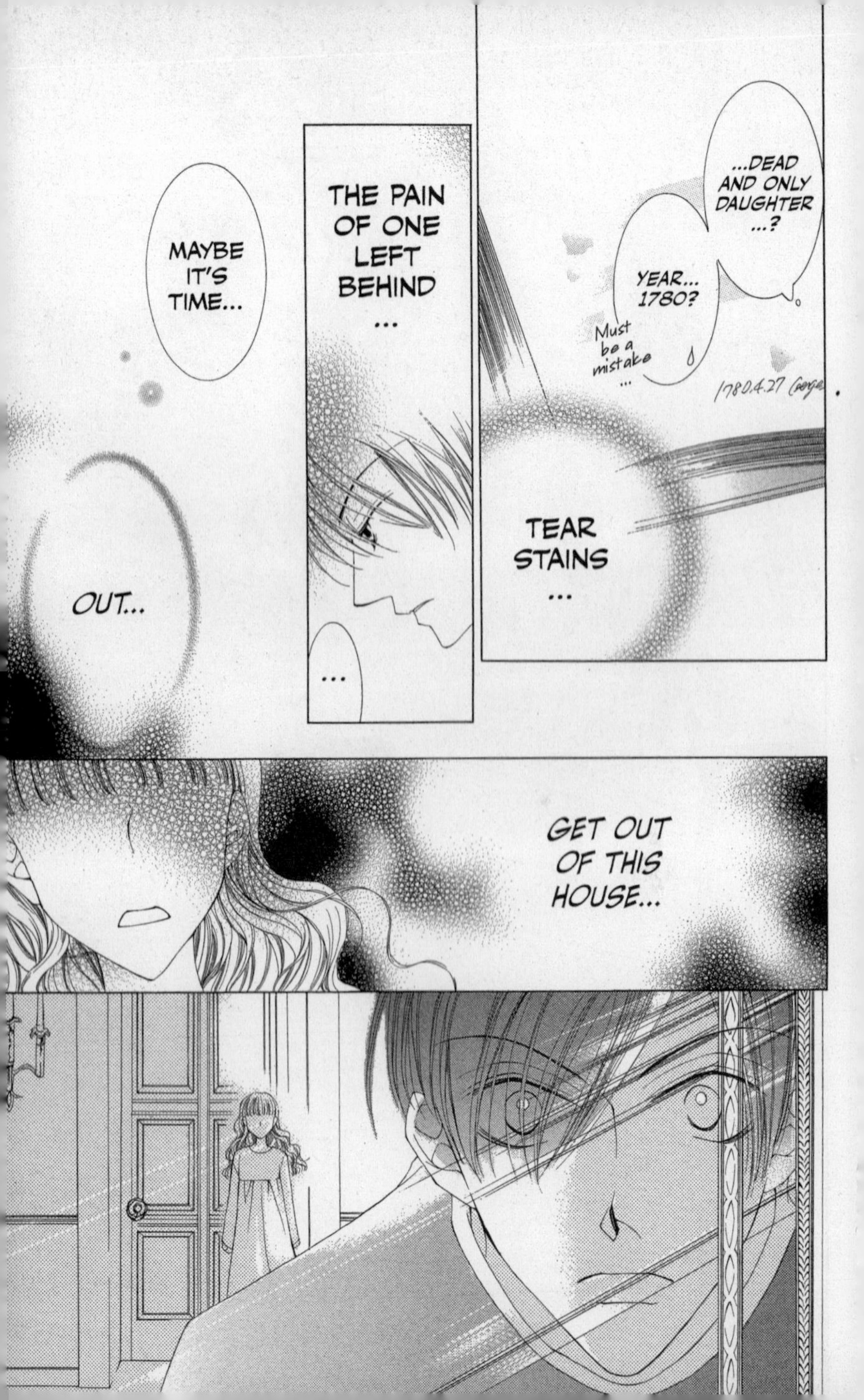
...DEAD AND ONLY DAUGHTER ...?
YEAR... 1780?
Must be a mistake ...
1780.4.27
TEAR STAINS ...
THE PAIN OF ONE LEFT BEHIND ...
...
MAYBE IT'S TIME...
OUT...
GET OUT OF THIS HOUSE...

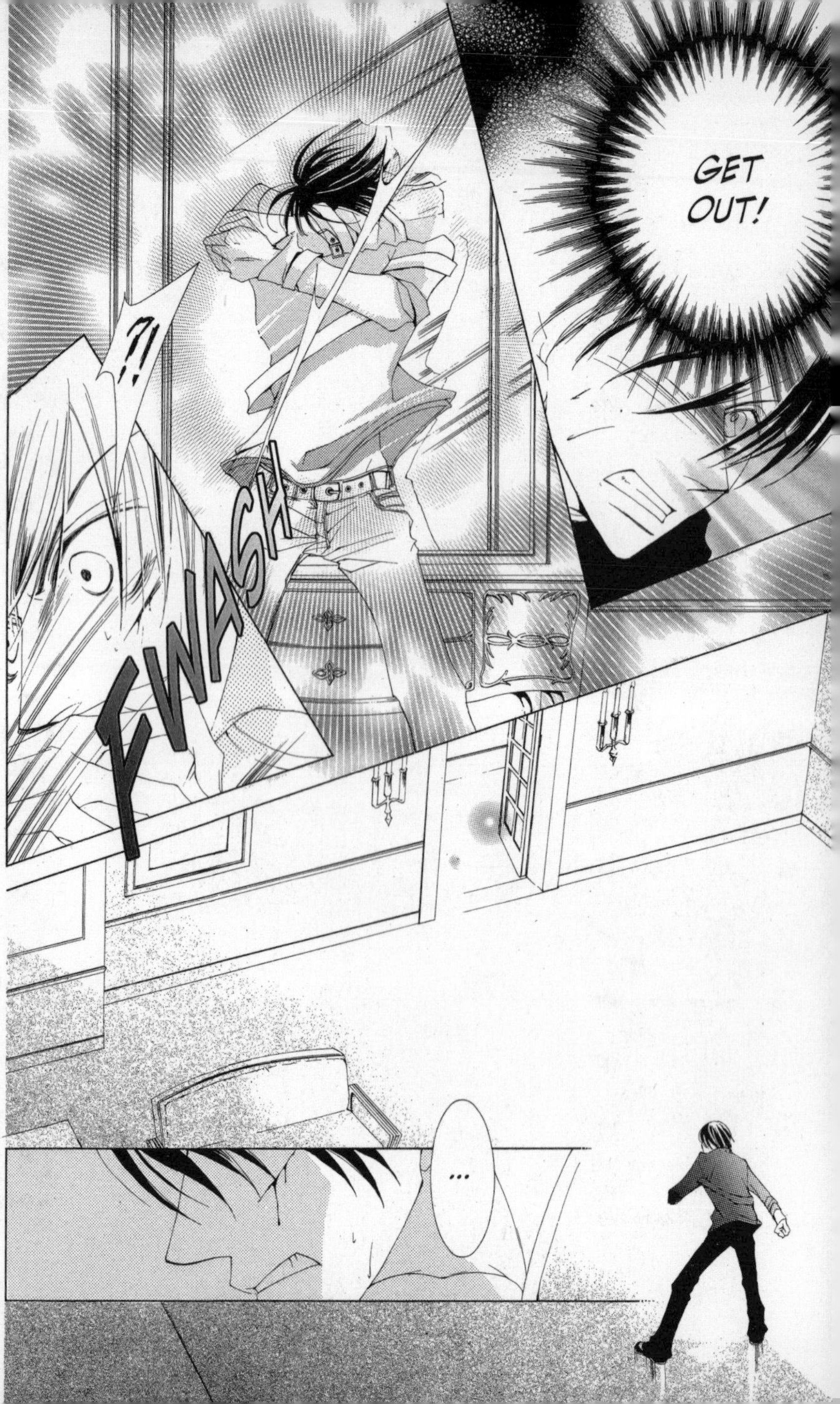
GET OUT!
?!
FWASH
...

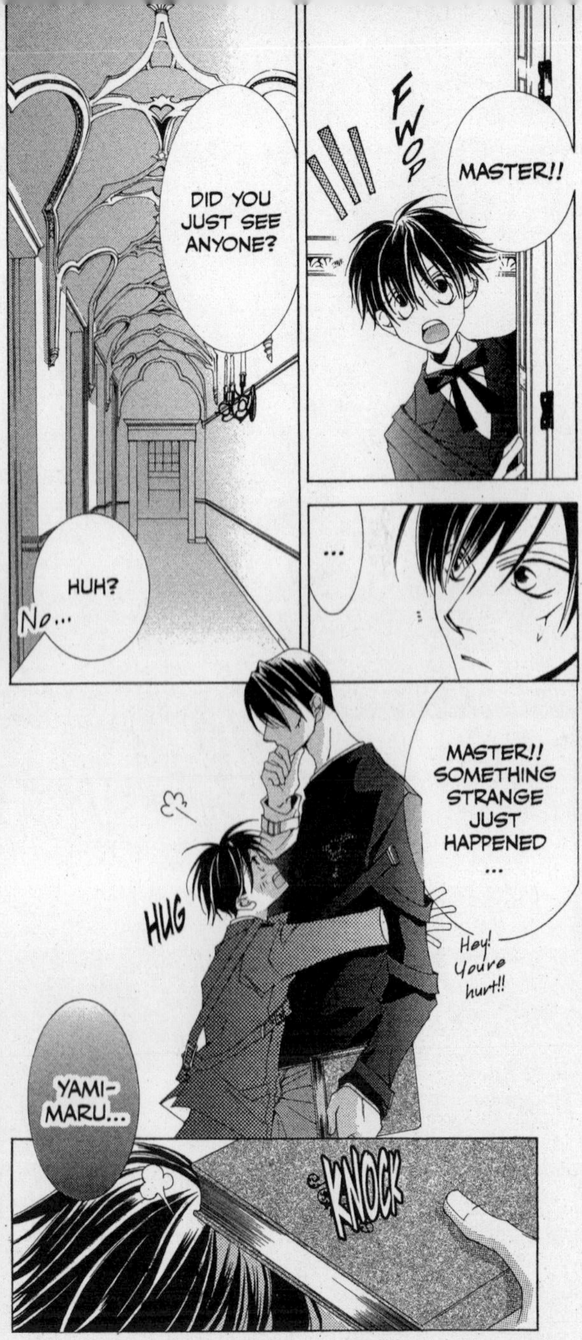
FWOP
MASTER!!
DID YOU JUST SEE ANYONE?
HUH?
No...
...
MASTER!! SOMETHING STRANGE JUST HAPPENED ...
Hey! You're hurt!!
HUG
YAMI-MARU...
KNOCK

松岡 千雪

CHIYUKI·MATSUOKA

5'2" tall
Blood type: A
She must have a strong skull. It's rare for a heroine to be hit on the head as much as Chiyuki is...

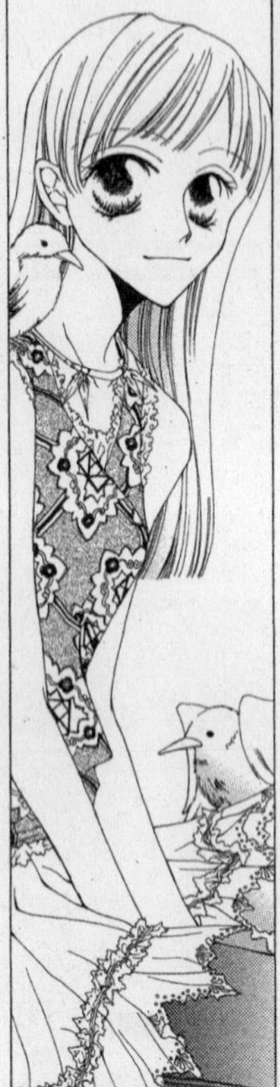

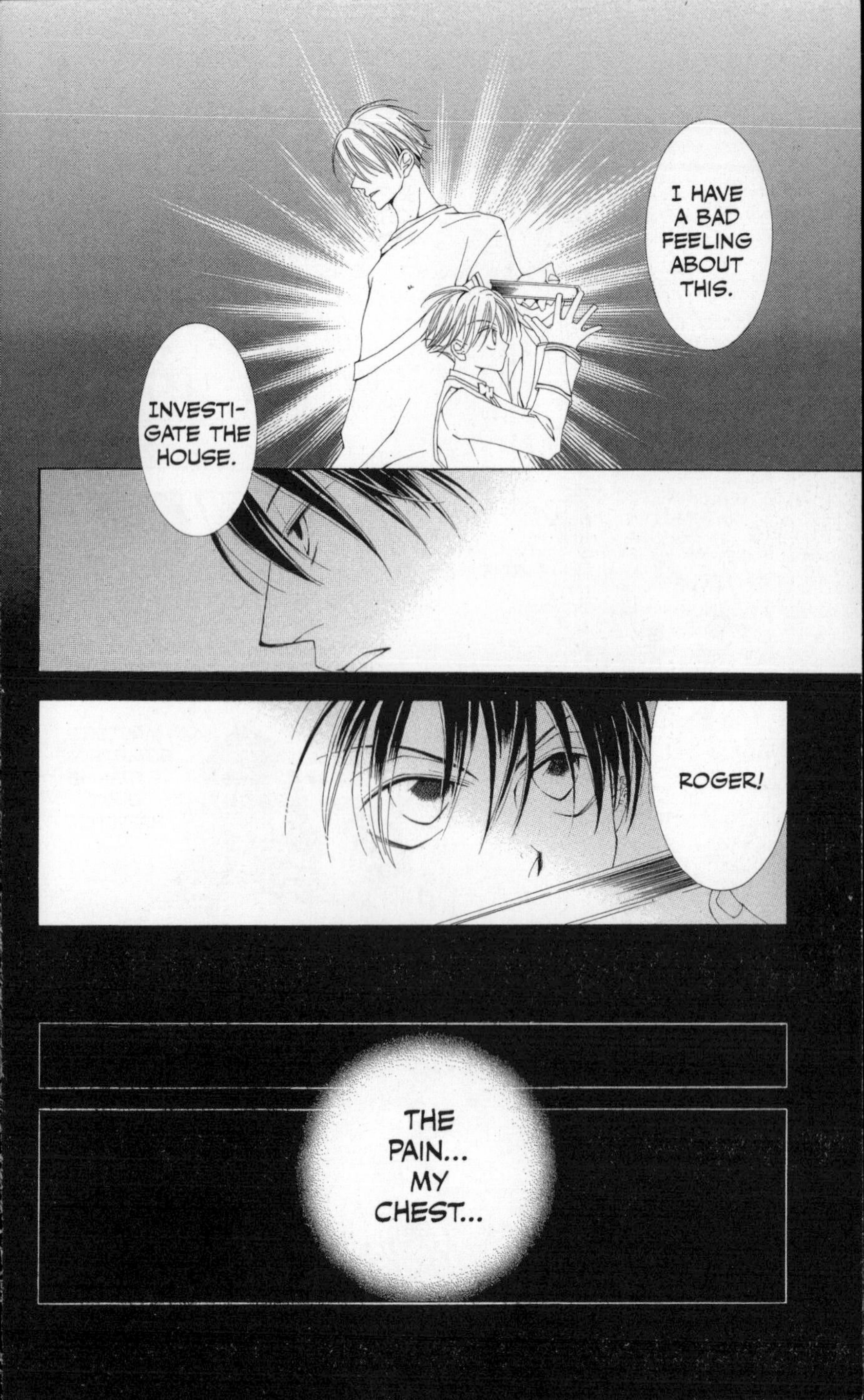
I HAVE A BAD FEELING ABOUT THIS.
INVESTIGATE THE HOUSE.
ROGER!
THE PAIN... MY CHEST...

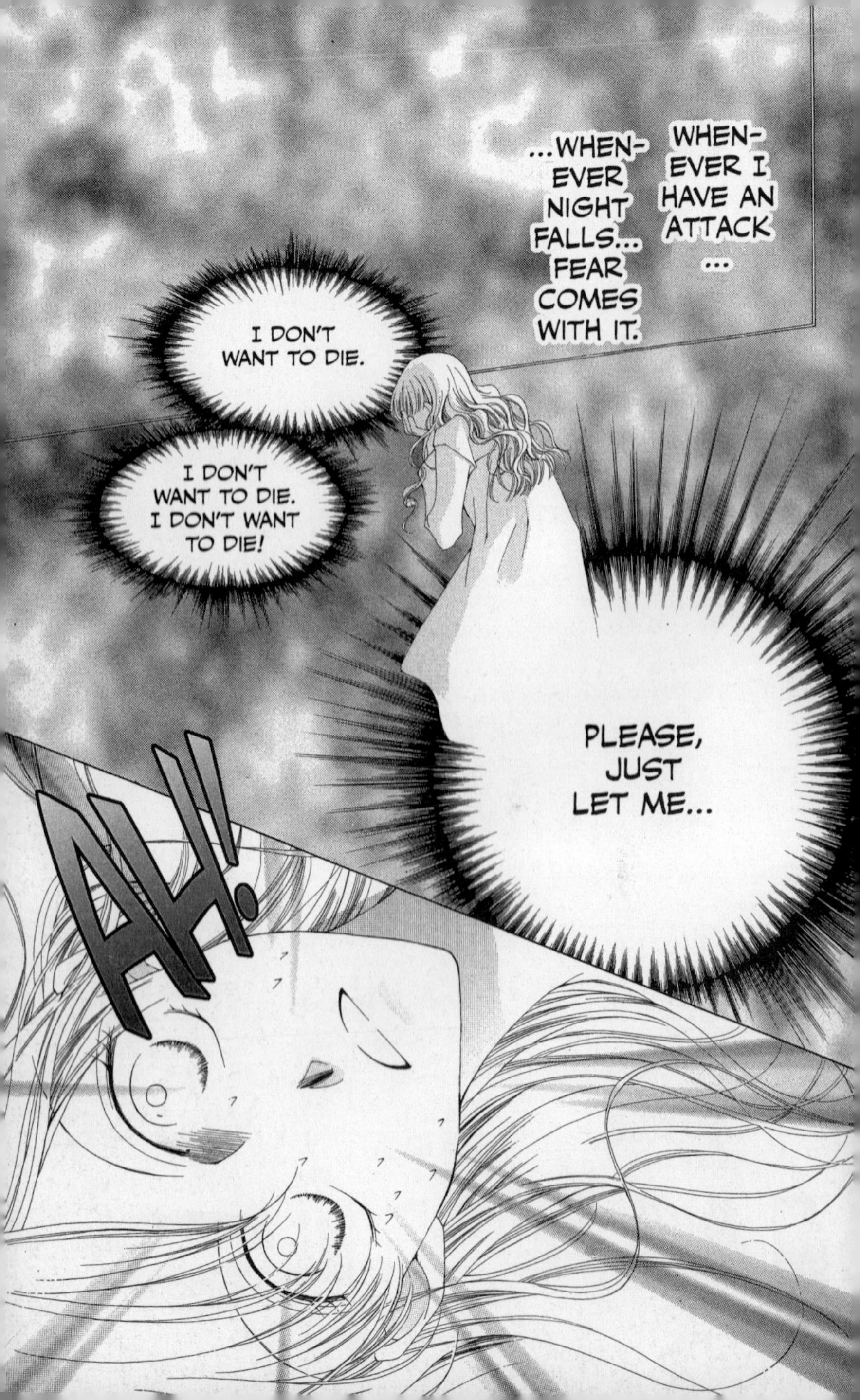
WHEN-EVER I HAVE AN ATTACK ...
...WHEN-EVER NIGHT FALLS... FEAR COMES WITH IT.
I DON'T WANT TO DIE.
I DON'T WANT TO DIE. I DON'T WANT TO DIE!
PLEASE, JUST LET ME...
AH!!

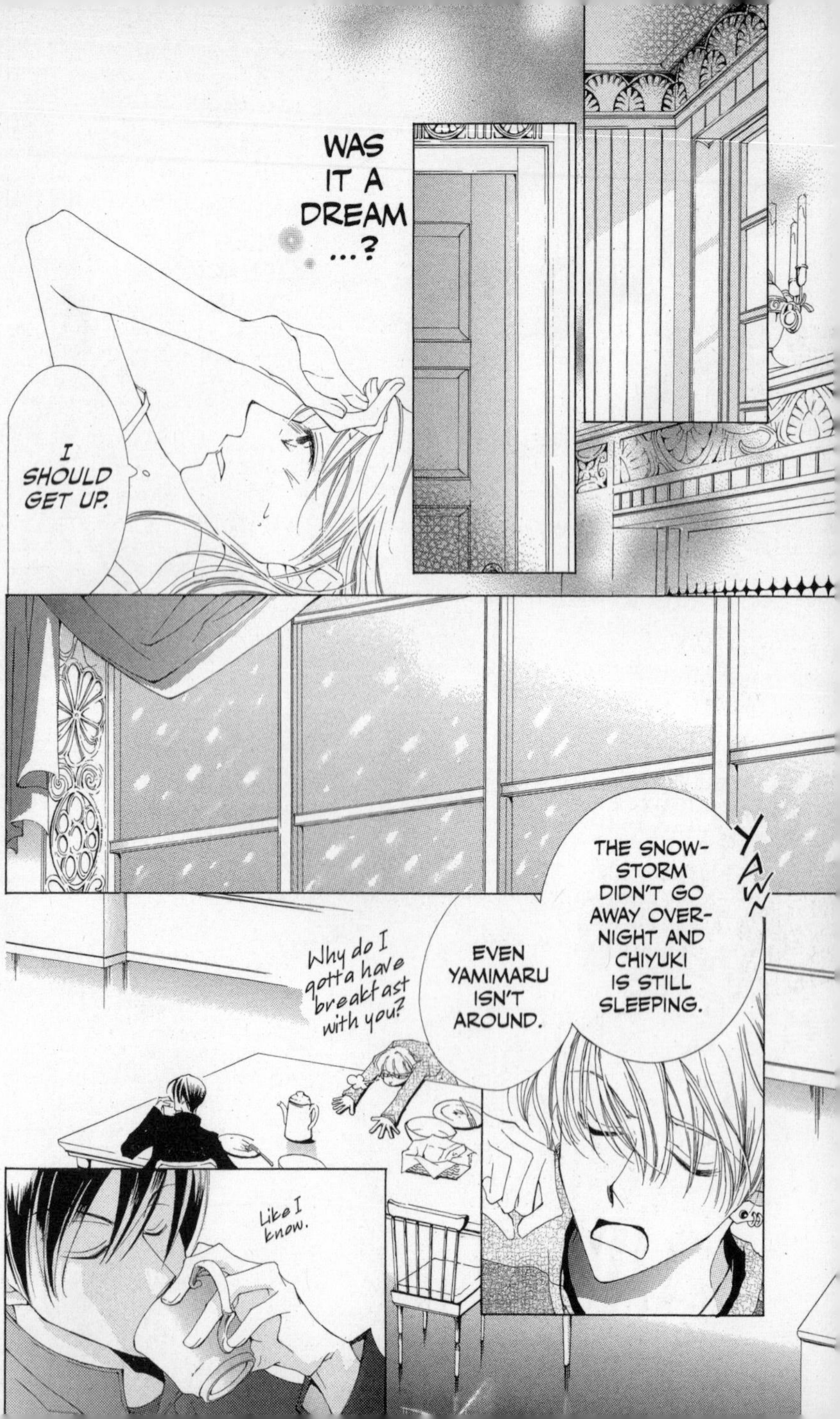
WAS IT A DREAM ...?
I SHOULD GET UP.
THE SNOW-STORM DIDN'T GO AWAY OVER-NIGHT AND CHIYUKI IS STILL SLEEPING.
YAWN
EVEN YAMIMARU ISN'T AROUND.
Why do I gotta have breakfast with you?
Like I know.

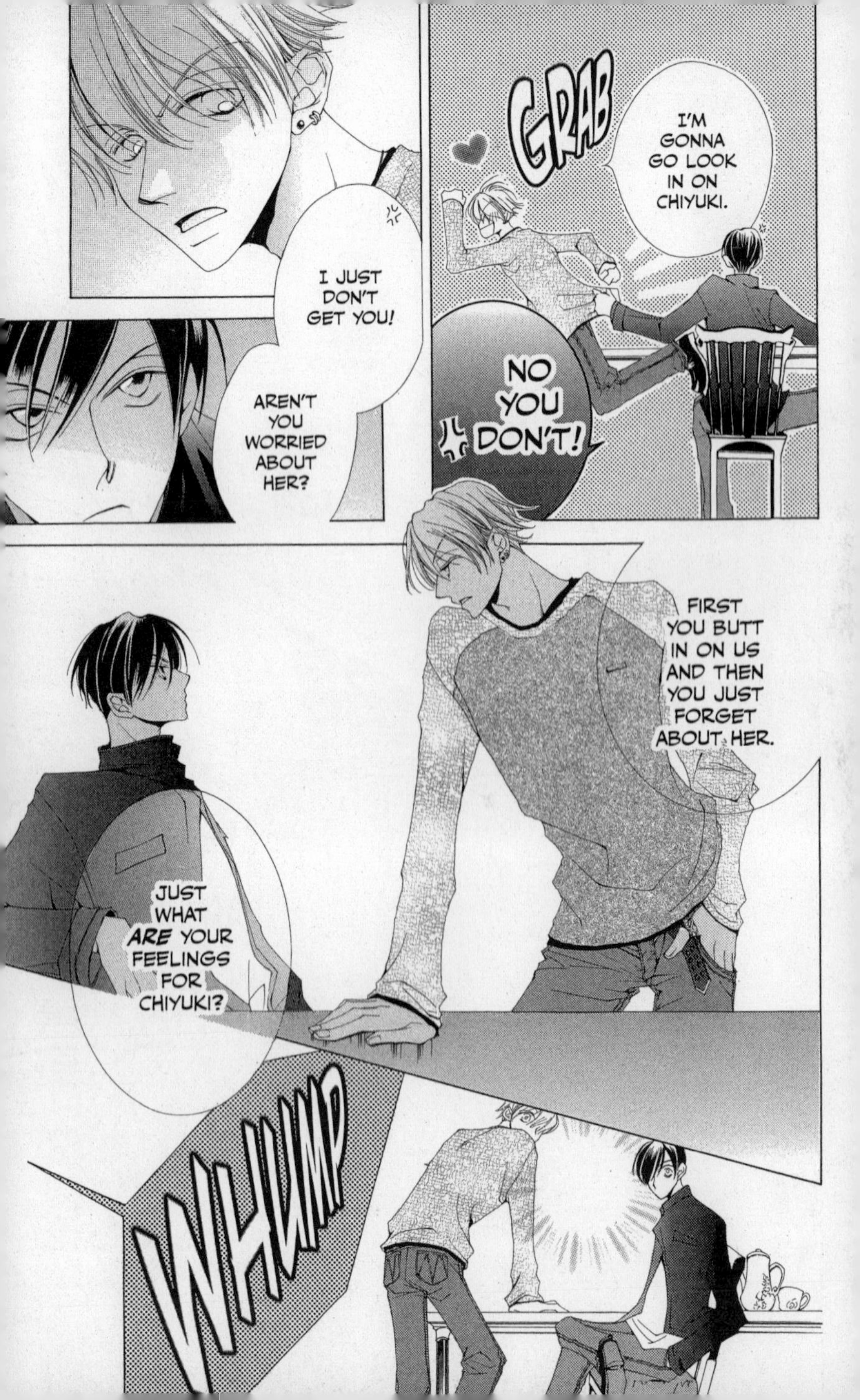
GRAB
I'M GONNA GO LOOK IN ON CHIYUKI.
NO YOU DON'T!
I JUST DON'T GET YOU!
AREN'T YOU WORRIED ABOUT HER?
FIRST YOU BUTT IN ON US AND THEN YOU JUST FORGET ABOUT HER.
JUST WHAT *ARE* YOUR FEELINGS FOR CHIYUKI?
WHUMP

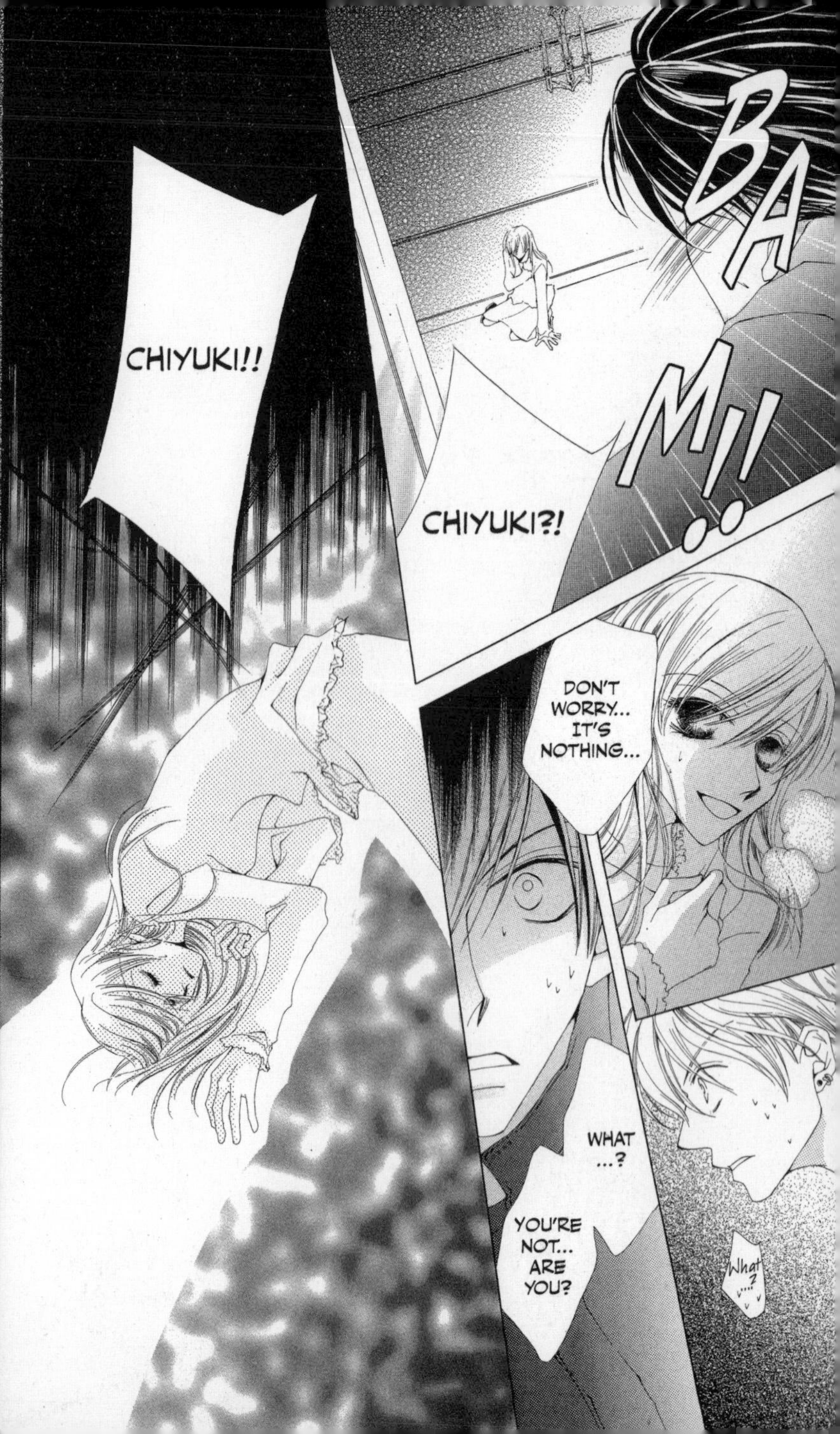
BAM!!
CHIYUKI?!
DON'T WORRY... IT'S NOTHING...
WHAT ...?
YOU'RE NOT... ARE YOU?
What ...?
CHIYUKI!!

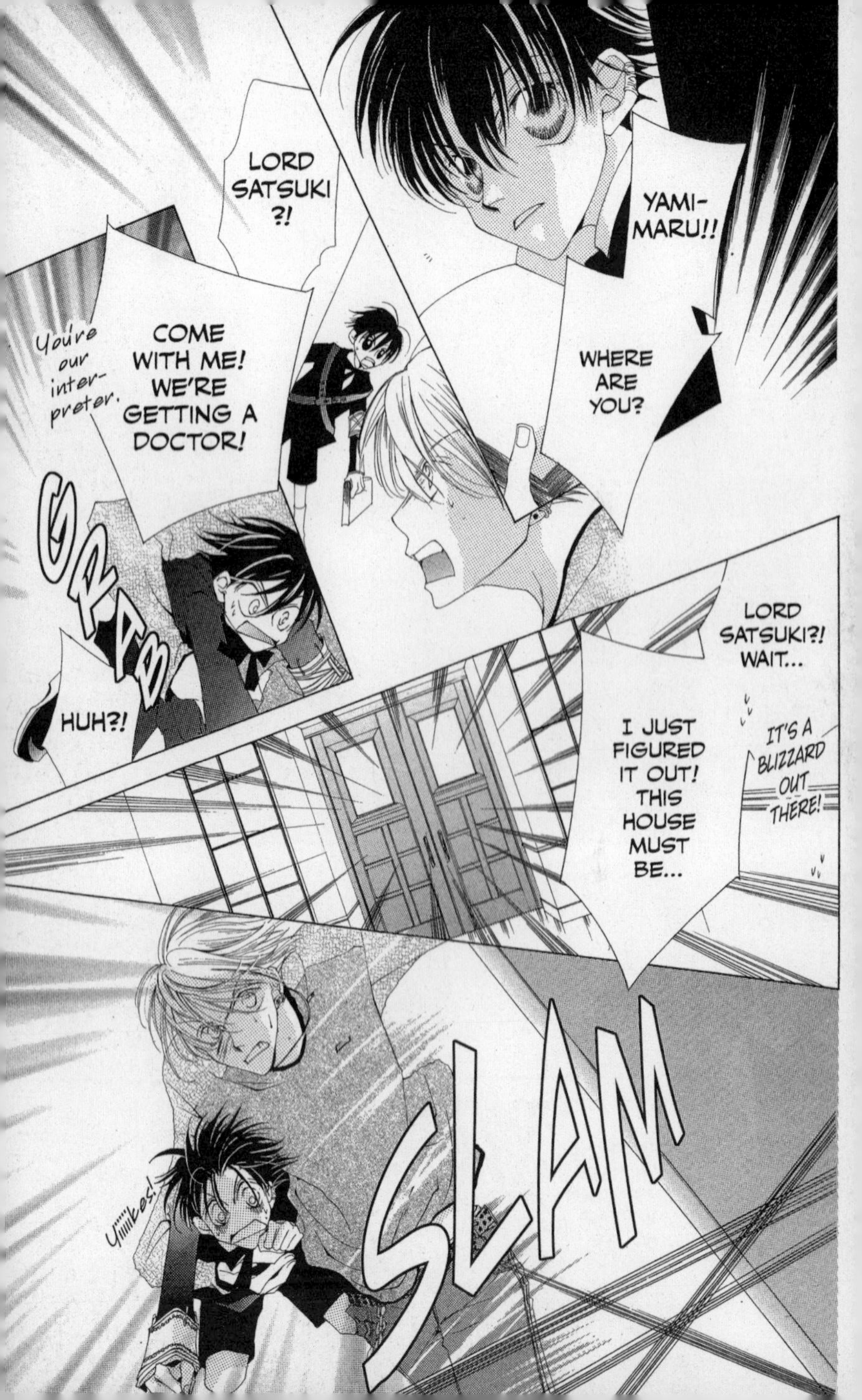
YAMI-MARU!!
WHERE ARE YOU?
LORD SATSUKI ?!
COME WITH ME! WE'RE GETTING A DOCTOR!
You're our inter-preter.
GRAB
HUH?!
LORD SATSUKI?! WAIT...
IT'S A BLIZZARD OUT THERE!
I JUST FIGURED IT OUT! THIS HOUSE MUST BE...
SLAM
Yiiiikes!

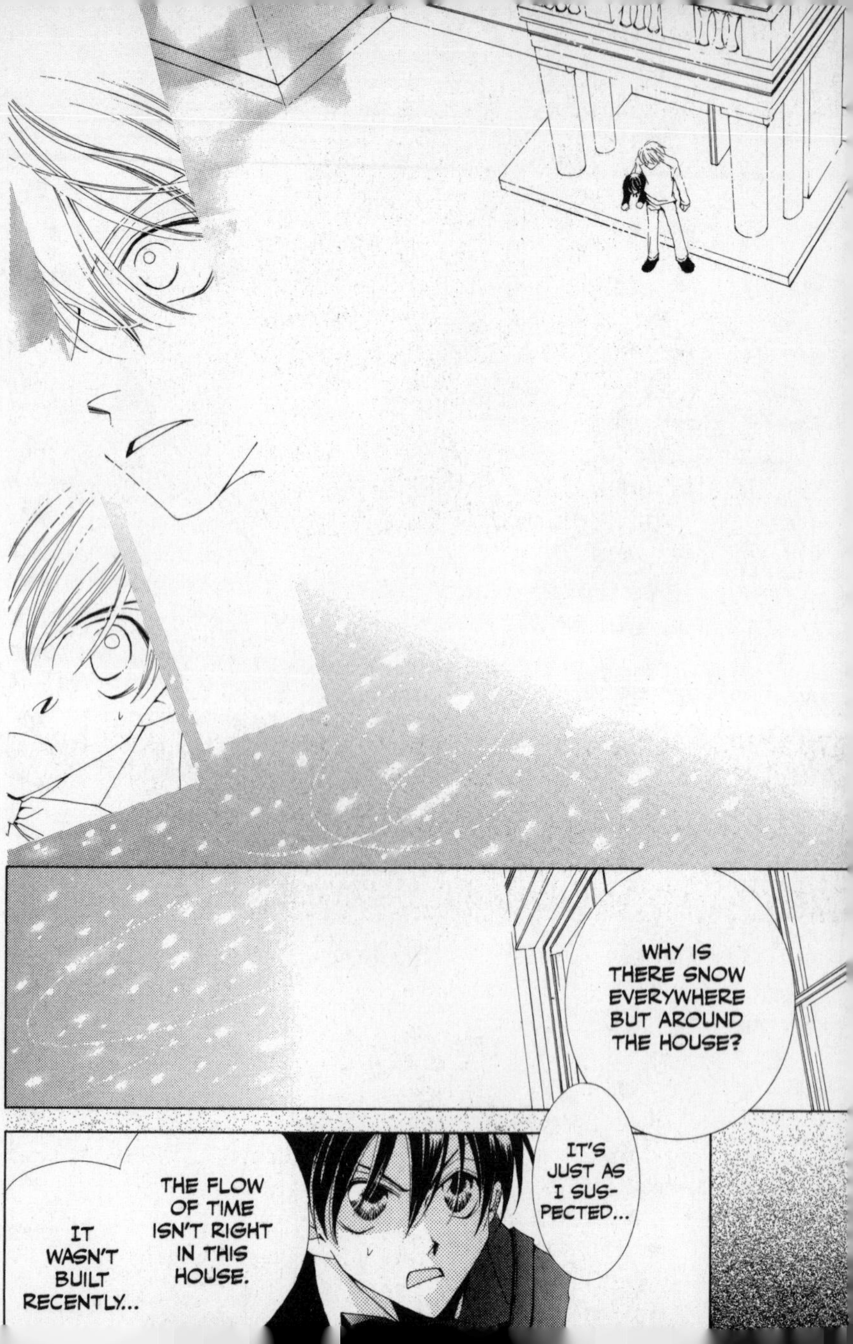
WHY IS THERE SNOW EVERYWHERE BUT AROUND THE HOUSE?
IT'S JUST AS I SUS-PECTED...
THE FLOW OF TIME ISN'T RIGHT IN THIS HOUSE.
IT WASN'T BUILT RECENTLY...

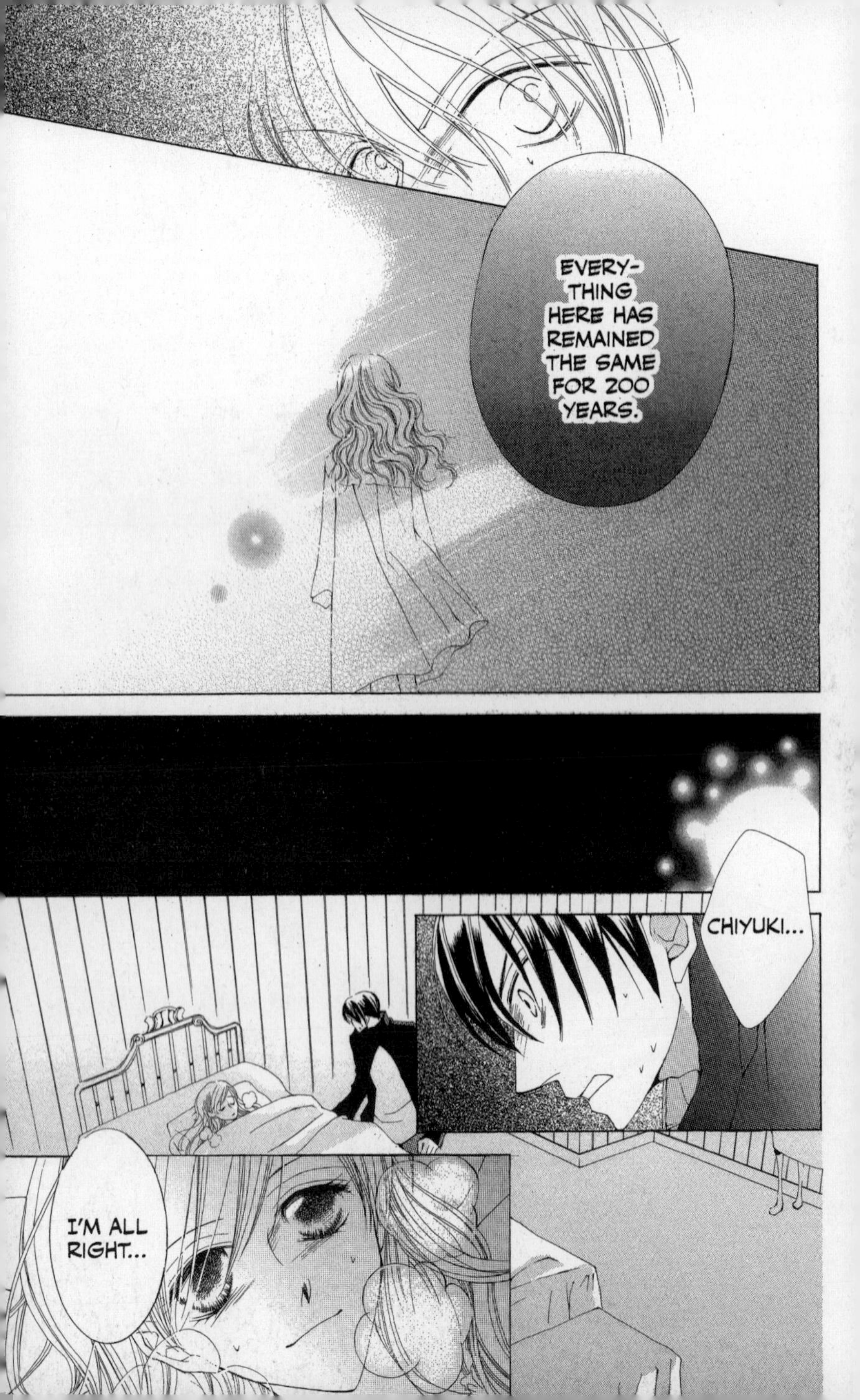
EVERY-THING HERE HAS REMAINED THE SAME FOR 200 YEARS.
CHIYUKI...
I'M ALL RIGHT...

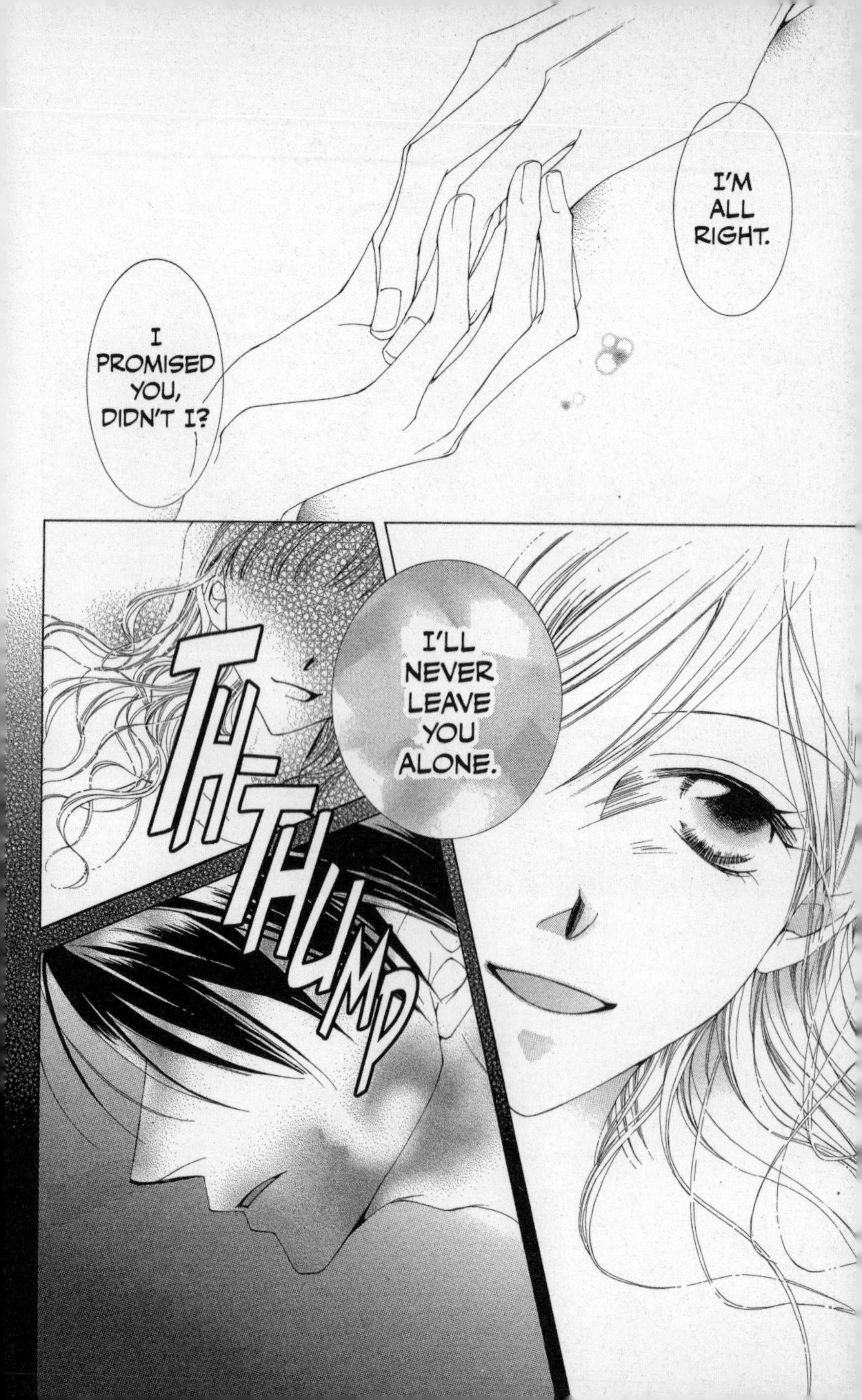
I'M ALL RIGHT.
I PROMISED YOU, DIDN'T I?
I'LL NEVER LEAVE YOU ALONE.
TH-THUMP

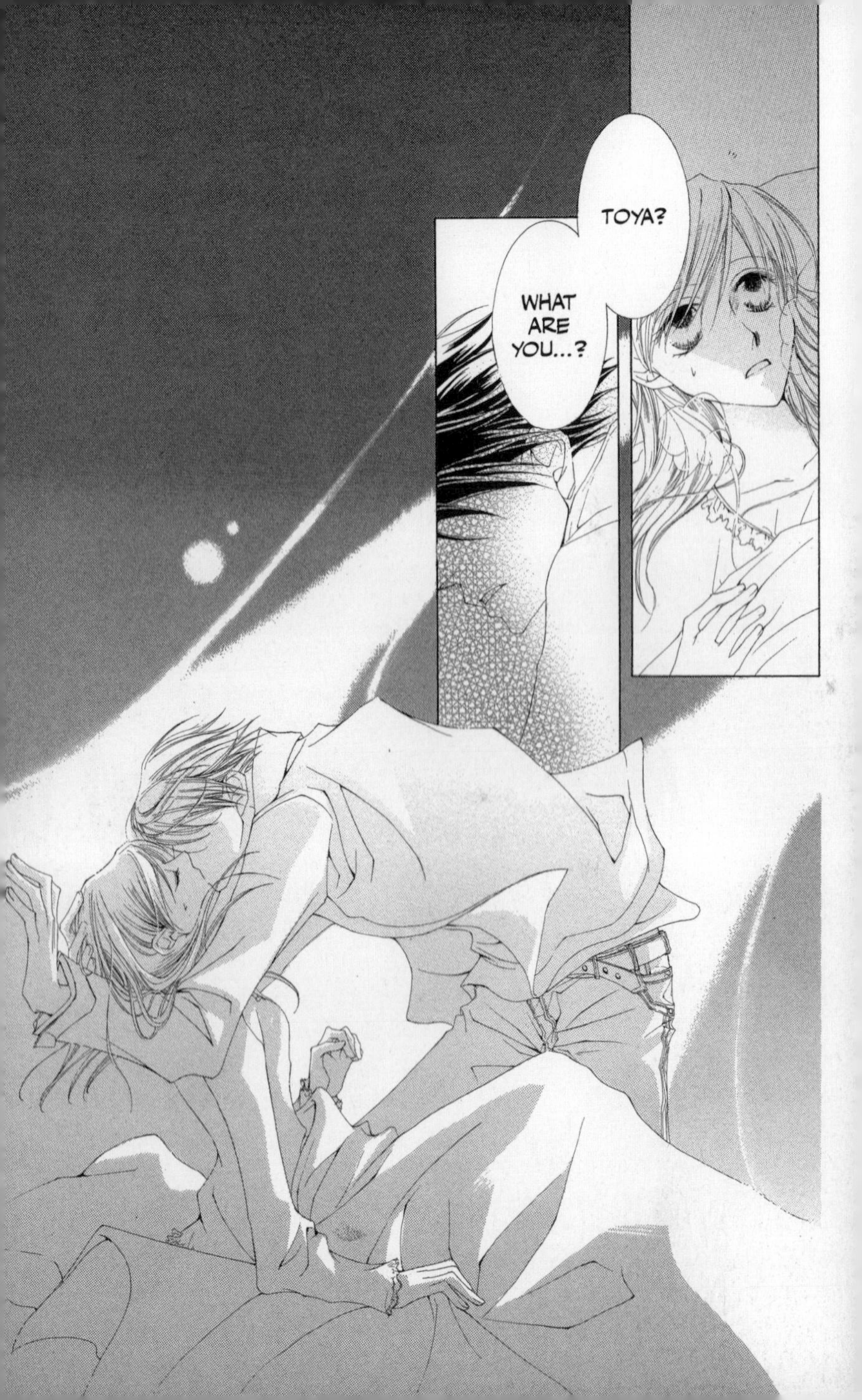
TOYA?
WHAT ARE YOU...?

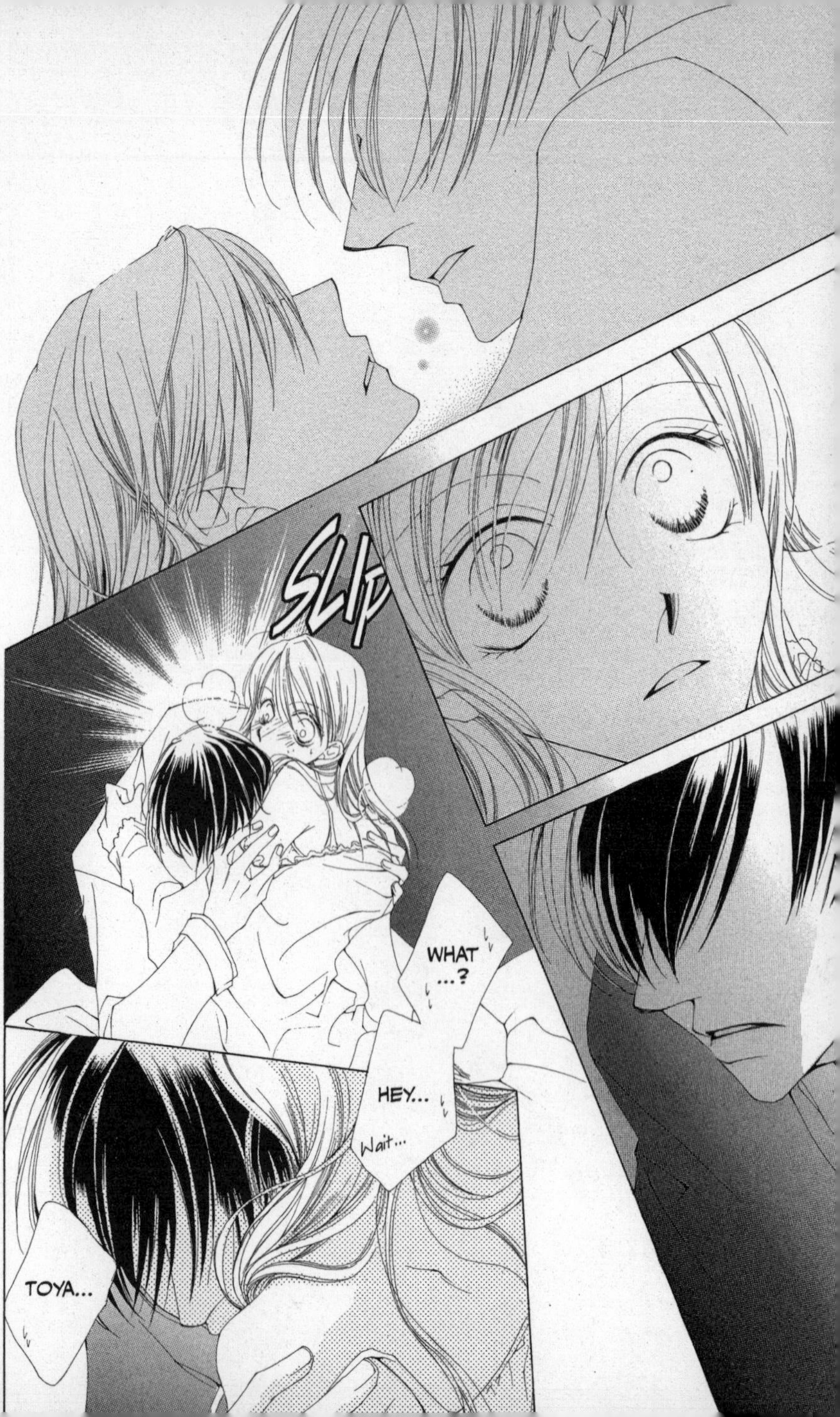
SLIP
WHAT ...?
HEY...
Wait...
TOYA...

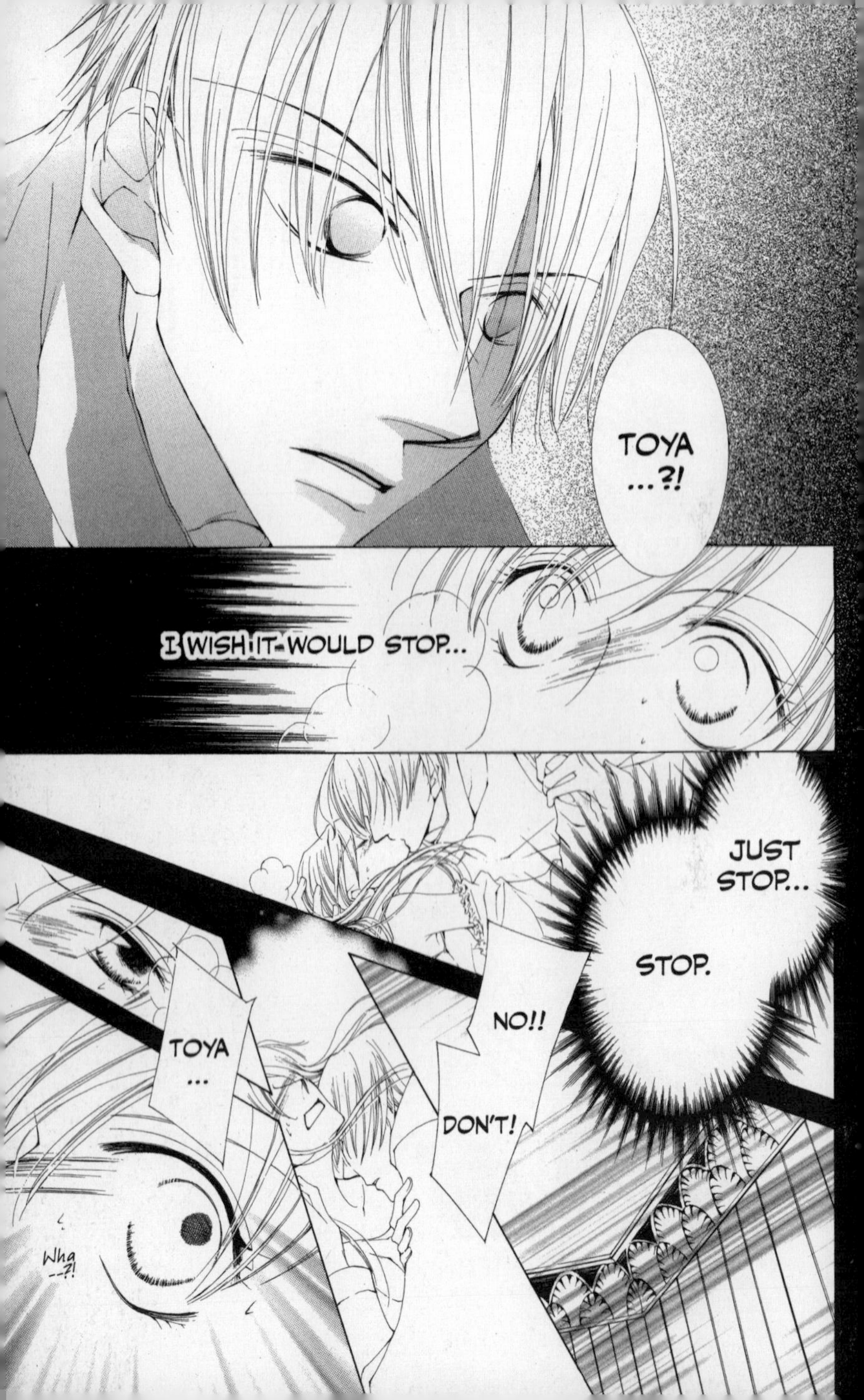
TOYA ...?!
I WISH IT WOULD STOP...
JUST STOP...
STOP.
NO!!
DON'T!
TOYA ...
Wha --?!

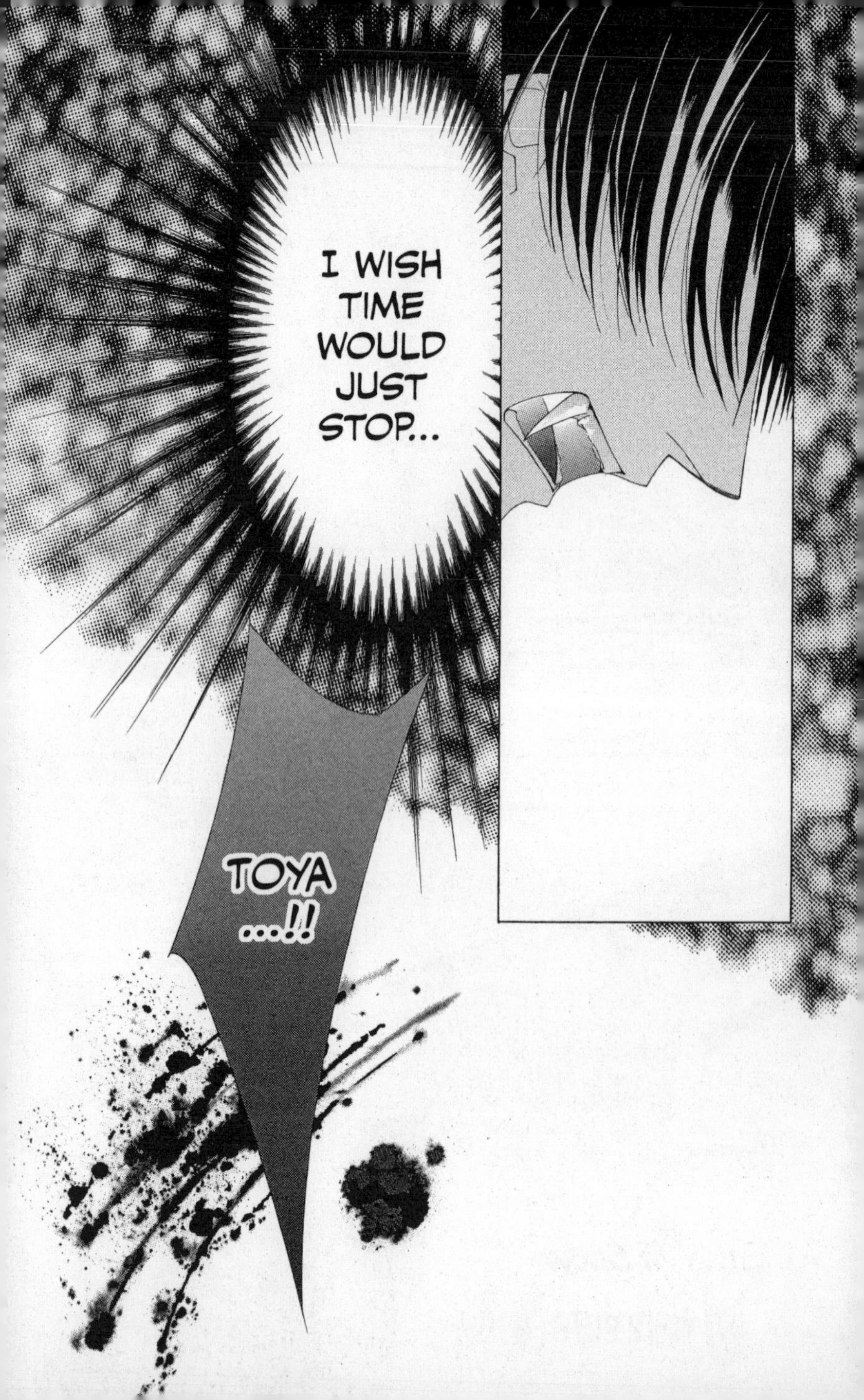
I WISH TIME WOULD JUST STOP...
TOYA ...!!

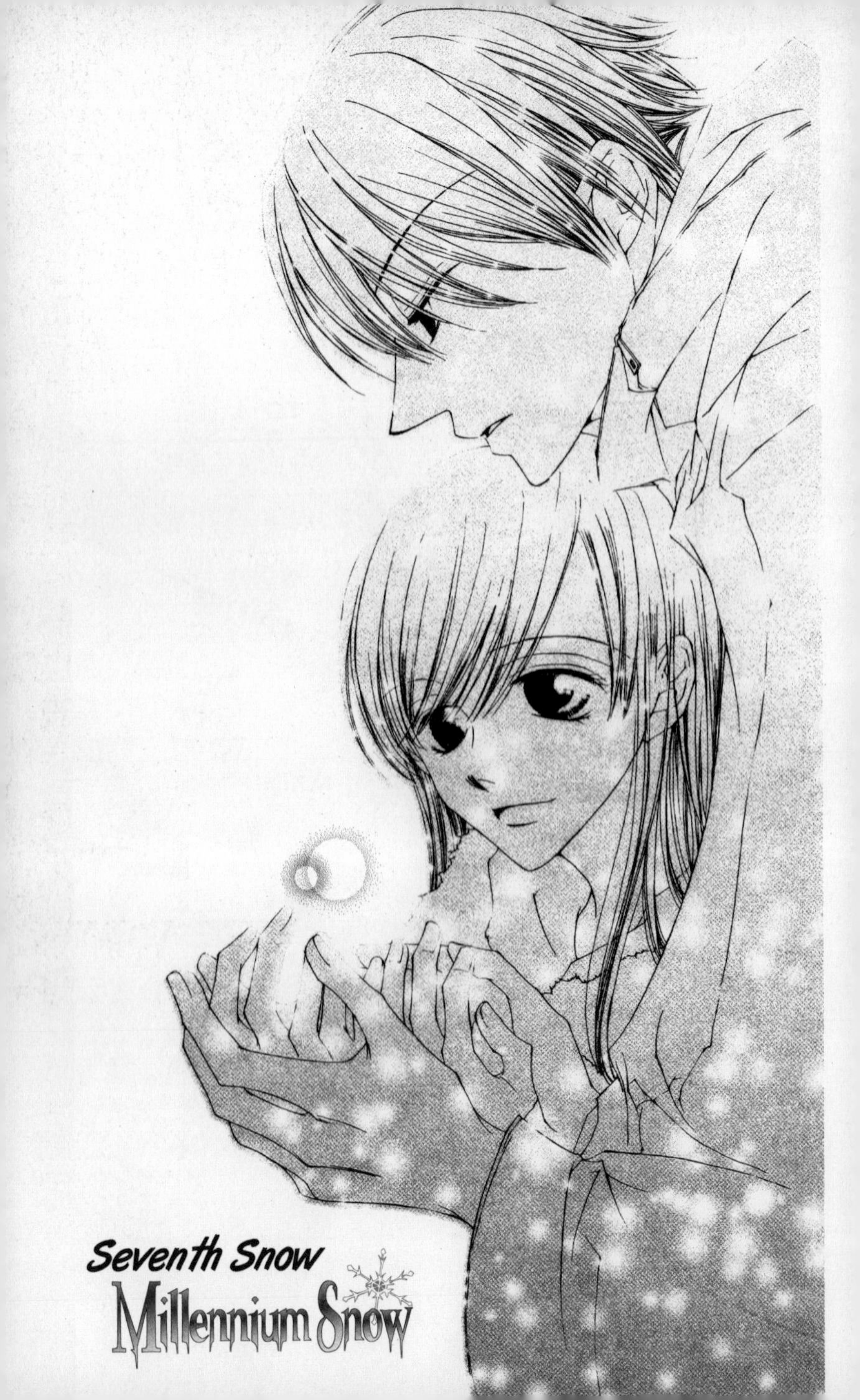
Seventh Snow
Millennium Snow

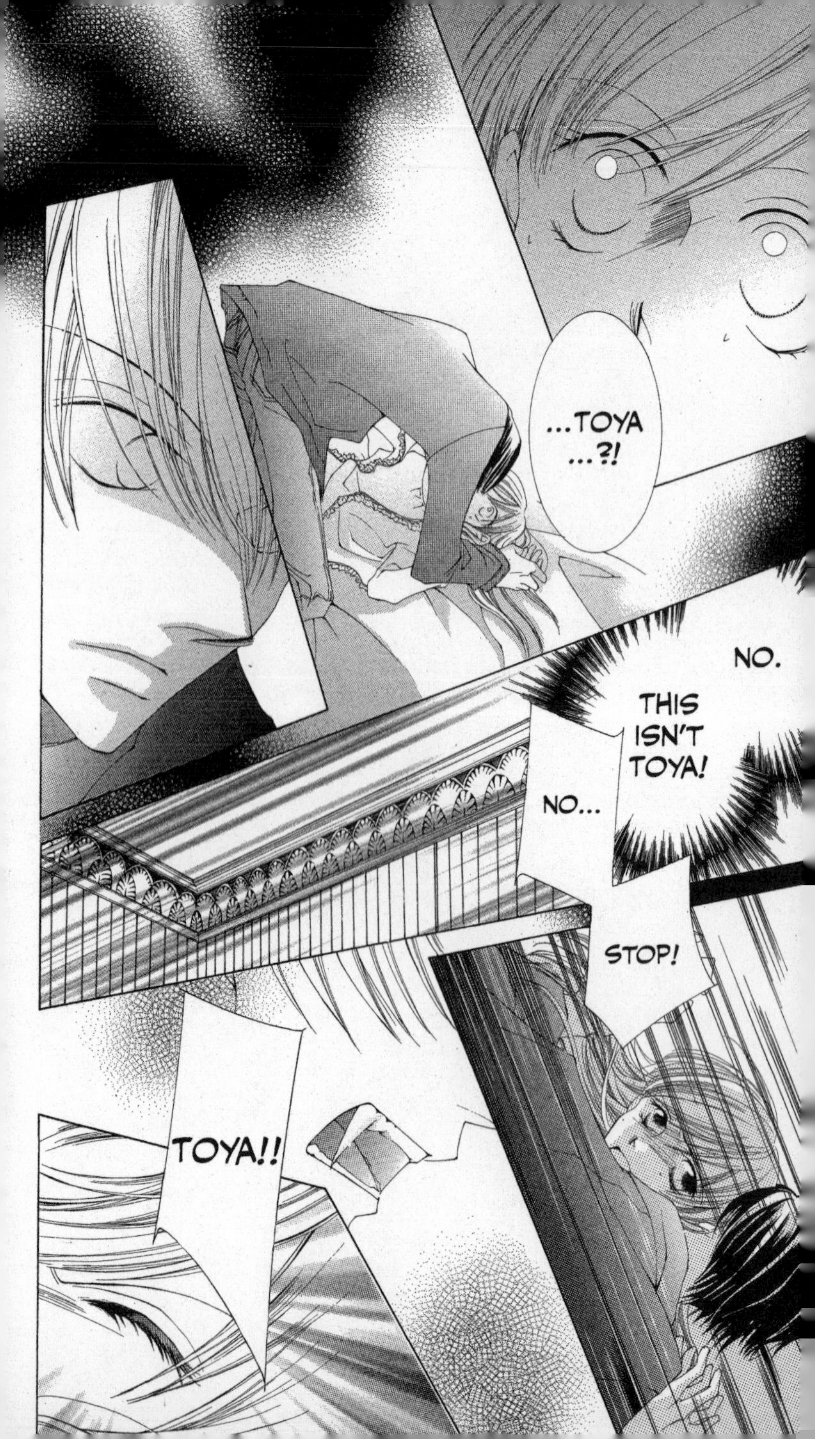
...TOYA ...?!
NO.
THIS ISN'T TOYA!
NO...
STOP!
TOYA!!

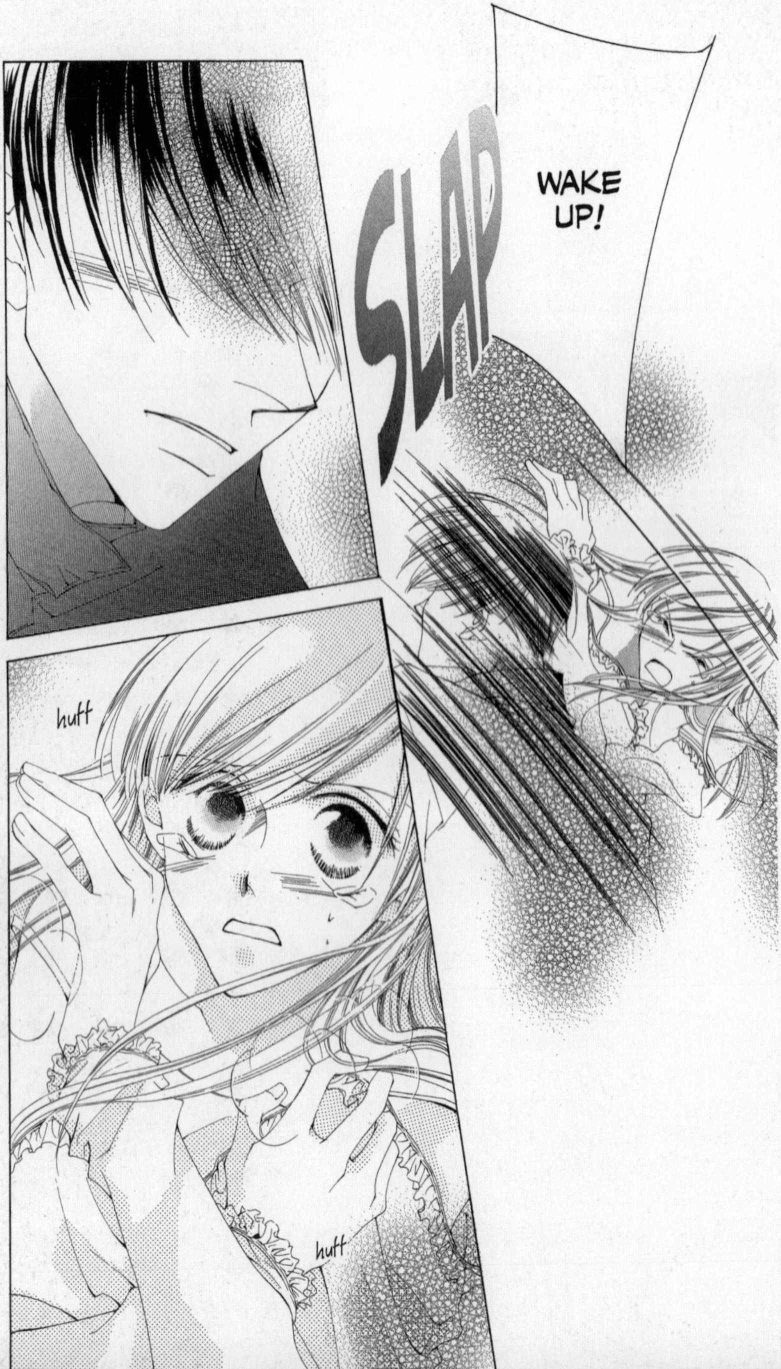
WAKE UP!
SLAP
huff
huff

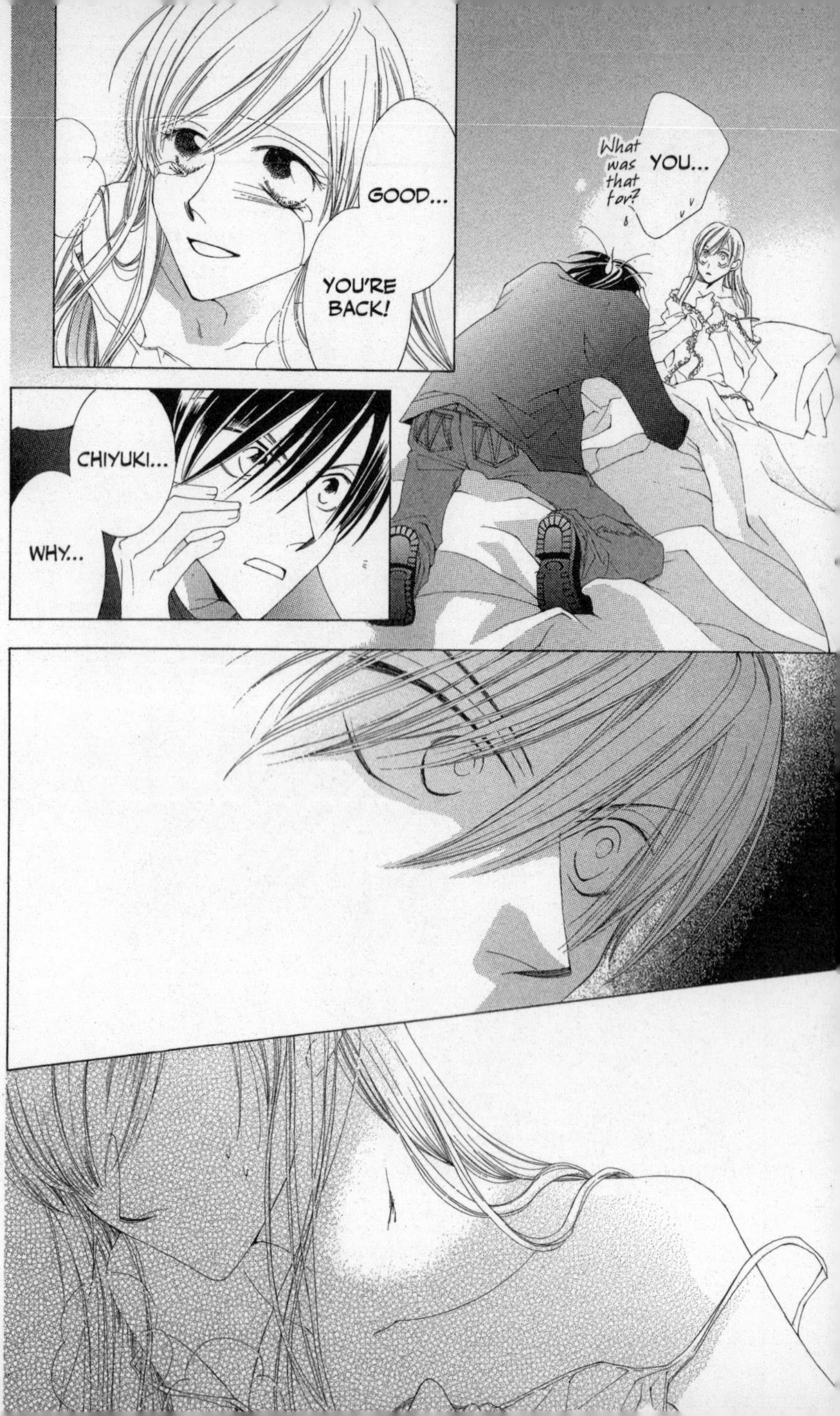
YOU...
What was that for?
GOOD...
YOU'RE BACK!
CHIYUKI...
WHY...

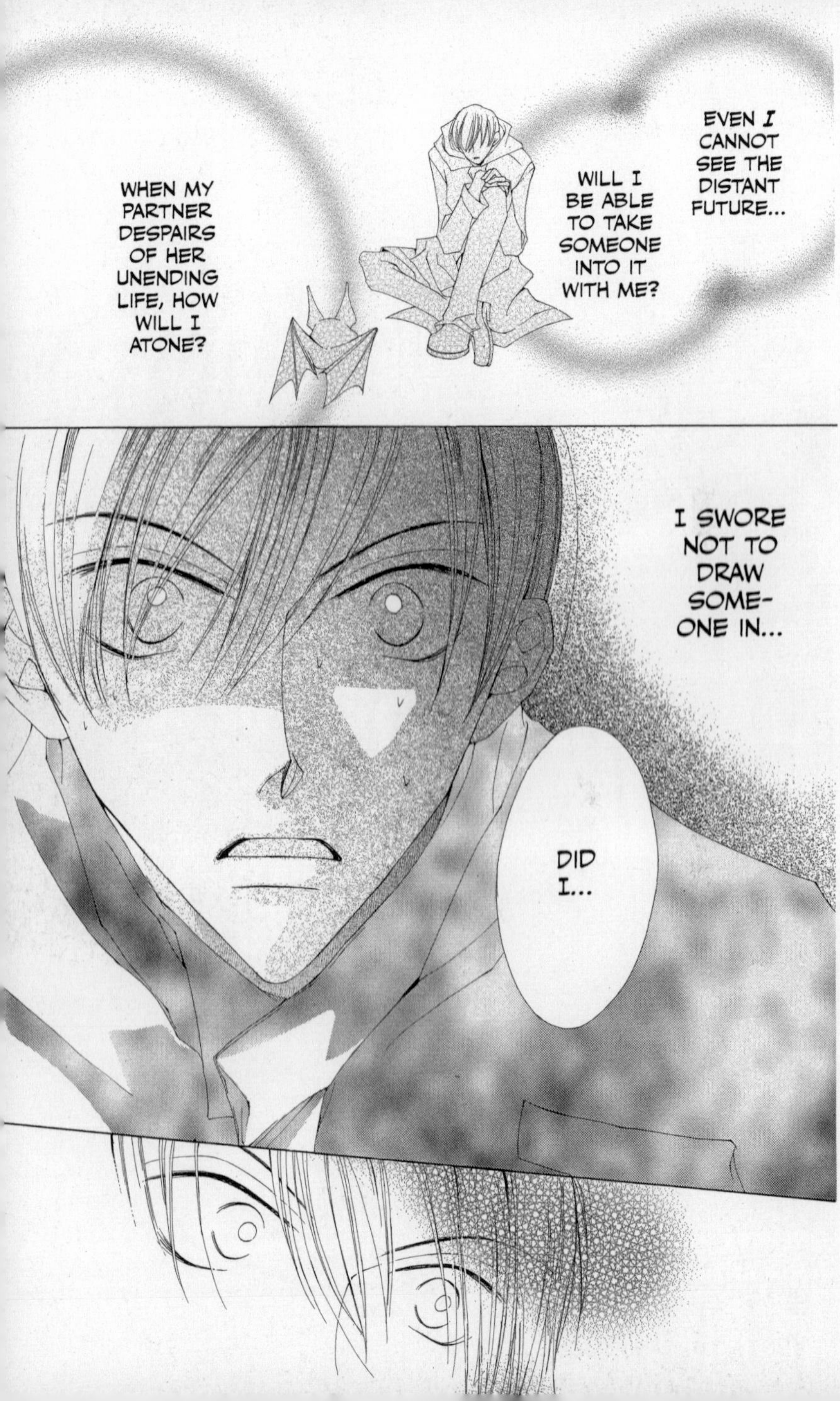
EVEN I CANNOT SEE THE DISTANT FUTURE...
WILL I BE ABLE TO TAKE SOMEONE INTO IT WITH ME?
WHEN MY PARTNER DESPAIRS OF HER UNENDING LIFE, HOW WILL I ATONE?
I SWORE NOT TO DRAW SOME-ONE IN...
DID I...

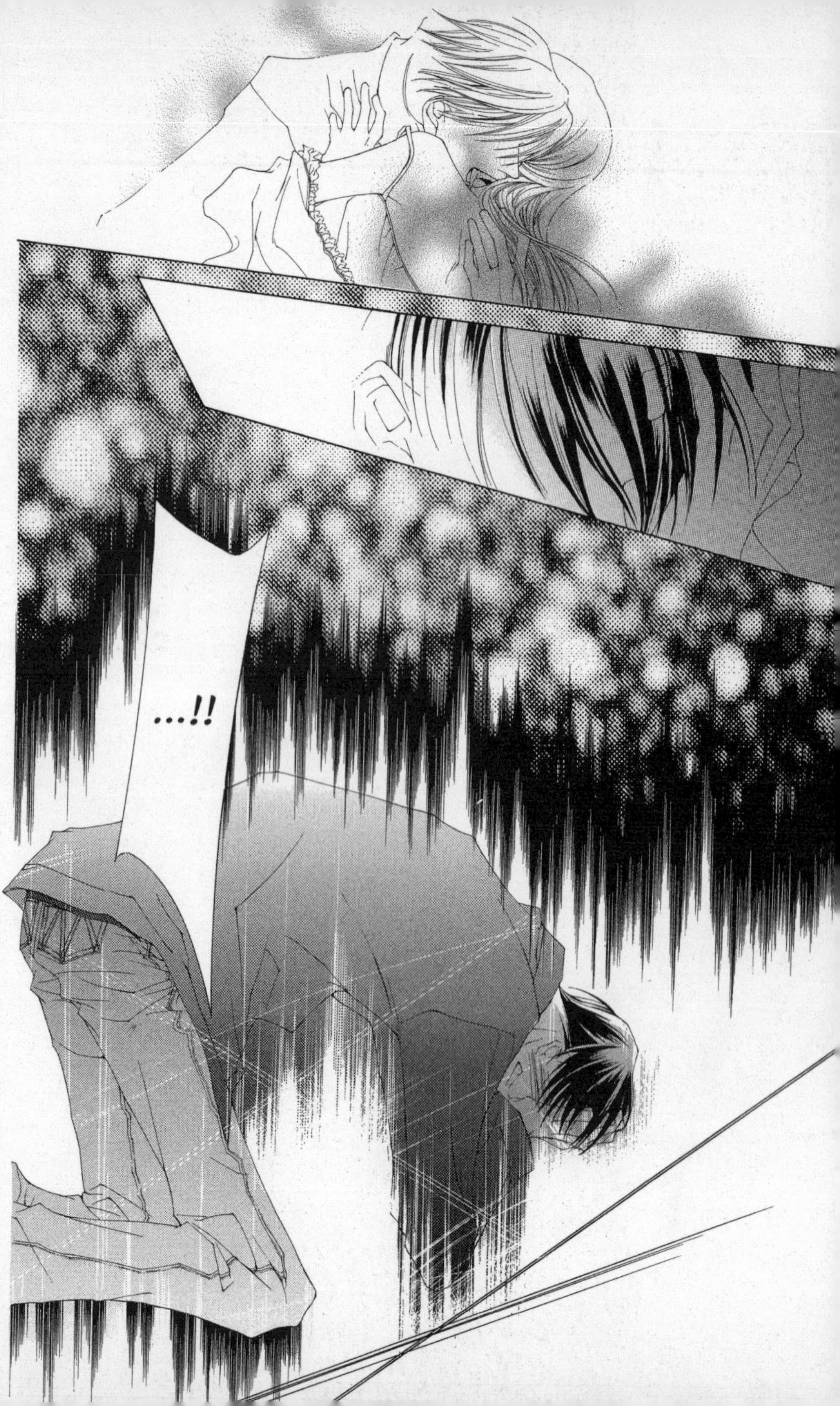
...!!

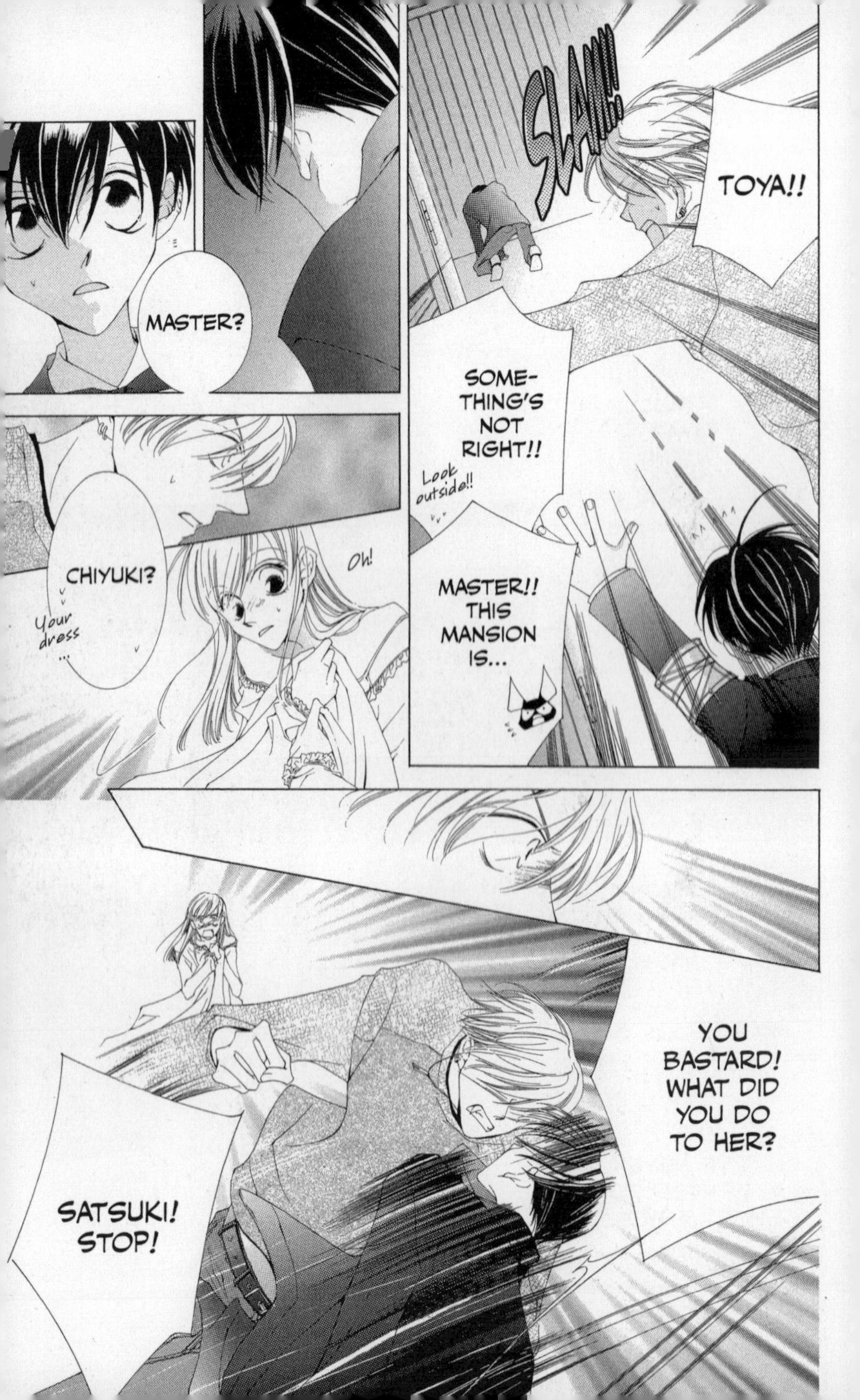
SLAM!!!
TOYA!!
SOME-THING'S NOT RIGHT!!
Look outside!!
MASTER!! THIS MANSION IS...
MASTER?
CHIYUKI?
Your dress...
Oh!
YOU BASTARD! WHAT DID YOU DO TO HER?
SATSUKI! STOP!

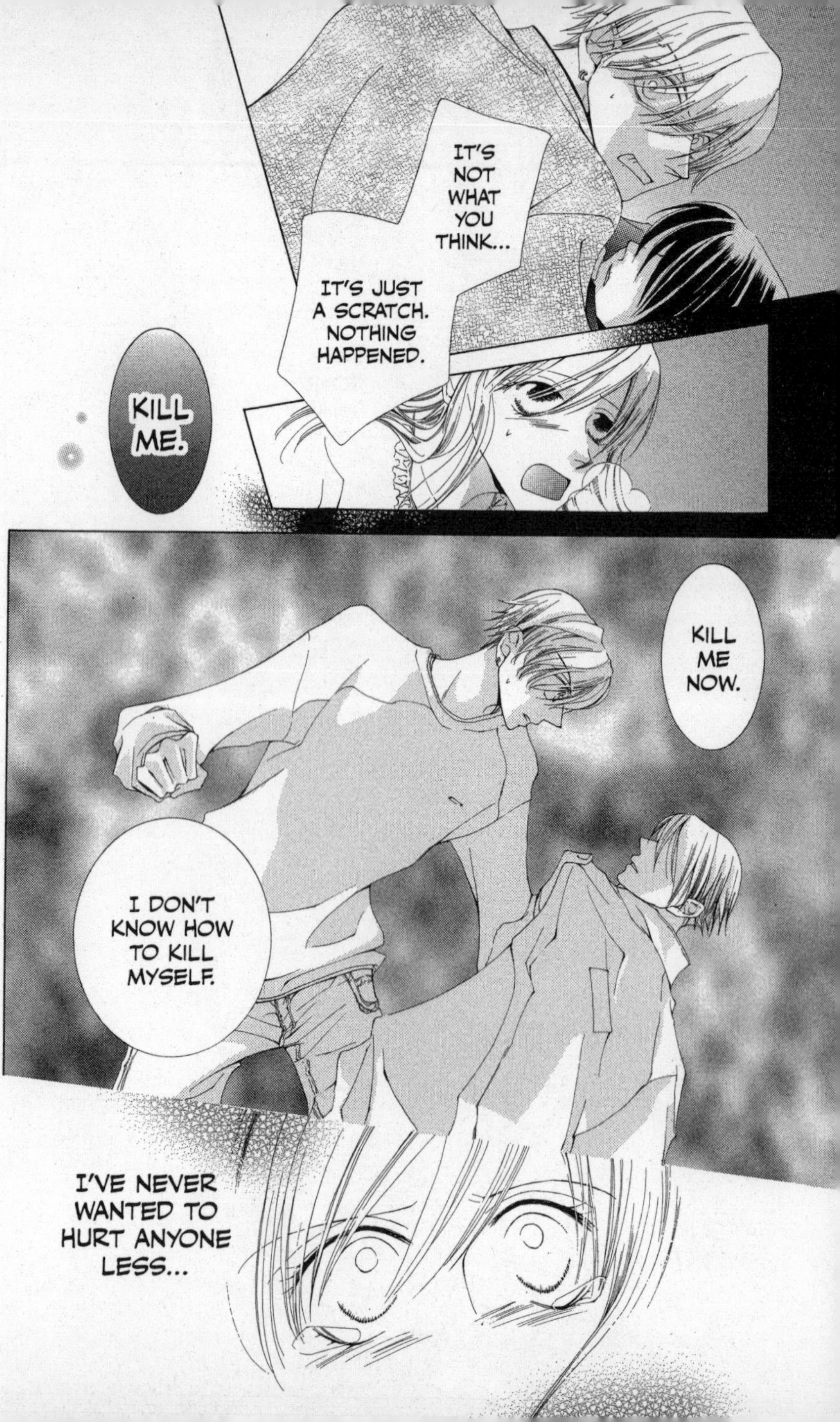
IT'S NOT WHAT YOU THINK...
IT'S JUST A SCRATCH. NOTHING HAPPENED.
KILL ME.
KILL ME NOW.
I DON'T KNOW HOW TO KILL MYSELF.
I'VE NEVER WANTED TO HURT ANYONE LESS...

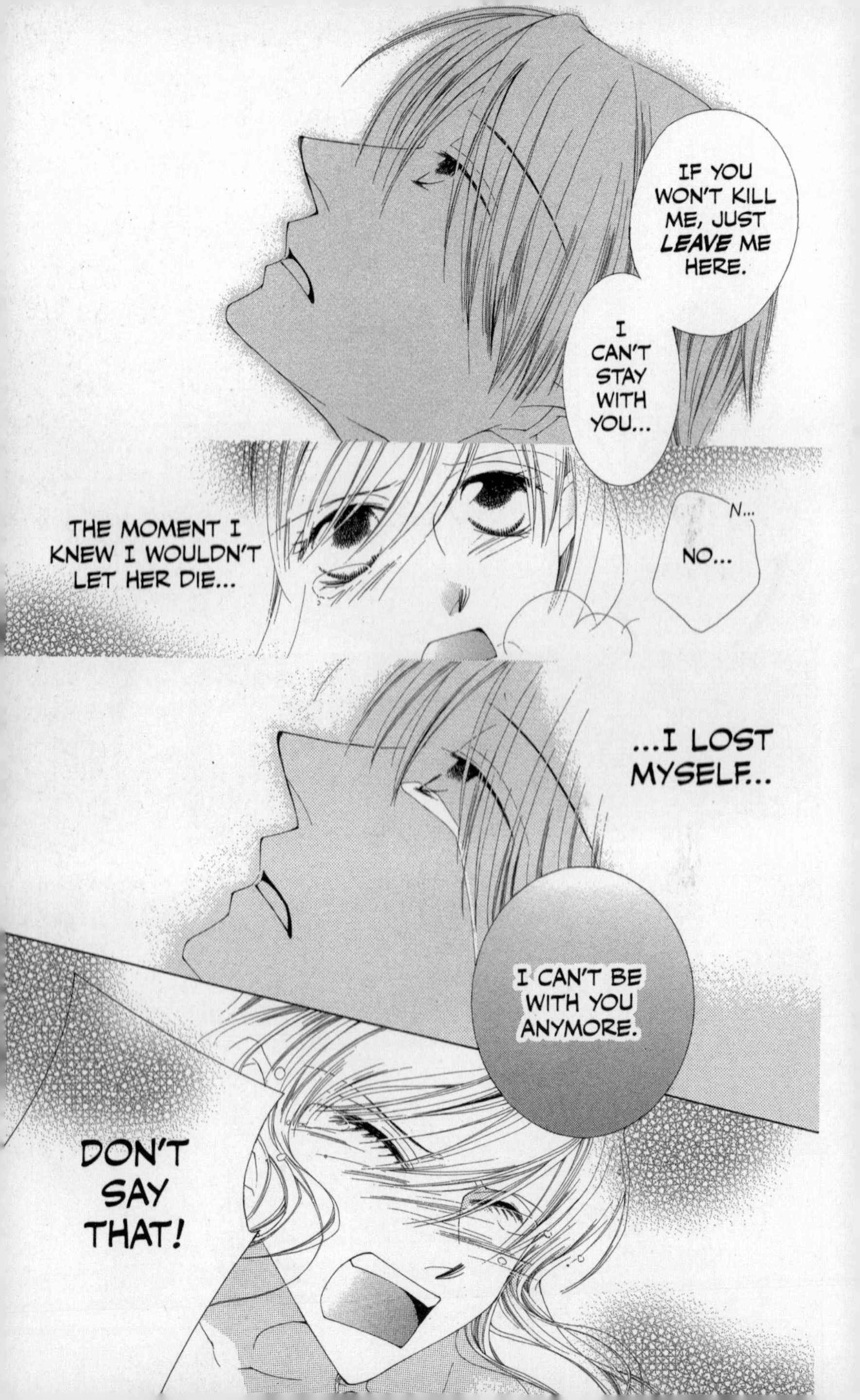
IF YOU WON'T KILL ME, JUST *LEAVE* ME HERE.
I CAN'T STAY WITH YOU...
N... NO...
THE MOMENT I KNEW I WOULDN'T LET HER DIE...
...I LOST MYSELF...
I CAN'T BE WITH YOU ANYMORE.
DON'T SAY THAT!

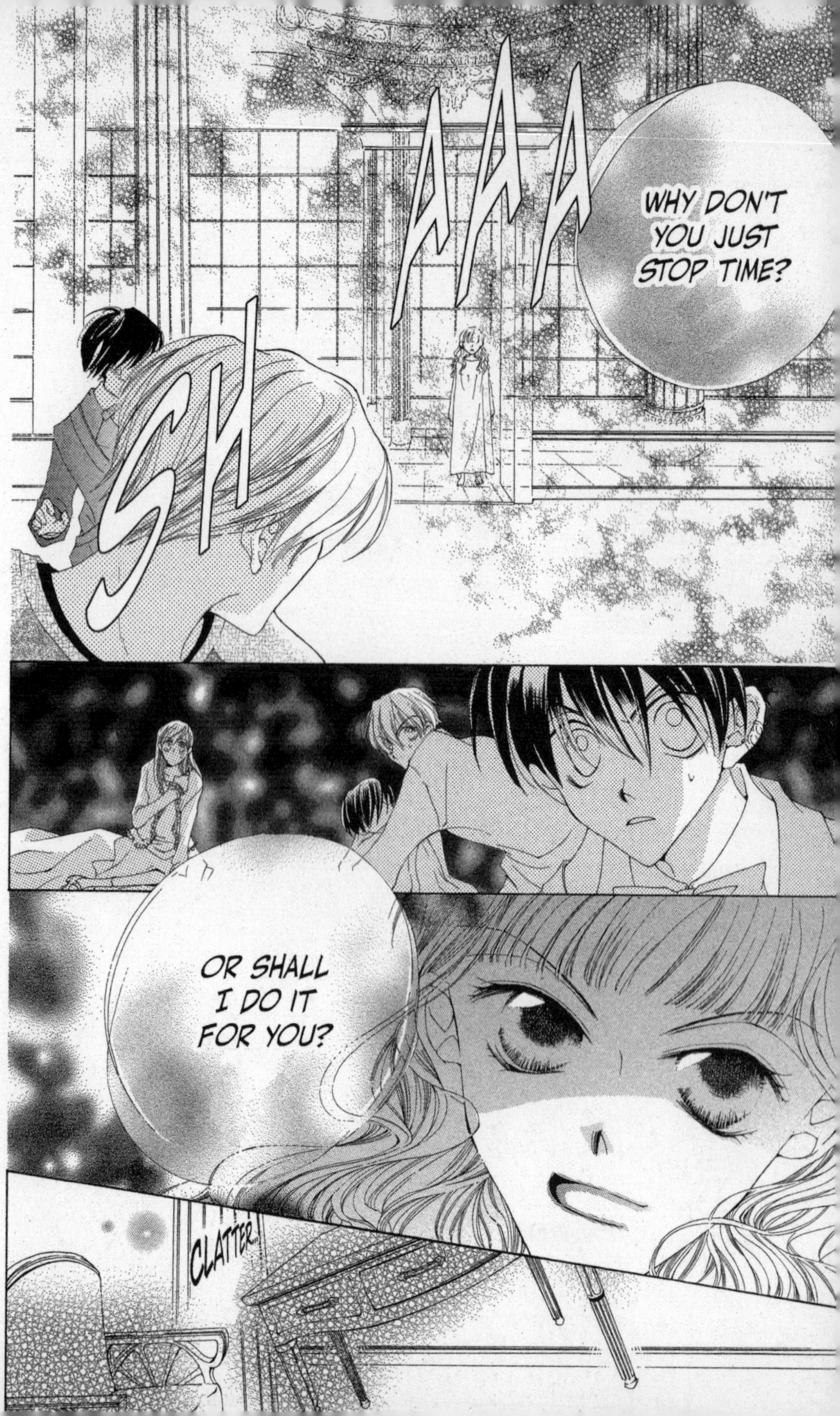
WHY DON'T YOU JUST STOP TIME?
AAA
SH
OR SHALL I DO IT FOR YOU?
CLATTER...

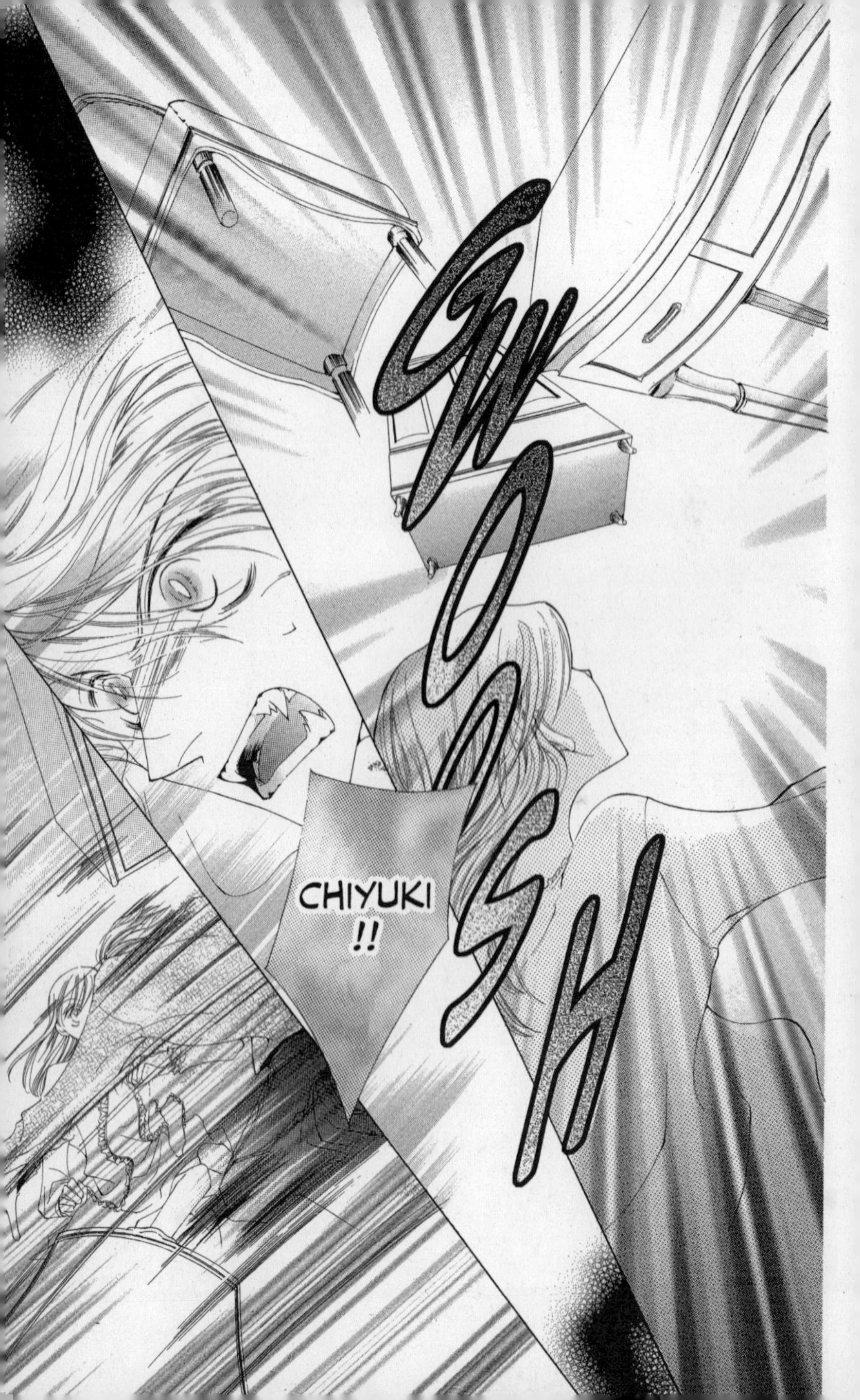
GWOOOSSH
CHIYUKI !!

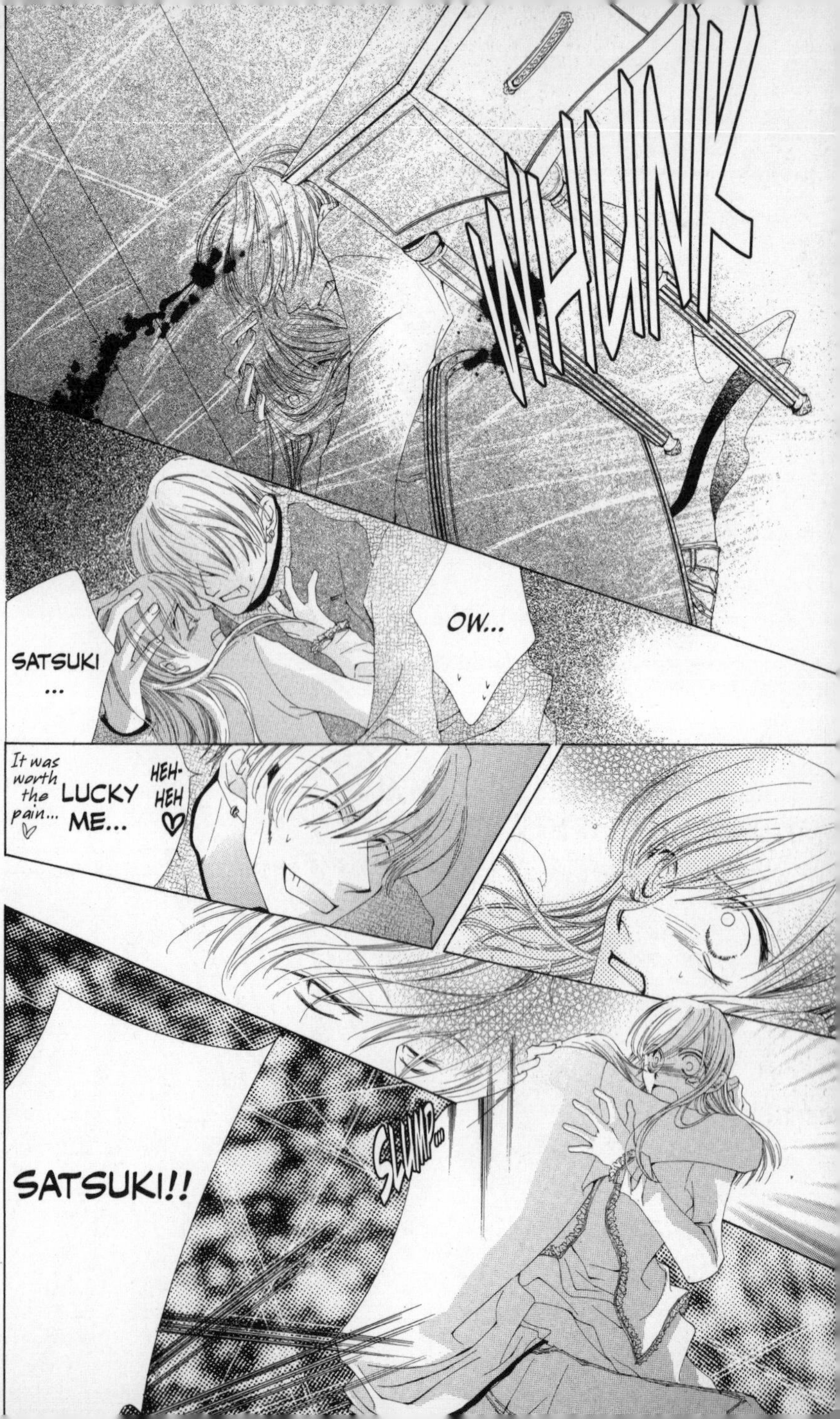
WHUNK
OW...
SATSUKI ...
HEH-HEH
LUCKY ME...
It was worth the pain...
SLUMP...
SATSUKI!!

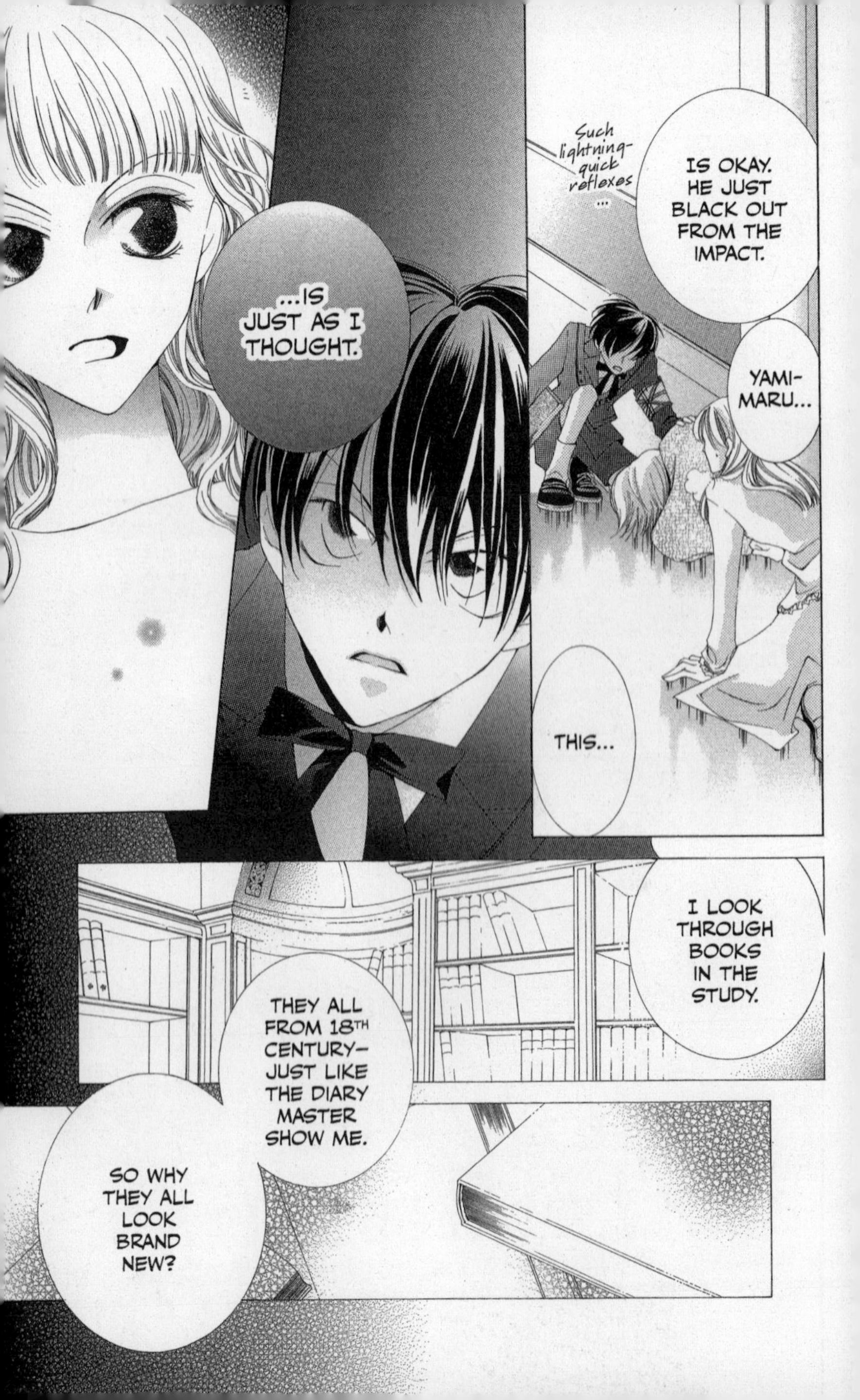
IS OKAY. HE JUST BLACK OUT FROM THE IMPACT.
Such lightning-quick reflexes...
YAMI-MARU...
THIS...
...IS JUST AS I THOUGHT.
I LOOK THROUGH BOOKS IN THE STUDY.
THEY ALL FROM 18TH CENTURY—JUST LIKE THE DIARY MASTER SHOW ME.
SO WHY THEY ALL LOOK BRAND NEW?

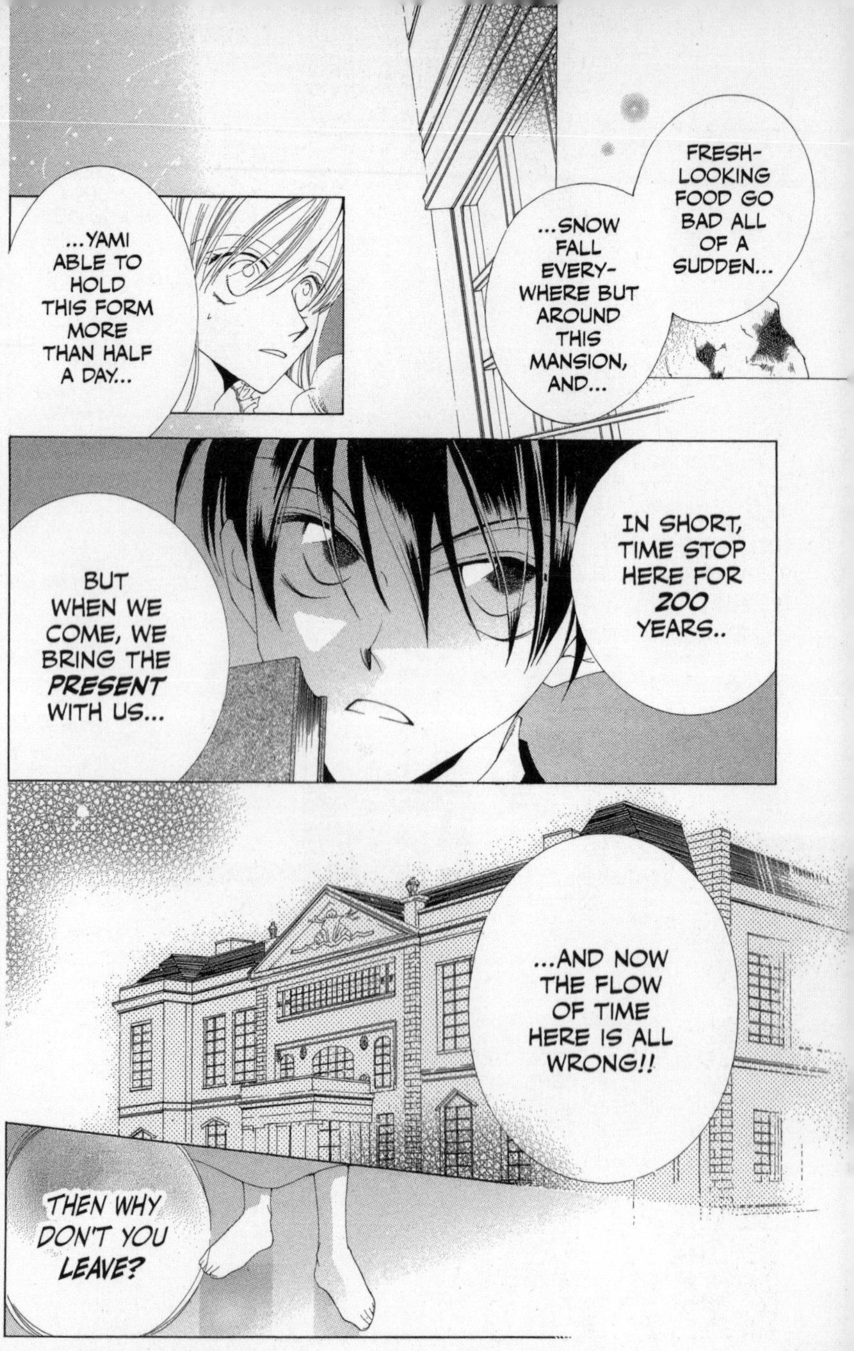
FRESH-LOOKING FOOD GO BAD ALL OF A SUDDEN...
...SNOW FALL EVERYWHERE BUT AROUND THIS MANSION, AND...
...YAMI ABLE TO HOLD THIS FORM MORE THAN HALF A DAY...
IN SHORT, TIME STOP HERE FOR 200 YEARS..
BUT WHEN WE COME, WE BRING THE PRESENT WITH US...
...AND NOW THE FLOW OF TIME HERE IS ALL WRONG!!
THEN WHY DON'T YOU LEAVE?

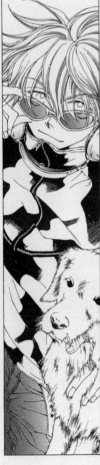

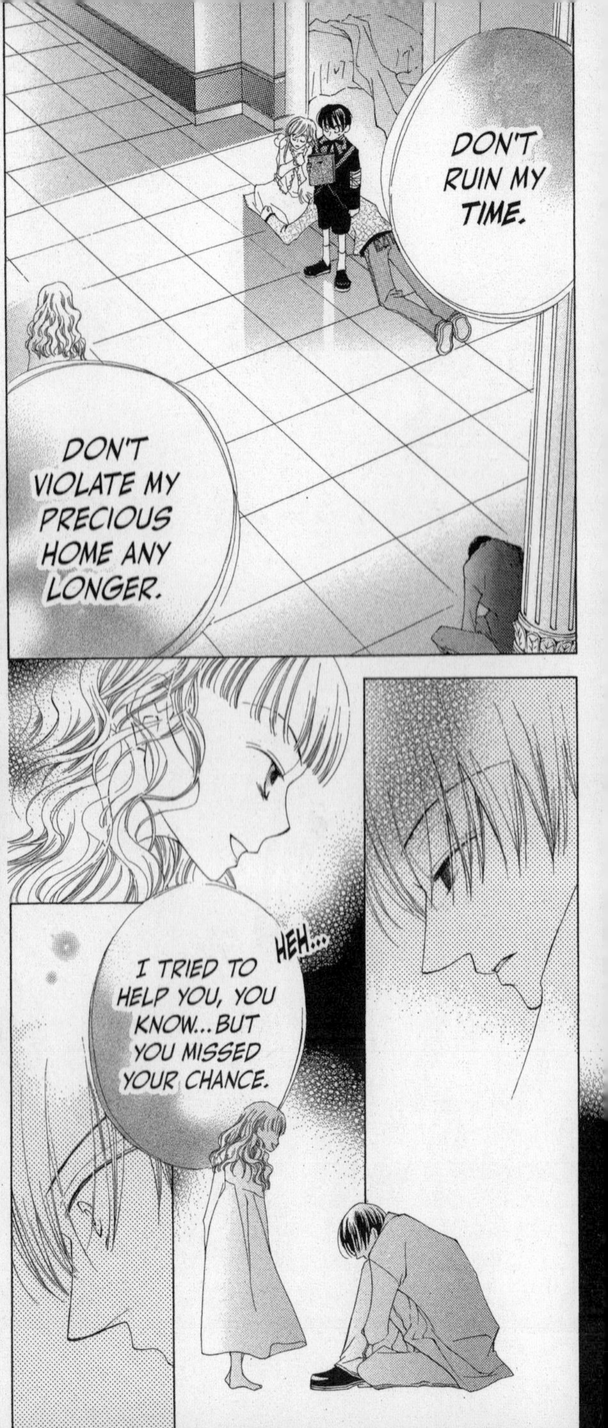
DON'T RUIN MY TIME.
DON'T VIOLATE MY PRECIOUS HOME ANY LONGER.
HEH...
I TRIED TO HELP YOU, YOU KNOW...BUT YOU MISSED YOUR CHANCE.

有吉 砂月

SATSUKI·ARIYOSHI

Height: 6'
Blood type: A
In this volume he's mostly just a big dummy, but I had wanted him to do more.

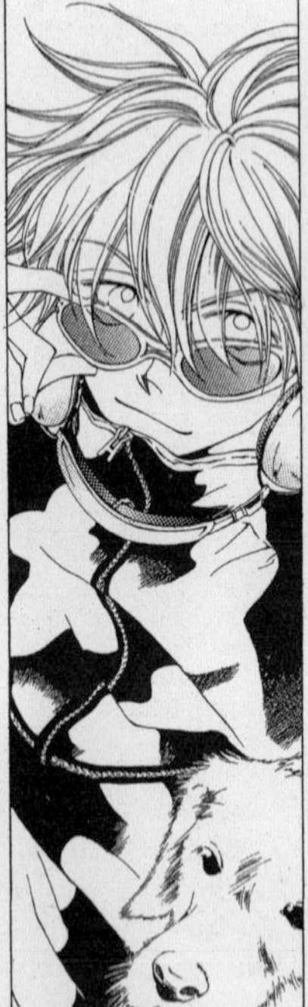

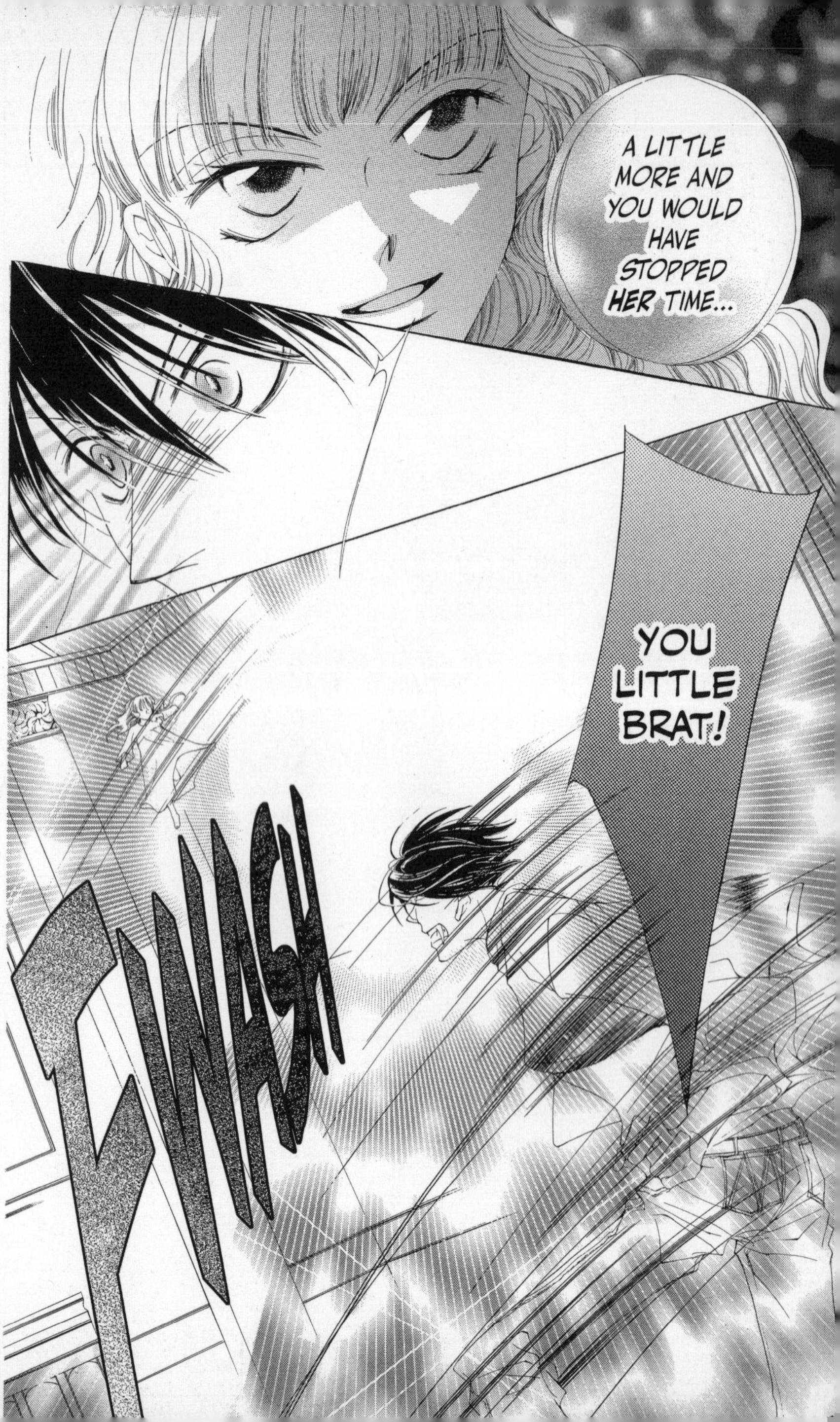
A LITTLE MORE AND YOU WOULD HAVE STOPPED HER TIME...
YOU LITTLE BRAT!
ZWASH

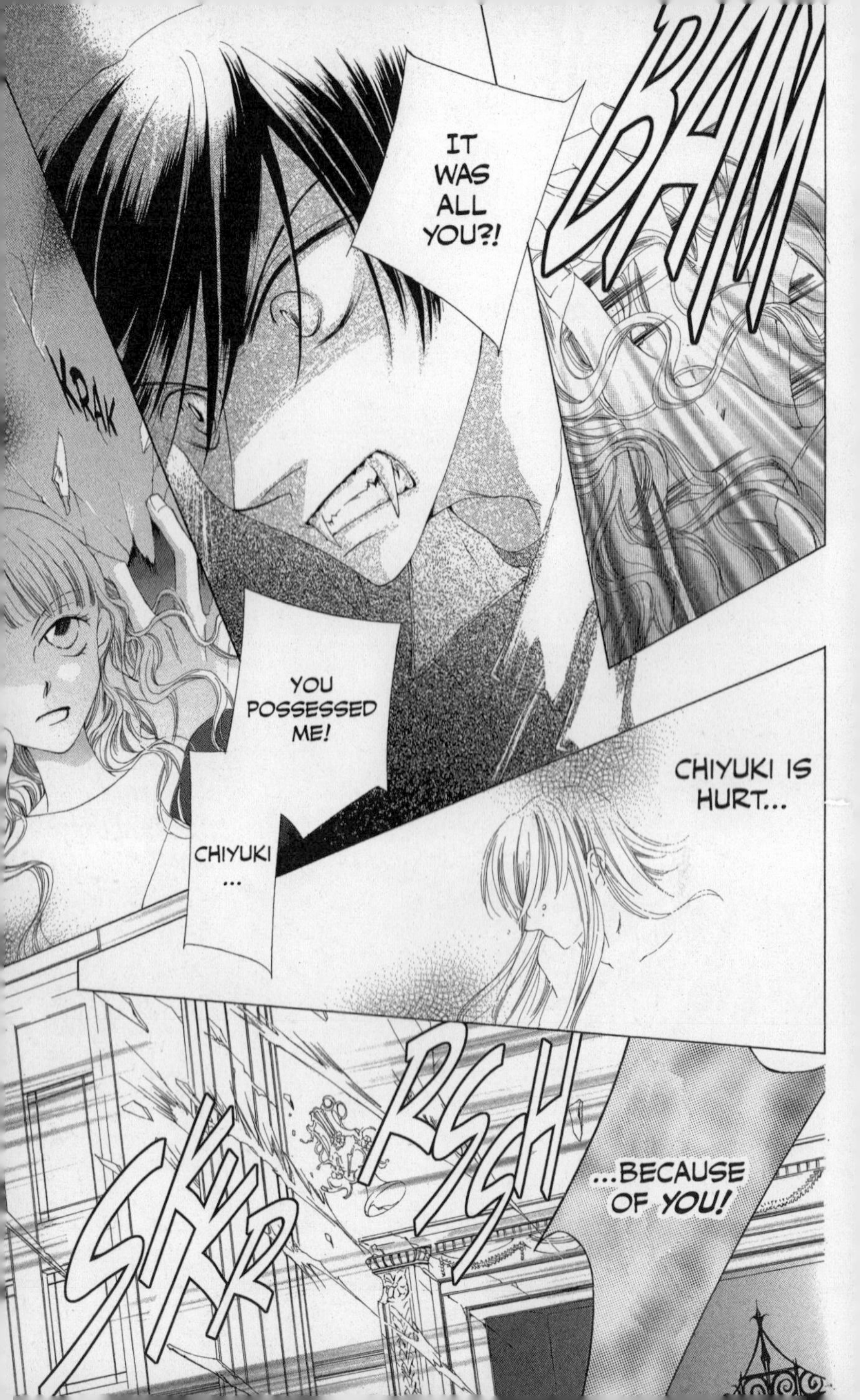
BAM
IT WAS ALL YOU?!
KRAK
YOU POSSESSED ME!
CHIYUKI ...
CHIYUKI IS HURT...
...BECAUSE OF YOU!
RSCH
SKRR

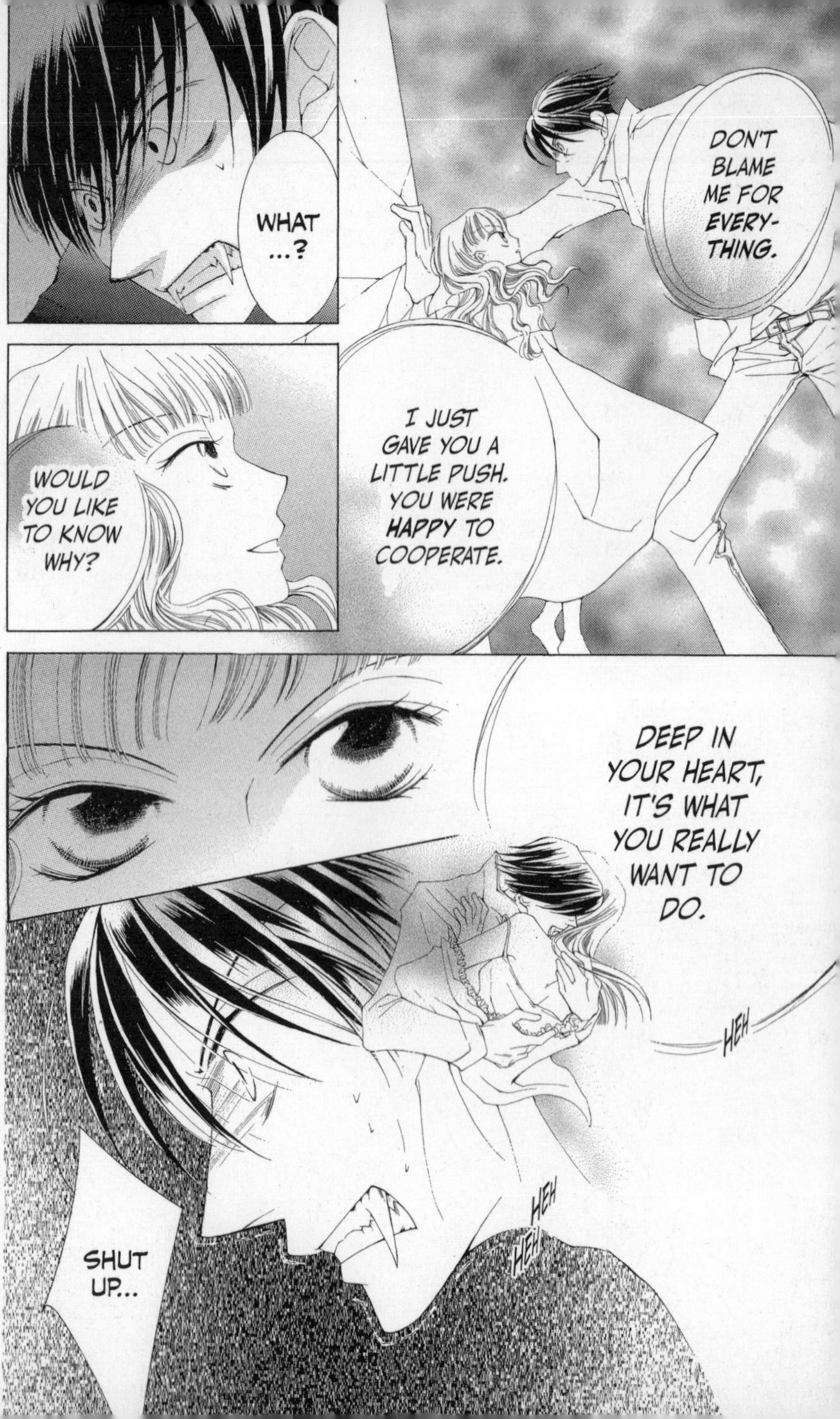
DON'T BLAME ME FOR EVERY-THING.
I JUST GAVE YOU A LITTLE PUSH. YOU WERE HAPPY TO COOPERATE.
WHAT ...?
WOULD YOU LIKE TO KNOW WHY?
DEEP IN YOUR HEART, IT'S WHAT YOU REALLY WANT TO DO.
HEH
HEH HEH
SHUT UP...

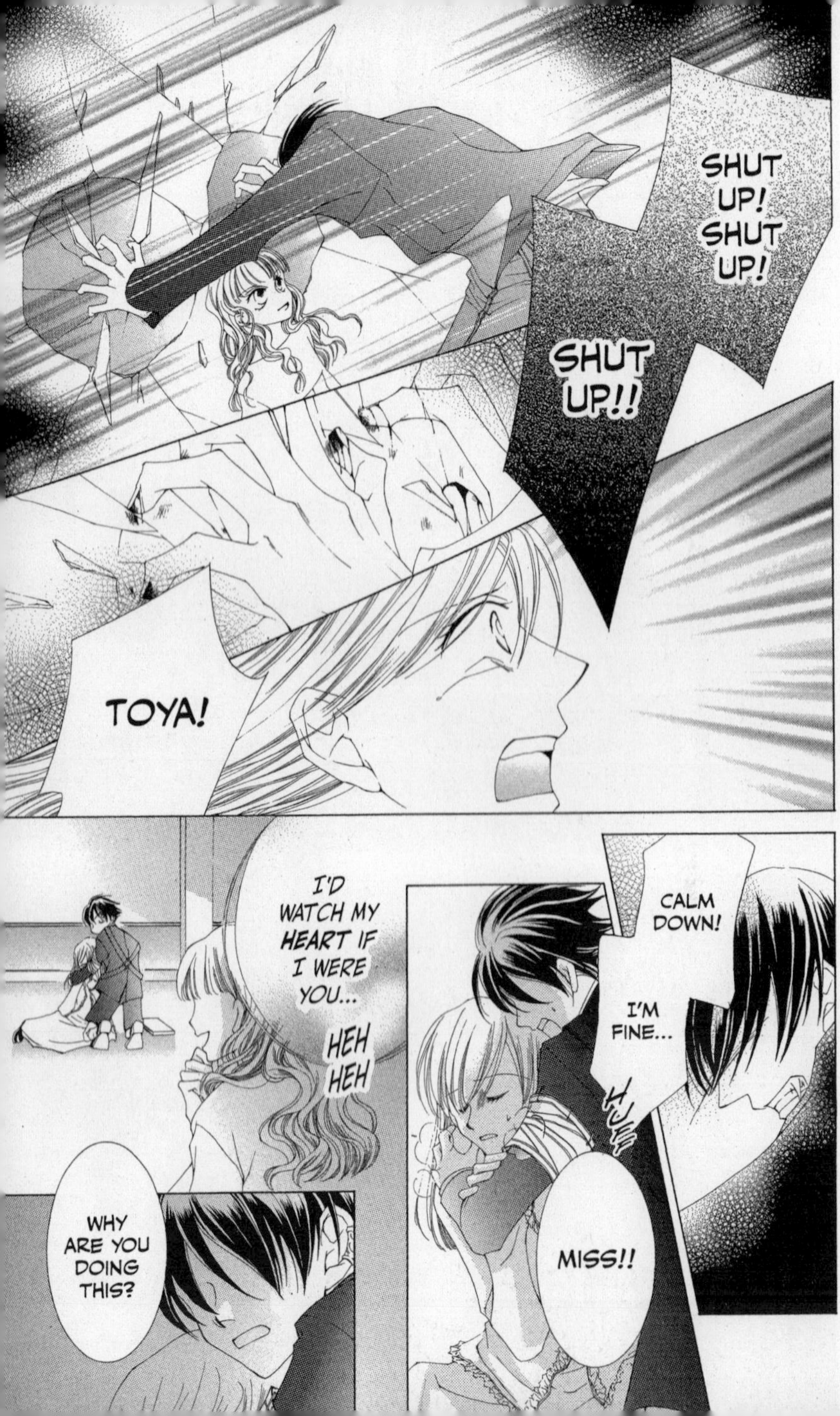
SHUT UP! SHUT UP!
SHUT UP!!
TOYA!
CALM DOWN!
I'M FINE...
MISS!!
I'D WATCH MY HEART IF I WERE YOU...
HEH HEH
WHY ARE YOU DOING THIS?

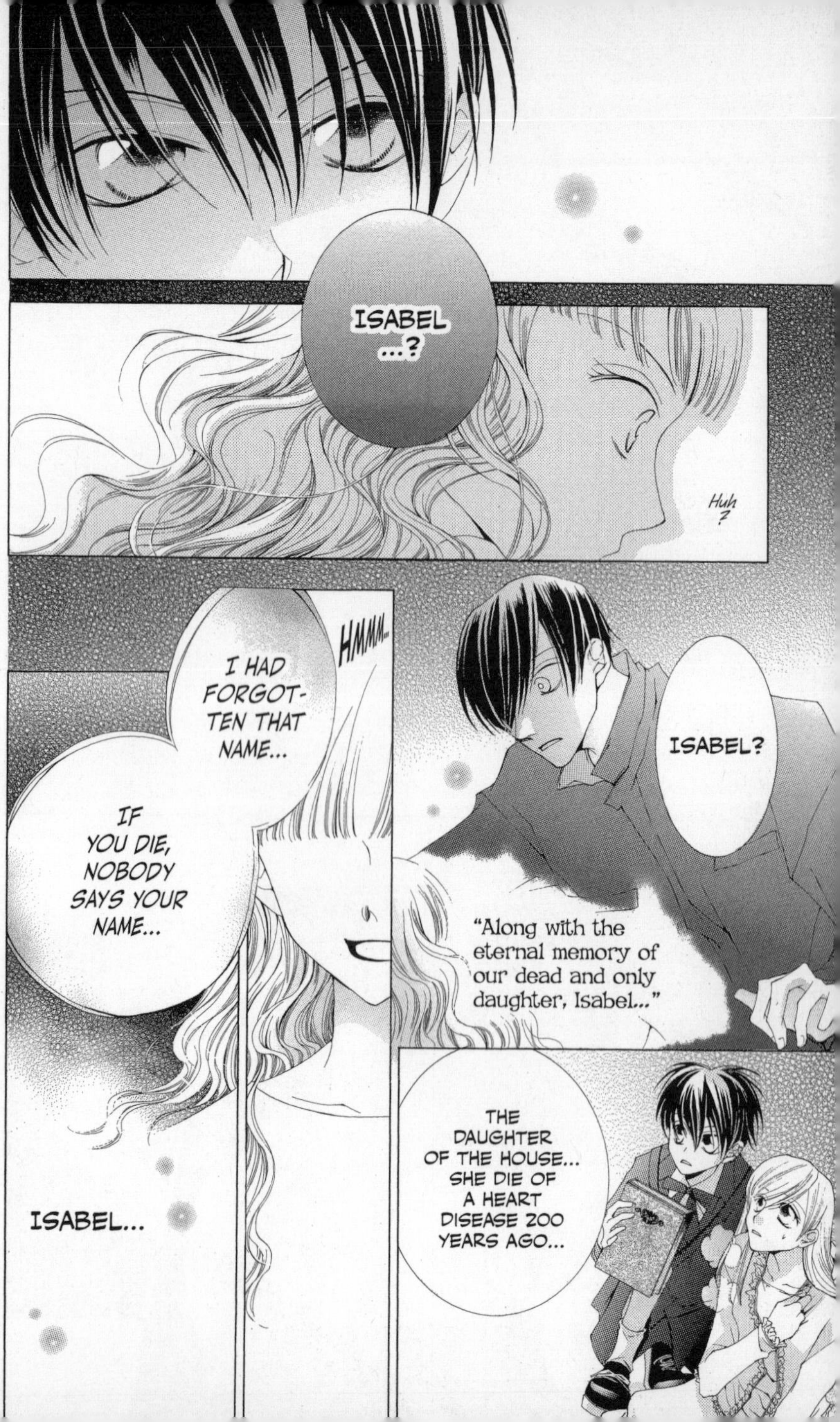
ISABEL ...?
Huh?
ISABEL?
"Along with the eternal memory of our dead and only daughter, Isabel..."
THE DAUGHTER OF THE HOUSE... SHE DIE OF A HEART DISEASE 200 YEARS AGO...
HMMM...
I HAD FORGOT-TEN THAT NAME...
IF YOU DIE, NOBODY SAYS YOUR NAME...
ISABEL...

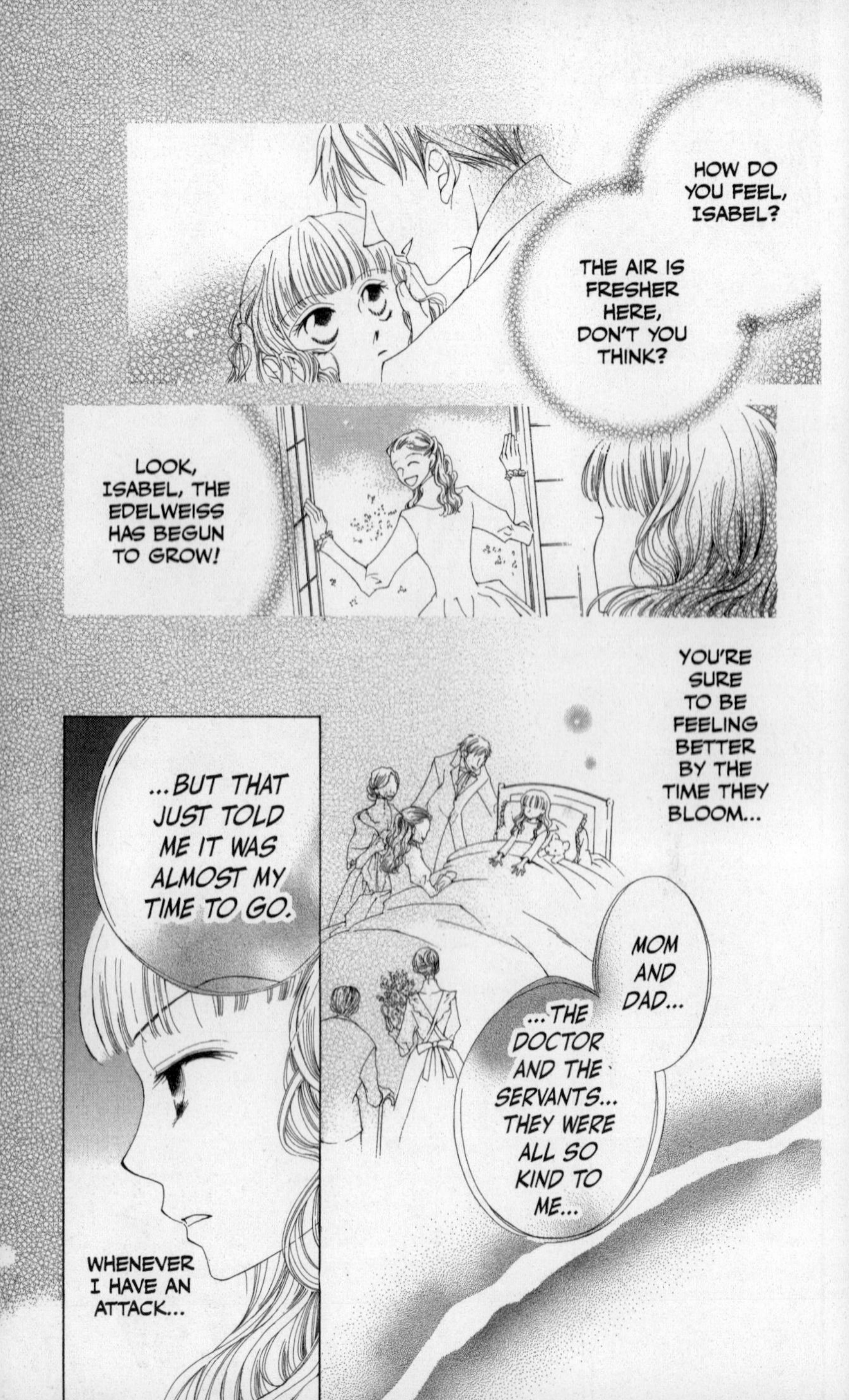
HOW DO YOU FEEL, ISABEL?
THE AIR IS FRESHER HERE, DON'T YOU THINK?
LOOK, ISABEL, THE EDELWEISS HAS BEGUN TO GROW!
YOU'RE SURE TO BE FEELING BETTER BY THE TIME THEY BLOOM...
WHENEVER I HAVE AN ATTACK...
MOM AND DAD...
...THE DOCTOR AND THE SERVANTS... THEY WERE ALL SO KIND TO ME...
...BUT THAT JUST TOLD ME IT WAS ALMOST MY TIME TO GO.

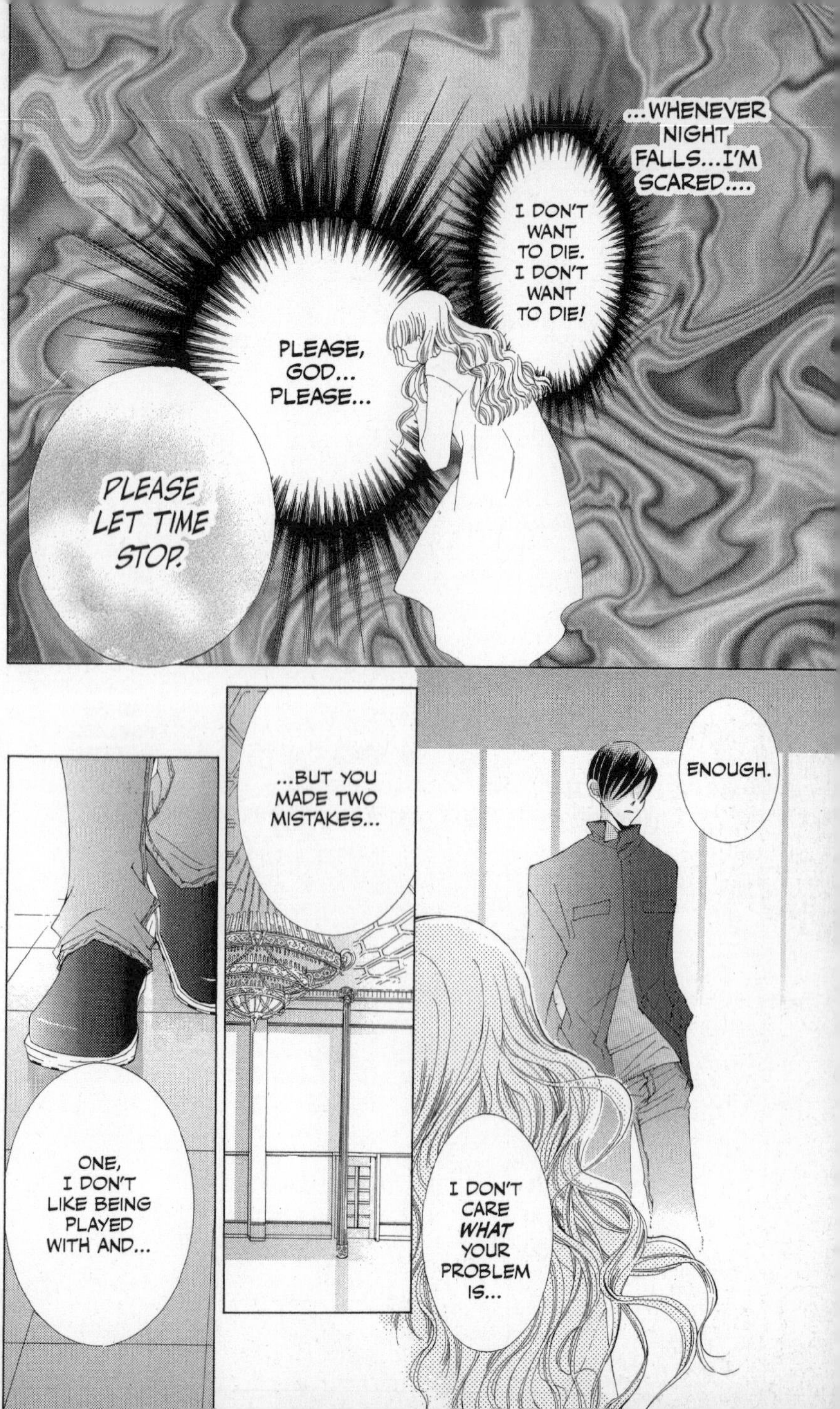
...WHENEVER NIGHT FALLS...I'M SCARED....
I DON'T WANT TO DIE. I DON'T WANT TO DIE!
PLEASE, GOD... PLEASE...
PLEASE LET TIME STOP.
ENOUGH.
I DON'T CARE *WHAT* YOUR PROBLEM IS...
...BUT YOU MADE TWO MISTAKES...
ONE, I DON'T LIKE BEING PLAYED WITH AND...

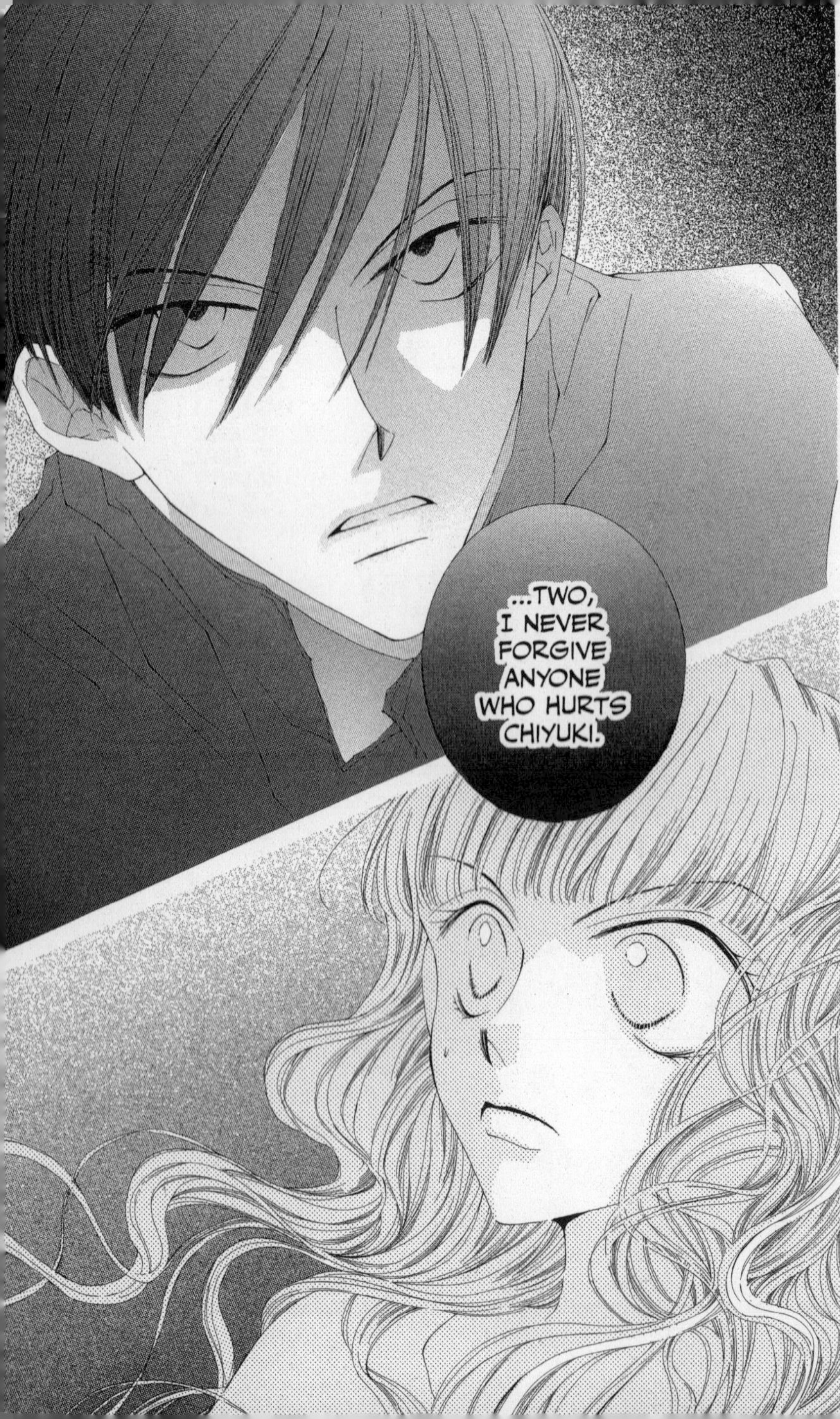
...TWO, I NEVER FORGIVE ANYONE WHO HURTS CHIYUKI.

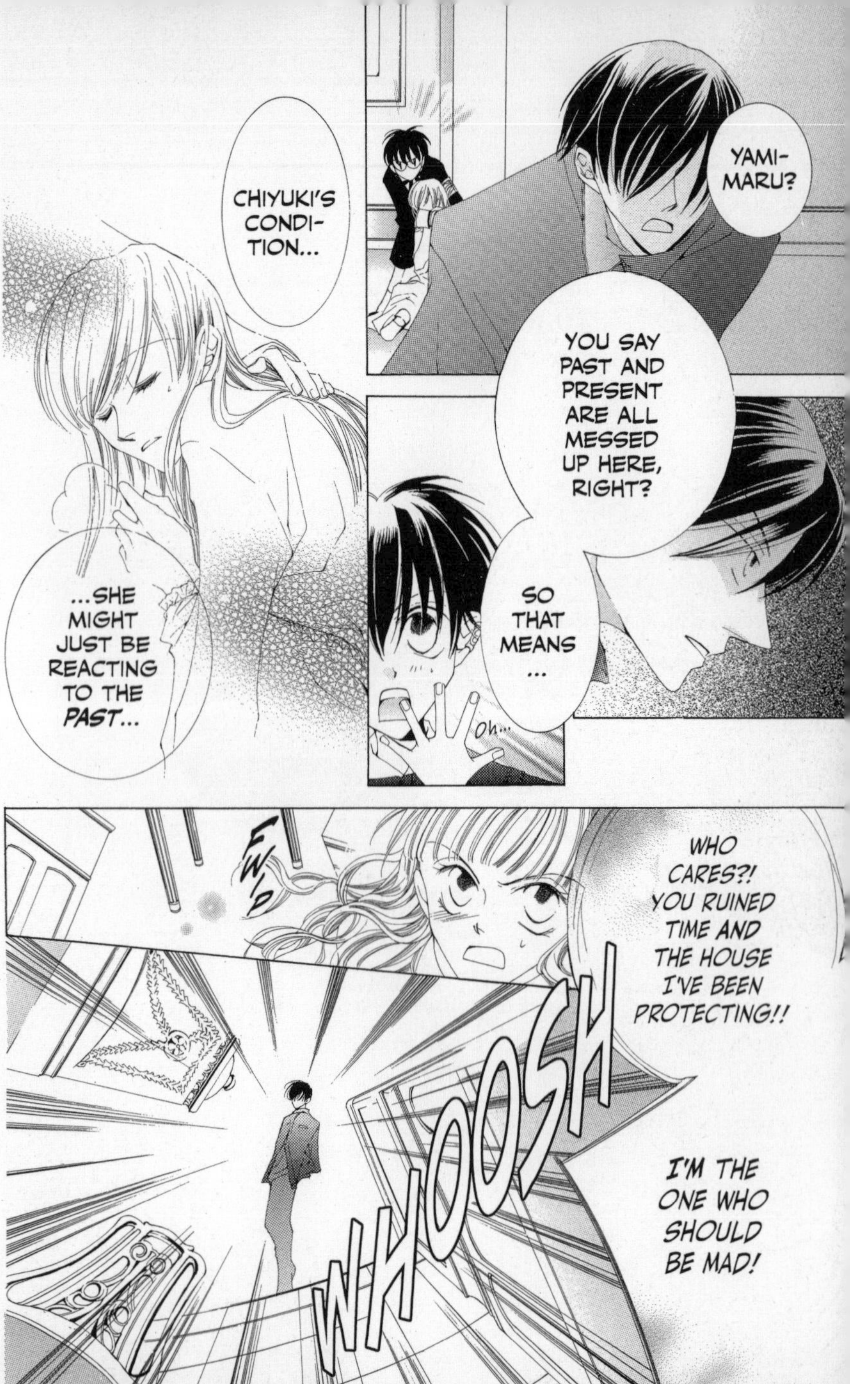
YAMI-MARU?
YOU SAY PAST AND PRESENT ARE ALL MESSED UP HERE, RIGHT?
SO THAT MEANS ...
Oh...
CHIYUKI'S CONDITION...
...SHE MIGHT JUST BE REACTING TO THE *PAST*...
FWIP
WHO CARES?! YOU RUINED TIME AND THE HOUSE I'VE BEEN PROTECTING!!
WHOOSH
I'M THE ONE WHO SHOULD BE MAD!

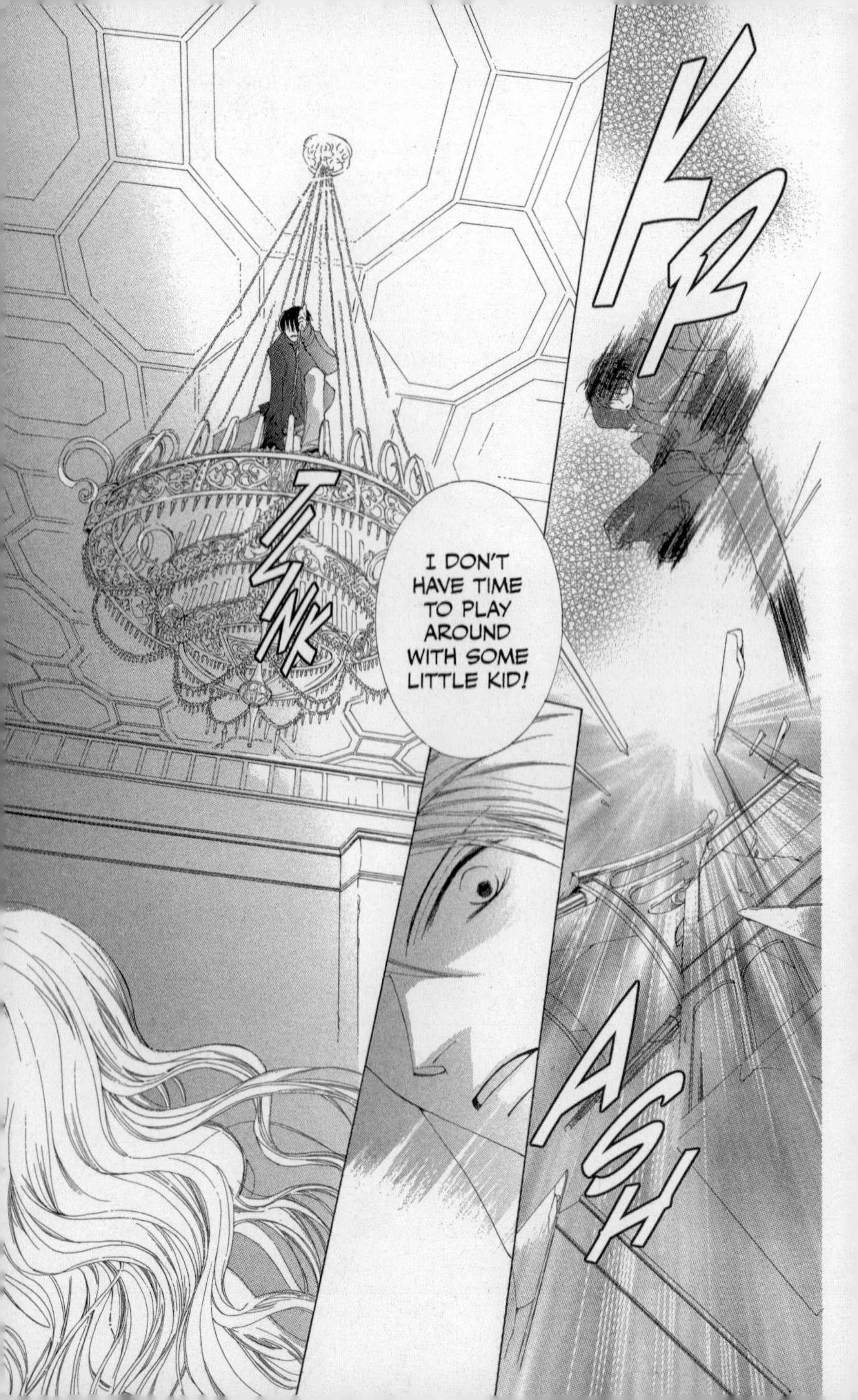
I DON'T HAVE TIME TO PLAY AROUND WITH SOME LITTLE KID!

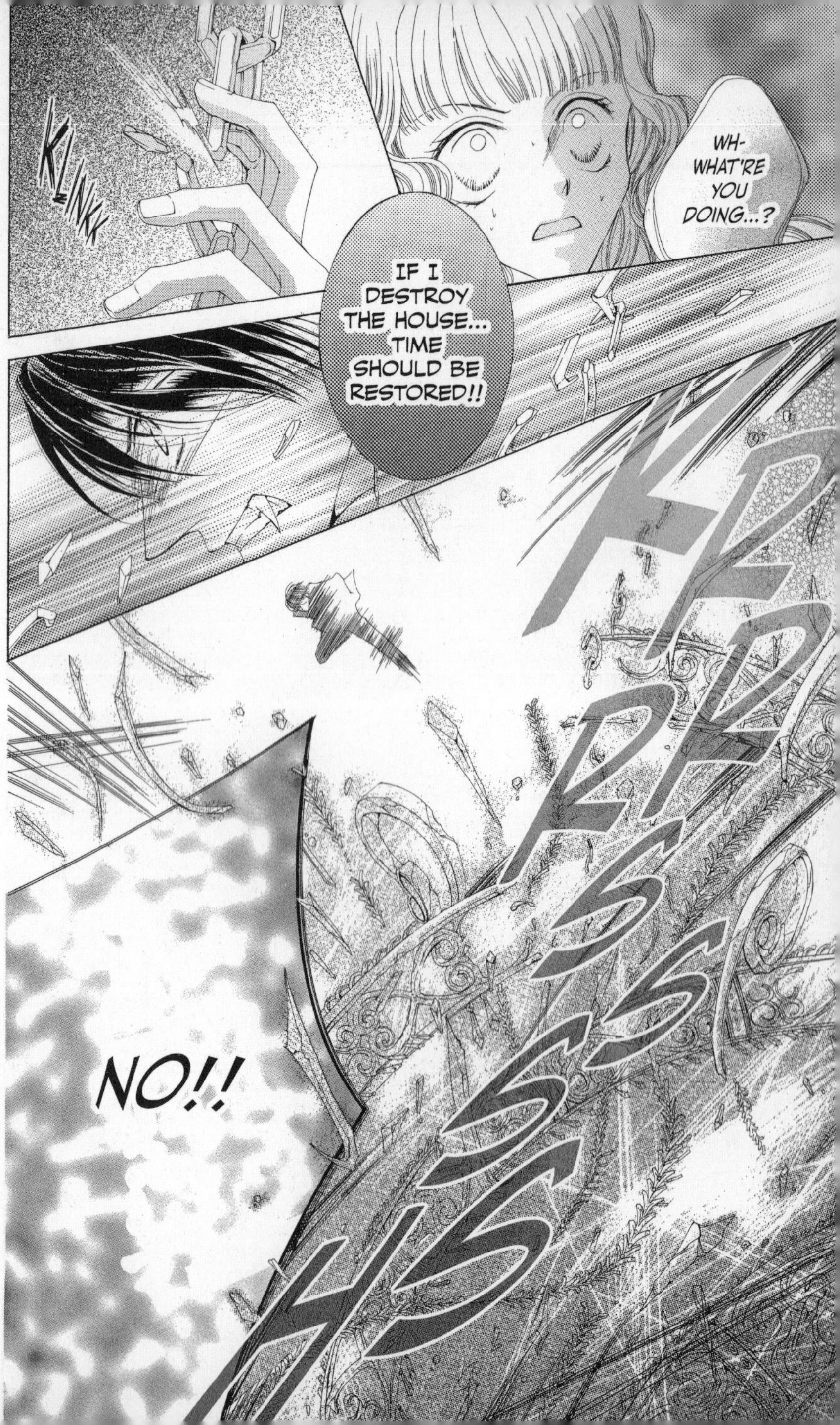
WH- WHAT'RE YOU DOING...?
KLINKK
IF I DESTROY THE HOUSE... TIME SHOULD BE RESTORED!!
NO!!

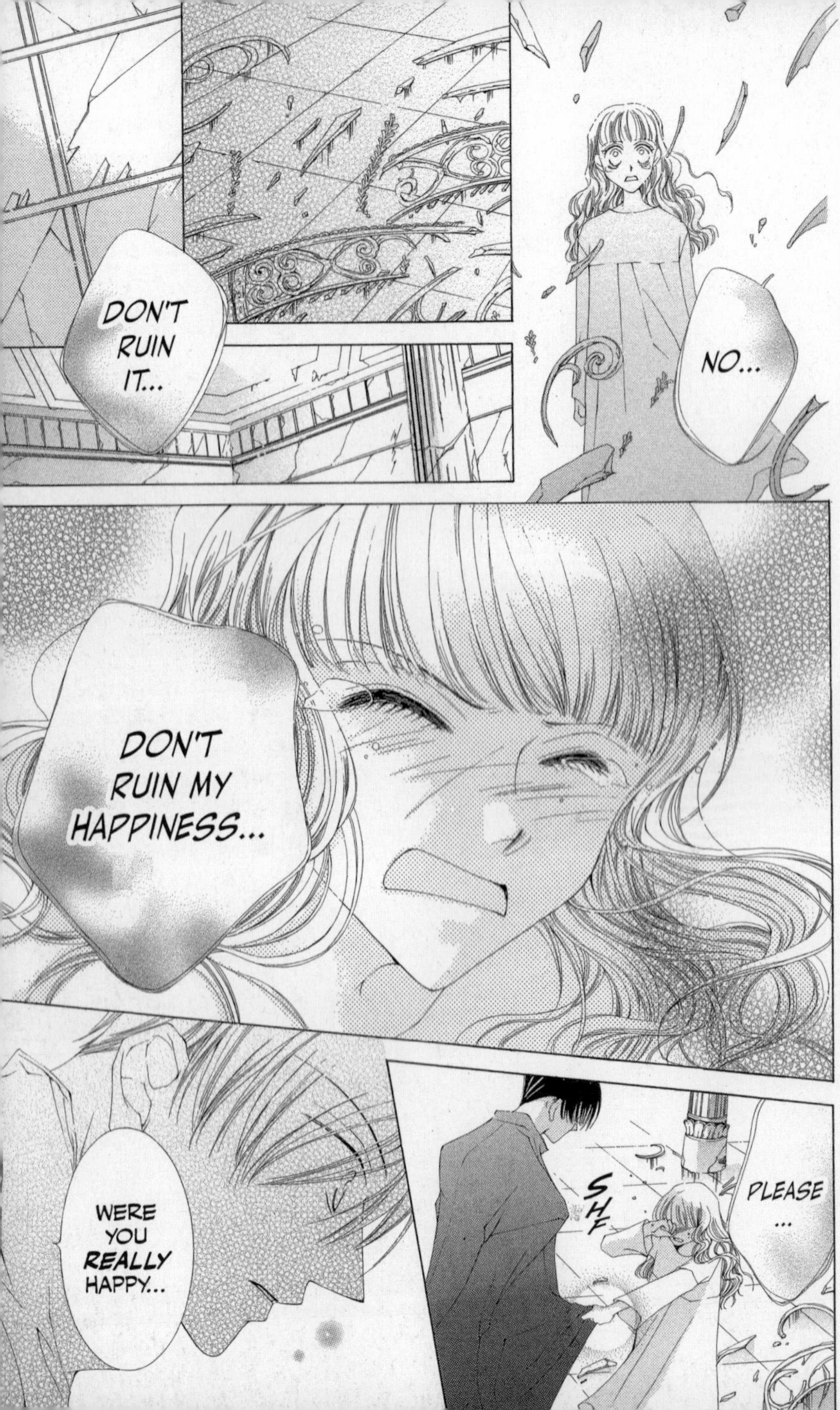
NO...
DON'T RUIN IT...
DON'T RUIN MY HAPPINESS...
PLEASE ...
SHF
WERE YOU REALLY HAPPY...

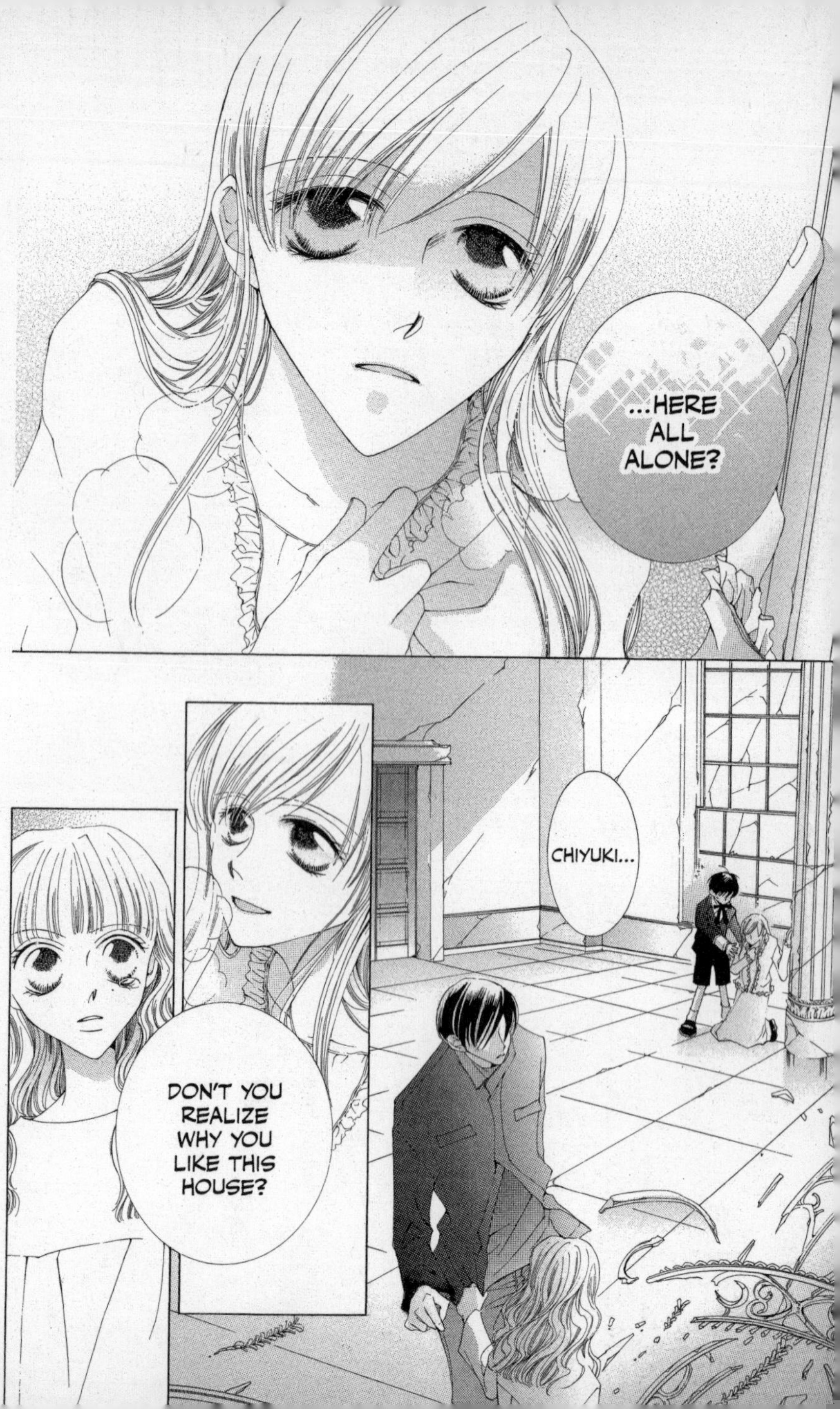
...HERE ALL ALONE?
CHIYUKI...
DON'T YOU REALIZE WHY YOU LIKE THIS HOUSE?

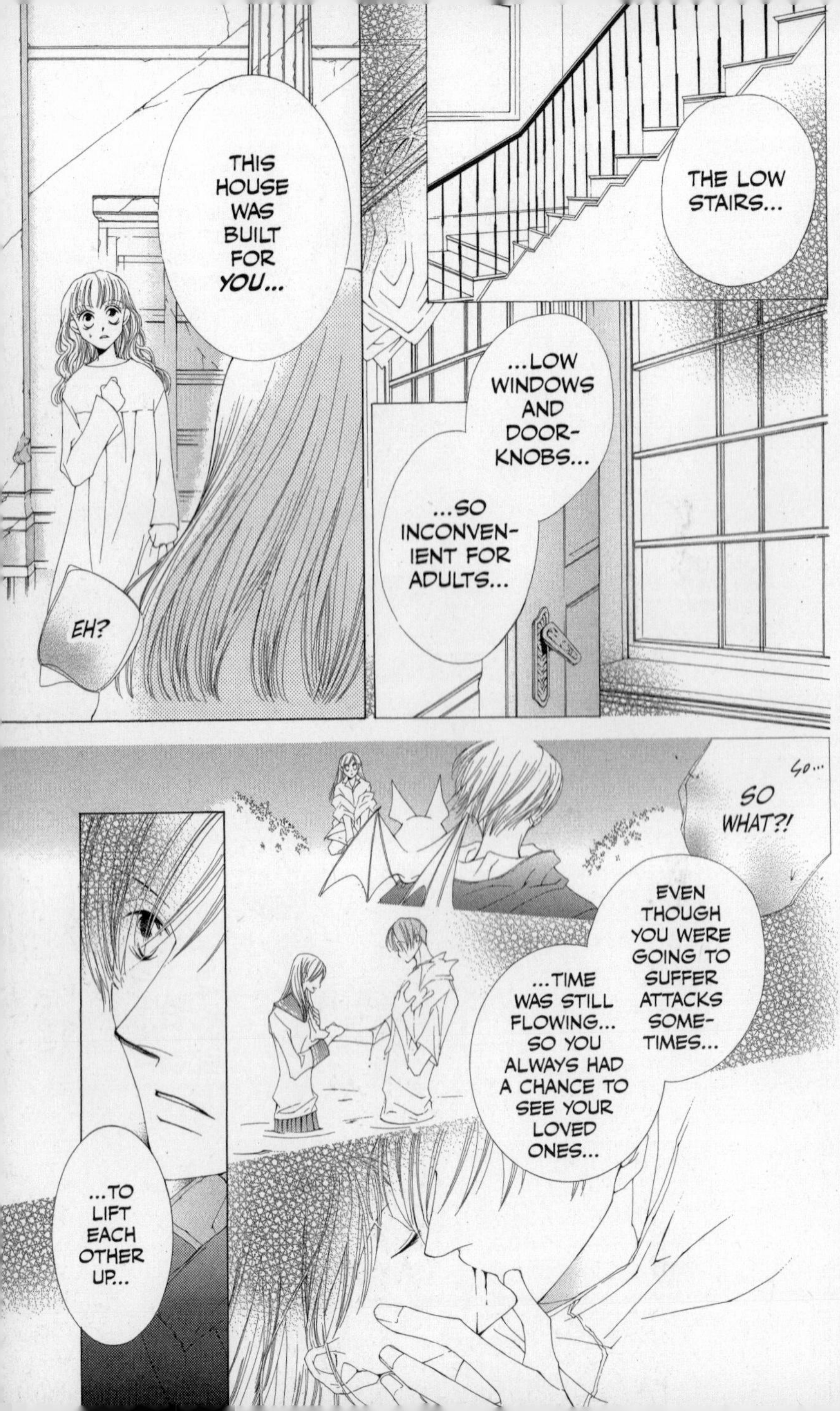
THE LOW STAIRS...
...LOW WINDOWS AND DOOR-KNOBS...
...SO INCONVEN-IENT FOR ADULTS...
THIS HOUSE WAS BUILT FOR *YOU*...
EH?
So...
SO WHAT?!
EVEN THOUGH YOU WERE GOING TO SUFFER ATTACKS SOME-TIMES...
...TIME WAS STILL FLOWING... SO YOU ALWAYS HAD A CHANCE TO SEE YOUR LOVED ONES...
...TO LIFT EACH OTHER UP...

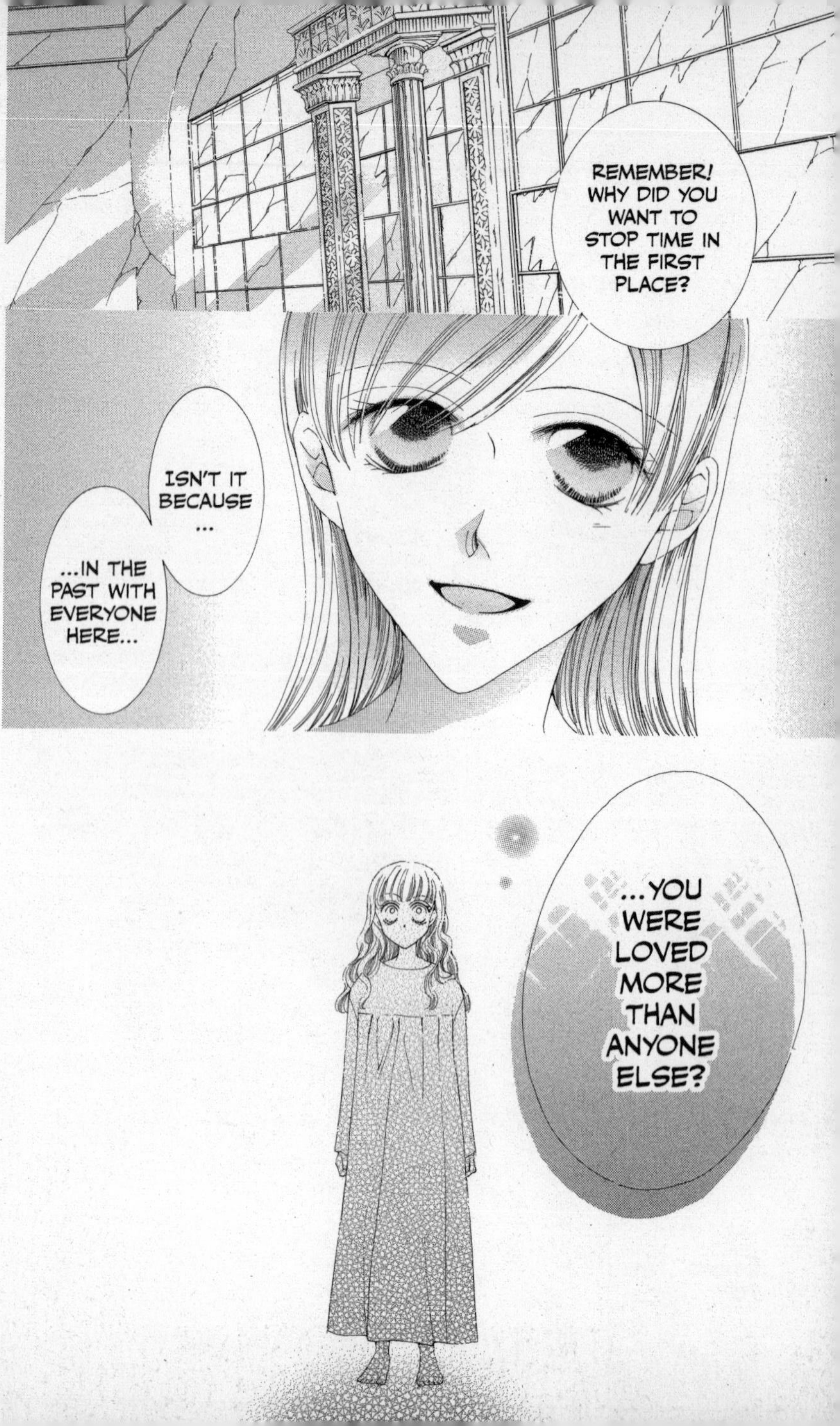
REMEMBER! WHY DID YOU WANT TO STOP TIME IN THE FIRST PLACE?
ISN'T IT BECAUSE ...
...IN THE PAST WITH EVERYONE HERE...
...YOU WERE LOVED MORE THAN ANYONE ELSE?

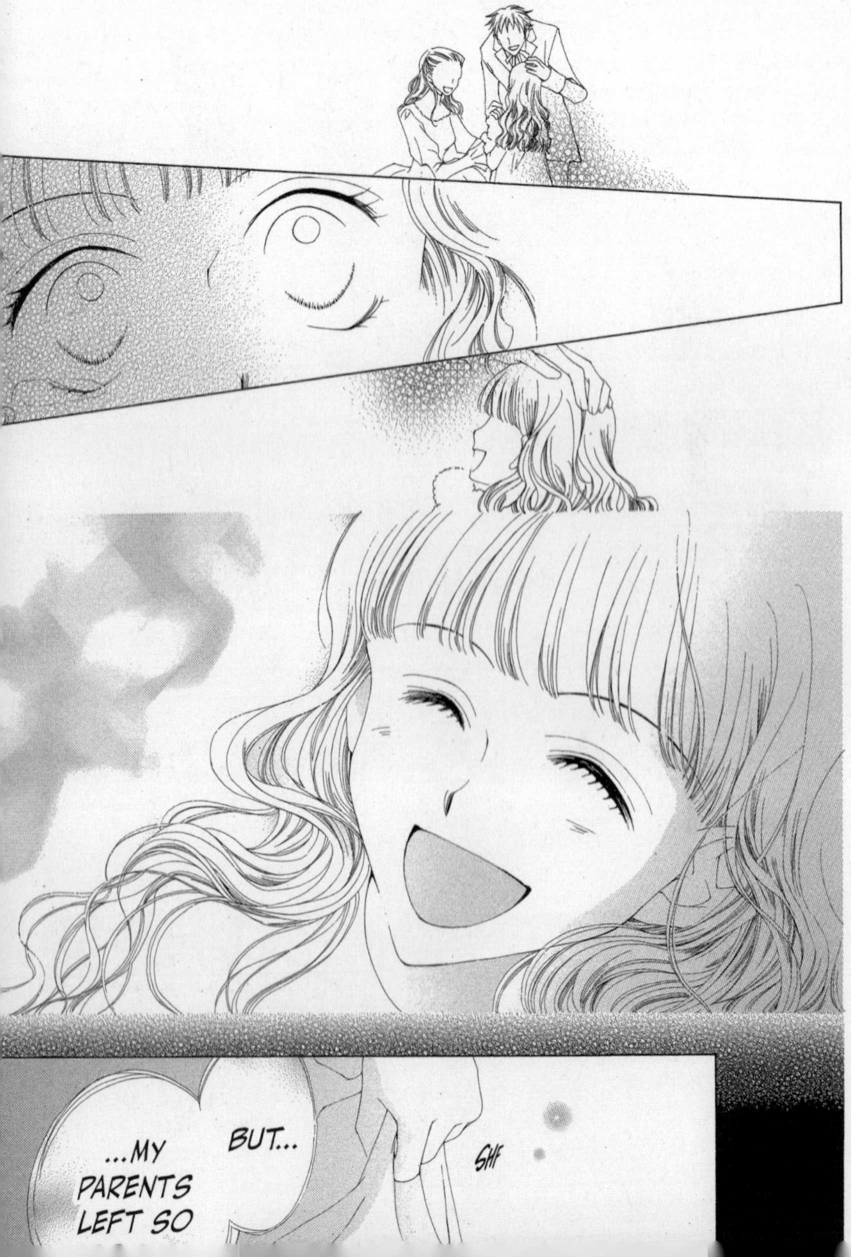
BUT...
SHF
...MY PARENTS LEFT SO

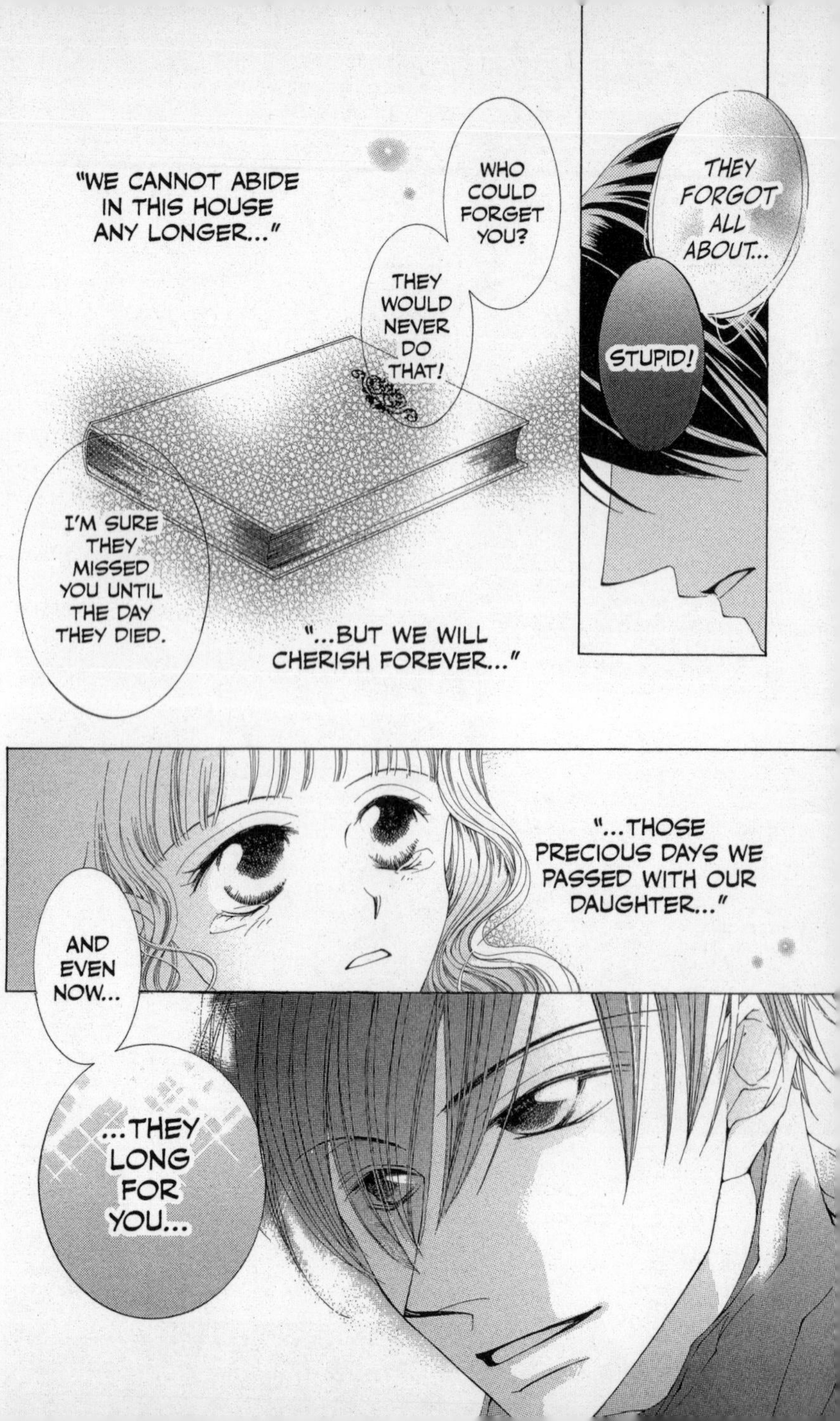
THEY FORGOT ALL ABOUT...
STUPID!
WHO COULD FORGET YOU?
THEY WOULD NEVER DO THAT!
"WE CANNOT ABIDE IN THIS HOUSE ANY LONGER..."
I'M SURE THEY MISSED YOU UNTIL THE DAY THEY DIED.
"...BUT WE WILL CHERISH FOREVER..."
"...THOSE PRECIOUS DAYS WE PASSED WITH OUR DAUGHTER..."
AND EVEN NOW...
...THEY LONG FOR YOU...

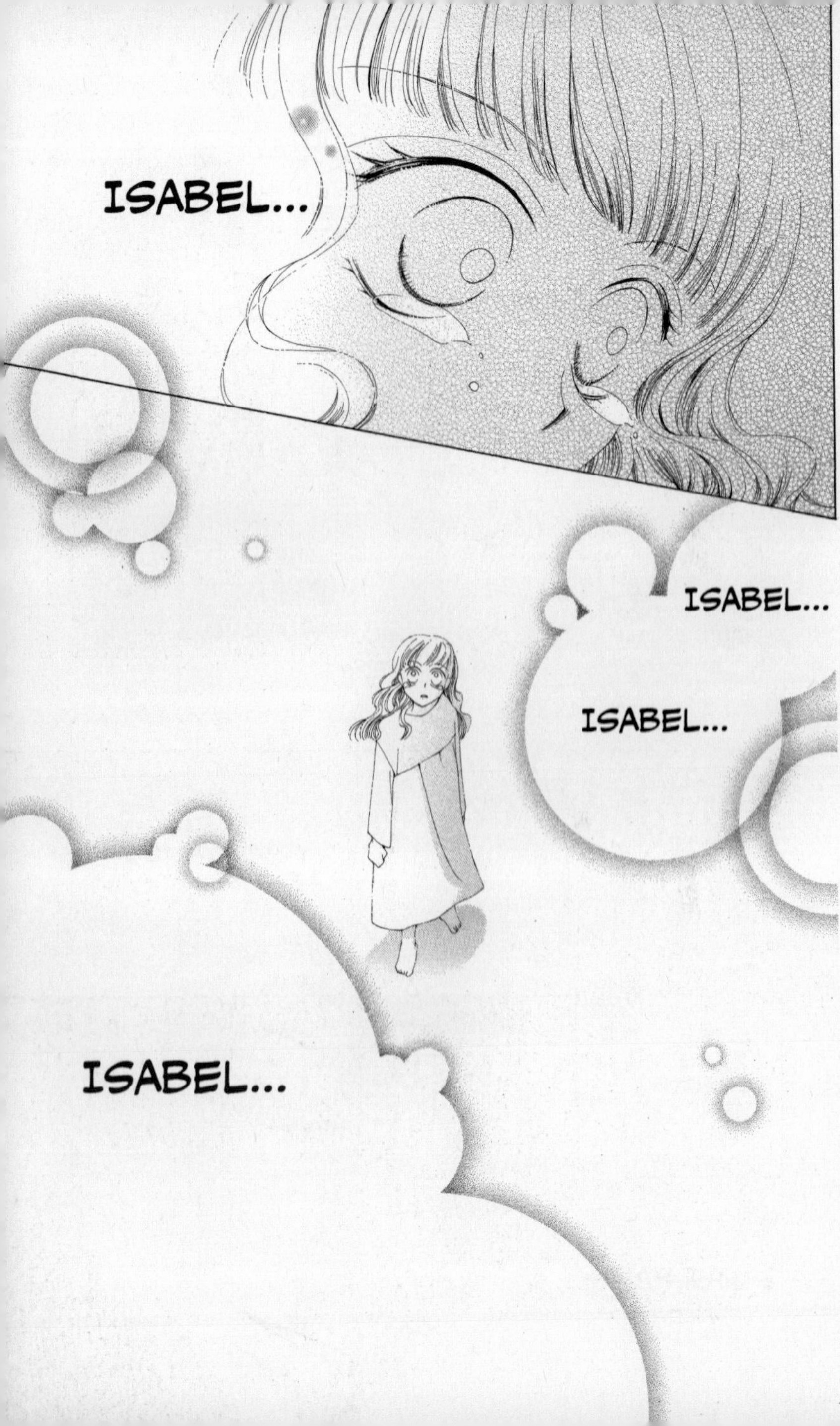
ISABEL...
ISABEL...
ISABEL...
ISABEL...

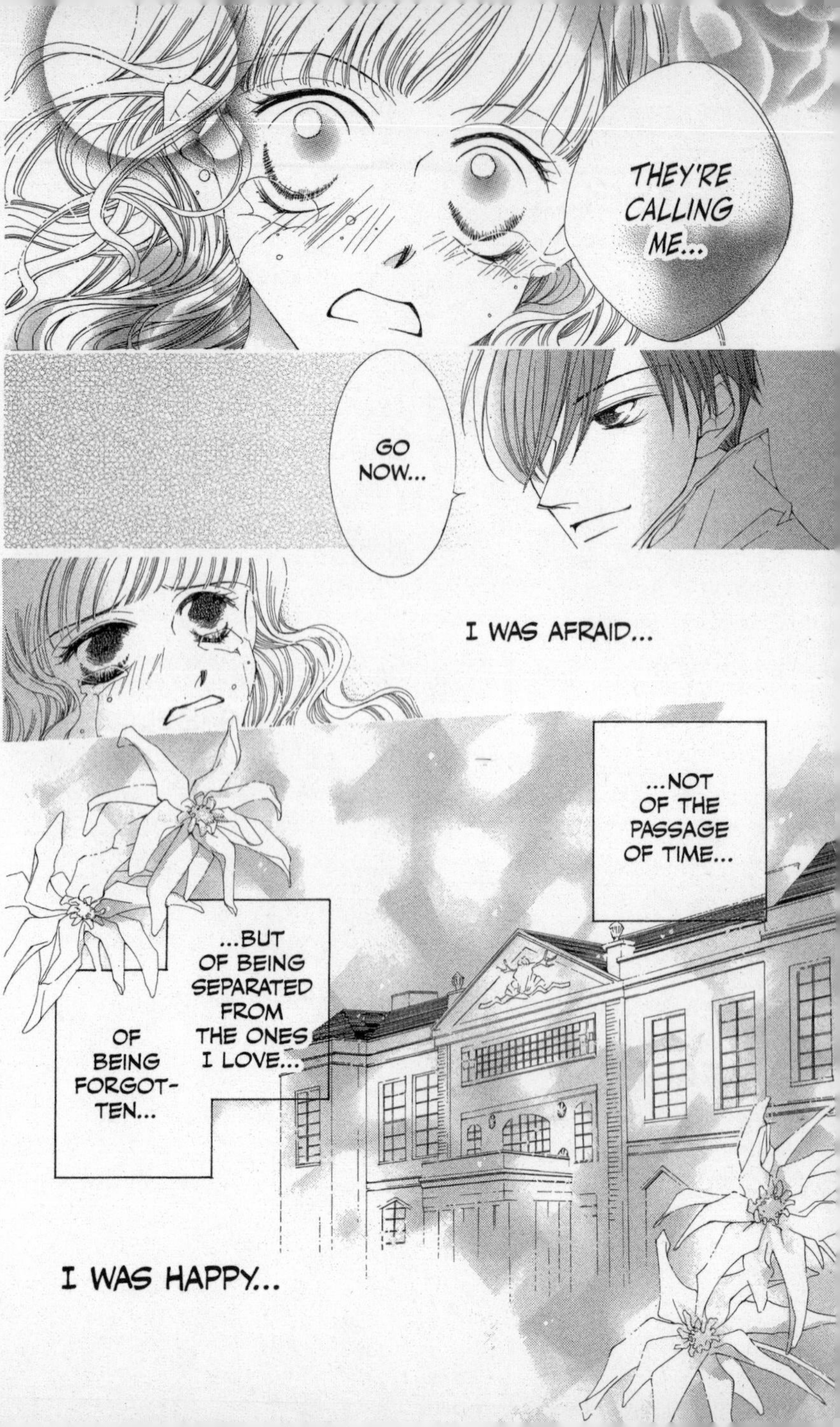
THEY'RE CALLING ME...
GO NOW...
I WAS AFRAID...
...NOT OF THE PASSAGE OF TIME...
...BUT OF BEING SEPARATED FROM THE ONES I LOVE...
OF BEING FORGOT-TEN...
I WAS HAPPY...

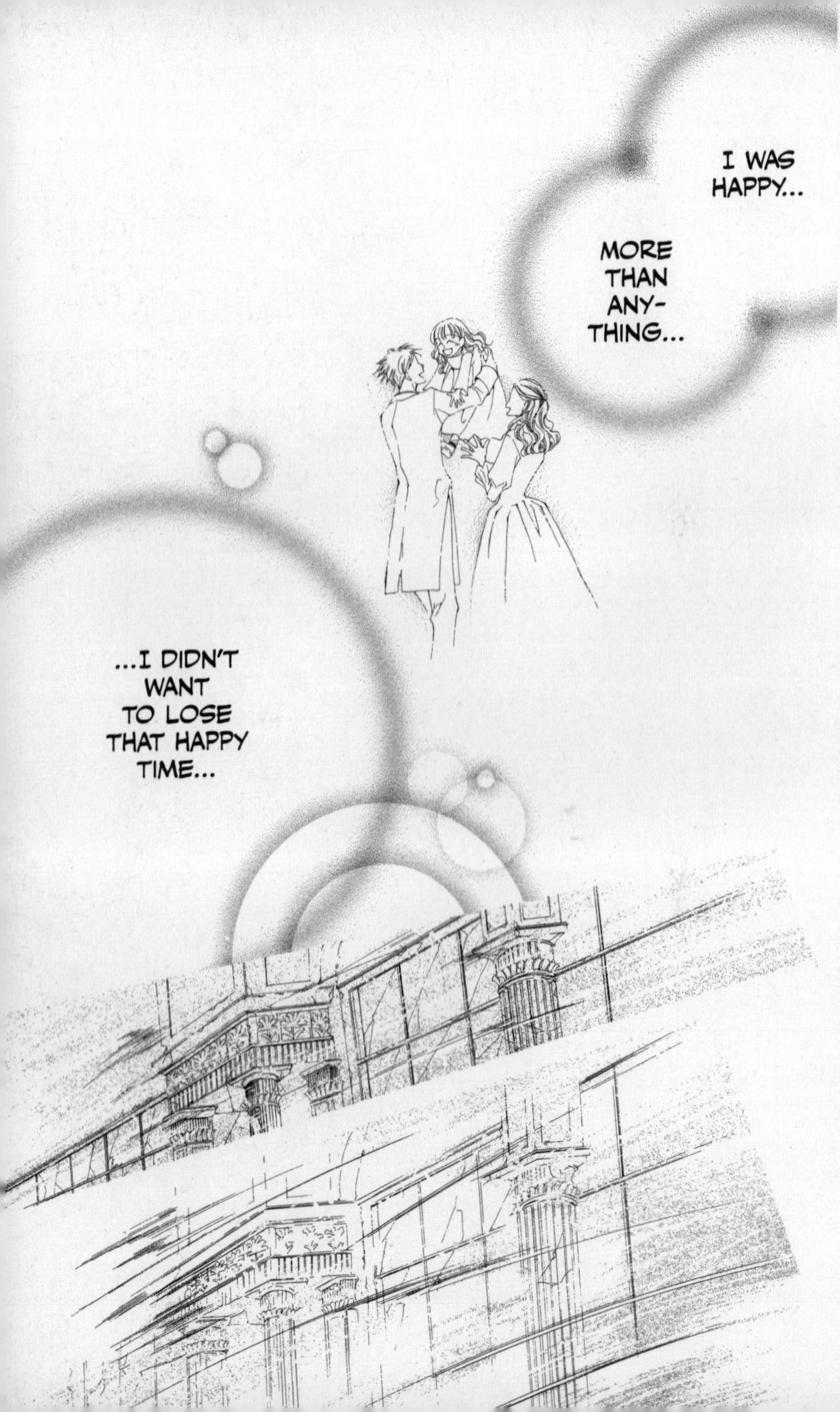
I WAS HAPPY...
MORE THAN ANY-THING...
...I DIDN'T WANT TO LOSE THAT HAPPY TIME...

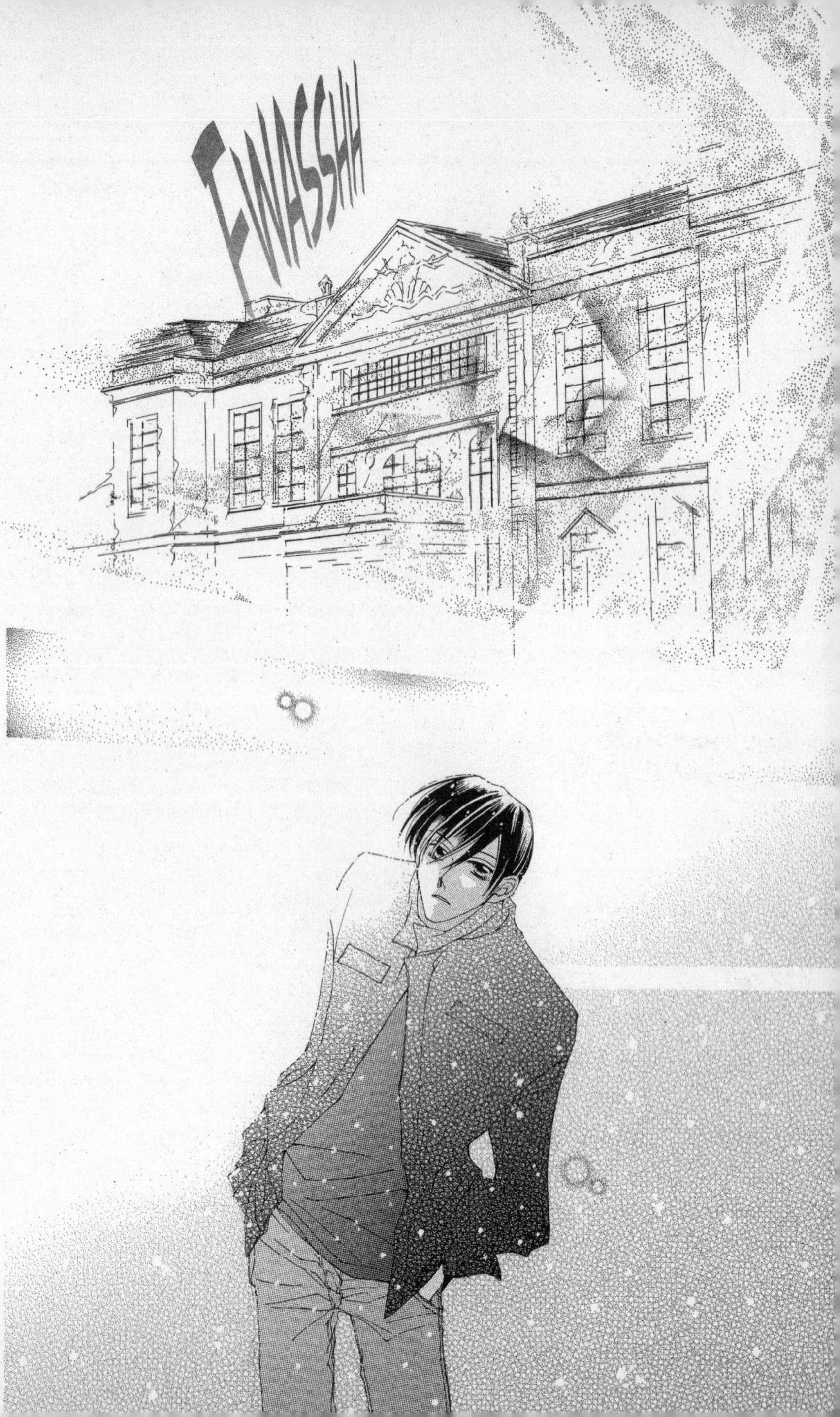
FWASSHH

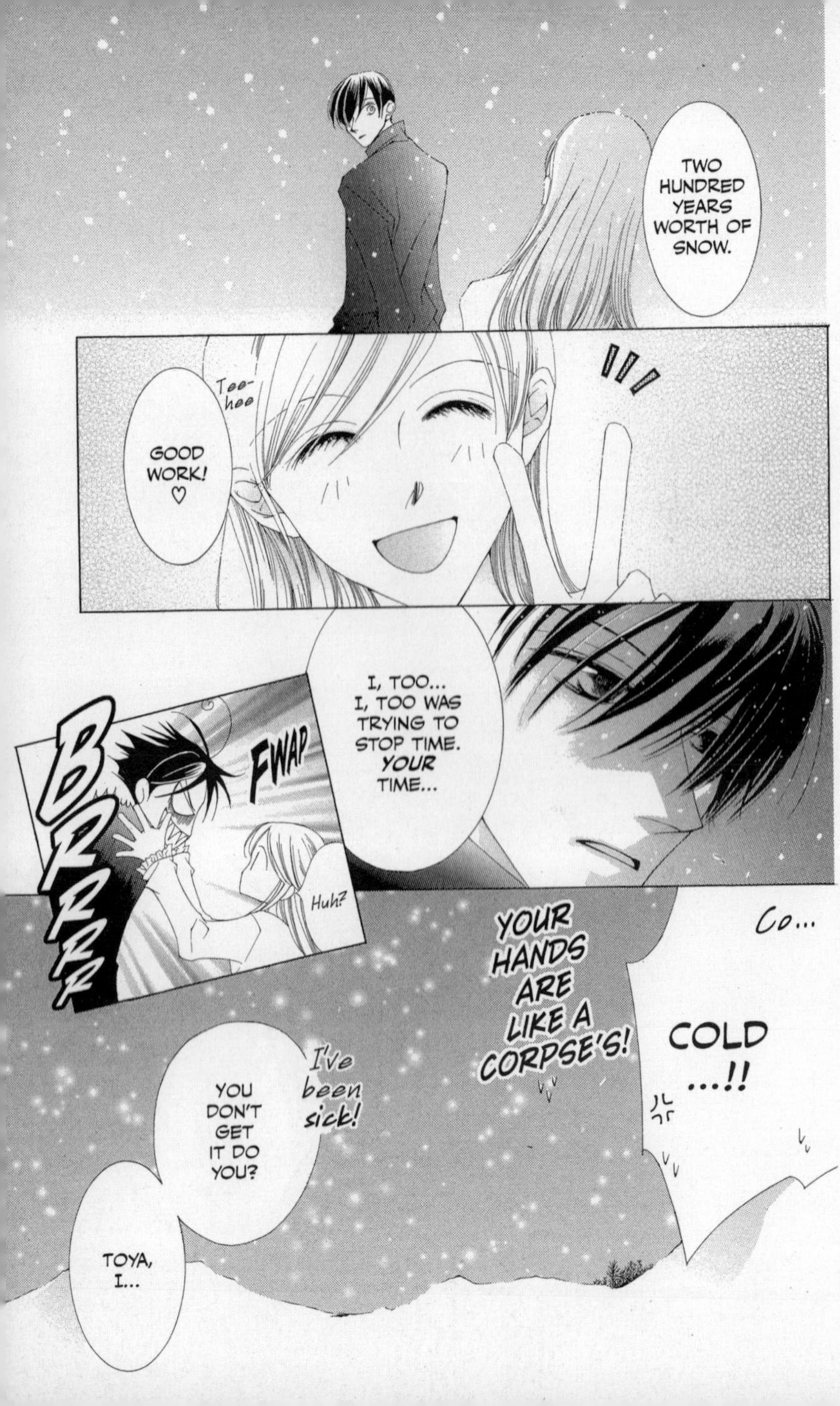
TWO HUNDRED YEARS WORTH OF SNOW.
Tee-hee
GOOD WORK! ♡
I, TOO... I, TOO WAS TRYING TO STOP TIME. *YOUR* TIME...
FWAP
BRRRR
Huh?
Co...
COLD ...!!
YOUR HANDS ARE LIKE A CORPSE'S!
I've been sick!
YOU DON'T GET IT DO YOU?
TOYA, I...

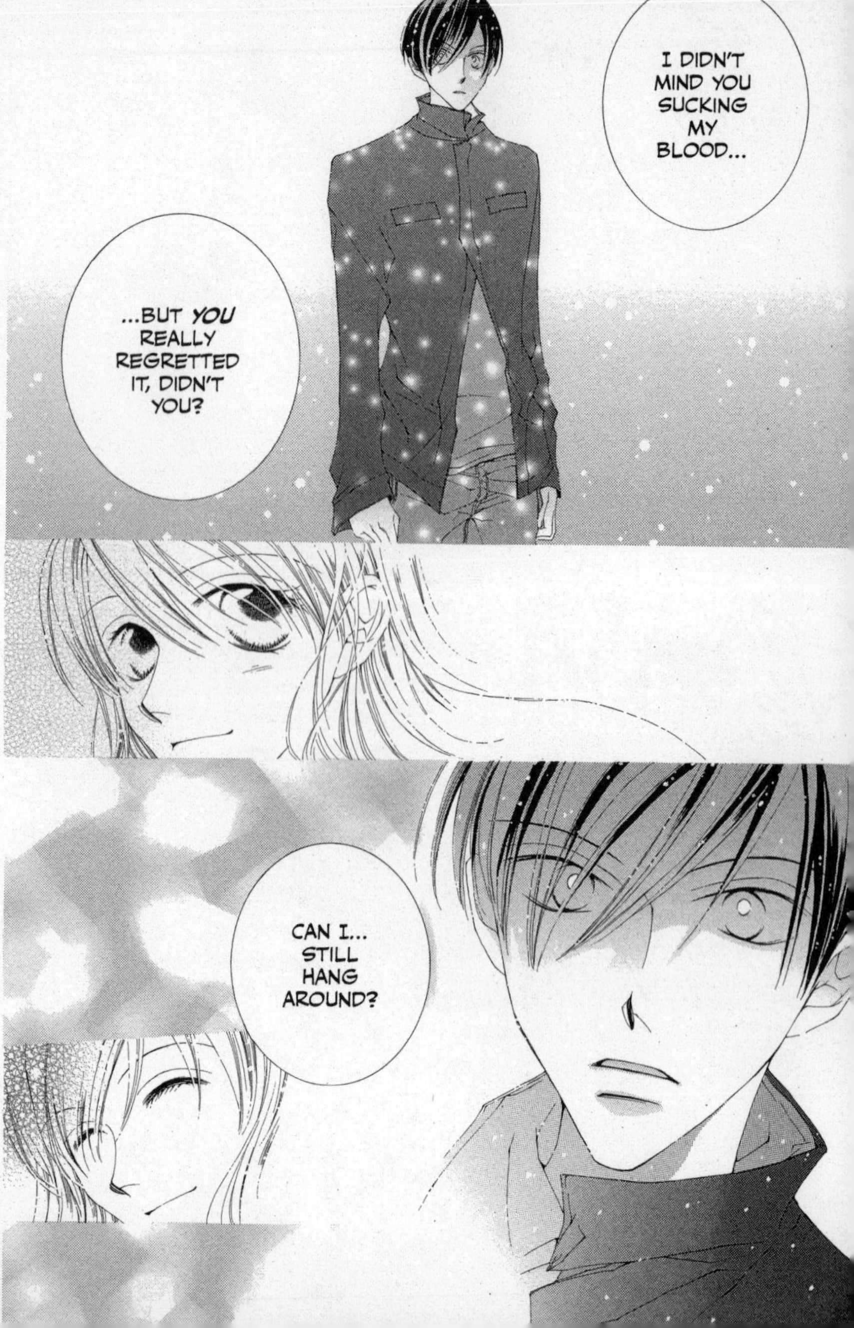
I DIDN'T MIND YOU SUCKING MY BLOOD...
...BUT *YOU* REALLY REGRETTED IT, DIDN'T YOU?
CAN I... STILL HANG AROUND?

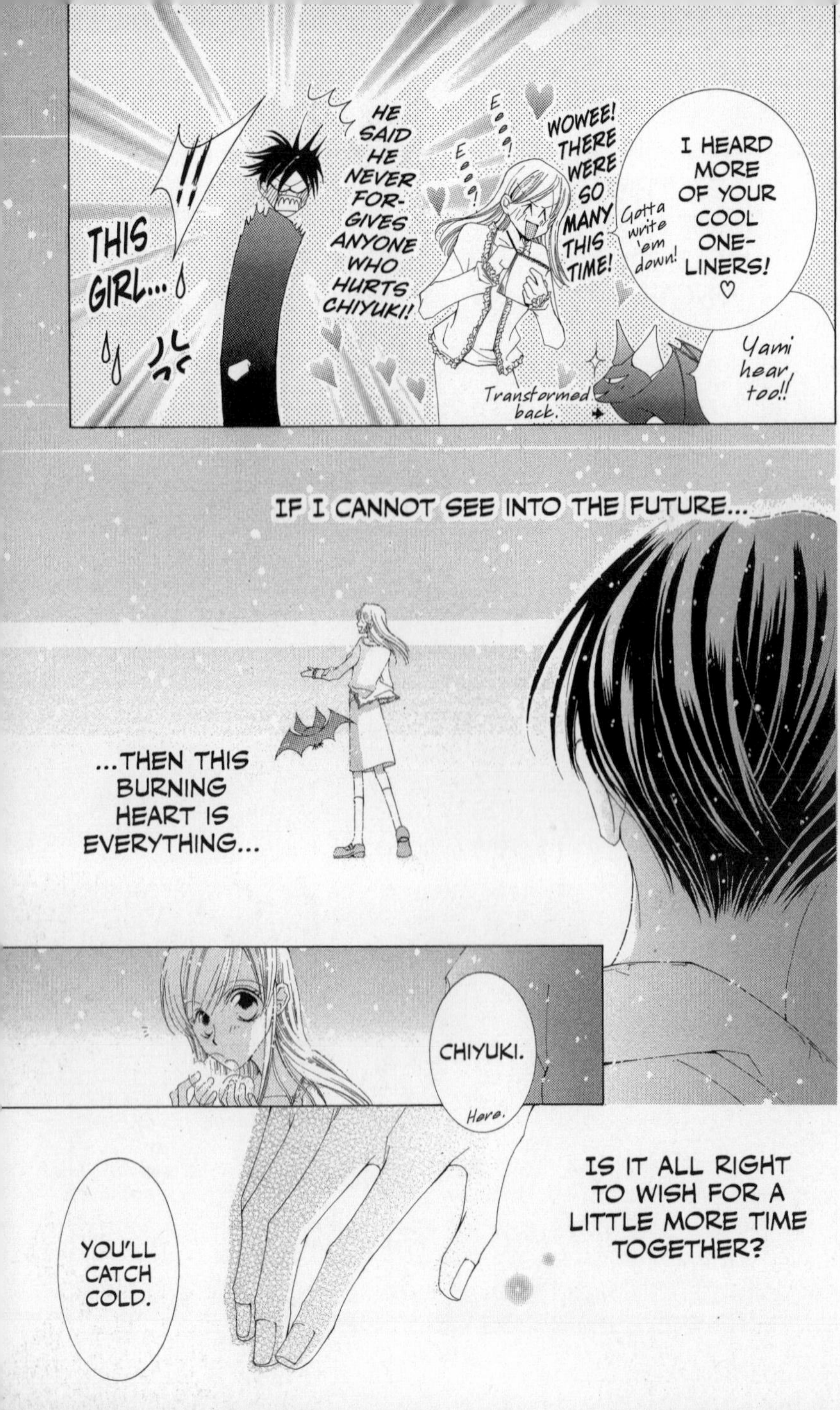
I HEARD MORE OF YOUR COOL ONE-LINERS! ♡
Yami hear, too!!
Gotta write 'em down!
WOWEE! THERE WERE SO MANY THIS TIME!
Transformed back.
HE SAID HE NEVER FOR-GIVES ANYONE WHO HURTS CHIYUKI!
!!
THIS GIRL...
IF I CANNOT SEE INTO THE FUTURE...
...THEN THIS BURNING HEART IS EVERYTHING...
CHIYUKI.
Here.
IS IT ALL RIGHT TO WISH FOR A LITTLE MORE TIME TOGETHER?
YOU'LL CATCH COLD.

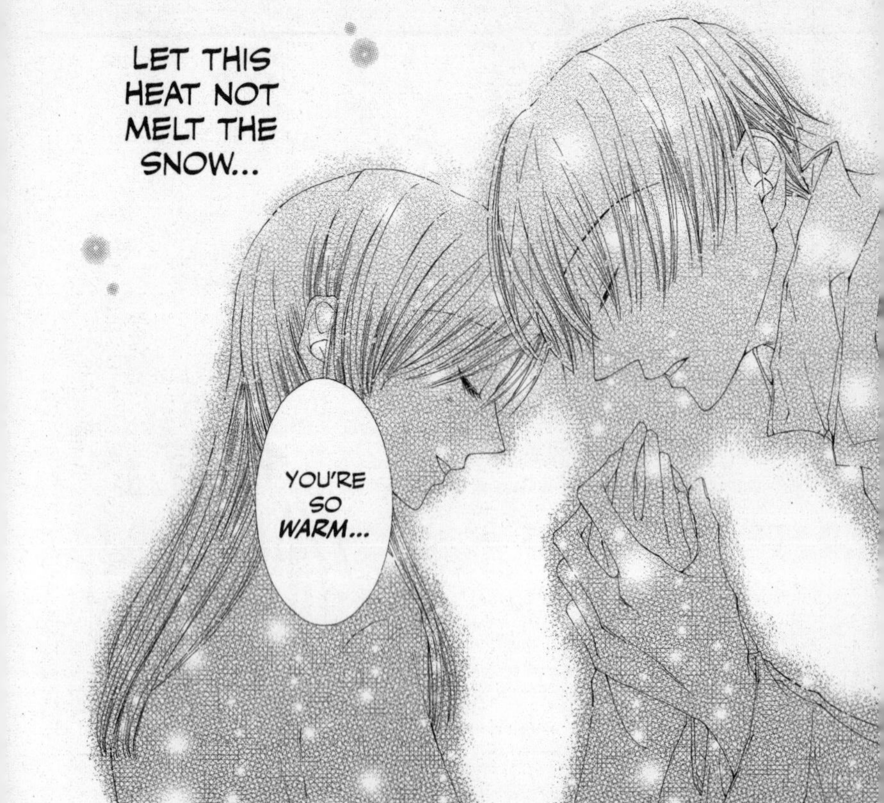
LET THIS HEAT NOT MELT THE SNOW...
YOU'RE SO WARM...

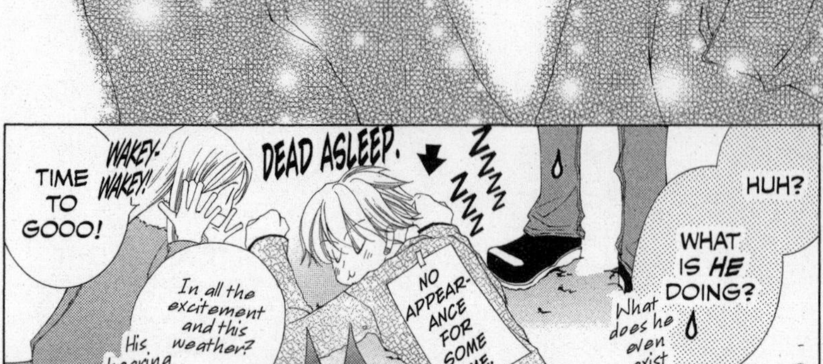
HUH?
WHAT IS HE DOING?
What does he even exist for?
NO APPEARANCE FOR SOME TIME.
ZZZZ ZZZ
DEAD ASLEEP.
WAKEY-WAKEY!
TIME TO GOOO!
In all the excitement and this weather?
His hearing must be bad...

After-bath cake.
The last snack of the day.

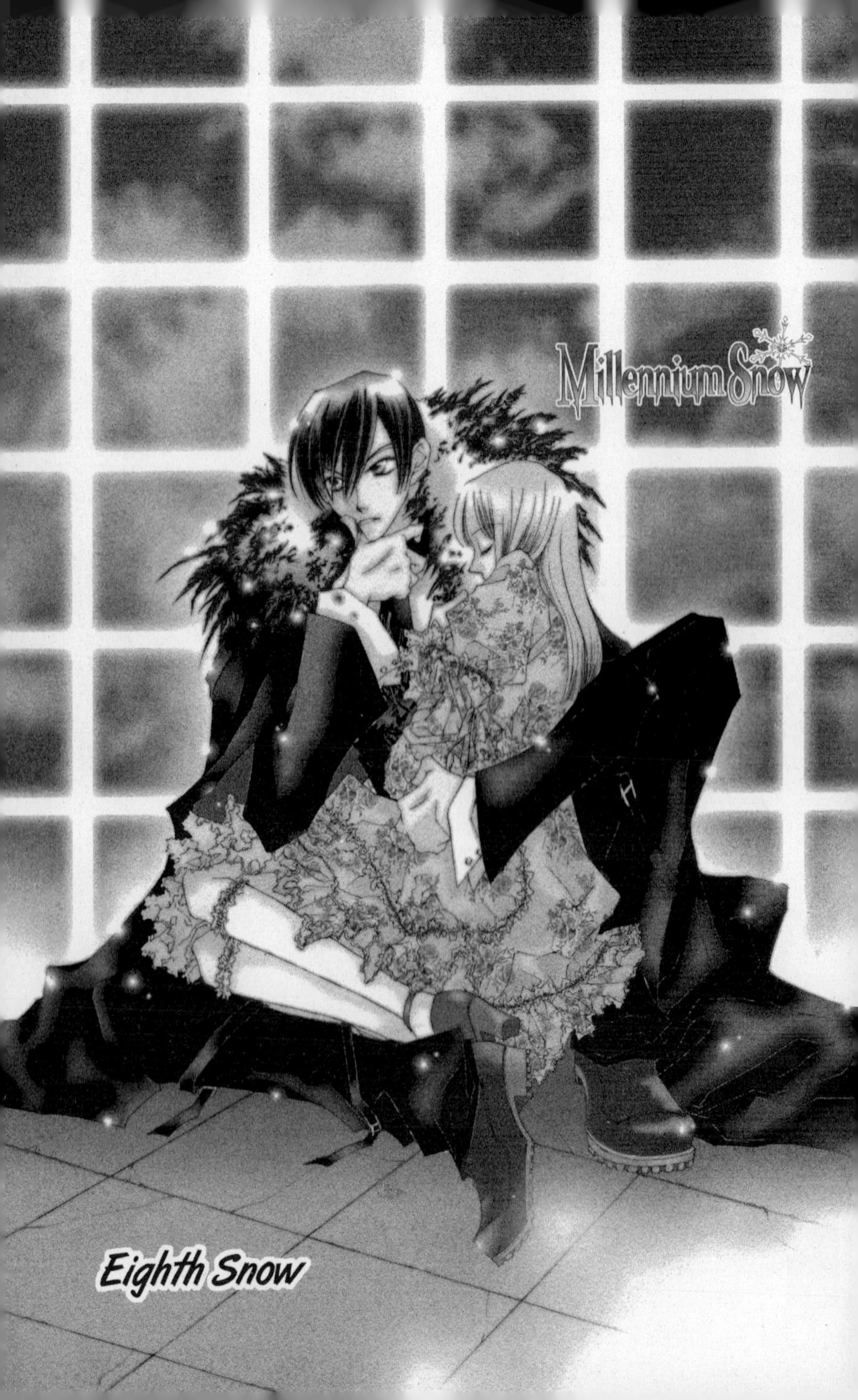
Millennium Snow
Eighth Snow

Go Go Shopping

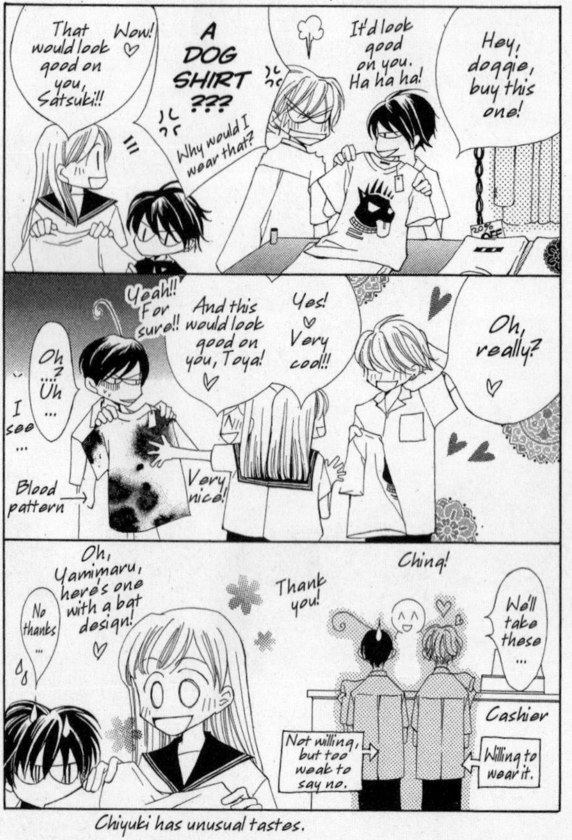
Hey, doggie, buy this one!
It'd look good on you. Ha ha ha!
A DOG SHIRT???
Why would I wear that?
Wow!
That would look good on you, Satsuki!!
20% OFF
Oh, really?
Yes! Very cool!!
And this would look good on you, Toya!
Yeah!! For sure!!
Very nice!
Oh...? Uh...
I see...
Blood pattern
We'll take these...
Ching!
Thank you!
Cashier
Willing to wear it.
Not willing, but too weak to say no.
Oh, Yamimaru, here's one with a bat design!
No thanks...

Chiyuki has unusual tastes.

← And now...

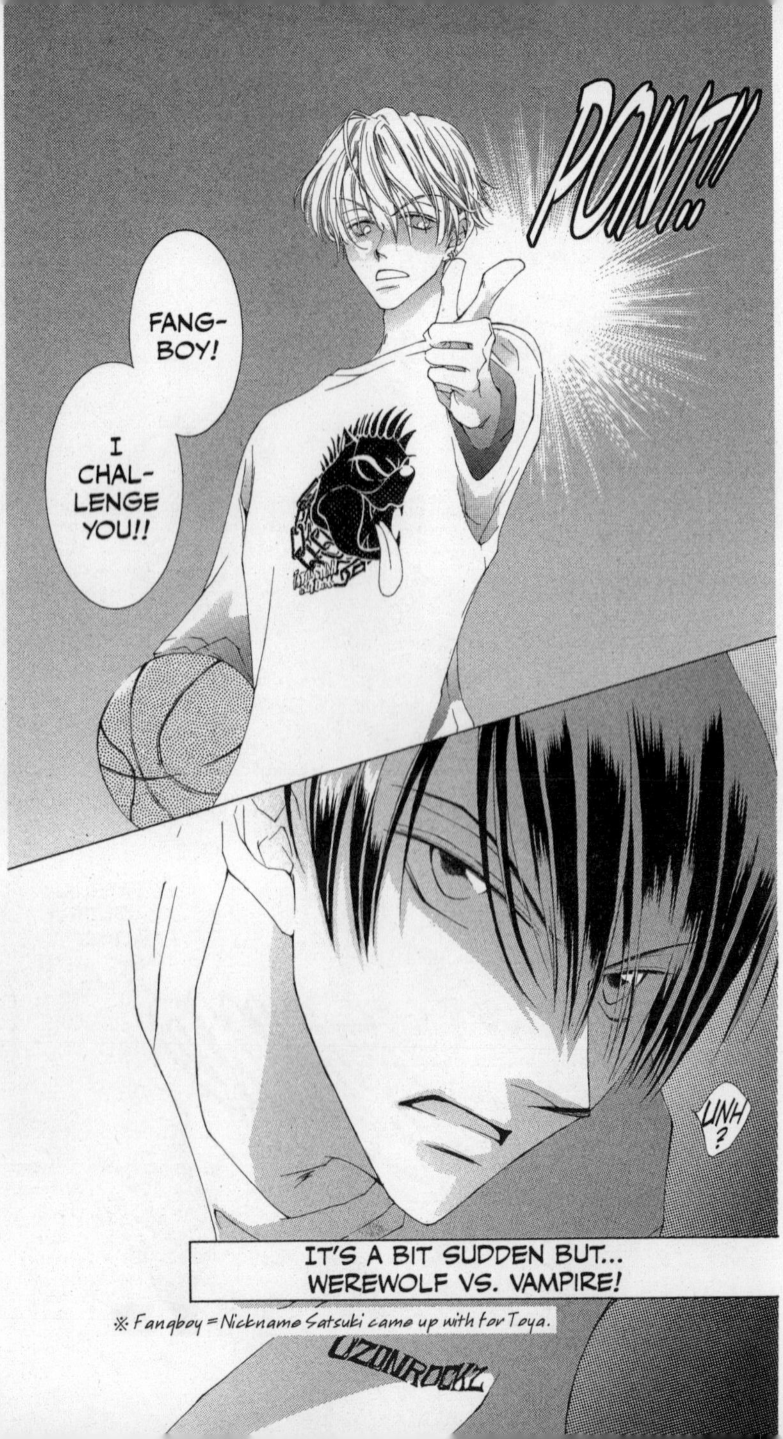
PON!!
FANG-BOY!
I CHAL-LENGE YOU!!
UNH?
IT'S A BIT SUDDEN BUT... WEREWOLF VS. VAMPIRE!
※ Fangboy = Nickname Satsuki came up with for Toya.
UZONROCKZ

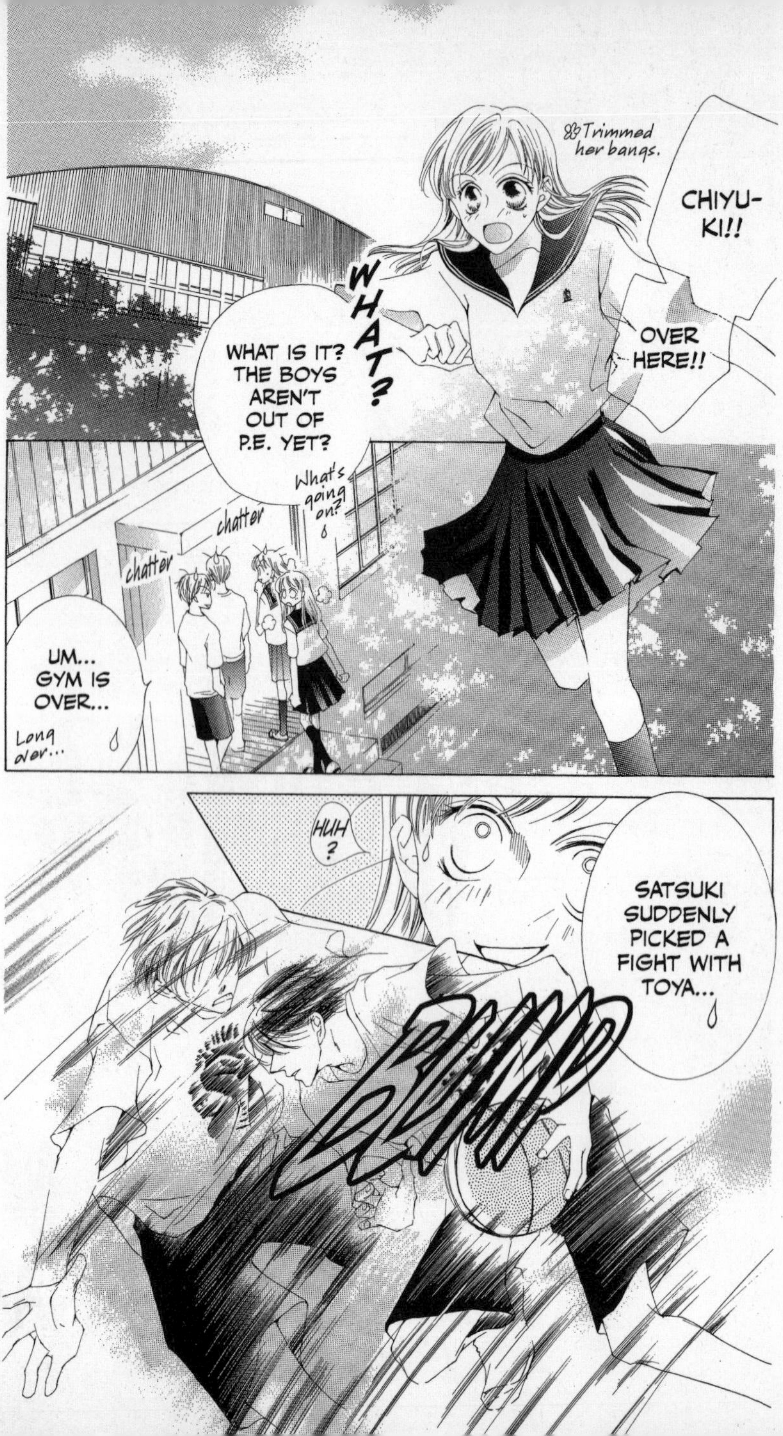
Trimmed her bangs.
CHIYU-KI!!
OVER HERE!!
WHAT?
WHAT IS IT? THE BOYS AREN'T OUT OF P.E. YET?
What's going on?
chatter
chatter
UM... GYM IS OVER...
Long over...
SATSUKI SUDDENLY PICKED A FIGHT WITH TOYA...
HUH?

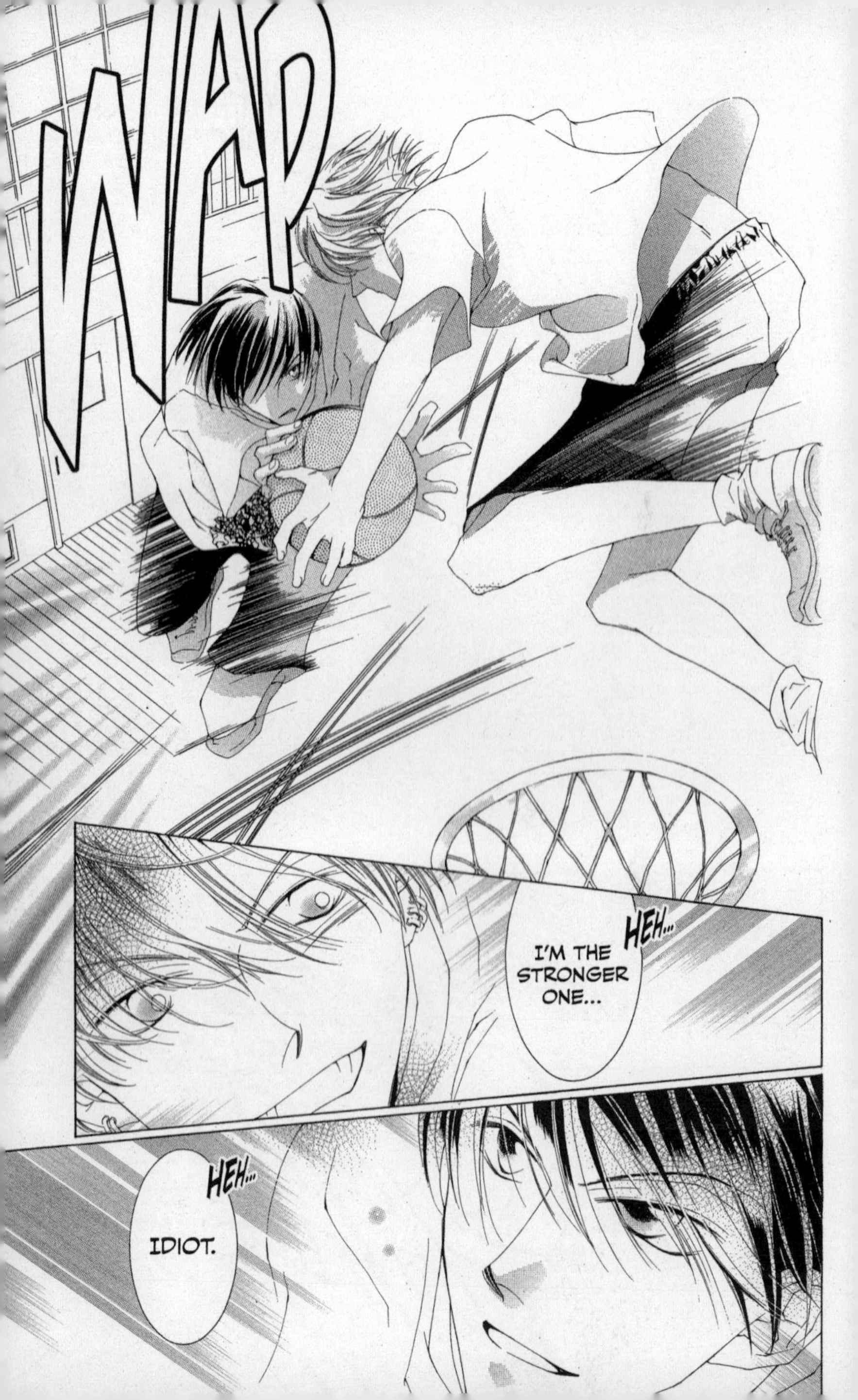
WAP
HEH...
I'M THE STRONGER ONE...
HEH...
IDIOT.

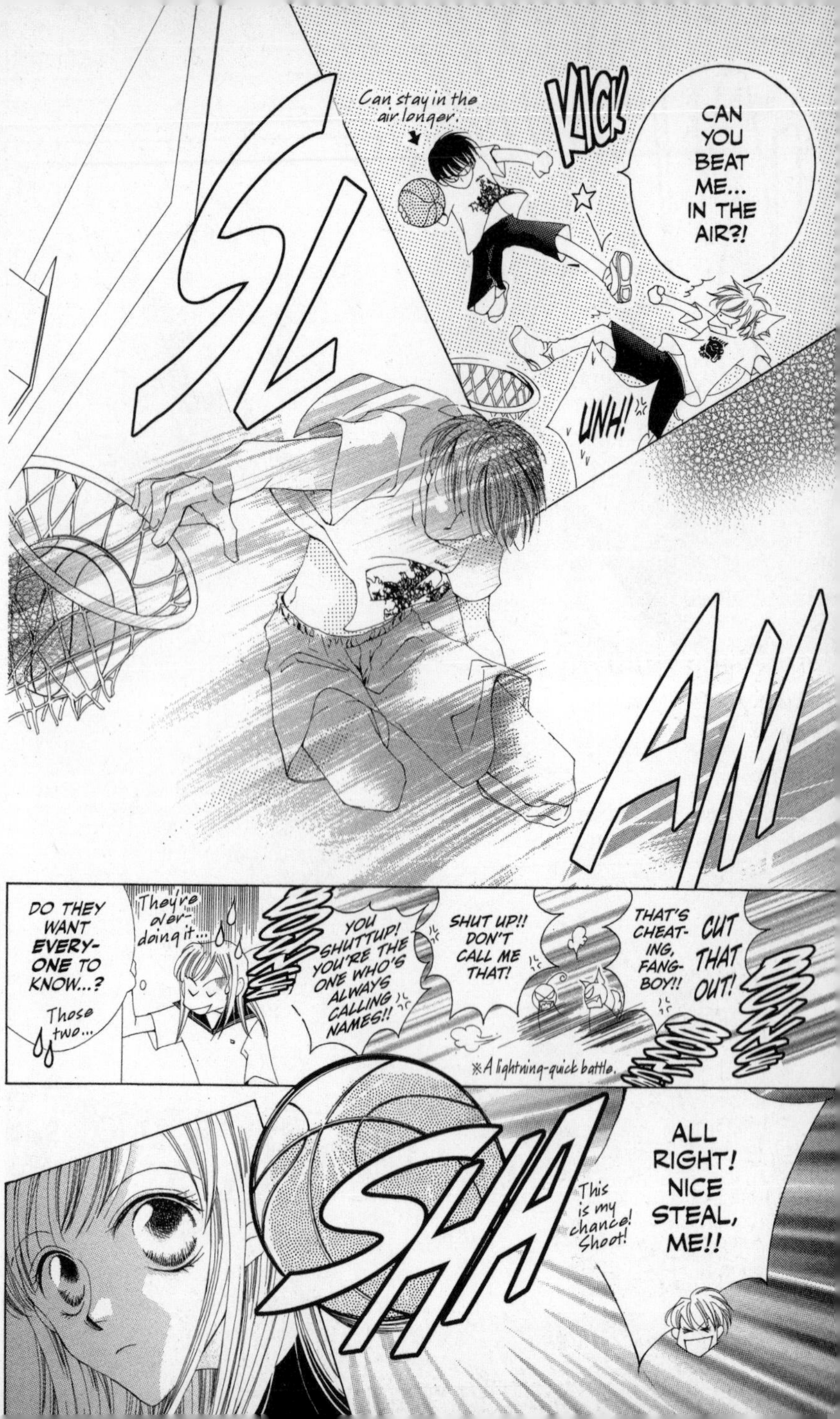
CAN YOU BEAT ME... IN THE AIR?!
KICK
Can stay in the air longer.
UNH!
SL
AM
CUT THAT OUT!
THAT'S CHEAT-ING, FANG-BOY!!
SHUT UP!! DON'T CALL ME THAT!
YOU SHUTTUP! YOU'RE THE ONE WHO'S ALWAYS CALLING NAMES!!
They're over-doing it...
DO THEY WANT EVERYONE TO KNOW...?
Those two...
※A lightning-quick battle.
ALL RIGHT! NICE STEAL, ME!!
This is my chance! Shoot!
SHA

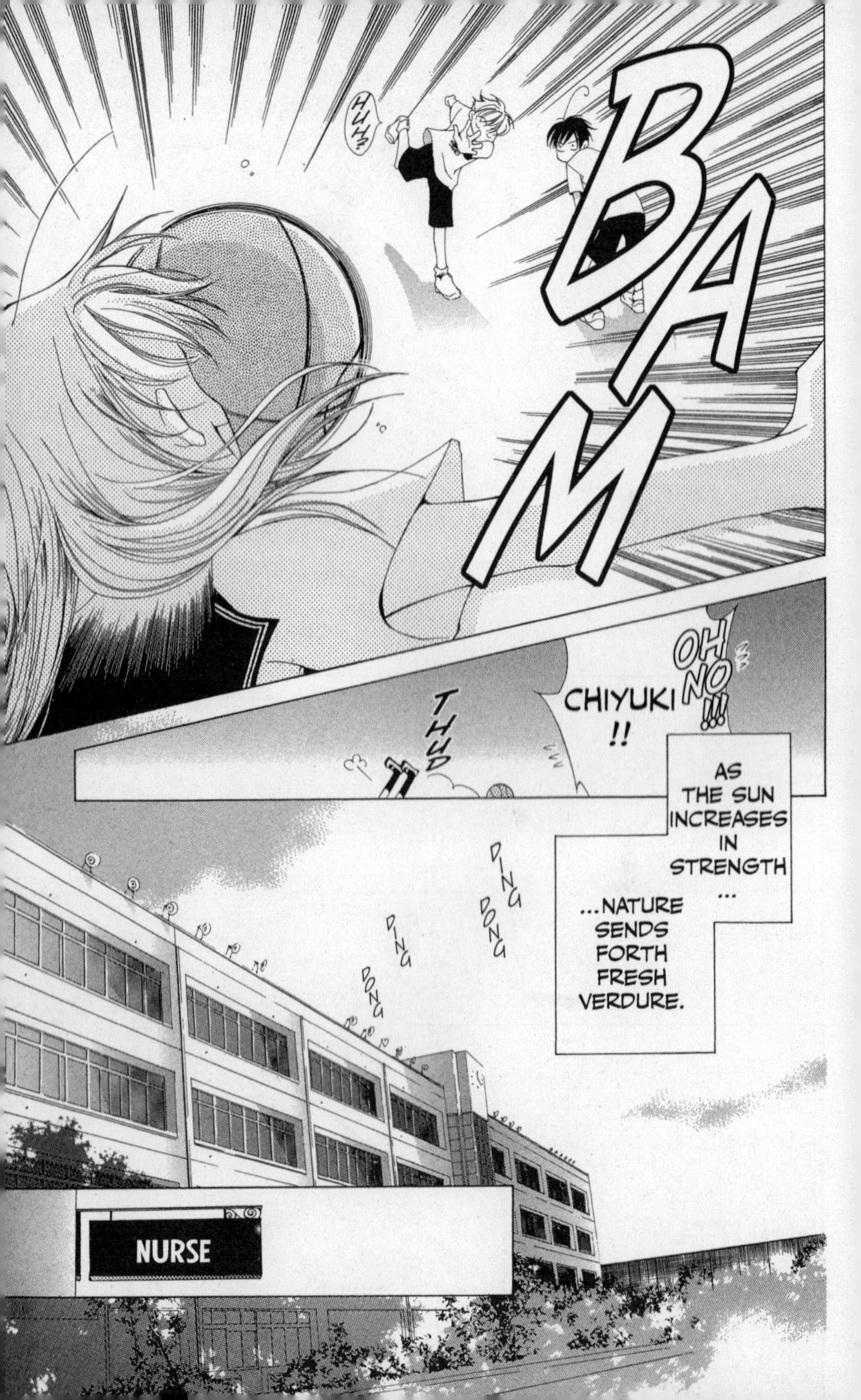
HUH?
BAM
OH NO!!!
CHIYUKI!!
THUD
AS THE SUN INCREASES IN STRENGTH...
...NATURE SENDS FORTH FRESH VERDURE.
DING DONG
DING DONG
NURSE

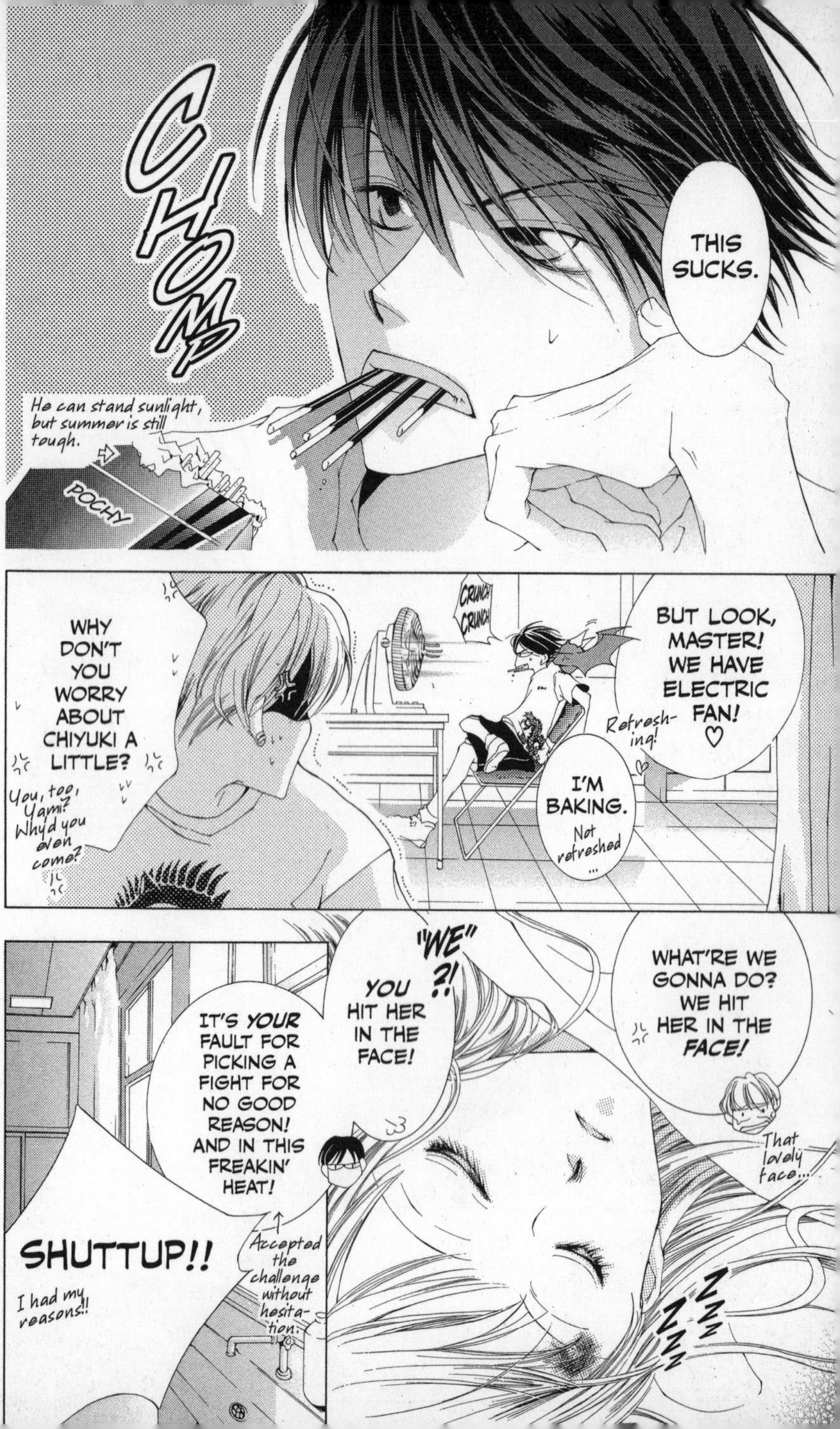
CHOMP
THIS SUCKS.
He can stand sunlight, but summer is still tough.
POCHY
BUT LOOK, MASTER! WE HAVE ELECTRIC FAN! ♡
Refresh-ing!
CRUNCH CRUNCH
I'M BAKING.
Not refreshed ...
WHY DON'T YOU WORRY ABOUT CHIYUKI A LITTLE?
You, too, Yami? Why'd you even come?
WHAT'RE WE GONNA DO? WE HIT HER IN THE FACE!
That lovely face...
"WE" ?!
YOU HIT HER IN THE FACE!
IT'S YOUR FAULT FOR PICKING A FIGHT FOR NO GOOD REASON! AND IN THIS FREAKIN' HEAT!
Accepted the challenge without hesita-tion.
SHUTTUP!!
I had my reasons!!
ZZZ

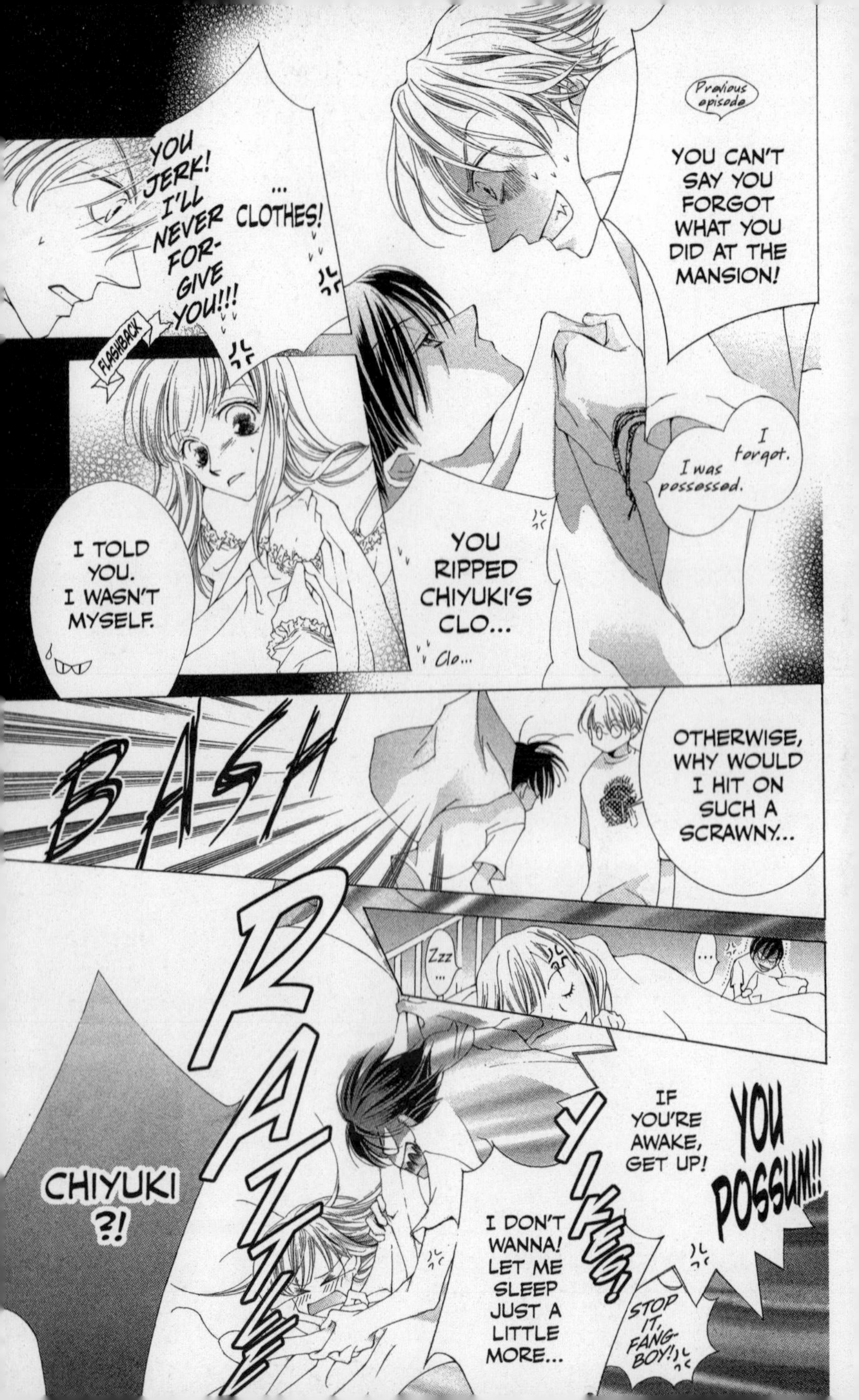
Previous episode
YOU CAN'T SAY YOU FORGOT WHAT YOU DID AT THE MANSION!
I forgot. I was possessed.
YOU RIPPED CHIYUKI'S CLO...
Clo...
... CLOTHES!
YOU JERK! I'LL NEVER FOR-GIVE YOU!!!
FLASHBACK
I TOLD YOU. I WASN'T MYSELF.
OTHERWISE, WHY WOULD I HIT ON SUCH A SCRAWNY...
BASH
...
Zzz ...
IF YOU'RE AWAKE, GET UP!
YOU POSSUM!!
I DON'T WANNA! LET ME SLEEP JUST A LITTLE MORE...
STOP IT, FANG-BOY!
CHIYUKI ?!

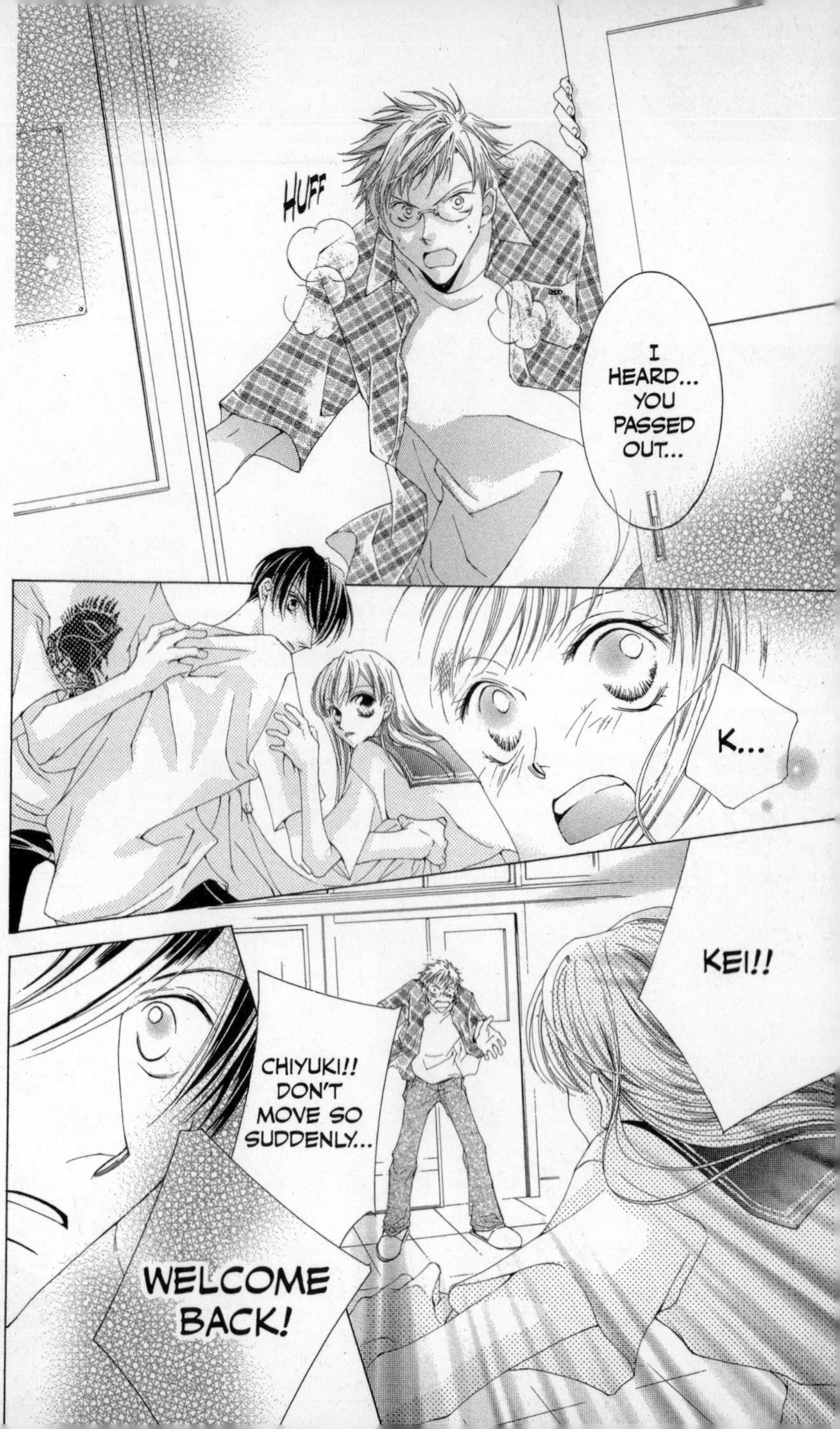
HUFF
I HEARD... YOU PASSED OUT...
K...
KEI!!
CHIYUKI!! DON'T MOVE SO SUDDENLY...
WELCOME BACK!

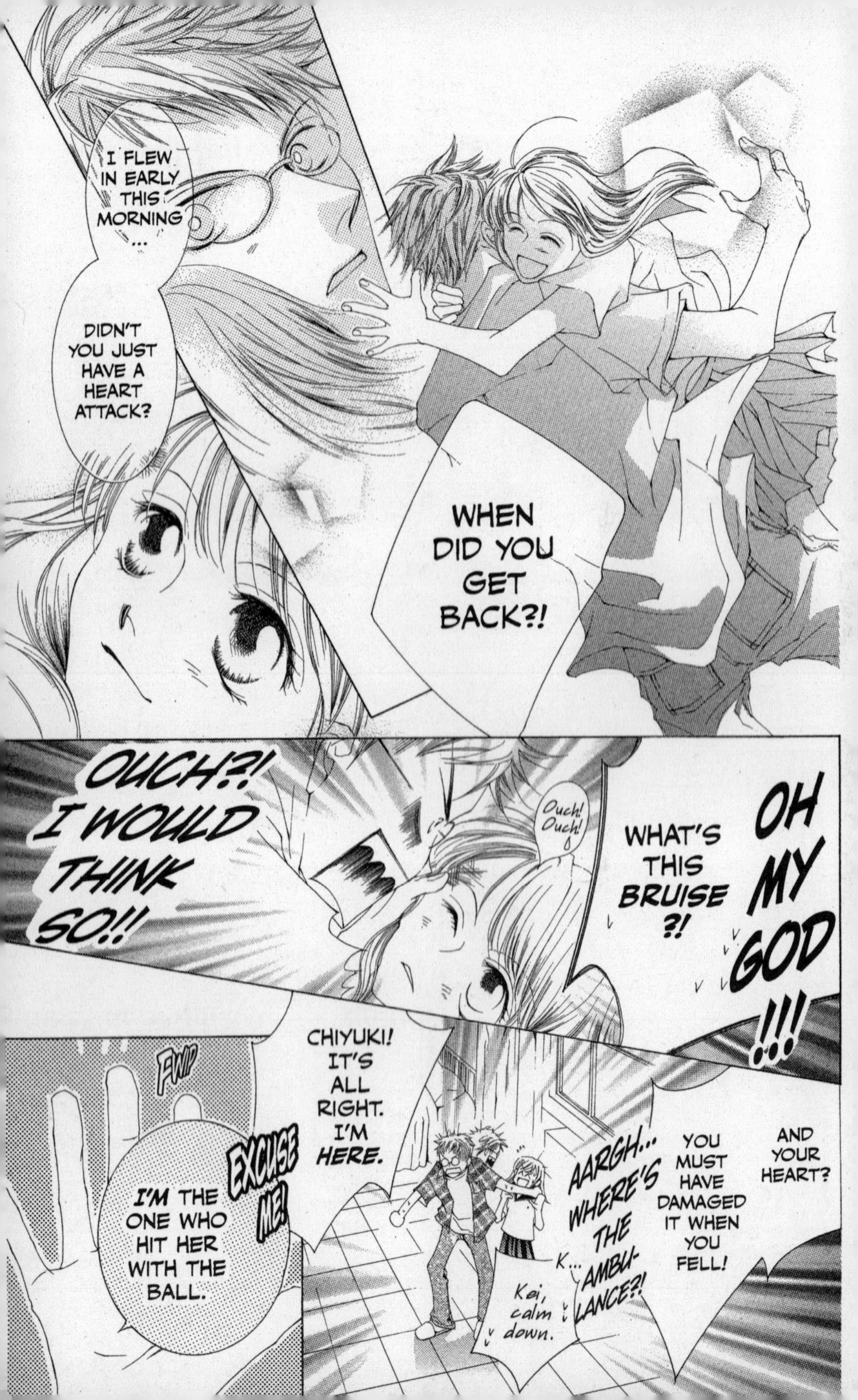
WHEN DID YOU GET BACK?!
I FLEW IN EARLY THIS MORNING...
DIDN'T YOU JUST HAVE A HEART ATTACK?
OH MY GOD!!!
WHAT'S THIS BRUISE?!
Ouch! Ouch!
OUCH?! I WOULD THINK SO!!
AND YOUR HEART?
YOU MUST HAVE DAMAGED IT WHEN YOU FELL!
AARGH... WHERE'S THE AMBULANCE?!
K...
Kei, calm down.
CHIYUKI! IT'S ALL RIGHT. I'M HERE.
FWIP
EXCUSE ME!
I'M THE ONE WHO HIT HER WITH THE BALL.

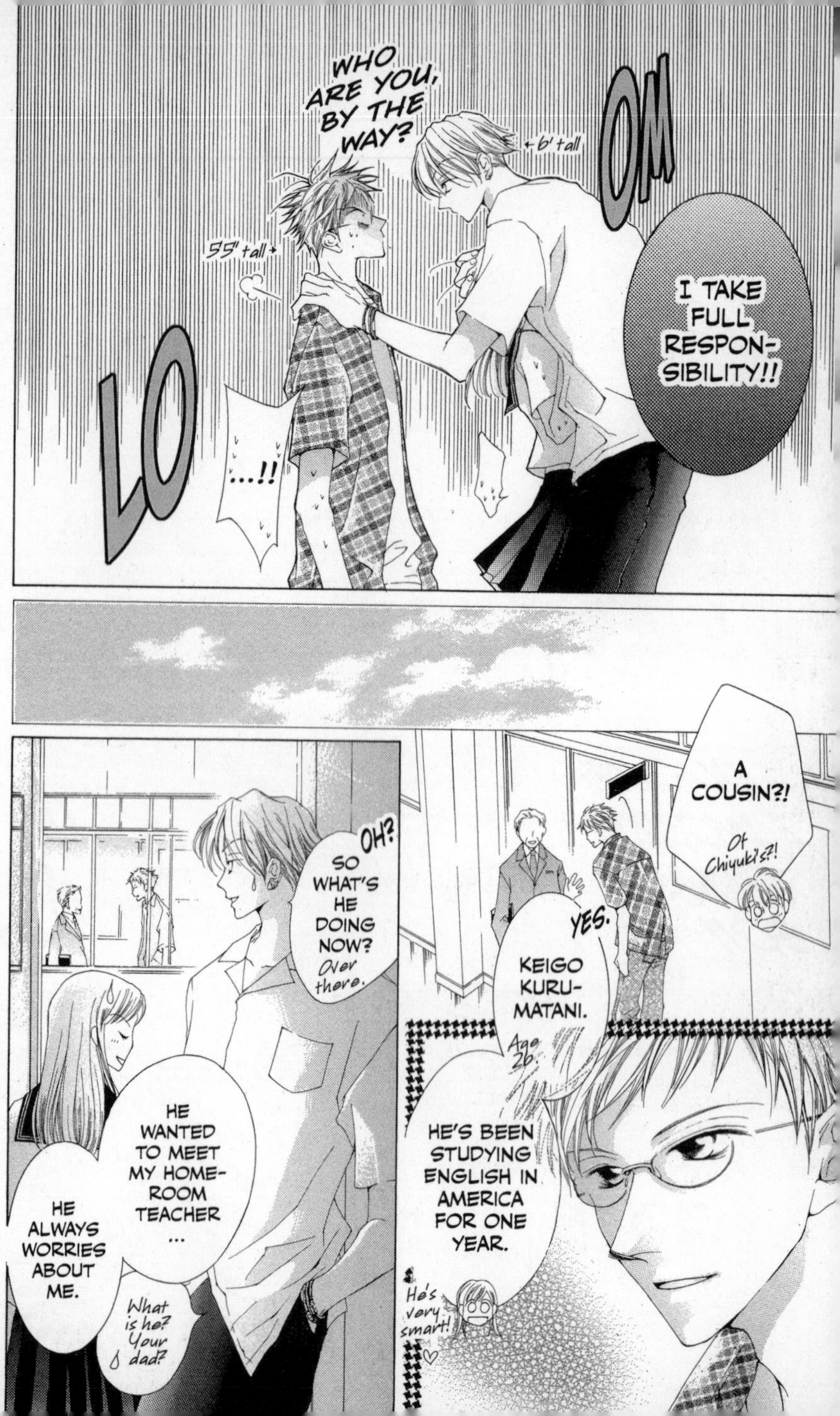
OM
I TAKE FULL RESPON-SIBILITY!!
←6' tall
WHO ARE YOU, BY THE WAY?
5'5' tall→
...!!
LO
A COUSIN?!
Of Chiyuki's?!
YES.
KEIGO KURU-MATANI.
Age 26.
HE'S BEEN STUDYING ENGLISH IN AMERICA FOR ONE YEAR.
He's very smart!
OH?
SO WHAT'S HE DOING NOW?
Over there.
HE WANTED TO MEET MY HOME-ROOM TEACHER ...
HE ALWAYS WORRIES ABOUT ME.
What is he? Your dad?

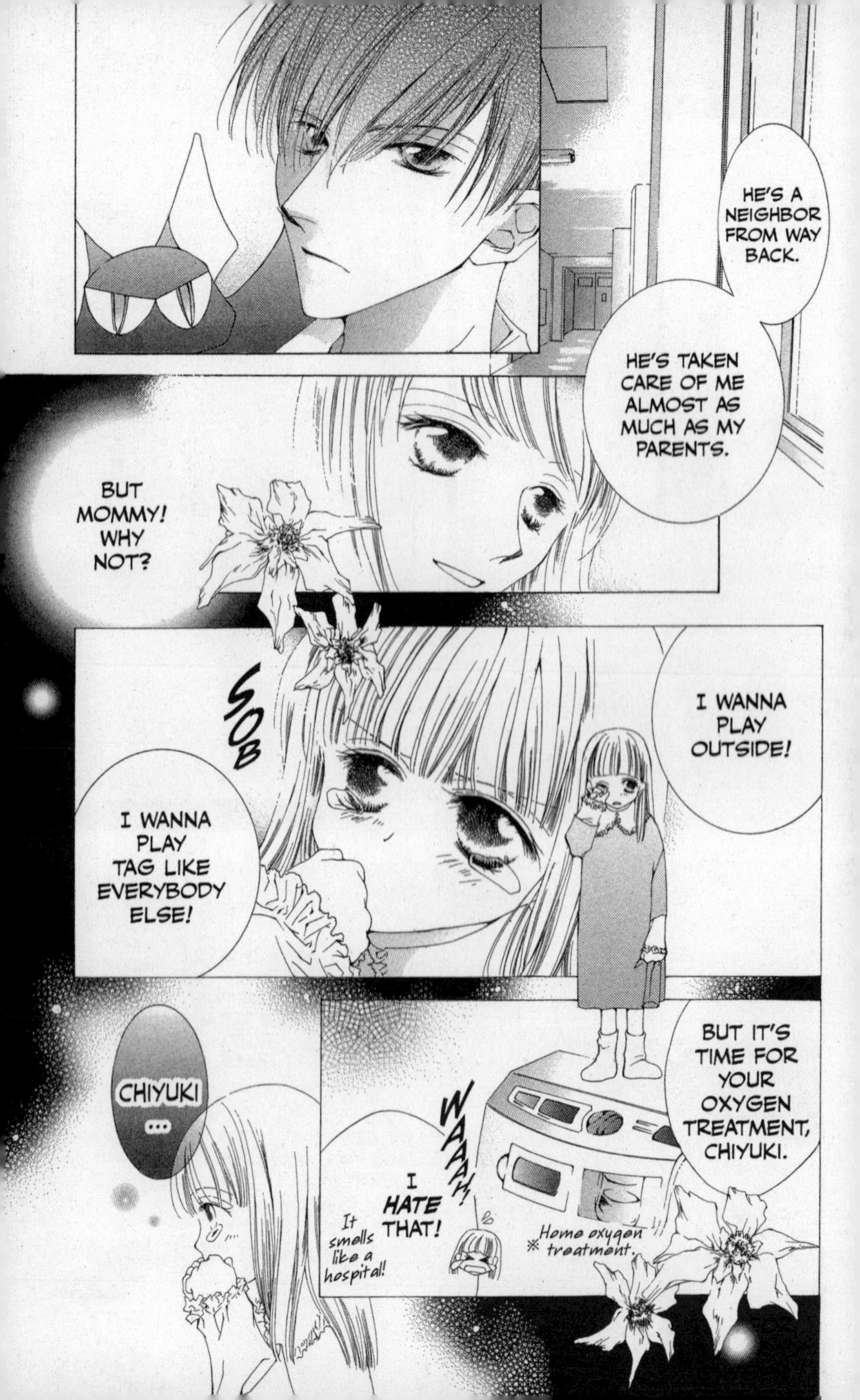
HE'S A NEIGHBOR FROM WAY BACK.
HE'S TAKEN CARE OF ME ALMOST AS MUCH AS MY PARENTS.
BUT MOMMY! WHY NOT?
I WANNA PLAY OUTSIDE!
SOB
I WANNA PLAY TAG LIKE EVERYBODY ELSE!
BUT IT'S TIME FOR YOUR OXYGEN TREATMENT, CHIYUKI.
※ Home oxygen treatment.
WAAAH!
I HATE THAT!
It smells like a hospital!
CHIYUKI ...

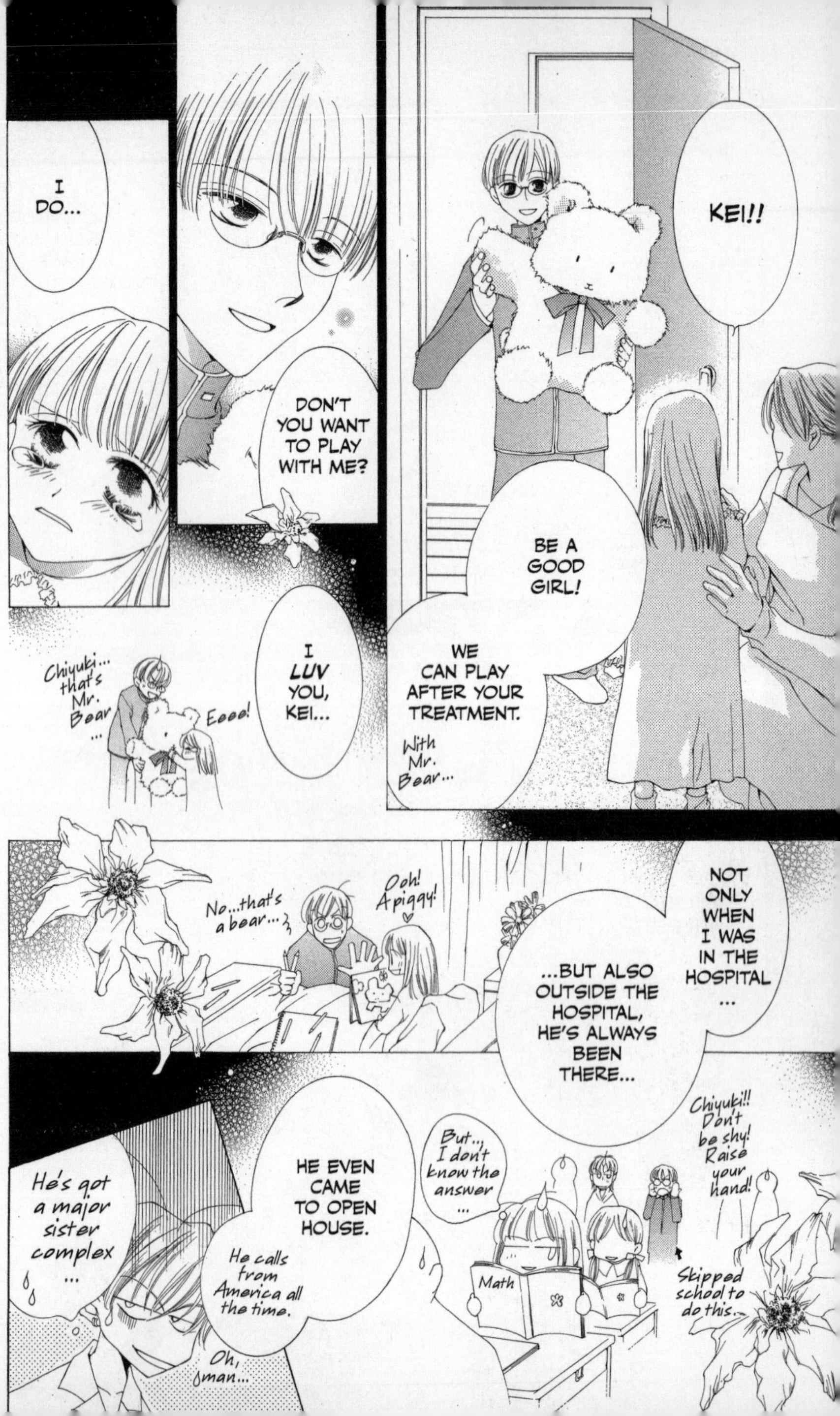
KEI!!
BE A GOOD GIRL!
WE CAN PLAY AFTER YOUR TREATMENT.
With Mr. Bear...
DON'T YOU WANT TO PLAY WITH ME?
I DO...
I LUV YOU, KEI...
Chiyuki... that's Mr. Bear...
Eeee!
NOT ONLY WHEN I WAS IN THE HOSPITAL...
Ooh! A piggy!
No...that's a bear...
...BUT ALSO OUTSIDE THE HOSPITAL, HE'S ALWAYS BEEN THERE...
Chiyuki!! Don't be shy! Raise your hand!
Skipped school to do this.
But..., I don't know the answer...
Math
HE EVEN CAME TO OPEN HOUSE.
He calls from America all the time.
He's got a major sister complex...
Oh, man...

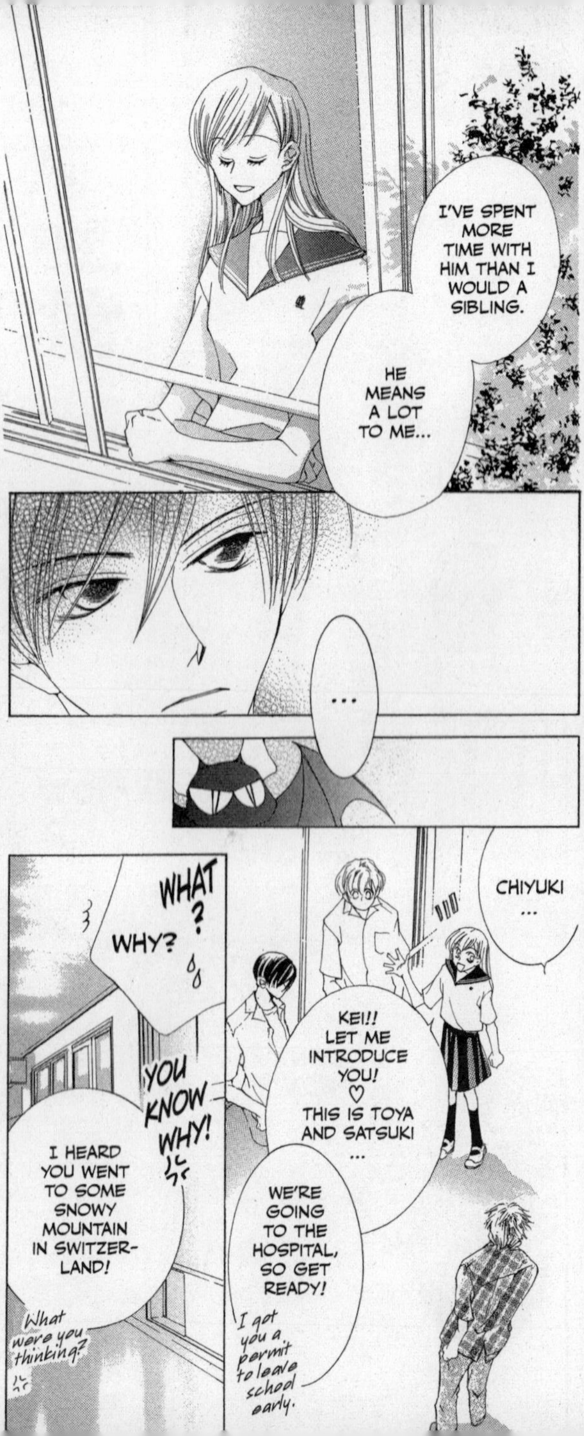
I'VE SPENT MORE TIME WITH HIM THAN I WOULD A SIBLING.
HE MEANS A LOT TO ME...
...
CHIYUKI ...
KEI!! LET ME INTRODUCE YOU! ♡ THIS IS TOYA AND SATSUKI ...
WE'RE GOING TO THE HOSPITAL, SO GET READY!
I got you a permit to leave school early.
WHAT?
WHY?
YOU KNOW WHY!
I HEARD YOU WENT TO SOME SNOWY MOUNTAIN IN SWITZER-LAND!
What were you thinking?

闇丸
YAMIMARU

"Yamimaru" is often written as "Ranmaru" in the letters I receive... Even my assistant, A-chan, calls him "Kuramaru." (lol) Out of all the characters of Millennium Snow, the little boy Yami is the easiest to draw. The hardest one is the grown-up Yami, so I guess everything balances out...? "Ranmaru" and "Kuramaru" each use a different first kanji for Yamimaru's name. "Ran" looks similar to Yamimaru's "Yami," which is why fans of Millennium Snow make this mistake. Incidentally, this "ran" is also the "ran" of "Ouran" of Ouran High School Host Club. It means "orchid." The "kura" of "Kuramaru" is similar in meaning to "yami." Thus, A-chan is calling him "Kuramaru" as a sort of pun.

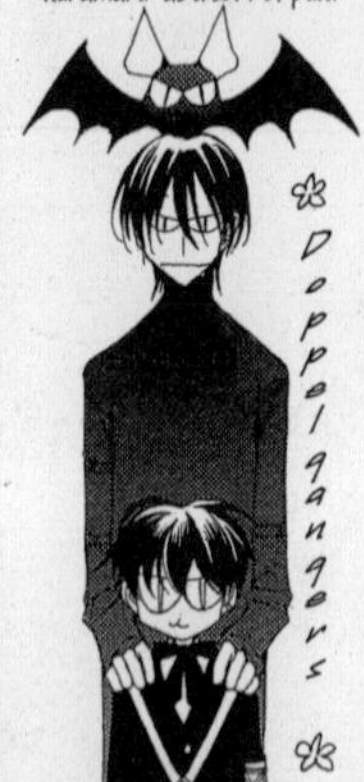
Doppelgangers

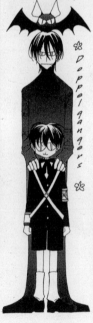

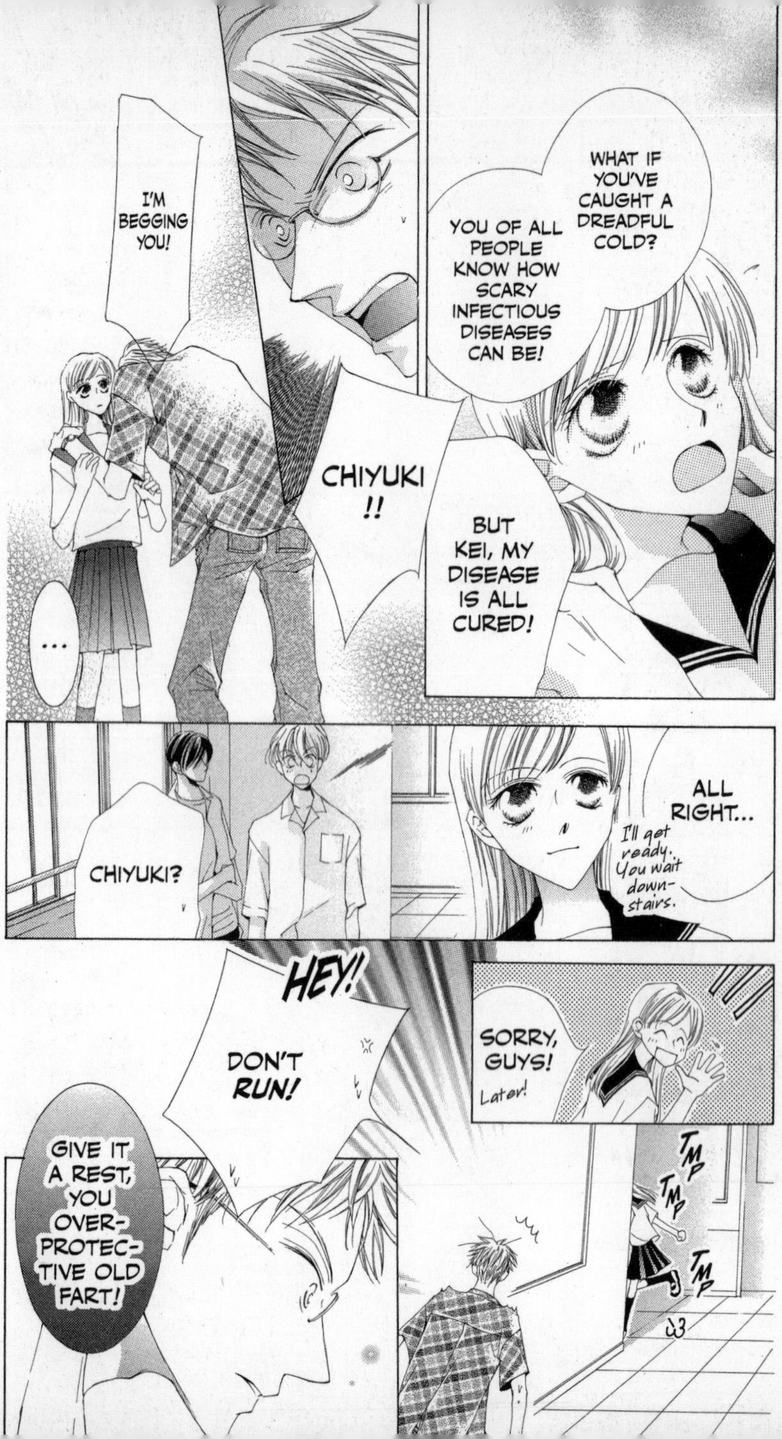
WHAT IF YOU'VE CAUGHT A DREADFUL COLD?
YOU OF ALL PEOPLE KNOW HOW SCARY INFECTIOUS DISEASES CAN BE!
BUT KEI, MY DISEASE IS ALL CURED!
CHIYUKI !!
I'M BEGGING YOU!
...
ALL RIGHT...
I'll get ready. You wait down-stairs.
CHIYUKI?
SORRY, GUYS!
Later!
HEY!
DON'T RUN!
TMP
TMP
TMP
GIVE IT A REST, YOU OVER-PROTEC-TIVE OLD FART!

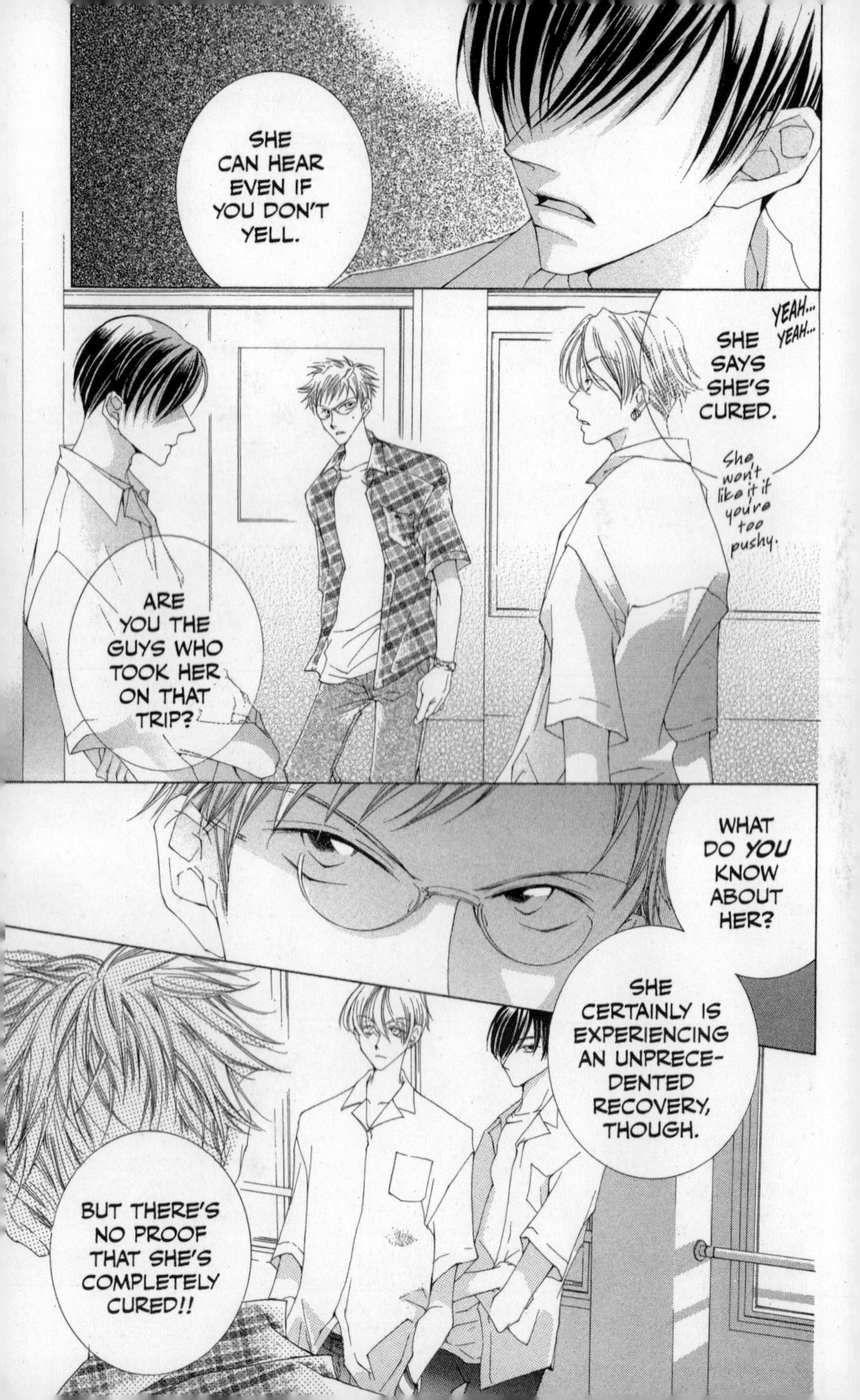
SHE CAN HEAR EVEN IF YOU DON'T YELL.
YEAH... YEAH...
SHE SAYS SHE'S CURED.
She won't like it if you're too pushy.
ARE YOU THE GUYS WHO TOOK HER ON THAT TRIP?
WHAT DO *YOU* KNOW ABOUT HER?
SHE CERTAINLY IS EXPERIENCING AN UNPRECE-DENTED RECOVERY, THOUGH.
BUT THERE'S NO PROOF THAT SHE'S COMPLETELY CURED!!

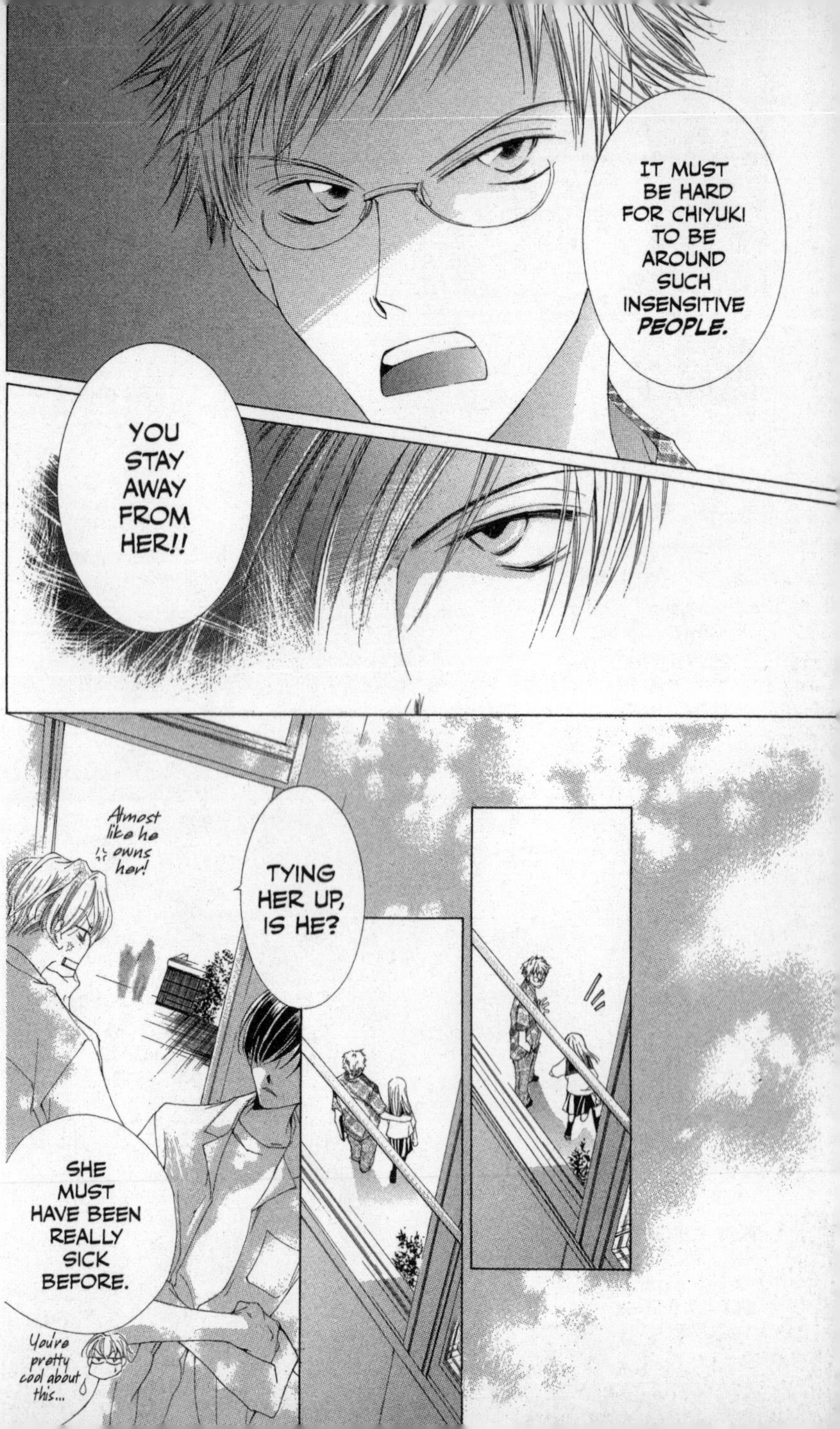
IT MUST BE HARD FOR CHIYUKI TO BE AROUND SUCH INSENSITIVE *PEOPLE.*
YOU STAY AWAY FROM HER!!
TYING HER UP, IS HE?
Almost like he owns her!
SHE MUST HAVE BEEN REALLY SICK BEFORE.
You're pretty cool about this...

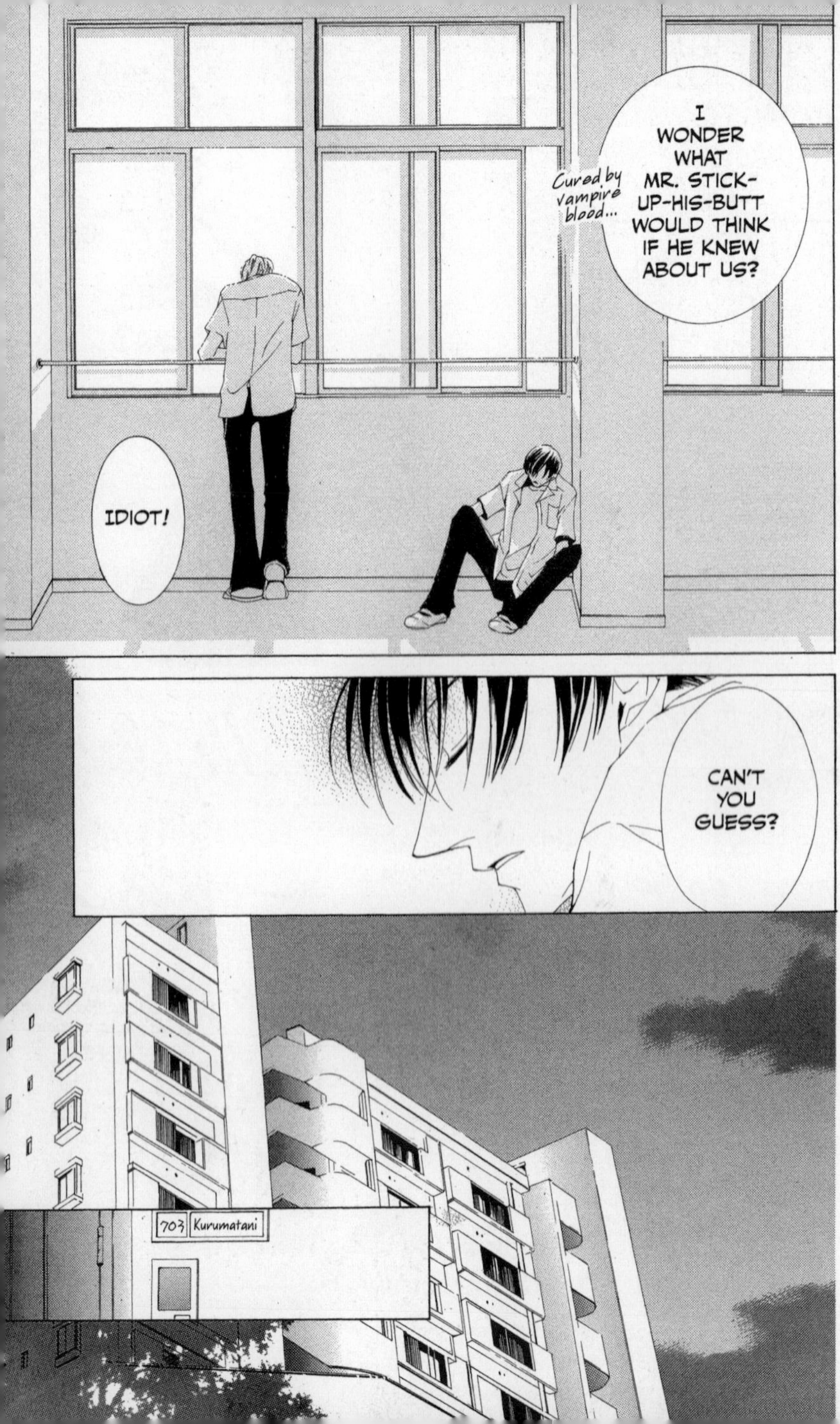
I WONDER WHAT MR. STICK-UP-HIS-BUTT WOULD THINK IF HE KNEW ABOUT US?
Cured by vampire blood...
IDIOT!
CAN'T YOU GUESS?
703 Kurumatani

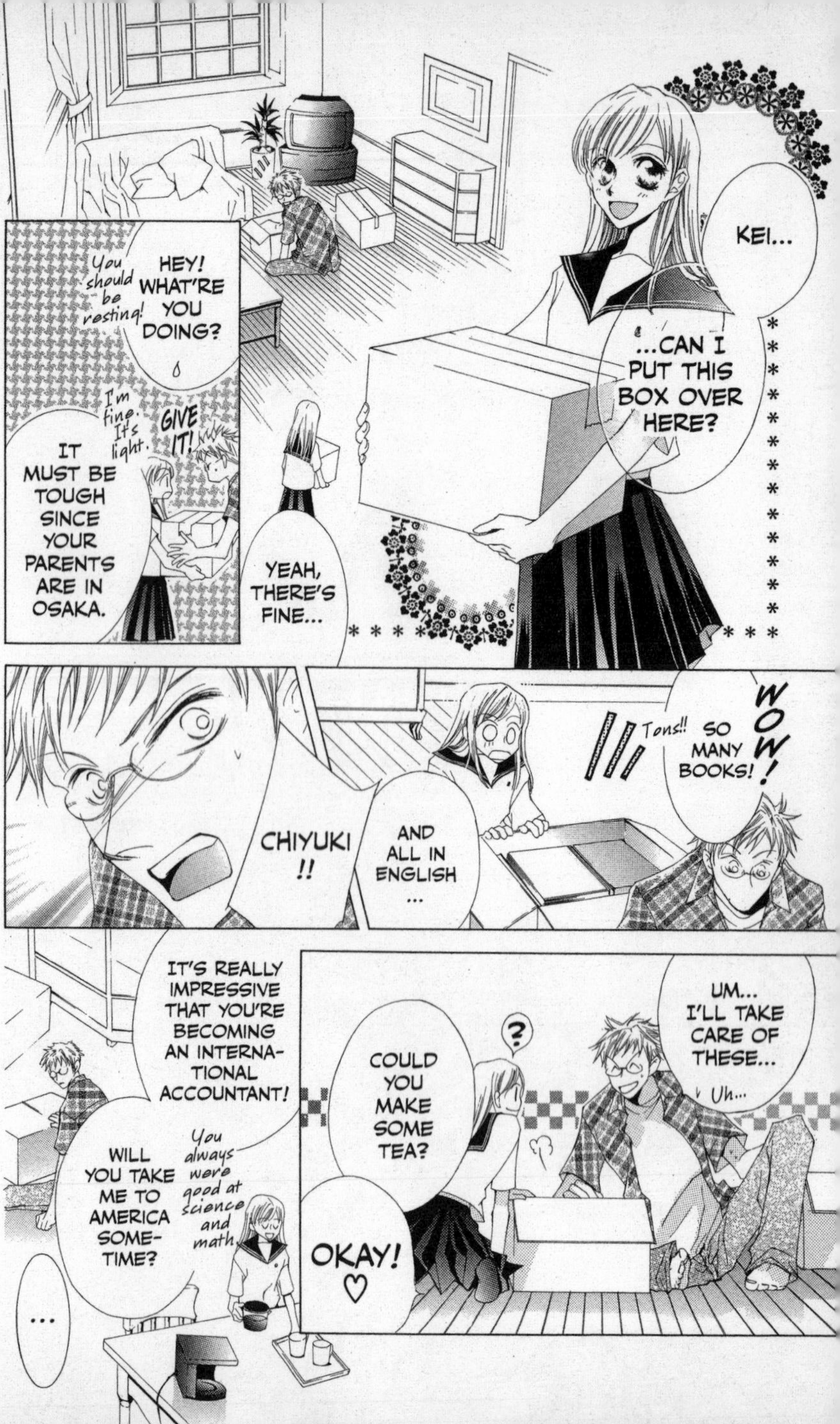
KEI...
...CAN I PUT THIS BOX OVER HERE?
YEAH, THERE'S FINE...
HEY! WHAT'RE YOU DOING?
You should be resting!
GIVE IT!
I'm fine. It's light.
IT MUST BE TOUGH SINCE YOUR PARENTS ARE IN OSAKA.
WOW!
SO MANY BOOKS!
Tons!!
AND ALL IN ENGLISH...
CHIYUKI!!
UM... I'LL TAKE CARE OF THESE...
Uh...
COULD YOU MAKE SOME TEA?
OKAY! ♥
IT'S REALLY IMPRESSIVE THAT YOU'RE BECOMING AN INTERNATIONAL ACCOUNTANT!
You always were good at science and math
WILL YOU TAKE ME TO AMERICA SOMETIME?
...

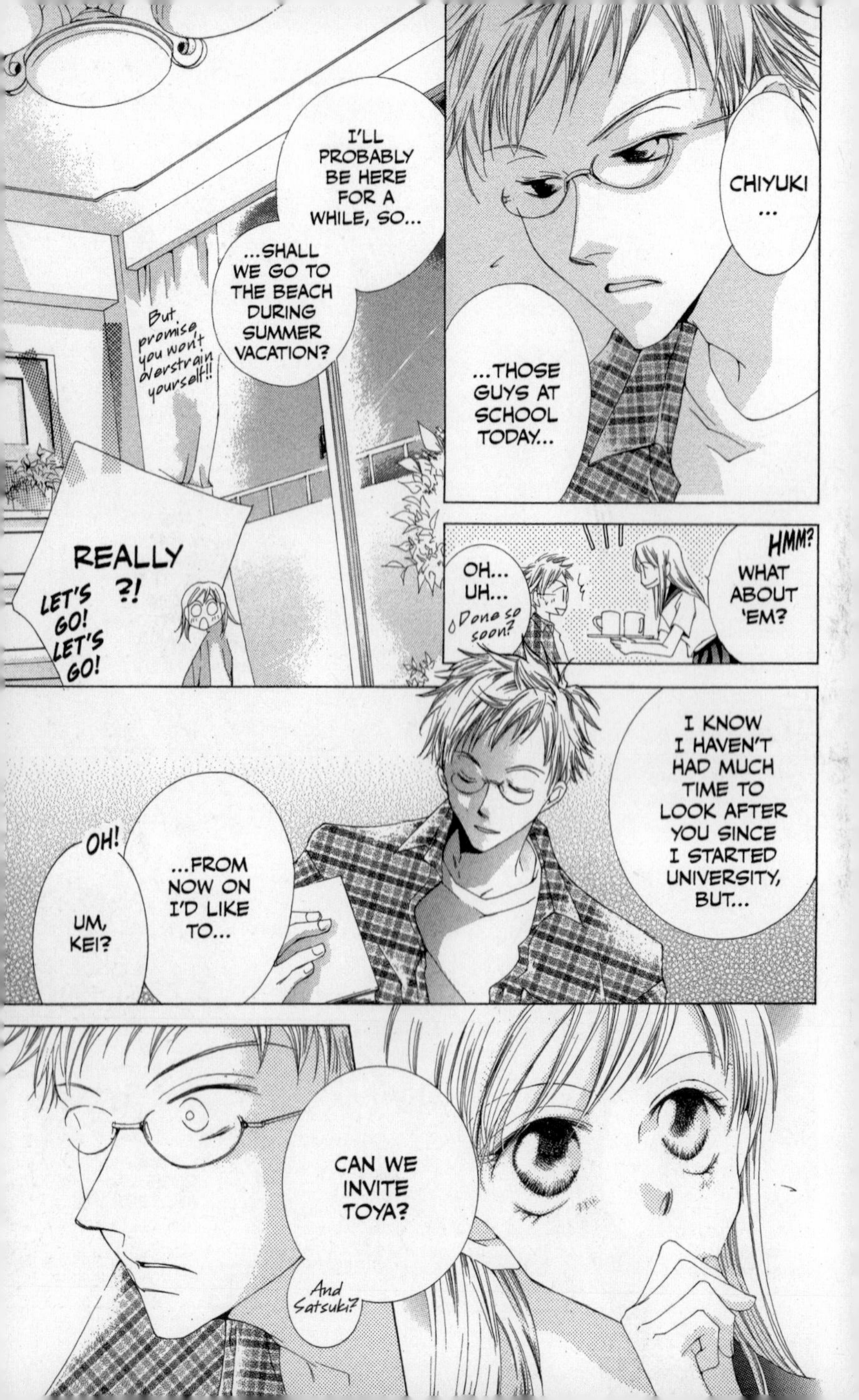
CHIYUKI...
...THOSE GUYS AT SCHOOL TODAY...
HMM? WHAT ABOUT 'EM?
OH... UH...
Done so soon?
I KNOW I HAVEN'T HAD MUCH TIME TO LOOK AFTER YOU SINCE I STARTED UNIVERSITY, BUT...
...FROM NOW ON I'D LIKE TO...
I'LL PROBABLY BE HERE FOR A WHILE, SO...
...SHALL WE GO TO THE BEACH DURING SUMMER VACATION?
But promise you won't overstrain yourself!!
REALLY ?!
LET'S GO! LET'S GO!
OH!
UM, KEI?
CAN WE INVITE TOYA?
And Satsuki?

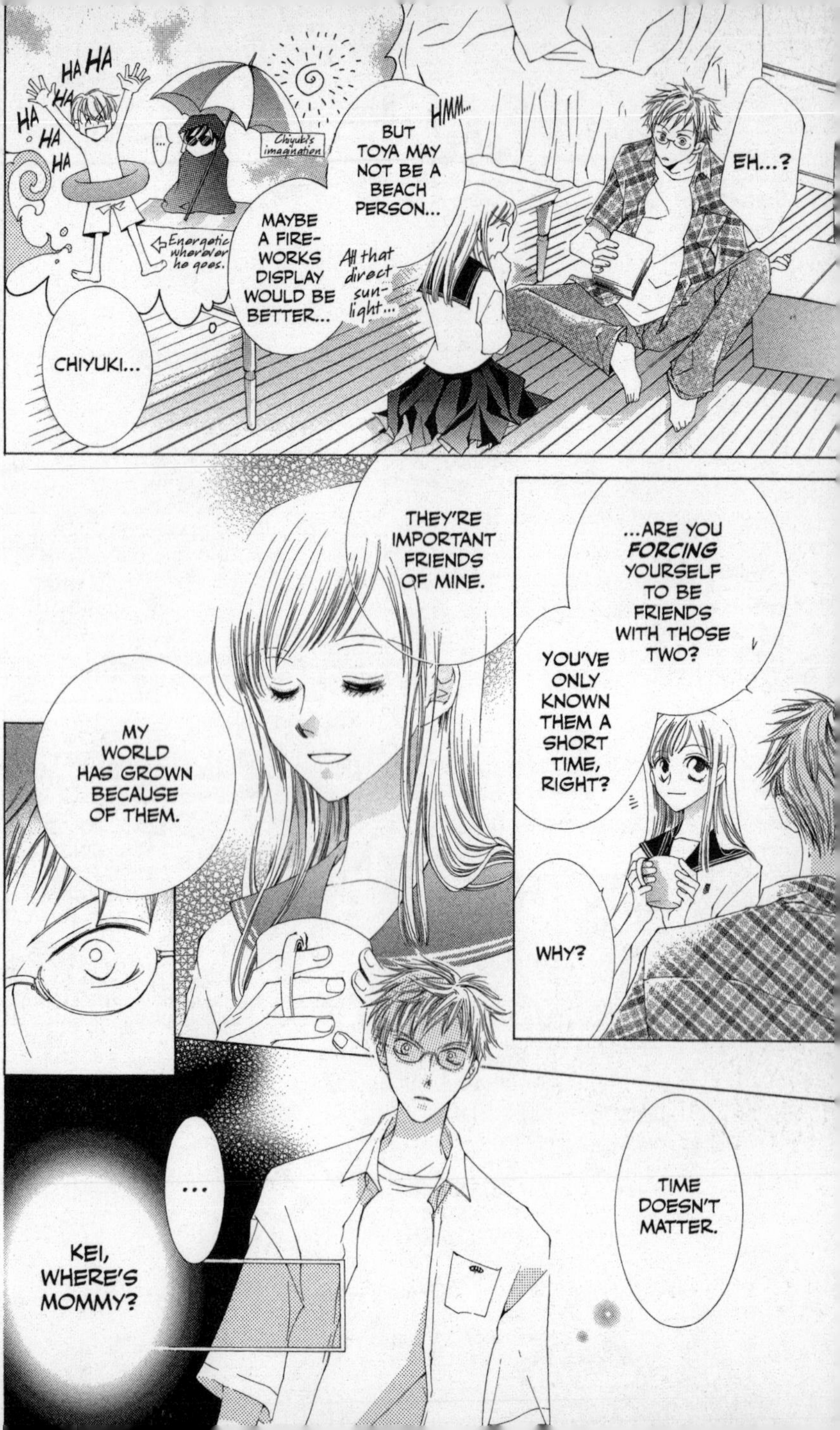
EH...?
HMM...
BUT TOYA MAY NOT BE A BEACH PERSON...
MAYBE A FIRE-WORKS DISPLAY WOULD BE BETTER...
All that direct sun-light...
Chiyuki's imagination
HA HA HA HA HA HA
...
Energetic wherever he goes.
CHIYUKI...
...ARE YOU *FORCING* YOURSELF TO BE FRIENDS WITH THOSE TWO?
YOU'VE ONLY KNOWN THEM A SHORT TIME, RIGHT?
WHY?
THEY'RE IMPORTANT FRIENDS OF MINE.
MY WORLD HAS GROWN BECAUSE OF THEM.
TIME DOESN'T MATTER.
...
KEI, WHERE'S MOMMY?

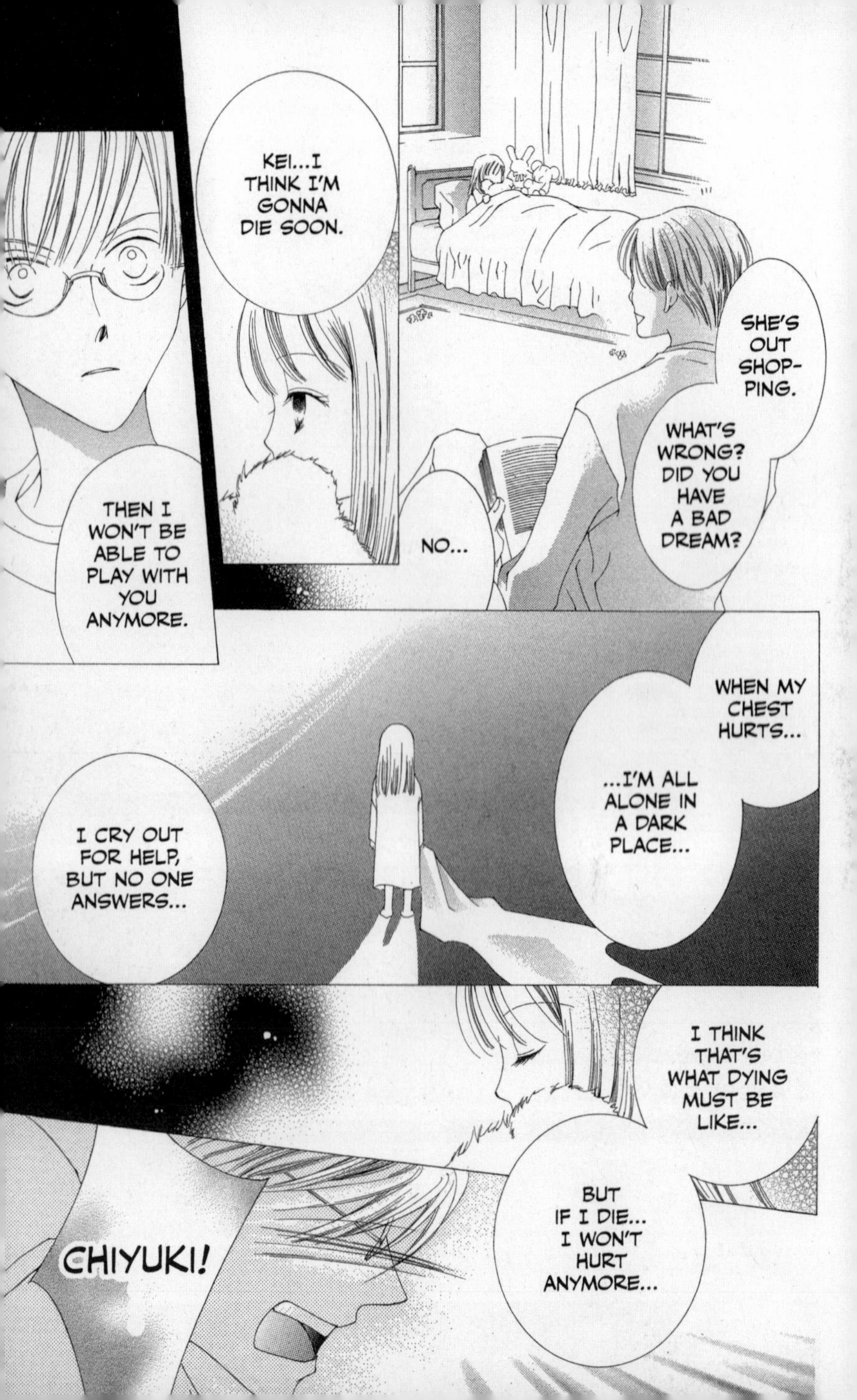
SHE'S OUT SHOP-PING.
WHAT'S WRONG? DID YOU HAVE A BAD DREAM?
NO...
KEI...I THINK I'M GONNA DIE SOON.
THEN I WON'T BE ABLE TO PLAY WITH YOU ANYMORE.
WHEN MY CHEST HURTS...
...I'M ALL ALONE IN A DARK PLACE...
I CRY OUT FOR HELP, BUT NO ONE ANSWERS...
I THINK THAT'S WHAT DYING MUST BE LIKE...
BUT IF I DIE... I WON'T HURT ANYMORE...
CHIYUKI!

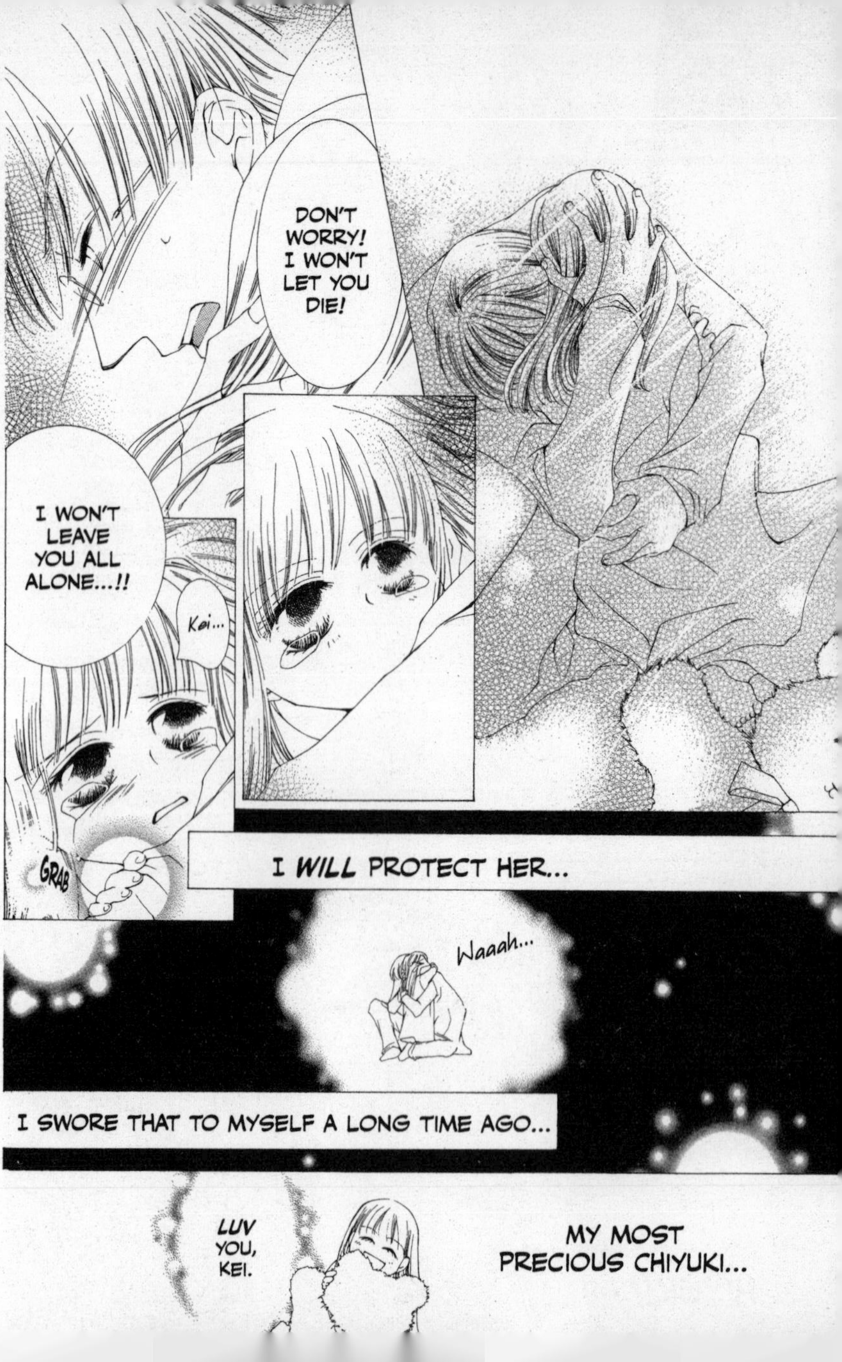
DON'T WORRY! I WON'T LET YOU DIE!
I WON'T LEAVE YOU ALL ALONE...!!
Kei...
GRAB
I *WILL* PROTECT HER...
Waaah...
I SWORE THAT TO MYSELF A LONG TIME AGO...
MY MOST PRECIOUS CHIYUKI...
LUV YOU, KEI.

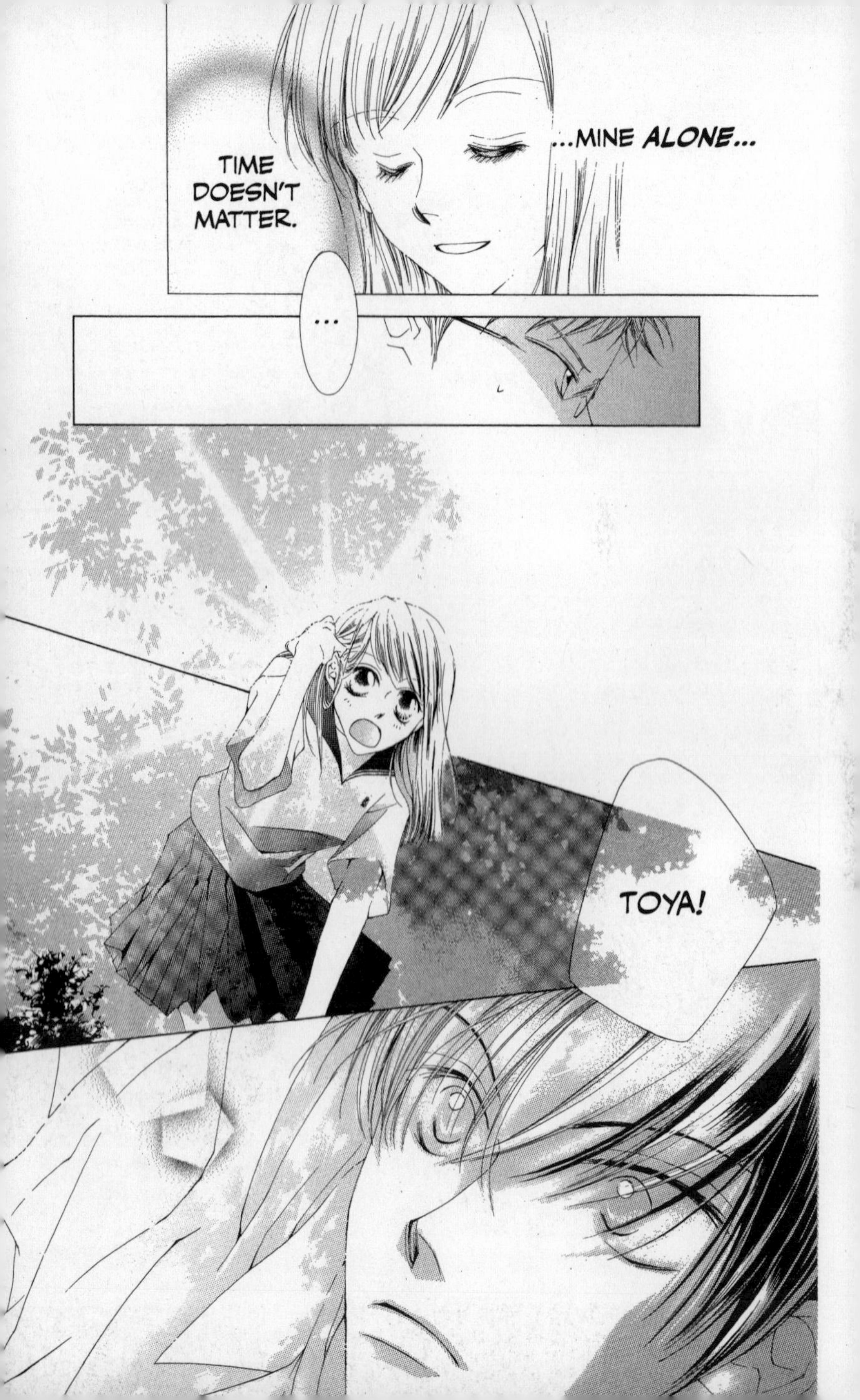
...MINE *ALONE*...
TIME DOESN'T MATTER.
...
TOYA!

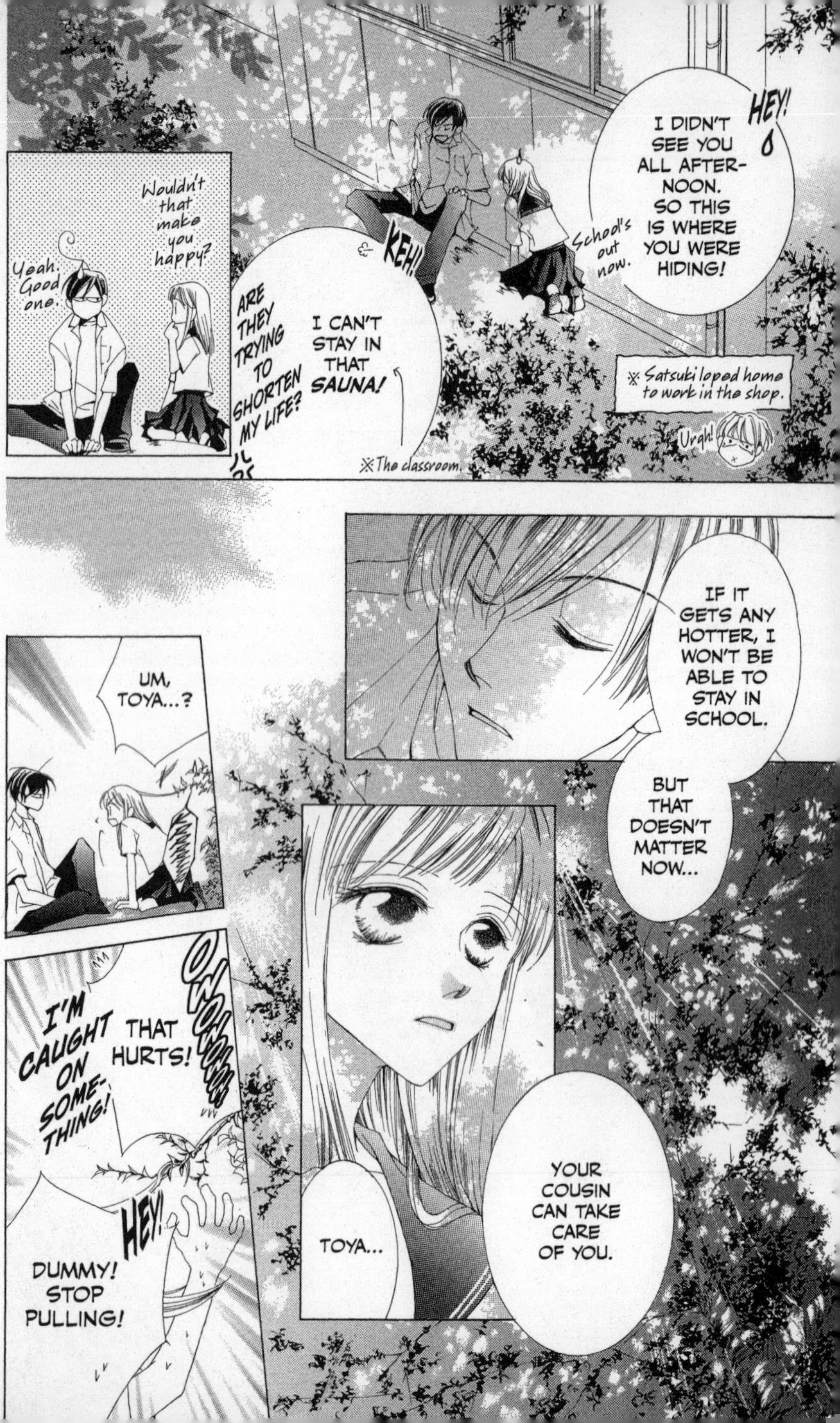
HEY!
I DIDN'T SEE YOU ALL AFTERNOON. SO THIS IS WHERE YOU WERE HIDING!
School's out now.
※Satsuki loped home to work in the shop.
Urgh!
KEH!
I CAN'T STAY IN THAT SAUNA!
※The classroom.
ARE THEY TRYING TO SHORTEN MY LIFE?
Wouldn't that make you happy?
Yeah. Good one.
IF IT GETS ANY HOTTER, I WON'T BE ABLE TO STAY IN SCHOOL.
BUT THAT DOESN'T MATTER NOW...
YOUR COUSIN CAN TAKE CARE OF YOU.
TOYA...
UM, TOYA...?
THAT HURTS!
I'M CAUGHT ON SOMETHING!
HEY!
DUMMY! STOP PULLING!

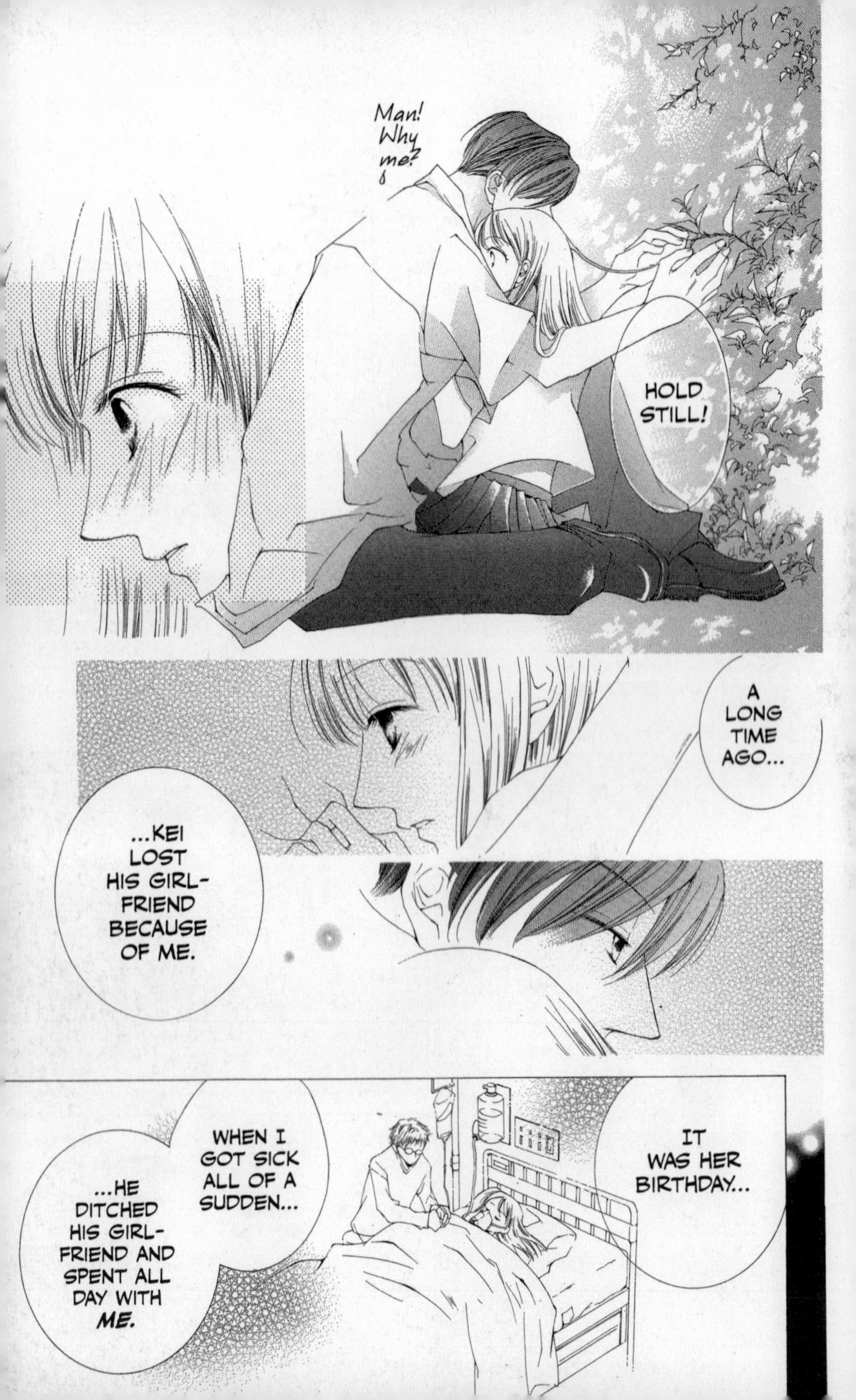
HOLD STILL!
Man! Why me?
A LONG TIME AGO...
...KEI LOST HIS GIRL-FRIEND BECAUSE OF ME.
IT WAS HER BIRTHDAY...
WHEN I GOT SICK ALL OF A SUDDEN...
...HE DITCHED HIS GIRL-FRIEND AND SPENT ALL DAY WITH *ME.*

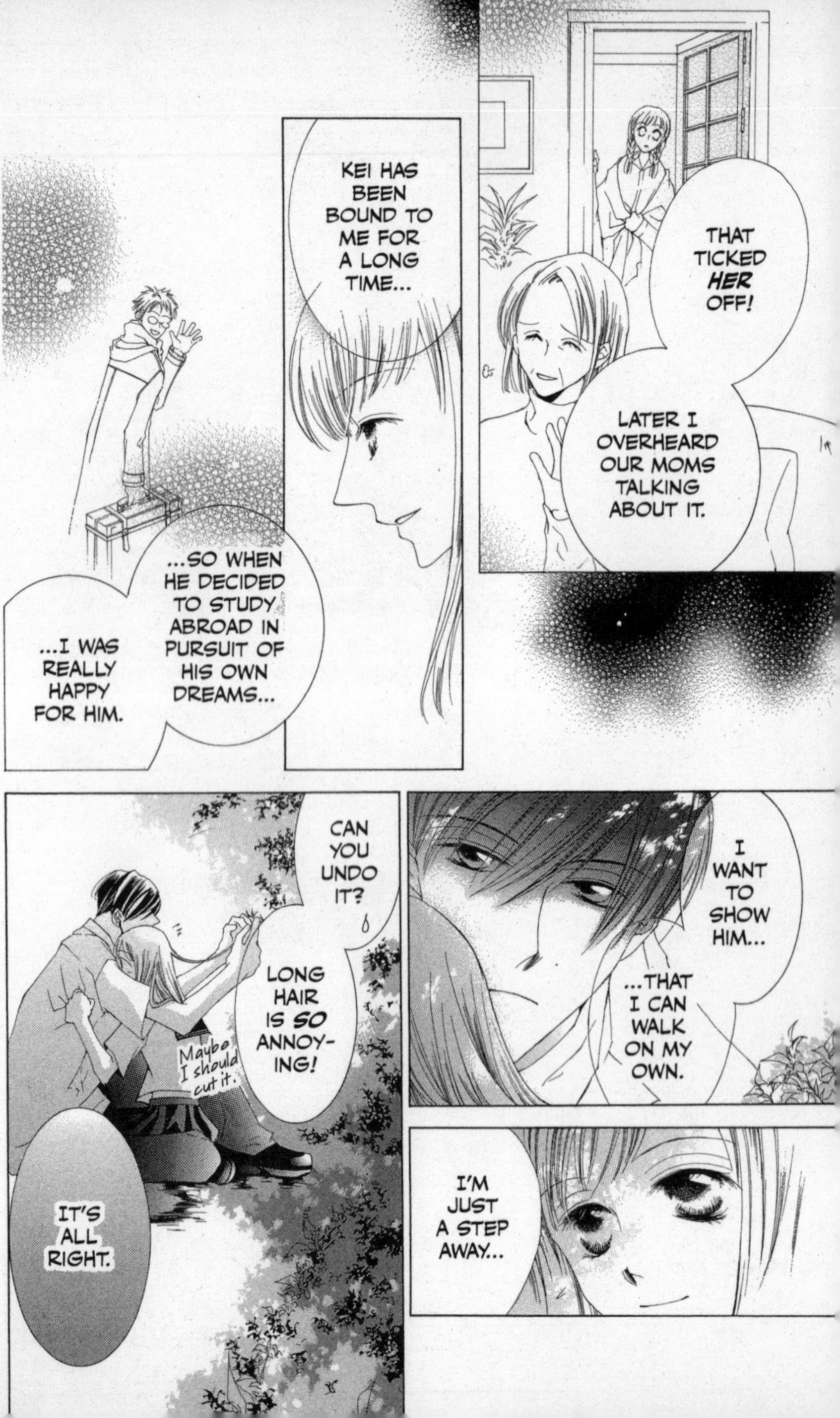
THAT TICKED *HER* OFF!
LATER I OVERHEARD OUR MOMS TALKING ABOUT IT.
KEI HAS BEEN BOUND TO ME FOR A LONG TIME...
...SO WHEN HE DECIDED TO STUDY ABROAD IN PURSUIT OF HIS OWN DREAMS...
...I WAS REALLY HAPPY FOR HIM.
I WANT TO SHOW HIM...
...THAT I CAN WALK ON MY OWN.
I'M JUST A STEP AWAY...
CAN YOU UNDO IT?
LONG HAIR IS *SO* ANNOY-ING!
Maybe I should cut it.
IT'S ALL RIGHT.

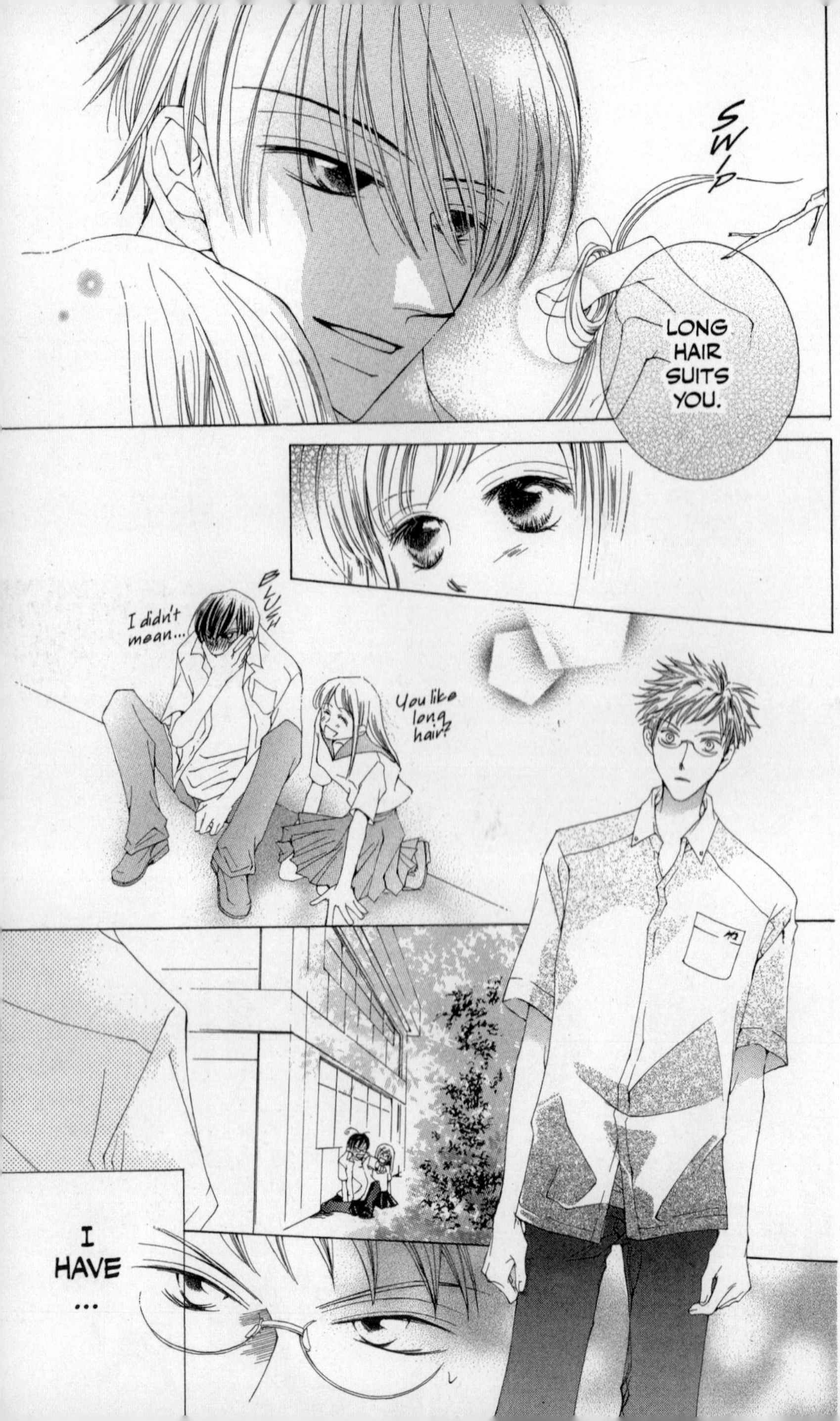
SWIP
LONG HAIR SUITS YOU.
BLUSH
I didn't mean...
You like long hair?
I HAVE ...

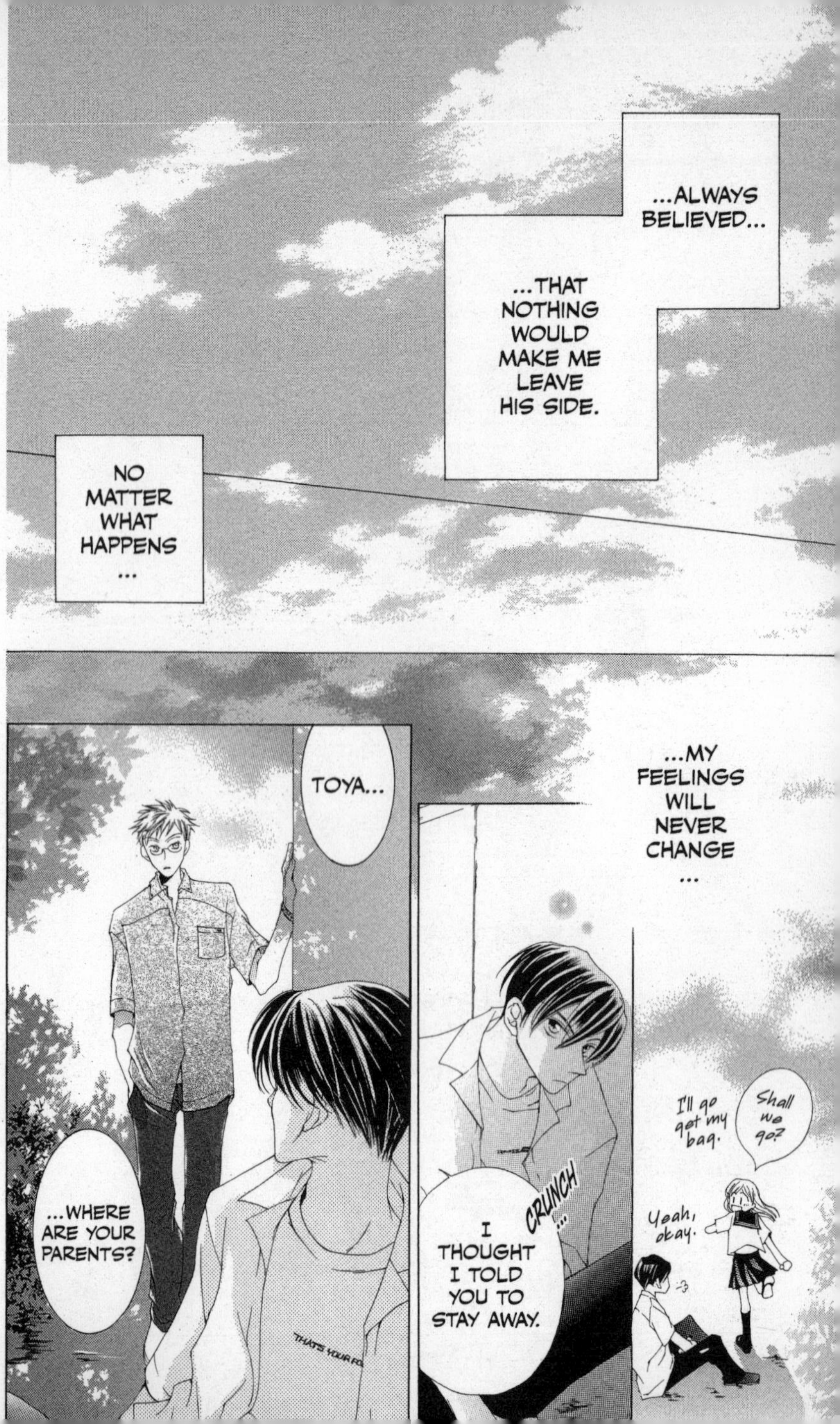
...ALWAYS BELIEVED...
...THAT NOTHING WOULD MAKE ME LEAVE HIS SIDE.
NO MATTER WHAT HAPPENS...
...MY FEELINGS WILL NEVER CHANGE...
Shall we go?
I'll go get my bag.
Yeah, okay.
CRUNCH...
I THOUGHT I TOLD YOU TO STAY AWAY.
TOYA...
...WHERE ARE YOUR PARENTS?

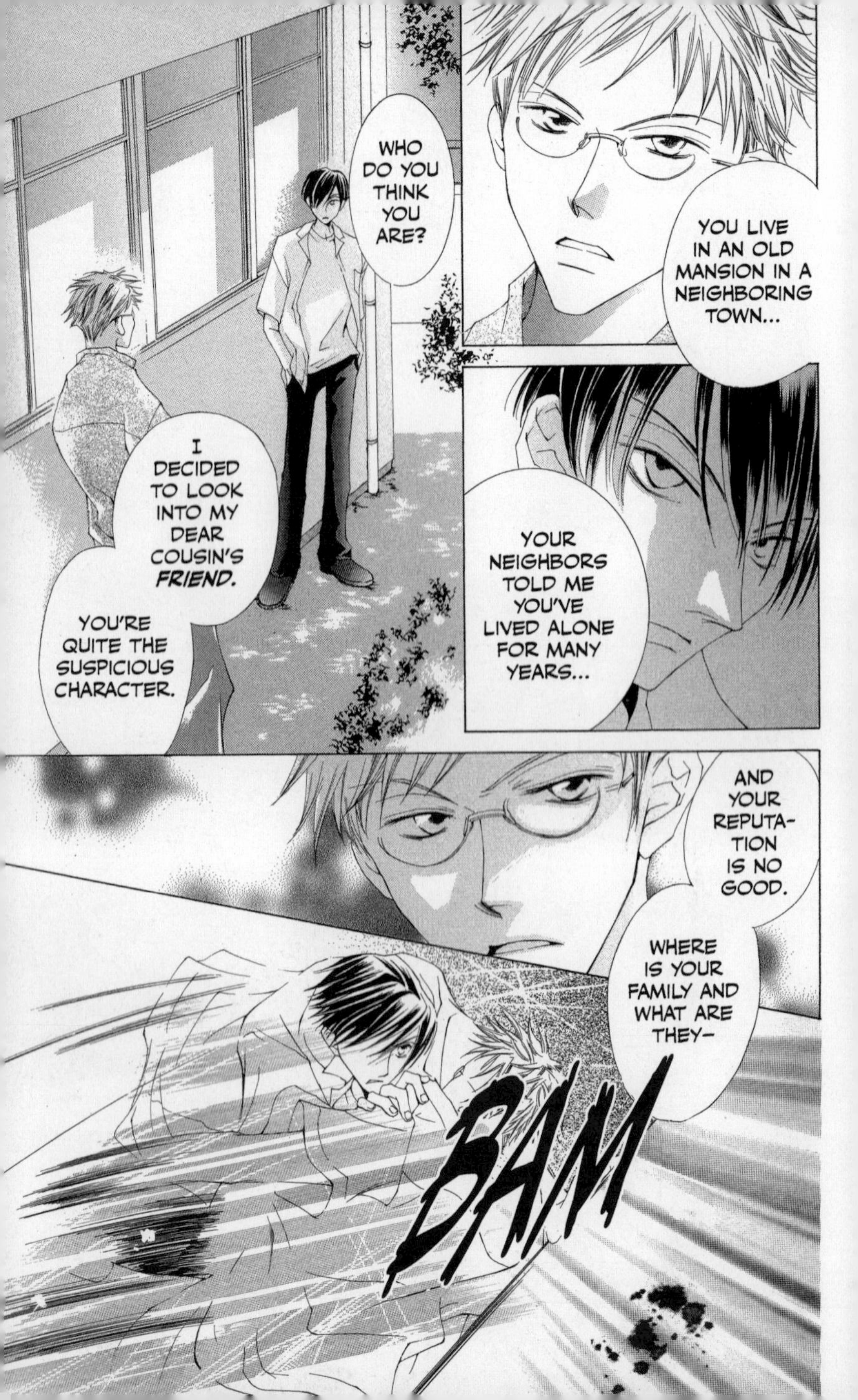
WHO DO YOU THINK YOU ARE?
I DECIDED TO LOOK INTO MY DEAR COUSIN'S *FRIEND.*
YOU'RE QUITE THE SUSPICIOUS CHARACTER.
YOU LIVE IN AN OLD MANSION IN A NEIGHBORING TOWN...
YOUR NEIGHBORS TOLD ME YOU'VE LIVED ALONE FOR MANY YEARS...
AND YOUR REPUTATION IS NO GOOD.
WHERE IS YOUR FAMILY AND WHAT ARE THEY—
BAM

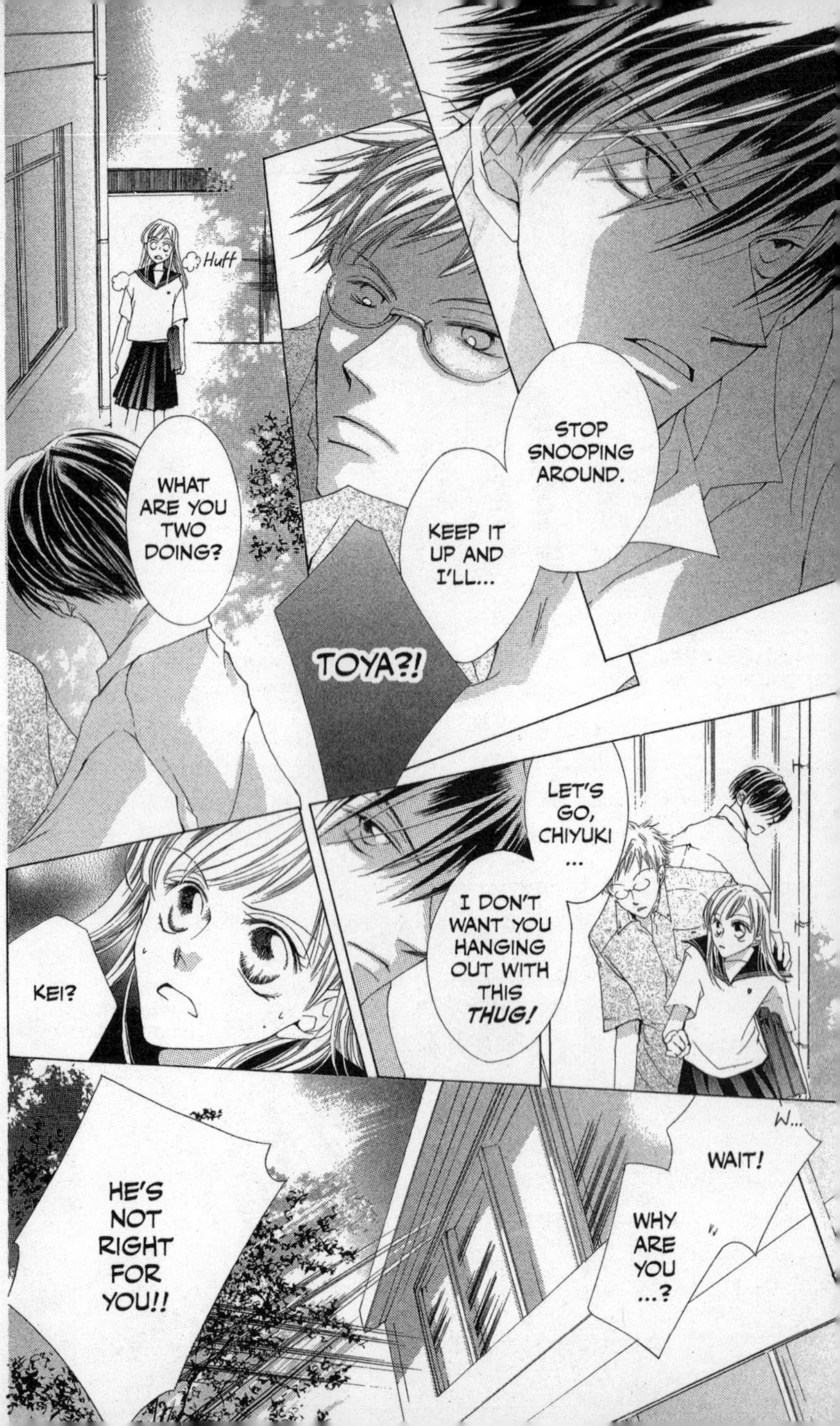
STOP SNOOPING AROUND.
KEEP IT UP AND I'LL...
Huff
WHAT ARE YOU TWO DOING?
TOYA?!
LET'S GO, CHIYUKI ...
I DON'T WANT YOU HANGING OUT WITH THIS *THUG!*
KEI?
W...
WAIT!
WHY ARE YOU ...?
HE'S NOT RIGHT FOR YOU!!

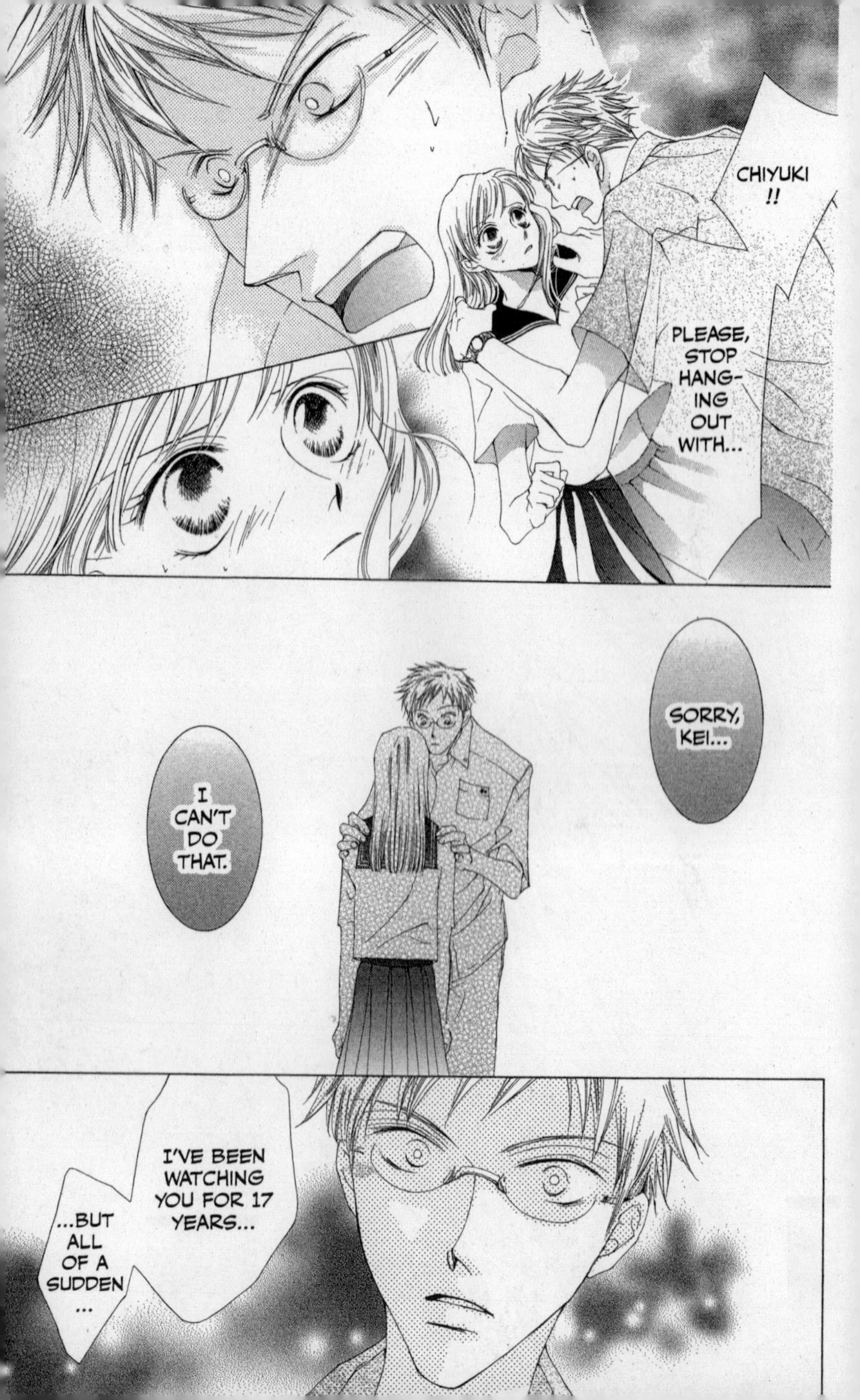
CHIYUKI !!
PLEASE, STOP HANG-ING OUT WITH...
SORRY, KEI...
I CAN'T DO THAT.
I'VE BEEN WATCHING YOU FOR 17 YEARS...
...BUT ALL OF A SUDDEN ...

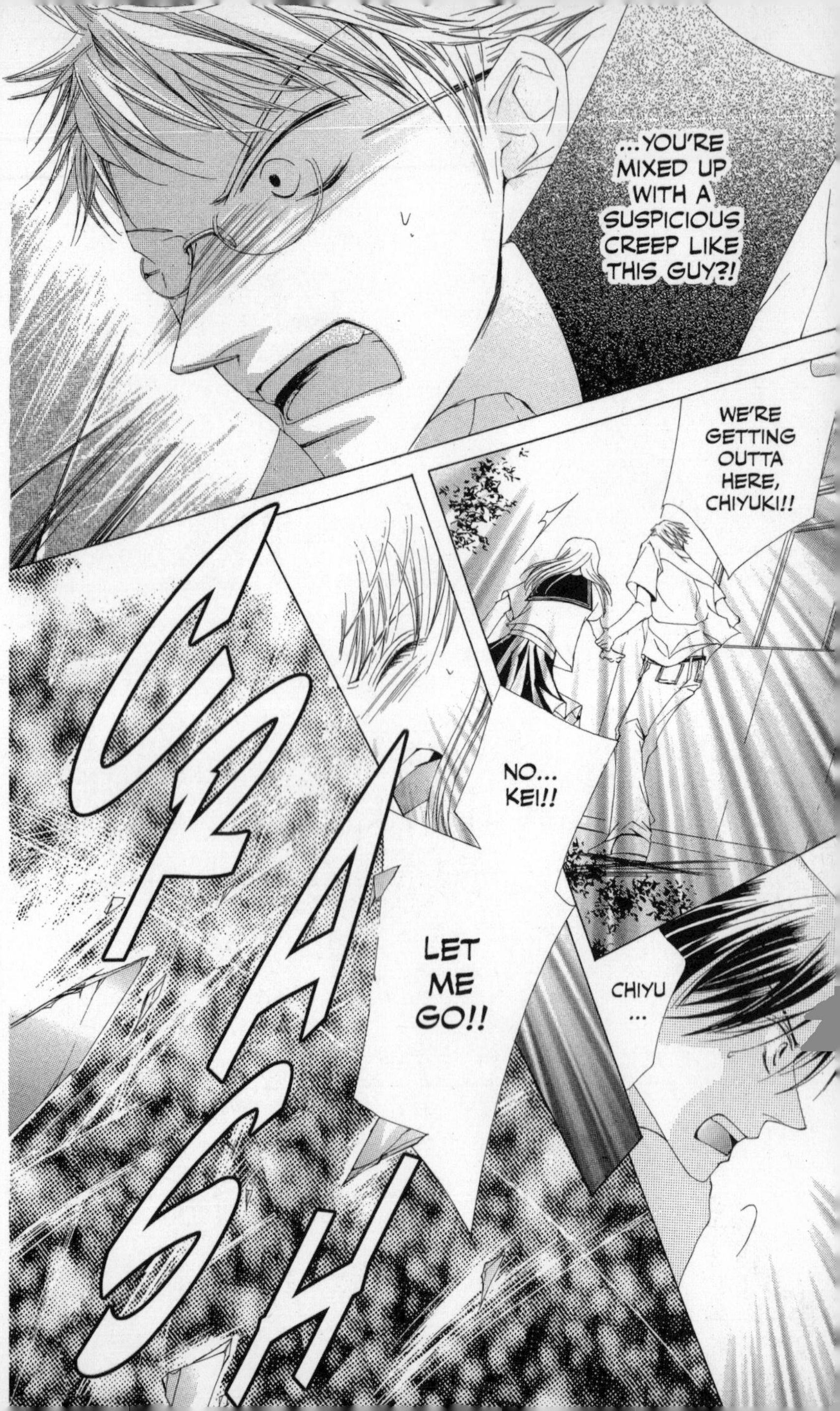
...YOU'RE MIXED UP WITH A SUSPICIOUS CREEP LIKE THIS GUY?!
WE'RE GETTING OUTTA HERE, CHIYUKI!!
NO... KEI!!
LET ME GO!!
CRASH
CHIYU ...

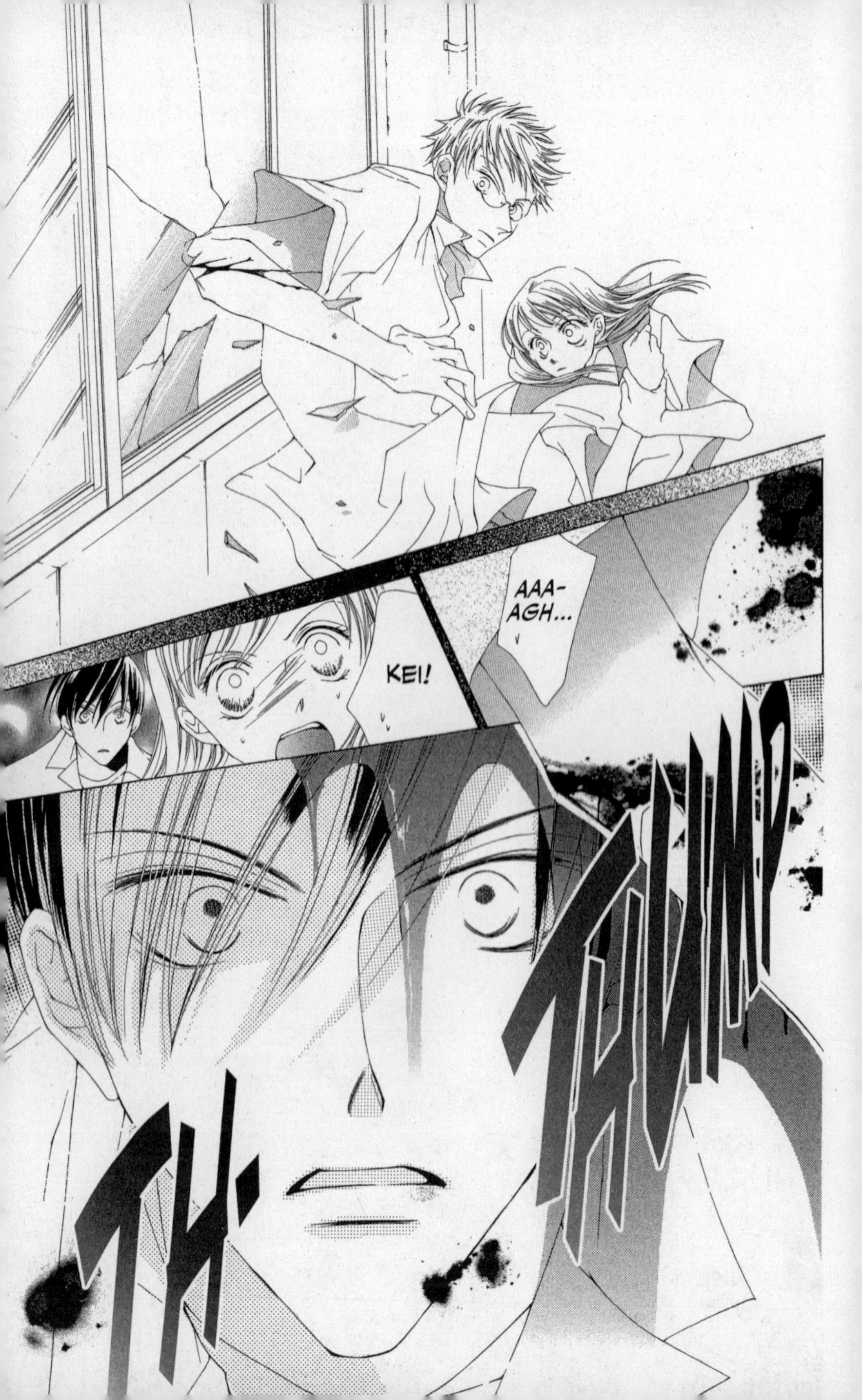
AAA-
AGH...
KEI!
THUMP
TH-

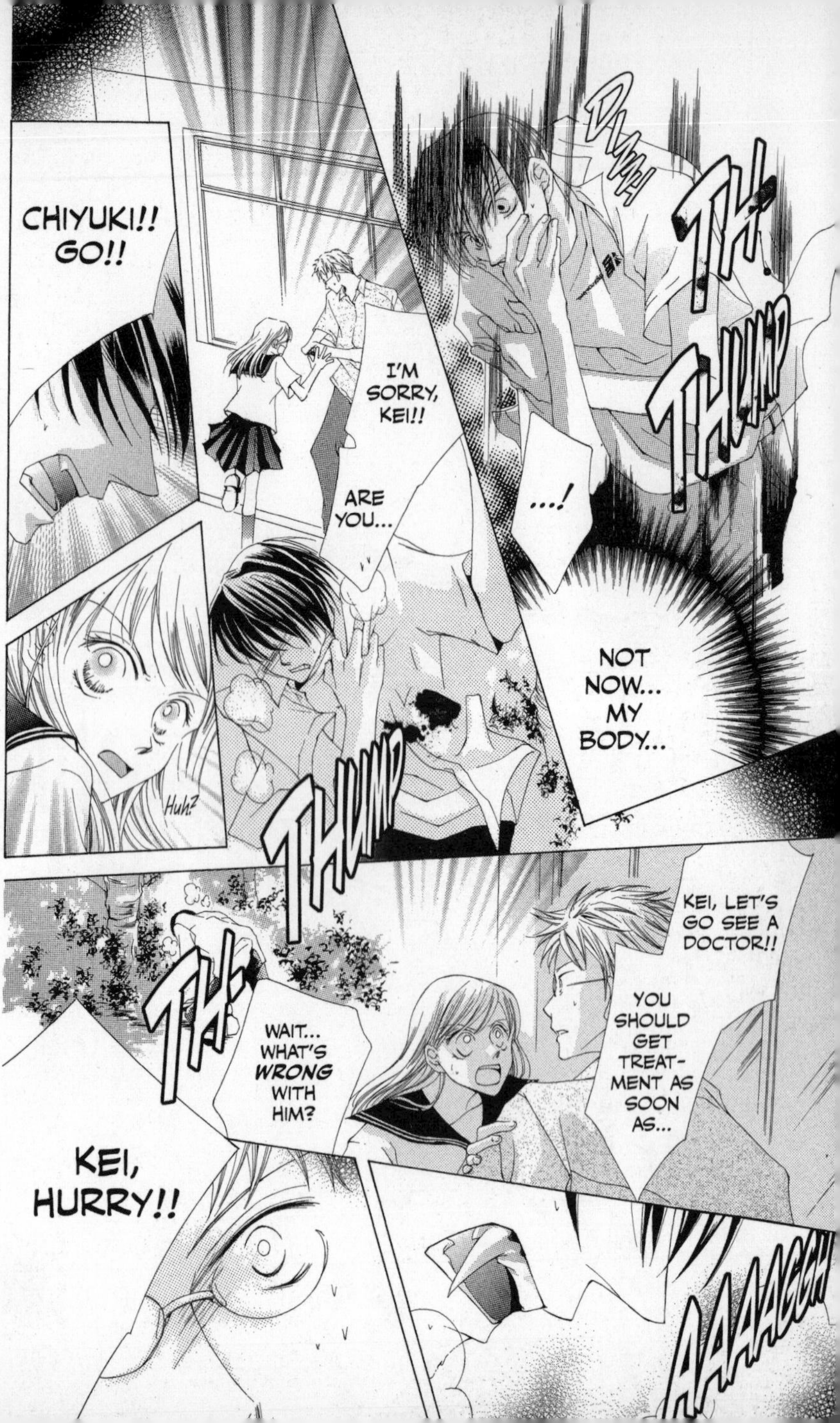
DWAH
TH-
THUMP
...!
NOT NOW... MY BODY...
CHIYUKI!! GO!!
I'M SORRY, KEI!!
ARE YOU...
Huh?
THUMP
KEI, LET'S GO SEE A DOCTOR!!
YOU SHOULD GET TREAT-MENT AS SOON AS...
WAIT... WHAT'S *WRONG* WITH HIM?
TH-
KEI, HURRY!!
AAAAGH

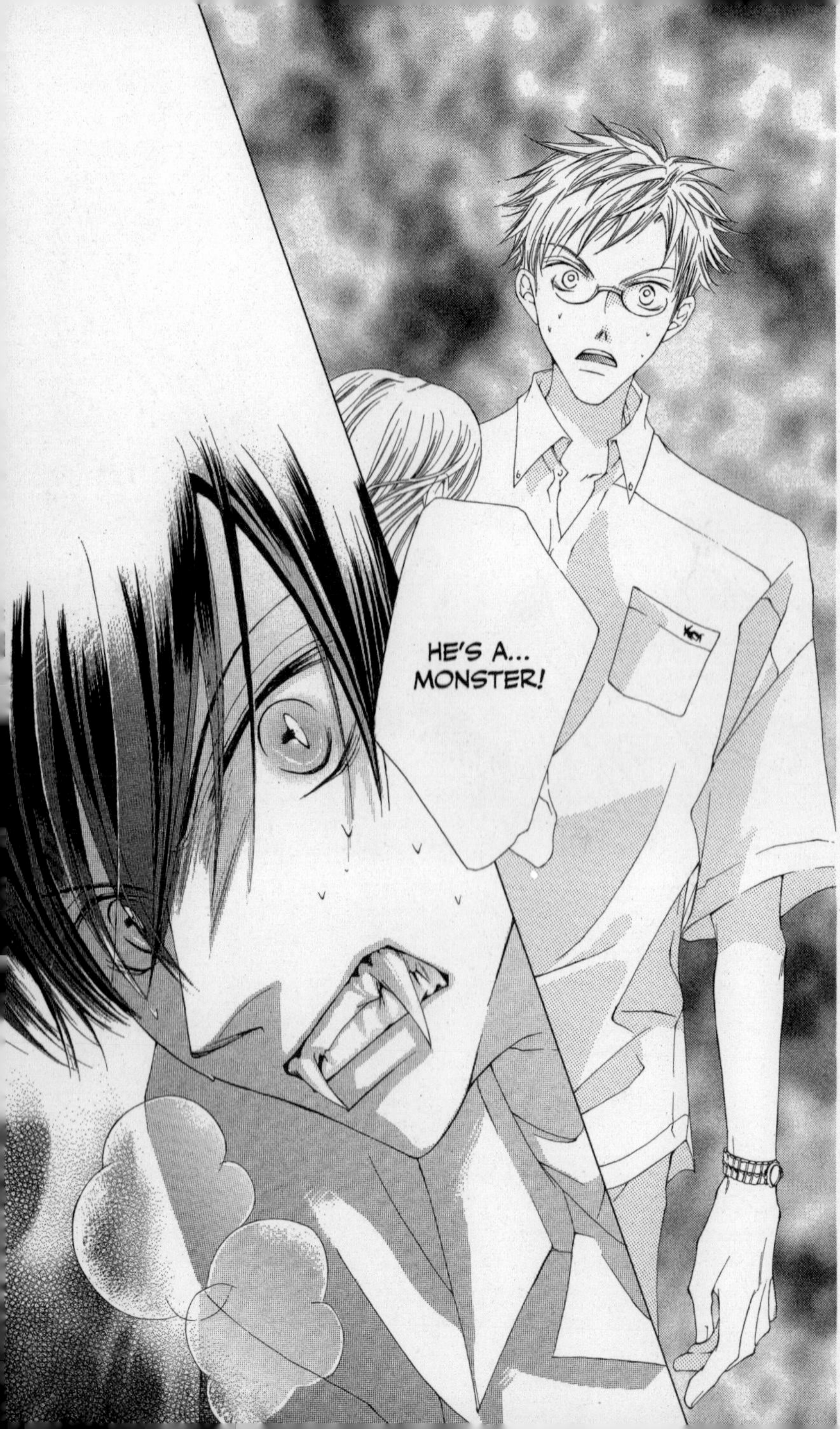
HE'S A... MONSTER!

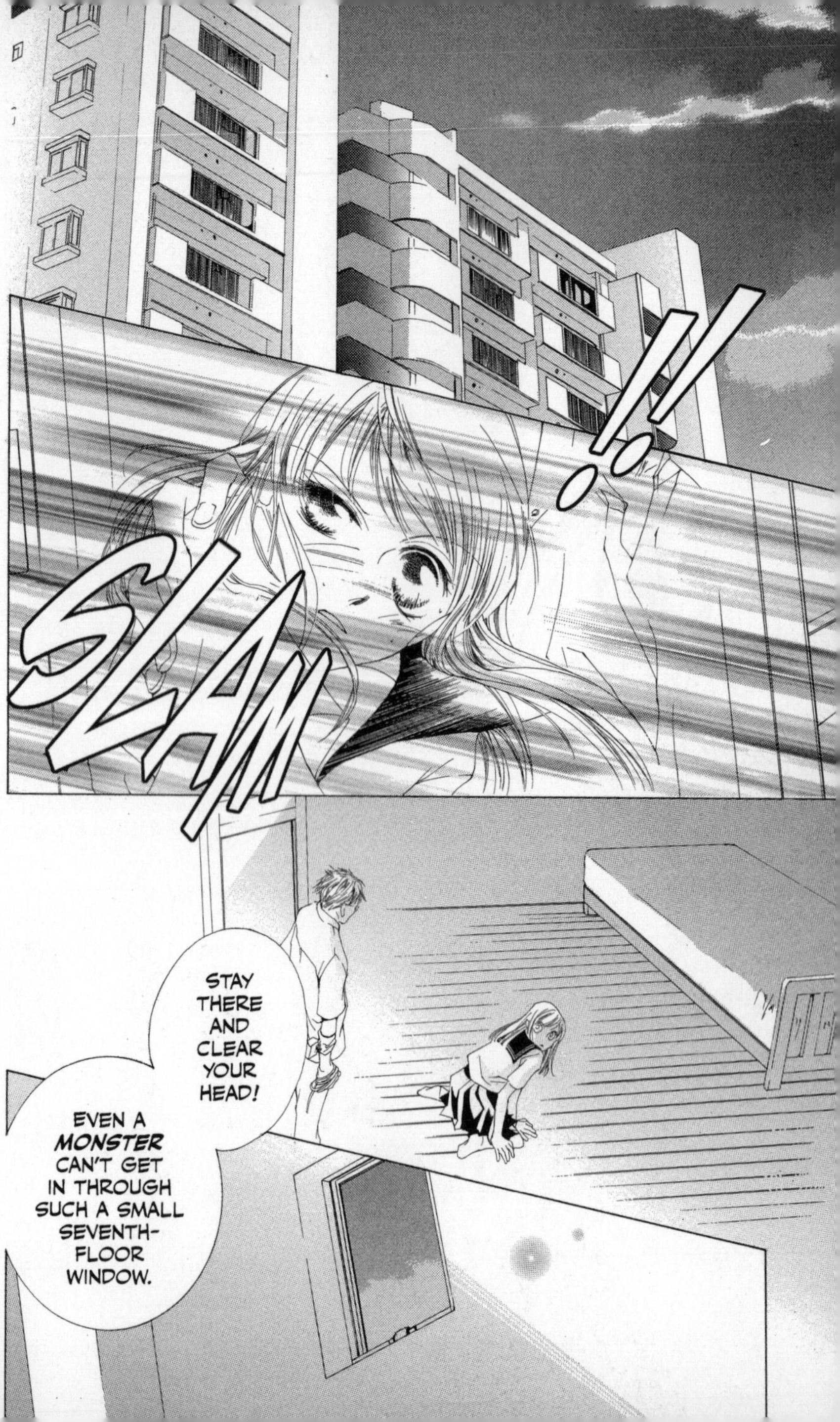
!!
SLAM
STAY THERE AND CLEAR YOUR HEAD!
EVEN A *MONSTER* CAN'T GET IN THROUGH SUCH A SMALL SEVENTH-FLOOR WINDOW.

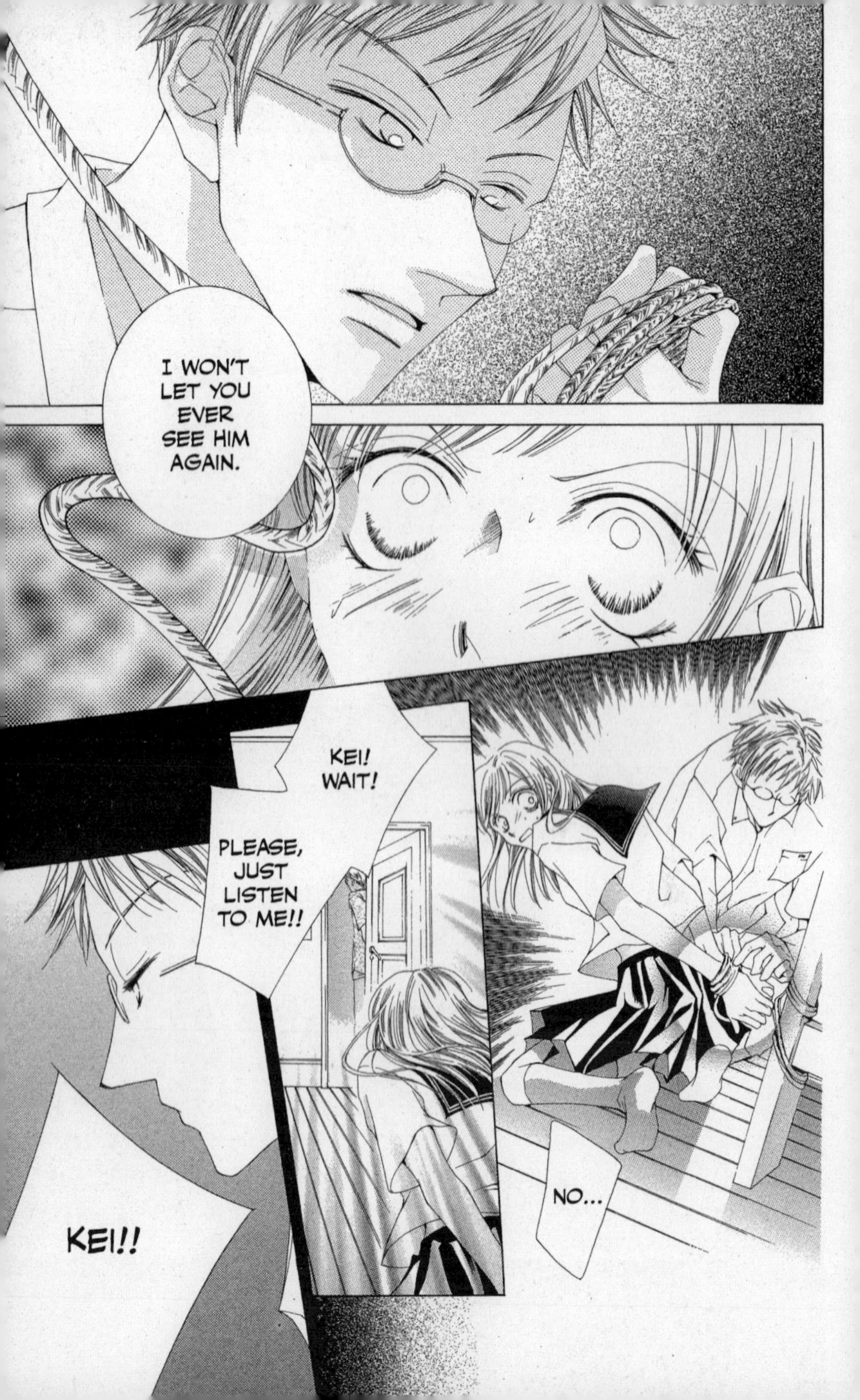
I WON'T LET YOU EVER SEE HIM AGAIN.
NO...
KEI! WAIT!
PLEASE, JUST LISTEN TO ME!!
KEI!!

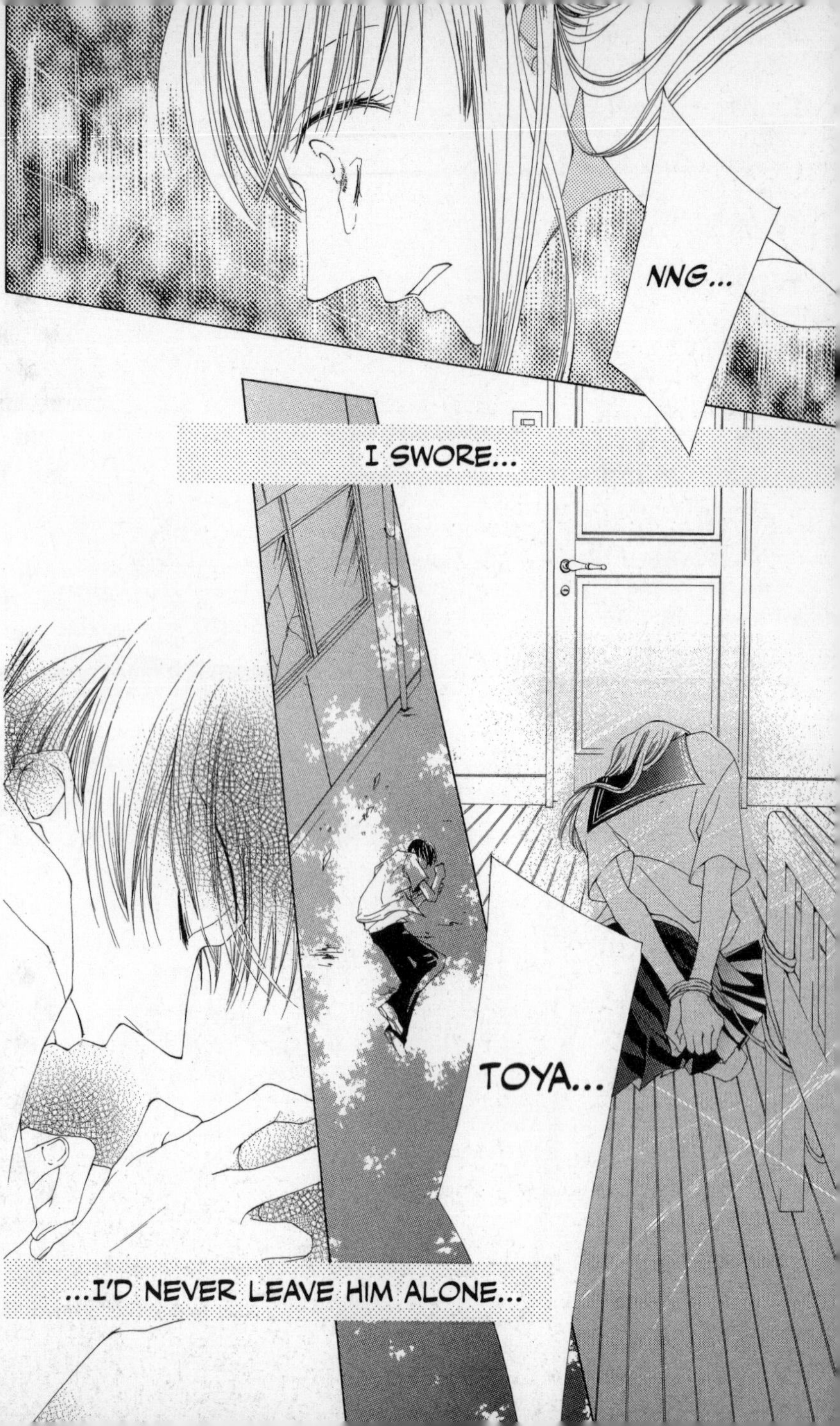
NNG...
I SWORE...
TOYA...
...I'D NEVER LEAVE HIM ALONE...

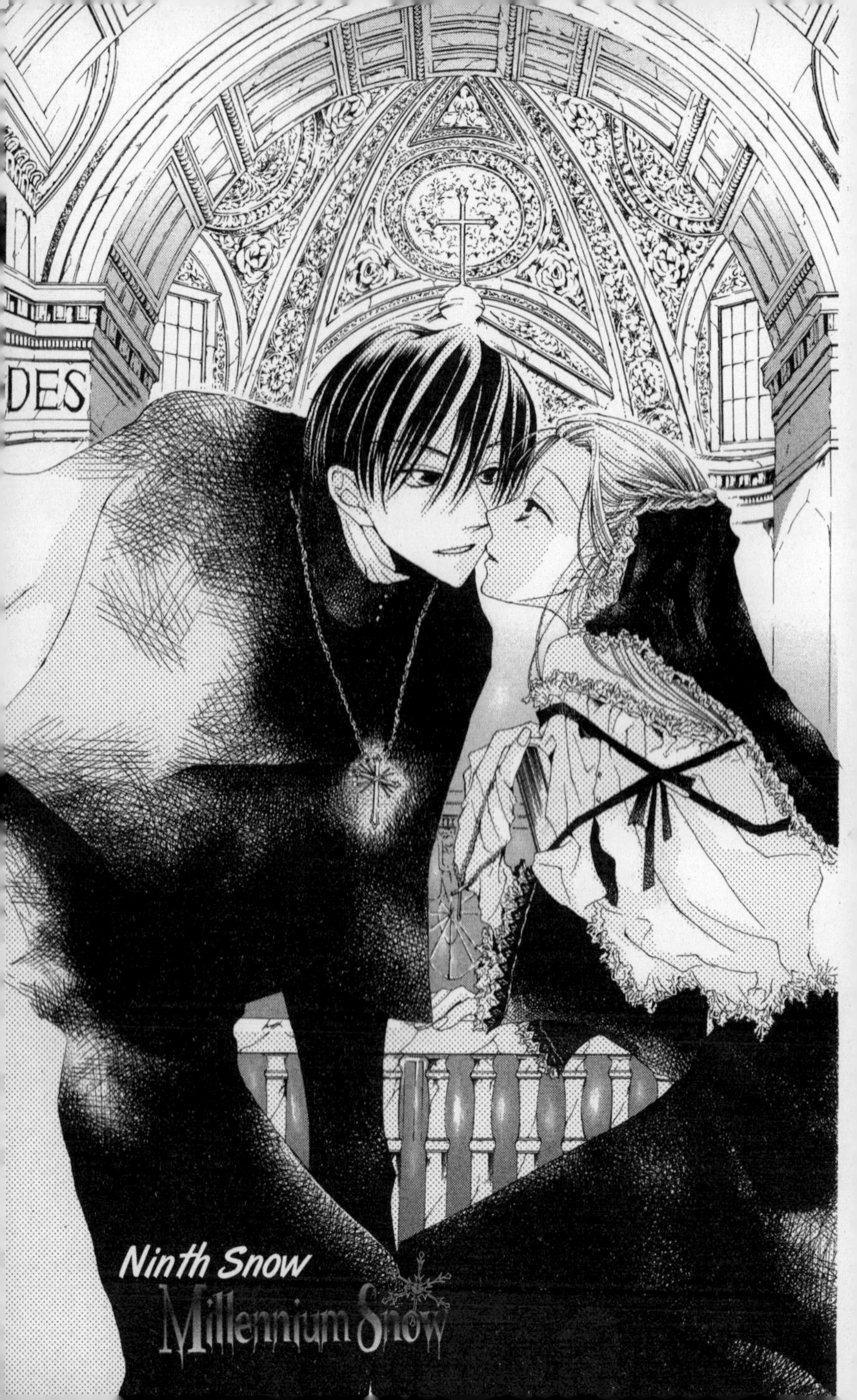
DES
Ninth Snow
Millennium Snow

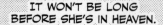

IT WON'T BE LONG
BEFORE SHE'S IN HEAVEN.

KEI,
LET'S
MAKE
A BET.

WHICH
CLOUD
DO YOU
THINK
WILL
SNOW
FIRST?

I KNOW THAT AS RAIN FALLS
AT LAST TO EARTH...

...SHE WISHES TO BECOME AS THE SNOW...

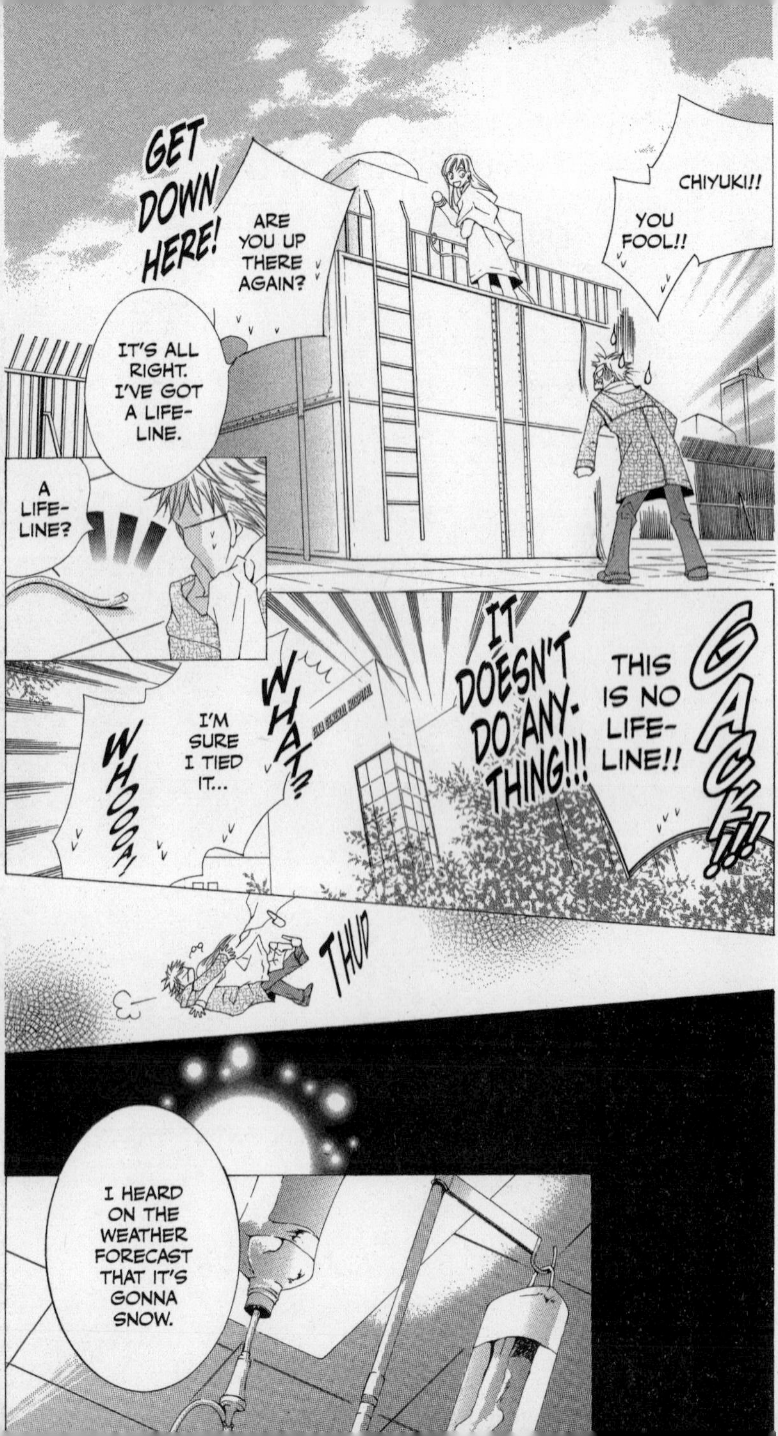
CHIYUKI!!
YOU FOOL!!
GET DOWN HERE!
ARE YOU UP THERE AGAIN?
IT'S ALL RIGHT. I'VE GOT A LIFE-LINE.
A LIFE-LINE?
GACK!!
THIS IS NO LIFE-LINE!!
IT DOESN'T DO ANY-THING!!!
WHAT!?
I'M SURE I TIED IT...
WHOOOA!
THUD
I HEARD ON THE WEATHER FORECAST THAT IT'S GONNA SNOW.

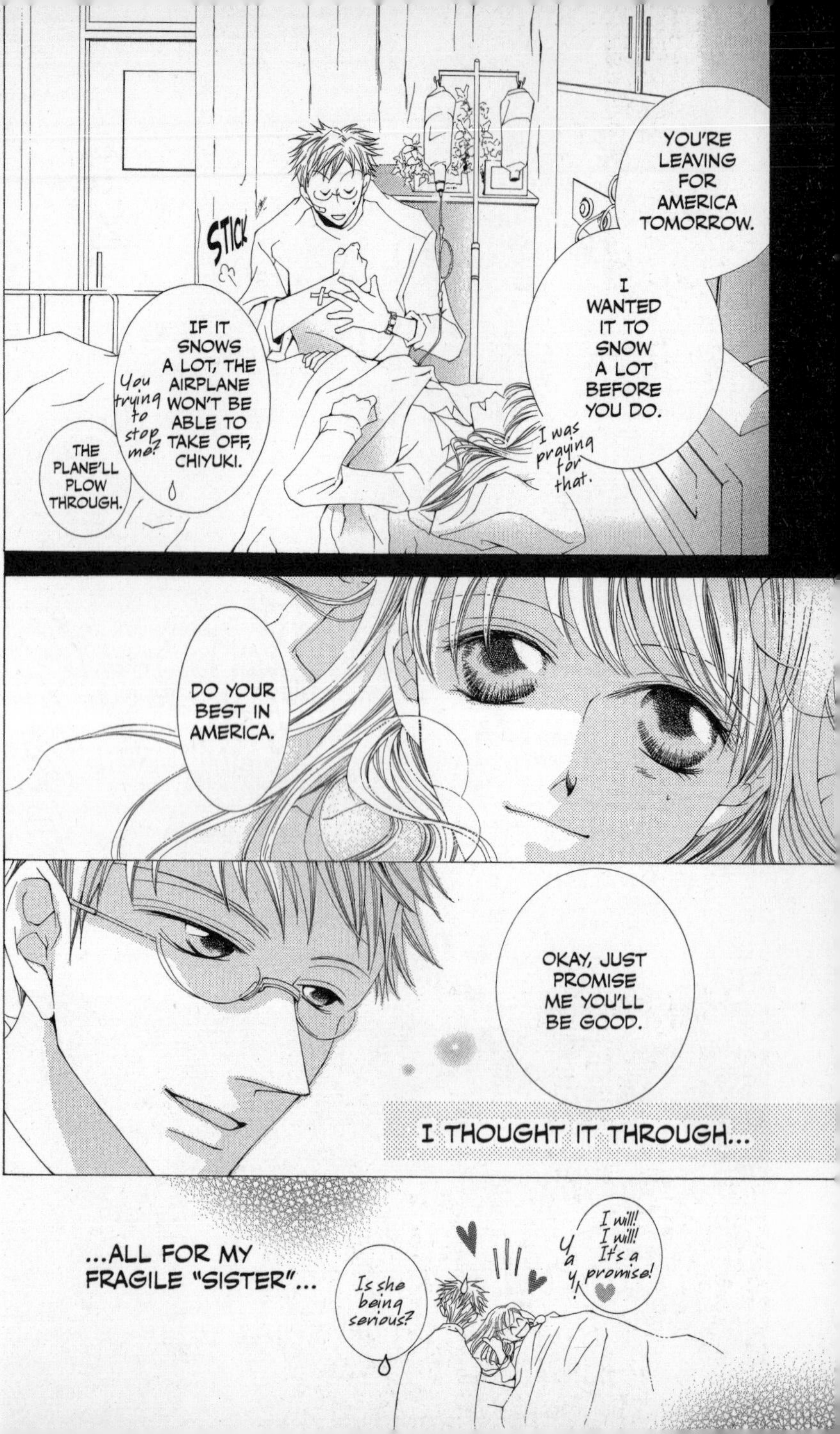
YOU'RE LEAVING FOR AMERICA TOMORROW.
I WANTED IT TO SNOW A LOT BEFORE YOU DO.
I was praying for that.
STICK
IF IT SNOWS A LOT, THE AIRPLANE WON'T BE ABLE TO TAKE OFF, CHIYUKI.
You trying to stop me?
THE PLANE'LL PLOW THROUGH.
DO YOUR BEST IN AMERICA.
OKAY, JUST PROMISE ME YOU'LL BE GOOD.
I THOUGHT IT THROUGH...
I will! I will! It's a promise!
Yay!
Is she being serious?
...ALL FOR MY FRAGILE "SISTER"...

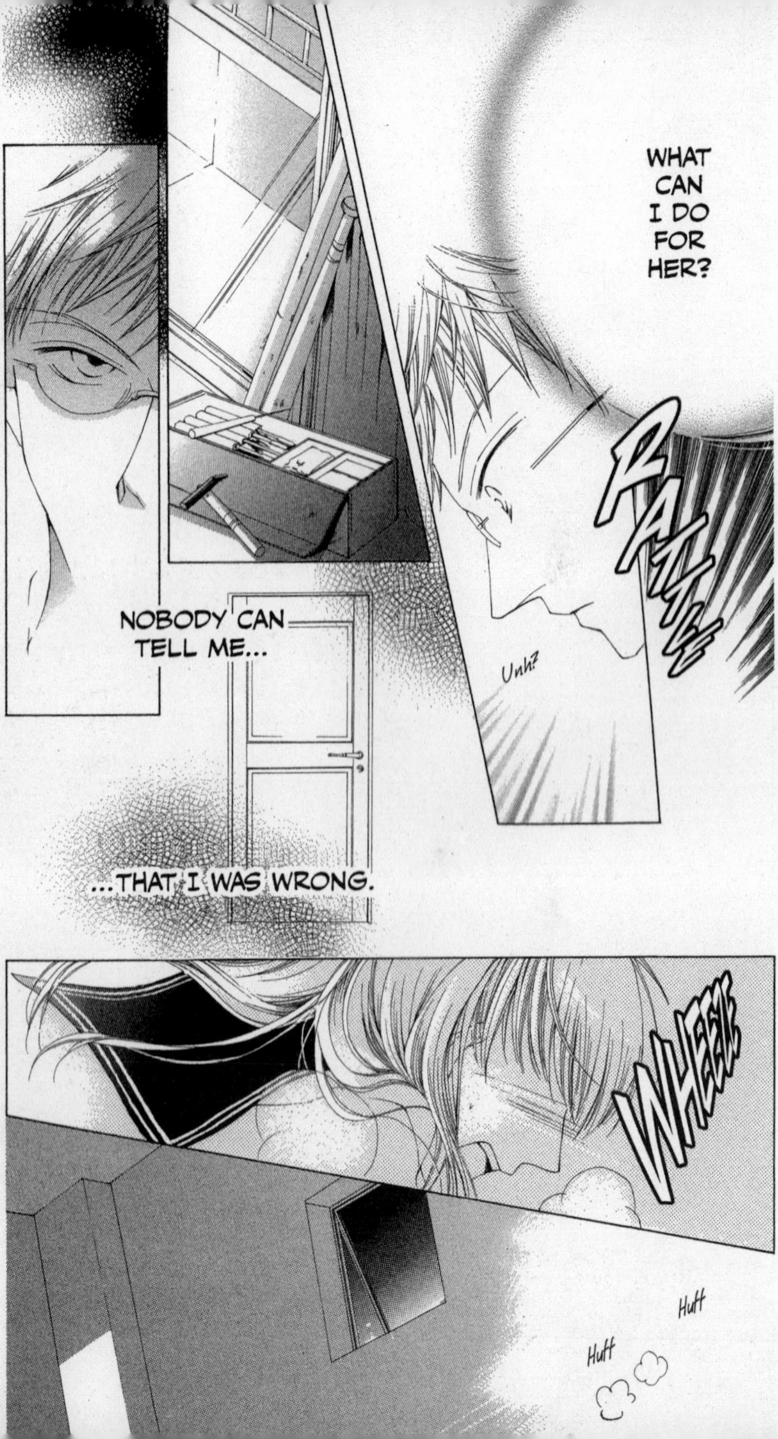
WHAT CAN I DO FOR HER?
Unh?
NOBODY CAN TELL ME...
...THAT I WAS WRONG.
WHEEZE
Huff
Huff

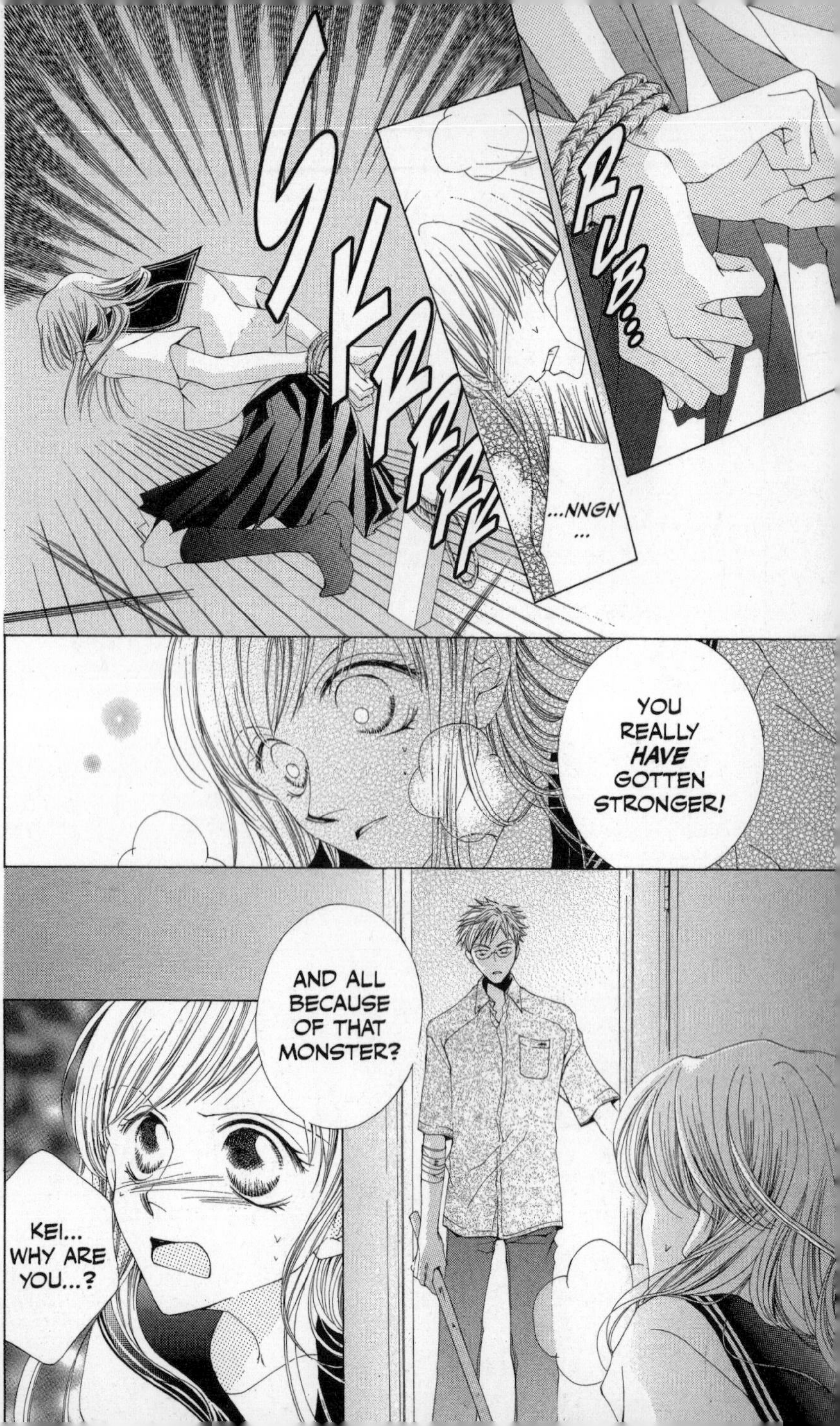
RUB...
...NNGN ...
SKRRRK
YOU REALLY HAVE GOTTEN STRONGER!
AND ALL BECAUSE OF THAT MONSTER?
KEI... WHY ARE YOU...?

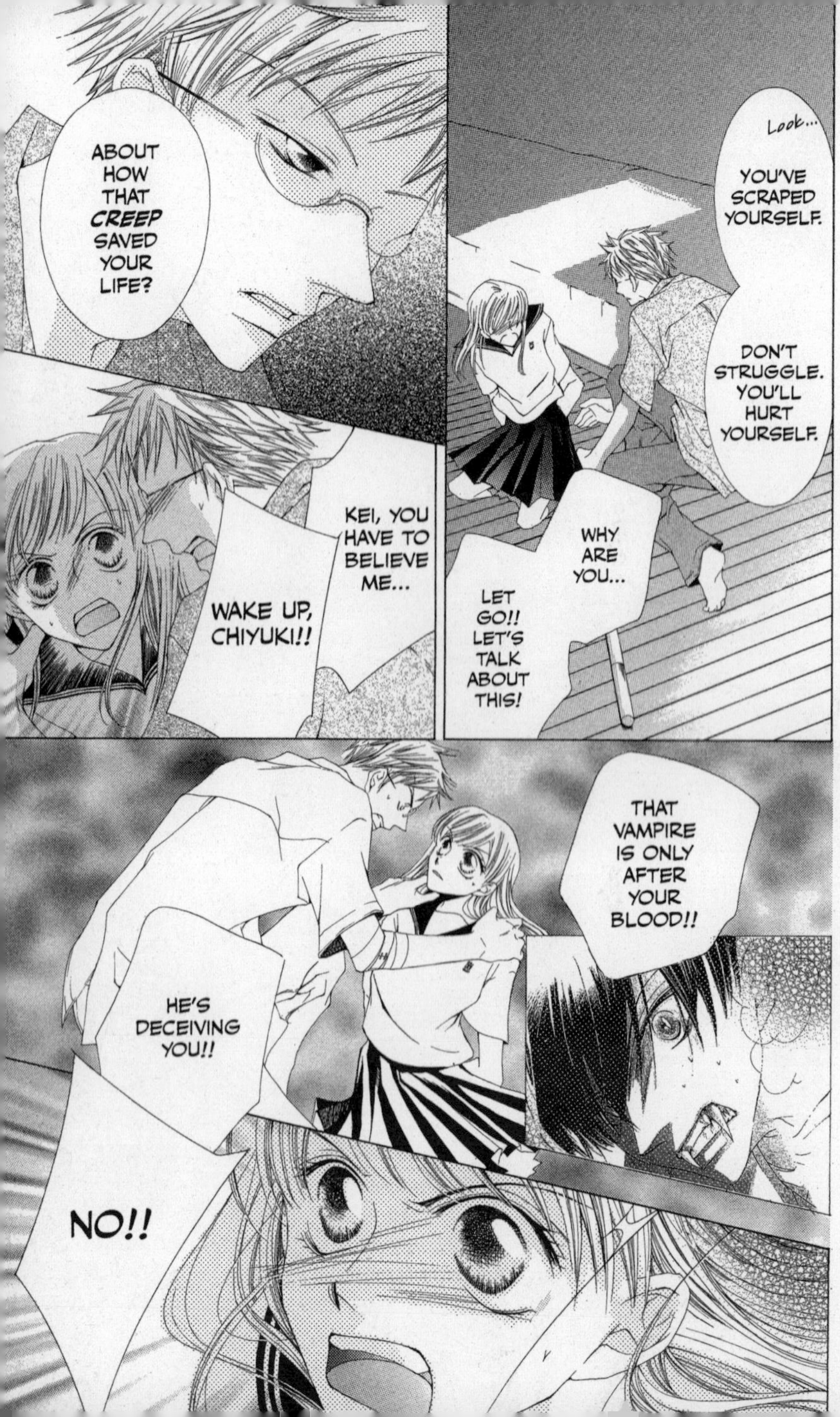
Look...
YOU'VE SCRAPED YOURSELF.
DON'T STRUGGLE. YOU'LL HURT YOURSELF.
WHY ARE YOU...
LET GO!! LET'S TALK ABOUT THIS!
ABOUT HOW THAT *CREEP* SAVED YOUR LIFE?
KEI, YOU HAVE TO BELIEVE ME...
WAKE UP, CHIYUKI!!
THAT VAMPIRE IS ONLY AFTER YOUR BLOOD!!
HE'S DECEIVING YOU!!
NO!!

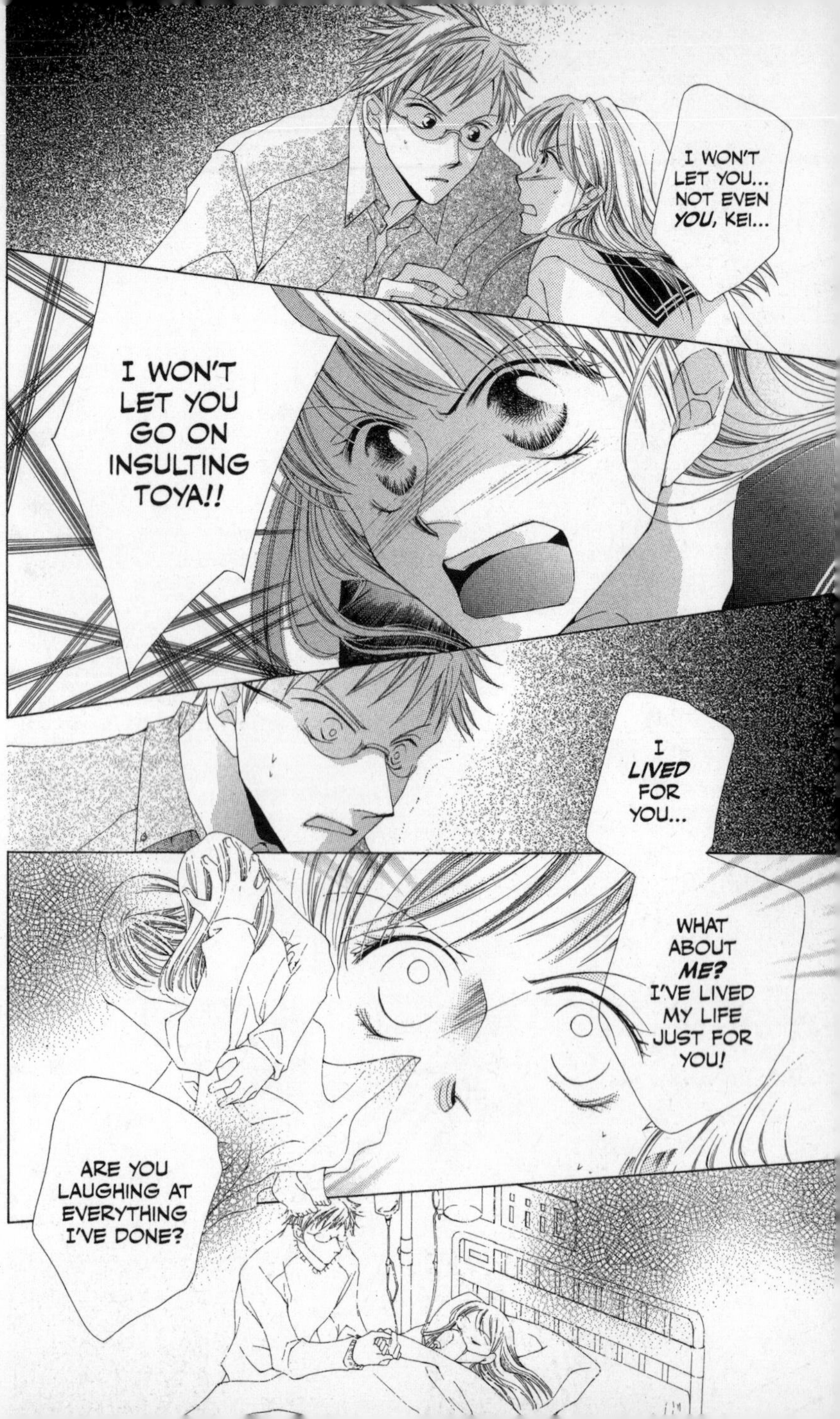
I WON'T LET YOU... NOT EVEN *YOU*, KEI...
I WON'T LET YOU GO ON INSULTING TOYA!!
I *LIVED* FOR YOU...
WHAT ABOUT *ME?* I'VE LIVED MY LIFE JUST FOR YOU!
ARE YOU LAUGHING AT EVERYTHING I'VE DONE?

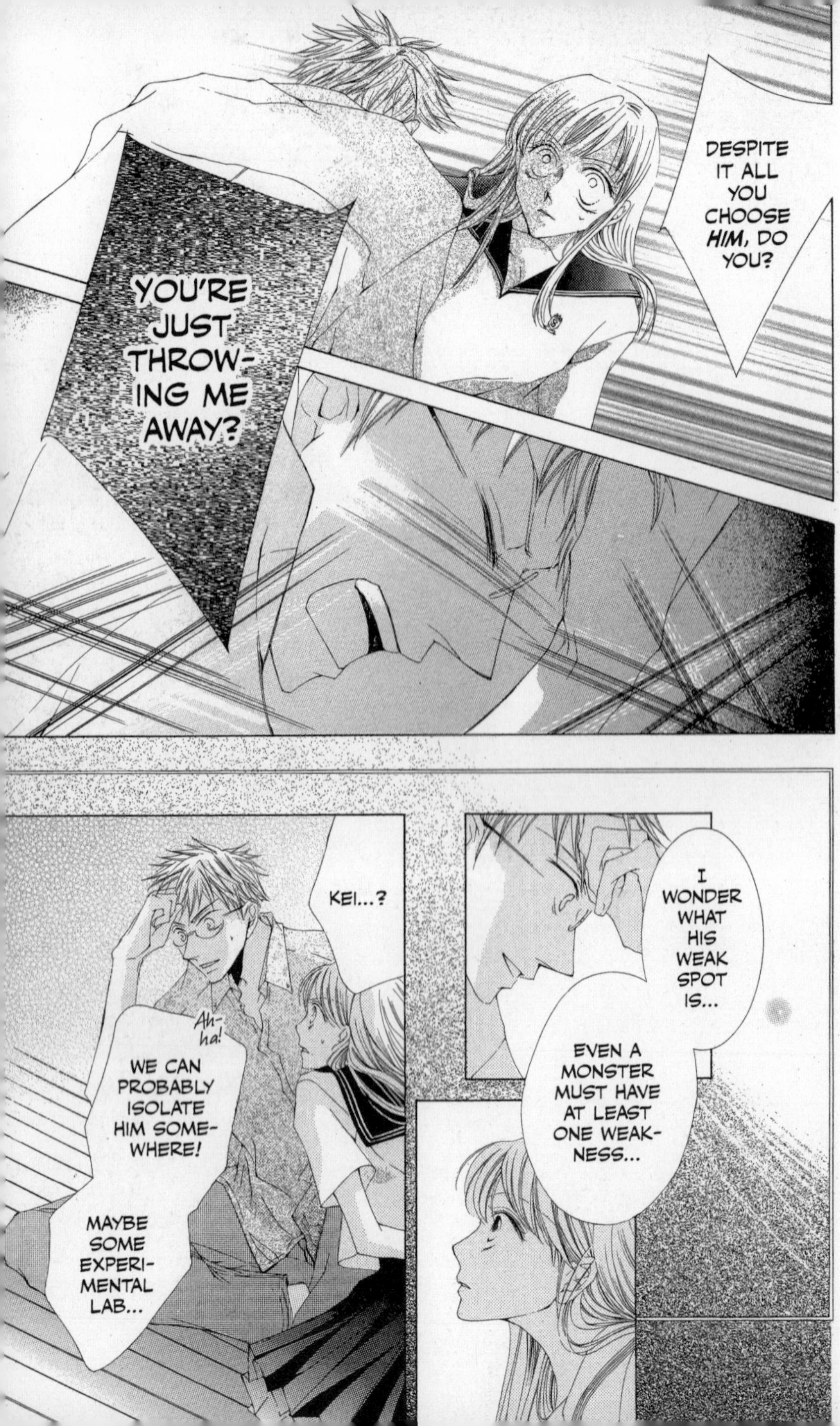
DESPITE IT ALL YOU CHOOSE *HIM*, DO YOU?
YOU'RE JUST THROWING ME AWAY?
I WONDER WHAT HIS WEAK SPOT IS...
EVEN A MONSTER MUST HAVE AT LEAST ONE WEAKNESS...
KEI...?
Ah-ha!
WE CAN PROBABLY ISOLATE HIM SOMEWHERE!
MAYBE SOME EXPERIMENTAL LAB...

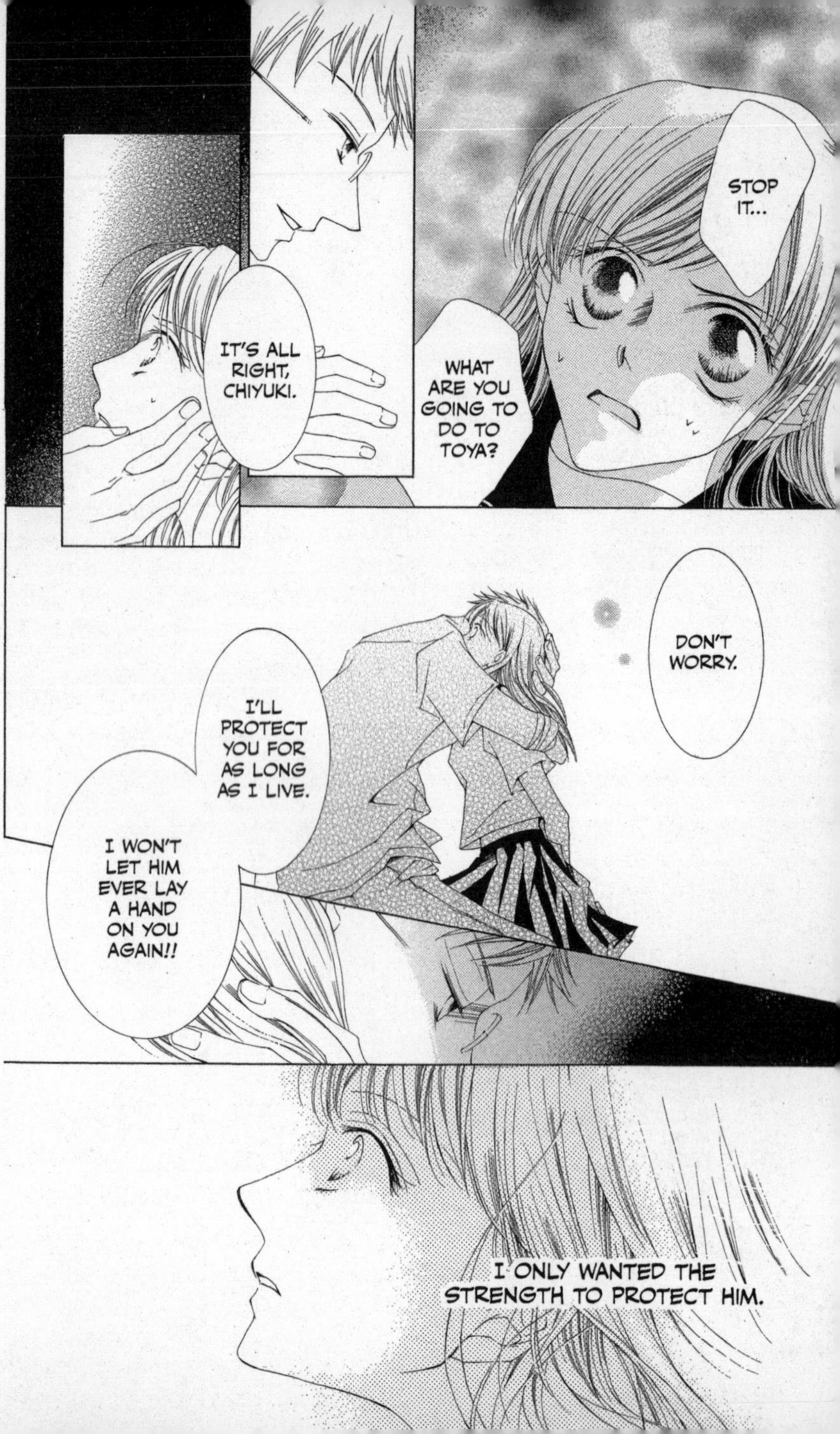
STOP IT...
WHAT ARE YOU GOING TO DO TO TOYA?
IT'S ALL RIGHT, CHIYUKI.
DON'T WORRY.
I'LL PROTECT YOU FOR AS LONG AS I LIVE.
I WON'T LET HIM EVER LAY A HAND ON YOU AGAIN!!
I ONLY WANTED THE STRENGTH TO PROTECT HIM.

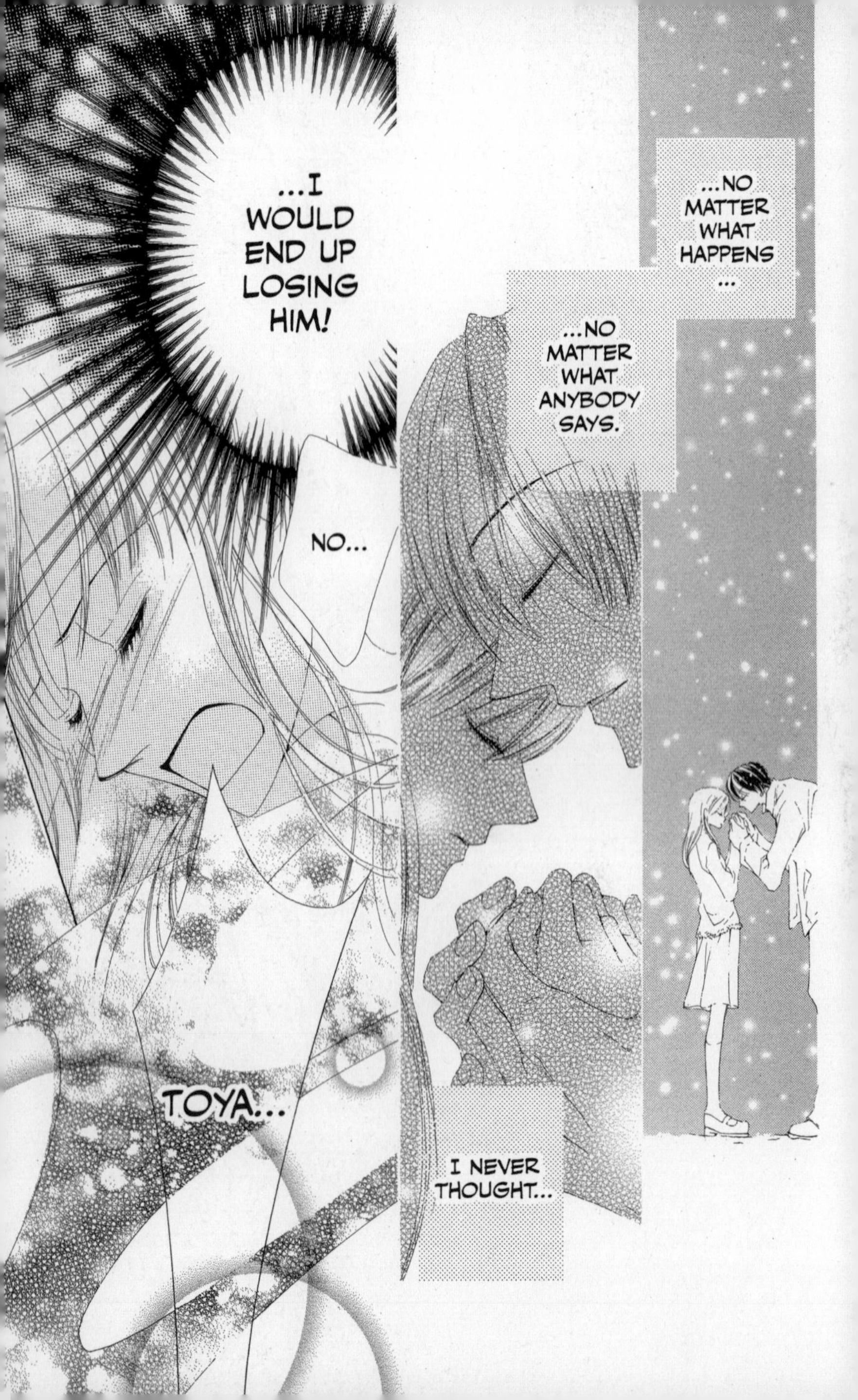
...NO MATTER WHAT HAPPENS ...
...NO MATTER WHAT ANYBODY SAYS.
I NEVER THOUGHT...
...I WOULD END UP LOSING HIM!
NO...
TOYA...

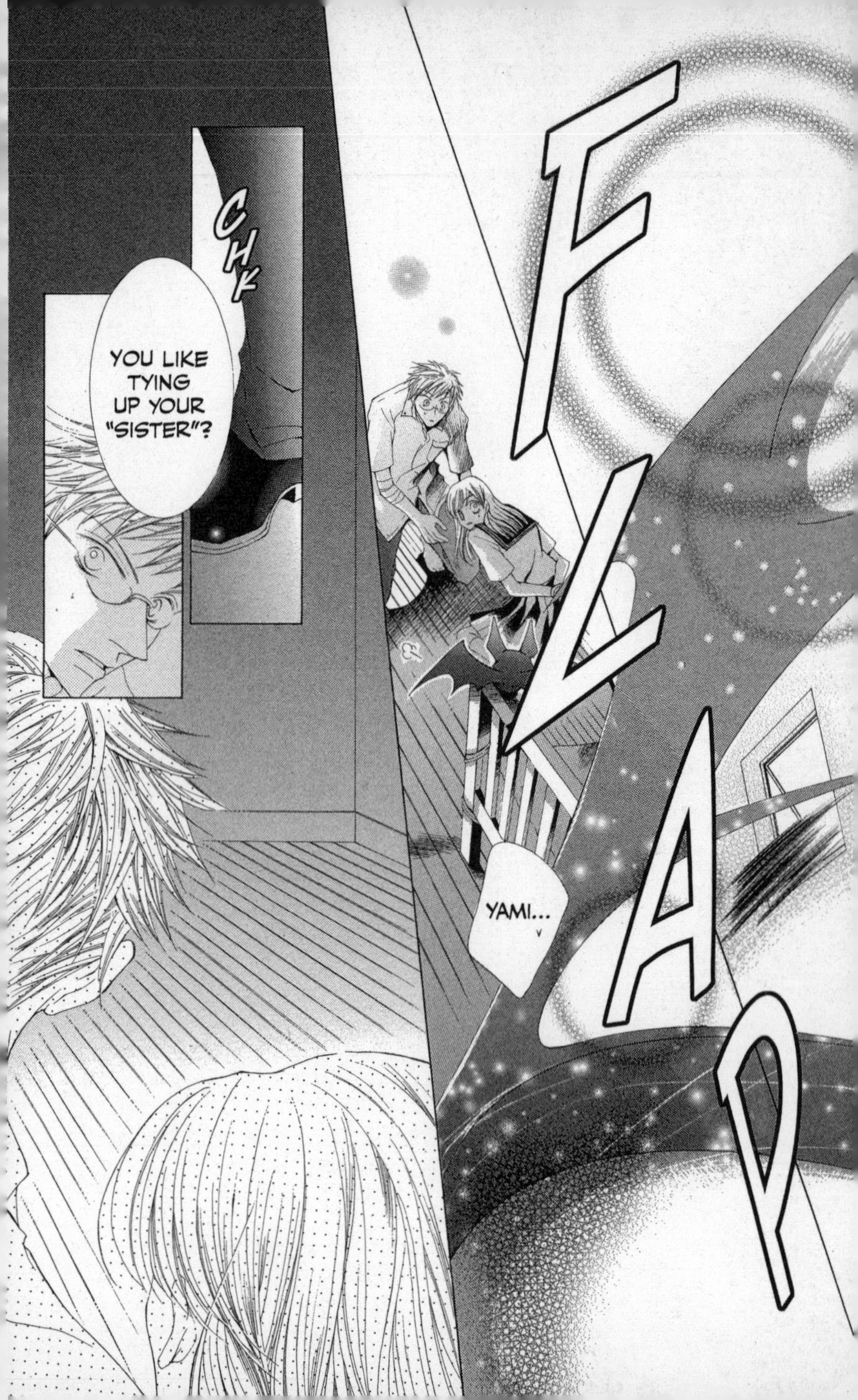
FLAP
YAMI...
CHK
YOU LIKE TYING UP YOUR "SISTER"?

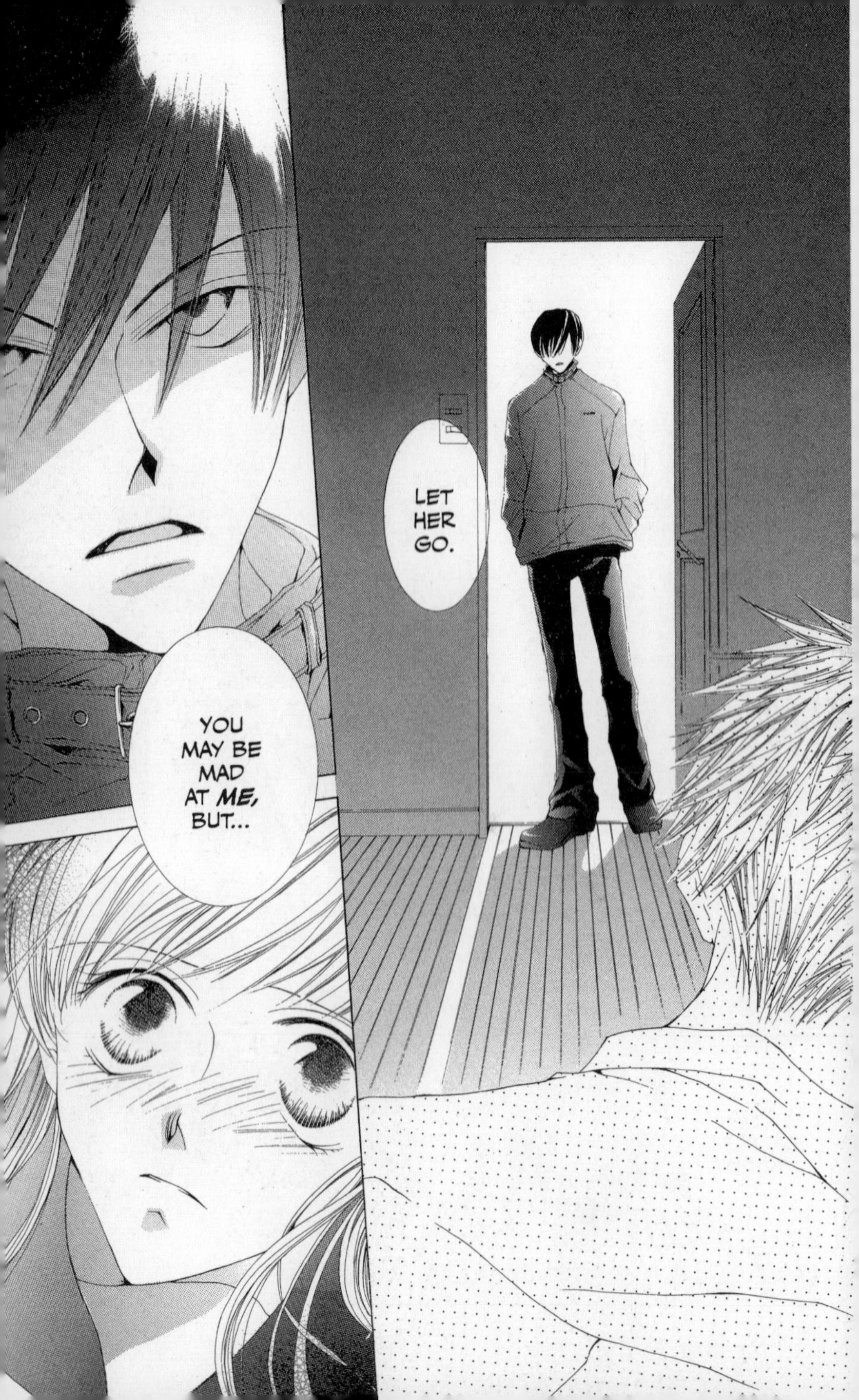
LET HER GO.
YOU MAY BE MAD AT *ME,* BUT...

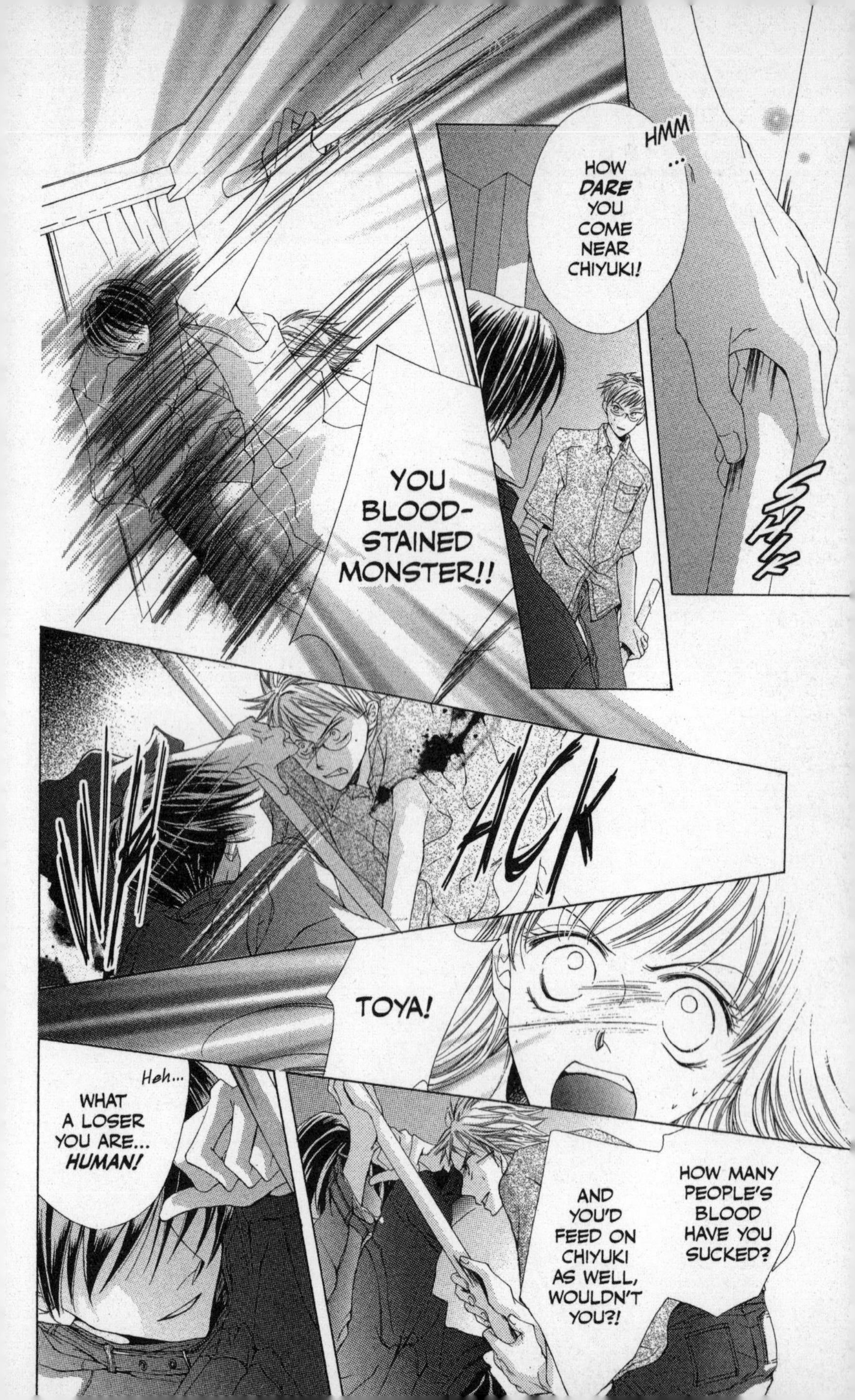
SHHK
HMM...
HOW DARE YOU COME NEAR CHIYUKI!
YOU BLOOD-STAINED MONSTER!!
ACK
WHAK
TOYA!
HOW MANY PEOPLE'S BLOOD HAVE YOU SUCKED?
AND YOU'D FEED ON CHIYUKI AS WELL, WOULDN'T YOU?!
Heh...
WHAT A LOSER YOU ARE... HUMAN!

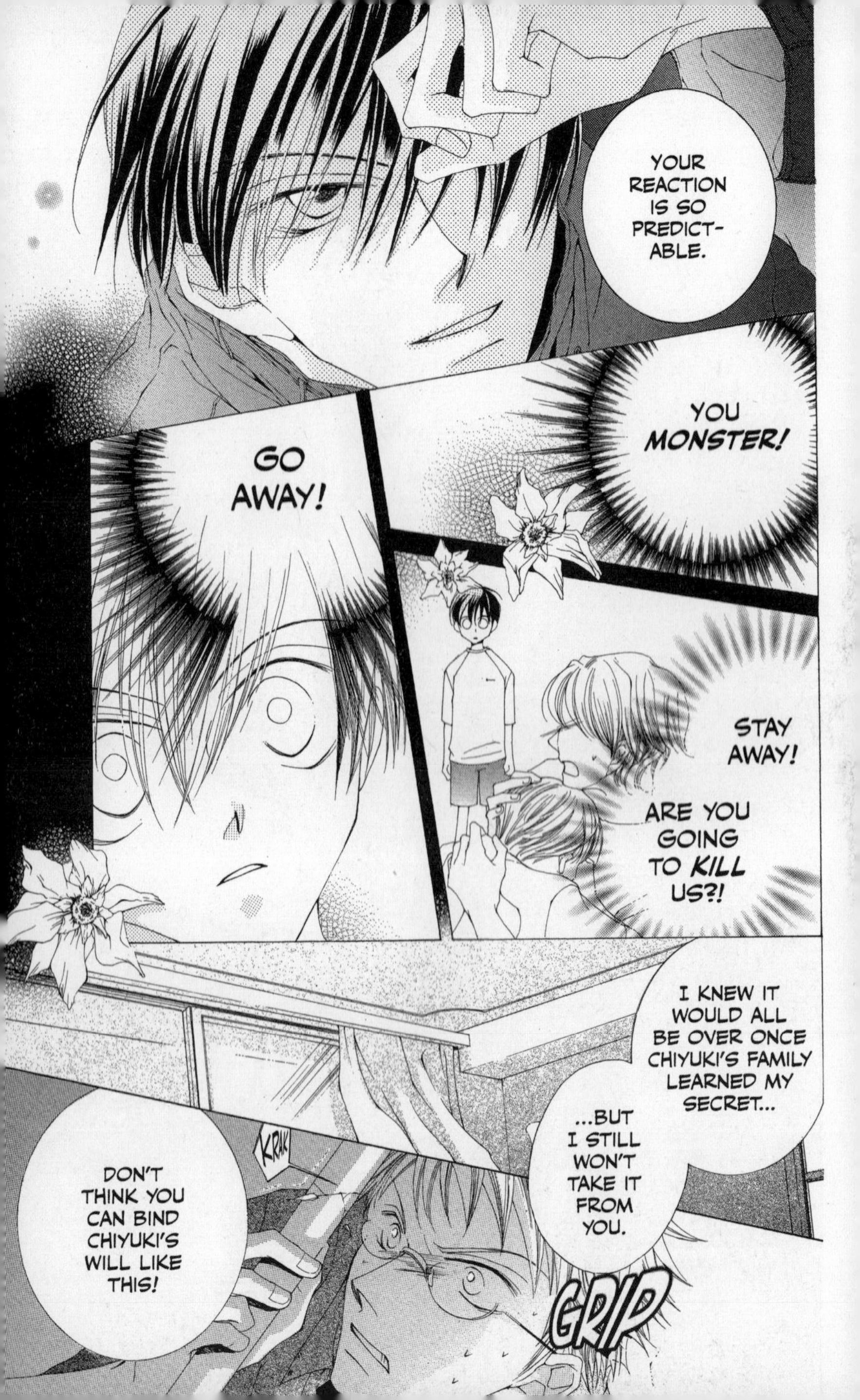
YOUR REACTION IS SO PREDICT-ABLE.
YOU MONSTER!
STAY AWAY!
ARE YOU GOING TO KILL US?!
GO AWAY!
I KNEW IT WOULD ALL BE OVER ONCE CHIYUKI'S FAMILY LEARNED MY SECRET...
...BUT I STILL WON'T TAKE IT FROM YOU.
GRIP
KRAK
DON'T THINK YOU CAN BIND CHIYUKI'S WILL LIKE THIS!

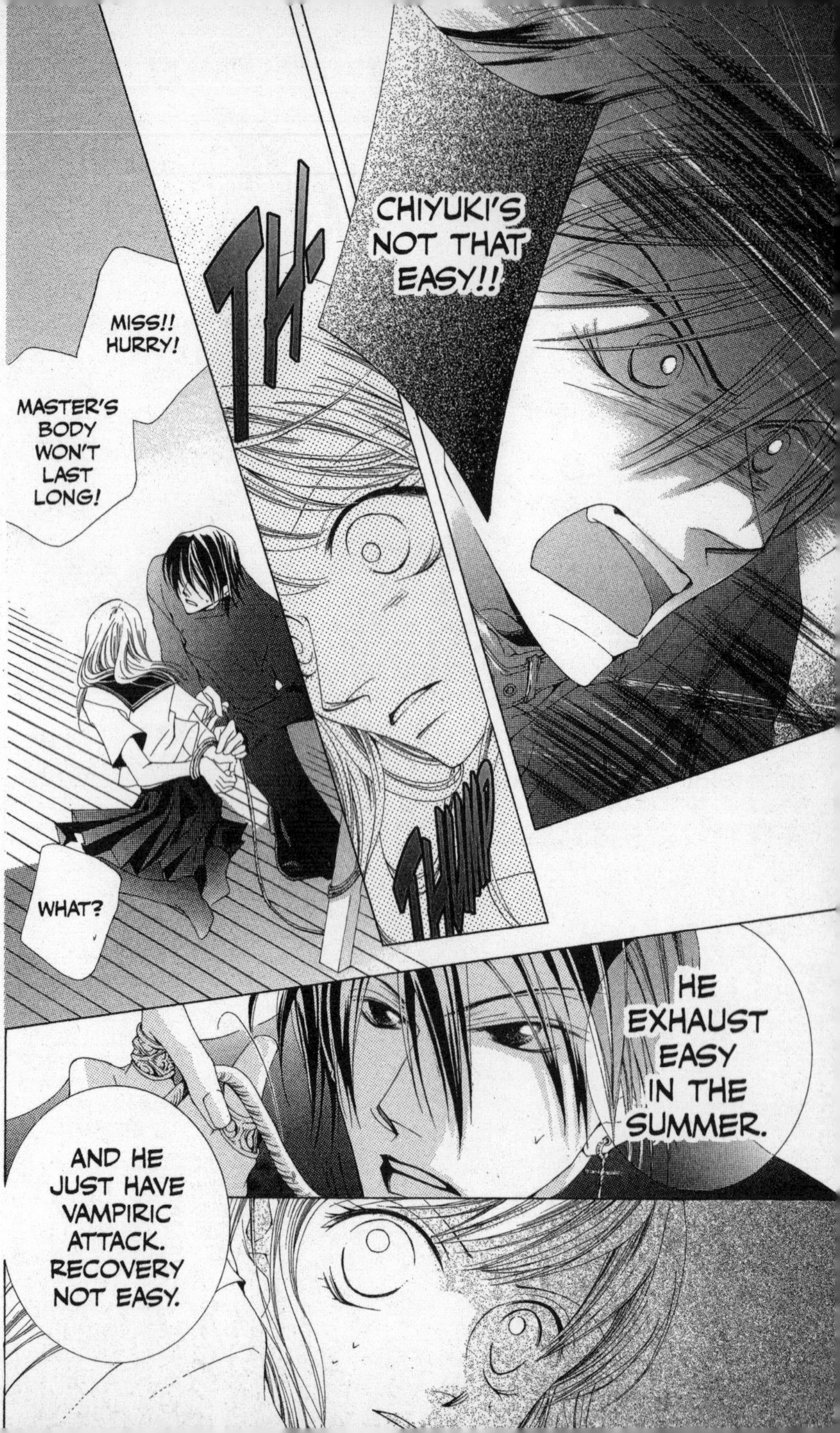
CHIYUKI'S NOT THAT EASY!!
TH-
MISS!! HURRY!
MASTER'S BODY WON'T LAST LONG!
WHAT?
HE EXHAUST EASY IN THE SUMMER.
AND HE JUST HAVE VAMPIRIC ATTACK. RECOVERY NOT EASY.

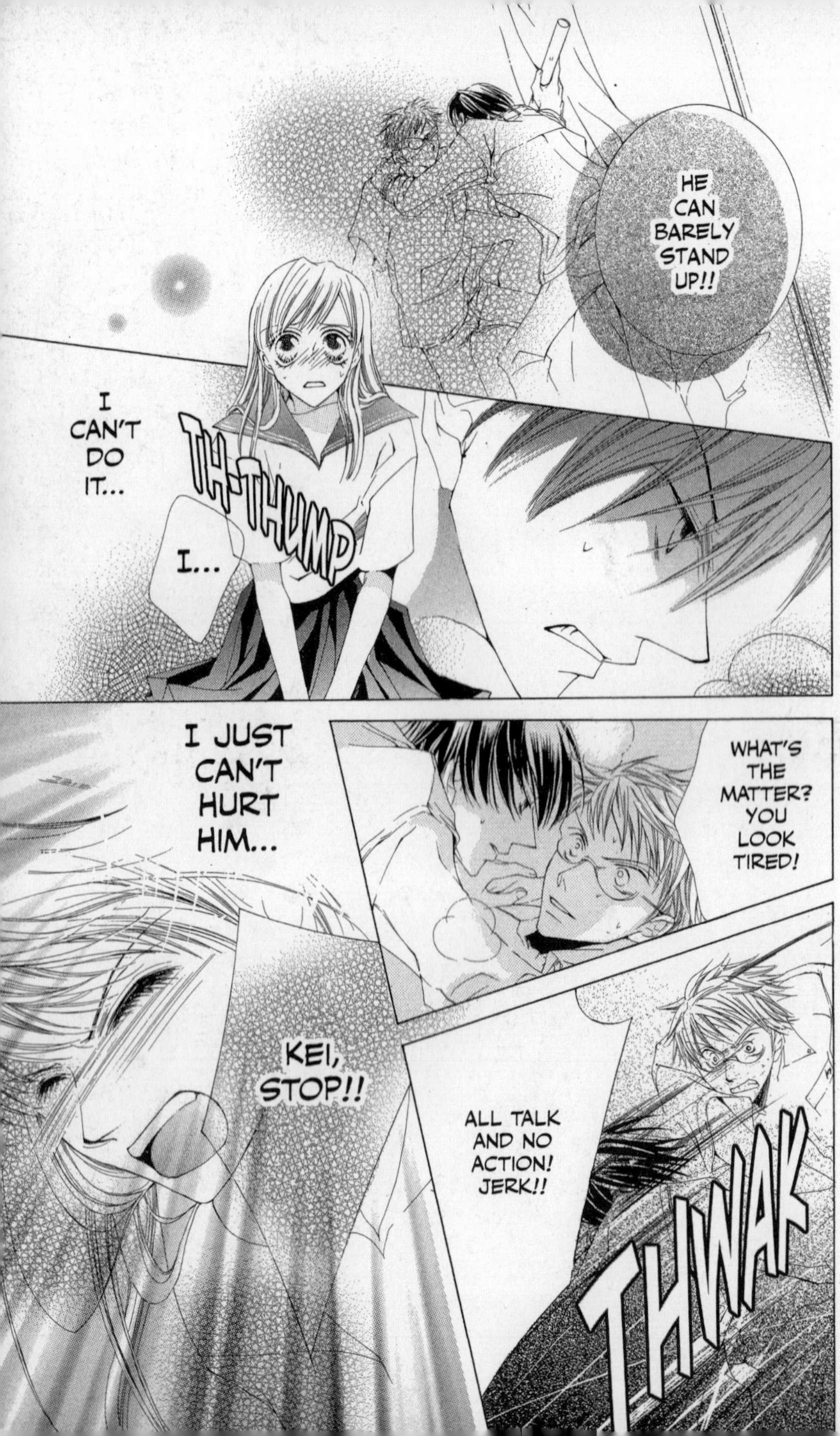
HE CAN BARELY STAND UP!!
I CAN'T DO IT...
TH-THUMP
I...
WHAT'S THE MATTER? YOU LOOK TIRED!
I JUST CAN'T HURT HIM...
ALL TALK AND NO ACTION! JERK!!
THWAK
KEI, STOP!!

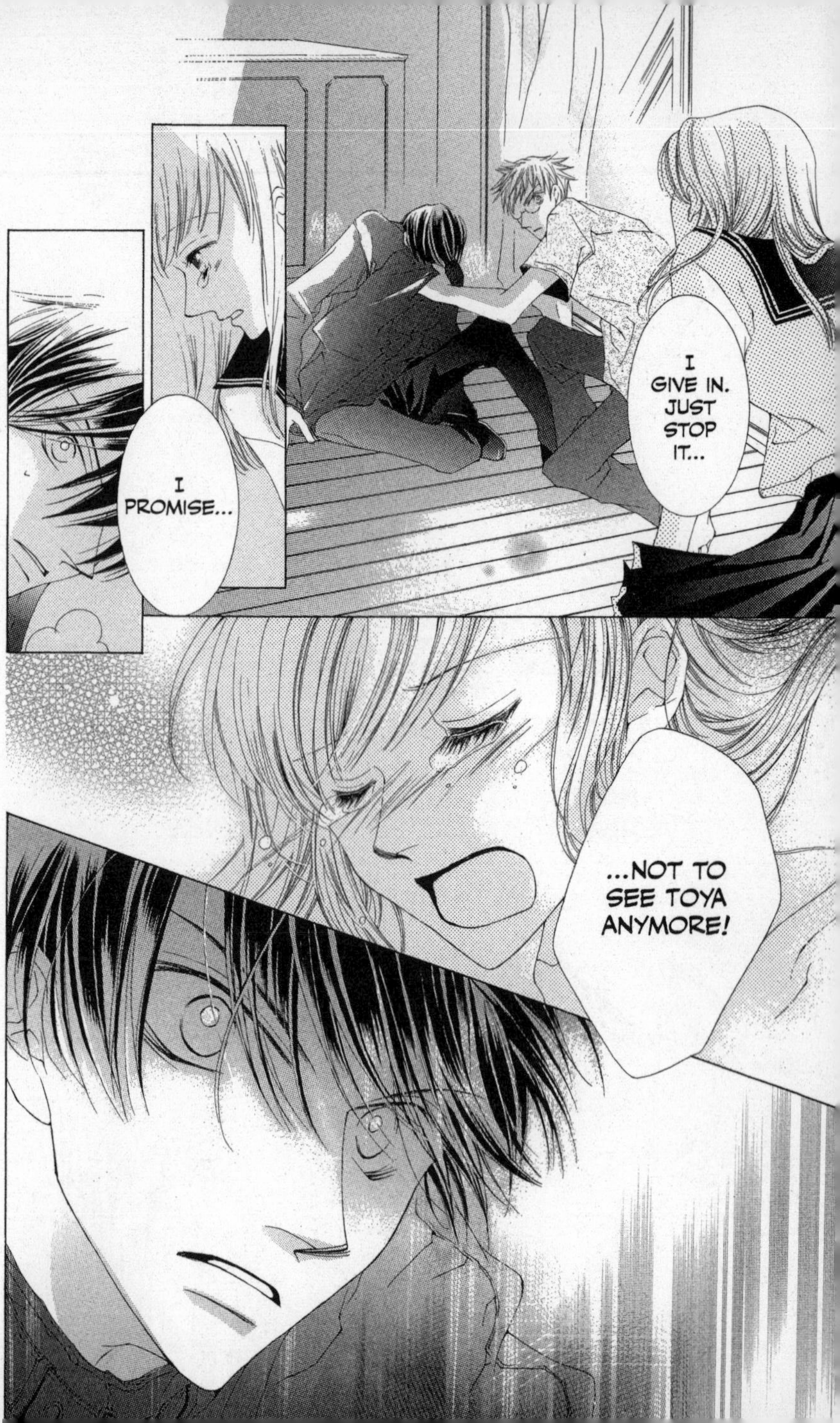
I GIVE IN. JUST STOP IT...
I PROMISE...
...NOT TO SEE TOYA ANYMORE!

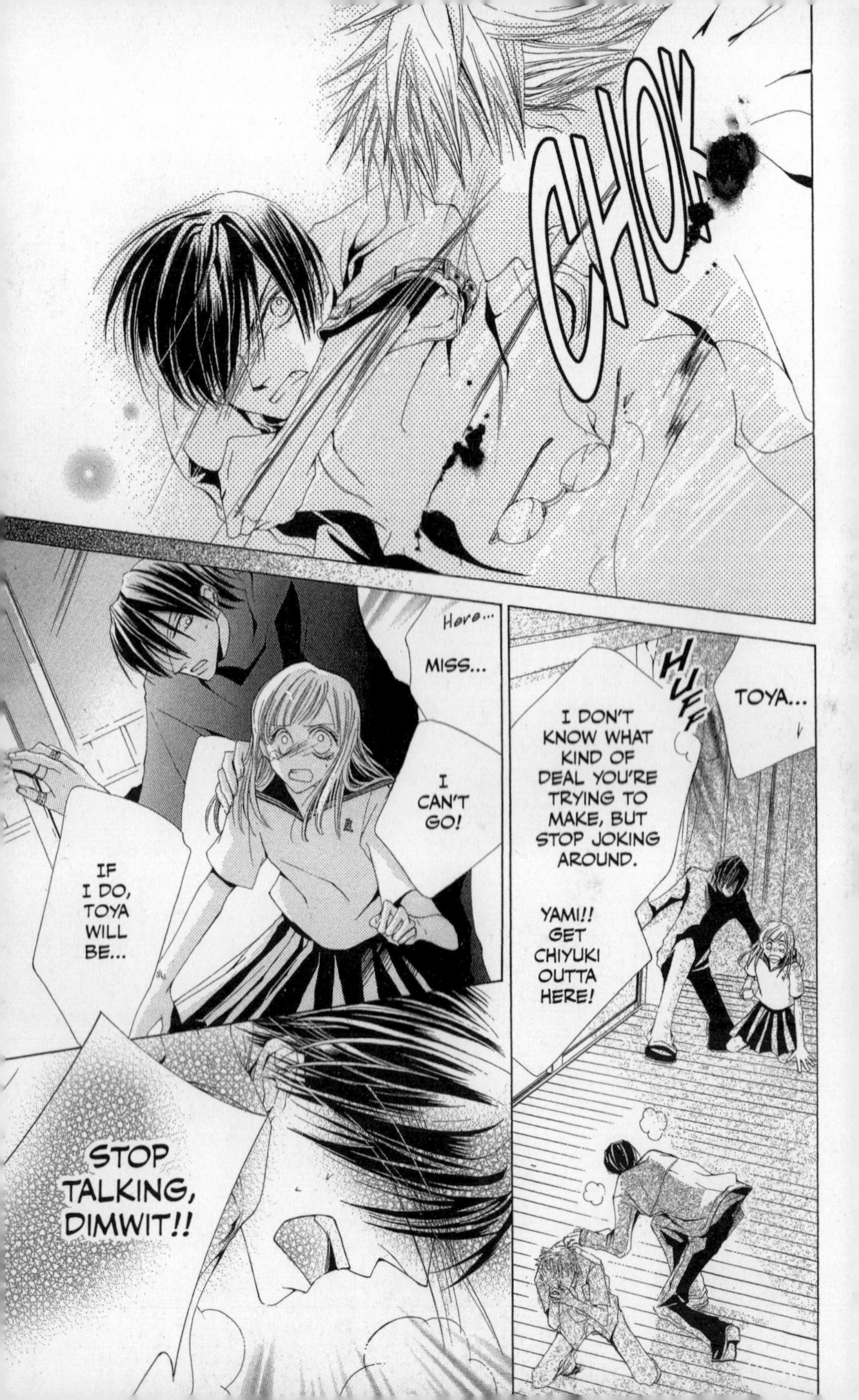
CHOK
HUFF
TOYA...
I DON'T KNOW WHAT KIND OF DEAL YOU'RE TRYING TO MAKE, BUT STOP JOKING AROUND.
YAMI!! GET CHIYUKI OUTTA HERE!
Here...
MISS...
I CAN'T GO!
IF I DO, TOYA WILL BE...
STOP TALKING, DIMWIT!!

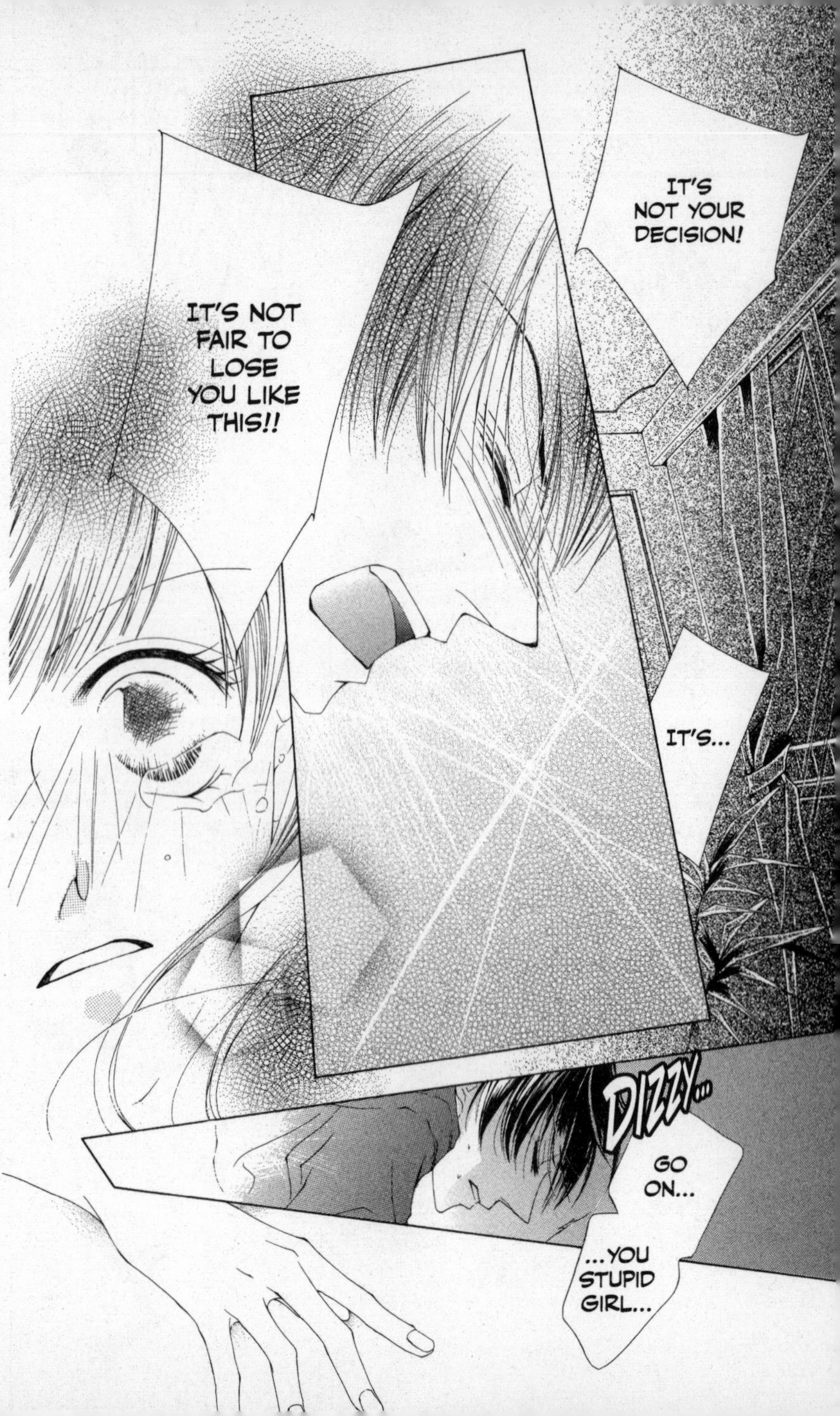
IT'S NOT YOUR DECISION!
IT'S NOT FAIR TO LOSE YOU LIKE THIS!!
IT'S...
DIZZY...
GO ON...
...YOU STUPID GIRL...

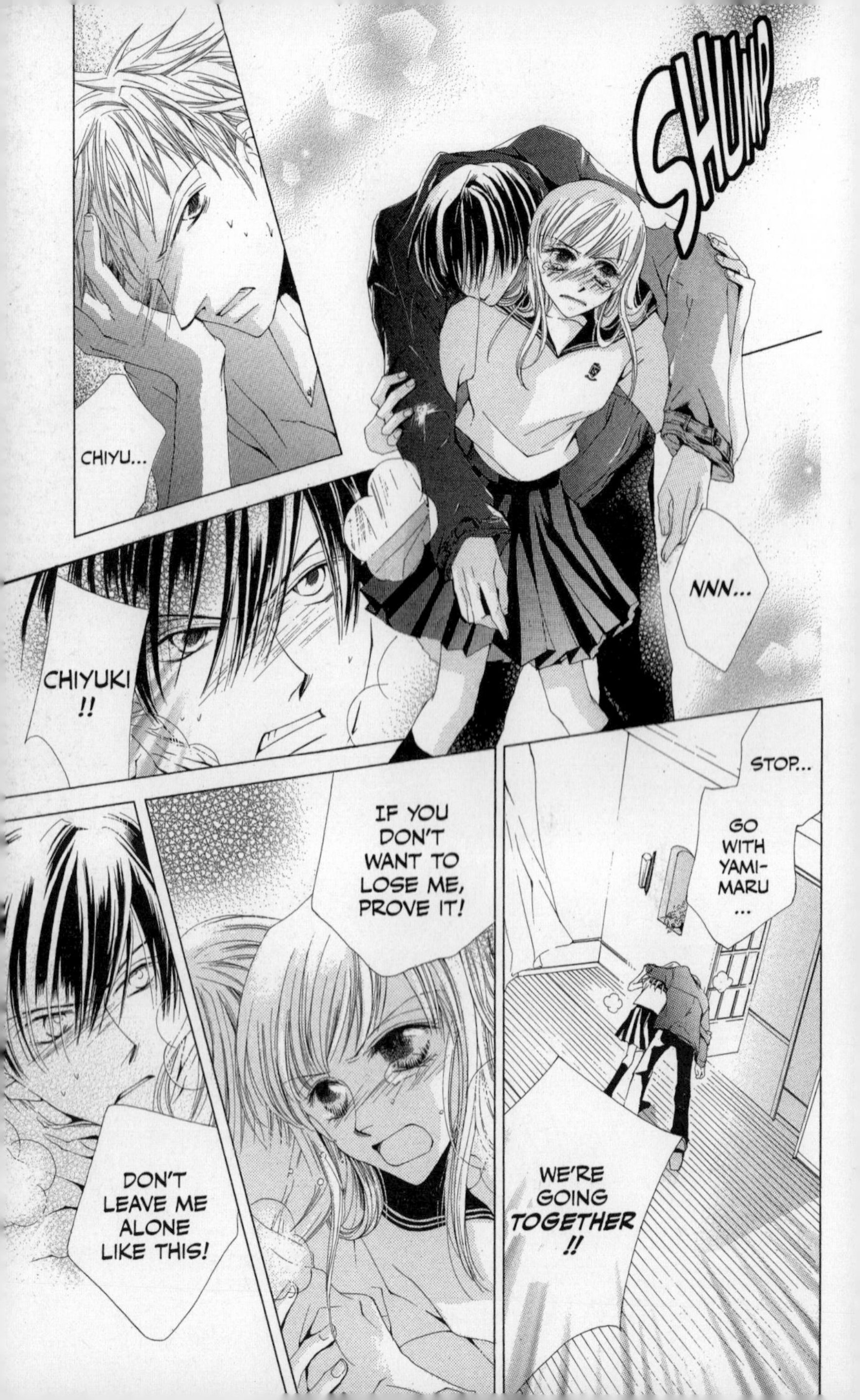
SHUMP
NNN...
CHIYU...
CHIYUKI !!
STOP...
GO WITH YAMI-MARU ...
WE'RE GOING TOGETHER !!
IF YOU DON'T WANT TO LOSE ME, PROVE IT!
DON'T LEAVE ME ALONE LIKE THIS!

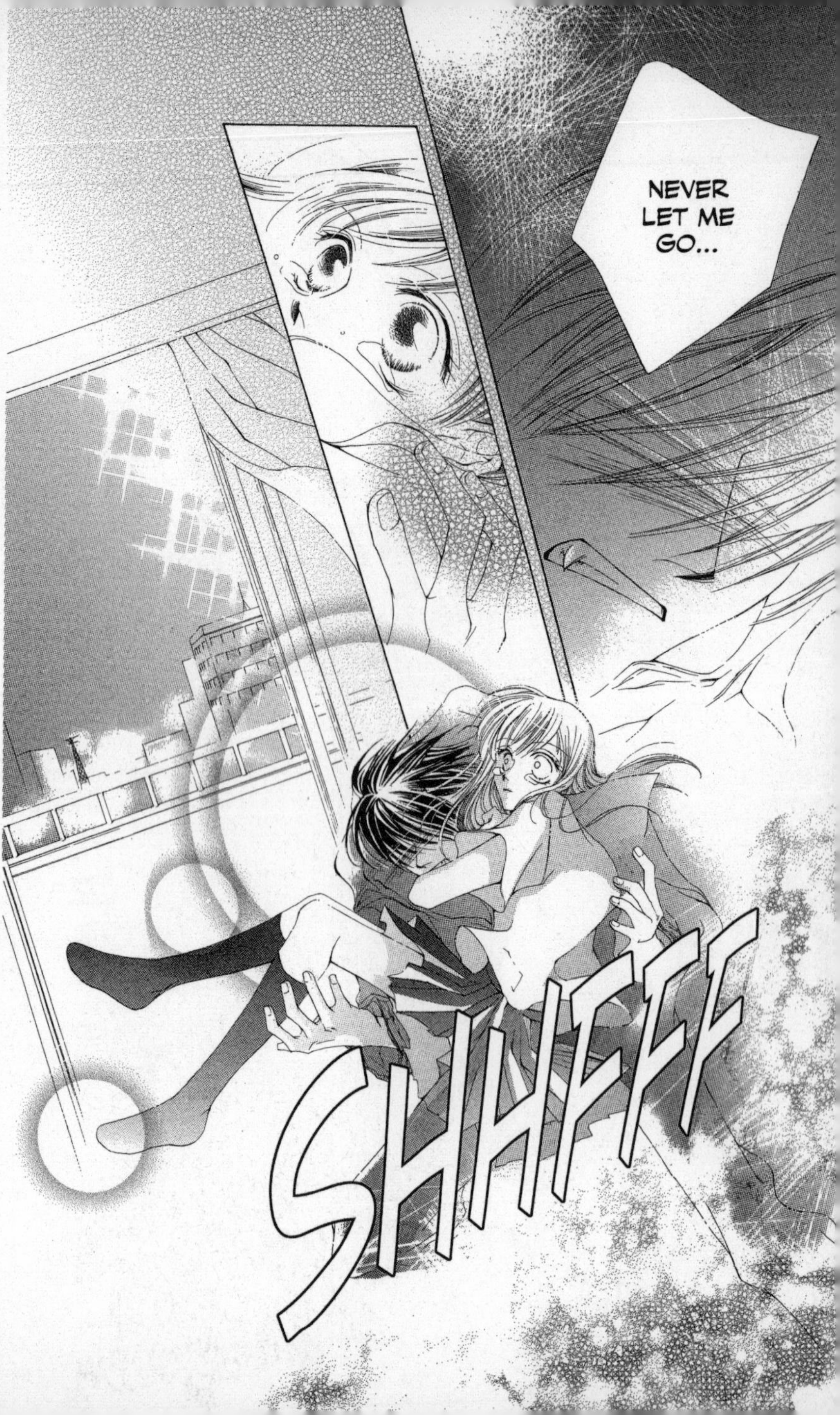
NEVER LET ME GO...
SHHFFF

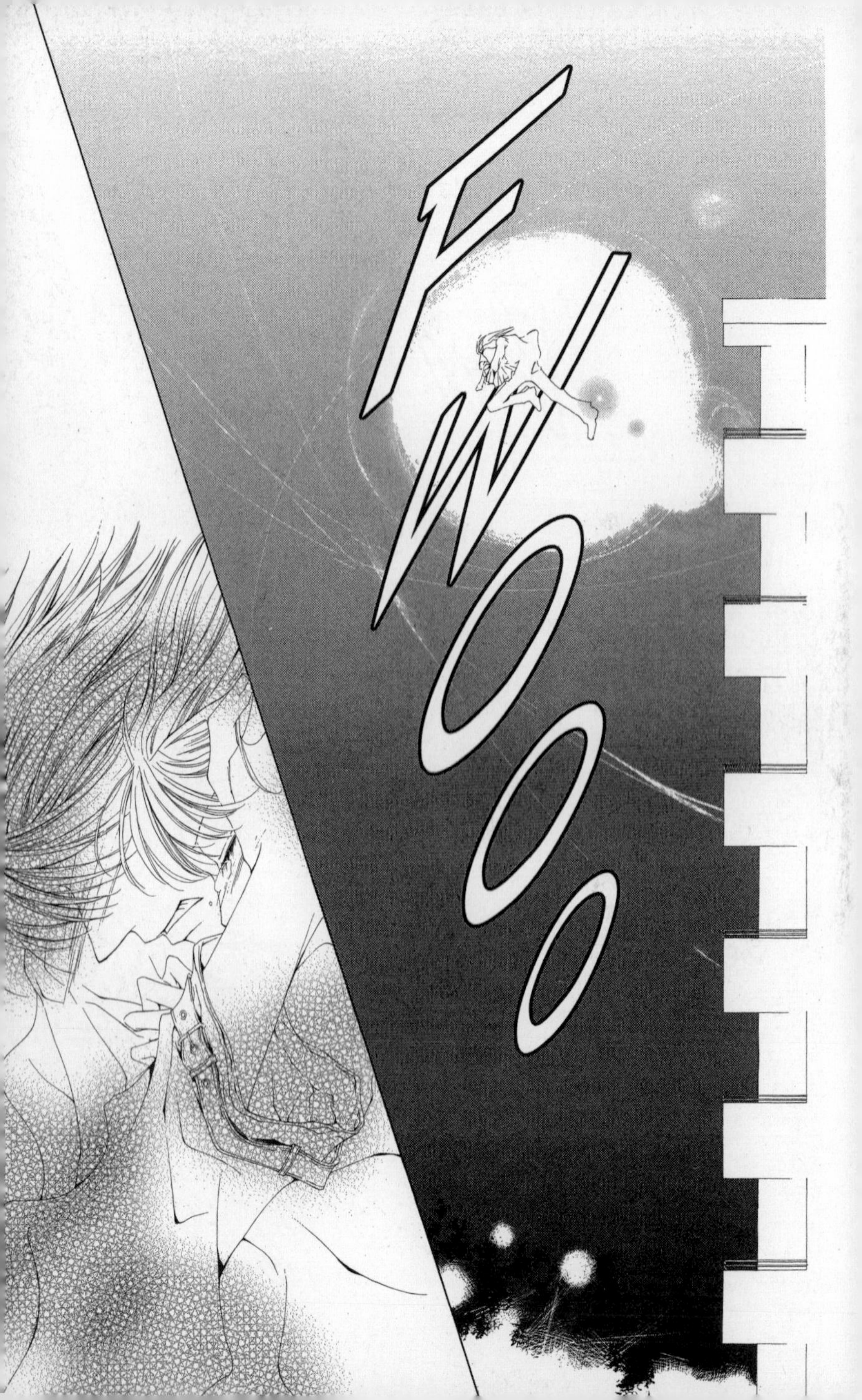
FWOOO

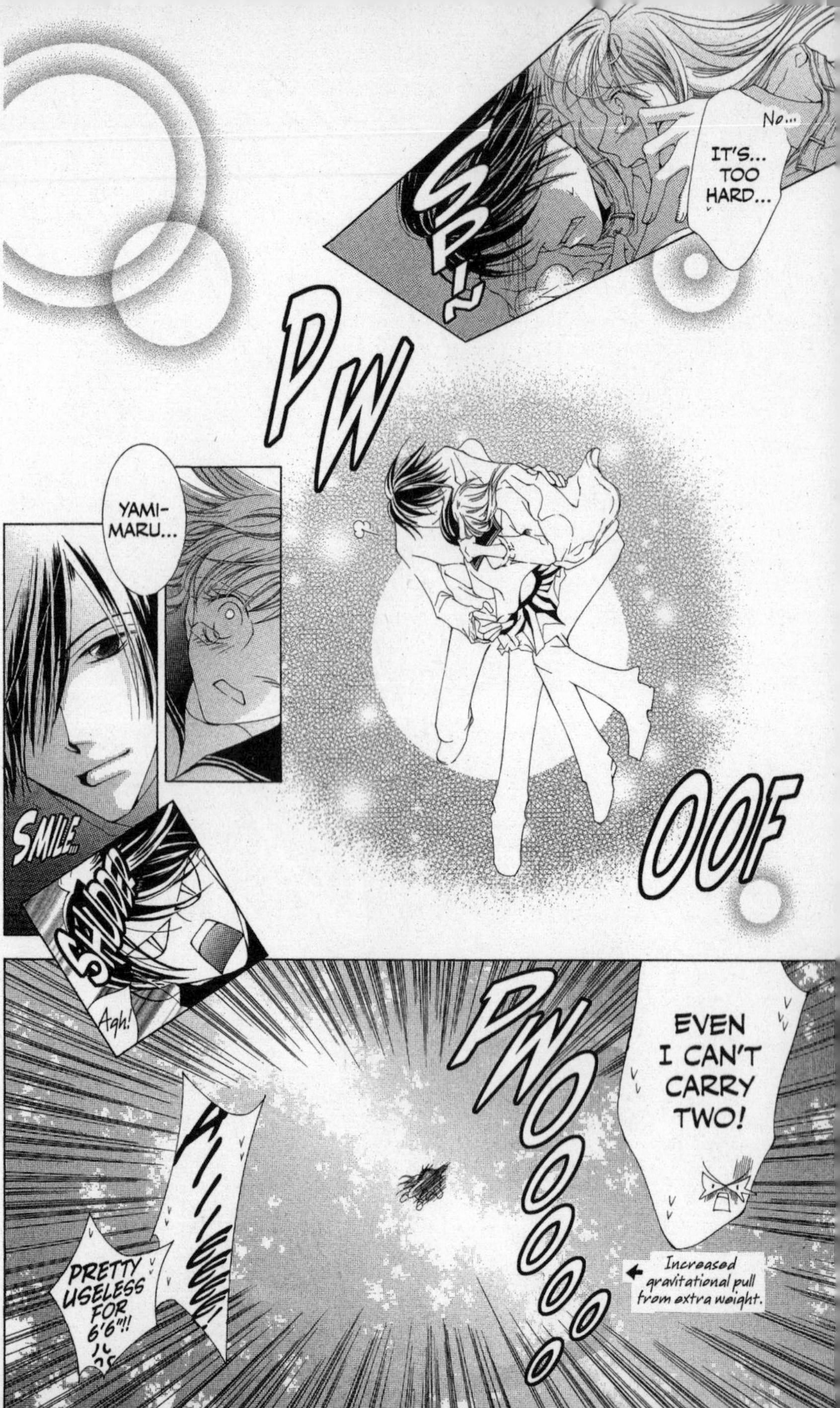
No...
IT'S... TOO HARD...
PW
OOF
YAMI-MARU...
SMILE
Agh!
EVEN I CAN'T CARRY TWO!
Increased gravitational pull from extra weight.
PRETTY USELESS FOR 6'6"!!

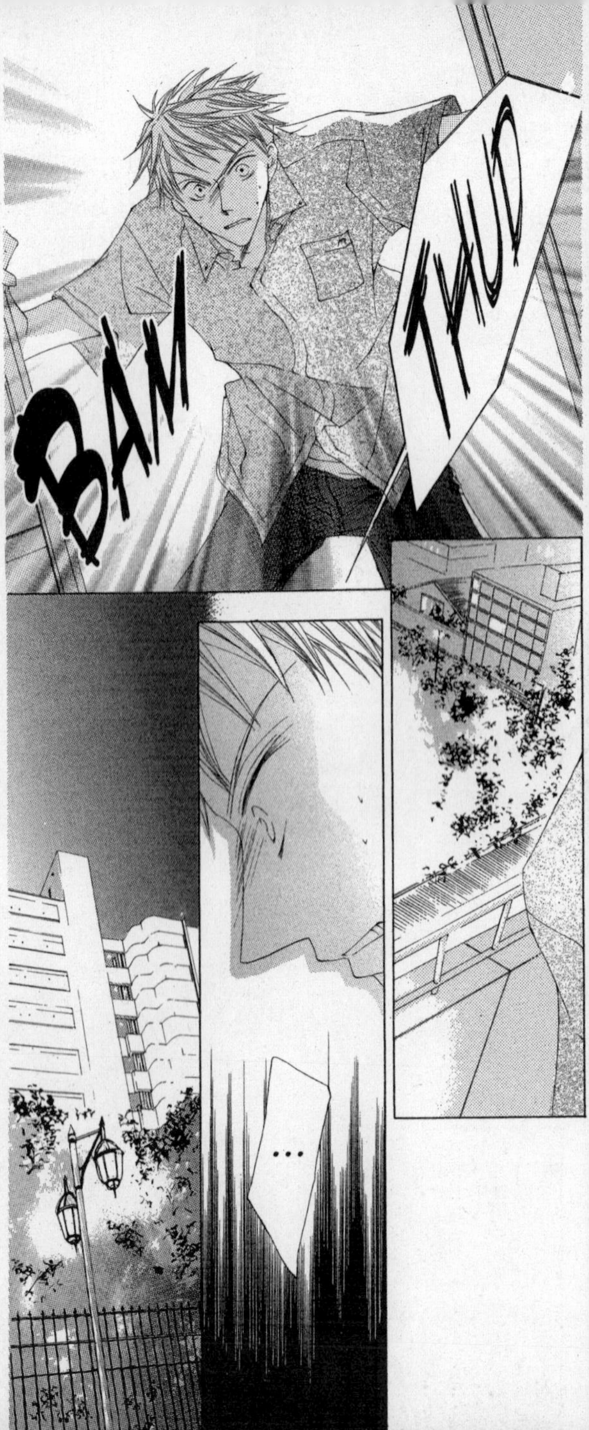
THUD
BAM
...

✧ 葉鳥ビスコ ✧
BISCO·HATORI

Lives in Tokyo
Virgo
Blood type: AB

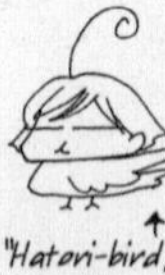

"Hatori-bird," thought up by Noriko Nagahama.

I love the images vampires conjure up, but I'm an extraordinarily faint-hearted person. I can't stand horror movies or even surgery scenes in television dramas. On top of hating bugs and dark places, I even hate bats. (They're too sinewy!)

I love anything written by Shuji Terayama and Ranpo Edogawa, but I can never watch them in visual form. Puppet animation, classic dolls, and deserted structures...the things I am attracted to and the things I am weak at are two sides of the same coin... That's Hatori. Cheers to a life of contradiction!

My latest crazes are Bump of Chicken and Ira Ishida's books. They're so great they make me cry!

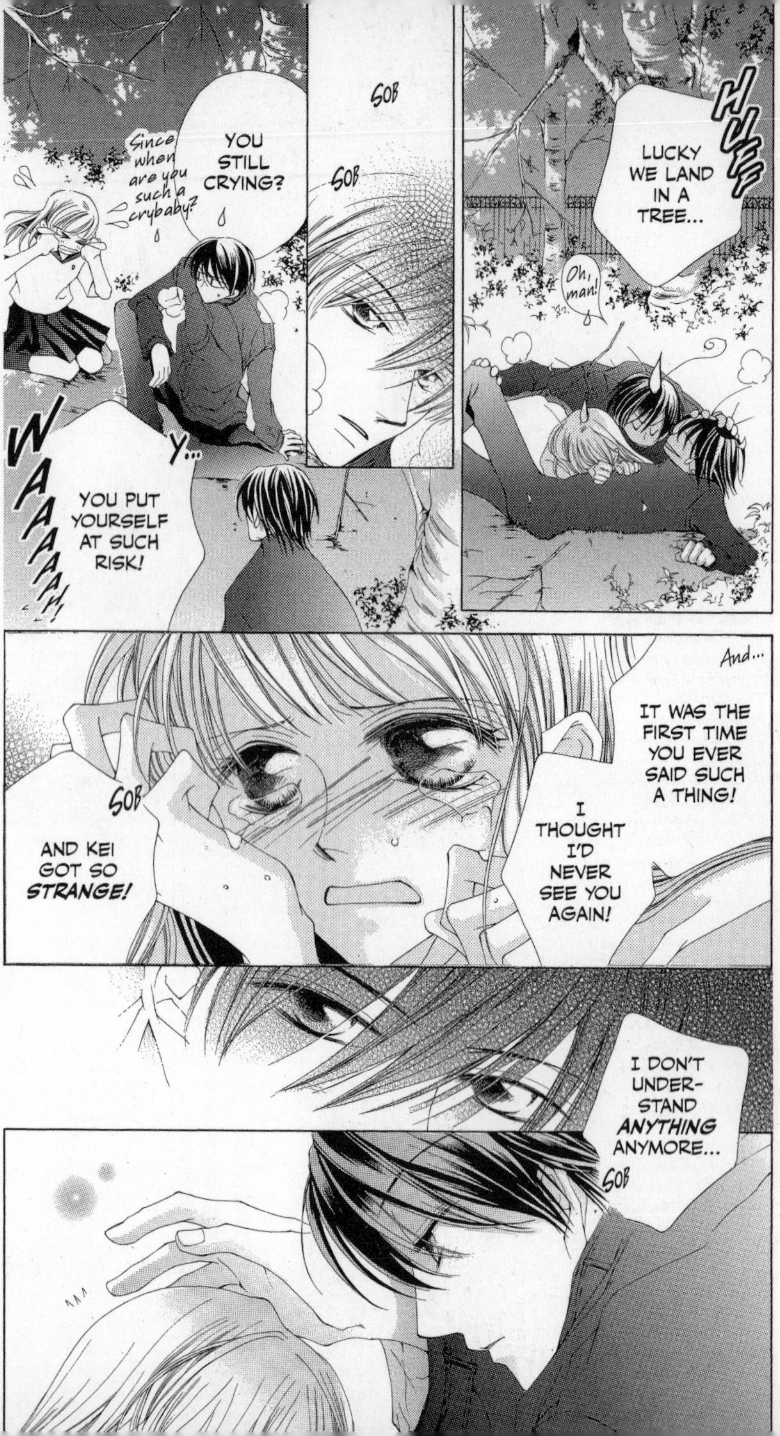
LUCKY WE LAND IN A TREE...
Oh, man!
SOB
SOB
YOU STILL CRYING?
Since when are you such a crybaby?
WAAAAAH!
Y...
YOU PUT YOURSELF AT SUCH RISK!
And...
IT WAS THE FIRST TIME YOU EVER SAID SUCH A THING!
I THOUGHT I'D NEVER SEE YOU AGAIN!
SOB
AND KEI GOT SO STRANGE!
I DON'T UNDER-STAND ANYTHING ANYMORE...
SOB

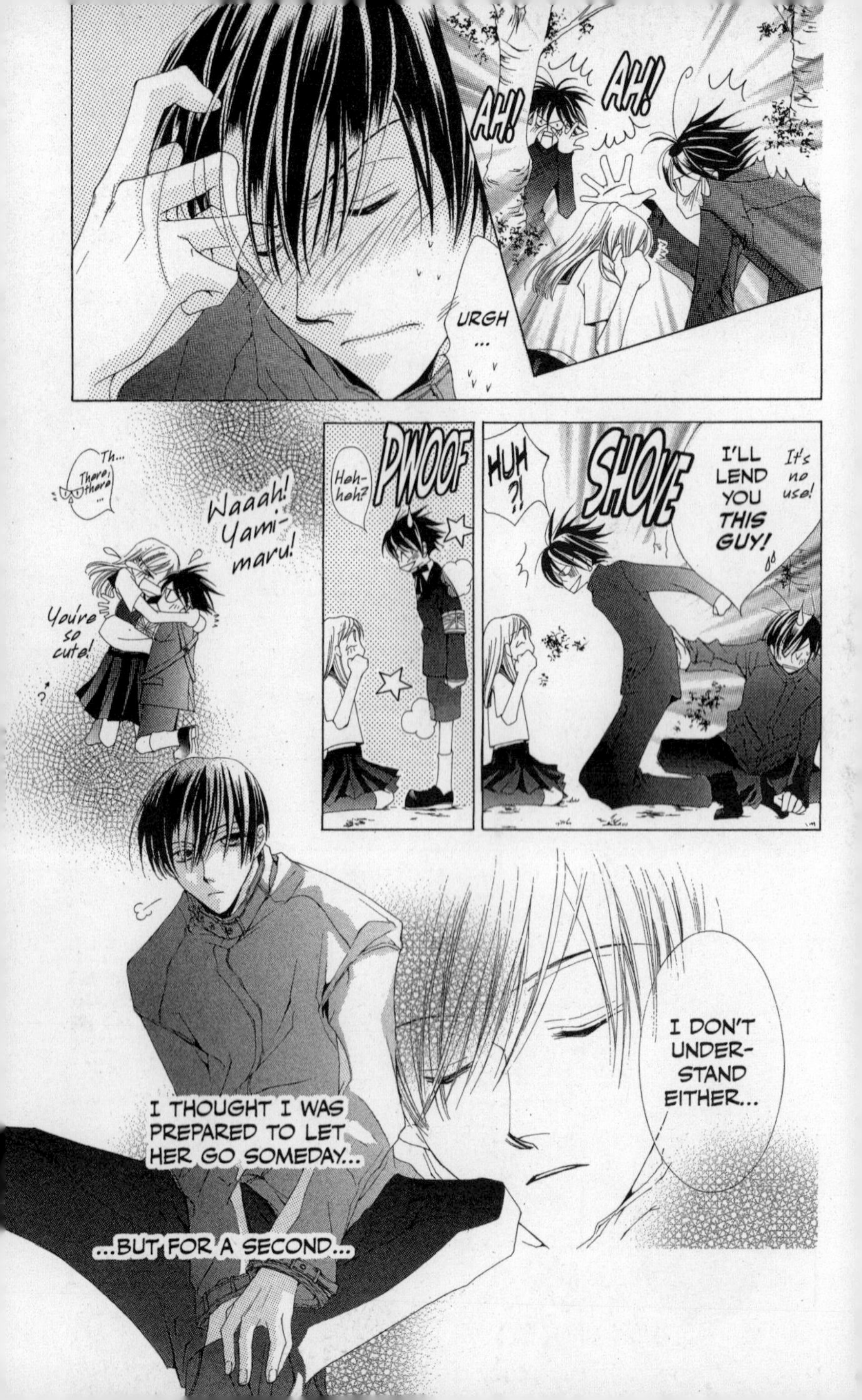
AH!
AH!
URGH ...
It's no use!
I'LL LEND YOU THIS GUY!
SHOVE
HUH ?!
PWOOF
Heh-heh?
Th... There, there ...
Waaah! Yami-maru!
You're so cute!
?
I DON'T UNDER-STAND EITHER...
I THOUGHT I WAS PREPARED TO LET HER GO SOMEDAY...
...BUT FOR A SECOND...

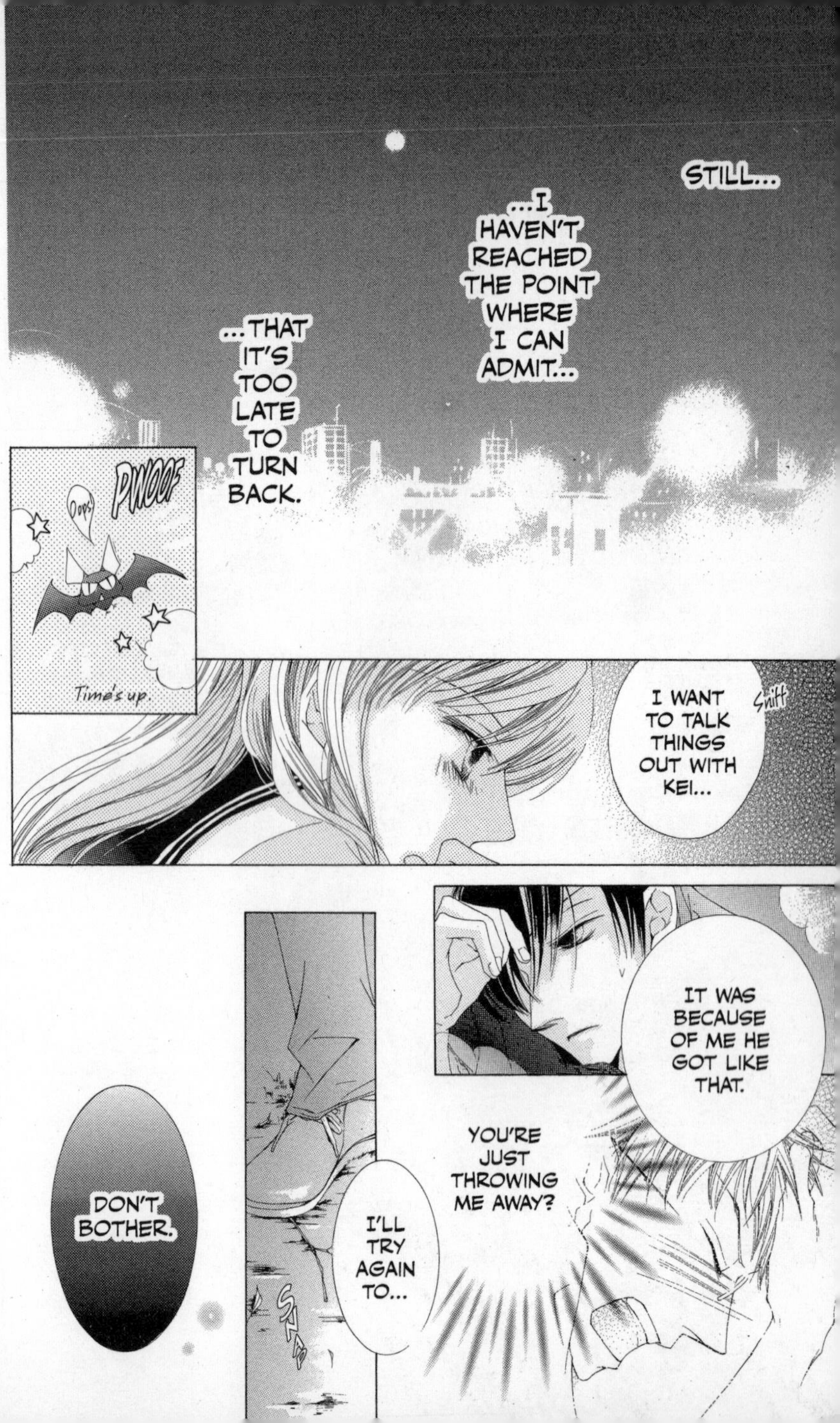
STILL...
...I HAVEN'T REACHED THE POINT WHERE I CAN ADMIT...
...THAT IT'S TOO LATE TO TURN BACK.
I WANT TO TALK THINGS OUT WITH KEI...
Sniff
PWOOF
Oops!
Time's up.
IT WAS BECAUSE OF ME HE GOT LIKE THAT.
YOU'RE JUST THROWING ME AWAY?
I'LL TRY AGAIN TO...
DON'T BOTHER.

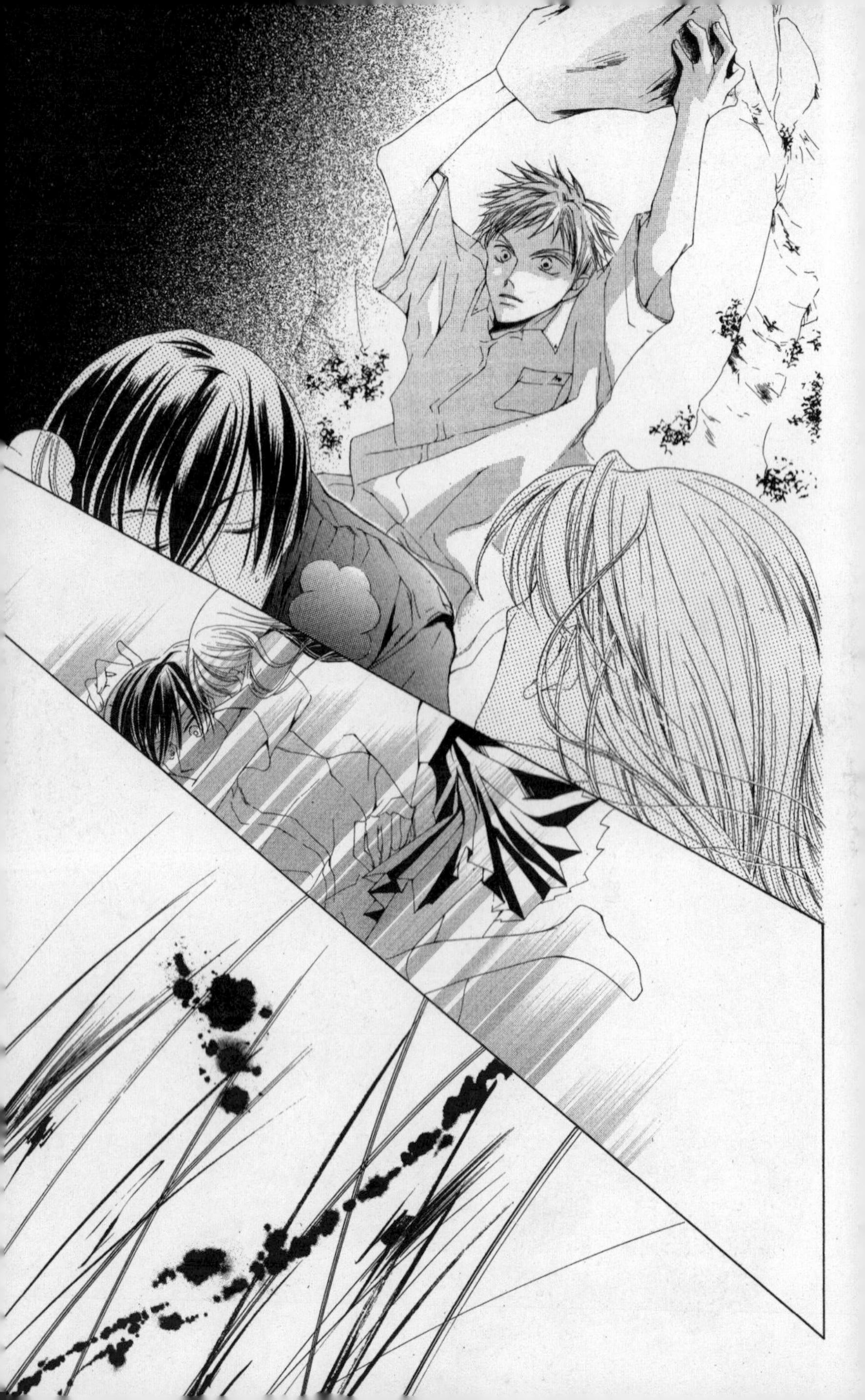

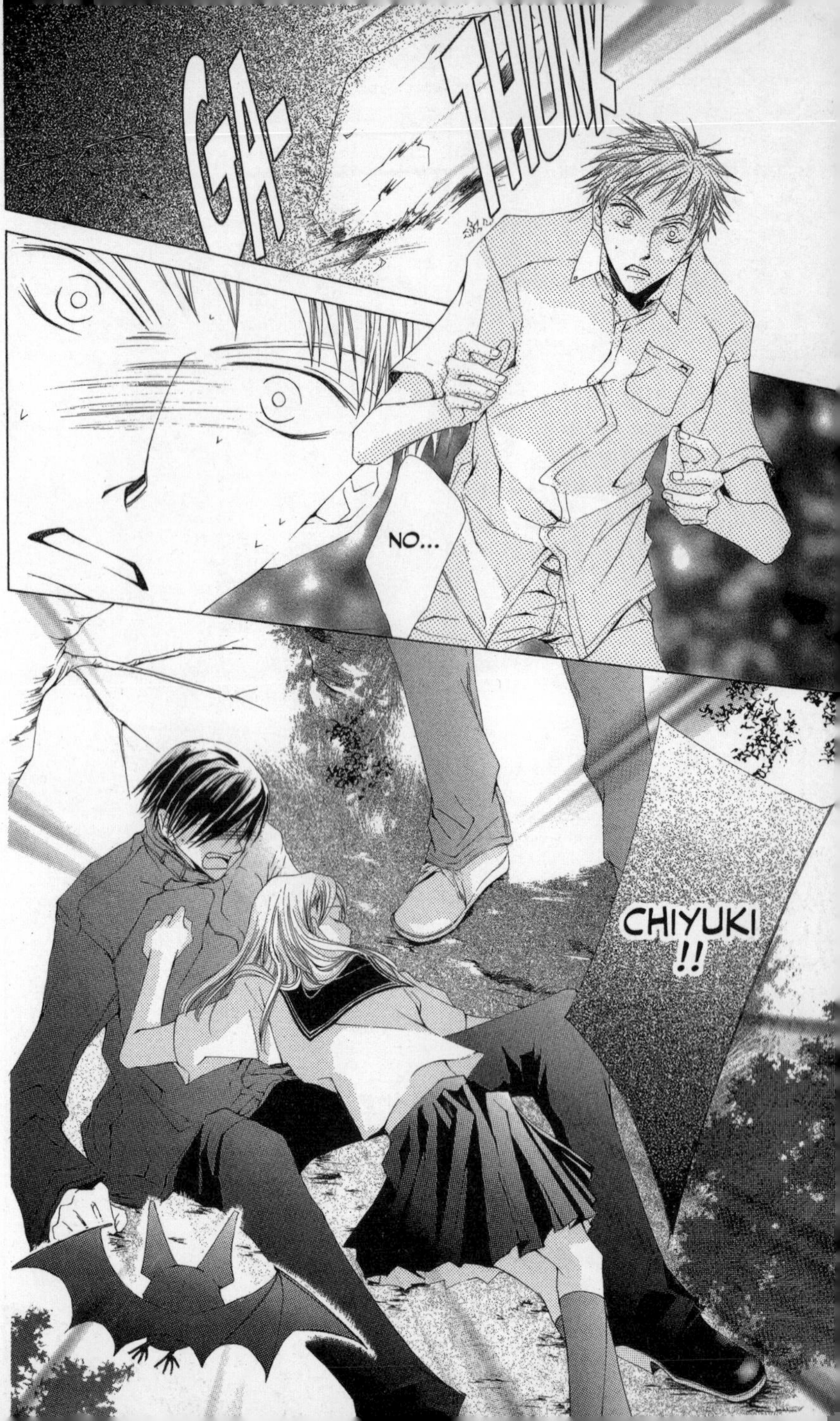
GA-THUNK
NO...
CHIYUKI!!

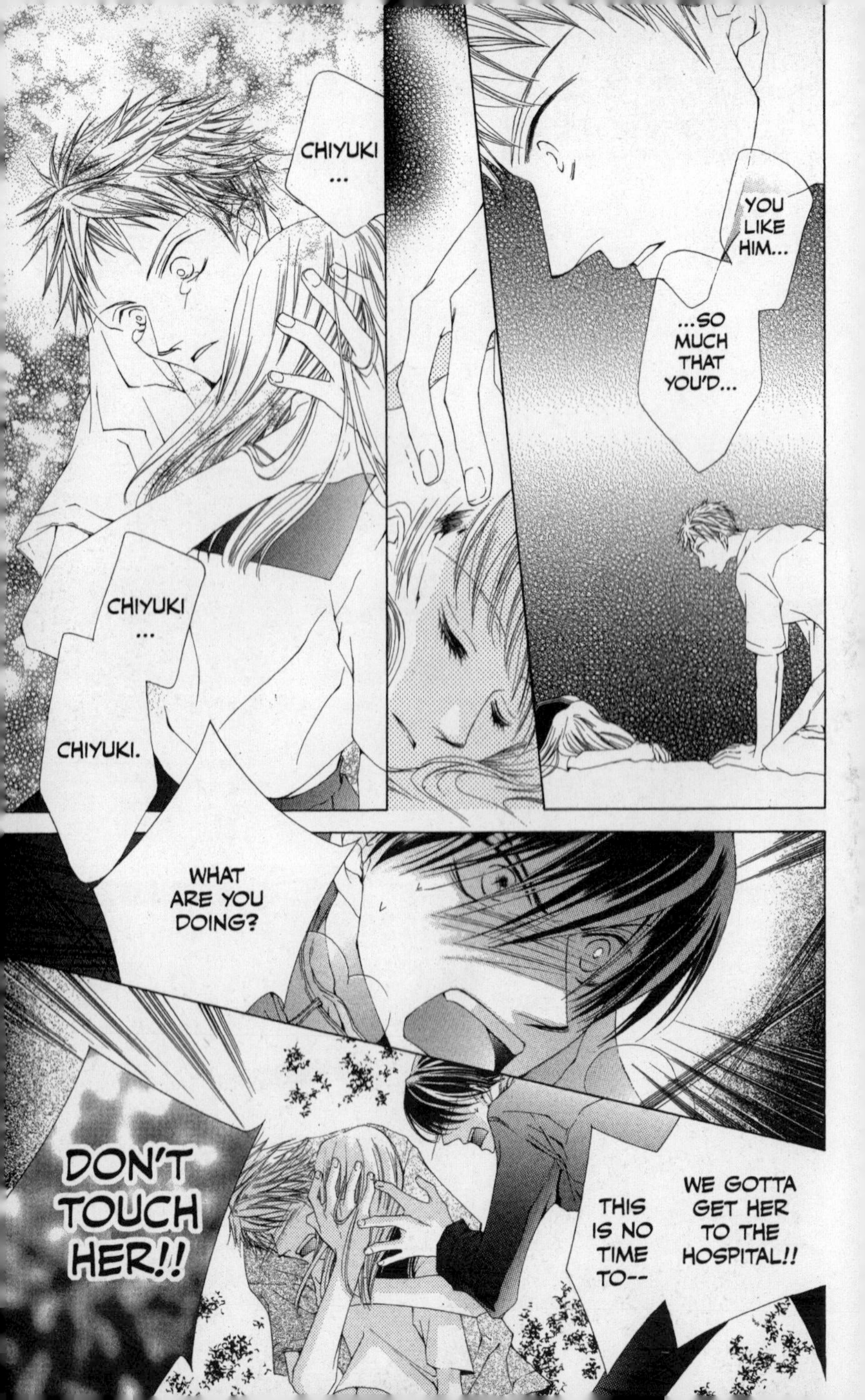
YOU LIKE HIM...
...SO MUCH THAT YOU'D...
CHIYUKI ...
CHIYUKI ...
CHIYUKI.
WHAT ARE YOU DOING?
WE GOTTA GET HER TO THE HOSPITAL!!
THIS IS NO TIME TO--
DON'T TOUCH HER!!

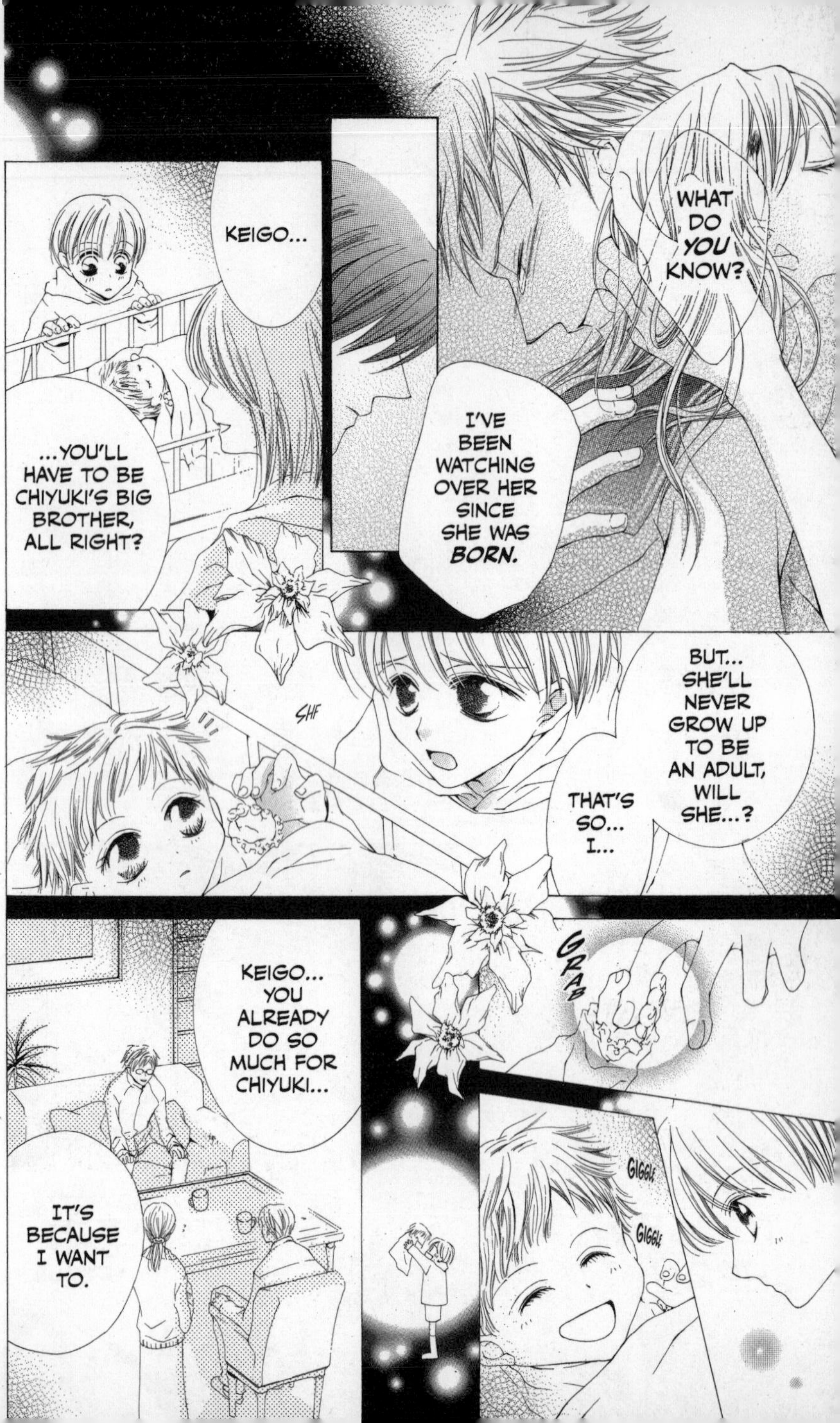
WHAT DO YOU KNOW?
I'VE BEEN WATCHING OVER HER SINCE SHE WAS BORN.
KEIGO...
...YOU'LL HAVE TO BE CHIYUKI'S BIG BROTHER, ALL RIGHT?
BUT... SHE'LL NEVER GROW UP TO BE AN ADULT, WILL SHE...?
THAT'S SO... I...
SHF
GRAB
GIGGLE
GIGGLE
KEIGO... YOU ALREADY DO SO MUCH FOR CHIYUKI...
IT'S BECAUSE I WANT TO.

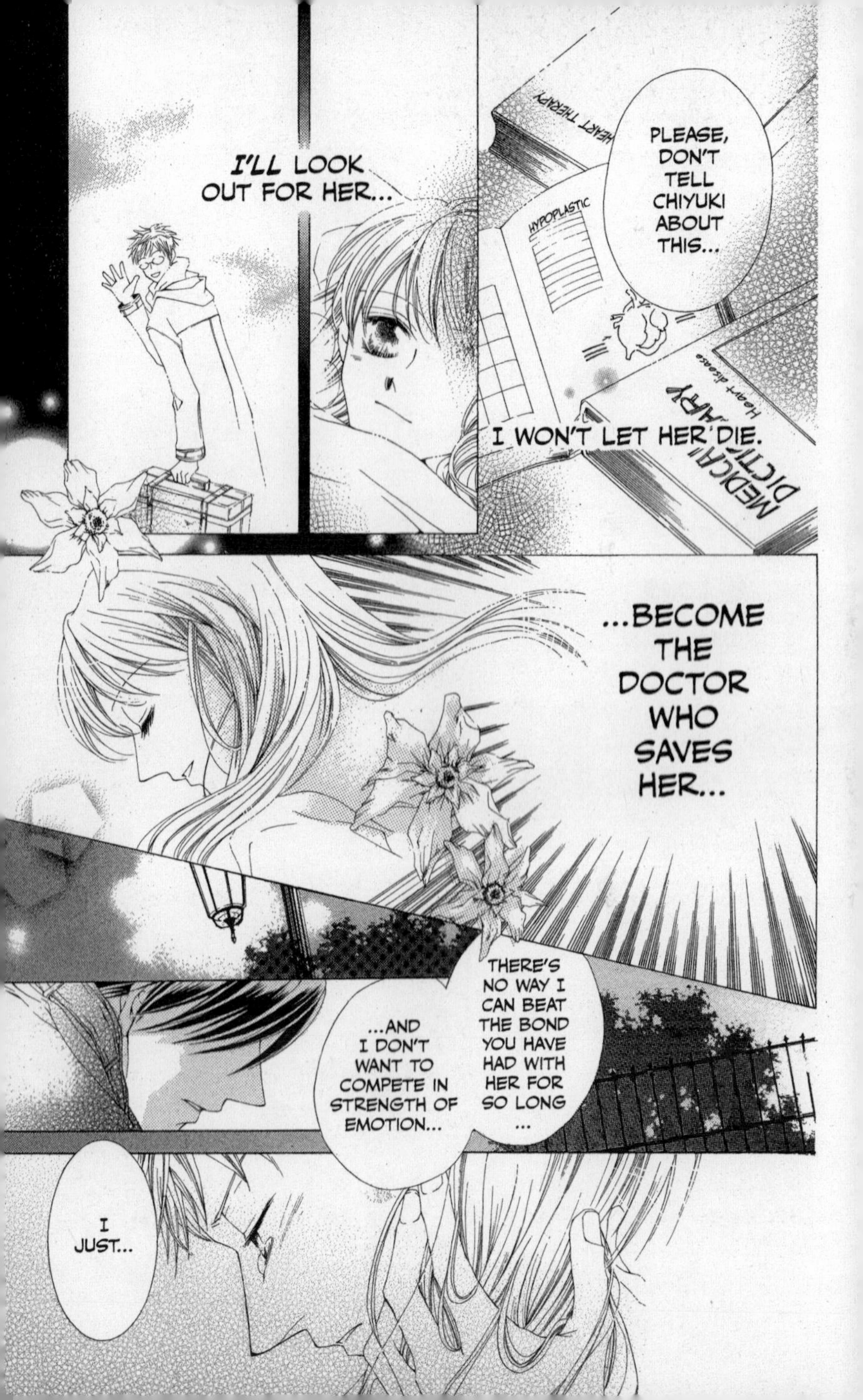
PLEASE, DON'T TELL CHIYUKI ABOUT THIS...
HEART THERAPY
HYPOPLASTIC
Heart disease
I WON'T LET HER DIE.
I'LL LOOK OUT FOR HER...
...BECOME THE DOCTOR WHO SAVES HER...
THERE'S NO WAY I CAN BEAT THE BOND YOU HAVE HAD WITH HER FOR SO LONG ...
...AND I DON'T WANT TO COMPETE IN STRENGTH OF EMOTION...
I JUST...

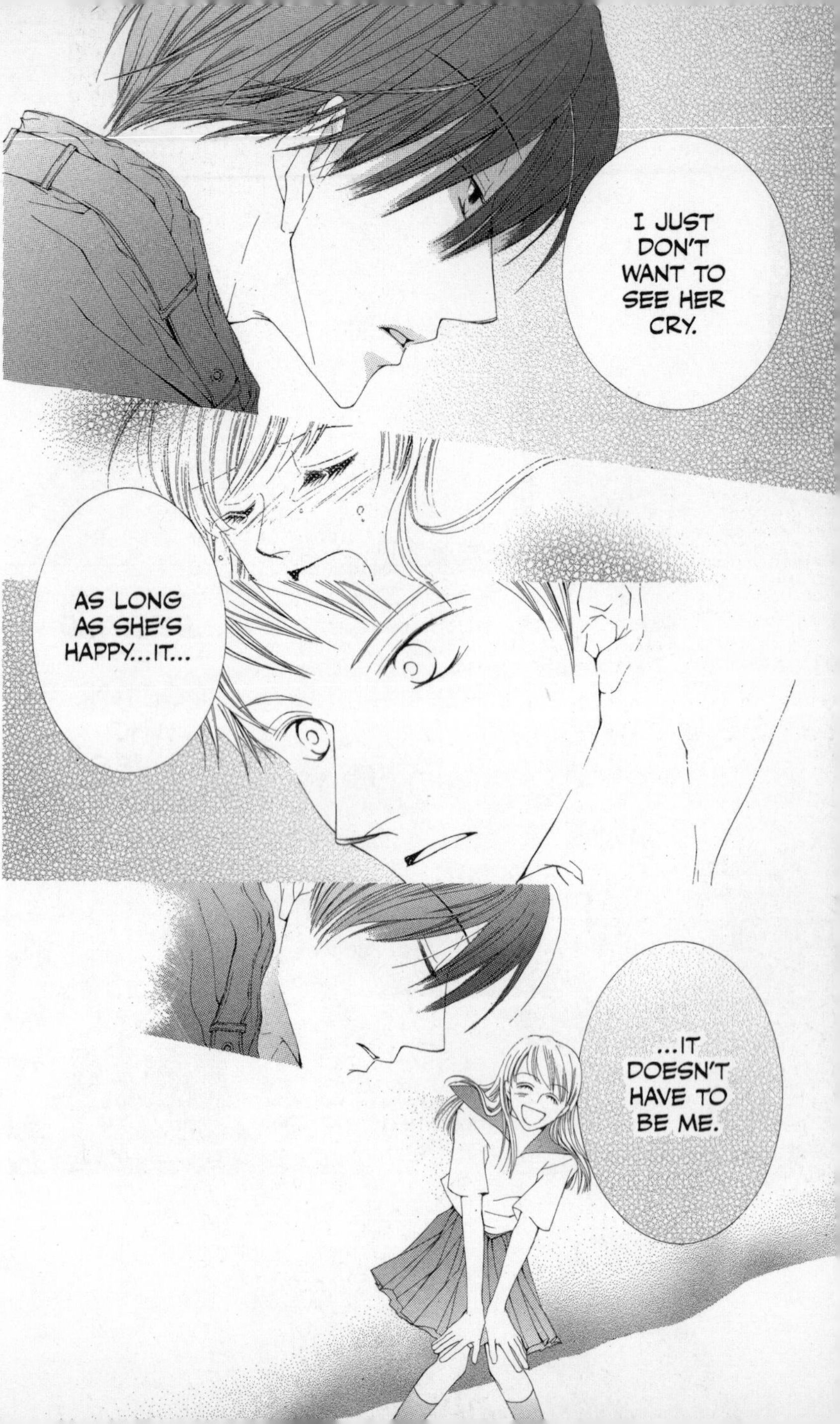
I JUST DON'T WANT TO SEE HER CRY.
AS LONG AS SHE'S HAPPY...IT...
...IT DOESN'T HAVE TO BE ME.

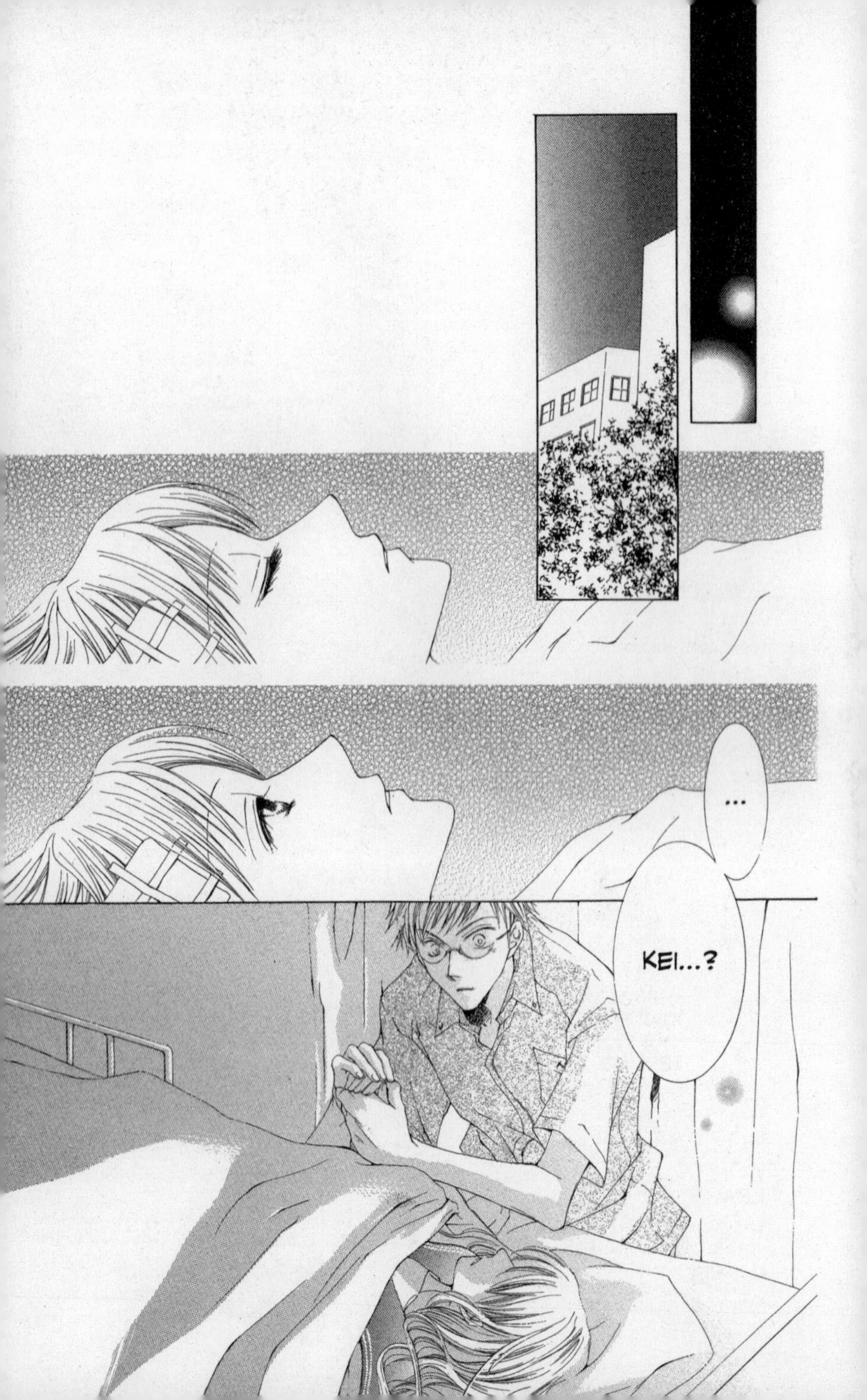
...
KEI...?

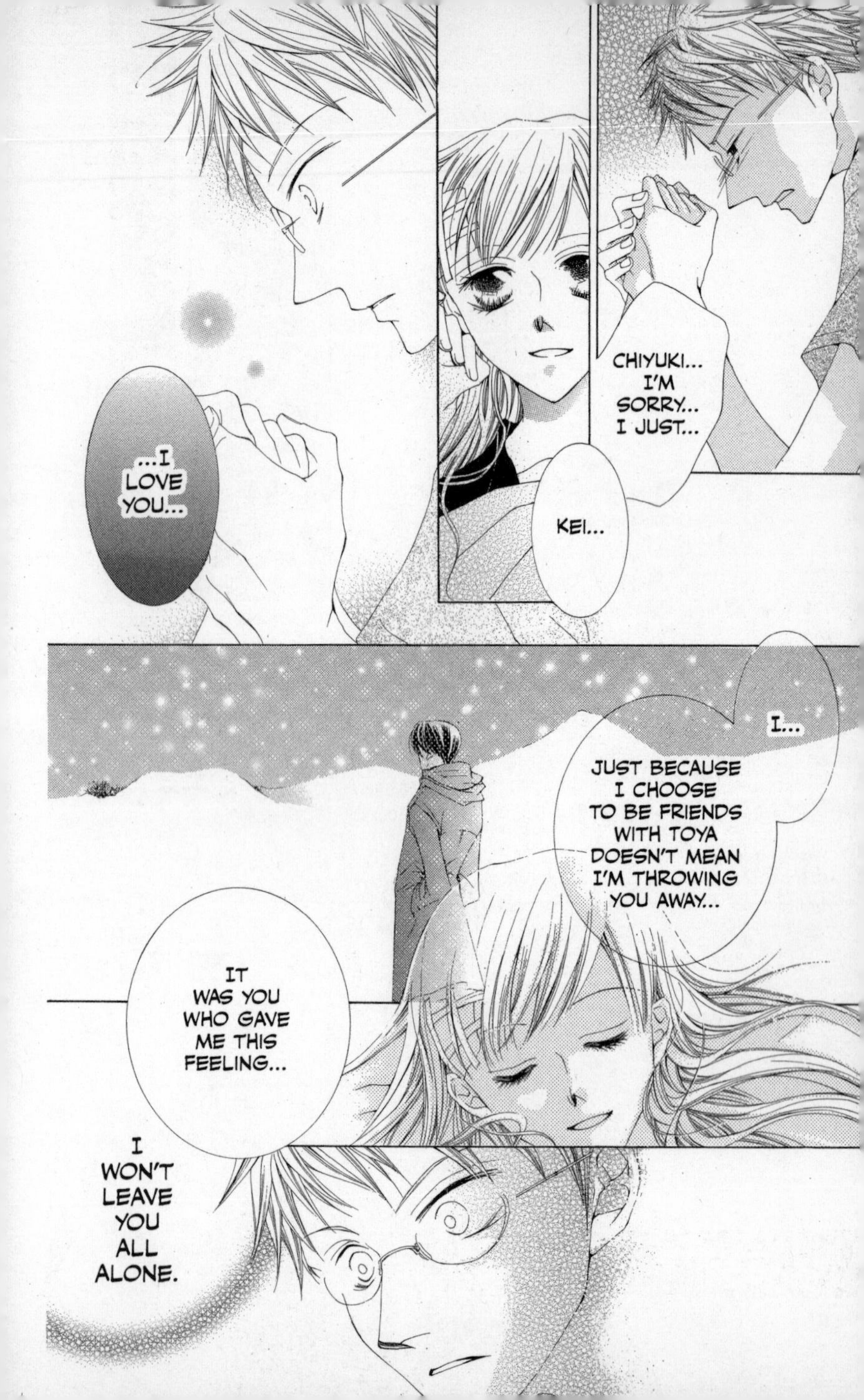
CHIYUKI... I'M SORRY... I JUST...
KEI...
...I LOVE YOU...
I...
JUST BECAUSE I CHOOSE TO BE FRIENDS WITH TOYA DOESN'T MEAN I'M THROWING YOU AWAY...
IT WAS YOU WHO GAVE ME THIS FEELING...
I WON'T LEAVE YOU ALL ALONE.

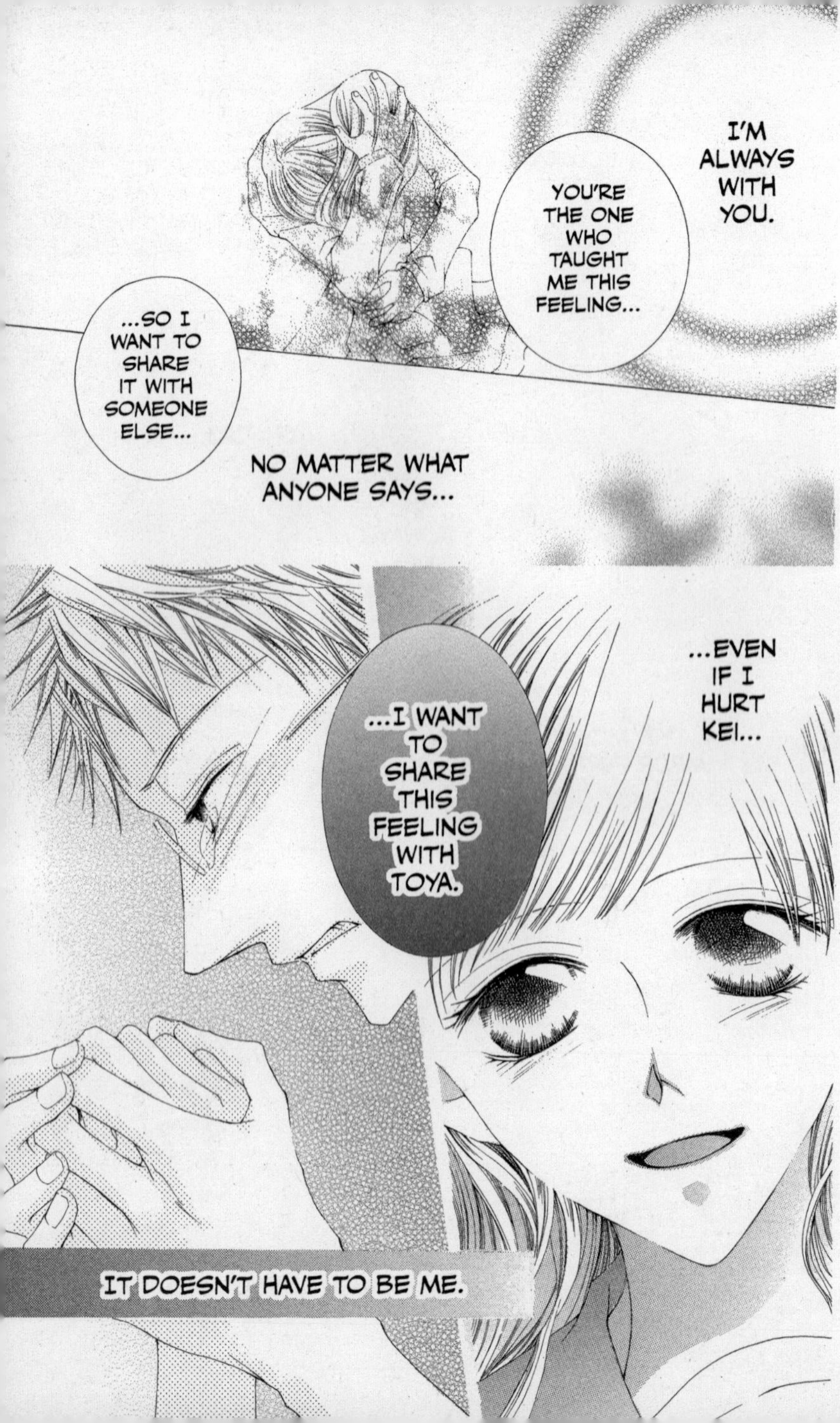
I'M ALWAYS WITH YOU.
YOU'RE THE ONE WHO TAUGHT ME THIS FEELING...
...SO I WANT TO SHARE IT WITH SOMEONE ELSE...
NO MATTER WHAT ANYONE SAYS...
...EVEN IF I HURT KEI...
...I WANT TO SHARE THIS FEELING WITH TOYA.
IT DOESN'T HAVE TO BE ME.

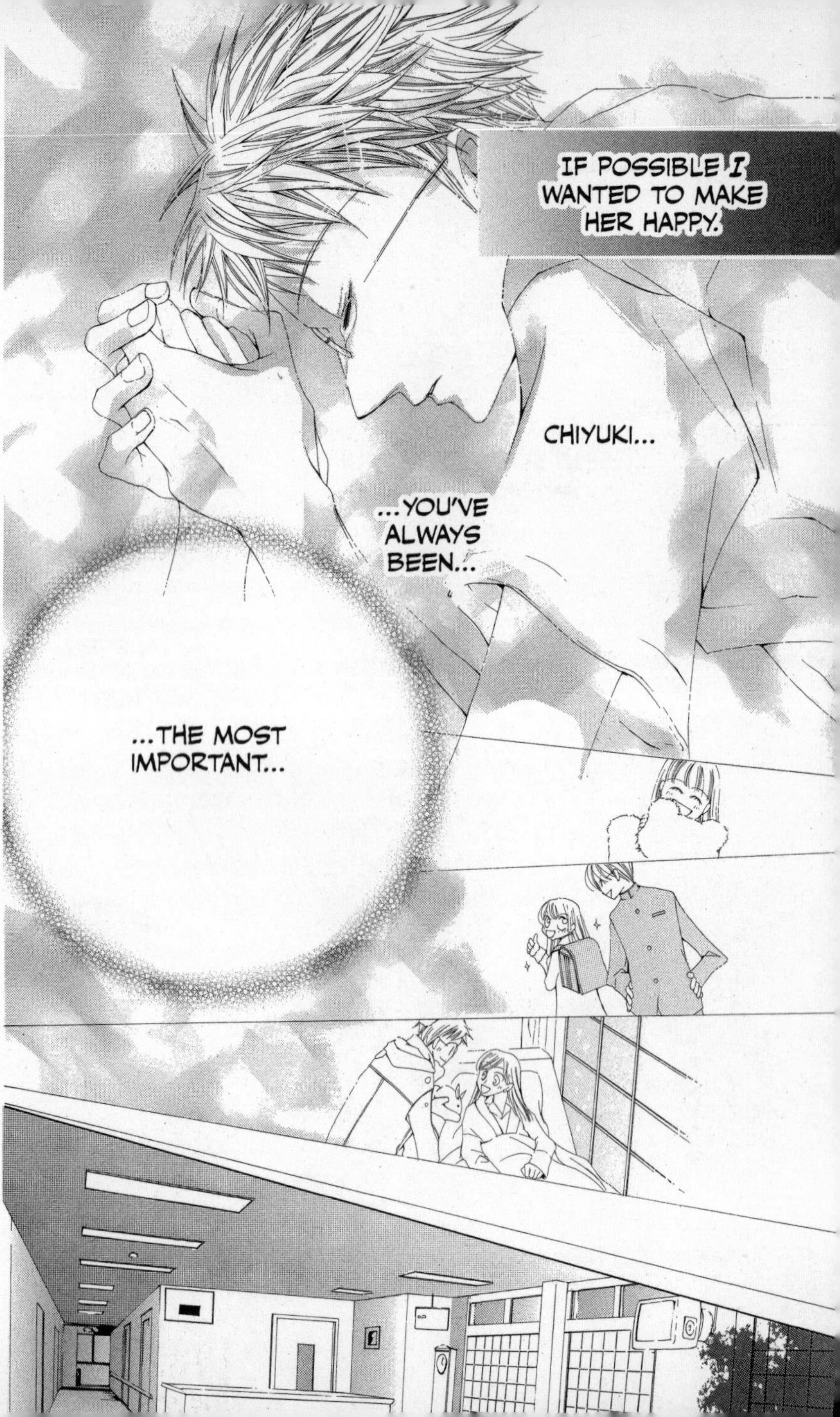
IF POSSIBLE I WANTED TO MAKE HER HAPPY.
CHIYUKI...
...YOU'VE ALWAYS BEEN...
...THE MOST IMPORTANT...

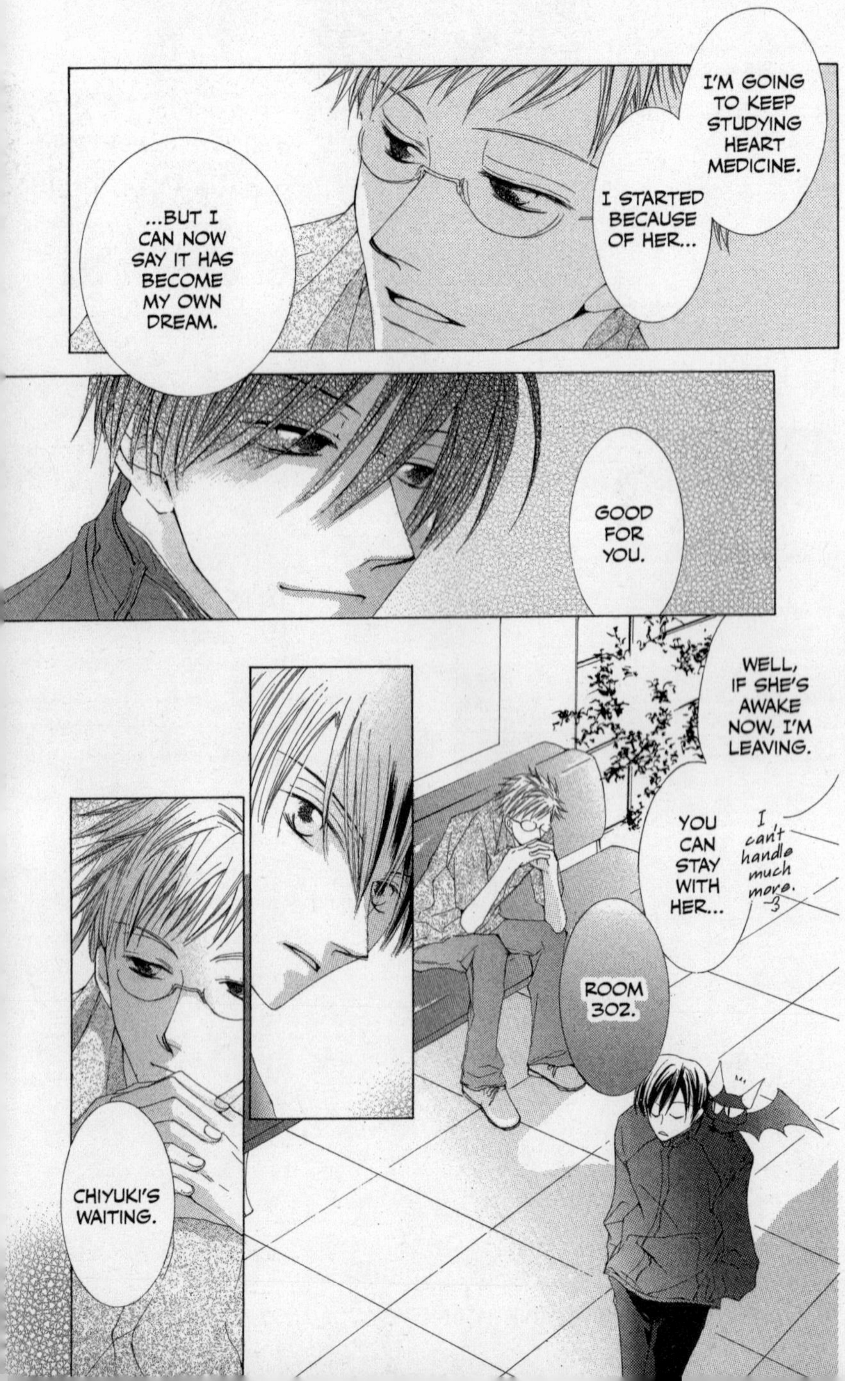
I'M GOING TO KEEP STUDYING HEART MEDICINE.
I STARTED BECAUSE OF HER...
...BUT I CAN NOW SAY IT HAS BECOME MY OWN DREAM.
GOOD FOR YOU.
WELL, IF SHE'S AWAKE NOW, I'M LEAVING.
YOU CAN STAY WITH HER...
I can't handle much more.
ROOM 302.
CHIYUKI'S WAITING.

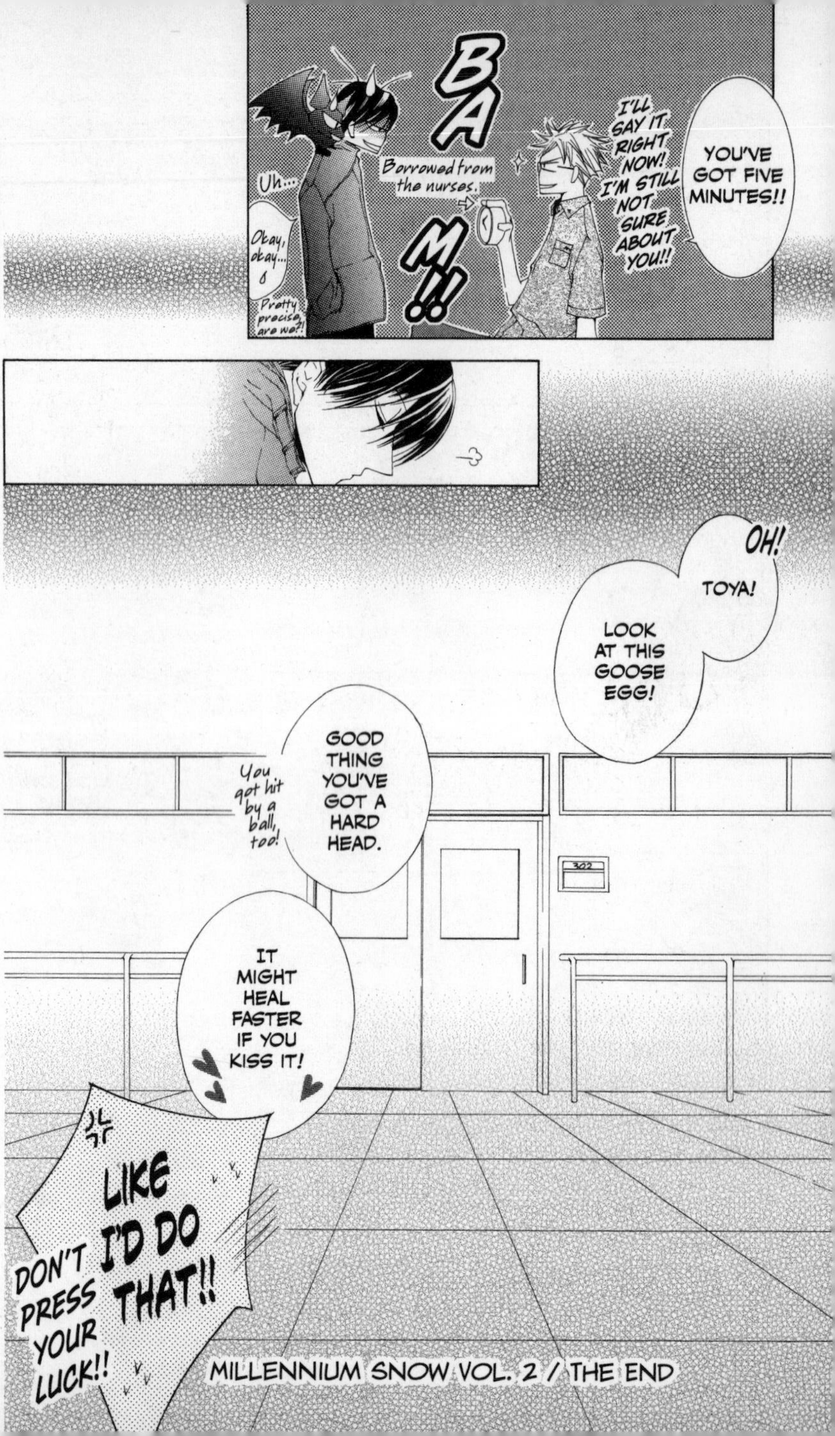
YOU'VE GOT FIVE MINUTES!!
I'LL SAY IT RIGHT NOW! I'M STILL NOT SURE ABOUT YOU!!
BAM!!
Borrowed from the nurses.
Uh...
Okay, okay...
Pretty precise, are we?!
OH!
TOYA!
LOOK AT THIS GOOSE EGG!
GOOD THING YOU'VE GOT A HARD HEAD.
You got hit by a ball, too!
IT MIGHT HEAL FASTER IF YOU KISS IT!
LIKE I'D DO THAT!!
DON'T PRESS YOUR LUCK!!

MILLENNIUM SNOW VOL. 2 / THE END

Dopplegangers ✿ Part 2

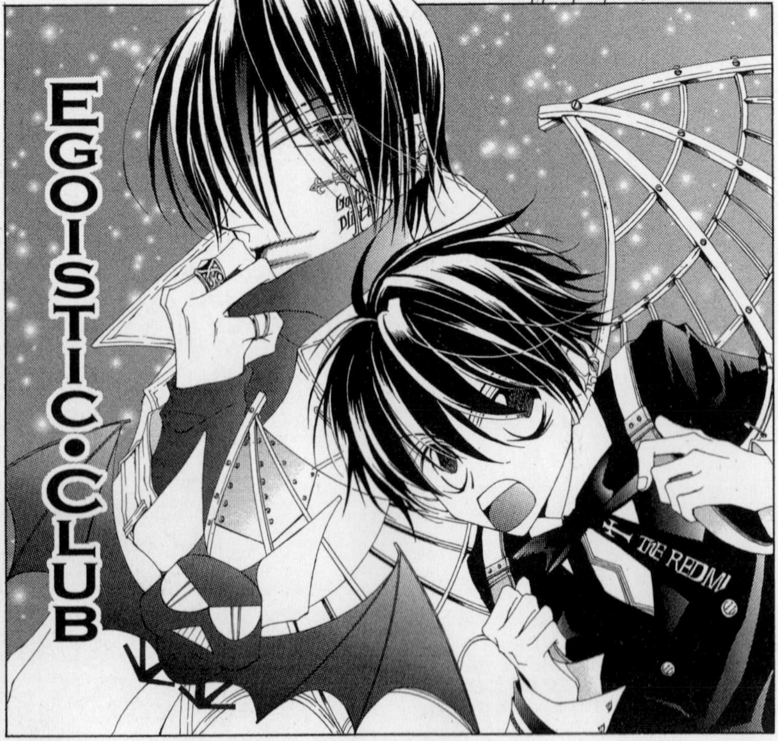
EGOISTIC•CLUB

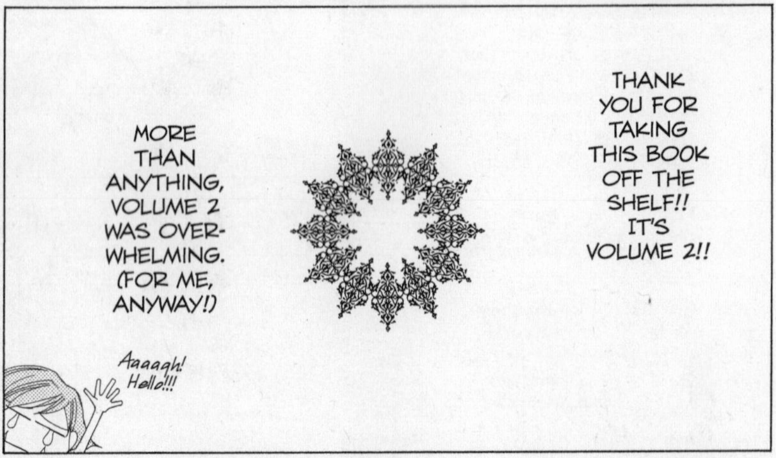
THANK YOU FOR TAKING THIS BOOK OFF THE SHELF!! IT'S VOLUME 2!!
MORE THAN ANYTHING, VOLUME 2 WAS OVER-WHELMING. (FOR ME, ANYWAY!)
Aaaagh! Hello!!!

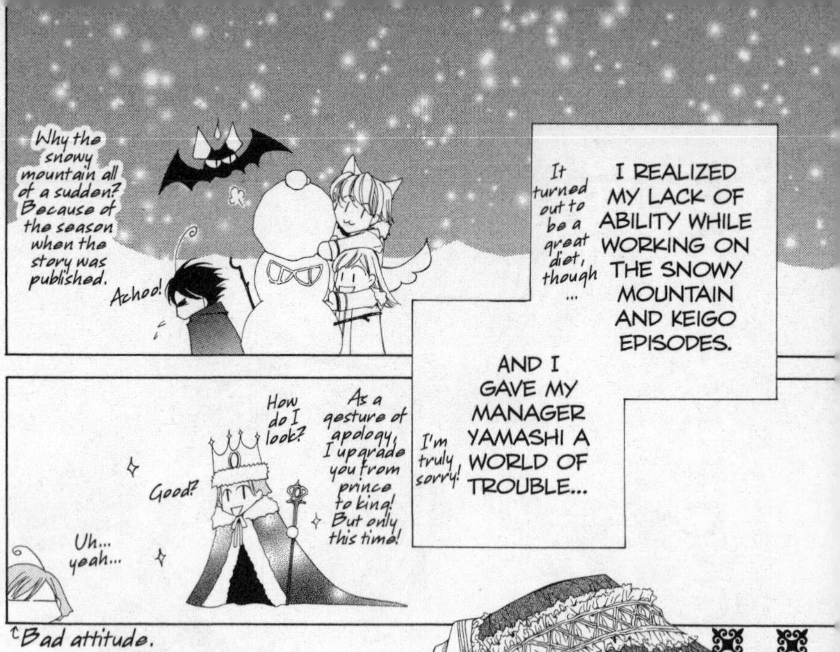
I REALIZED MY LACK OF ABILITY WHILE WORKING ON THE SNOWY MOUNTAIN AND KEIGO EPISODES.
It turned out to be a great diet, though...
Why the snowy mountain all of a sudden? Because of the season when the story was published.
Achoo!
AND I GAVE MY MANAGER YAMASHI A WORLD OF TROUBLE...
I'm truly sorry!
As a gesture of apology, I upgrade you from prince to king! But only this time!
How do I look?
Good?
Uh... yeah...
Bad attitude.

ISABEL'S NAME CAME FROM THE *TWINS AT ST. CLARE'S* CHILDREN'S NOVEL SERIES, WHICH I LOVED BACK WHEN I WAS IN ELEMENTARY SCHOOL. COME TO THINK OF IT, I HAD A WEAK SPOT FOR STUFF LIKE ENGLAND, BOARDING SCHOOLS AND TWINS AT THAT TIME. (THE MAIN CHARACTERS OF THE NOVEL ARE TWIN SISTERS.) I WAS ALSO INTO *CHARLIE & LOUISE* ABOUT THE SAME TIME. THEY'RE BOTH MASTERPIECES.

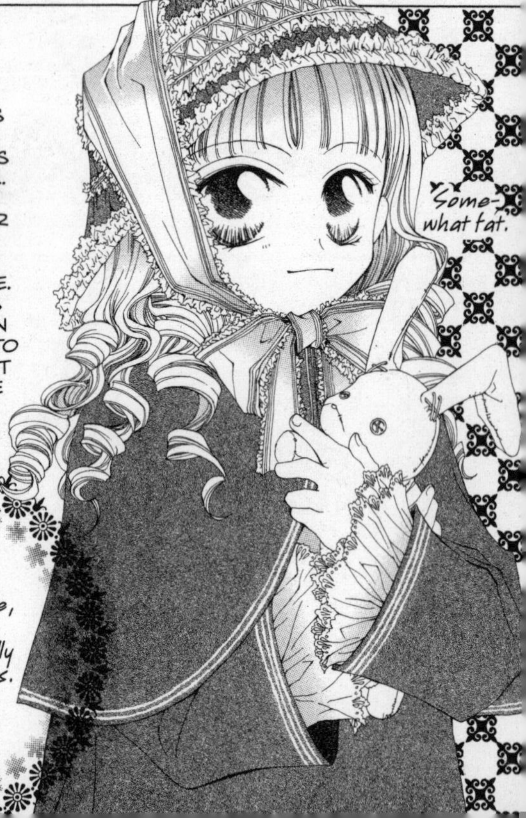
Some-what fat.

During the making of the snowy mountain episode, I realized I like drawing frilly dresses and ruins. I'm in seventh heaven when absorbed in detail.

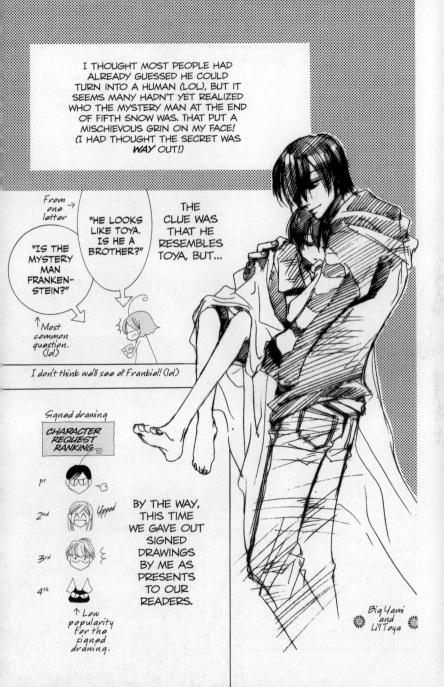

I THOUGHT MOST PEOPLE HAD ALREADY GUESSED HE COULD TURN INTO A HUMAN (LOL), BUT IT SEEMS MANY HADN'T YET REALIZED WHO THE MYSTERY MAN AT THE END OF FIFTH SNOW WAS. THAT PUT A MISCHIEVOUS GRIN ON MY FACE! (I HAD THOUGHT THE SECRET WAS *WAY* OUT!)

Big Yami and Li'l Toya

THE CLUE WAS THAT HE RESEMBLES TOYA, BUT...

From one letter →

"HE LOOKS LIKE TOYA. IS HE A BROTHER?"

"IS THE MYSTERY MAN FRANKEN-STEIN?"

↑ Most common question. (lol)

I don't think we'll see ol' Frankie!! (lol)

Signed drawing

CHARACTER REQUEST RANKING

1st
2nd
Yippee
3rd
4th

↑ Low popularity for the signed drawing.

BY THE WAY, THIS TIME WE GAVE OUT SIGNED DRAWINGS BY ME AS PRESENTS TO OUR READERS.

I was relieved when Toya won first place!

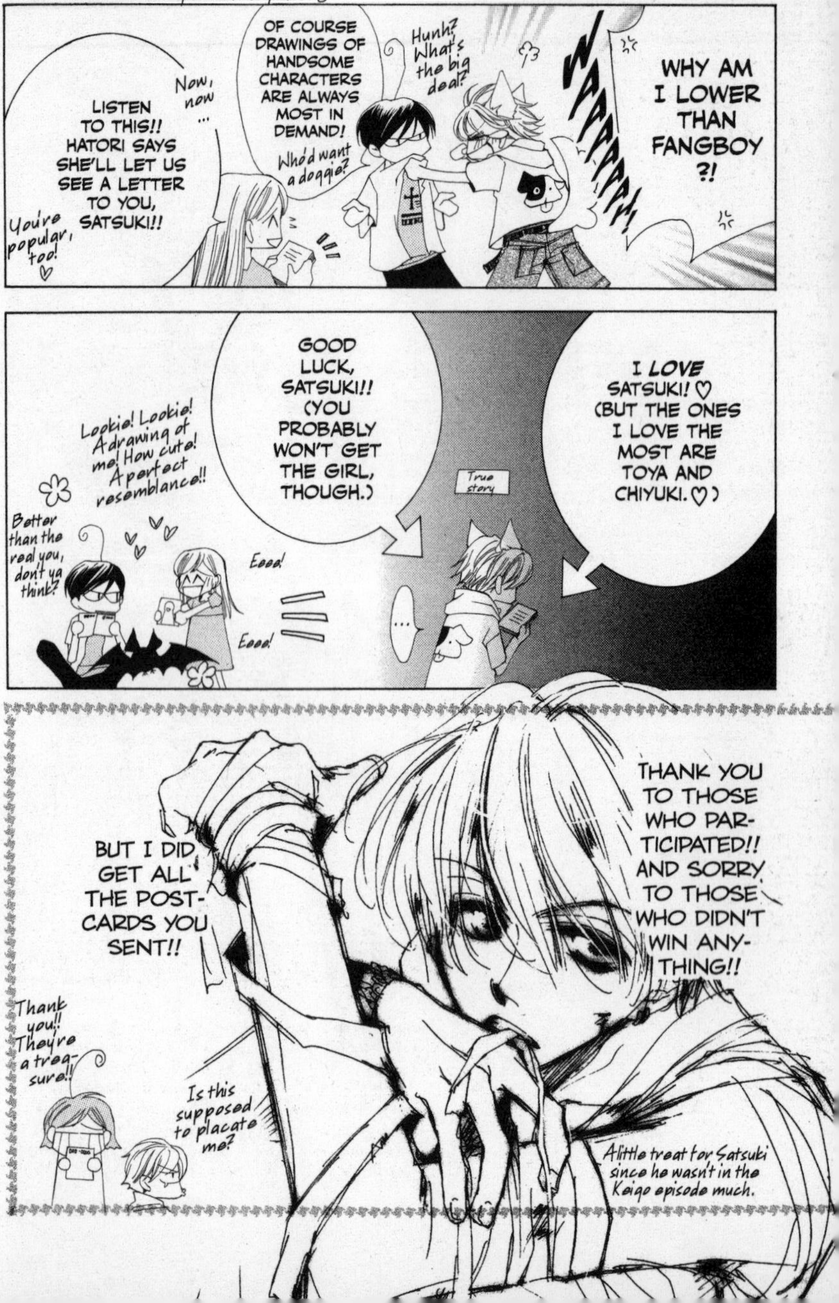
WHY AM I LOWER THAN FANGBOY ?!
Hunh? What's the big deal?
OF COURSE DRAWINGS OF HANDSOME CHARACTERS ARE ALWAYS MOST IN DEMAND!
Who'd want a doggie?
Now, now ...
LISTEN TO THIS!! HATORI SAYS SHE'LL LET US SEE A LETTER TO YOU, SATSUKI!!
You're popular, too!
I LOVE SATSUKI! ♡ (BUT THE ONES I LOVE THE MOST ARE TOYA AND CHIYUKI. ♡)
True story
GOOD LUCK, SATSUKI!! (YOU PROBABLY WON'T GET THE GIRL, THOUGH.)
...
Eeee!
Eeee!
Lookie! Lookie! A drawing of me! How cute! A perfect resemblance!!
Better than the real you, don't ya think?
THANK YOU TO THOSE WHO PAR-TICIPATED!! AND SORRY TO THOSE WHO DIDN'T WIN ANY-THING!!
BUT I DID GET ALL THE POST-CARDS YOU SENT!!
A little treat for Satsuki since he wasn't in the Keigo episode much.
Is this supposed to placate me?
Thank you!! They're a trea-sure!!

THE KEIGO EPISODE

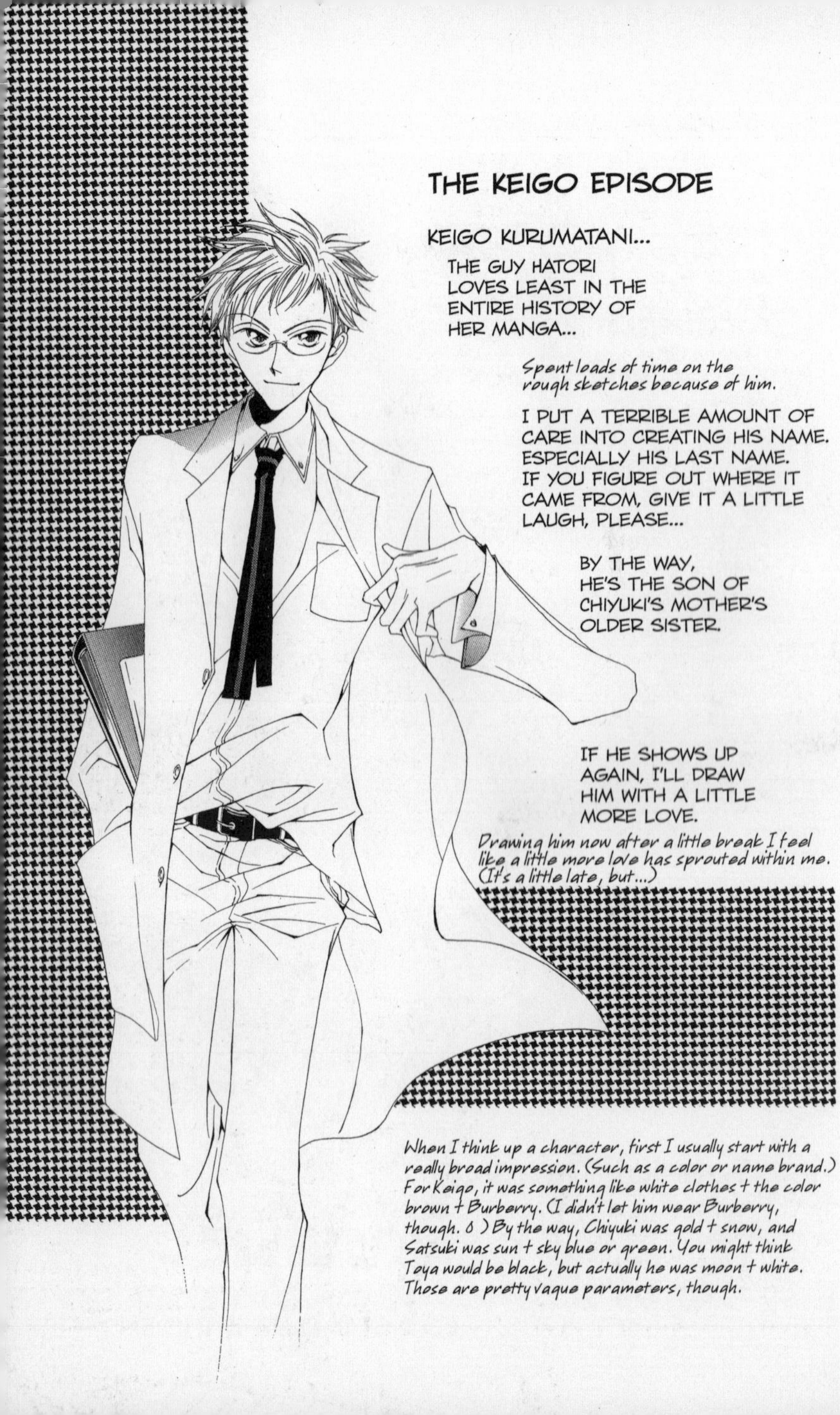

KEIGO KURUMATANI...

THE GUY HATORI LOVES LEAST IN THE ENTIRE HISTORY OF HER MANGA...

Spent loads of time on the rough sketches because of him.

I PUT A TERRIBLE AMOUNT OF CARE INTO CREATING HIS NAME. ESPECIALLY HIS LAST NAME. IF YOU FIGURE OUT WHERE IT CAME FROM, GIVE IT A LITTLE LAUGH, PLEASE...

BY THE WAY, HE'S THE SON OF CHIYUKI'S MOTHER'S OLDER SISTER.

IF HE SHOWS UP AGAIN, I'LL DRAW HIM WITH A LITTLE MORE LOVE.

Drawing him now after a little break I feel like a little more love has sprouted within me. (It's a little late, but...)

When I think up a character, first I usually start with a really broad impression. (Such as a color or name brand.) For Keigo, it was something like white clothes + the color brown + Burberry. (I didn't let him wear Burberry, though. δ) By the way, Chiyuki was gold + snow, and Satsuki was sun + sky blue or green. You might think Toya would be black, but actually he was moon + white. Those are pretty vague parameters, though.

THANKS TO YOU THE READERS, I PLAN TO CONTINUE *MILLENNIUM SNOW* FOR A LITTLE WHILE MORE. I'M NOT SURE HOW FAR I'LL GET, BUT HOPEFULLY TO THE END...

PLEASE LET ME HEAR WHAT YOU THINK.

BISCO HATORI
C/O SHOJO BEAT
VIZ MEDIA
P.O. BOX 77010
SAN FRANCISCO, CA 94107

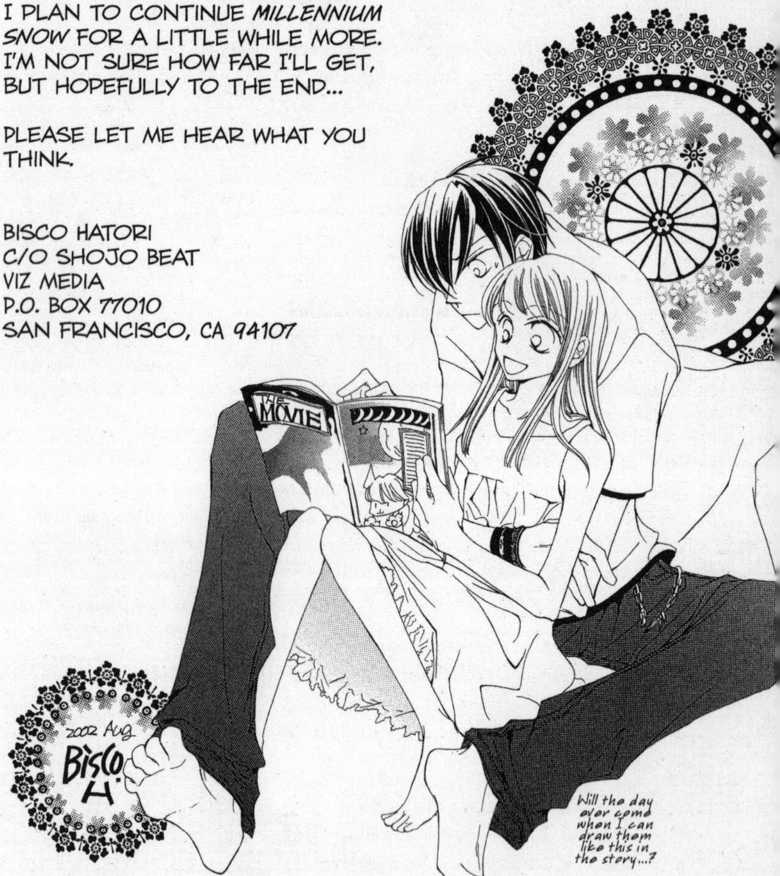
THE MOVIE
2002 Aug.
Bisco H.
Will the day ever come when I can draw them like this in the story...?

Special Thanks!!

YAMASHITA, ALL THE EDITORS, EVERYONE INVOLVED IN PUBLISHING THIS BOOK, FAMILY, FRIENDS, YUI NATSUKI, AYA AOMURA, AKIRA HAGIO, MECA TANAKA, AND MOST OF ALL YOU READERS!!

EGOISTIC CLUB / THE END

Glossary

While the appeal of the vampire needs no help to cross the language barrier, here are a few terms that could use a little extra explaining.

Page 230, panel 3: Miso
Fermented soybean paste used to flavor many Japanese dishes, including soup. The nutritional value of miso has been widely touted; it has been considered efficacious against radiation sickness and was fed to patients in Nagasaki and Chernobyl.

Page 231, panel 1: Boiled veggies
In the original Japanese, it is *nimono*, or foods that have been simmered and seasoned simply.

Page 329, panel 6: Possum
In Japan, "playing possum" is called *tanukineiri*. It is named after the *tanuki* (raccoon dog), which is rumored to pass out or pretend to sleep when surprised.

Page 385, side bar: Hatori-bird
Hato means "pigeon" in Japanese.

Page 385, side bar: Shuji Terayama
Author, dramatist, and director who published almost 200 works and directed over 20 short and feature length films. Terayama was co-founder of the avant-garde theater Tenjo Sajiki and founder of the experimental cinema Universal Gravitation. He was born December 10, 1935 and died May 4, 1983 of cirrhosis of the liver.

Page 385, side bar: Ranpo Edogawa
Pen name of Taro Hirai, author and literary critic, he is most famous for his detective fiction featuring the character Kogoro Akechi. He derived his pen name from the Japanese spelling of Edgar Allan Poe. He was born October 21, 1894 and died July 28, 1965.

Page 385, side bar: Bump of Chicken
A J-rock band. The members are Motoo Fujiwara, Hiroaki Masukawa, Yoshifumi Naoi, and Hideo Masu.

Page 385, side bar: Ira Ishida
An author whose stories are published bi-weekly in the Japanese culture magazine *R25*.

Page 402, panel 3: *Twins at St. Clare's*
The first of a series of six books written by Enid Blyton, set at the St. Clare's Boarding School. The eponymous twins are Patricia and Isabel O'Sullivan, who have myriad adventures.

B isco Hatori made her manga debut with *Isshun kan no Romance (A Moment of Romance)* in *LaLa DX* magazine. The comedy *Ouran High School Host Club* is her breakout hit. When she's stuck thinking up characters' names, she gets inspired by loud, upbeat music (her radio is set to NACK5 FM). She enjoys reading all kinds of manga, but she's especially fond of the sci-fi drama *Please Save My Earth* and *Slam Dunk*, a basketball classic...

MILLENNIUM SNOW
2-in-1 Edition

Volume 1
A compilation of graphic novel volumes 1-2

STORY & ART BY
BISCO HATORI

Translation & English Adaptation/Honyaku Center
Touch-up Art & Lettering/Gia Cam Luc
Design/Izumi Evers
Editor/Pancha Diaz

Sennen no Yuki by Bisco Hatori © Bisco Hatori 1998
All rights reserved.
First published in Japan in 2001, 2002 by HAKUSENSHA, Inc., Tokyo.
English language translation rights arranged with HAKUSENSHA, Inc., Tokyo.

Published by VIZ Media, LLC
P.O. Box 77010
San Francisco, CA 94107

10 9 8 7 6 5 4 3 2 1
2-in-1 edition first printing, June 2014

Hana-Kimi
HISAYA NAKAJO
VOLUMES 1·2·3

Hana-Kimi
HISAYA NAKAJO
VOLUMES 4·5·6

Hana-Kimi
Story & Art by HISAYA NAKAJO
VOLUMES 7·8·9

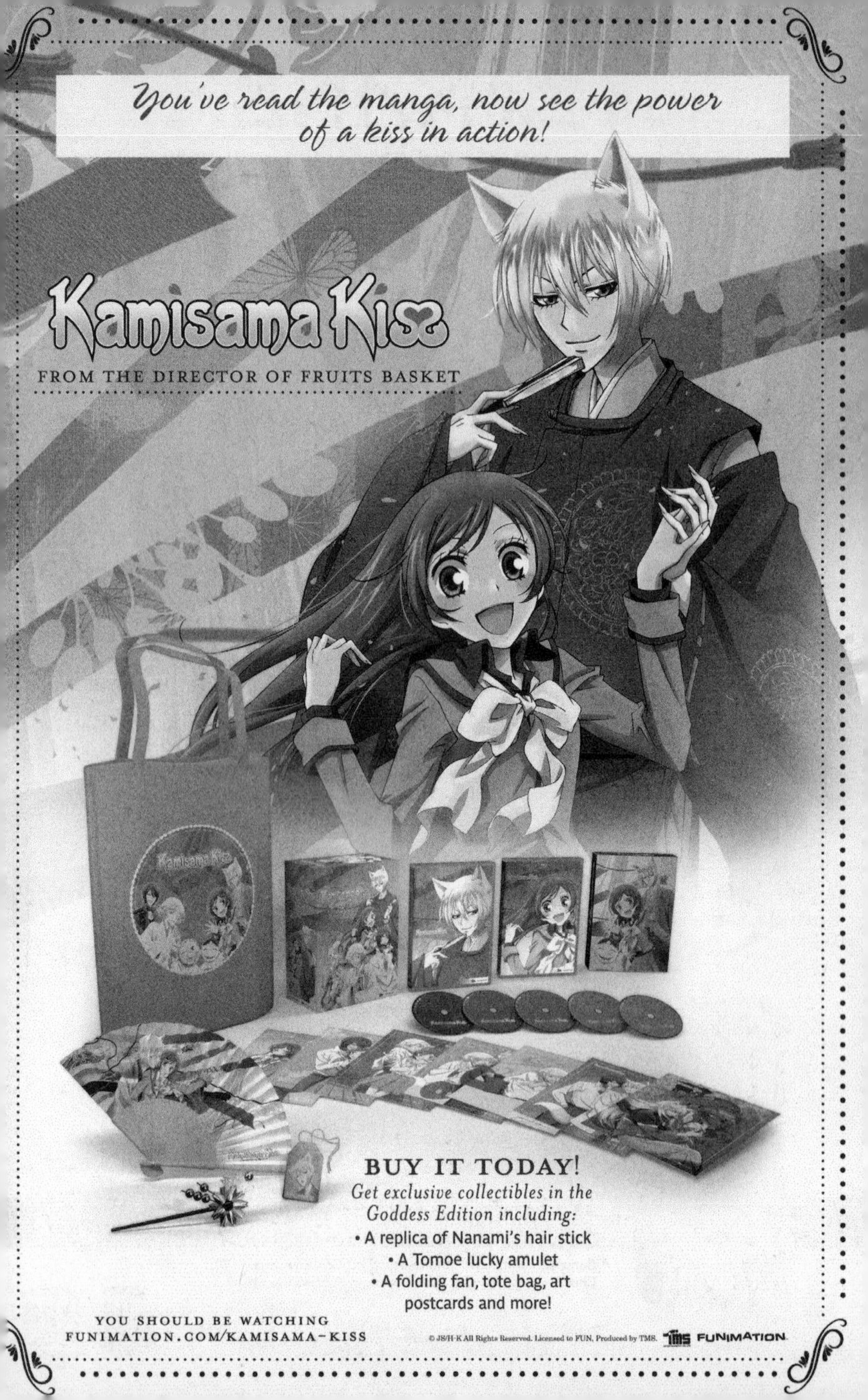

You've read the manga, now see the power of a kiss in action!
Kamisama Kiss
FROM THE DIRECTOR OF FRUITS BASKET
BUY IT TODAY!
Get exclusive collectibles in the Goddess Edition including:
• A replica of Nanami's hair stick
• A Tomoe lucky amulet
• A folding fan, tote bag, art postcards and more!
YOU SHOULD BE WATCHING
FUNIMATION.COM/KAMISAMA-KISS
© JS/H-K All Rights Reserved. Licensed to FUN, Produced by TMS.
FUNIMATION

SURPRISE!

You may be reading the wrong way!

It's true: In keeping with the original Japanese comic format, this book reads from right to left—so action, sound effects, and word balloons are completely reversed. This preserves the orientation of the original artwork—plus, it's fun! Check out the diagram shown here to get the hang of things, and then turn to the other side of the book to get started!

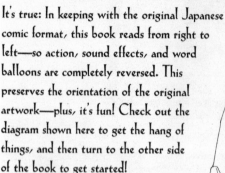

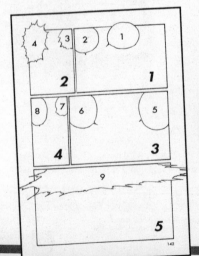